Forgetful of Their Sex

Jane Tibbetts Schulenburg

Forgetful of Their Sex

Female Sanctity and Society

ca. 500–1100

The University of Chicago Press
Chicago & London

Jane Tibbetts Schulenburg is professor of history in the Department of Liberal Studies, Continuing Studies Division, University of Wisconsin-Madison.

The University of Chicago Press, Chicago 60637
The University of Chicago Press, Ltd., London
© 1998 by The University of Chicago
All rights reserved. Published 1998
Printed in the United States of America
06 05 04 03 02 01 00 99 98   1   2   3   4   5
ISBN: 0-226-74053-6 (cloth)

Library of Congress Cataloging-in-Publication Data

Schulenburg, Jane Tibbetts.
    Forgetful of their sex : female sanctity and society, ca. 500–1100 / Jane Tibbetts Schulenburg.
        p.   cm.
    Includes bibliographical references and index.
    ISBN 0-226-74053-6 (cloth : alk. paper). — ISBN 0-226-74054-4 (paper : alk. paper)
        1. Women in Christianity—History—Early church, ca. 30–600.
    2. Women in Christianity—History—Middle Ages, ca. 600–1500.
    3. Sex—Religious aspects—Christianity.   4. Celibacy—Religious aspects—Christianity.   5. Virginity—Religious aspects—Christianity.   I. Title.
    BR195.W6S38   1998
    270.3'082—dc21   97-18646
                                                                                          CIP

Dedicated in loving gratitude to
my mother, Alice M. Sperberg Tibbetts,
who instilled in me a love of history,
and in memory of my father,
Jay Leslie Tibbetts, who encouraged
me to be "forgetful of my sex."

Contents

Illustrations follow pages 132 and 218

Acknowledgments

Over the long period involved in the writing and publishing of this book I have benefited greatly from the help and support of many friends and colleagues. One of the true pleasures of publishing this book is the public acknowledgment of these special people and sources of support.

First I owe a particular debt to William Chaney (Lawrence University), who introduced me to the field of medieval history. His passion for his work, his excellence in teaching, and his guidance and support convinced me to pursue a career as a medievalist. I especially owe profound thanks to the late David Horlihy, who was my major professor in graduate school and whose pioneering work in social and economic history and women's history has greatly influenced my own work. His immense love of the field, his kindness, gentle humor, counsel, and encouragement also served as an inspiration. I am indebted to James Brundage for his long friendship and continuing interest in and support of this project. I want to thank Penelope Johnson and Richard Kieckhefer for their careful reading of my manuscript for the University of Chicago Press. Their thoughtful questions, suggestions, and corrections were extremely helpful and improved the final version of this book. I should also like to express my deep gratitude to a number of scholars who have been involved in the history and literature of medieval women. Over the years I have learned a great deal from them, leaned heavily on their works, and valued their friendship and support. They include, especially, Suzanne Fonay Wemple, Jo Ann McNamara, Mary Martin McLaughlin, Penelope Johnson, Barbara Newman, Constance Berman, Joyce Salisbury, Caroline Walker Bynum, and Penny Schine Gold.

I owe a great debt to my colleagues in the Department of Liberal Studies, University of Wisconsin-Madison. Special thanks to Margaret Bogue, who over the years has been an important mentor, friend, and supporter of my research; the late Katherine Jones for her friendship, encouragement, and help; to Robert Wilson and Rosalie Wood for their invaluable assistance with computer problems; and to Irene Geller, Victoria Meyer, and Hope Hague for their generous help with translations. I would like to express my gratitude to the UW Women's Studies program and to Susan Friedman and Elaine Marks for their many kindnesses and support over the years. This book would never have been possible without the UW Memorial Library and the assistance of its excellent staff. I would particularly like to thank Judith Tuohy and her Interlibrary Loan staff for their efficient and good-natured help in procuring the many rare volumes needed for this project; Edward Van Gemert, User Services, for his special assistance; and the reference librarians and the staff of the Special Collections/Rare Book Room.

Over the years I have been generously provided with a number of fellowships and institutional support from the University of Wisconsin. I am particularly grateful to the National Endowment for the Humanities for a twelve-month fellowship (1981–82); to the Ford Foundation for a travel grant (1980); to the UW Institute for Research in the Humanities for a fellowship (spring semester 1991); and to the UW Graduate School for two summer research awards (1986 and 1992). I would also like to thank Dean Howard Martin for his support.

In the various stages of the production of the book I owe a special debt to a number of people, including Matt Hogan, for all of his assistance with the Latin translations of the saints' *vitae* (unless otherwise indicated, the Latin translations in the book are those of Hogan and Schulenburg); Sara Richards, for her help in the collection of some of the data on the saints and a translation; Elizabeth "Dolly" Weber, for her work on the bibliography; and Kimberly Seymour, Kathleen Suchenski, Diane Balmer, and Chris Schulenburg for their careful work in reading through the entire manuscript and saving me from numerous stylistic errors and embarrassments of inconsistency. I am also deeply grateful to the following for their help with the illustrations in the book: Judith Martin, for the wonderful etching of the heroics of St. Ebba and her nuns of Coldingham; Virginia Blanton-Whetsell, for her kindness in allowing me to reproduce her photograph of St. Etheldreda's installation, Ely Cathedral; and Anneke B. Mulder-Bakker and Mireille Madou for the photograph of the carving of St. Notburga with her nonaplets. I also want to thank the libraries and museums who have so generously allowed photographs of their holdings to be reproduced in this book. Specific acknowledgments appear in the captions accompanying the plates.

I also wish to express my gratitude to the University of Chicago

Press, especially to Doug Mitchell for his interest in this project, and to Kathryn Krug, Matt Howard, and Marianne Jankowski for all their work in producing this book.

I have profited immensely from the many opportunities I have had to try out some of the ideas of this book at various colleges and universities and at conferences—especially the International Congresses on Medieval Studies at Western Michigan University, Kalamazoo, Michigan, and the Berkshire Conferences on the History of Women. I have gained much from the questions asked and suggestions offered by the participants on these occasions. I also want to thank my students past and present, and particularly my continuing education students and those who have accompanied me on our many UW medieval pilgrimages. Over the years I have shared with them my collection of stories of medieval saints and want to thank them for their unflagging interest, encouragement, and inspiration.

I owe special gratitude to a group of colleagues, friends, and relatives who have been a constant support throughout this project and have assisted me in innumerable ways. They include Merry Wiesner-Hanks, Jane Endter, Patricia Flynn Wilcox, Helena Hamerow, Suzanne Desan, Barbara Kreutz, Marcia Parker, Sherry Reames, Marilyn Chavera, Lynn Courtonay, Eileen Seifert, Grethe Jacobsen, Ingrid Åkerlund, Mary Ann Rossi, and Jay and Sandi Tibbetts. Other colleagues and friends too numerous to name have also provided assistance. For all of the help from so many over these years, my sincere thanks.

Most importantly, I should like to acknowledge the special involvement of my husband, Eric, in this project. For part of the time while I was busy teaching and working on this book, he cared for the children and did the cooking. Without his strong encouragement and support (and homemade bread), this book would not have been written. I also want to express my appreciation to my long-suffering sons, Chris and Ben, for their patience, especially when subjected to the telling and retelling of the stories and miracles of the medieval saints, and for their delightful sense of humor throughout. The book is dedicated to my mother and the memory of my father.

Parts of this book have previously been published and appear here, in revised form, with the publishers' permission. Chapter 1 was first published in *Medieval Women and the Sources of Medieval History*, edited by Joel T. Rosenthal, pp. 285–320 (Athens: University of Georgia Press, 1990); chapter 2 in *Women and Power in the Middle Ages*, edited by Mary Erler and Maryanne Kowaleski, pp. 102–25 (Athens:

University of Georgia Press, 1988); chapter 3 in *Women in the Middle Ages and the Renaissance: Literary and Historical Perspectives,* edited by Mary Beth Rose, pp. 29–72 (Syracuse, N.Y.: Syracuse University Press, 1986); and portions of chapter 5 in *Sex in the Middle Ages: A Book of Essays,* edited by Joyce E. Salisbury, 203–31 (New York: Garland, 1991).

Introduction

The title of this book, *Forgetful of Their Sex,* is taken from a letter written by St. Jerome in 404. The purpose of this letter was to console Eustochium on the recent death of her mother, St. Paula. In this panegyric, Jerome provides a detailed biography of Paula's life which includes a fascinating account of Paula and Jerome's travels to Egypt and their visits to the monasteries of Nitria, as well as their pilgrimages to the sacred places of the Holy Land. It is then in his firsthand description of Paula's experiences among the Desert Fathers and monks of Egypt that Jerome notes with perhaps an element of surprise or incredulity as well as praise: "Her enthusiasm was wonderful and her endurance scarcely credible in a woman! [*Mirus ardor, et vix in femina credibilis fortitudo!*] Forgetful of her sex and of her weaknesses [*Oblita sexus et fragilitatis corporeae*] she even desired to make her abode, together with the young women who accompanied her, among these thousands of monks." [1]

In their praise of women, many ecclesiastical writers of the Middle Ages expressed similar sentiments regarding some women's special ability to deny or transcend the "natural frailty" of their own sex; this type of behavior set them apart from ordinary women and singled them out as candidates for sainthood. Gregory of Tours (d. 594), in his *Life of the Fathers,* comments on how Christ "exhorts us to live after the example of the saints and to fortify ourselves by His incessant precepts. He gives us as models not only men, but also the lesser sex, who fight not feebly, but with a virile strength; He brings into His celestial kingdom not only men, who fight as they should, but also women, who exert themselves in the struggle with success." [2] Or Leander of Seville (d. 600) notes in "The Training of Nuns," "Forgetful of her natural feminine weakness, she [the virgin] lives in manly vigor and has used virtue to give strength to her weak sex." [3]

The lives of these women saints were, then, to serve as inspiration as well as *exempla* for the faithful: they provided role models of proper deportment, which were to be admired and in some cases (i.e., if not too "extreme") imitated.[4] However, this heroic and strong, or "virile," behavior which was encouraged in certain cultural contexts proved to be problematic in others. Seen as a serious threat to male order or authority, actions which had once won the approbation of the Church and society came to be perceived as extreme and dangerous. Instead of attracting praise and elevation to sainthood, the transcendence of the limitations and temptations of female sexuality and their proper gender roles (i.e., acting in a manner which was "forgetful of their sex") brought suspicion and contempt to women. Viewed as exercising profoundly threatening, transgressive, or disturbing roles, such women were seen as the dangerous "other"; they needed to be contained, marginalized, or punished. The daring, defiant conduct, or acts of insubordination of these women thus served as a convenient arsenal of negative role models for ecclesiastical writers. Consequently, with the cultural relativity of sanctity, fluctuating attitudes toward women and their valuation in the Church and society, as well as the sometimes subtle hagiographic distinction between *admiranda* and *imitanda,* there frequently existed only a very fine line separating contemporary notions of "sanctity" from perceptions of aberrant or deviant modes of behavior.

The term *saint* has its origins in the Latin word *sanctus.* In its early pagan context, *sanctus* originally meant "sacred" or "inviolable"; as applied to character, it denoted the morally pure, good, innocent, pious, holy, just, etc.[5] In the Middle Ages *sanctus* brought these earlier meanings into a Christian context, and was applied to those who were "holy, sacred, dedicated to God," "saintly, living a religious life," or "holy, worshipped as a saint." The special role of women within the context of sanctity can be found in the term *sanctimonialis* which meant, in general, "holy, dedicated to God," "devout": this term was also used specifically to designate a nun.[6] And it appears that in the making of saints, women religious had a special advantage, as the majority of women saints of the early Middle Ages were recruited from the cloister.

There are many definitions of what constitutes a saint. In his important study, *Hagiography and the Cult of Saints: The Diocese of Orleans, 800–1200,* Thomas Head notes: "The saints were people who had entered heaven—for that is the simplest definition of sanctity—through the exercise of spiritual power in their lives. They continued to exhibit that *virtus* posthumously, most particularly at their tombs. . . . This exercise of *virtus,* whether during the lifetimes of the saints or at their tombs, resulted in miracles. Lives of the saints described their original holiness, while collections of posthumous miracle stories described the *virtutes* which they performed in contemporary times."[7]

Hippolyte Delehaye's classic essay *Sanctus* provides the following concept of sanctity: "the saint belongs to an elite. In the sphere of intelligence man bows before genius. In the sphere of energy and will, he venerates the hero. A person whom the Christian places at the pinnacle of his respect and admiration is one who in the service of God lives the superior life. The saint is a hero in the moral and religious order; he is a perfect Christian."[8]

John Mecklin, in his fascinating work *The Passing of the Saint: A Study of a Cultural Type,* discusses the terminology of sanctity and its contexts. The saint is first of all a cultural type and as such is "the product of prejudices wise or unwise, of the masses."[9] According to Mecklin, "the saint was the source of spiritual power and social reform, the special receptacle of divine wonder-working energy, the mysterious citizen of two worlds, the savior-god of the benighted lower classes. Yet he was an integral part of society. . . . The term 'saint' is singularly meaningless in our modern world. . . . For the saint in the classic sense is a spiritual aristocrat and presupposes a society with fixed and fundamental class distinctions. A democracy of saints is unthinkable. . . . In the absence of the medieval setting which has given the term its characteristic meaning, it has for us today mainly a historical significance. . . . But for the best part of the history of Christendom the 'saint' embodied the highest ideal—moral, spiritual, and social—of the age. Saintliness was the last word in the catalogue of virtues."[10]

In her study, *Body and Soul: Essays on Medieval Women and Mysticism,* Elizabeth Alvilda Petroff offers an especially perceptive description of the particular nature or characteristics of medieval women saints: "The women saints of the Middle Ages were transgressors, rule-breakers, flouters of boundaries, and yet they were also saints. Of course, in a way all saints are transgressors, in the sense that a saint lives by excess, lives in a beyond where ordinary measure does not hold; all saints, by their lives, stretch the boundaries of what we have conceived of as human possibility, and their zeal in breaking through conventional limitations can be both attractive and repellent, pointlessly mad and unshakeably sane at the same time. Women saints, it seems to me, were doubly transgressors—first, by their nature as saints and, second, by their nature as women."[11]

For the period of the sixth through the eleventh centuries (the general focus of this book), those who won recognition of sainthood were essentially local, popular saints rather than candidates formally canonized by the papacy. It was during these centuries that specific procedures developed for the making of saints.

During the Merovingian and Anglo-Saxon era, canonization remained a very informal process. It entailed the inscription of the name of the candidate for sainthood in the local catalogue of saints along with the subsequent issuance of an order by the Church that the faithful publicly recognize or venerate the new saint. The making of a saint thus originated on the local level. Frequently it sprang spontaneously from the local community and expressed the will of the populace and/or that of special interest groups such as a bishop and his chapter, an abbot or abbess and his or her community, or a royal or noble family. Thus this informal process of canonization did not provide an occasion for any kind of judicial investigation or intervention of higher ecclesiastical authorities; nor did it require formal authorization of the cult similar to the later process of canonization.[12]

Beginning with the Carolingian reforms of the mid-eighth century, however, there is a reappearance of Roman influence and an attempt on the part of the Church to eradicate local tendencies and corruption of the later Merovingian period. A series of canons emerge from the reform councils which were meant to regularize the veneration of saints and the establishment of their cults through extending episcopal control and power over this procedure. These regulations were specifically aimed at halting the immense proliferation of new popular saints and abolishing the growing abuse connected with saints and their relics. By the end of the eighth century the "formal" authorization of sanctity and public veneration, or the "normal outward sign of canonization" had been the translation (*translatio*) or elevation (*elevatio*) of the saint, that is, moving the remains to a more exalted position in the church where the body of the holy dead would more easily serve as an object of veneration for the faithful. However, the Carolingian reform legislation now specified that translations were to be carried out in a more formal or regularized way: namely, no translations were to be effected without the express sanctions of the local bishop and synod; one canon even required the intervention of the bishop, synod, and secular ruler.[13]

From the Carolingian period onward there was a tendency toward greater regularization and formalization in the procedure of recognizing saints: specifically, there was a much greater involvement of higher ecclesiastical authorities and an increased use of synods. Through these changes the Church attempted to determine and secure the legal status of the new candidates for sainthood, as well as to enhance the impressiveness of the translation and provide greater visibility and splendor to the cult.[14]

The first papal canonization took place in 993, and thereafter the papacy became increasingly involved in this procedure. This shift was brought about by the church reforms of the eleventh and twelfth centuries, the increasing centralization of the Church after the Gregorian Reform, and the growth in papal power and prestige. Very generally, between 1159 and 1234 the papacy attempted to establish complete control over canonization. In 1234 the policy which theoretically reserved canonization to the pontifical domain was defined in the *Decretals* of Pope Gregory IX. However, in practice it was only with the Counter-Reformation and the decrees of Pope Urban VIII in 1625 that the cult of saints was finally brought under full papal authority.[15]

Thus, despite their attempts, the reformers, canonists, and theologians of the eleventh and twelfth century did not fully succeed in placing canonization strictly within the realm of the papacy. And for the six centuries under consideration in this study, saints remained basically "local products." At the most, these candidates, who were recruited from specific monasteries or dioceses, received formal authorization of their sanctity and cult from their local bishops and synods through the procedure of translation. Most of the saints were therefore venerated with "something short" of official, papal confirmation. And in this they perhaps reflect more accurately the popular collective religious mentality of the period than those officially canonized or beatified by the Holy See.[16] (For the eleventh century, for example, out of a total of approximately three hundred popular saints, the papacy officially designated or canonized only twenty-six: twenty-three male saints and three *mulieres sanctae* or women saints.)[17]

Moreover, of importance for this period and particularly for the making of women saints was the basic shift in procedure from the rather loose and spontaneous designation of sainthood by the *vox populi* (which included the *vox feminae*) found in the Merovingian and Anglo-Saxon societies, to the increased episcopal and synodic control of canonization required by the Carolingian reforms. These reforms attempted to introduce a crucial change in designating who controlled the rights to determine which candidates would ultimately win recognition of sanctity. This preoccupation with *ordo*, regularization, and formalization, this ordering of the process, shifted the power of selection essentially to the male ecclesiastical hierarchy—specifically to the episcopal and metropolitan level. Thus beginning with the Carolingian period, these procedural changes would have a detrimental effect on the promotion and ultimate selection of female saints.[18]

The making of saints did not occur within a social or cultural vacuum. In addition to being affected by changing structural and ecclesiastical processes of selection, official membership in the heavenly city indirectly reflected the values of the hierarchically ordered and gender-based earthly societies of the Middle Ages. Clearly, celestial prominence had a very definite "this-worldly" or terrestrial base. The powerful on earth were therefore seen to be the powerful in the heavenly kingdom. That is, in order to achieve a visibility which could lead to fame of sanctity, it was necessary for candidates to be provided with opportunities which would lend them this prominence and recognition. Would-be saints needed, for example, wealth and access to positions of prestige and power within the Church and society. They also required a supportive environment in which to build up their spiritual dossiers.

One might perhaps conclude from the Church's insistence on a policy of spiritual egalitarianism—based, for example, on St. Paul's statement that "there is neither Jew nor Greek . . . slave nor free . . . male nor female . . . for you are all one in Christ Jesus" [19]—that there would be no barriers of gender or discrimination in the selection of saints. In his study, "La statut de la femme en droit canonique médiéval," René Metz has argued that "woman is the absolute equal of man by virtue of the fundamental principles of Christianity with regard to the human being, redemption and sanctity." He also noted that "sanctity, which constitutes the veritable scale of values, is not the privilege of a particular category; men and women, weak and powerful are able to achieve it equally.[20] However, despite the egalitarian rhetoric of the Church, a definite gender-based asymmetry (sometimes exaggerated) existed among the membership of the holy dead (see plate 1). Invariably it was much more difficult for women than for men to enter the ranks of the celestial hierarchy. For example, for the period from the sixth through the eleventh century, only approximately one out of seven, or 15 percent, of the saints were female, while 85 percent were male. This rather wide discrepancy among the spiritual elect can be explained in part by the traditional exclusion of women from leadership roles in the secular church hierarchy. Nevertheless, certain periods as well as geographic regions seemed to be more receptive to women's active participation in Church and society; they therefore provided favorable circumstances or opportunities by which women could gain importance and recognition and thence the concomitant honors of sainthood.

It was, however, essentially within the context of the irregular powers of the early medieval family, with the intersection of public and domestic spheres, that women could achieve positions of power and authority as well as direct control over wealth and property.[21] With the coming of Christianity, especially to the northern regions of Europe (approximately the sixth through eighth centuries), new opportunities appeared for women. Women with power and wealth were actively recruited by churchmen to aid in missionary work and to establish churches, monasteries, and centers of education. These noblewomen were also called upon to assume leadership positions within their new foundations. Many of them became strong, charismatic figures of these early religious communities. Their essential contributions and roles in the establishment of Christianity in turn provided them with a visibility and prominence which frequently led to rewards of sainthood. Thus during this initial period of women's active participation in the Church and society along with their high valuation, approximately one out of every three saints was female.

But beginning with the development of the Carolingian Empire and the Carolingian reforms, followed by the reforms of the tenth and eleventh centuries (the situation being further exacerbated by the devastation and disruption caused by the Viking, Saracen, and Hungarian invasions), these earlier pragmatic arrangements which had encouraged, or certainly allowed, the exercise of power by women were transformed. The Church became increasingly concerned with hierarchy, *ordo;* it became more regularized and structured. The initial enthusiasm for women's active participation and visibility in religion, and particularly within monasticism, began to wane. Church councils formulated policies of strict enclosure for female religious. In practice, these gender-specific regulations affected women's autonomy and independence; they precipitated economic hardship as well as a decline in education in many of the women's communities. A definite preference for male leadership made itself felt within the Church. The various reform movements, with their emphasis on clerical hierarchies, celibacy, ritual purity, and sacramental formalism, fostered an exaggerated fear of women and in some cases a blatant misogynism.

Furthermore, in the eleventh century, economic and formal political power among women of the elite classes began to deteriorate in many regions of Europe. Basic changes occurred within the family—such as the replacement of bilineal kinship networks by patrilineage—which would have serious repercussions for women.[22] In some regions, an increasingly rigid separation of public and domestic spheres, of male and female activities, also began to emerge. Attempts were made by the Church and government to move women out of public roles and to marginalize them. Corresponding to these changes, new ideals of sanctity emerged for women: with the new "privatized" domestic saint or the obedient, subservient wife-saint, for example, the Church attempted to popularize and promote passive virtues for women. Very briefly, through these and other basic changes of this period, women were now frequently denied opportunities for the prominence in both

Church and society which they had previously assumed; and one of the end results was to decidedly curtail their options for the sort of visibility upon which the recognition of sanctity was predicated.

The present book is based on a collective study of over 2,200 male and female saints. In addition to saints' Lives or *vitae,* this study utilizes many other contemporary sources that corroborate evidence found in the *vitae,* including chronicles, cartularies, secular and ecclesiastical legislation, correspondence, penitentials, liturgical collections, handbooks of ecclesiastical offices, art, and architectural and archaeological evidence. This rich variety of sources provides narrative, anecdotal, visual, and statistical evidence for a study of sanctity and society during this period.

The time frame of the book is the sixth through the eleventh century. This is an especially formative period in the history of women and sanctity which has not received the attention from scholars that it deserves.[23] As noted, it is an epoch which witnessed a great deal of change in society, the economy, and the Church, as well as shifts in attitudes and mentalities. Bounded on one side by the collapse of the Roman Empire, with the "new beginnings" of the successor states, and the spread of Christianity and monasticism to the north of Europe, it was bounded on the other side by the twelfth century—an age of renaissance and reformation. On one level a culmination of what came before, the twelfth century also saw the emergence of a much more complex society with the development of feudal monarchies, the rise of urban centers and culture, the Crusades, a new imperial papacy, a proliferation of new religious movements, shifts in education, etc. Thus our concentration on the sixth through the eleventh century provides us with an opportunity to look at change over a long period of time, and—while there is always something arbitrary involved in selecting one's chronological framework—there also seems to be a certain coherence in the six centuries prior to the twelfth century.[24]

Although the major focus of this study is on women saints, or *mulieres sanctae,* this work also looks at gender and has an important comparative element: the data includes information about male saints along with that of female saints. For in order to offer broad interpretations of change during this period, it is frequently necessary to measure women's "condition"—their various opportunities and experiences, as well as restrictions and exclusions—against that of their male contemporaries. In addition, the *vitae* of male saints are particularly rich sources for information on the medieval family, motherhood, brother-sister relationships, friendship, women's monastic life, and miracles concerning women; moreover, they provide many fascinating examples of "negative role models" for women and of female "transgressive" or "deviant" behavior.

While dealing for the most part with the exceptional, highly visible, and sometimes rather eccentric individuals who achieved recognition of sainthood, this study is not simply about this minute portion of society or an elite core of women saints; that is, it is not merely a survey of plaster-cast saints or a "nimbus count." Rather, its purpose in focusing on this select group is to study larger questions about changing attitudes toward women, various opportunities available to them in the Church and society, and some of the commonalities of female experience, as well, across these critical six centuries of history. It is an attempt to trace a number of aspects of the physical, social, economic, and spiritual setting out of which these women saints emerged. It endeavors to offer a broad interpretation of the complex of inter dependent forces of society and the Church that were involved in either encouraging the recognition of female saints or hindering this process. It is an attempt to provide a sympathetic perspective on different types, models, or notions of female saintliness and variants of anti-social, "aberrant," or "deviant" behavior, transcending the boundaries of permissible diversity, which emerged at this time.

NOTE ON SOURCES AND METHODOLOGY

When I began this study in the early 1970s, my original intention was to write an article with a general focus on women and the early medieval Church. I wanted to reconstruct some aspects of women's religious experience during this early period, to explore their opportunities for leadership roles and power, to look at change in the perceptions of women, and, in general, to gain an impression of how women fared within society and the Church. Preferring to get away from the strictly prescriptive literature of the period, such as patristic writings, canon laws, monastic *regulae,* sermons, etc., I decided to focus on what was then a little-investigated source—the Lives of women saints. The clear interest in women as saints and the preoccupation with female "transgressive" or "deviant" behavior made saints' Lives an extremely attractive source. Moreover, the sheer numbers of the *vitae* provided a rough data base with unlimited possibilities.

Thus my first rather uncharted foray into the field of "nimbus counts," or "hagiometrics," began with a census of the saints found in the *Bibliotheca hagiographica latina antiquae et mediae aetatis.* This two-volume work, plus supplement, was published by the Bollandist Society (1898–1903; Supplement, 1913) and is the classic bibliography of Latin hagiographical works. Although it is an invaluable compilation, highly convenient and manageable in regard to the numbers and entries of saints, I soon realized that this collection did not include a number of the popular saints for this early period who had important cults but lacked official *vitae;* moreover, being primarily a bibliographic tool, it provided limited biographical data for each saint.[25]

I then turned to what is at present the most comprehensive collection or encyclopedia of saints, the twelve-volume *Bibliotheca Sanctorum* published by the Istituto Giovanni XXIII della Pontificia Università Lateranense (Rome, 1961–70). This Italian encyclopedia of saints contains a wealth of information, "factual" and legendary, on famous and little-known saints of the East and West and their cults; it also has useful bibliographic entries for each saint. Thus in the process of collecting basic statistical data compiled in the *Bibliotheca Sanctorum,* I was introduced to an incredible amount of fascinating detail, "incidental information" about women's experiences and lives. At this point I decided that the richness of these sources required a much more extensive study; little did I realize what this might lead to!

I subsequently turned to a number of other collections of saints' lives and worked my way through the thirteen-volume collection of the *Vies des saints et des bienheureux, selon l'ordre du calendrier avec l'historique des fêtes,* by the RR. PP. Bénédictins de Paris (1935–59); *Butler's Lives of the Saints, Complete Edition,* edited, revised, and supplemented by H. Thurston and D. Attwater, 4 vols. (1956); the rather problematic collection *Les Petits Bollandistes,* 14 vols. (7th ed., 1876); Dunbar's *Dictionary of Saintly Women,* 2 vols (1904–5); and David Hugh Farmer's *Oxford Dictionary of Saints* (1982). Although there was a great deal of repetition or overlap in these works, each collection seemed to favor the saints of certain geographic areas, or specific orders, and neglect others; moreover, each provided additional perspectives and unique details which proved to be very useful. Dunbar's *Dictionary of Saintly Women,* although somewhat outdated, was extremely helpful.

After consulting these various encyclopedic collections of saints, I then turned to the major collections of primary sources for medieval saints: the *Acta Sanctorum, Acta Sanctorum Belgii Selecta, Acta Sanctorum ordinis Sancti Benedicti, Patrologia Latina, Monumenta Germania Historica, Scriptores rerum merovingicarum* and *Scriptores,* Plummer's *Vitae sanctorum Hiberniae* and his *The Lives of Irish Saints,* as well as many other individually edited or translated *vitae,* in order to study in some depth and detail certain selected Latin Lives of these saints.

However, the statistical aspect of this study, the census or general distribution of the holy dead, is based on information collected from the twelve-volume *Bibliotheca Sanctorum*. In amassing data on the number and distribution of female and male saints of this period, I have attempted to include only "real" saints (if one can use this term)—that is, saints with some sort of historical authentication attested by a combination of sources, including contemporary or later *vitae,* chronicles, liturgical or cultic evidence, sermons, letters, inscriptions, and archaeological data. Although this process involved some rather subjective choices, I did not include in my count those saints whose existence appeared to be highly improbable or undatable, nor those saints who have been totally discounted by a number of historians. (Perhaps to avoid confusion, I should add here that although I attempted to eliminate the especially questionable saints from my rough statistics, I have included a number of these marvelous figures and their folklore traditions in the narrative of the book.)

In general, I have tried to be more inclusive than exclusive in this exercise. I have therefore not adopted, for example, the criterion utilized by Michael Goodich in his *Vita Perfecta: The Ideal of Sainthood in the Thirteenth Century,* where he included in his study only those saints whose veneration was attested by at least two independent contemporary or near contemporary sources. Because of the fragmentary nature of our documentation, as well as the special conditions and problems surrounding the transmission of saints' lives—which seemed to favor male saints—this criterion would be extremely difficult to apply to this early period. Thus the application of Goodich's standard would have the end result of excluding a number of important early medieval women saints for whom we no longer possess contemporary *vitae* or other contemporary sources.

In collecting information about the distribution of the holy dead, entries for each saint have been collated and recorded according to the saint's date of death. In many cases we know the exact year of death; however, when we are provided with only the century of the saint's death, the saint is entered in our data base as dying in the middle of the period: for example, when the date given is the sixth century, for our statistics it would be assigned the arbitrary date of 550. It should also be noted that in our tabulations of the holy dead, only individual saints are recognized and recorded. The tradition of large groups of saints/martyrs (perhaps the most blatant example being that of St. Ursula and her 11,000 virgins—whose exaggerated numbers have been attributed to a scribal error), if incorporated in our count, would have substantially skewed our statistics! And while there is some fluctuation in base numbers and percentages in the distribution of women saints over this six-hundred-year period, the sex ratio among the holy dead is approximately seven males for every female, or 15 percent women saints. (It is interesting to note that the percentages in my original calculations, based on the smaller number of entries recorded in the *Bibliotheca hagiographica latina,* turned out to be approximately the same as those taken from the *Bibliotheca Sanctorum.*)[26]

This study is also geographically limited to the general areas of modern-day France, Belgium and the Low Countries, Germany, Austria, Switzerland, Italy, and Britain. In the rough numerical survey of the distribution of saints according to country, I limited this further to focus specifically on Italy, France, Belgium, Britain, and Germany. Moreover, in assigning the *loca sanctorum* for the holy dead of this period, the country designated is that in which the saint died and where her or his first cult originated. In some cases this was the saint's country of origin; in others, especially those of the missionary saints, the country associated with the saint was a foreign land. Because of the enormous confusion and difficulties involved in identifying, naming, and dating Irish saints in general, I decided not to attempt to include this important group in my "nimbus count"—with the exception of those who died and had cults in other, "foreign," countries. I also did not incorporate in my general statistics the early saints of Spain or Portugal. Nevertheless, because of the richness of many of the Irish and Spanish *vitae,* I have included in this study a number of examples or incidents from these Lives which further corroborate information found in other hagiographic sources of the period.

In addition to the gathering and collating of material from the collections of saints' lives, I have also incorporated in this study some rough statistics on monasticism for women during this formative period. Since many of the monasteries played a primary role in the recruitment and promotion of the *mulieres sanctae,* it seemed important to look briefly at the development of this institution for women in order to see the relationship between female patronage and the foundation of new monasteries and the making of saints. Rough data on the establishment, distribution, and demise of women's monastic communities are based on information from the following collections: L. H. Cottineau, *Répertoire topo-bibliographique des abbayes et prieurés,* 2 vols., (1935–37); E. de Moreau, *Histoire de l'église en Belgique: Circonscriptions ecclésiastiques, chapitres, abbayes, couvents en Belgique avant 1559* (Brussels, 1948); David Knowles and R. Neville Hadcock, *Medieval Religious Houses: England and Wales* (1971); and the Ordnance Survey, *Monastic Britain* (1978). Although these sources are incomplete and not without problems, they provide us with much invaluable information which further corroborates our statistics on women saints.[27]

In the final analysis, perhaps any attempt at quantification of membership in the celestial gynaeceum remains risky at best. Because of the many ambiguities and difficulties inherent in our sources as well as the inability to quantify the unique or atypical, these statistics remain only approximate and must therefore be used with caution. While the numbers might provide a false precision to the information, as rough indicators they serve as an indirect index, a reinforcement for other evidence; they are supplemental to the many illustrations and examples, another yardstick by which to compare and assess women's opportunities and visibility during this early period. They allow us to judge how these *incomparabiles feminae* were evaluated and how they fared in the recognition of sainthood through the various fluctuations of society and the Church.

Over the past twenty-five or thirty years, there has occurred a great resurgence of interest in hagiography or the study of sainthood and the cult of saints. Especially during the 1980s and early 1990s, there has been a veritable explosion of scholarly works on medieval saints.[28] Similarly, during this same period, there has been a burgeoning of impressive research on women in medieval society and the Church.[29] Thus my study, *Forgetful of Their Sex: Female Sanctity and Society, ca. 500–1100,* is located at the intersection of these two new, increasingly popular, and immensely productive directions of historical research. And while this work has been in process during these past twenty-five years, it has been the beneficiary of many of these new ideas, approaches, discoveries, editions and translations of *vitae,* and the general excitement and generosity shared by scholars in the fields of hagiography and women's history. I am especially grateful to the many scholars who have contributed so much to these new areas of research and who have succeeded in legitimating these fields of study.

This book surveys a number of aspects of the making of women saints for the period ca. 500–1100. It is organized around the general concept of the changing social contexts of female sanctity (women saints as embodiments of cultural models) as well as of various kinds of extravagant, "transgressive," anti-social female behavior which frequently challenged the *ordo* of the Church. It explores some of the major factors, such as power, influence, patronage, and special relationships, involved in the making of women saints. The chapters therefore focus, for example, on the importance of public roles, visibility, and the recognition of female sanctity; the significance or cost of virginity in the making of saints; the critical roles of the family and circles of friendship in establishing reputations of sanctity and promoting their candidates; as well as the general importance of longevity in the making of saints. It looks at various cultural traditions, as well as social functions of saints and their lives which come into play during this period. Because of the sheer numbers of *vitae,* the richness of our source material, its openness to a wide variety of interpretations, and the complexities of these topics, each chapter of this study could easily be expanded into a book-length manuscript. Thus in many ways this has been a rather difficult and perhaps perilous undertaking. As an initial attempt, it has merely scratched the surface. It is my hope that this project will serve as a useful beginning and will encourage further questions, debate, and additional research in this incredibly fascinating and promising area of medieval history and society.

For the profit of many and as her perpetual memorial, we shall undertake with true and faithful pen to produce a truthful narrative from what we have learned from her followers. Therefore, animated by the merits of this glorious patron who rejoices in her happy marriage with the Celestial Emperor, obeying your orders with pious devotion, I shall now put my mind to writing of her holy birth, customs, and death and how through her the Lord made signs of miracles.

Prologue, De S. Austrebertae virgine in Belgio et Normannia (*SWDA*, 2:307)

Therefore, for the edification of the faithful, we have been pleased to write here a few of the many deeds in the life of the servant of God, Bertilla of blessed memory. Then anyone who likes may carefully consider and imitate, as in a clear mirror, those examples of virtue.

Vita Bertilae abbatissae Calensis (*SWDA*, 9:288)

Saints' Lives as a Source for the History of Women, ca. 500–1100

Our sources for the years 500–1100 are incomplete, fragmentary, and rather limited. Hagiography, the most common and prolific form of writing during this early period, is frequently the only source to have survived in any substantial quantity.[1] While the chronicles, histories, laws, charters, wills, contracts, correspondence, heroic epics, poems, art and archaeological evidence, and other sources of the time provide glimpses of women in medieval society, saints' Lives hold a remarkable potential for historians of medieval women. The *vitae* focus a great deal of attention on women. They are directly concerned with female roles in the Church and society: they also provide contemporary perceptions, ideals, and valuations of women. The sheer numbers of extant female and male Lives (quantities unlike those of any other source) afford us the extraordinary opportunity to observe broad patterns of change across the centuries and to discern shifts in access to power and sainthood, ideals of saintly behavior, and the construction and manipulation of sanctity as related to gender. Saints' *vitae* provide an excellent condensing lens (although filtered and not without its own particular perspective) through which to view medieval perceptions of women as well as various indices of women's opportunities, experiences, and lives.

Yet it is necessary to note that hagiographers were not necessarily historians or biographers. Their works were panegyrics, conscious programs of persuasion or propaganda, meant to prove the particular sanctity of their protagonists. Frequently motivated by the particular interests of the monasteries or churches which claimed the holy dead as their patrons and possessed their relics, hagiographers attempted to demonstrate the efficacy of their saints and their exceptional worth as special friends of God.

Delehaye, in his classic study *Les Légendes hagiographiques* (1906), warned scholars that "the important thing to be emphasized at the outset is the distinction between hagiography and history. The work of the hagiographer may be historical, but it is not necessarily so. It may take any literary form suited to honoring the saints, from an official record adapted to the needs of the faithful to a highly exuberant poem that is completely removed from factual reality."[2] Kathleen Hughes has argued in her study of sources of early Christian Ireland,

> Hagiography is not history. The author is not concerned to establish a correct chronology. He is not interested in assembling and examining evidence and coming to a conclusion which takes all the evidence into account. He is rather writing the panegyric of a saint, stressing in particular his holy way of life and the supernatural phenomena which attended it. Sometimes the aim is didactic, sometimes more crudely financial. What he praises will depend on his audience and on the society for which he is writing. Hagiography will thus give reliable contemporary evidence about the aspirations and culture of a people.[3]

Also David Rollason in his work *The Mildrith Legend: A Study in Early Medieval Hagiography in England* has noted in regard to hagiography, history, and the study of medieval society:

> Far from being primarily a devotional genre out of touch with life beyond the monastery's or church's walls, hagiography appears as intimately concerned with wider attitudes and aspirations, a living genre which in some cases may have as much claim to have been in touch with the society in which it was written or read as medieval historical writing itself. The cults too appear as intimately connected with that society, although in a subsidiary role.[4]

Saints' Lives thus present incredible richness and an untapped wealth of information for historians studying early medieval society.

TWO SAMPLE LIVES

At the outset it might be useful to provide a preliminary sketch or brief synopsis of the lives of two women saints: one who lived at the beginning and the other at the end of the period under consideration in this study. It is hoped that this exercise will help the reader to make sense of how the disparate details related in this and the following chapters fit together to form the life of a *mulier sancta*.

The first case study is that of the famous sixth-century Frankish saint Radegund (ca. 520/25–87). The life of this queen-saint is one of the best documented of this early period. Two contemporary saints' Lives, as well as Gregory of Tours' *History of the Franks* and the

Glory of the Confessors, describe the events of Radegund's life as royal ascetic and model nun.[5] These works, then, represent the Merovingian cultural tradition of hagiography.

Radegund was the daughter of Bertechar, king of Thuringia. Captured by the Franks during a war with the Thuringians, Radegund and her young brother were taken as prisoners by Clothar and brought up at the royal court at Athies in the Vermandois (Picardy). There she received her early education. Already as a child Radegund showed a predilection toward saintly activities. She discussed with the other children her desire to become a martyr if the opportunity presented itself. At approximately eighteen years of age, learning of her impending marriage to the king, Radegund fled from the court with a few companions. She was captured, however, and married to King Clothar (who was in his forties and had been married several times before). During her marriage, Radegund led a double life: that of a queen and a nun manqué. She practiced a life of extreme austerities and self-mortification: under her royal garments she wore a haircloth; she fasted and spent her nights outside of the royal bed prostrated in prayer on the cold stone floor. Charitable activities occupied a major part of Radegund's life as a queen-saint. She built a hospital at Athies for indigent women and personally cared for the sick and poor. Around the year 550, Clothar had Radegund's brother, of whom she was very fond, killed. Shortly thereafter the queen, probably in her late twenties and no longer able to tolerate the marriage, left her husband. She went to Noyon and begged Bishop Medard to give her the veil and consecrate her as a deaconess. After leaving Noyon she went on pilgrimage to Tours where she visited the tomb of St. Martin; she also established in this city a monastery for men. She then went to Candes where St. Martin had died. At each of these places she divested herself of her royal garments and jewels, which were divided among the churches and the poor. She then went to live on her dower or *morgengabe* lands at Saix. Here she followed an ascetic life devoted to charity: dispensing alms, caring for the sick and lepers. After learning that the king wanted to take her back as his wife, Radegund fled from Saix to Poitiers. It was in Poitiers that she founded a monastery for women, originally dedicated to Notre Dame. (After the acquisition of her prized relic of the Holy Cross brought from Constantinople, the name of the monastery was changed to Ste-Croix.) Under Radegund's influence as royal founder/patron, spiritual leader, and charismatic figure, Ste-Croix became a very popular monastic foundation. Although retired from the court, and formally adopting the Rule of Caesarius of Arles and the cloistered life of a nun at Ste-Croix, Radegund was not cut off from the world; rather, she maintained an active involvement

and interest in the activities and politics of the period. She was especially dedicated to peacemaking efforts in the Frankish kingdom. During her years in the monastery, Radegund regularly retired to a private
cell where she multiplied her austerities, which included self-inflicted
bodily tortures. She also experienced a number of visions and brought
about several miracles; even during her lifetime, she was recognized as
a saint. At her death in 587, at the age of approximately sixty-two to
sixty-seven years, there were some two hundred nuns in Radegund's
community. Her style of piety or program of sanctity as queen and
monastic saint was ascetic and antimatrimonial, with an emphasis on
such themes as the *militia spiritualis, regina ancilla,* and *"martyre non
sanglant."* Her Life would provide an important exemplum for royal
and aristocratic women of the following centuries and would become
a model, with different inflections, for, among others, the Lives of
Sts. Balthild, Mathilda, and Margaret of Scotland.

The second case study concerns another queen-saint, Margaret of
Scotland (1046–93), who lived at the end of the period under consideration in this study. Her remarkable biography was written by her
contemporary and confidant, Turgot, prior of Durham and bishop
of St. Andrews.[6] One of the last survivors of Anglo-Saxon royalty,
Margaret was the daughter of Edward the Atheling and the granddaughter of King Edmund Ironside. While England was under the rule
of Danish Kings, Edward the Atheling and his family found asylum
in Hungary, at the king-saint Stephen's newly converted court, and it
was here that Margaret spent her early years. In 1057 Margaret and
her family were recalled to Britain and spent some nine years at the
court of Edward the Confessor. With the Norman Conquest, this
Anglo-Saxon princess, along with her mother, sister, and brother, fled
for safety to the court of the king of Scotland. In 1070 Margaret married Malcolm III, king of Scotland, and from this marriage, which was
described as successful and happy, there came six sons and two
daughters.

In her public role as queen, Margaret assumed a prominent, truly
collaborative position as partner and indispensable counselor of the
king. She was involved in improving the image and honor of the royal
court. She encouraged the business of foreign merchants. She played a
significant role as a supporter of Gregorian reform policies in Scotland
and occupied a prominent position in the reform councils of the period. The queen was also active as a generous patron of the Church
and founded or restored a number of monasteries and churches. Dunfermline, one of her major foundations, was built to serve as a mausoleum for the royal family. In her role as queen, one of her main tasks
involved dispensing charity to the poor, and she was also passionately

occupied with freeing Anglo-Saxon captives. Another of her projects was providing hostels, as well as ships, for pilgrims traveling to
St. Andrews.

While her public role as queen and generous donor afforded Margaret much visibility in the spheres of politics and religion, the saint
was also recognized for her strong and positive influence as wife and
mother. Unlike Radegund, Margaret did not retire to a monastery
and become a nun, but lived out her life in the secular world, at court.
King Malcolm was very much under the queen's influence and "what
she rejected, he rejected . . . what she loved, he for love of her loved
too."[7] While Margaret was well educated and an avid collector of
books, Malcolm, on the other hand, could not read. In order to please
his wife, the king would have her favorite books covered with gold,
silver, and jewels. Margaret was also very much preoccupied with her
children and concerned with their proper upbringing and education.
And it is under her influence that the Scottish court during this period
has been described as "something of a nursery of saints."[8] The careers
of a number of her children reflect the continuity of Margaret's interest in the conduct of church life as well as her good works and practical piety. While publicly adhering to the requirements of the life of the
court, Margaret, in the tradition of St. Radegund, and influenced by
the Benedictine Rule, followed a quasi-monastic life of humility and
austerity, marked by long fasts and vigils.[9] Shortly before her death in
1093, worn out by excessive fasting, as well as a long illness filled with
suffering, Margaret learned that both her husband and son had been
killed in a military expedition against William Rufus. The queen was
then buried alongside of her husband in her beloved church at Dunfermline. Her *vita,* in contrast to that of Radegund, emphasizes the
conjugal comportment of the queen as one of the main factors of her
fama sanctitatis.

After these brief outlines of the lives of two major women saints of
this period, it is necessary to take a look at the *vitae* collectively, their
purpose, and their audience.

THE *VITA*: PURPOSE AND AUDIENCE

In *Sociologie et canonisations,* Pierre Delooz emphasizes the fact that
one is only a saint "for others" as well as "by others." That is, the
value of sanctity is first of all situated in the collective memory of the
community; it is the saintly reputation recognized by one's peers that
is of primary importance. Second, one becomes a recognized saint
only as a result of the energetic expression of this opinion, namely
through a pressure group which formulates a public cult.[10] Therefore,

in the process of the "making of a saint," it was of primary importance to procure a worthy propagandist or biographer to redact a *vita*
of the candidate for sainthood, for it was this dossier of the holy dead
that became the main official vehicle by which the saintly reputation
was transformed into a public cult. Over time, the *vita* also served the
very important historical function of keeping alive the memory of the
saint and inspired among the faithful an expectation of the saint's
miraculous power. As noted by Thomas Head in his work *Hagiography and the Cult of Saints: The Diocese of Orleans, 800–1200:*

> Without the memory of the saints contained in stories—both
> those stories which the authors 'set down on pages' and the
> oral traditions on which they depended—the relics would have
> been simply bones and ashes buried in the earth rather than
> holy persons alive in the community. Their audience used the
> stories told about the saints to interpret the relics of those
> saints. Miracles were crucial to this hermeneutic interaction of
> relics, text, and audience. As evidence of a close relationship
> with God, they served as an authentication of sanctity.[11]

The alleged purpose or expressed end of all saints' Lives was, however, pastoral and didactic: to edify the faithful, to teach Christian
virtue, and strengthen Christian resolve. According to Delehaye, "To
be strictly hagiographical the document must be of a religious character and aim at edification. The term, then, must be confined to writings inspired by religious devotion to the saints and intended to increase that devotion."[12] The Church hoped that through the use of
exempla, or models of saintly behavior, the faithful might modify
their behavior or bring about "conversions" in their own spiritually
deficient lives.[13] Many of the saints' Lives specifically mention edification as their primary purpose. The prologue of the *vita* of St. Gertrude
of Nivelles noted that "we believe and we hold with steadfast and in-
violate faith, that it will help those who seek the road to the heavenly
fatherland and utterly to relinquish earthly profit in order to win the
eternal prize, if I strive to record in writing or preaching some small
part of the lives and conduct of holy men and women, virgins of
Christ, for the advancement and edification of my neighbors. Thus the
examples of holy virgins, men and women, who came before us may
illuminate the darkness in our hearts with the flames of charity and the
heat of holy compunction."[14] The prologue to the Life of St. Balthild
stressed that, rather than being addressed primarily to scholars, the
vita, through its "plain and open style" was to be accessible for the
advancement and edification of the many.[15] In his *vita* of St. Aldegund,
Hucbald of St. Amand wrote, "Behold, here you have the deeds of

a saint which you have read or heard piously that you may imitate
them. . . . Therefore, imitate what you have read. Live as she lived.
Walk as she walked and there is no doubt that you will go where she
has gone with the help of the Creator who works His mercy in His
saints and gives virtue and fortitude to His people." [16] Similarly, the
prologue to the Life of St. Waldetrude concluded, "so we draw examples from the lives of holy men and women who preceded us on
this road, led by grace, and left their own footprints behind. Thus all
that may have seemed impossible to them has been made easy to the
hopeful who can see how others made the same crossing. Often, the
saint's example excites the hearts of the sluggish and torpid to love of
God and desire for eternal life better than preaching." [17] The author of
the Life of St. Leoba also mentioned the instructive purpose of his
work: this *vita* was dedicated to Hadamout in order that she "may
have something to read with pleasure and imitate with profit." [18] At
the end of the letter of dedication to the *vita* of Adelaide, the author,
Odilo, abbot of Cluny, noted that the work was to be a *speculum reginarum,* a mirror or model of conduct for queens and princesses.
Through his description of the empress's exalted deeds, they were to
follow the saint on roads of honesty; moreover, the work was to serve
as an exemplum for queens or sovereigns especially dedicated to the
cura domestica.[19] The *vita* of St. Margaret of Scotland was commissioned by and dedicated to Margaret's daughter, Queen Matilda II
(wife of Henry I of England). The author, Turgot, addressed her, saying "[you desired] not only to hear of the life of the queen your
mother, who ever aspired to the realm of angels, but also to have it
constantly before you in writing: so that, although you knew but little
your mother's face, you may have more fully the knowledge of her
virtues." [20] As Lois Huneycutt has observed, the Life of St. Margaret
was a didactic work, a "teaching text," and it served as an exemplum
or model: it provided ideals of queenly deportment, a pattern of behavior for Matilda to follow.[21] Honeycutt notes:

> The ideals presented in the *Life of St Margaret* and reinforced
> in the other literature written for Matilda were reflected in her
> behaviour. And, although this behaviour could have arisen
> independently of the *vita,* Matilda's clear interest in her ances-
> try makes it likely that she did indeed commission and read the
> biography, then patterned herself after the mother presented
> so compellingly in the *Life.*[22]

Although the encouragement of moral or spiritual improvement was
the expressed purpose of hagiographic literature, *vitae* were in fact often written with more pragmatic, self-serving political and economic

ends in mind. Some were inspired or commissioned by the great families of the period and served to legitimize and to exalt their noble lineage, reputations, or influence. (These *vitae* glorified a very prominent type of early medieval saint called the *Adelsheilige* by the German historians.)[23] Many of the Lives reflected institutional concerns. They focused on the religious communities who possessed the relics of the saint and had placed themselves under the saint's special patronage.[24] We can see, for example, a combination of these traditions in the Ottonian Lives of St. Mathilda. As noted by Corbet, the *Vita Mahthildis antiquior* was written to glorify and bring prestige to Otto II, while the second redaction, the *Vita Mahthildis posterior,* was composed to glorify Henry the Young and to tie his fame to the ascendency of the new king, Henry of Bavaria, grandson of Henry the Young. Nevertheless, the subtext of these works was to remind the ruling prince of Otto I's promise to his mother that her favored foundation, the monastery of Nordhausen and its possessions, were always to benefit from imperial protection.[25]

However, in general, the *vitae* served as propaganda for the promotion or expansion of the cult of the saint and the exaltation of a religious center. Thus, through the *fama sanctitatis,* or celebrity of the saint and her miracles (as advertised by the *vita*), churchmen and churchwomen hoped to inspire devotion and to attract crowds of pilgrims, material donations, and special privileges to the monasteries or sanctuaries which "owned" and guarded the precious remains of the holy dead.[26] This program of persuasion was of primary importance for churches and monasteries: in some cases their very survival depended on their ability to win over the faithful to believe in the superiority and special efficacy of their saint.

As a genre of didactic literature, the *vita* aimed at universal appeal: it addressed a very broad medieval audience composed of all Christians and especially those viewed as sinners. In their attempt to appeal to all social classes, the authors of the Lives often portrayed their protagonists, who at this time were invariably recruited from the nobility, as classless, "socially amphibious" individuals.[27] Through a certain noblesse oblige, the saints accommodated themselves to the social diversity of the faithful. During their lifetime they came into contact with the local serfs, peasants, and townspeople, as well as the nobility and royalty. And after their death—now as a citizens of both worlds—they remained faithful to their same earthly constituency. With their enhanced spiritual *potentia,* the holy dead continued to assist their supporters through the working of miracles; they served as patrons and protectors of their monasteries—along with their properties and rights—as well as heavenly interceders for their souls.

Despite ideological attempts at universal appeal, many of the cults of the holy dead remained rather localized, reflecting local roots and regional interests. This seems to have been especially true for female saints, who frequently had limited posthumous cults.[28] Christine Fell has shown, for example, that the cult of St. Hild/Hilda of Whitby was geographically and chronologically restricted. Her fame was limited largely to her own generation and her posthumous cult remained very localized. Fell observes: "It would be foolish to expect any kind of equation between magnitude of a saint's cult and the magnitude of a saint's achievement, but in the case of St Hild they seem almost to be in inverse proportion."[29] The Belgian *Vita Berlindis* appears to have been written for the parishioners of Meerbeke, the burial place of St. Berlinde. The hagiographer specifically notes that "the saints must be particularly honored where they are buried."[30] In this context, the favors or miracles of the holy dead remained rather specific and localized. They used their special intercessory powers, for example, to quiet local storms, extinguish fires, free the area of drought, famine, or pestilence; or they promoted bountiful crops and healthy livestock. Thus the audience of the saint's Life was often geographically limited to a provincial or even microregional level. Many of the *vitae* seem to have been tied to the zone of influence of the monastery in which they were written; others were directed to the inhabitants of the specific locale or parish where the saint was buried.

Further distinctions were sometimes made in regard to the audience of the saint's Life. The early Lives were generally written in Latin and therefore required a certain level of education and proficiency in Latin among the listeners or readers in order to comprehend these works.[31] It also appears that the material of some of the *vitae* was recognized as much too subtle for the appreciation of the masses: it incorporated formal theology and dogma that supposed a level of sophistication, a capacity of abstraction too complex for a general audience. Therefore, many of the saints' Lives seem to have been especially directed to the more restricted interests and needs of religious specialists and the educated elite, namely churchmen and churchwomen.[32] Since the majority of female saints for this period acceded to sanctity by means of the cloister—specifically as founders/patrons and abbesses of monasteries—many of the *vitae* were clearly intended for religious communities. These Lives were often directed to the abbess or sisterhood of a particular saint's community, who, in turn, were responsible for promoting her cult. In some cases a number of *vitae* of female saints were condensed, collected, and then incorporated as exempla in a larger didactic work. This was the case, for example, of Aldhelm's famous prose treatise, *De virginitate* (ca. 680). This work, which contains the condensed lives of some twenty-two virginal female saints and twenty-nine virginal male saints, was addressed to Abbess Hildelith and a number of her nuns at the double monastery of Barking.[33]

Further evidence of the makeup of the audience of the *vitae* can be found in the content of these Lives. In spite of their attempts to appeal to all levels of society, in many of the Lives we can see a bias toward a socially elite audience and its values. (This is consistent with the social composition of these early monastic communities.) On the one hand, the *vitae* portray in some detail royal or noble saints as models of *humilitas,* assuming some of the most humble tasks within their convents. These activities would especially endear these highborn women to the lower classes and allow them to identify with them. Radegund, for example, is shown carrying out her weekly chores which entailed hauling firewood, transporting water from the well and distributing it to different basins in the monastery, cleaning and peeling herbs and vegetables, caring for the fire, cooking and serving food, washing dishes, and cleaning the kitchen. We also learn that Radegund made candles and spun wool: she swept the monastery's corridors, and washed and mended the linens. During Lent she ground fresh flour, which was then distributed to local religious communities, perhaps for altar breads.[34] According to her *vitae,* Radegund loved to wash the feet of her sisters, and also, when all the nuns were sleeping, she cleaned their shoes—rubbing them with oil and then returning them to each cell.[35] Apparently not repelled by the most repugnant of household tasks, the saintly queen was said to clean the latrines and carry out the fetid excrement herself.[36] However, coinciding with this image of humility, in which the *regina ancilla* assumed a certain sympathy or identification with common women and their tasks, there was also an underlying assumption of hierarchy and social propriety which existed within these early monasteries. We learn, for example, that after Radegund's death a certain servant woman named Vinoberga had the audacity to sit on the saint-queen's special throne (*cathedra*). Radegund was then said to have reached down from heaven to exact swift punishment on this woman for her extremely unseemly or improper behavior.[37]

Another prominent case which underscores this bias toward the values of a socially elite audience can be found in the twelfth-century Life of the royal Anglo-Saxon saint Edburga of Winchester.[38] Following in the tradition of Christ's ministry of washing the feet of his disciples, Edburga also exhibited this virtue of *humilitas* through secretly cleaning the shoes of her sisters. Like Radegund, every night Edburga would secretly carry off the nuns' shoes in order to clean them and soften them with oil. When she was ultimately identified as the one responsible for this shoe-cleaning service, the royal saint was brought before the community. Instead of winning praise for her humble service to the nuns, she was severely reprimanded. The community viewed this act as highly inappropriate and beneath her "privileged position": it was a "betrayal of her royal status." "It is unseemly," they said, "for a royal child to bow her neck to such humble service and to set about the work of a common slave; it is harmful to the dignity of her illustrious birth."[39]

Many of these Lives were, then, directed toward a monastic community and had special appeal and relevance to audiences of female religious, as well as noblewomen who followed a life of monastic virtue within the confines of their home. They served to validate certain monastic virtues and religious behavior and lent authority to lives spent in the cloister. In praising monastic spirituality, with its requirements of alienation from the world, humility, harsh asceticism, a fascination with the passion of Christ, readiness for martyrdom, the cultivation of mystical experiences, and so forth, these *vitae* provided spiritual lessons or models of the holy life for nuns (or nuns manqué) to imitate.[40]

As guides for female religious, the Lives of the *mulieres sanctae* formed an integral part of women's monastic experience. These biographies of edification, for example, were recited in their monastic choirs; they were read to the nuns in chapter and in the refectory during their meals as well as in their workrooms while they occupied themselves with various manual tasks such as weaving, sewing, and embroidery. The Lives of saints were also available for private reading and meditation by the nuns. Female religious wrote, transcribed, and illuminated the *vitae* in their monastic *scriptoria*. The especially dramatic events of the saints' lives, or saints accompanied by their special symbols, were visually captured in the iconographic programs of the monastery which included sculptural cycles, wall paintings, tapestries, liturgical vestments, altarcloths, and reliquaries.

The *vitae* were incorporated into the monastic liturgy: prayers, hymns, and readings extolled the saints' virtues. Sermons focused on the lives of popular saints. The holy dead were catalogued in church calendars, legendaries, and martyrologies. The *vita* assumed special importance on the anniversary of the saint or her *dies natalis* (that is, on the day of her death) when the extraordinary acts of her life as well as posthumous miracles provided the focal point of the celebration. Aldhelm, for example, notes in his *De virginitate* that the "fame and uniqueness" of the miracles of the virgin saints Anatolia and Victoria "spread far and wide through all the corners of the world so long as their names are read out from the written characters (of service books)

from the pulpit of the Church, when Catholic (Christians), in the re-
volving circle of the year celebrate their birthdays."[41]

HAGIOGRAPHERS AND THEIR CRAFT

Although there has been severe scholarly criticism of hagiography and
the authors of the early medieval saints' Lives, many of these authors
were in fact rather well-informed biographers. It appears that a good
number of the *vitae* were actually compiled by contemporaries or
near contemporaries of the candidate for sainthood. Writing as eye-
witnesses to many of the events ("iuxta id quod vidimus" or "iuxta id
quod vidimus vel per idoneos testes audivimus"), they have left us numerous careful works describing female saints and their milieu.[42] In
general, the closer the *vita* can be dated to the saint's own lifetime, the
greater our chances for retrieving reliable information about the saint
and her cult; stories introduced years after the saints' death are less
likely to contain accurate social detail, which can be corroborated by
other sources, than are contemporary Lives. Many of the *vitae* were
redacted shortly after the saint's death; others are of an uncertain date
and appear to be essentially retrospective works.[43] In their consistency
with other sources of the period, some of these retrospective Lives appear to have been written only a few generations after the death of the
saint; others can be dated a century or more after the saint's death.

Although some of these legends of ancient saints are total fabri-
cations based on an amalgamation of popular hagiographic *topoi,*
among the later versions of saints' Lives, one frequently finds revisions
or sometimes amplified editions of older *vitae,* which in many cases
appear to remain rather faithful to the original texts. For example,
during the Carolingian period and that of the French and English reforms or revivals of the tenth and eleventh century, there occurred a
renewal in the veneration of saints, and with this resurgence came
a proliferation of saints' Lives produced in monastic *scriptoria.* It
appears that in rewriting the *vitae,* many of these hagiographers did
not alter the basic information of the sources but were "enterprising
textual editors" concerned with stylistic changes and shifts in tastes in
hagiographical material. Some added new materials: they provided
more elaborate description, adding *topoi* to flesh out portraits as
well as classical and scriptural allusions.[44] Jo Ann McNamara has
argued in regard to the tradition of revised *vitae* produced by Carolingian scribes: "In most cases, their contributions chiefly consist of
repairing barbarities of literary style and embellishing the original
with pious reflections and scriptural citations designed to heighten the

didactic value of the story."[45] As Patrick Corbet has noted in his study
Les Saints ottoniens, the second *vita* of St. Mathilda (written between
1002 and 1014) remained essentially faithful to the *Vita Mahthildis
antiquior* of 974. It retained the same themes and a similar order. Although one chapter was cut, the second version was more important
for its additions than its deletions. Essentially most chapters were
amplified or embellished in the second *vita:* while the ancient *vita*
consisted of some 350 lines, or seven pages, the second Life had
900 lines, or eighteen pages. Greater attention was given to details
which clarified and added precision to the original redaction. According to Corbet, the initial facts were adapted, spiritualized, and rationalized. The roughness of the first *vita* was ameliorated by more
elegant and rhymed prose as well as a more careful and smooth composition. And although the second biography was faithful to the spirit
of the first, the basic tone and encoded message or political inflection
shifted in the second redaction from the glorification of Otto II to that
of Henry the Young.[46] Goscelin, who rewrote the Life of St. Mildred/
Mildrith, notes in his prologue to the *vita* that his account was based
on an earlier version of the saint's life and miracles. According to
David Rollason, this redaction was based on a mid-eleventh-century
version which Goscelin regarded as stylistically deficient. Goscelin
observed that Mildrith's glories were like "the sun behind a cloud,
gold in the earth, a jewel besmeared with mud, a nut in its shell, wheat
encased in chaff."[47] While Goscelin kept the same details and the
narrative order of the earlier Life, he clarified the style and the Latin,
added scriptural and classical references, and brought to the work "a
touch of grandeur."[48]

Nevertheless, while we find a renewed interest in the composition
of saints' Lives during, for example, the Carolingian and Cluniac reforms, it is important to note that a disproportionately small part of
this work focused on women saints. The interest in promoting new or
contemporary women saints during this period appears to have been
minimal. As Julia M. H. Smith has argued, "the major distinctions between hagiography about men and about women in the Carolingian
period concern not so much types of text as number and distribution.
In contrast to the many hundreds of lives or miracle-books concerning
male saints, only a handful have women as their subject and they constitute a small fraction of the total. . . . In Carolingian Aquitaine,
Provence, and still more so in Italy, saints' lives concerned primarily
bishops, occasionally monks, but certainly never women. To locate
women's *vitae* composed in the Carolingian period, we have to turn to
a small part of the area beyond the Loire and the Alps. The churches

in which lives of women were composed mostly cluster in the zone
between the Seine and the Meuse, but with outliers from the Rhineland
and further north from the areas of missionary activity in Saxony."[49]

The process involved in the selection of the hagiographer, the collection of information, and the actual redaction of the *vita* is of special
interest to the historian. It appears that few authors of *vitae* began
their holy biographies without having their "hand forced" or without receiving a formal commission to undertake the work.[50] The
process usually began when those involved in the promotion of the
saint and the development of her cult center (this could be the abbess
or abbot of a monastery, the whole community, or the local bishop)
approached a monk, cleric, or nun to write the *vita* of their candidate
for sanctity. We learn, for example, that the *vitae* of Saints Radegund,
Gertrude, Rictrude, Austreberta, Aldegund, Adelheide, and a number
of others, were written at the request of the abbess or monastic community of the saint. The Life of St. Gertrude, for example, was commissioned by Abbess Dominica, the third abbess of Nivelles. The *vita*
was then written by one of the Irish priests of the double community
of Nivelles. As a contemporary of the saint, he presents himself as a
well-informed eyewitness to the events which he describes, "iuxta id
quod vidimus."[51] The first of six Lives of St. Aldegund, abbess of
Maubeuge (d. 684), was also written shortly after the saint's death.
Again, the author appears to have been a contemporary of the saint
and was present at many of the events he describes, including her
funeral, at which he assisted. It has been suggested that the author was
perhaps a monk at Nivelles and was commissioned by his community
to write the *vita*. (This life is also of special interest since it incorporates Aldegund's visions, which the saint had originally related to
Abbot Subnius of Nivelles and to another anonymous brother.)[52] The
prologue to the Life of St. Austreberta, abbess of Pavilly (650–703),
also notes the process involved in commissioning a *vita*. The author,
a contemporary of the saint, and perhaps a nun, monk, or chaplain
attached to Pavilly, or a monk from the nearby brother-house of Jumièges, begins the prologue by making excuses for the delay in writing
the Life: "Venerable mother Julia, disciple of Christ: for a long time
now you have begged me with all your might, in importunate prayers,
to try with my pen to compose the most blessed virgin Austreberta's
life so that the publicity might bring that bright gem to a wider audience. Often have you urged this upon me, admonishing me and accus-
ing me of torpor and idleness. . . ."[53]

The abbess or community, then, usually approached someone of
their own monastery or of an affiliated institution who was preferably

both a writer and an acquaintance of the candidate for sainthood to compose the *vita*. However, if for some reason there was no one believed to be competent to undertake this task within one's own community, it was necessary to solicit a writer from another house or from the "outside." [54] Therefore, in some cases, professional hagiographers were sought out and commissioned to write the prescribed Life. The primary *vita* of St. Rictrude and the fourth Life of St. Aldegund, for example, were commissioned by their communities to be written by Hucbald, a monk of Saint Amand. At this time he was apparently "l'hagiographe à la mode" of their region.[55] It is interesting to note that sometimes the *vitae* commissioned of "strangers" from outside of the community did not prove to be entirely successful in the long run. Such was the situation, for example, at Liessies, where the canons solicited a monk of Waulsort to redact a Life of St. Hiltrude. The chroniclers of Liessies later came to regret this choice of biographer, for, although he had been adept in hagiographic literature, he was ignorant of the abbey's unique history.[56]

Delehaye has noted that hagiography from its beginnings was an impersonal literature—the product of anonymous authors.[57] Although the majority of authors remain in the anonymous tradition, a good number of hagiographers of this period can in fact be identified. From a collective study of some 1,130 saints' Lives catalogued in the *Bibliotheca hagiographica latina* for the years 500–1100, we know the names of the redactors of approximately 41 percent of the male *vitae* and 39 percent of the female *vitae*. It is indeed significant to note that with the exception of two *vitae*, all of the Lives of women saints with identifiable authors (found in the *Bibliotheca hagiographica latina*) were written by men. Also, as catalogued by this collection, only two of the Lives of male saints have been officially attributed to female authors.[58] Hrotswitha of Gandersheim, in her *Gesta Ottonis* (ca. 965–68; not strictly in the hagiographic genre but recording the lives of women saints), provides biographical information on Mathilda, Edith, and Adelaide. In addition, St. Oda and her daughter St. Hathumoda are the heroes of Hrothswitha's poem on the origins of the monastery of Gandersheim, *Primordia coenobii Gandeshemensis,* written in 970.[59] Other collections of saints' Lives have mentioned a few additional women hagiographers. These female authors redacted the Lives of male saints who were either the founders or patron saints of their monastic communities. For example, St. Cecile, a seventh-century abbess of Remiremont, is credited with writing the Life of St. Romaric; St. Gebetrude, a late seventh-century abbess of Remiremont, wrote the Life of St. Adelph; and Leutwithe, abbess of Auchy (eighth century?), rewrote the life of St. Silvin, in which she notes that she corrected the previous author's errors in language and style while at the same time preserving the sense of detail.[60]

Thus, despite the high level of education and literary competency of female religious during this early period, it seems that in many cases nuns were relegated to the function of copyists, and only infrequently were they designated as authors of *vitae*.[61] It would seem reasonable that the authorship of female saints' Lives (as was the case for male *vitae*) would have been assigned to those closest to the holy candidate and most knowledgeable in regard to her attributes and activities, namely, female members of the saint's community. Nevertheless, it was apparently traditional for churchmen to assume the redaction of the "official" *vitae* of the female candidates for sainthood. It appears that this practice can already be found among the early Church Fathers. The letters of St. Jerome, *The Lausiac History* by Palladius, and *The Dialogues* of Pope Gregory the Great all contain early biographies of female saints.[62] It is of interest to note that in St. Odilo of Cluny's contemporary *vita* of the empress-saint Adelaide (d. 999), he comments on this tradition of learned men assuming the responsibility of recording the lives of holy women. He specifically refers to St. Jerome and his descriptions of the holy acts of Paula, Eustochium, Marcella, Melania, Fabiola, and others. Odilo comments that if Jerome had been a contemporary of the empress, he would also have consecrated works in praise of Adelaide. Odilo's own *vita* is then influenced by Jerome's program of female sanctity and particularly his epitaph of St. Paula.[63]

Therefore, in general, the authors of female saints' Lives of ca. 500–1100 appear to have been recruited from among educated churchmen. While the majority of the *vitae* were products of monastic hagiography, a few of the Lives were written by popes, bishops, priests, and chaplains. It seems quite possible that the preference for churchmen as propagandists of female saints might have been perceived as politically and pragmatically expedient by communities wishing to promote their candidate's cult; that is, the close association of churchmen (sometimes prominent figures in the church hierarchy) with the *mulieres sanctae* and their *vitae* no doubt provided a greater authoritativeness or lent additional credence, as well as enhanced visibility, to the new saints' cults. It served perhaps as a type of validation of female sanctity by the Church and its male hierarchy. Often faced with the skepticism and contempt of *detractores* toward the holy dead (and this seems to have been especially problematic in regard to the *mulieres sanctae* and their cults), hagiographers had to rigorously defend the extraordinary acts and miracles of their saints.[64] The refutation of perceived objections or the bolstering of saintly credentials was perhaps believed to be strengthened by a male-authored defense of the holy dead as compared to the testimony, for example, of a "simple nun."

Stephanie Hollis, in her important work *Anglo-Saxon Women and the Church* has argued that "the lack of early female saints Lives written by women is not a reflection of the general level of their literary skill; rather, even if female religious did not believe that an abbess worthy of written commemoration was, by definition, one whose Life was written by a man, interest in the Lives written by women was insufficient to generate enough copies to ensure their survival." That is, according to Hollis, the *vitae* written by women's communities which celebrated the lives of their founding abbesses "generally held so little interest for the world beyond their monasteries that they failed to gain sufficient currency to ensure their preservation; unless the relics chanced to pass into the possession of monks." [65] This tendency was no doubt further exacerbated by a lack of continuity in memory and tradition frequently associated with many of these female communities. As a result of the destruction and dislocation caused by the invasions, as well as the policies of the reform movements which favored male ecclesiastics over female religious, a substantial number of these monasteries which had formerly been occupied by women were reestablished for monks. In those instances in which the cults of women saints were now dependent on the vested interests of male ecclesiastics, a cleric would be hired to redact a new Life. Frequently the new *vitae* were based on these earlier works, now lost or forgotten, which had been written by women. This was the case, for example, of Goscelin's late eleventh-century Lives of Anglo-Saxon women saints.[66]

Although it appears from our survey of *vitae* with identifiable authors that it was traditional for churchmen to compose the Lives of women saints, a closer study of historical context and internal clues of the *vitae* might in fact reveal an increased possibility of female authorship. A fascinating case in point concerns the discovery by B. Bischoff of the identity of the anonymous author of the Lives of Saints Willibald and Wynnebald. Through the interpretation of a cryptogram which had been placed between these two *vitae* in an early manuscript, Bischoff was able to identify Huneberc, an Anglo-Saxon nun of Heidenheim, as the author.[67] Although in the past scholars assumed that anonymous authors of saints' Lives were male ecclesiastics and therefore searched for textual indicators which might help to identify them with certain monasteries or positions within the Church, these sources need to be reexamined with the underlying assumption that "anonymous" could in fact also be a woman, especially a female religious. Cases in which there are a series of several *vitae* commissioned over time for the same saint could prove to be especially important

in the discovery of female authorship. It is in this context that Janet
Nelson, for example, has come to the conclusion that the early
"*A*" *vita* of St. Balthild, originally attributed to a monk, was in fact
redacted by a nun of Balthild's monastery of Chelles and commissioned by a community of monks—perhaps that of Corbie.[68] Corbet
has also noted that the first Life of the Ottonian queen-saint Mathilda
was redacted in the queen's monastic foundation of Nordhausen by an
anonymous biographer. He argues that nothing indicates that this author was a cleric of the community, rather he is inclined to attribute
the *vita* to a female author, specifically Abbess Richburge of Nordhausen. Richburge was the faithful servant of the queen, eyewitness
to the events of her life, as well as frequently cited in a sympathetic
manner in the biography, and therefore appears to be the logical biographer of the saint.[69]

DOSSIERS OF THE HOLY DEAD: PATTERNS AND CONTENT

While many of the *vitae* conform to a general pattern or schema, there
still remains a great deal of variety in these spiritual biographies. In
general, the early hagiographers wrote in Latin and in prose. However, many vernacular saints' Lives date to the ninth through eleventh
centuries. For example, in Ireland the early *vitae* of the seventh and
eighth centuries were written in Latin. Beginning in the eighth and
ninth centuries the Latin literary tradition gave way to the use of the
Irish language.[70] One of the especially popular works in the vernacular was Aelfric's *Lives of Saints,* written in Anglo-Saxon, ca. 996.[71]
These early Lives in the vernacular were rather widespread, but the
use of vernacular in the writing of *vitae* became especially popular in
the twelfth century. In a few cases, a second life, based on the first,
would be written in meter: *vita metrica* or *rhythmica*. Aldhelm, for example, followed his prose work *De Virginitate* with a version in verse.
It has been suggested that the metrical form of the *vita* was perhaps
used in a less official or more popular context. It appears to have
served pedagogical purposes, specifically as exercises for young students.[72] It seems that this form was also used for purposes of private
meditation and for acquiring more profound or deeper meanings from
these Lives. Alcuin, for example, notes the different uses of his three
versions of the Life of St. Willibrord: his prose Life was to be read out
publicly to the monks in church, his verse Life was for meditating on
"in the privacy of one's room," while the homily was for preaching to
the people.[73]

Many of the saints' Lives of this period begin with a prologue
which is particularly valuable for historians. Although it incorporates

formulae and stereotypic language, the prologue nonetheless places the *vita* in the political and religious context of the age. It sometimes reveals the identity of the author, the commissioner(s) of the *vita,* and to whom the work was dedicated. In the prologue the biographer also attempts to bolster the credibility of the *vita* by carefully identifying the various sources of information. The alleged purpose of the *vita* and protestations of incompetence on the part of the author are also found in the prologue.[74]

In the hagiographers' attempts to scrupulously identify their sources of information, the prologues of some of these Lives are of special interest to historians. As noted, in the "naming of sources" the authors intended to provide unassailable proof to the skeptics of the validity of the virtues and supernatural acts of their protagonists.[75] In this context Susan Ridyard argues that "the purpose of this literary device was the establishment of authority by appeal to witness: it was among the most common hagiographical topoi"; therefore, both the written and oral sources cited by these hagiographers must also be handled with care.[76]

It appears from the prologues that the hagiographers generally relied on a combination of sources—written and oral—in the redaction of their *vitae.* The monk Rudolf, in his Life of St. Leoba (written ca. 836), provides us with wonderful detail on the procedure of collecting material for his *vita* as well as his specific sources of information. He laments that

> I have been unable to discover all the facts of her life. I shall therefore recount the few that I have learned from the writings of others, venerable men who heard them from four of her disciples, Agatha, Thecla, Nana and Eoloba. Each one copied them down according to his ability and left them as a memorial to posterity.
>
> One of these, a holy priest and monk named Mago, who died about five years ago, was on friendly terms with these women and during his frequent visits to them used to speak with them about things profitable to the soul. In this way he was able to learn a great deal about her life. He was careful to make short notes of everything he heard, but, unfortunately, what he left was almost unintelligible, because, whilst he was trying to be brief and succinct, he expressed things in such a way as to leave the facts open to misunderstanding and provide no basis for certainty. This happened, in my opinion, because in his eagerness to take down every detail before it escaped his memory he wrote the facts down in a kind of shorthand and

hoped that during his leisure he could put them in order and
make the book more easy for readers to understand. The reason why he left everything in such disorder, jotted down on odd
pieces of parchment, was that he died quite suddenly and had
no time to carry out his purpose.

   . . . I have tried to collect together all the scattered notes
and papers left by the men I have mentioned. The sequence of
events . . . is based on information found in their notes and on
the evidence I have gathered from others by word of mouth. For
there are several religious men still living who can vouch for the
facts mentioned in the documents, since they heard them from
their predecessors, and who can add some others worthy of remembrance. These latter appeared to me suitable for inclusion
in the book and therefore I have combined them with material
from the written notes.

Rudolf then concludes his fascinating discussion of sources, the justification for their use, as well as his underlying preference for male
authority, with the following argument:

For it seems to me that there should be no doubt in the minds
of the faithful about the veracity of the statements made in this
book, since they are shown to be true both by the blameless
character of those who relate them and by the miracles which
are frequently performed at the shrine of the saint.[77]

The Life of St. Rictrude (d. ca. 688) also provides some fascinating
details on the process of gathering information and problems of
hagiographic production. Apparently during the Norman invasions
(ca. 879), the old *vita* or acts of the saint had been destroyed along
with Rictrude's monastery of Marchiennes. At the beginning of the
tenth century (ca. 907), Stephen, bishop of Liège, and the clerks and
nuns of the community then approached Hucbald, a monk of the
neighboring monastery of Saint Amand and a "professional hagiographer," to write a new biography of their patron saint. However, they
were able to provide him only with fragmentary written information
about the saint which corroborated facts found in the oral tradition.
Thus, in the preface to the *vita,* Hucbald carefully relates that some individuals worthy of trust provided guarantees, that is, affirmed to him
under sworn oath, that the oral facts which they recounted conformed
to those of the ancient sources which had disappeared with the Norman pillaging of the monastery.[78]

   As recorded by a variety of sources of the period, many of the *vitae* were in fact lost, misplaced, and destroyed over time. Some perished through fires, flood, or other "natural" disasters. Many, no doubt, fell victim to the devastation wrought by the Viking, Saracen, and Hungarian invasions. The loss of *vitae* of the *mulieres sanctae* seems to have been especially great. In this context Kathleen Hughes noted that in the *Martyrology of Tallaght* at least 119 Irish women saints or groups of women are mentioned; however, the Lives of only four of these women saints are still extant.[79] There is other scattered evidence of lost *vitae* of women saints of this early period. In her study of Hilda of Whitby, Christine Fell has traced evidence for a lost Life of the saint: for example, Bede was supposed to have had access to a copy of Hilda's *vita,* the Old English Martyrology contains information that attests to a lost Life, and the compiler of the Anglo-Saxon Chronicle relied on sources from Whitby that are no longer extant.[80]

We also learn of a few cases where saints' *vitae* were said to have been intentionally destroyed. The author of one of the Lives of St. Withburga explains that his ignorance in regard to the details of her life was based on the fact that an early written source had been destroyed by the inhabitants of Dereham after the loss of their saint. His *vita* was then based on limited evidence found in chronicles and ancient works.[81] Another interesting example concerns St. Rotrude, a ninth-century virgin who was venerated at Andres. According to later sources, nothing was known of St. Rotrude because the original documentation, which provided this information, had been intentionally destroyed by Count Baudoin II. This feudal lord was allegedly afraid that the monastery of Andres, founded in 1084 by Baudoin I (count of Boulogne and Guines), would become too powerful—thanks to the patronage of St. Rotrude. Therefore, fearing that St. Rotrude's monastery would take over all of his property at Andres, he hoped that through the destruction of the Life he would be able to reduce this patron saint's fame and power as well as that of her monastery.[82]

The *vita* of St. Adelheid, first abbess of Vilich (d. ca. 1015), is also of interest in regard to the hagiographer's sources (see plate 2). This Life is one of the very few which has preserved the name of its female author. It was written by Bertha, a noblewoman and nun of the abbey of Vilich, around the year 1057. In the *vita* the author notes her reliance on the oral tradition: she received her source material from the nuns who had been taught by the saint "through instruction and example," and especially from the testimony of Engilrada, the faithful servant woman of Adelheid (*cubicularia fidelis*). As noted by Bertha, Engilrada "has outstripped you (i.e., the nuns) all in age and thus could remember more of the story and better than any of you. She has revealed certain ancestral connections to royalty and many of the family's great honours."[83]

The situation surrounding the writing of the contemporary *vita* of the empress-saint Adelaide (d. 999) appears to have been rather unusual. The Life was written by the empress's friend, Abbot Odilo of Cluny. According to the author, it was based on a narrative of facts which the candidate for sainthood, Adelaide herself, had related to Odilo about the events of her own life.[84]

In addition to providing information on the source material used by the hagiographers in redacting their *vitae,* the prologues or introductory chapters also contain the authors' protestations of humility and incompetence. Because of their "perceived" unfitness for the task, some hagiographers requested that their work be corrected or amended as necessary. Although these protestations of incompetence were essentially formulaic and part of hagiographic convention, one of the *vitae* attributed to a woman writer (i.e., the nun Huneberc), notes the author's awareness of her own scholarly "disabilities" as well as her special vulnerability based on her gender. Perhaps recognizing that the writing of saints' Lives was essentially a masculine prerogative, she was aware of the gender-specific criticism which her work might arouse simply because it was written by a woman. Yet her admission of "weakness" or female frailty could perhaps be read as a pretended or feigned diffidence, for beneath it all there appears to have been a great self-assurance and conviction of purpose.[85] She felt after all "compelled" as a relative of Saints Willibald and Wynnebald to use her talent to keep alive their saintly memory. In the preface to her biography of Saint Willibald, the nun Huneberc writes, in self-deprecating, submissive *topoi:*

> I, an unworthy sister of Saxon origin, last and least in life and
> manners, venture to write for the sake of posterity and present
> to you who are religious and preachers of the Gospel a brief
> account of the early life of the venerable Willibald. Although I
> lack the necessary experience and knowledge *because I am but
> a weak woman,* yet I would like as far as lies in my power, to
> gather together a kind of nosegay of his virtues and give you
> something by which you may remember them. And here I re-
> peat that I am not urged on through presumption to attempt a
> task for which I am so ill fitted. . . . I know that it may seem
> very bold on my part to write this book when there are so
> many holy priests capable of doing better, but as a humble rela-
> tive I would like to record something of their deeds and travels
> for future ages.[86]

The prologue of the Life of St. Austreberta also notes the author's protestations of ignorance and "untutored eloquence," as well as the fear that his or her patron would rewrite or revise the text:

> For I fear lest I suffer what I have heard happened to another author. Someone asked him to write the life and habits of the most reverend Philibert, former abbot of the monastery of Jumièges, and with diligent pen he strove to do so. And when it came to the patron's hand to be read, he despised and mocked it and finally changed it into quite a different sort of text.[87]

Bertha, the author of the *vita* of St. Adelheid of Vilich, adopts the humility *topos* to excuse her rustic style and poor written form. Moreover she notes the need to circulate her *vita* among learned men in order to seek their approval of her work: "Not to presume on my power, but rather in humble reverence have I submitted to him [i.e., Anno, Archbishop of Cologne, to whom the *vita* is dedicated], so that, if later a devoted admirer should bring this life into the light with an elegant style, he would find a truthful record already written. So that your verdict of this work, which cannot support itself on the grace of fulsome words, would not condemn it on the basis of the lowness of my person, upon which in truth all look down, I decided to circulate it among some credible men who are sufficiently knowledgeable in the liberal arts. These men have approved it after repeated reading and have declared it worthy to be seen by the public." [88]

The prologues also frequently contained an expression of the public piety of the communities who commissioned the *vita*, as well as the private piety of the authors. The authors hoped that through the act of writing the saint's Life and therefore establishing a special bond with one's protagonist, they would subsequently win eternal rewards.[89] In addition, the hagiographers asked those who commissioned the Life, or those to whom the Life was dedicated, to intercede for their souls and to pray that their work be successful.

In a few *vitae* of women saints, the prologue was also seen as an appropriate place to discuss issues of gender and sainthood. Gregory of Tours, in his *Life of the Fathers*, argues in the introduction to the life of Blessed Monegund that Christ provided us with *exempla* of saintly behavior which were taken from both genders:

> He gives us as models not only men, but also the lesser sex,
> who fight not feebly, but with a virile strength; he brings into
> his celestial kingdom not only men, who fight as they should,
> but also women, who exert themselves in the struggle with
> success.[90]

Fortunatus, in his prologue to the Life of St. Radegund, for example, writes:

> So great is the munificence of our Redeemer that he multiplies *even among women* brilliant victories, and that despite the weakness of their bodies, He makes them glorious by the courage and elevation of their souls. To these beings who are born so delicate, Christ gives the strength of the faith, and, despite their apparent frailty, He who created them in crowning them for their merits bestows on them the greatest praise, for hidden within a frail external appearance they have guarded the treasures of heaven, and their heart is the abode where the king, Jesus Christ, lives with his riches.[91]

The prologue of the *vita* is then followed by the saint's dossier per se. It is a type of spiritual itinerary, a biographic "ladder of perfection" which documents the saint's pursuit of the *vita perfecta*. Here the hagiographer consciously shapes the life of the saintly hero or "special friend of God" into a coherent whole with the purpose of swaying the readers or listeners to the saint's cause.[92] As consciously calculated works of propaganda, *vitae* were meant to promote their candidate's *auctoritas*, build her reputation, authenticate her history, and provide irrefutable evidence of her sanctity. While many of the *vitae* are arranged in a chronological and progressive order, others follow a less regular form and provide disconnected fragments and sporadic episodes of the saint's life. The organization of the sacred biography was aimed at providing a biographic image and emphasizing or highlighting the virtues, attainments, and special miracles of the saint.[93]

The "typical" Life contains a combination of the following biographical information: the saint's origins, parents, and social status; birth, infancy, and adolescence (often accompanied by a life crisis); the adoption of a religious vocation within the cloister or the decision to pursue a holy life "in the world"; and the advancement and recognition of the candidate for sanctity within her chosen career. The *vita* also provides a catalogue of the saint's virtues, temptations or trials, miracles, visions, and prophecies. Many of the saintly dossiers furnish rather limited descriptions of the saint's early life and activities, and concentrate in some detail on the final illness of the *mulier sancta,* with the climax of the *vita* recounting the premonitions surrounding the saint's death, the death itself, and the burial. (Since the cult of the saint focused on the tomb and the saint's "invisible living presence" within this sacrosanct place, the events surrounding the actual death and burial of the holy dead played an extremely significant role for the propagandist as well as the faithful.)

The dossier of the holy dead is frequently followed by an appendix called the *miracula*. It is in this section of the *vita* that the posthumous miracles of the saint are recorded. For many of the *mulieres sanctae,* the collection of miracles formed one of the most important elements—the raison d'être—in the propagation of their Lives and cults. Miracles were especially used to provoke the veneration of the faithful and to attract crowds and material advantages to the saints' tombs. And in the face of the skepticism and contempt voiced by the *detractores* toward the holy dead, miracles provided irrefutable evidence of their sanctity.[94]

In addition to the *miracula,* a final section called the *translatio* or *elevatio* was frequently appended to the *vita*. This appendix sets forth how the relics of the saint were acquired or recounts the process, events, and miracles surrounding the official elevation or translation of the saint's body to a new, more worthy place of burial. David Rollason describes the procedure in Anglo-Saxon England: "In cases where the remains had been buried outside a church, the grave was opened and the relics were brought into the church ('translated' into it in technical parlance) and usually placed not in a new grave but in some sort of shrine on the floor of the church. Where the remains had been buried in the church from the start, the grave was nevertheless opened and the relics were placed on the floor of the church (i.e. they were 'elevated')."[95] During this early period it was, then, the act of translation or elevation which publicly recognized the sanctity of the individual and the establishment of her cult: it was in effect an informal canonization for these popular saints. The saint's translation frequently provided the occasion for the redaction of the *vita,* as a coordinated promotional effort of advertising or "selling" the saint and her cult. Frequently the building of a new church, which provided a more magnificent setting for the saint's tomb, furnished the impetus for the translation of the saint's body and the writing of the *vita*.[96]

Although many of the *vitae* followed a predictable pattern or schema, their actual content and orientation varied considerably. In the creation, elaboration, and reconstitution of hagiographic material a number of forces were involved. As we have noted, the *vita* was shaped by its general purpose, its patronage, and its audience, as well as by the information available to the author. In addition, the special economic and political interests, the values, perspectives, and "space" in which the author worked, played a decidedly influential role in molding the *vita*.

To underscore the significant discrepancies which could occur in
the content, ideals, and values of saints' Lives, we are especially fortunate to have two contemporary *vitae* which were commissioned for
the same sixth-century female saint, the Frankish queen Radegund.
The original "official" *vita* was written in about 587 by Fortunatus,
poet, friend, and spiritual adviser to St. Radegund and later the bishop
of Poitiers.[97] The "second *vita*," as it was called, was written some
twenty years later, after Fortunatus's death, by the nun Baudonivia,
confidante, companion, and witness to the events of Radegund's life
(see plate 3).[98] It is interesting that Baudonivia's redaction was written
at the insistence of Deidimia, abbess of Radegund's monastery of
Ste-Croix, to fill the many lacunae which Fortunatus had left in his
vita. Her charge was specifically to broaden or enlarge upon that
which he had passed over. She therefore notes that she does not wish
to repeat those things which Fortunatus had written about in his *vita*.
Baudonivia also begins her *vita* by underscoring the difficulty of the
assignment: "To accomplish the task imposed upon me, to presume
to say something of the life of the saintly Lady Radegund, is no less
impossible than for the sky to be touched with our fingers."[99]

In the past, scholars in general have failed to take seriously the *liber
secundus* by Baudonivia. They have frequently dismissed this *vita* as
an invalid or unauthoritative source or have viewed it as merely a
complementary text, a simple appendix or addition to the primary
vita by Fortunatus.[100] The general disdain for, and lack of trust in,
Baudonivia's Life seem to have been based on the author's rusticity of
language (as she herself notes, "non polito sed rustico"), the digres-
sions and lack of rigorous ordering in her presentation of facts, as
well as discrepancies between some of her perceptions and "facts"
and those of Gregory of Tours.[101] However, the lack of interest in Baudonivia as an early hagiographer and the devaluation of her *vita* as
an authoritative text seem also to have been predicated, at least
in part, on Baudonivia's position as female author, a simple nun
(who describes herself as "less learned but more devoted"), in contrast to the prestige of the renowned and eloquent author and bishop,
Fortunatus.[102]

In the "avant-propos" of his *Sainte Radegonde* (1918), René Aigrain noted the differences between the contemporary *vitae* of Fortunatus and Baudonivia. While commenting on Baudonivia's weakness
in expressing herself, Aigrain nevertheless wrote that she deserves recognition. "Without her we would know nothing or nearly nothing of
that which gives the life of Radegund its individual character, its particular charm: neither the resistance to the attempts of Clothar, nor
the cult of relics, nor the apparitions, nor the last moments. . . . Not

that that of Fortunatus does not have its value, but it falls more in the common framework of hagiography, expanding on the virtues and series of miracles."[103] Later, in his classic work *L'Hagiographie* (1953), Aigrain commented upon such "strange lacunae of Fortunatus's *vita* that the nuns of Ste-Croix requested that one of their own make good on it and complete it." He noted that Baudonivia undertook the task of completing this insufficient narration by recording her precious memories of the saint's intimate life, which had been revealed to her, as confidante, by the queen.[104]

In his fascinating study, "Sainte Radegonde, son type de sainteté et la chretienté de son temps," Etienne Delaruelle has argued that the two *vitae* of St. Radegund reflect in fact the age's opposing conceptions of sanctity. In his view, a sharp dichotomy existed between these two works: "Fortunatus saw in Radegund only the nun whose human horizon was voluntarily limited. Baudonivia, on the contrary, portrays for us a figure as expansive as the world of her time, caring about all that happens and continuing to use her royal power to intervene."[105]

It was this pioneering study by Delaruelle which sparked a lively debate among scholars on the interpretation of the basic variations found in these *vitae*. Delaruelle's hypotheses of the strong opposition in the conceptualization of Radegund and the epic tradition underlying the political action of the queen have been criticized by František Graus. In stressing a general continuity of the *vitae*, Graus minimized the differences between Fortunatus's portrayal of Radegund as "ascetic" and Baudonivia's depiction of the saint as "nun and patron of a royal monastery."[106]

Jacques Fontaine, in his perceptive study "Hagiographie et politique," has traced the development of this scholarly controversy. Very briefly, while recognizing the merits of Delaruelle's arguments, Fontaine stresses the continuity of the literary and spiritual influence of the popular model *Vita Martini* on Radegund's sanctity, as well as on the style and content of the biographies written by Baudonivia and Fortunatus. He argues that this Martinian archetype—both spiritual and literary—allowed Fortunatus and Baudonivia to portray the Frankish queen as the type of complex reincarnation of most of the *virtutes Martini*. While Fortunatus emphasized Radegund's imitation of the ascetic and thaumaturgical roles of St. Martin (in praising her heroic exercise of self-abnegation, penitence, and miracles), Baudonivia accentuated the active aspects of a "militant sanctity"—also present among the *virtutes* of Martin. Thus Baudonivia introduced a number of major episodes of the queen's active intervention in political affairs outside of the cloister of Ste-Croix, events absent from Fortunatus's account of the saint.[107] In praising Radegund's active, public role, for example, as peacemaker, proselytizer, and acquirer of relics, Baudonivia introduced a new concept, that of the queen-saint's service to her country.[108] It is, then, in this active political role as "militant saint" that Baudonivia depicted Radegund as sharing in the impressive historic legacy of other great female saints. Thus, in light of her protagonist's successful procurement of the relics of the Holy Cross and in an attempt to further strengthen her royal and saintly credentials, Baudonivia placed Radegund in the great imperial tradition of the first Christian empress, St. Helena (who is credited with discovering the "true cross"). Baudonivia then argued that what St. Helena did for the East, Blessed Radegund accomplished for Gaul.[109] And it was through the acquisition of the piece of the "true cross" that Radegund hoped to promote her monastery of Ste-Croix as the center of a dynastic cult which would serve as "an agency of intercession on behalf of kings."[110] According to Baudonivia, Radegund envisioned the relic of the Holy Cross "as an instrument through which the salvation of the kingdom could be secured and the welfare of the country assured."[111]

In addition to describing the active, public aspects of Radegund's sanctity, the *liber secundus* also focuses in some detail on the saint's private virtues. Here Baudonivia utilized personal information which she had learned as a confidante of the saint. Fontaine suggests that the choice of episodes found in Baudonivia's *vita* "is at the same time more interior and more exterior than in the first Life. More interior in the sense of confidences on the interior life of the queen, on her visions and mystical graces; but also more exterior, in the sense of an exercise of this 'active sanctity' in the world. . . ."[112] Fontaine then argues persuasively that the biographers' distinct choices in selecting different Martinian archetypes with which to present the virtues of Radegund were based on changes in the functional orientation required of each Life. Fortunatus's *vita,* written shortly after the queen's death in 587 and the establishment of her cult, had the purpose of preserving the memory of the founder of the monastery. In contrast, Baudonivia's Life, written some twenty years later, reflects a rather different milieu with different needs. The monastery of Ste-Croix had suffered a serious revolt of its nuns in 589 and was experiencing problems with the episcopacy and local powers. Faced with these critical threats, a new image of the saintly founder-protector was required. Fontaine argues that the second *vita* by Baudonivia might be seen as a type of "hagiographic reconstruction," which, in light of the present difficulties at Ste-Croix, insisted on the active, political aspects of Radegund's "militant sanctity"—namely, her forceful intervention outside of the cloister.[113]

Suzanne Wemple has also observed the differing conceptions of sanctity found in the two Lives of Radegund. She, however, argues convincingly that the preference for certain styles of sanctity—the diversity in ideals and values—was at least in part gender-based. She writes: "Female authors writing about women introduced feminine values and ideals into hagiography. They replaced the ideal of the asexual female saint, the 'virago,' whose greatest accomplishment was the imitation of male virtues, with a heroine who relied on female attributes to achieve sanctity." [114] Wemple notes that Baudonivia was the first to emphasize typically female attributes. Her characterization of Radegund as mother figure, peacemaker, and promoter of a dynastic cult was an unusual theme in hagiography at that time. Wemple argues that Baudonivia's presentation of the Frankish queen as a prototype of the ideal nun was not "a self-effacing and sexless abstraction. In contrast to Fortunatus' portrayal of Radegund as the withdrawn wife and reluctant queen whose main objective was to transcend her femininity and escape from her husband, Baudonivia described Radegund as an outgoing and emotional woman, who was as concerned about the affairs of the convent as about the developments in the kingdom." [115]

Both *vitae*, the *liber primus* by Fortunatus and the *liber secundus* by Baudonivia, are extremely useful in reconstructing the life and society of this fascinating Merovingian saint. They provide complementary information, which, as Baudonivia notes, was the reason her second Life was commissioned. The *vitae* also reflect the special interests, orientations, institutional needs, ideals, and values of the authors. They are especially invaluable for historians, for they allow us to compare these two contemporary visions or programs of sanctity. Fortunatus, influenced by the early Church Fathers, promotes an image of Radegund as a cloistered *regina ancilla* with a privatized existence of self-abnegation and penitence. Baudonivia provides us with, in some ways, a more complex view of the various intersections of the saint's public and private life. Clearly, the *vita* by the nun Baudonivia should not be dismissed as an unauthoritative source (as it has been in the past), nor should it be considered as merely an appendix or supplement to Fortunatus's "official" *vita*. Rather, this Life should be recognized and studied on its own merits, for it is especially through Baudonivia's candid, "nonprofessional" *vita*, with its personal details, observations, and strength of characterization, that we are able to transcend Fortunatus's more learned and abstract portrayal of the saint and to understand the unique aspects of Radegund's personality, strategies, and experiences. Also, and very importantly, through her original portrayal of a female saint, Baudonivia furnishes us with the first extant sacred biography written by a woman who has left us her name. Indeed, her *vita* of St. Radegund is at the beginning of medieval women's biographic tradition—"in praise of women worthies"—which culminates in Christine de Pizan's monumental historical work, *The Book of the City of Ladies*.[116] Baudonivia's Life provides us with the unique opportunity to examine female perceptions, ideals, and values of this early period. It is, then, this *vita secunda*, studied against a background of Fortunatus's work as well the writings of Gregory of Tours, which is of particular value to those interested in women's history.

POSSIBILITIES AND LIMITATIONS

Only recently—with the increased respectability of hagiography and the growing interest in social history, women's history, and the history of mentalities—have scholars recognized the dossiers of saints to be an invaluable source for the study of women in the medieval church and society. (For a brief discussion of these developments, see notes 28 and 29 to the Introduction.) The *vitae* have proved to be especially useful for the early medieval period, when other documentation is scarce enough for the study of traditional male-oriented, political history but frustratingly absent for the reconstruction of women's lives and experiences as well as attitudes toward women. Thus, despite their complexities, problems, and special difficulties, the immense possibilities and promise afforded by this extensive body of material far outweigh their disadvantages.

Before turning to the many aspects of this source which make it so attractive to historians, let us look at some of the classic complaints leveled against saints' Lives. In general, the past's often hypercritical evaluation of the *vitae* of saints was based on its rather narrow view of history (essentially political history), with its obsession with the recreation of events, with ascertainable "facts," evidence, and authenticity. Some historians of the nineteenth and early twentieth century were perhaps also reacting to the contemporary field of hagiography, with its pious polemics and embarrassing credulity. The study of saints was viewed as off-putting; it was perceived as neither a respectable nor legitimate area of research. Thus many historians remained highly suspicious of saints' Lives as sources and of the field in general. Some summarily dismissed the *vitae* of the holy dead as totally unreliable, "entirely worthless," as works of "pious fiction," worthy of neither trust nor the expenditure of scholarly effort. They saw saints' Lives as embarassingly repetitious, stereotypic, essentially clichés; as sources, they were "devoid of content," as well as tedious and boring.[117]

A few of the more extravagant responses which discounted the use of saints' Lives as historical sources can be found in early studies by French scholars. For example, in his work on Saint Martin of Tours (1912), E. C. Babut claimed that most of the *Vita Martini* was an "anthology of unbelievable facts of diverse sources . . . most of which without doubt have come from fiction, plagiarism, or from a hundred-fold exaggeration." According to Babut, the Life of St. Martin was "a tissue of untrue tales." [118] Ferdinand Lot, in his classic work, *The End of the Ancient World and the Beginnings of the Middle Ages* (1927), argued: "The study of the lives of saints of the East and West (there are thousands of them) has in store for us great critical difficulties and also painful literary disappointments. Very few of these vitae are sincere and have real emotion. The vast majority of them are abominable trash. Hagiography is a low form of literature like the serial novel in our own days." In another work Lot observed that the Lives of Breton saints were "entirely devoid of historical value." [119] T. Wright (1861) condemned saints' Lives and miracles as "the most ridiculous and disgusting portions of religious belief of the Middle Ages." [120] And more recently, Hubert Silvester, in his study "Le Problème des faux au moyen âge" (1960), condemned much of medieval hagiography, claiming that it was essentially forged by clerics for the purpose of deceiving an audience of lay pilgrims. [121]

However, in contrast to these scholars who summarily dismissed saints' Lives as a historical source, Marc Bloch, in *The Historian's Craft* (1953), emphasized their special value as unintentional evidence and perhaps anticipated the new directions to be adopted by scholars in the study of saints and society. As noted by Bloch: "At least three fourths of the lives of the saints of the high Middle Ages can teach us nothing concrete about those pious personages whose careers they pretend to describe. If on the other hand, we consult them as to the way of life or thought peculiar to the epoch in which they were written (all things which the biographer of the saint had not the least intention of revealing), we shall find them invaluable." [122]

Nonetheless, it should be noted that despite the frequent condemnations of saints' Lives, this subject was not neglected; in fact, many scholars of the nineteenth and the early decades of the twentieth centuries worked in this area and produced an impressive body of literature. [123] Some of these earlier scholars, along with those presently working in the field, have written extensively on the specific problems involved in the use of these sources, which include the often substantial time lapse between the redaction of a Life and the events it purported to record; the uncritical approach and analysis of the hagiographers; incompetence of style accompanied by blatant plagiarism from earlier saints' Lives or borrowings from the Bible; problems of authenticity and the attribution of the actions of a well-known saint to an unknown or spurious figure; invention of false information; distortion of events, actions, and virtues; the use of vague, abstract types and pious generalities rather than individualized depictions and particular details; and the frequent incorporation of *topoi,* legends, and popular fantasy. Other problems concern the transmission of the *vitae* and the added difficulties involved as a result of copying, rearranging, and various interpolations and editions. Thus dismissing the dossiers of the holy dead as primary sources unworthy of serious historical consideration, scholars in the past frequently restricted their use of saints' *vitae* to providing unusual anecdotes, incidental information, or notes which could then be gathered to support "real" historical evidence.[124]

"Even today," as Aviad Kleinberg has noted, "saints' Lives are only reluctantly accepted as historical evidence by the modern historian. Some historiographers do not even consider them part of historical writing in the Middle Ages. Hagiography is presented more as an aberration of history than a special branch of it." [125]

However, for social historians studying this early period, the impressive numbers of *vitae* with their possibilities for a comparative approach, as well as the intrinsic interest of these sources, override the potential drawbacks or problems.

The sheer numbers alone, the hundreds of female and male saints' *vitae* for this period, allow us to study on a macrolevel women in medieval society. Through a collective study of these sources, we can look at gender relations and compare the experiences of the *mulieres sanctae* with those of their male contemporaries. The Lives provide us with the unique opportunity, not available in any other sources of the period, to observe broad changes across the centuries and geographic boundaries in regard to female and male sanctity. Through the collection of rough statistical data, enough information is available to form a rather crude but accurate evaluation of some of the following: shifts in the typology of sanctity; the density and distribution of female saints; sex ratios of saints; geographic disparities in the selection of *mulieres sanctae;* social and economic status; and demographic information, including, for example, family size, age of first marriage, as well as data on longevity and sanctity. These rough data can be used to bracket continuity and change over time and to test various theories of change.

However, some of the most fascinating and little-known information which can be gleaned from the *vitae* consists of unique, unconventional details: data not at all easily categorized and essentially unquantifiable. These details frequently appear in the *vitae* as accidental or incidental facts. This type of hagiographic information falls into the category of unconscious or "unintentional evidence," perhaps often more reliable than other, "intentional," evidence found in the *vitae*.[126] Since these details are not central to the eulogistic or propagandist purposes of the hagiographer, they are perhaps less likely to be exaggerated or purposefully falsified. Thus, through a collective treatment of these inadvertent or accidental details, patterns frequently emerge which shed new light on many aspects of the medieval female experience.

The *vitae* are particularly useful for providing insights on women and the early medieval family. Since it was through the irregular powers and landed wealth of the family that noblewomen of this early period could achieve a certain visibility which frequently led to sanctity, the saint's family was of central importance to the hagiographer.[127] The *vitae* thus provide information on the saint's parents and her noble genealogy. (It is interesting that during this early period we find several instances in which all of the members of a family came to be recognized as saints.) The Lives sometimes describe the economic status of the family, especially noting the great generosity of the saint and her relatives in making donations to the church. The *vitae* also provide observations on many details of everyday family life, including, for example, information on marriage, friendship within marriage, sexual practices, problems of infertility, childbirth, naming of infants, care of premature infants, infanticide or abandonment of infants, child abuse, adolescence, incest, stepmothers, mother-daughter relationships, sibling bonds, economic independence of women, domestic roles, violence toward women (e.g., attempted rape and wife beating), repudiation or separation, widowhood, death, burial, and other topics.

Moreover, since the majority of women saints of this early period were recruited from the cloister, the *vitae* offer a unique glimpse into the female monastic experience. (Some of the details provided by the hagiographers can be used to complete the basic information found in monastic *regulae*, charters, and chronicles.)[128] The Lives, for example, describe the "founding" of monasteries (factual or "invented"), recruitment practices and problems, admission policies, vows, size of communities, organization of double monasteries and affiliated houses (as well as the relationships between nuns and monks), the special bonds of confederation established between communities and churches, monastic administration, the role of the abbess, adoption of monastic rules, and policies of enclosure. The Lives include precious information about monastic churches, the arrangement of the cloister and its buildings, along with descriptions of special funerary churches and monastic cemeteries. They discuss the activities of the female communities, noting monastic education and curricula, reading, manuscript illumination, needlework and painting, the *laus perennis,* care of the sick, and charity work. In addition, the *vitae* tell of the dress of female religious, tonsure of nuns, hygiene, diet, bloodletting, along with ascetic practices of fasting and sleep deprivation which were frequently carried to extremes by these early "spiritual athletes."[129]

The Lives are also extremely informative in regard to the economic aspects of female monastic communities and the increasing concern for income, material support, and the well-being of such institutions.[130] They provide information on the constitution of land holdings and agricultural and commercial activities, data which is again often confirmed by monastic charters, diplomas, and chronicles. Many of the *vitae* include evidence used to validate land holdings and privileges of monasteries as well as their possession of relics. They describe the special privileges promised to those buried in the saint's cemetery or church. (These burial privileges in turn brought economic advantage to the church in the form of fees and bequests.) Other Lives emphasize the role of patron saints in inspiring the generosity of the faithful to give landed estates to churches or monasteries, or they relate the saints' miraculous intervention in the retrieval of usurped properties and their "just" punishment of usurpers. The *vitae* also tell of the invasions and their devastating effects on female monastic life. Some Lives describe growing problems of poverty, famine, and plague, with the decimation and ultimate dissolution of entire female communities.

Another area of fascinating detail provided by the *vitae* and *miracula* concerns female unconventional, transgressive behavior, viewed by the hagiographer and Church as sometimes admirable and praiseworthy, and at other times as a challenge or threat to the order of society and thus condemned as aberrant or "deviant" behavior. In some cases, these activities appear perhaps rather bizarre or even repulsive to the modern reader. The Lives describe instances of women adopting various creative strategies in defense of their virginity, including those of "self-disfigurement" and feigned illness and insanity. A few of the *vitae* (in the "regendering" or "virago" tradition) portray examples of *mulieres religiosae* disguised as men—wearing male dress with short hair or tonsure—in order to experience lives denied them as women or as a protective strategy to defend their virginity. There are instances of women's covert attempts to enter male monasteries, or sanctuaries (forbidden to females), and of the subsequent miracles which they brought about, or the severe punishments which they suffered for their audacious behavior. The *vitae* describe women continuing to foster pagan beliefs and observances. There are accusations found in the saints' Lives of various moral improprieties, such as incest between brothers and their saintly sisters, adultery, the breaking of vows of virginity as well as enclosure by recalcitrant nuns, or the determined attempts by nuns at "abbessicide." The active role of the *mulieres sanctae* in the acquisition of relics, including their direct involvement in the actual "furta sacra," or "theft" of the remains of the holy dead, are also described in some detail in the *vitae*.

Moreover, the *miracula* of the saints' Lives also provide rich data for the study of popular mentalities and the belief in the miraculous intervention of the holy dead. The "miracles" frequently furnish extraordinary descriptions of physical and mental illnesses, as well as medical beliefs and practices, miraculous cures, and exorcisms. In addition, the *miracula* tell of those seeking the saint's assistance at her cult center and therefore provide invaluable data on gender, class, and age of the pilgrims along with their specific illnesses.[131]

Nevertheless, despite their incredible wealth, the *vitae* are complex sources to be used with caution, and we should not attempt to claim for them a greater degree of historical accuracy than is warranted. The *vitae* should be placed within the political and historical context in which they were read, copied, and revised. Since saints' Lives did not remain static but changed with ecclesiastical and societal perceptions and needs, scholars should study and compare, when possible, a series of subsequent Lives for the same saint. They should then apply textual criticism to the *vitae* in order to see how the matter itself was manipulated and transformed over time, and how encoded information indirectly reflected the special interests or purposes of the hagiographers and their institutions. Ideally each Life should be tested for internal consistency of fact and language. Also, in the exploration of patterns of female sanctity within the broad context of culture and society, the value of the *vita* as a historical source is much greater when the Lives are studied collectively rather than in isolation. In addition, the information of the *vitae* can often be supplemented by other hagiographic information, such as calendars, martyrologies, liturgies, panegyrics, homilies, and *lectiones* for the festivals of the saints. This information is further strengthened when it is checked for external consistency or conformity against other sources of the period. Therefore, for the most complete or successful reconstruction of the female experience in the early medieval church and society, hagiographic literature should be used in collaboration with other contemporary historical sources, such as chronicles, canon and secular laws, penitentials, monastic *regulae,* cartularies, correspondence, treatises, archaeological and epigraphic evidence, and iconography. And indeed, through this collective approach one finds, for example, reinforcing or corroborative evidence that many of the behavioral modes and strategies attributed to female saints—previously dismissed by scholars as wildly implausible, mere hagiographic exaggeration, fantasy, or *topoi*—are in fact in the realm of "real" contemporary behavior.

However, despite these various strategies which attempt to extrapolate useful historical data from the *vitae* and to supplement it with other contemporary sources, one constantly needs to be reminded that saints' Lives are ultimately reflections of the mind-set and world of the hagiographer and the particular occasion which provided the impetus for the redaction or revision of the Life. Indeed, as Richard Kieckhefer has noted, one cannot assume in all cases that the information or data described in the *vitae* necessarily refers to specific social realities. Rather, as works of propaganda, the Lives reflect the hagiographers' intense views of these realities, their own (frequently biased and skewed) personal visions of sanctity and society. Indeed, on one level the *vitae* frequently tell us as much or perhaps even more about the mind-sets of the hagiographers and their world, the ideas and stereotypes prevalent in their own society, or the concerns with institutional power and increasing the prestige of a church, monastery, or royal house, than factual information about the saint.[132]

It is then in this context that one must ask how trustworthy the *vitae* are as evidence for specifically women's experiences and lives. And how does one interpret them? Since the majority of saints' Lives appear to have been written by men—medieval clerics—are the Lives of female saints merely reflections of male worth and their notions and fantasies of ideal women, or do they describe "real" women's roles and the religious and social expectations of women of the period?[133] Briefly, the very nature of sainthood required that the *mulieres sanctae* be somewhat extraordinary or "atypical" women. Through their aristocratic birth, families, and exercise of autonomy and power, they belonged to an elite group within which they were further singled out for their piety, religious dedication, and zeal. While the lives of these holy heroines do not seem to have been fully coterminous with the experiences of religious women in general, it appears that especially during the early stages of conversion to Christianity and the development of monasticism, when aristocratic women were particularly well placed to play a central role as generous patrons and founding abbesses of monasteries, there were a great many women with more power and visibility in the Church and society than usual. They were then rewarded for their leadership roles in the Church by being elevated to sainthood. These female saints and their *vitae* therefore provided society with some idea of the ideals and the kind of life being practiced by this very special holy elite.

For this early period churchmen advocated, as the preferred life-style or career for women, a life of dedicated professional virginity. Thus the Church endorsed these female symbols of virtue (outstanding for their virginity, martyrdom, etc.) as exempla, whose behavior was then to be admired and, in some cases, imitated or emulated, by the women of the Christian community. Through this means, the Church hoped to inspire a certain modification in behavior, a religious conformity, and to mold "social copies." [134] Thus, through the use of saints' Lives, churchmen attempted to reinforce their own concepts of ideal female behavior. They endeavored to socialize women according to contemporary religious ideals, to shape and control women and female sexuality by dictating how women should think and behave. On this level, the *vitae* might be viewed as oppressive tools utilized by the clergy to control or restrict women's activities and visions.

Although the Lives of women saints often reveal much about male clerical hagiographers and their perceptions of female sanctity and conventional behavior, according to Jocelyn Wogan-Browne these "portrayals contribute to female self-images, and for all the authorial dominance of one gender, do not necessarily cease entirely to encode self-perceptions and historical experience for the other." [135] In her study of women and Anglo-Norman hagiography, Wogan-Browne has argued that these male-authored hagiographical portrayals had a great deal to say to women:

As with many other bodies of evidence, Anglo-Norman hagiography would seem more liable to yield information about clerical and seigneurial mentalities than to represent or address the experience of Anglo-Norman noble and gentry women (let alone women of lower class.) Nevertheless, just as literary representation has implications for, but is not precisely commensurate with, socio-economic standing, so there is often, even in stereotypical representation of women, the potential of slippage between particular hagiographic texts and their readers' responses to them. Identification between martyrdom and female asceticism can be used in different ways. Some women, most famously Christina of Markyate, seem to have used hagiography for their own purposes, and in (especially) the genre's sophisticated examples, meaning is in any case complex and to a significant extent negotiable between reader and text, rather than automatically fixed by the text. Though

a clerical and aristocratic culture allowing access to privileged
women may remain 'overwhelmingly male', this does not mean
that the saints' lives have nothing to say to women or that
women can say nothing in, through, or in response to them.[136]

Thus the meaning of the *vitae* is not set or fixed but could be negotiated between reader and text. These Lives of female saints provided
women with "multivalent messages" and a certain flexibility in their
"use" as religious symbols. For as Clarissa Atkinson has noted, these
sacred symbols can be used "at different times by different persons
for totally different needs."[137] Women with religious leanings seemed
to have learned what they wanted to learn from the *vitae,* and they
frequently took some liberties in creatively adapting these behavioral
models to their own specific situations and needs. Therefore, in addition to serving as vehicles of ecclesiastical and societal control, saints'
Lives provided a variety of remarkable roles and experiences for the
female imagination to act upon. Women seemed to have a special sympathy as well as admiration for the concerns and achievements of
the *mulieres sanctae*. They inspired women with new possibilities for
their own lives of spiritual perfection. They provided active strategies
and roles which could be used or adapted to transcend the social and
ecclesiastical restrictions of the period. And not infrequently these
creative adaptations or improvisations seem to have been in direct opposition to the conventional behavior the Church had hoped the Life
would inspire.

As *exempla* of holy behavior, the *vitae* of saints therefore seem to
have profoundly influenced the lives of religious women and men in
medieval society. The lessons of the female saints' Lives were not lost
on the *mulieres religiosae* of the period. In his *History of the Kings,*
William of Malmesbury, for example, noted that St. Cuthburga
"embraced the profession of holy celibacy from the perusal of Aldhelm's book on virginity."[138] (As previously noted, Aldhelm's treatise
contained an important collection of the lives of virgin saints.) An
example of the profound influence the lives of saints could exercise on
medieval women can be found in one of the *vitae* of St. Radegund. As
a young child she was apparently very much moved by the lives of the
martyrs and often "played at" being a saint. She would discuss with
the other children her desire to be a martyr if she were offered the
chance in her lifetime. And although the church at this time was experiencing peace, Radegund suffered persecution from her own household. (In her later life, when martyrdom was not forthcoming, she
inflicted on herself various austerities and corporal punishments as a
type of self-martyrdom.)[139]

The author of the *vita* of St. Sadalberga/Salaberga, founder and abbess of the monestary of St. John of Laon (d. ca. 670), notes that her saintly virtues "imitated" the humility, charity, and moral goodness of the noble women saints Melania and Paula, whose lives were written by St. Jerome. The blessed Salaberga also repeated the behavior of others, imitating, for instance, Helena, the mother of Constantine, by "mortification of the flesh," disdain of the worldly, and her behavior as a submissive servant of God.[140]

Jocelyn Wogan-Browne has also noted in the case of Christina of Markyate the potential relation between virgin models provided by saints' Lives and the experience of women who read them: "Apart from citing the life of St Caecilia to her betrothed, Christina had added to the calendar of her psalter the feasts of Amalburga (virgin or chaste spouse), Etheldreda (virgin spouse and abbess), Frideswide (virgin), Hild (abbess and patron of recluses and hermits), Christina, Faith, Felicity and Juliana (virgin martyrs). Four of these saints, like Christina herself, rejected suitors for religious careers."[141]

Joan of Arc was perhaps one of the most famous historical figures who experienced the strong influence of saints on her life and used their authority for her own purposes. She claimed to have been inspired by St. Catherine of Alexandria, St. Margaret of Antioch, and St. Michael. The female saints provided role models of virgin martyrs who had refused marriage, as had Joan of Arc; their lives also promoted courage, autonomy, defiance of authority, and heroic martyrdom. According to Joan, the saints provided her counsel and comfort; she followed their voices in "everything good" that she accomplished. Sts. Catherine and Margaret, for example, ordered her in God's name to wear men's clothing; they also promised to lead her to Paradise provided she preserved her virginity which she had vowed to them.[142]

It is interesting to note the continuity in the influence of saints' lives on women in the modern world. Dorothy Day, one of the founders of the Catholic Worker, describes how in their childhood she, her sister, and a friend would "practice being saints." In her autobiography, *The Long Loneliness,* she writes:

> I don't remember what we talked about, but I do remember one particular occasion when she [her friend, Mary Harrington] talked to me about the life of some saint. I do not know which saint it was, and I cannot remember any of the incidents of the life; I only remember my feeling of lofty enthusiasm, and how my heart almost burst with desire to take part in such high endeavor. . . . I was filled with natural striving, a thrilling recognition of the possibilities of spiritual adventure.[143]

The writer Kay Hogan, in reminiscing about her childhood, notes:

> The day Ann Cunningham told me the facts of life I decided to
> become a saint. . . . I draped myself in white curtains with a
> rope tied around my waist and practiced looking saintly. The
> saints I read about died defending their virginity, whatever that
> was. The dying I could handle but the mechanics of defense
> eluded me.[144]

The novelist Kathryn Harrison recalls the major influence the lives
of women saints assumed in her own life:

> I still had my little books of the female saints. I looked at them
> before bed some nights, stared at their little portraits, at bleed-
> ing hands and feet, at exultant faces tipped up to heaven.

In her youth she aspired to imitate the fourteenth-century mystic,
St. Catherine of Siena. Like the saint who starved herself, "eating only
bread and uncooked vegetables" and began to experience ecstasies,
Harrison "ate raw vegetables, multivitamins, No-Doz and . . . when
[she] climbed stairs, [she] saw stars." [145]

Thus in these medieval and modern examples we see a remarkable
continuity in the influence of the *vitae* of female saints upon women's
powers of imagination and their lives. And while over the centuries
the *vitae* served as a vehicle by which the Church attempted to mold
or control women, the Lives also allowed for alternative readings.
They provided sources of inspiration, authority, and empowerment
for women by suggesting a variety of relevant role models and experiences for them to admire, imitate, or to modify in order to fit their special needs or situations.

Saints' Lives, then, are especially rich in providing an indirect index
of social and ecclesiastical values, perceptions, and collective mentalities of the hagiographer's world. The *vitae* also furnish information on
the commonalities of female experience as well as a wide variety of
unique details on women's lives found in no other records of the period. As a source, they still remain relatively unexplored. As a nearly
inexhaustible resource for social historians, they are open to a great
variety of interpretations dependent on our changing interests and
views of medieval society. They present a myriad of possibilities for research in women's history. We need to study the *vitae* collectively in
light of the complex relationships between the ideal models proposed
by the hagiographers, the collective mentalities, and the social and
political structures of this early period.[146] We need to approach these
lives in a sympathetic yet critical manner. We need to ask new ques-

tions and make an imaginative effort in our reexamination of these sources.

The hundreds of *vitae* of the *mulieres sanctae* still have a great deal to tell us about women's images, experiences, and traditions in the early medieval church and society, if we are willing to make the effort and take the time to listen.

*At that time throughout the provinces of Gaul, a multitude of
monks and swarms of virgins [sacrarum puellarum examina] under
the rule of the blessed fathers Benedict and Columbanus began to
spread not only in the fields, towns, villages, and castles, but also in
the desert of the hermits, whereas before this time scarcely a few
monasteries were found in these places.*

Vita Sadalbergae Abbatissae
Laudunensis [1]

*The first order of Catholic saints was in the time of Patrick; and
then they were all bishops, famous and holy . . . 350 in number,
founders of churches. . . . They rejected not the services and society
of women; . . . they feared not the blast of temptation. This order
of saints continued for four reigns [432–544]. The second order
was of Catholic Presbyters . . . in number 300. . . . they refused the
services of women, separating them from the monasteries. This order . . . lasted for four reigns [544–98]. The first Order was most
holy [sanctissimus]; the second Order, very holy [sanctior] . . ."*

The Catalogue of the
Three Orders of Irish Saints [2]

The Making of the Mulier Sancta: Public and Private Roles

Saints, as we have noted, were "made." In modern, rather crass, terms, they were often popular "products": they were "packaged," "promoted" or "advertised," and then "sold" to the faithful. Although their promoters frequently focused on the "otherworldly" and intercessory aspects of their invisible patrons, sainthood in itself was a very "this-worldly" and public business. A halo of sanctity was not won by simply leading a quiet, private, "otherworldly" life in blissful seclusion. No matter how exemplary or holy they were, without some sort of public role, or visibility, and the presence of others as witnesses and supporters, these uncommon lives would have been lost. Escaping the collective memory of their age, they would have faded into oblivion. Sainthood therefore required a public: a dedicated company of friends, relatives, or faithful to witness and provide evidence of one's extraordinary acts or miracles. In many cases, the success of a candidate for sainthood initially relied on a public groundswell, an organized local pressure group or lobbyists—including churchmen and women—who over time promoted the cult of their patron saint. While many of the early medieval cults had popular origins, they were then formalized, organized, and given their official shape and direction by the Church. However, the fame of sanctity and cults of the holy dead were frequently precarious and ephemeral. The collective memory could be frail and short-lived. Saints and their cults often needed intermittent revalidation; they required the remobilization of popular support through the introduction of fresh proof of their efficacy by means of new miracles and other evidence of the saint's presence. Thus the continued success of the saint and her cult was never assured; rather it depended on a sustained "advertising" campaign waged by the church or community which guarded the saint's remains. Through such a concerted effort, cult centers attempted to continue to attract the support of the local faithful, as well as pilgrims, who flocked to the saint's tomb in expectant hope of a personal miracle.

In the making of women saints, however, an environment or milieu
favorably disposed toward members of their sex—one which encouraged and valued their participation in the Church and society—was
required. Opportunities which would lend women a certain prominence or visibility had to be available. They needed the chance to excel
in the various professions they had adopted in their pursuit of the *vita
perfecta*. Furthermore, in order to attract the attention of the faithful
and to fuel their imaginations, the actions and miracles of the would-
be saints had to be perceived as extraordinary, in some cases extravagant and extreme; yet, at the same time, they could not transcend the
boundaries of permissible diversity, but needed to conform on some
level in order to be "acceptable" to the Church and society. It was
therefore imperative that the social and religious climate of the period
allow, or encourage, the saintly candidates to function in a manner
that would accentuate the exceptional aspects of their behavior and
provide them with the visibility, the "power profile," necessary for
promotion to sainthood.

A study of the typology of women saints is thus able to reveal
significant patterns with regard to female power, prominence, and
visibility in society and the Church. In general, for the early Middle
Ages, access to sainthood came essentially through worldly power,
high status, public office, and social and economic prominence. Power
on earth frequently provided entrée to power in heaven. At this time
popular sanctity was often predicated on "public" acts—exterior
actions, often practical in nature—rather than the more "private" interior, mystical traits which would become so important during the
later Middle Ages.

Male saints were recruited from among the upper secular clergy
(popes, archbishops, and bishops). By far the greater number of these
early male saints were bishops: they assumed immense secular and
religious power in their dioceses and won special recognition as
founders or builders of new churches. André Vauchez has noted that
the high percentage of bishops recognized as saints during this early
period stems in part from the practice of attaching "blessed" to the
names of many of these early bishops. Thus in the following centuries,
these figures continued to be recognized among the ranks of the
saints.[3] A high concentration of male saints was also recruited from
the cloister, from among the abbots and monks, while only a very few
male saints for this early period came from the ranks of kings and emperors.[4] Women, in contrast, denied access to the secular church hierarchy, were rewarded with recognition of sainthood for their roles as
generous patrons of religious projects, pious queens, abbesses, consecrated virgins, nuns, hermits, and martyrs.

What social and cultural arrangements provided the necessary opportunities for women to achieve positions of power and visibility which could in turn promote *fama sanctitatis* and candidacy for sanctity? During this period, in the absence of strong, impersonal governmental institutions, royal or aristocratic families assumed the political, economic, and social authority in Europe. Thus within the context of the irregular powers of the early medieval family, women could achieve positions of authority and control over landed property and movable wealth. With political and economic power situated within the family, aristocratic women were particularly well placed, and their households became the locus of power. The early medieval household therefore provided nearly limitless opportunities for women whose families were politically and economically powerful. It is, then, through the family that women were able to achieve a prominence and visibility which could lead to recognition of sanctity.[5]

In recent years there has been a proliferation of scholarship, especially among anthropologists, sociologists, and historians, on the roles and status of women as defined by the public/private paradigm. In their pioneering studies, Michelle Rosaldo, Nancy Chodorow, and Sherry Ortner, for example, argued that "in all human societies," as summarized by Rosaldo, "sexual asymmetry might be seen to correspond to a rough institutional division between domestic and public spheres of activity, the one built around reproduction, affective, and familial bonds, and particularly constraining to women; the other, providing for collectivity, jural order, and social cooperation, organized primarily by men. The domestic/public division as it appeared in any given society was not a necessary, but an 'intelligible' product of the mutual accommodation of human history and human biology."[6] Thus in the cultural evaluation of the sexes, power, authority, and prestige were attached to the activities of men and the public sphere. In contrast, women—as wives and mothers—were confined to the private or domestic sphere, where they were denied access to the sorts of public roles and exercise of power that were viewed as the special prerogatives of men.[7]

This public/private dichotomy has then been used to explain women's "lower" status in society, and specifically their lack of access to public power and positions of authority. It has served to account for the devaluation or "invisibility" of their activities. "This model has also been used to explain why women took different avenues from men to gain prestige or influence and why the exercise of public authority by women is often viewed as illegitimate."[8]

While scholars continue to explore these gendered spheres and the ideologies of sexual stratification, the universal applicability of the public/private construct has been challenged. There are problems, for example, in applying this model in an unqualified or inflexible way to social realities and to total cultural systems. There are difficulties in attempting to establish rigid or unchanging boundaries between public and domestic spheres, or of allocating women on a permanent basis to one domain or to the other.[9] Furthermore, there are questions in regard to the relative value of the "spheres," and whether the domestic or private sphere should be viewed as secondary, or subordinate, to the public realm. However, while scholars perhaps agree that this universal bipolar model of gender inequity does not fully capture the complexities of social relationships of a given period, the paradigm still remains a useful analytical device for studying the relationships between women, men, and power.[10]

In the medieval period, for example, the social, economic, and institutional arrangements which affected public/private dichotomies and women's roles and conditions appear to have shifted dramatically from the early to the late Middle Ages. The newly established Church and society of the early Middle Ages failed to designate strict divisions between public and domestic spheres of activity; rather, the conditions of the period seemed to promote a basic intersection of public and private rights, powers, and space. This arrangement in turn, seemed to favor the acquisition of power by women and worked to enhance their status and visibility. But with the development of the Carolingian Empire and a growing concern with Church reform, and especially with the multiplicity of changes of the eleventh and twelfth centuries, these early conditions seem to have been fundamentally transformed. A greater emphasis was now placed on institutional organization, regularization, and reform, an increased sacramental formalism and liturgical specialization, with a concurrent attempt to rigidly delineate public and private spheres, male and female activities. These changes were strongly biased in favor of the augmentation of men's roles in the Church. They promoted an exaggerated sexual asymmetry: they worked (although without total success) to gradually exclude women from the public sphere and to relegate them to the personal, private, or domestic realm.[11]

This chapter will focus on the importance of women's public roles, power, and disposable wealth in their selection as saints. It will explore some of the channels though which women had access to power and how they used this power. The important roles of queenship and royal patronage, as well as peacemaking efforts, reforming practices of slavery, and the freeing of captives will be examined. However, considering that the majority of female saints were recruited from the cloister, this chapter will especially focus on monasticism and the

TABLE 1 Women Saints in the Middle Ages, 500–1099

YEARS	TOTAL NUMBER OF SAINTS	MALE SAINTS	FEMALE SAINTS	PERCENTAGE OF FEMALE SAINTS*
500–49	236	213	23	9.7
550–99	304	281	23	7.6
600–49	201	180	21	10.4
650–99	365	292	73	20.0
700–49	230	176	54	23.5
750–99	194	157	37	19.1
800–49	128	109	19	14.8
850–99	151	132	19	12.6
900–49	64	49	15	23.4
950–99	105	88	17	16.2
1000–49	132	117	15	11.4
1050–99	164	148	16	9.8
Total	2,274	1,942	332	—

Source: Saints listed in the *Bibliotheca sanctorum.*
Note: Because of the nature of our sources, the figures shown are only approximate.
*Average = 14.9

various opportunities which this institution provided to women as patrons, abbesses, and nuns. Primary roles in administration, education, building campaigns, the collection of relics, hospitality and the dispensing of charity, and prophecy helped to enhance their dossiers and move these monastic candidates for sainthood closer in their quest for holiness. This chapter will also look at the growth of gender-based restrictions beginning with the Carolingian reforms of the ninth century as well as some of the basic shifts in the ideals of female sanctity.

PERIODIZATION AND TOPOGRAPHY OF FEMALE SANCTITY

Several years ago in an article entitled "Sexism and the Celestial Gynaeceum," I attempted to provide a general statistical overview of the holy dead from ca. 500 to 1200.[12] Based on a collective examination of some 2,680 male and female saints listed in the *Bibliotheca Sanctorum,* this study surveyed changes in the ratio of female to male saints who lived in the regions of Britain, France, Germany, the Low Countries, and Italy.[13] Very briefly, I found that despite claims of spiritual egalitarianism by the Church, it was clearly much more difficult for women to be recognized as saints than it was for men. Over this period of some seven centuries, women represented less than 15 percent of the recognized saints. Table 1 summarizes this information for the years 500–1099. Although overall, the percentage of *mulieres sanctae* remains quite low, it appears that certain periods during this time

TABLE 2 General Geographical Distribution of Saints at Death,
500–1099

COUNTRIES WHERE SAINTS DIED	MEN	WOMEN	TOTAL	PERCENTAGE OF FEMALE SAINTS*
Italy	411	31	442	7.2
France	873	101	974	10.4
Britain	167	65	232	27.6
Germany	285	77	362	21.2
Belgium	146	50	196	25.5
Total	1,882	324	2,206	

Note: Approximate numbers based on the saints in the *Bibliotheca sanctorum*.
*Average = 14.7

were more conducive than others to the making of female saints. The years 650–750, for example, emerge as a rather flourishing period for female saints. Then, in general, after 751, with the establishment of the Carolingian dynasty and the subsequent Church reforms, the total number of both male and female saints fell, as did the relative proportion of female saints. This downturn is temporarily modified in the tenth century, which witnessed an increase in female sanctity tied to ecclesiastical developments in Saxony and a revitalization of monasticism in England. But after the year 1000, the decline was further exacerbated and the percentage of female saints reached its nadir between 1050 and 1100, when only approximately 9.8 percent of all saints were female. This approximate data, then, provides an indirect index of a progressive deterioration in the valuation of women and their active roles in the Church.[14]

Moreover, just as some periods proved to be more favorable than others in the recognition and making of women saints, there also seems to have been a certain topography of female sanctity, with some geographic areas more conducive than others to the recruitment of the *mulieres sanctae*. Table 2 presents a rough statistical survey of the geographical distribution of the *loca sanctorum* (based on the saint's recorded place of death and burial for this period of ca. 500–1100).[15] Out of a total of approximately 2,206 popular saints, the great majority, some 974 male and female saints, were recruited from France. This is more than twice the number claimed by Italy (442 saints), followed by Germany with some 362 saints, Britain with 232 saints, and Belgium with 196.

Thus in the general distribution of saints for this early period there appears to be a basic split between Italy and France on the one hand— which together produced nearly two-thirds of all the saints—and the northern countries of Britain, Germany, and Belgium. This disparity in numbers can perhaps be explained, at least in part, by the fact that during this early period France supported the greatest population in Europe, followed by Italy.[16] Nevertheless, it is especially noteworthy that while France and Italy clearly produced the greatest number of saints during these centuries, they also provided the lowest percentage of female saints: only 8.8 percent of their total number of saints were female (7.2 percent for Italy and 10.4 percent for France) in comparison to the average percentage of 14.7. In contrast, while the total number of saints promoted by the northern countries of Britain, Germany, and Belgium did not equal those of France, their percentages of female saints were more than twice that of France. Britain, over all, emerged as the country most favorable to the making of *mulieres sanctae* with over 27 percent women saints, followed by Belgium with 25.5 percent female saints and Germany with 21.2 percent. (Although we need to be careful not to give too much credence to some of these statistics, since they are frequently based on less than thirty saints per fifty-year period.)

For France, the most favorable period in the promotion of female saints occurred between 650 and 799 when slightly over 17 percent of those elected to sainthood were women. It is important to emphasize that during this period the *mulieres sanctae* came primarily from the areas of the north of France, in contrast to those in the sixth and early seventh century from the south of France.

In Britain the "golden age" of female sanctity occurred between 650 and 750 when nearly 40 percent of the saints were female. It should perhaps be noted that the percentages of women saints in Britain would have been further enhanced if one "counted" in this number the Anglo-Saxon women who came to be recognized as saints by their adopted monastic communities of France and Germany. In general, throughout this six-hundred-year period, the numbers and percentages of women saints remained rather high and impressive in Britain.

The statistics for Germany were in some ways similar to those of Britain. Although its initial "flood" of women saints occurred ca. 700–799 (39 percent *mulieres sanctae*), the later part of the ninth century and the eleventh century also provided impressive percentages of women saints. These increases or resurgences in sanctity were, again, related to new opportunities provided for women in the Church through the expansion of monastic life into various "frontier" regions of Germany.

The rough statistics for Italy do not seem to indicate that any age during this early period was particularly favorable to the promotion of women saints. It is important to note, however, that this is in contrast to the impressive number of women found among the early Christian

saints and martyrs, and also the high percentages of female saints of
the late Middle Ages (especially the fourteenth and fifteenth centuries)
which would be recruited from Italy. Also, perhaps in light of the
wealth of early Christian saints and martyrs, and impressive collections of relics, Italy did not experience the same pressing need to
"make" new saints during this period, as was the case, for example,
for the countries of the north of Europe and Britain.

An important indirect index of the *loca sanctorum* (the sites where
the saints "chose" to leave their mortal remains) can be seen in the use
of place-names. Many saints have left an indelible imprint on the
topography of medieval and modern Europe in the form of place-
names. As the saints were impressed on the consciousness of their age
or that of subsequent periods, various forms of their names came to be
attached to settlements, villages, towns, as well as the natural features
of the countryside such as hills, forests, streams, etc. It appears that
many of these place-names containing the names of saints were appropriated by villages or towns which grew up around monasteries and
which then adopted the name of the monastery's patron or titular
saint. Although, through popular usage, many of these place-names
have been altered over time and are sometimes rather difficult to
recognize, the number of towns in Europe which still bear these
hagiographic traces is indeed amazing. For example, a simple perusal
of a geographic dictionary of France, a French postal dictionary, or
the Michelin Tourist Guides, or a trip through the French countryside,
serves to remind us of the great numbers of localities which have
adopted saints' names. (It should also be noted that through the tenth
century the Latin terms *domnus* and *sanctus* were frequently inter-
changeable and therefore many French place-names with the prefix
of "dom" or "don" can also be attributed to saints.)[17] The following brief sampling of French place-names contains the names of a few
male saints of our period: St. Gildas, St. Amand, Donnement (Domnus
Amandus), St-Antonin-Noble-Val, St-Guilhem-le-Désert, St. Aubin,
St. Malo, Domremy (Domnus Remigius). In Britain, there is Boston
(named for St. Botolph) or Congresbury (St. Congar).[18] Examples of
place-names identified with female saints in France include Faremoutiers (St. Fara), Baignes-Ste-Radegund, Ste-Enimie, Ste-Geneviève-
des-Bois, Ste-Maure-de-Touraine, Ste-Avoye, or Getruydenberg (Brabant), and Odilienberg (St. Odilia, Rhine); and in Britain, Peakirk
(St. Pega), St. Bees (St. Bega), or Ebb's Head (St. Ebba of Coldingham).
The adoption of these place-names, then, provides another indication
of the prominence of the holy dead and their cults in various regions
of Europe and Britain. However, as might be expected in light of our
other indices in regard to women saints, place-names based on the

names of women saints (excluding those identified with Mary) form only a small proportion of these place-names.[19]

In general, the broad patterns related to the topography of sanctity indirectly reflect the movements of expansion of Christianity and especially of monasticism in medieval Europe. Beginning in the south, in Italy and southern France, the new faith spread into the north of Europe and Britain. It is, then, these new frontiers which frequently provided a combination of favorable circumstances, a climate of exceptional opportunity for women in the Church and society which was particularly conducive to the making of saints.

QUEEN-SAINTS AND ROYAL PATRONAGE

During this period, women's power or office on earth was frequently translated to power in heaven. For the early Middle Ages, the household served as the royal or noblewoman's "powerhouse." With the intersection of the domestic and public spheres, the household was located at the very center of power and authority.[20] It is therefore within the context of the family and household that a substantial number of noblewomen and queens of this period achieved sainthood. The early queens were recognized, for example, for their successful work as "domestic proselytizers."[21] While such missions might in some ways be viewed as "privatized," they were in fact part of a concerted "public" strategy of conversion carried out in close cooperation with contemporary popes and bishops. Their indispensable roles in the missionary effort were clearly recognized by the church hierarchy. The queens' success in their proselytizing activities had immense public/ political repercussions, for the freshly baptized Christian king was followed in his new faith by all of his retainers and the entire realm. Thus, for example, through her successful work in converting her husband, Clovis, to Christianity, St. Clotilda, queen of the Franks, established a precedent which would be followed by many other queens and noblewomen who would also win recognition of sainthood.[22] (See chapter 4, "Marriage and Domestic Proselytization," for a more extensive look at this topic.)

The early medieval queen-saint achieved prominence or visibility through her role as *consors regni, consocia* or partner to the king, as regent, and especially as dowager queen. In these positions, queens actively participated in the king's council (*curia regis*) which was small, personal, and itinerant.[23] Through their royal offices, pious queens appointed bishops and abbots; they worked to formulate alliances between the crown and bishoprics or monasteries; they influenced and effected religious policy and organization. These queens also seemed to exercise an inordinate amount of power over royal revenues and essentially held the "purse-strings" of the realm. Thus, they assumed major roles as patrons of the church. This proved to be an especially important way for them to leave their mark on society, and it clearly provided visibility and a route to fame. These queens and noblewomen endowed churches, founded monasteries and hospitals, and ransomed slaves, as well as dispensed substantial amounts in charity toward the needy. In this context Gregory of Tours, for example, praised St. Clotilda's pious activities: "She endowed churches, monasteries and other holy places with the lands necessary for their upkeep; her giving was so generous and so eager that already in her lifetime she was looked upon not as a Queen but as the handmaiden of God whom she served with such zeal." [24]

Clotilda's impressive patronage of the Church, however, was eclipsed by several other royal saints. The Merovingian queen-saint Radegund was especially famous for her extravagant donations. Fortunatus provides us with detailed accounts of her acts of generosity toward the Church and the poor. He notes, for example, that while she was still queen and at court, she dedicated her time and wealth to charity. The king handed over to Radegund a portion of the tribute which he had levied. This she distributed to monasteries, and when she could not carry these gifts in person, they were sent in her name. In underscoring her great generosity, Fortunatus states that even the hermits were not able to escape from the queen's largess! [25] After fleeing from the court and demanding the veil from Bishop Medard at Noyon, Radegund removed all of her expensive clothing, costly jewels, and ornaments, and placed them on the altar. She broke her heavy gold belt and distributed it among the poor. [26] As she made her way to Poitiers, Radegund provided rich donations to all of the churches and monasteries on her route. While in Tours, for example, the saintly queen visited all of its churches, and after hearing Mass she deposited on the altars the rich clothing and ornaments she had carried with her from the court. Thus in order to avoid this heavy burden, Fortunatus notes, she distributed all that was given to her. She never ignored the voice of the poor; she even disposed of her own clothing, seeing in the indigent bodies that she clothed the body of Christ. Fortunatus then observes that her charity was indeed great in order for it not to be overwhelmed by the pressing demands of the poor: while the requests were not lacking, so, too, the queen did not lack alms for distribution. According to Fortunatus, it was a miracle that Radegund was continually able to meet this demand. How as an exile, he asks, was she continually provided with such stores of treasure and wealth? [27] Radegund also established in Tours a monastery for men, and in Poitiers she founded her major monastery for women which was financed by her ex-husband, King Clothar.[28]

The Merovingian queen-saint Balthild (d. ca. 680) also won recognition for her generous patronage of the Church and acts of charity. According to her *vita,* "she loved the bishops as her fathers, monks as her brothers, and was the mother of the poor." She therefore provided for them all with large donations and charitable works. In fact, the *sancta regina* became so preoccupied with the administration and distribution of charity that the king provided her with a special officer, Abbot Genesius, to serve as her minister of largess. He was directed to serve the bishops and poor: he was to nourish the indigent, clothe the naked, bury the dead, and distribute gold and silver to monasteries of monks and nuns. The saintly queen proved to be especially generous toward monastic communities, and her hagiographer provides extensive information on the scope of her patronage in this area: "Who can enumerate the wealth that Balthild bestowed on the monasteries; how many entire estates and vast forests she gave them? . . . She considered them as God's own dwelling places."[29]

The queen's generosity was aimed at the promotion of both male and female monasticism. Among her many bequests were rich endowments for the rebuilding of the monastery for women at Chelles, and extensive lands, including Villa Nova, for the female community of Jouarre; she also enriched the women's houses of Logium and Faremoutiers with impressive grants and donations. Moreover, Balthild used her influence over her son Clothar III, as well as her own resources, to establish the male monastery of Corbie, where she selected Theudofred to be abbot. The queen-saint provided Abbot Philibert of Jumièges with a large forest and pastures, as well as other landed properties; to Abbot Laumer of Corbion (modern St-Laumer-de-Moutier) she gave a rich villa, large sums of silver and gold, and her royal girdle, along with other presents; to Fontenelle (St-Wandrille-Rançon) she donated many estates, and in response to their desperate straits, she sent them carts filled with provisions when their cellars were empty. Balthild also gave several villas and substantial sums of money to Luxeuil, as well as to other monasteries in Burgundy. She similarly enriched the churches and monasteries of holy men and holy women of Paris. According to her hagiographer, her charity even extended beyond the frontiers of the kingdom: the Roman basilicas of Sts. Peter and Paul, for example, received considerable donations from the queen, while the poor of Rome were also recipients of her abundant and frequent charity. In sum, notes the author of her *vita,* it is impossible to enumerate even half of Balthild's good works.[30]

In addition to her generous donations to monasteries and churches,

Queen Balthild also exercised a strong public role in attempting to regulate monastic life in the kingdom. According to her *vita:* "Nevertheless, we must not be silent about that which she did for the abbeys of St. Denis, St. Germain, St. Medard, St. Peter, St. Aignan, and St. Martin, and all of those where she was able to intervene. She wrote to the bishops and abbots in order that they establish among the monks a regular, common order, the *sanctus regularis ordo*. To the weight of her royal word she added privileges and immunities liberally granted to the communities which obeyed her and those that she recommended to pray to Christ for the king and for the peace of the kingdom."[31] By granting special immunities and privileges to these monasteries, Balthild freed them from episcopal authority and placed them directly under royal control, making them dependent on and answerable only to the Crown. Moreover, one of the major areas of her ecclesiastical policy concerned the appointment of bishops. Balthild appears to have exercised her influence in the appointment of at least four bishops: Erembert to the bishopric of Toulouse; Genese to the bishopric of Lyons, Leodegar to the bishopric of Autun, and Sigobrand to the bishopric of Paris.[32]

While the queen's extensive donations for the advancement of monasticism provided her with public recognition and a significant reputation as a patron of the Church, it was, however, her restoration of the monasteries of Corbie and Chelles that would be of special importance for the future promotion of her candidacy for sainthood. For these great monastic communities would preserve the memory of her political life, her social and religious work: they would become the primary foyers of the cult of the *sancta regina* Balthild.[33]

A number of other saintly queens and noblewomen won public recognition and praise for their patronage, and particularly for their generous benefactions toward the establishment of churches and monasteries. The queen-saint Richarde (d. ca. 909), wife of Charles III (the Fat), assumed an important role in the royal diplomas involving economic interventions in a number of monasteries and churches of the Frankish kingdom. As noted by Robert Folz in his important study, *Les Saintes reines du moyen âge en occident (VIᵉ–XIIIᵉ siècles)*, Queen Richarde received the usufruct of the monasteries of Sackingen and Sts-Felix-et-Regula at Zurich; she obtained in life annuity the Abbey St-Marin at Pavia and the monastery of Zurzach; she also intervened on behalf of the churches of Liège, Aix-la-Chapelle, and Langres. Richarde's major contribution, however, was the royal monastery for nuns, which, with the consent of her husband, she established on her own lands at Andlau. She provided a special privilege for her house, freeing it from local episcopal authority and placing it directly under the protection of the pope. And it was here at Andlau that Richarde spent her final years. The queen also provided a substantial donation to the abbey of Etival and received from the king the small monastery of Bonmoutier; both monasteries were then placed under Andlau. It is, therefore, the monastic communities of Andlau and Etival which became the main centers of promotion of the cult of their patron saint, Richarde.[34]

The Ottonian queen-saint Mathilda (ca. 895–968) wife of Henry I, was provided by her husband with a very generous dowry which consisted of Quedlinburg, Nordhausen, Pöhlde, Grona, and Duderstadt. Along with the right to alienate any of these properties as she pleased was the specific condition that she was not to remarry after her husband's death. A strong supporter of the Church, Mathilda used her influence and extensive wealth and lands to establish a number of very important *Familienklosters*. Clearly convinced of the value of, and need for, female houses, Mathilda therefore founded three impressive royal monasteries for women located at Quedlinburg, Enger, and Nordhausen, as well as monasteries for men at Pöhlde and Quedlinburg. She also exercised a strong influence over her son, Otto I, and "encouraged" him to provide donations and special privileges to the monasteries of St. Maurice of Magdeburg, Nordhausen, and Hilwartshausen. Although toward the end of her life she appears to have especially favored her new community of Nordhausen, she chose to die and to be buried beside her husband in her model foundation of Quedlinburg which was under the rule of her granddaughter, Abbess Mathilda.[35]

The tenth-century empress St. Adelaide (d. 999) was also well known for her generous donations to various churches and monasteries, as well as for the commissioning of a number of new monastic foundations. She had a particular interest in the great center of reform, the monastery of Cluny, which became the privileged beneficiary of her royal patronage. In his *vita* of St. Adelaide, Odilo of Cluny notes several of the great abbeys which were recipients of her munificence. We also learn that in her later years, as a thank-offering to God, Adelaide founded a monastic church or community for each of the three crowns worn by her husband and son (namely, those of Germany, Italy, and the Empire). According to Odilo, the first of these foundations for monks was at Payerne, Burgundy. (It had originally been established by her mother and was her mother's place of burial.) Adelaide then undertook the actual construction of the monastery. She placed this community under the care of St. Mayeul, who subsequently became abbot of Cluny. Her second major foundation was the monastery of St-Sauveur, located near Pavia. She extravagantly endowed this male community and also gave it to Cluny. And finally, toward the end of her life, she built the monastery of St. Peter and Paul at Selz in the Alsace. As a royal abbey for monks, it was given an immunity and placed directly under the papacy. The empress provided this foundation with a considerable endowment consisting of landed estates, buildings, gold, jewels, precious vestments, and various household furnishings. According to Odilo, she made generous donations to many other monasteries and churches including Monte Cassino and Souvigny; she also provided assistance for the restoration of the abbey of St. Martin of Tours, as well as bestowed the emperor's best cloak to the shrine of St. Martin of Tours.[36] It is, however, interesting to note that Adelaide, with her great fondness for the very masculine reform order of Cluny, apparently did not have any special commitment toward assisting female religious. Thus, unlike several other queen-saints for the period, Adelaide did not move to establish any monasteries for women. And in line with this masculine preference, at the end of her life she elected to retire to her monastery at Selz, and it was here among its monks that she chose her place of burial.[37]

The queen/empress-saint Cunegund (ca. 975–1033), wife of St. Henry (duke of Bavaria, king of Germany, and emperor), assumed the position of partner in rule. In collaboration the saintly couple endowed and built many churches, monasteries, and hospitals throughout Germany. Cunegund's advice was frequently sought and she was involved in many of the charters of the period concerning ecclesiastical matters such as the establishment of bishoprics and donations to the Church. At least partially through the empress's initiative and encouragement, Henry established the monastery and cathedral of Bamberg. However, Cunegund seemed to be especially interested in furthering monasticism for women and established her own foundation at Kaufungen in Hesse. In 1024, on the anniversary of her husband's death, Cunegund arranged for the dedication of her church at Kaufungen. During the ceremony, she provided the church with a piece of the "true cross" and took the veil. Cunegund thus spent her last years living as a nun at Kaufungen, where she died on March 3, 1033.[38]

Another public religious role and responsibility assumed by these aristocratic and royal women, which was related to patronage and charity, was that of providing prayers for their family and remembering its dead. These women were believed to possess a special efficacy as intercessors for their families' this-worldly and otherworldly needs. As noted by Karl Leyser in regard to the women of the Saxon aristocracy: "Their good works and prayers were felt to secure the successes of their menfolk, fathers, uncles, brothers, husbands and sons, in this life and they were responsible for the welfare of their souls in the next.

The two *vitae* of Queen Mathilda were as deeply concerned with this
duty and its performance as was Thietmar in his *Chronicon*. Mathilda's
prayers, pious works, endowments and personal sanctity secured
Otto's safe return from his second Italian expedition and by them she
expiated Henry I's sins as did Adelheid those of the emperor." [39] In this
crucial female religious tradition of securing the salvation of the souls
of one's family, providing the family *memoria,* Queen Mathilda
shortly before her death (d. 968) entrusted this function to her young
granddaughter, Mathilda, abbess of Quedlinburg. She turned over to
her a calendar containing the names of the dead Saxon princes and
asked her to pray for the soul of her husband, Henry, and for her own
soul as well as all of those the queen had formerly commemorated in
her prayers. [40] Thus, many of these queens and noblewomen assumed
this primary role of remembering the dead through their own prayers,
fasting, and penance, and on the anniversary of a relative's death, they
provided special charity to the poor to keep his or her memory alive.
These gender-specific functions were sometimes carried out by aristocratic women while they lived in the secular world; however, frequently the liturgical acts of *memoria* and intercession for the dead
were assumed by noblewomen who retired to convents to serve as
abbesses or as simple nuns in their family monasteries. [41]

Thus, through these few selected examples, we can note the extremely important role that many of these queens and empresses
played as generous donors and patrons of the Church. (The case of
St. Margaret of Scotland, also in this tradition, will be discussed later
in this chapter.) Their donations were often tied to the establishment
of family monasteries which provided opportunities for family members to assume the office of abbess, or a place of retirement at the end
of one's secular career; the cloisters also furnished special privileges of
burial in the family mausoleum and liturgical acts or perpetual prayers for the "safety" of the souls of the founders and their kin. These
queens and empresses were therefore particularly active in using their
resources and influence in the building of churches and promotion of
monasticism for both men and women. And it is in this context that
Jo Ann McNamara has so aptly noted: "God's work on earth needed
money as well as holiness and the road to sanctity for the women of
Merovingian Gaul was paved with their familial fortunes." [42]

PEACEMAKING ROLES OF THE MULIERES SANCTAE

During this early period, queens and noblewomen assumed significant public roles in the strategies of securing peace for their lands or
kingdoms. In many ways "peacemaking" and the maintenance or

protection of peace came to be viewed as a special female responsibility for early medieval society: only later did this activity come
increasingly under the auspices of the Church. As an ideal, it seemed
to be especially attached to royal and noblewomen. It was viewed as
one of their proper Christian duties: they were looked to as protectors
of the peace or "peace-weavers." This same activity also came to be
viewed as an important criterion for female sanctity.[43]

On one level, as peace-pledges, queens or noblewomen became the
principals involved in strategic marriage negotiations which were contracted between various kingdoms or countries that wished to effect
peace. Leaving their families and homelands behind to become princesses and queens of other kingdoms, these women, as instruments
of peace, also enhanced the strength and connections of the families
involved in these marriage alliances.[44]

A number of women saints also assumed active roles in the peace
initiatives of their period. The life of St. Radegund is again particularly
informative in regard to this queen-saint's peacemaking role in her
realm. Although at this point in her life she had left the court and
resided within the cloister of Ste-Croix, Radegund still managed to
remain well-informed in regard to the political climate: she followed
with great concern the intrigues, factionalism, and disorders of the
time. In the interests of her monastery and its holdings, as well as her
country, she continued to maintain close ties with those who wielded
power. As noted by Baudonivia, she was always concerned with these
relations, *semper de pace sollicita, de salute patriae curiosa.* Greatly
disturbed by the violence and devastation brought about by the kings
Sigebert and Chilperic in their disputes over their landed inheritance
(which included Poitou—the area in which Ste-Croix was located),
Radegund attempted to intervene as an agent of peace. According to
Baudonivia, she wrote letters of emotional appeal begging these rulers
to make peace in order to avoid the risk of ruining their common
country. Radegund also addressed the kings' circle of advisors and attempted to enlist their assistance "in order to assure the safety of the
people and of the country." In addition, the queen's acquisition of the
important relic of the Holy Cross was closely tied to her role as promoter of peace. She hoped that her treasured piece of the "True
Cross" would serve as "an instrument through which the salvation of
the kingdom could be secured and the welfare of the country assured."
Moreover, the queen called on her own monastic community of Ste-
Croix (which was to serve as "an agency of intercession on behalf of
kings") to assist in furthering the cause of peace: its nuns prayed without interruption; they undertook vigils and inflicted upon themselves
corporal penances for peace. Baudonivia then concludes, rather opti-

mistically and in the tradition of hagiographic license, that it was in fact through her protagonist—through St. Radegund's intercession—that peace was ultimately brought to the realm. Thus relieved of war, the country had been saved by the saintly queen.[45]

Similarly the Italian queen-saint Theodolinda also received praise for her peacemaking efforts in Lombardy. In a letter to the queen (598), Pope Gregory the Great wrote: "We have learned by the report of our son the abbot Probus, how kindly and zealously, according to your wont, you have exerted yourself for the conclusion of peace. We knew that we might reckon on your Christianity for this, that you would by all means apply your labour and your kindness to the cause of peace."[46]

The Life of Queen Balthild, which was influenced by St. Radegund's *vitae*, also credits this queen for her initiatory role as peacemaker in the kingdom of the Franks. According to her biographer, it was specifically through Balthild's faith and God's rule that peace was effected between Austrasia, Burgundy, and the Franks.[47]

Similarly Odilo of Cluny's *vita* of the empress-saint Adelaide notes her commitment to her responsibility as peacemaker. According to the Abbot of Cluny, she was always a friend of peace, "pacis ut semper amica," and therefore, at the end of the empress's life, during her last voyage, she traveled to Burgundy in order to reestablish peace.[48] Thus, for a number of these women saints, peacemaking activities assumed an important role in their programs of sanctity.

THE REFORM OF PRACTICES OF SLAVERY

Another significant public role which provided visibility for a number of these early women saints was that of reforming practices of slavery, as well as the actual buying of captives or slaves and restoring their freedom.

Among the *mulieres sanctae* who were depicted in their *vitae* as actively involved in this area of social reform and charity was St. Genovefa/Geneviève (d. 502). According to her Life, King Childeric had planned to kill a group of prisoners. Although the king had great respect for Genovefa, he also realized that she would attempt to rescue some of his captives and thus thwart his plans. He therefore left Paris and took his prisoners along with him. Warned by messengers, Genovefa followed him and, through her powers of persuasion, she was able to convince the king to spare the prisoners.[49]

In this same tradition Radegund, through her prayers, was said to have broken the chains of captives and freed them from their prisons. Radegund also appeared in a dream to a certain tribune named

Domnolenus who was ill. In curing him she asked that he release all of his prisoners.[50] St. Waldetrude was also involved in arranging for the freedom of captives. According to her *vita,* "prompted by divine compassion [she] took up the pious intention under vow to free captives. She arranged the ransom price [*pretium*], weighed out the silver. . . . When the captives had been bought back with the ransom money out of her own purse, at her command they returned to their families and homes." [51]

The queen-saint Balthild also showed a special concern for the freeing of captives and slaves. In this context it is interesting to note that Balthild was said to have been of low social origins. While the vast majority of saints of this early period were selected from the noble classes, Balthild's social background is quite unusual. As a young child she had been captured and sold into slavery in Britain. She was then exported to France and bought by the mayor of the palace at a "cheap price." [52] Thus until her marriage to the king, she had lived as a servant among the lower classes at the Frankish court. These early experiences perhaps made her more sympathetic to the problems and needs of the poor and unfree classes as well as to the plight of captives. As queen, for example, she ordered the abolition or reduction of a very unpopular tax which had weighed especially heavily upon the poor. According to her *vita,* unable to escape the heavy exactions of this tax, many of the desperately poor wished for the death of their children rather than the expense involved in having to nourish and raise them. Balthild was particularly remembered, however, for her attempts to reform the practices of slavery of her time. Her hagiographer comments on her significant role in this area: "It is necessary to make known that which crowns all of her merits. By orders dispatched to all the cities, she forbade the trading of Christian slaves so that henceforth not any [slaves] could be sold. She also bought a great number of captives; she restored freedom to some, placing others in monasteries and applying herself to rescue those of her country and *especially young girls whom she fondly nurtured and whom more readily still, she guided toward the cloister.*" [53]

The ransoming of slaves and captives provided, then, another important public role which was highlighted in the holy dossiers of these women and satisfied another criterion for their *fama sanctitatis.* (See also Margaret of Scotland's role in the ransoming of slaves, discussed later in this chapter.) A charitable activity, it also served a missionary function as the newly freed slaves were sometimes incorporated into the church or given over to monastic life. These groups of freed captives, no doubt, expressed their special gratitude to these saintly women—who had "saved their lives"—by becoming their loyal supporters and promoters of their cults.

MONASTICISM AND THE RECRUITMENT OF WOMEN SAINTS

While some of the most famous saints of this early period were princess- or queen-saints who were recruited from the royal courts, in many cases their primary claims to sanctity were in fact based on their "second careers," or the roles which they assumed as patrons or founding abbesses after their retirement from the court to monastic life. (This close identification or the overlapping of categories of queens and abbesses was noted, for example, in the ninth-century *Liber vitae* of Lindisfarne, which classified queens and abbesses together: *nomina reginarum et abbatissarum.*)[54]

For this period, more than one-half of the female saints were abbesses and nuns of the newly founded monasteries. The early flourishing of female saints of the mid-seventh through mid-eighth century in France, Belgium, and Britain, and the resurgence in tenth-century Britain and Germany, were intimately connected with new opportunities for women in the Church—specifically with the early popularity of female monasticism and the enthusiastic establishment of convents by the nobility. The Life of St. Sadalberga/Salaberga (d. ca. 670), for example, notes the expansiveness of this movement in the Frankish countryside under the influence of the Irish monks: "At that time throughout the provinces of Gaul, a multitude of monks and swarms of virgins under the rule of the blessed fathers Benedict and Columbanus began to spread not only in the fields, towns, villages, and castles, but also in the desert of the hermits, whereas before this time scarcely a few monasteries were found in these places."[55] Similarly the *vita* of St. Leoba describes the charismatic role of women saints in inspiring conversions and the adoption of monastic life in Germany: "The people's faith was stimulated by such tokens of holiness, and as religious feeling increased so did contempt of the world. Many nobles and influential men gave their daughters to God to live in the monastery in perpetual chastity; many widows also forsook their homes, made vows of chastity and took the veil in the cloister."[56] Thus the proliferation of new monastic communities for women—with the concomitant opportunities for patronage coupled with women's direction of these new foundations—is in turn reflected in the increasing number of women saints.

I have explored in another study some of the general patterns of the expansion and decline of female monasticism from ca. 500 to 1100.[57]

TABLE 3 New Religious Foundations: France/Belgium, 500–1099

| | | | WOMEN'S HOUSES | |
| | | | | PERCENTAGE |
YEARS	TOTAL	MEN'S HOUSES	NUMBER	OF TOTAL*
500–49	108	100	8	7.4
550–99	156	137	19	12.2
600–49	102	77	25	24.5
650–99	159	107	52	32.7
700–49	63	55	8	12.7
750–99	91	80	11	12.1
800–49	146	134	12	8.2
850–99	107	99	8	7.5
900–49	136	130	6	4.4
950–99	232	219	13	5.6
1000–49	543	515	28	5.2
1050–99	979	946	33	3.4
Total	2,822	2,599	223	—

Source: Based on the monastic foundations listed in L. H. Cottineau, *Répertoire topo-bibliographique des abbayes et prieurés* (Mâcon, 1935–37), 2 vols., and E. de Moreau, *Histoire de l'église en Belgique: Circonscriptions ecclésiastiques, chapitres, abbayes, couvents en Belgique avant 1559* (Brussels, 1948).

*Average = 7.9 percent.

Very briefly, according to our rather rough statistics, collected in tables 3 and 4, for the period from 500 to 1100, the total number of new religious houses established for male and female religious in France/Belgium and Britain was approximately 3,178. Of these settlements, fewer than 300 foundations were established for women; that is, less than 10 percent of the total number of new houses were founded for female religious. The era of most intense activity for women in monastic life in France/Belgium and Britain (as reflected in the founding of new female houses) was the seventh century. During the first half of the seventh century approximately 24.5 percent of the new foundations established in France/Belgium were women's communities. For the years 650–99, this increased to 32.7 percent. For the first half of the seventh century in Britain it appears that new foundations for women comprised approximately 31 percent of the total number of monastic foundations, and for the period 650–99, approximately 40.4 percent of new houses belonged to women. The proliferation of new monasteries in France/Belgium and Britain were closely tied to the expansion of the fledgling Church in the north, and new missionary activities of these regions. Also many of these new communities were coeducational, double houses, or affiliated com-

TABLE 4 New Religious Foundations: Britain, 500–1099

| | | | WOMEN'S HOUSES | |
| | | | | PERCENTAGE |
YEARS	TOTAL	MEN'S HOUSES	NUMBER	OF TOTAL*
500–49	8	8	0	0
550–99	39	39	0	0
600–49	29	20	9	31.0
650–99	94	56	38	40.4
700–49	26	19	7	26.9
750–99	16	15	1	6.3
800–49	12	8	4	33.3
850–99	11	9	2	18.2
900–49	22	19	3	13.6
950–99	26	21	5	19.2
1000–49	16	15	1	6.3
1050–99	57	51	6	10.5
Total	356	280	76	—

Source: Based on the monastic foundations listed in David Knowles and R. Neville Hadcock, *Medieval Religious Houses: England and Wales* (London, 1971), and the Ordnance Survey, *Monastic Britain* (Southampton, 1978).
*Average = 21.3

munities (which housed nuns and monks), and were located in the countryside or suburbs. These monasteries then provided important institutional frameworks in which royal and noble women, as patrons, founding abbesses, and nuns could exercise power and wealth and win promotion to sainthood.

As Karl Leyser has noted in regard to the impressive development of monasticism for women in Saxony, the nobility's eagerness to establish often lavishly endowed family monasteries seems to have owed much of its momentum to the opportunities provided by the new frontiers of these freshly Christianized lands—the rapid influx of landed wealth, spoils of war, and the enhancement of power and lordship. In part, this initial desire to establish convents seems to have been the response of a self-protective aristocratic caste to its own special needs.[58] The family monastery in this early period was in many ways regarded as simply an extension of the noble household. From the perspective of the founders of these new communities, the often substantial endowment did not constitute a permanent alienation of property; rather, it was viewed as perhaps a temporary "loan" or investment in a complementary sphere of influence. Therefore, as a type of strategy, the founding families often attempted to maintain control over their monasteries and properties by safeguarding the election of the abbesses and advocacy of the convent for their heirs.[59] These communities also answered the practical concerns of the noble households by providing a proper place of security or refuge for daughters who did not wish to marry, or for whom marriages were perhaps inexpedient in light of family strategies. Moreover, they provided a convenient place of retirement for widows or repudiated wives of the court.[60] Finally, these family houses furnished privileged space for the burial of their founders and family members; their communities also provided prayers and liturgical *memoria* for the salvation of their souls.

Thus many of the saints of this early period were recruited from the cloister, specifically from among founding abbesses and their immediate heirs. We can, then, see a correlation between the flurry of activity in the founding of new communities for female religious and the designation of these royal/noble patrons and founding abbesses as saints.

At the outset it is interesting to note that despite the very practical or "this-worldly" basis of these women's sanctity, one of the ideals frequently underscored in the monastic *vitae* is the dramatic withdrawal from the world by these saintly queens or noblewomen. Their hagiographers focus in some detail on the severing of their "this-worldly" connections and cares, as well as their remarkable renunciation of wealth and status. They are called *regina ancilla* or *ancilla dei*. Moreover, the pious acts of these women of privilege, now under monasticism, are described as "disinterested" and apolitical. In reality, however, as noted in the case of St. Radegund, and as Susan Ridyard has argued in regard to royal Anglo-Saxon saints, this "renunciatory ideal" strayed rather far from the truth and it had little in the way of practical consequences.[61] In fact, far from "cutting themselves off" from the political life of the court, these royal saints/abbesses continued to maintain close ties with their families and friends. For example, as Ridyard has noted in regard to St. Edburga, this saint's royal foundation was physically located only a "short stroll" from her father's palace in Winchester.[62] Other abbesses occupied monasteries located within cities held by their families, or within family defenses or castles, or on family lands. This physical proximity of their new foundations then encouraged their continual involvement in the political and economic affairs of their families; and not infrequently these saintly queens used their special connections to provide, for themselves, further access to corridors of power (e.g., the king, bishop, etc.), or to bring additional privileges, wealth, and property to their communities.[63]

The biographer of St. Balthild, for example, notes this queen's forced retirement into her monastic foundation at Chelles. The queen is described as publicly adopting the attributes of humility and sub-missiveness in her relationship with the abbess of the community. On the other hand, the author also provides us with a fascinating descrip-tion of Balthild's continuing preoccupation with the prosperity of her monastery and how she often discussed matters of strategy, power, and reputation with the abbess. "Thus she demanded that they maintain good relations with the king, queen, and the worthy nobility of the palace, that they give them offerings of eulogies, according to the custom, so that the house that she had established for the glory of God did not lose any of its fame, but, on the contrary, it was more beloved and valuable to those who loved it." [64]

The critical relationship between economics (landed wealth) and sanctity was clearly not lost on the hagiographers. In addition to praising the saint's great generosity in favor of the Church, the lives frequently provide detailed accounts of the extensive landed estates which the saint or her parents had employed in the establishment of their family monastery. While many of these early family houses were created for daughters of kings or queens, aristocrats, or, frequently, sisters of bishops or abbots, who would then assume the position of founding abbess, a good number of religious houses were established by widows acting in their own names. They founded these monas-teries on their dower lands as places of retirement and security. Many of these noble widows became abbesses of their new communities or as patrons continued to exercise an immense amount of influence and control over their establishments without officially assuming the position of abbess. A number of these women handed their founda-tions over to their daughters or nieces who subsequently assumed the position of abbess.

The *vitae* frequently underscore the immense autonomy and power found among these early medieval widows whose use, and, in some cases, manipulation of power were manifested in a number of ways. [65] Many of the holy widows refused remarriage and insisted on taking the veil and entering monastic life. For example, through the use of a clever ruse—(acting "not womanlike but manlike")—the seventh-century St. Rictrude, founding abbess of the monastery of Marchi-ennes in Hainault was said to have tricked the king (perhaps Dago-bert), and escaped from a forced second marriage. She then used her vast resources to build a monastic foundation for women at Marchiennes, alongside the monastery for men that her husband and St. Amand had previously built. Assuming the position of abbess of her popular new foundation, she then ruled Marchiennes for some forty years. [66]

The autonomy of these widows became especially apparent in their rather liberal alienations of family properties in favor of the establishment of new monastic communities and churches. While the saints' Lives praised and encouraged their independent acts—that is, the generous or extravagant donations in favor of the Church—in reality, many of these bequests appear to have been accomplished as overt acts of defiance, acts of "holy robbery" carried out against the express wishes of the widow's family. These actions emphasize the helplessness of the family at this time to effectively control widows' activities—specifically, their inability to prevent widows from making what appeared to some as impulsive or excessively generous donations, at odds with family strategies and at the expense of the future interests of the patrimony.[67]

The *vitae* also tell of the success of the founding abbess-saints and their successors in augmenting their community's original endowment, especially through attracting additional bequests and donations from the local nobility. Women of the aristocracy who wished to join monasteries were expected to bring with them landed estates and other wealth which were then deeded over to the community. The initial popularity of the movement, along with the widespread fame of the founding abbess-saints, served to attract impressive numbers of noblewomen to some of these newly established communities. Although a good number of these proprietary houses appear to have been fairly small, with communities of only a dozen or so female religious, and survived only a generation or two, other monasteries were extremely large and successful, and housed several hundred inmates. According to Baudonivia's *vita* of St. Radegund, the foundress wanted her new monastery to be able to accommodate the greatest possible number of nuns (see plate 4).[68] Therefore, at the death of St. Radegund in 587, her monastery of Ste-Croix at Poitiers had approximately two hundred nuns, plus clergy and monastic *familia.*[69] Some three hundred women flocked to live under the rule of the founding abbess-saint Aurea in her monastery in Paris while approximately three hundred nuns joined Salaberga's monastery in Laon. St. Sexburga's new foundation at Sheppey had some seventy-seven inmates, and St. Mildred's monastery at Minster-in-Thanet had seventy. St. Tetta, an eighth-century abbess of Wimborne, was said to have had approximately fifty nuns under her care.[70] Many other *vitae* mention the large communities of nuns, and monks in the case of the double monastery, over which these abbess-saints ruled. Thus in the early enthusiasm of monastic life for women, a number of these communities were very large and impressive religious centers. Filled with women from wealthy and powerful families, they provided a significant power base for the rulers of these communities. They would also prove to be immensely important in promoting the cults of their founding abbesses or patron saints.

FEMALE SAINTS AND BUILDING CAMPAIGNS

The early medieval founding abbess-saints, like their male cohorts, also exercised their authority and won immortality through impressive building campaigns. The significant role which they assumed as patrons of major building campaigns or as "builder-saints" is again related to the special needs and opportunities, as well as the early fervor, found in these newly Christianized lands. The great numbers of new churches and monastic buildings, as well as the rapidity with which many of these construction projects were completed, appear to be truly amazing—indeed "miraculous" in themselves. Although today very little remains of these early medieval buildings, archaeological finds, the *vitae* of saints, chronicles, and cartularies all provide hints as to the size, numbers, and extent of these structures.[71]

It was apparently traditional for many of these early monastic complexes to have several churches: one specifically for the nuns (or for the nuns and monks, or nuns and parishioners), another which served as a funerary basilica or a mausoleum for the community, and perhaps another for the male component of the monastery, the priests and monks.[72] The abbess-saint Salaberga, for example, was said to have built a large monastery with six churches for her nuns. For the men attached to the community, she constructed a smaller monastery with its own church.[73] The female communities at Nivelles and Soissons each had four churches. We learn from our sources that in the seventh century St. Begga made a pilgrimage to Rome and on her return she built a monastery at Andenne. In imitation of the seven churches of Rome she built seven churches at her new foundation at Andenne.[74] According to the *vita* of St. Austreberta, abbess of Pavilly (d. 703), she "built a wonderful monastery dedicated to Mary, God's mother. She also constructed basilicas to Saint Peter, Saint Martin and other saints, housing them as saints should be, with all prepared swiftly and properly."[75] Toward the end of her career, St. Bertha, eighth-century abbess and founder of Blangy, enlarged and redecorated her monastic buildings. She was also said to have built ten churches (chapels?), eight of which were dedicated to St. Martin, one to St. Audomar, and the other to St. Vedast.[76]

The abbess "builder-saints," like their contemporary abbots and bishops, appeared as commissioners of ecclesiastical buildings. Many oversaw the actual construction of these buildings.[77] An eleventh-century text, for example, praises St. Sexburga for her building activities. "Then for delight and for honour, it pleased the holy woman Seaxburh to found and build a minster for herself there [on the island of Sheppey] so that men of old said that the sound of creaking cart and complaining harrow never stopped for thirty years."[78] The German saint Hadeloga, founder and abbess of Kitzingen, was also remembered for her building activities. According to tradition, she was responsible for having built a stone bridge over the river Main at Kitzingen, one which took some thirty-two years to be constructed.[79]

A few of the *vitae*, however, tell of a more direct involvement in these building activities by female saints. The Life of St. Rusticula, abbess of Arles (d. ca. 632) is especially illuminating in regard to her role as a "builder-saint." According to the *vita*, Rusticula was an extremely successful abbess and she was inspired by the Holy Spirit to provide her nuns with "a larger place for prayer." "Meanwhile she built churches and put up walls for the holy [nuns]. At the commencement of the church, when the foundations were being laid, the most holy mother rejoiced with her own hands to carry stones to the workmen; when the building was complete with the Lord's favor and inspiration, she dedicated the church to the Holy Cross." We then learn that "after this, Rusticula had a vision of a church of huge dimensions built in heaven, and as she gazed upon it she received a command from the Lord to build one like it on earth. She therefore hastened with joy faithfully to fulfill the Lord's command and she built a church of resplendent loveliness. She likewise decided that since this church was the larger, to dedicate it to the Holy Cross and the church she had built earlier she rededicated in honor of St. Michael the Archangel." We also learn that she established seven altars in her new church. "Thus indeed in accord with the Apostle's instruction, Rusticula, as a wise builder, laid her foundation; she built on earth what afterwards she found in heaven, because those saints whom she venerated with such love on earth, prepared celestial habitations for her in paradise through their intercession."[80]

The seventh-century abbess-saint Landrada was also said to have worked with her own hands in the construction of her church in honor of the Virgin Mary. According to our sources, she worked "like a man" in preparing the foundations. After clearing away the briars, she dug up and transported stones, and personally erected the altar of her church.[81] The *vita* of the eighth-century abbess-saints Herlinda and Renilda also describes the building activities of these two sisters. Each morning they would get up early to work on the family monastery at Eyck, where they carried sand and immense stones for the building. According to their hagiographer, their monastery was completed with amazing rapidity.[82]

St. Hathumoda, founding abbess of the famous monastery of Gandersheim, wanted to construct for her community an impressive church of stone rather than of wood, as was traditional at this time. And allegedly, through a miracle she was led to an area which held all of the stone that she needed to build her new church.[83]

In the Life of King Edward the Confessor we learn that the king and queen competed with one another in the construction of their special churches. The author then provides the very important observation: "Also, nowhere did she [Queen Edith] believe alms better bestowed than where the weaker sex, less skilled in building, more deeply felt the pinch of poverty, and was less able by its own efforts to drive it away." Edith then began rebuilding the royal abbey of Wilton (previously built in wood) in stone. "Impetuously she urged the workmen to make haste. . . . But the prudent queen's building, because it was more modestly planned, was completed more quickly. No delays she wove for this undertaking; and when a few years had slipped by it was finished nobly with all things necessary to, and becoming, such a work and also royal honour and glory." The *vita* also notes that together with the bishop, Edith presided over the dedication of her new church at Wilton.[84] This source then underscores two important gender-based differences: the poverty indigenous to many female houses as well as the smaller scale of their churches in comparison to male foundations.

A number of abbess-saints won recognition for enlarging their churches and monastic buildings; others were lauded for their work in decorating and enriching their new foundations. The *vita* of the seventh-century abbess-saint Eustadiola, founder of the large monastery of Moyen-Moutiers at Bourges, notes that she embellished the walls of her church with magnificent embroidered wall hangings and covered the altar with expensive cloth fringed with gold. With their own hands the abbess and her nuns had made these works of art. St. Eustadiola also commissioned crosses, candelabra, chalices, and reliquaries for the adornment of the church.[85]

Several founding abbess-saints were remembered for assisting their new foundations in other ways. We learn, for example, that St. Eanswith's monastery, built on a cliff at Folkestone, experienced serious problems with its water supply. Thus, according to legend, St. Eanswith dug a canal with the tip of her crozier (the symbol of abbatial power) and made the water run uphill to her foundation![86] A similar incident is associated with St. Bertha, the founder of a convent near Avernay. This monastery also lacked access to a water supply. Through a vision, however, St. Bertha learned of a nearby garden with a spring. She then purchased this land for one pound of silver and traced with her crozier a small ditch which connected this spring to her monastery. According to tradition, the saint called the stream "Libra" since it had been bought for a pound.[87]

Thus another important area of activity of these abbesses and patrons of the early church, which aided the progress of the conversion movement in the Church as well as being among the criteria of individual sanctity, was the patronage and the actual construction of churches and monasteries. These works then provided a certain visibility and fame to those who had initiated the building campaigns, and strongly contributed to these women's saintly dossiers.

COLLECTORS OF RELICS

Building campaigns were frequently associated with the procurement of precious relics by monastic communities and churches and the establishment of pilgrimage centers. For many houses the acquisition of a major relic could mean the difference between the economic survival or well-being of a religious community, and its neglect and ultimate oblivion.[88] However, the acquisition of holy relics also provided an occasion for public visibility, for prestige—another criterion for sanctity—for the person who obtained them. As noted by Peter Brown, relics were believed to discern the personal status or merits of their owner and could declare in no uncertain terms whether or not they approved of this relationship. Thus success in acquiring relics was viewed as a sign of the special merit or holiness of the person who obtained them.[89]

A number of *vitae* and other sources describe the prominent role female saints assumed in the collection of relics of the holy dead. According to the early tradition attached to the fourth-century Empress St. Helena, she discovered the True Cross during her pilgrimage to Jerusalem. Subsequently she promoted the cult of the Cross. Helena was then to exercise an important role as an exemplum for medieval queens and other women in regard to the acquisition of relics.[90]

Perhaps one of the most celebrated cases of a female saint involved in the procurement of major relics and the establishment of a cult center is that of St. Radegund. While she was still living at the villa of Saix, Radegund began her collection, which was to include relics of all of the saints. She petitioned a priest named Magnus to bring her relics of St. Andrew and a number of other saints, which she then placed above the altar. However, according to Baudonivia's *vita*: "Since her entry into the monastery, the East is able to attest, the North, South, West are able to say, what an immense quantity of relics she had diligently requested and amassed. For these precious pearls, hidden in heaven, for these joys of Paradise, from all sides her devotion multi-plied the presents and requests and she ended by obtaining them." In her desire for the relics of the martyr Mamas of Caesarea, she sent a certain priest named Reoval to Jerusalem. Baudonivia notes that the patriarch of Jerusalem received the priest, and three days later, after celebrating Mass, he approached Mamas's tomb along with his con-gregation. He then requested of the holy martyr that if Radegund was truly a handmaid of the Lord, he would make it known by permitting her to receive the relic she requested. The patriarch touched each finger of the right hand and the little finger came away easily. The petition of the queen was successful and her wish fulfilled. And with fitting honors he sent the finger to the blessed Radegund and God's praises were sung in her honor from Jerusalem even to Poitiers. As stated by Baudonivia: "For God does not refuse to his faithful servants those things which they ask of him."[91]

Radegund's greatest coup, however, specifically followed in the tra-dition of the imperial legacy of St. Helena, namely, her acquisition of a piece of the Holy Cross from the court at Constantinople. As noted in the *vita:* "Thus, like Saint Helena, imbued with wisdom, full of the fear of God, glorious with good works, she eagerly sought to salute the wood where the ransom of the world was hung for our salvation that we might be snatched from the power of the devil. . . . That which [Helena] did in the East, the blessed Radegund accomplished in Gaul." Through the use of her political connections, Radegund was success-ful in acquiring this important relic, as well as the relics of a number of other apostles and martyrs. After the relics were finally placed in Radegund's convent with all due honor, the monastery changed its name from Saint Mary to Ste-Croix or Holy Cross, and the relic be-came the focus of a local cult. It was responsible for attracting crowds of pilgrims and also contributed to the fame of Radegund's thau-maturgical powers through the working of miracles. According to her *vita,* anyone who came to the cult center with faith, whatever the infirmity, would leave healed by the special *virtu* or *potentia* of the relic of the cross. Thus, despite the lamentations of the nuns on Rade-gund's death and their fear for their future lives without the benefit of their holy patron, according to Baudonivia's *vita,* Radegund did not leave her daughters bereft or in disorder but rather was the *provisatrix optima* ("the best provider"). For through the procurement of the precious and important relic of the Holy Cross, she had in fact made provisions for their continuing economic security.[92]

The seventh-century Belgian saint Reyneldis/Reineldis also won recognition for her important role in acquiring relics. As related by her *vita,* she embarked on a pilgrimage to the Holy Land and after some seven years was said to have procured a number of precious relics, including a splinter of the True Cross, a piece of the Holy Sepulchre, and a fragment of the tunic of the Virgin Mary. According to tradition, on her return home all of the inhabitants of the neighborhood of Saintes welcomed Reyneldis and the relics with great joy.[93]

There are a number of other sources which mention women saints and their acquisition of relics. The eighth-century Anglo-Saxon saint Mildred was said to have obtained a number of relics of saints, including the nail of the cross of Christ, while she was a nun at the monastery of Chelles. She then brought these relics with her when she returned to Britain and entered the monastery of Minster-in-Thanet.[94] The parents of the ninth-century St. Hathumoda, the *sancta mater* Oda and her husband, Liudolf, duke of the Saxons, went on a pilgrimage to Rome and brought back to their new monastery of Gandersheim the sacred relics of popes Anastasius and Innocent.[95] The sources also note that St. Adela, countess of Flanders (eleventh century), as a widow traveled to Rome where she received the veil from the pope as well as some relics of St. Sidronius. She brought these precious relics back to her monastic foundation of Meesene.[96] The saintly reputation of Irmgardis, countess of Zutphen (late eleventh to early twelfth century) was also enhanced by her involvement in procuring relics. Irmgardis apparently made three pilgrimages to Rome. On her first trip the pope asked her to bring him relics of the 11,000 virgins of Cologne; in return she was given part of the head of St. Silvester which she then carried back to Cologne.[97]

In contrast to these cases of authorized, or at least somewhat legitimate, acquisition of relics, there are a number of fascinating transactions which occurred under somewhat nefarius circumstances in the tradition of the *furta sacra*.[98] One of the earliest and most detailed accounts of the theft of relics concerns the indefatigable popular sixth-century St. Tygria/Tigre of Maurienne whose activities are described in several works, including Gregory of Tours's *Libri miraculorum*. Tigre's sanctity seems to have been essentially predicated on the fame and visibility which she achieved in procuring a valuable relic of St. John the Baptist for the church at Maurienne. According to tradition, excited by the stories related by several Irish monks of miracles which had occurred on the site of the relics of St. John the Baptist, Tigre made a pilgrimage to Alexandria for the specific purpose of acquiring a relic of the saint. However, after spending two years of extraordinary austerities and prayer at the tomb of St. John the Baptist, she was still unable to convince the guards to part with any of their precious relics. At the beginning of the third year, while prostrated on the ground before the tomb, she vowed that she would neither eat nor leave this position until her mission was accomplished. We are told that on the seventh day, weakened by fasting, she received an answer to her prayers: apparently the thumb of St. John the Baptist miraculously appeared on the tomb. Tigre promptly deposited this relic, which she believed was a gift from God, in a gold reliquary which she had prepared for this occasion. And according to tradition, she then returned to Maurienne with her precious relic. Her successful venture in procuring the relic for Maurienne made Tigre a local celebrity. She died (ca. 565) a few days after having assisted in the consecration of the new cathedral of St. John of Maurienne.[99]

There are also a number of cases of nuns involved in the stealing of relics. One interesting example concerns the relics of St. Werburga (d. ca. 700), abbess of Ely and founder of the monasteries of Hanbury, Threckingham, and Weedon. According to the sources, St. Werburga's final request was to be buried at the monastery of Hanbury. However, the abbess died at Threckingham and the nuns of this monastery, unwilling to lose this valuable possession—the body of their founding abbess—prepared to bury her in their own church. In order to safeguard their holy relics, they locked their gates and kept a close watch over St. Werburga's body. The community of Hanbury, aware of their foundress's last wishes and also wanting possession of her relics, came to Threckingham. Surprisingly, when they arrived, they found the gates of the monastery and church open and the watchman in a deep sleep. They therefore were able to remove the saint's body from Threckingham without any resistance, and they brought it back to Hanbury for burial.[100]

The economic impact of relics can be clearly seen in a mid-ninth-century case which concerned Ermentrude, abbess of Jouarre. Apparently moved by the desperate economic straits of her monastery, she approached her relative, the bishop of Sens, to ask him to assist her in securing the relic of St. Potentien for her community. The bishop ultimately acquiesced to this request; nevertheless, he realized that he was acting against the interests of his own city in giving this relic to Ermentrude. He therefore advised the abbess to secretly transport the famous relic to Jouarre, which she then did in all haste. At Jouarre the saint's body was welcomed by the congregation with transports of joy. And hereafter, we learn, the monastery no longer experienced indigency nor troubles; rather, it became famous through their new saint's exorcisms and cures.[101]

Similarly the *vita* of St. Gislenus notes that ca. 930 the nuns of Maubeuge stole the body of St. Gislenus from the neighboring monastery of Mons. It was only through threats of excommunication that they were forced by Stephen, bishop of Cambrai, to return the body.[102] (See also chapter 7 for the attempted *furta sacra* of the relics of St. Attala.)

We therefore see in our sources many examples of saints and other female religious actively involved in the procurement of relics. The successful acquisition of an important relic would provide an important economic base for their monastic community, church, or town through the establishment of a pilgrimage or curative center; this activity would also contribute to their own *fama sanctitatis*.

MONASTIC CHARITY AND HOSPITALITY

Like their secular sisters at court, many of these patron saints or abbesses also won praise for their active roles (and frequently extravagant behavior) in dispensing charity and hospitality. This area of pious activity was one of the highest priorities in the criteria for sanctity. Descriptions of saints' numerous acts of charity occupy a substantial portion of many of the *vitae*. As wealthy patrons of their new monasteries, these women distributed their wealth freely to those in need who visited their foundations. They provided the indigent with food, clothing, and money. However, for many communities, this emphasis on charity placed a definite strain on their limited resources. And in a number of cases, these saints appear to have been "generous to a fault," or economically irresponsible (at least from our perspective); for their acts of charity frequently had the end result of dissipating their monastery's resources and leaving their nuns in a state of very real poverty. A number of saints' Lives, in fact, underscore rather clearly the ambivalence or even strong resentment on the part of the community toward their patron's excessive generosity or profligate behavior toward "strangers." Nevertheless, these open-handed acts of charity were unanimously endorsed by the *vitae* of the period as one of the important measures or "signs" of sanctity. The Lives also strongly condemned calculated or cautious policies in regard to the sharing of one's food or wealth as mean-spirited or selfish.[103]

An interesting example can be found in the life of the Irish St. Brigid who was especially renowned as a profligate saint. She was said to have bestowed on the poor the monastery's only milk cow as well as the very oxen used for ploughing their fields. On one occasion, according to tradition, the queen of Crimthan gave Brigid a silver chain with a human image on one end and an apple on the other. Brigid then turned this chain over to the nuns of her monastery who immediately hid it, since they knew that the saint would inevitably share it with the poor. When a leper came to Brigid, she gave him the chain without her nuns' knowledge. When they learned of this, they confronted her with anger and bitterness: "Little good have we from thy compassion to everyone, and *we ourselves in need of food and raiment!*" Brigid then reprimanded them for their "sinful behavior" and told them to go into the church to the place where she traditionally prayed, and there they would find their chain. They did as they were told, and according to tradition, although it had been given to the poor man, the chain was miraculously restored to the nuns.[104]

It is, then, following in this tradition of extravagant behavior, or open-handed generosity or charity, that many of the miracles of these abbess-saints focus on the very real poverty of these early monastic foundations. The *vitae* describe various miraculous "antidotes" provided by the saint in response to the general poverty of the foundation, which, in some cases, was due to her own profligate behavior. These miracles, frequently in the biblical tradition, concern the fortuitous appearance of fish, bread, wine, milk, water, clothing, and so forth at their time of desperate need.[105]

In addition to their reputations of extravagant charity, many of these abbess-saints were renowned for their hospitality and the personal care and attention which they showered on their guests. We learn, for example, that every day St. Radegund dispensed charity to the poor and received them at her table. On Wednesdays and Saturdays, with her head wrapped up in a linen cloth, she prepared a bath and washed the heads of the indigent. According to Fortunatus, she was not repulsed by the various diseases of the scalp which she encountered; she did not turn away, for example, from the sight of crust, scabies, ringworm, or abscessed sores from which she sometimes extracted worms. She removed from their sores the rot which ate away at them. When she had finished washing her guests' heads, she then combed their hair. Moreover, according to Fortunatus, like the Good Samaritan, she covered their wounds with an unguent or oil. If a guest were female, Radegund had the woman step into the bath where she then washed her from head to foot. Afterwards Radegund served them a meal: she personally waited on each of them—cutting their bread and meat. When they left, if their clothing was too worn, Radegund provided them with new robes.

The saintly queen was particularly concerned with the welfare of leprous women. Fortunatus tells us that when lepers approached the monastery and had announced themselves according to their ordinary signal, Radegund sent someone to greet them and to inquire as to where they had come from and how many there were. When Radegund received this information, she set the table for her guests and secretly retired to a place where no one would see her. Fortunatus notes that she then took into her arms these leprous women, covered with sores, and with great love kissed their faces. Radegund then proceeded to wash their faces, hands, and fingernails in warm water; she also cleaned their sores and served them food. When they retired, she gave them gifts of gold or clothing, while barely admitting one of her nuns as witness. It appears that at Ste-Croix there existed a certain ambivalency, or, actual physical revulsion on the part of some members of her community of noblewomen in regard to Radegund's extravagant behavior toward women with leprosy. For, according to Fortunatus, one day one of Radegund's nuns got up the courage to ask her: "Most holy woman, in the future who would wish to kiss you, you who have kissed in a like manner lepers?" "In truth," responded Radegund with enjoyment, "if you do not wish to kiss me, I am already consoled." [106]

The Life of St. Odilia, first abbess of Hohenbourg (d. ca. 720) describes her hospitality to pilgrims. The location of her monastery on Mont-Sainte-Odile, rising over two thousand feet above the Rhine valley, discouraged the visits of many pilgrims. Thus with the approval of her community, Odilia built a new foundation at the base of the mountain which housed some of the members of her large community. It was later called Niedermünster. Here the saint received many women pilgrims from Ireland and Britain as well as religious men from various provinces.[107]

The *vita* of St. Leoba also notes that "she was extremely hospitable. She kept open house for all without exception, and even when she was fasting gave banquets and washed the feet of the guests with her own hands, at once the guardian and the minister of the practice instituted by our Lord." [108]

The *vitae* and chronicles of the early Middle Ages then recognized these *mulieres sanctae* for their many "public" activities—especially their broad economic roles and their practical talents, as well as their extravagant acts of generosity and hospitality. The dossiers of these holy women also endorsed their administrative skills, prudence, and wisdom.

SANCTITY AND MONASTIC ADMINISTRATION

During this early period, many of the abbesses, and perhaps especially those ruling over double monasteries or affiliated houses, had an impressive amount of public power and authority. Although they could not be consecrated priests and celebrate Mass (which was indeed a critical gender-based disability), many of the administrative roles which these early abbesses assumed closely approximated those of abbots or bishops of the period. The early ceremonies of ordination or investment emphasize this near equality of office (see plate 5).

Abbesses were invested with insignia indicative of their public office, which included the pallium, alb, stole, crozier (staff), pectoral cross, ring, gloves, and miter. For example, the fifth-century Visigothic Sacramentary, which provides instructions for the ordination of abbesses, notes that the candidate is to be clothed in sacred religious vestments and crowned with a miter. While investing the abbess with a pallium before the altar, the bishop was to repeat a prayer which stated that before God there was no discrimination of sex (*apud quem non est discretio sexuum*) and that women, like men, are called to collaborate in the spiritual struggle. According to the Moissac Sacramentary (ca. 800), the ordination rite for abbesses was the same as that for abbots. They were to be given an alb and stole and then prostrate themselves before the altar.[109]

An especially interesting case which has caused some controversy concerning the power, authority, or position of these early abbesssaints is that of the late fifth-/early-sixth-century Irish saint, Brigid. Cogitosus, writing approximately a century and a quarter after Brigid's death, describes the immense popularity, among both men and women, of the saint's early monastic foundation at Kildare. He then explains Brigid's role in the designation of a churchman to assist her in her administrative and sacramental duties: "wishing to provide in a wise manner and properly in all things for the souls of her people, and anxious about the churches of the many provinces that had attached themselves to her, she realised that she could not possibly do without a high priest (bishop) to consecrate churches and supply them with clergy in various grades. She sent accordingly for a distinguished man, adorned with all virtues, then leading a solitary life in the desert. Going herself to meet him, she brought him back in her company to *govern the church with her in episcopal dignity*, that nothing which depends on orders should be wanting in her churches. Thereafter the anointed head and chief of all bishops and the most blessed chief of virgins, in pleasant mutual agreement and with the directing aid of all the virtues, erected her principal church. At the same time, through the merits of both, her see, episcopal at once and virginal, spread like a fruitful vine, rich in growing branches, and took root in the whole island. In Ireland, therefore, the archbishop of the Irish bishops, and the abbess whom all the abbesses of the Irish revere, hold a preeminent position in a prosperous line and in perpetuity."[110]

A number of scholars have discussed the relationship of Brigid, as abbess, and her bishop in regard to power and authority. Todd, for example, has argued that "it is equally clear that she had her bishop under her own jurisdiction. She engaged him to govern the church with her."[111] In contrast, other scholars have concluded that this relationship was more of a partnership where the abbess and bishop exercised a type of joint rule.[112]

It is, however, interesting to note that according to the anonymous ninth-century Life of St. Brigid, Brigid was ordained as a bishop. This claim that the saint had received the episcopal order was perhaps an attempt to explain Brigid's unique position of honor and authority in the Church, as well as that of her successor abbesses at Kildare. According to the *vita,* as Brigid knelt to receive the nun's veil, Bishop Mel "being intoxicated with the grace of God there did not recognise what he was reciting from his book, for he consecrated Brigit with the orders of a bishop. 'This virgin alone in Ireland,' said Mel, 'will hold the episcopal ordination.' While she was being consecrated a fiery column ascended from her head."[113] Later versions of this story, however, attempted to discredit or dismiss this incident, arguing that it had clearly been a mistake: Bishop Mel had consecrated Brigid while he was drunk, thus making it invalid![114]

Lisal Bitel has argued in regard to this event: "Everything historians know about religious women in the age of conversion makes it unlikely that Brigit or any other woman actually became a bishop, and no other document described a woman performing recognizable episcopal duties. The literary incident in which Brigit became a bishop is hard to reconcile with the wives and sisters of historical reality, but it was no accident. Brigit's hagiographer meant for Mel to bungle the ordination, for although male hagiographers described women saints of the conversion period as wifely surrogates, they also sometimes cast them as ecclesiastical chiefs, landowners and the lords of clients. What better illustration of the complex, contradictory ideas about gender interaction flourishing among the early Irish: most women were guided into traditional roles of wife and mother, and Christian theology limited its female professionals to chaste imitations of these real-life roles; yet the most admirable and saintly nuns were not real women at all, at least by early Irish standards, but ersatz men."[115]

Thus, taken together, these sources clearly serve to underscore the immense authority, the prominence, and the preeminent public position—equal to that of abbot or a "quasi-episcopal" power—which some of these abbesses assumed during this early period. Moreover, the strong denial of the validity of Brigid's episcopal ordination by churchmen of a later period might perhaps reflect a changed atmosphere or tolerance in the Church toward women. It might also have expressed the need to allay any potential fears, on the part of churchmen, in regard to Brigid's successors at Kildare, or other abbesses, who might have recourse to this rather irregular "historical precedent" which could be used to justify their attempts at usurping male power and prerogatives.

Many of these early abbesses, then, like their male colleagues, held extensive power as well as landed properties and rights. A number of these abbesses received privileges or special political immunities which freed them from the overlordship of their bishop or local lord and placed them directly under the protection of the pope or king. They collected "taxes" from their lands as well as tithes from the churches under their control. They held court and dispensed legal decisions concerning civil and criminal cases. They had their own seals which they affixed to their official charters, diplomas, and letters. Some of these abbesses received grants of economic immunity, along with rights of marketplace and coinage. They also exercised "quasi-sacerdotal" functions: they preached, heard confession, and gave absolution and benediction to their nuns and monks.[116]

Many of these abbess-saints were singled out for their exceptional administrative abilities. In the tradition of the virile woman, Abbess Bertilla of Chelles was said to govern her monastery very well, "like a man with great sanctity and piety" (*viriliter cum summa sanctitate et religione*). Or, Abbess Ethelburga was praised for running her convent "in a manner worthy of her brother." [117] The early abbess-saints were called upon to attend royal councils and synods. In one of the Lives of St. Brigid we learn, for example, that Brigid along with Bishop Mel attended "an assembly of the men in Ireland" held in Teltown. There they were confronted by a difficult case in which a woman accused Bishop Bron of fathering her child. The question was brought to Brigid to be resolved, and it was then through Brigid's intervention that Bishop Bron was exonerated.[118] The great Synod of Whitby (663/64) was held at the double monastery founded and ruled by St. Hilda. Abbess Ebba, aunt of the king, participated in the deliberations of a Northumbrian council of 680–81. St. Mildred, abbess of Minster-in-Thanet, along with four other abbesses, attended a council (ca. 696–716) at Baccanceld, in Kent.[119] In the description of Abbess Aelffled's attendance at the Synod on the Nidd (706), she is called "the best of advisers, and a constant source of strength to the whole province." At this synod she addressed and advised the archbishop, king, bishops, abbots, and chief nobility of the kingdom "with inspired words." [120] In the *vita* of St. Cuthbert, St. Aelffled is involved in an important political discussion with St. Cuthbert and is described as appearing with "womanly daring" (*audacia feminea*) (see plate 20).[121] While the dignity of the position of abbess enhanced the prestige of these noblewomen, it also extended their networks beyond the family into the hierarchy of the Church, providing increased access to further sources of power. Frequently, through these important connections, abbess-saints were able to secure special monastic privileges and immunities which helped to ensure their communities' continued autonomy and to safeguard their landholdings.

MONASTIC EDUCATION AND SANCTITY

In addition to providing abbesses with opportunities to achieve a visibility in administration as well as an active involvement in the political activities of the period, the early monasteries were also important centers of learning and education. Many of these monasteries were located in the newly converted regions of northern Europe and Britain where they served as local missionary centers or stations, with their abbesses and nuns assisting in conversion efforts through the establishment of schools. These women were also active, well-educated scribes who produced an impressive number of liturgical books and other works for their own use as well as aiding the missionary effort by providing the new churches of their region with the necessary texts.[122]

A rather large number of female saints of this period were singled out in their *vitae* for their impressive learning and teaching. The Life of St. Ita of Ireland (d. ca. 570) notes the important role she played in establishing a school in her monastery of Cell Ide. Both boys and girls were educated here. St. Brendan of Clonfert, for example, received his formative education from St. Ita and spent five years studying under her. At this point, according to her hagiographer, Ita was said to have told the young Brendan to "go off now and learn the rules of holy men, who have practised what they preached; and do not study with virgins lest evil should be spoken of you by men." According to tradition, St. Mochoemoc spent twenty years studying under St. Ita, after which time he completed his studies in Bangor.[123]

The Life of Caesarius of Arles notes the scribal activities carried out by the successor of Caesarius's sister, Abbess Caesaria the Younger, and the nuns of her community. "Her work with her companions is so outstanding that in the midst of psalms and fasts, vigils and readings, the virgins of Christ beautifully copy out the holy books, with their mother herself as teacher."[124]

Fortunatus, in a letter to a friend, praises Radegund's intellectual attributes: her mental superiority, he claims, surpassed even St. Jerome's circle of learned women, including Eustochium, Fabiola, Melania, and others. "She exemplifies whatever is praiseworthy in them." According to Fortunatus, "I come across deeds in her such as I only read about before. . . . All pious teaching is food to her." He then enumerates her wide acquaintance with the major sources written by both Greek and Latin Fathers—Gregory, Basil, Athanasius, Hilary, Ambrose, Jerome, Augustine, Sedulius, and Orosius.[125] Baudonivia, in her *vita* of Radegund, notes that during the nighttime hours the holy queen stayed awake and spent her time reading—*semper lectio lege-batur*.[126] Gregory of Tours mentions that after Radegund's funeral he returned to the convent and visited the particular sites and relics asso-ciated with the saint—where she had been accustomed to read or pray as well as the book which she read.[127]

The *vita* of St. Rusticula, abbess of Arles (d. ca. 632), notes that she had committed to memory all of the Scriptures.[128] St. Gertrude of Nivelles (d. ca. 658) was also recognized for her intellectual abilities. We learn from her *vita* that both day and night she occupied herself with holy readings. She was especially famous for having memorized nearly the entire body of the divine law and for her ability to lecture to her nuns on the obscure mysteries of scriptural allegories. When establishing her monastery of Nivelles as a center of conversion and learning, St. Gertrude recruited monks from Ireland to teach the nuns of her new community divine law in verse and psalmody. She also sent messengers to Rome for sacred books for her community's library.[129]

The Life of St. Aurea, seventh-century abbess of a Parisian monas-tery founded by St. Eloi, notes in passing an incident which perhaps sheds light on this saint's education. On one occasion, after hearing the deacon of her convent stumble through a reading of the Gospels, Abbess Aurea lost all patience. She seized the book out of the incom-petent churchman's hands and read it herself to the congregation. (Later, we learn, she imposed a stiff penance on herself for this "irrev-erent" act!)[130]

The *vita* of St. Anstrude (late seventh-century abbess) notes that in the early years of her childhood she learned her letters and learned to sing praises to Christ. "Through divine clemency, she also waxed strong of memory in listening and reading, and she exercised herself in the teaching of doctrine . . . she was full of eloquence, but much more of wisdom."[131]

St. Bertilla, abbess of Chelles (d. ca. 705), was also renowned for her learning in Holy Scripture. She was summoned by Queen Balthild from Jouarre, which had a reputation for its quality education, to be-come abbess of the queen's newly refounded community of Chelles. At Chelles she continued to be recognized for her learning and for pro-ducing erudite disciples. In fact, according to her biographer, "even from over the seas, the faithful kings of the Saxons, through trusted messengers, asked her to send some of her disciples for the learning

and holy instruction they heard were wonderful in her, that they
might build convents of men and nuns in their land. She did not deny
these religious requests which would speed the salvation of souls. In
a thankful spirit, taking counsel with her elders and heeding her
brothers' exhortations, with great diligence and the protection of the
saints, she sent many volumes of books to them. That the harvest of
souls in that nation might increase through her and be multiplied by
God's grace, she sent chosen women and devout men." [132]

It was, then, the early Frankish monasteries that served as centers
of education for the aristocratic women of Anglo-Saxon England.
Bede notes in his *History of the English Church and People* that "for
as yet there were few monasteries built in English territory, and many
who wished to enter conventual life went from Britain to the Frankish
realm or Gaul for the purpose. Girls of noble family were also sent
there for their education, or to be betrothed to their heavenly Bridegroom, especially to the houses of Brie, Chelles, and Andelys." [133]
Thus, according to tradition, the Anglo-Saxon saint Mildred (later
abbess of Minster-in-Thanet) was sent abroad to Chelles for her education. And from this monastery she sent her mother a psalter she had
copied.[134] Many other noble Anglo-Saxon women with religious leanings crossed the channel to pursue their education; some even became
abbesses of their adopted Frankish communities. The princesses of
East Anglia—Ethelberga and Saethryd, daughter and stepdaughter of
King Anna, for example, both became abbesses of Faremoutiers-
en-Brie and later won recognition of sanctity. Their niece, Ercongota,
daughter of St. Sexburga, was also sent to Faremoutiers to be educated. Later, she too was elected abbess of this prominent Frankish
house and, following in the footsteps of her aunts and mother, she
also came to be recognized as a saint. Hereswith, sister-in-law of King
Anna of East Anglia and sister of St. Hilda of Whitby, became a nun at
the monastery of Chelles. Hereswith also won popular recognition of
sainthood.[135] The English St. Hildelith had apparently received her
education in France and then, at the request of Bishop Earconwald of
London, returned to Britain to settle at Barking Abbey where she was
named abbess. The fame of her erudition as abbess-saint has been preserved by Aldhelm's prose treatise, *De virginitate,* which was dedicated to Abbess Hildelith and her companions at Barking Abbey. In
this tract Aldhelm thanks the nuns of the abbey for the various writings which they sent to him and praises their high degree of learning,
calling them "gymnosophists" in the arena of discipline. Aldhelm uses
the analogy of the chaste bee to describe their prodigious educational
activities: like bees they collect everywhere material for study. He
also describes in some detail their curriculum, which includes the

study of the prophets, the ancient laws, the four Gospels, history, grammar, verse, and other topics. He concludes his treatise with the appropriate designation of these learned inmates at Barking as *alumnae scholasticae*.[136] (See plate 21.)

There are many other examples of Anglo-Saxon *mulieres sanctae* who were recognized by their contemporaries for their impressive learning. One of the most famous figures is that of St. Hilda of Whitby. Hilda had originally planned to follow her sister, Hereswith, to the Frankish monastery of Chelles, but she was summoned by Aidan of Lindisfarne, who requested that she remain in her newly converted native Northumbria. Here Hilda was to establish a monastic center of education and life similar to that found among the Franks.[137] The Venerable Bede describes the school which she established at Whitby as one of the first and greatest centers of learning in the North of England. He says of the learned Hilda, "so great was her prudence that not only ordinary folk, but kings and princes used to come and ask her advice in their difficulties and *take it*. Those under her direction were required to make a thorough study of the Scriptures and occupy themselves in good works, to such good effect that many were found fitted for Holy Orders and the service of God's altar."[138] Bede then notes, as testimony to her excellence in education, that five men who had studied under Hilda later became bishops.[139] In his Life of St. Cuthbert, Bede also praised the abbess-saint Aelffled of Whitby for her extraordinary erudition. He described her as a "wise woman and learned in holy scriptures" (*sapiens femina et in sanctis erudita scripturis*).[140]

The Anglo-Saxon missionary abbess-saint, Leoba, was also singled out for her impressive learning and her excellence in teaching. According to her biographer, she had been educated by Abbess Tetta of Wimborne Abbey. Here she was taught to have a primary interest in "the pursuit of sacred knowledge" and "fixed her mind always on reading or hearing the Word of God. Whatever she heard or read she committed to memory, and put all that she learned into practice." Moreover, while Leoba was a nun at Wimborne, she was said to have had a marvelous dream which foretold her special role as a great counselor and teacher. According to her hagiographer, in this dream "she saw a purple thread issuing from her mouth. It seemed to her that when she took hold of it with her hand and tried to draw it out there was no end to it; and as if it were coming from her very bowels, it extended little by little until it was of enormous length. When her hand was full of thread and it still issued from her mouth she rolled it round and round and made a ball of it." A nun who could foresee the future was called upon to interpret this dream. She explained that this vision revealed that because of Leoba's "teaching and good example" she would "confer benefits on many people. The thread which came from her bowels and issued from her mouth, signifies the wise counsels that she will speak from the heart. . . . the ball . . . signifies the mystery of the divine teaching, which is set in motion by the words and deeds of those who give instruction and which turns earthwards through active works and heavenwards through contemplation." It was, then, because of Leoba's "reputation for learning and holiness . . . [which] had spread far and wide" that Boniface requested her assistance in his mission to convert the Germans.[141]

In Germany, Leoba became abbess of an important monastic community at Bischofsheim where she dedicated herself to education. Here she "made such progress in her teaching that many of them [her nuns] afterwards became superiors of others, so that there was hardly a convent of nuns in that part which had not one of her disciples as abbess." Her biographer provides us with this wonderful, detailed description of Leoba's commitment to learning and her extensive curriculum: "So great was her zeal for reading that she discontinued it only for prayer or for the refreshment of her body with food or sleep: the Scriptures were never out of her hands. For, since she had been trained from infancy in the rudiments of grammar and the study of the other liberal arts, she tried by constant reflection to attain a perfect knowledge of divine things so that through the combination of her reading with her quick intelligence, by natural gifts and hard work, she became extremely learned. She read with attention all the books of the Old and New Testaments and learned by heart all the commandments of God. To these she added by way of completion the writings of the Church Fathers, the decrees of the Councils and the whole of ecclesiastical law. . . . When she lay down to rest, whether at night or in the afternoon, she used to have the Sacred Scriptures read out at her bedside, a duty which the younger nuns carried out in turn without grumbling." He then adds, "It seems difficult to believe, but even when she seemed to be asleep they could not skip over any word or syllable whilst they were reading without her immediately correcting them." It is also significant to note that Leoba's fame, respect, and authority among contemporaries were in fact closely tied to her education. Her hagiographer observes, "and because of her wide knowledge of the Scriptures and her prudence in counsel they [i.e., bishops, princes, and the nobility] often discussed spiritual matters and ecclesiastical discipline with her."[142]

The eighth-century Belgian abbess-saints Herlinda and Renilda won praise from their biographer for their wide learning. They were educated at the monastery of Valenciennes where "they were instructed in reading, chanting, psalmody, and also in what today is

considered wonderful, writing and painting, a task considered labori-
ous even for the strong men of this day and age" (*scribendo atque pin-
gendo, quod hujus aevi robustissimis viris oppido onerosum videter*).
Their biographer also noted that they transcribed the four Gospels, a
psalter, as well as many other works of Divine Scripture which still (in
the ninth century) remained "splendid in new and shining gold and
glowing with jewels" in their monastery.[143]

Another example of the impressive tradition of monastic learning
for this early period can be found in the *vita* of St. Hathumoda, the
first abbess of Gandersheim. According to her biographer, from childhood, Hathumoda, of her own free will, wanted to be admitted to
serious study. "No one could have shown greater quickness of perception, or a stronger power of understanding in listening to or in
expounding the Scriptures."[144]

A number of these early female saints who were recruited from the
cloister were also famous for their practical medical knowledge and
their successful cures. The early Irish St. Daveca was said to be an
expert in medicine: "For the Most High gave to her the grace of con-
ferring health upon the sick and of driving out demons."[145] The Lives
of St. Radegund provide interesting detail on this saint's successful
treatment of a number of patients. One case in particular, related by
Fortunatus, concerned a nun at Radegund's monastery of Ste-Croix
(see plate 6). This woman had suffered with a serious fever for a year;
for six months she had not been able to walk and lay stretched out on
her bed like a corpse. When Radegund learned of this nun's illness, she
had a warm bath prepared and had the woman brought into her own
cell where she immersed her in a tub of water. Sending away all of her
companions, Radegund, in the capacity of a physician, remained
alone with the nun for about two hours. Examining her entire body
from head to foot, she touched the nun's sore limbs one after the
other. Everywhere that Radegund's hands passed, the pain disappeared. Thus, according to this account, the sick woman, who had
required two nuns to help her into the bath, was able to leave on her
own—restored to perfect health.[146] Queen Balthild, while an inmate
at Chelles, devoted much of her time and energies to personally nursing the sick.[147] According to tradition, the popular Anglo-Saxon saint
Milburga was endowed with a special gift of healing. Like Radegund,
she restored sight to the blind, brought children back to life, and
effected other miraculous cures.[148] The abbess-saint Leoba was also
celebrated for her healing abilities. For example, she cured a nun of
her community who had been incapacitated by her bleeding hemor-
rhoids and pain of the bowel.[149] In this same tradition, St. Walburga,
abbess of the monastery of Heidenheim, was known for her medical

abilities (see plate 7). Our sources describe how Walburga was called upon by a nobleman to make a "house call" and to care for his daughter who was dying. Walburga not only restored the young girl to perfect health, but through this act the saint also achieved the conversion of the father.[150]

The significant role of women saints as experts in health care and medicine, and their special concern for the care of other women, then provided another valued attribute for their spiritual dossiers. And while their "miraculous" cures were directed toward both sexes, we find in many of the Lives of female saints that a heavy preponderance of cures especially effected during the saint's lifetime were aimed at women's health problems. For example, Fortunatus's *vita* of St. Radegund reports that among her miracles of healing while still in the world, ten concerned women (several of whom were nuns) and only two pertained to men. A similar concern of women saints for the diseases of members of their own sex can be found in a number of collections of posthumous cures: for example, all of the twenty miracles which were recorded as taking place at the tomb of St. Anstrude (monastery of Laon) applied to women (with eleven of the beneficiaries nuns), and of the recipients of the posthumous miracles attributed to St. Austreberta (abbess of Pavilly), twenty-one were women and four were men.[151] This very important role of saint as healer, as miracle-worker—using her special *potentia* or *virtu* to effect astonishing or wondrous cures (while alive or posthumously)—would therefore become one of the basic criteria for recognition of sanctity.

POWER AND PROPHECY

Another special ability providing visibility and empowering abbess-saints and other *mulieres sanctae* was that of prophecy. This role was traditionally open to women in both early Christian and pagan Germanic societies. Members of early Christian communities believed that the Spirit could be given to all Christians, regardless of their gender. Women prophets therefore functioned as charismatic, inspired leaders with their special authority based on divine revelation. A number of women prophets are mentioned, for example, in the New Testament, and in *The Acts of Paul and Thecla*.[152] Among the Germanic tribes, women seemed to hold a near monopoly of prophetic powers, and they were held in extremely high esteem for their possession and exercise of this special "gift." Tacitus, in his *Germania*, explained that the Germans "believe that there resides in women an element of holiness and the gift of prophecy; and so they do not scorn to ask their advice, or lightly disregard their replies." (This observation is amazingly similar to those already noted in regard to the special wisdom of the abbess-saints Hilda of Whitby and Leoba, for example.) Tacitus then notes, "In the reign of the emperor Vespasian we saw Veleda long honoured by many Germans as a divinity; and even earlier they showed a similar reverence for Aurinia and a number of others—a reverence untainted by servile flattery or any pretence of turning women into goddesses." In his *Histories,* however, Tacitus explains, "it is an ancient custom in Germany to credit a number of women with prophetic powers, and with the growth of superstition these develop into goddesses." [153]

We find an impressive number of women in leadership roles, particularly among early Frankish and Anglo-Saxon saints, who were also involved in prophesying. Frequently the visions of these saints foretold the time of their own death or that of other prominent individuals. According to Bede, for example: "Some say that [Etheldreda, abbess of Ely] possessed the spirit of prophecy, and that in the presence of all the community, she not only foretold the plague that was to cause her death, but also the number who would die of it in the convent." [154] According to Baudonivia, St. Radegund, before her own death, had experienced a vision of Christ appearing to her as bridegroom. During his visit he assured her that she would be a precious gem in his crown.[155] Balthild was said to have experienced a remarkable vision shortly before her death. In this vision she saw before the altar of the Virgin Mary a ladder which seemed to touch the sky: she then climbed this bright ladder accompanied by angels of God. According to her *vita,* this revelation clearly demonstrated to the saintly queen that through her merits, patience, and humility she would soon be transported to the throne of the eternal king and receive her heavenly rewards.[156]

The seventh-century St. Aldegund, founding abbess of the monastery of Maubeuge, gained a certain amount of fame for her rather extensive visions of Christ and the heavenly kingdom. According to her *vita,* Aldegund had been favored with celestial visions from the time of her early childhood. She dictated her visions and spiritual revelations to Abbot Subinius of nearby Nivelles, who then wrote them down. We learn that her visions were also read aloud to the nuns of her community at Maubeuge. Unfortunately, Aldegund's book of visions is no longer extant, although her biographer, who claimed to know Aldegund, states that he has summarized their contents in her *vita.* Her earliest vision was one in which Christ appeared to her and called her to a life of monasticism. Her visions also provided glowing details on the heavenly kingdom with its mansion, fragrant aroma, angels, Christ as bridegroom, St. Peter, and others. A few of her visions focused on the devil who appeared to Aldegund as a fierce lion and as a wolf. When the devil tried to persuade Aldegund to turn away from the ascetic life, an angel appeared to her and exhorted her to "act like a man"; for by preserving her virginity she would gain the crown which God had shown to her.[157] In another vision, Aldegund witnessed the ascent of her friend St. Amand into heaven, where he received his rewards for his earthly labors. She was also warned of her own impending death by St. Peter, who reassured her that she would be counted among the elect and she should not fear death, as "perfect love casts out fear." [158] As Suzanne Wemple has noted, Aldegund's visions emphasized the theme of love rather than fear. "Unlike the visions of the female saints described by men," Wemple argues, "Aldegund's experiences were not designed to convey instruction on how women might overcome the weaknesses of their sex. Aldegund's heavenly messengers intended to draw the messages of love, a lesson that was also proclaimed in the lives of Radegund and Balthild." [159]

There are a number of other saints of the period who gained a certain fame or reputation for their prophetic visions. This special, gender-free "gift" provided its recipients with an inspired "voice" and power, or authority, which was believed to come directly from God. These women saints were seen as "instruments of God's purpose" or channels of divine authority. For many of these abbess-saints, this special ability furnished further proof of their holiness. With the decided curtailment of other approved channels or opportunities for female power in the central and later Middle Ages, this gift would be used increasingly by religious women as a means to exercise influence within the Church and society.[160]

MIRACLES OF PROTECTION

As public figures and leaders of their communities and of the surrounding areas, these women saints were also frequently called upon in times of disaster to provide miracles of protection. An early hagiographic exemplum of a woman saint assuming a strong protective leadership role can be found in the Life of Saint Genovefa. According to the *vita*, threatened by an imminent invasion by Attila the Hun, the inhabitants of Paris were terror-stricken. Assuming the initiative, St. Genovefa called together the matrons of the city and proposed that, in the tradition of the biblical examples of Esther and Judith, they might ward off this impending disaster. Following her plan, the Parisian women spent a number of days in the baptistery fasting, praying, and keeping a vigil. Genovefa also convinced the male citizens of Paris not to take their goods and money out of Paris to the safety of other cities, as she foresaw that Paris, guarded by Christ, would not be attacked by the invaders. Thus by her prayers she was said to have repelled the Huns from Paris and saved the city.[161]

Similarly, the seventh-century abbess-saint Godeberta assumed an important protective role while a devastating plague raged in Noyon. She recommended that in order to placate the divine wrath responsible for the plague, the people of Noyon observe a fast for three days, wearing sackcloth and ashes. They followed her advice and, according to our sources, the plague was dissipated. On another occasion, while Godeberta was extremely ill, she was carried by the faithful to the scene of a great fire at Noyon. According to her saint's Life, with the sign of the cross she was able to extinguish the fire.[162]

In this tradition St. Leoba was called upon to organize the village of Bischofsheim in order to extinguish a threatening fire. Her hagiographer notes that when the village was inundated by fire, "the terrified villagers . . . ran in a mob to the abbess and begged her to avert the danger which threatened them. Unruffled and with great self-control, she calmed their fears and without being influenced by their trust in her, ordered them to take a bucket and bring some water from the upper part of the stream that flowed by the monastery." She then sprinkled some salt which had been blessed by St. Boniface into the water and told them to pour this special mixture back into the river. They were then ordered to gather water from the lower part of the stream (which had absorbed this "holy salt") and throw it onto the fire. We learn that after they followed the abbess's directions, the fire was miraculously extinguished and the buildings were saved. And the *vita* concludes: "At this miracle the whole crowd stood amazed and broke out into the praise of God, who through the faith and prayers of his handmaid had delivered them so extraordinarily from a terrible danger." Leoba's miracle-working abilities were also sought out to calm a devastating storm. Fearing for their lives and convinced that the last judgment was at hand, all of the villagers took refuge in the convent's church. Leoba tried to calm their fears and asked them to join her in prayer. Through her intercession, we are told, the storm changed its direction and the village was miraculously saved. According to the *vita*, "thus did divine power make manifest the merits of His handmaid. Unexpected peace came to His people and fear was banished."[163]

Although special privileges and immunities, as well as the presence of *advocati*, bishops, and abbots designated as guardians, provided a certain level of security and protection for the monasteries, the female communities still faced frequent attempts of usurpation on the part of the local nobility and bishops—in some cases from those who were designated as their protectors. It was then particularly at these times—when their monasteries' lands were threatened—that the abbess-saints displayed their formidable powers and appeared as protector saints.

It should be noted, however, that while most of the saintly activities we have been tracing thus far occurred while the saint was still living "in this world," many of the cases in which patron saints exhibited protective powers over their properties were accomplished posthumously, from the saint's tomb. It was generally believed that the saint, although deceased, remained a living force, as powerful (or perhaps even more so) in death as in life. The *vita* of St. Waldetrude, for example, notes that "daily she is entreated that what she did when she was alive may be continued by her dead bones. For it is no wonder that her dead bones still live in wonder-working when she did such wonders in her life."[164] Thus residing in her tomb, the saint continued to watch over and protect her foundation, its lands, and its people—generally the same constituency she had served during her lifetime. And from this most sacred vantage point she could easily reveal herself (in many marvelous ways), and make her feelings or position quite clear to all involved. Therefore in times of dire necessity, the patron saint could be invoked to use her special *potentia* on behalf of her community of nuns.[165] And as can be noted in the *vitae,* the supernatural powers of these female patron saints (and particularly their vengeance) were clearly recognized and feared by men and women of all classes of medieval society.

A fascinating incident of the exercise of power and protection by the holy dead over their properties can be found in the case of the popular late-seventh-century Belgian saint Aya. A wealthy noblewoman who had taken the veil at Mons under the abbess-saint Waldetrude, Aya donated extensive properties to the monastery. According to tradition, however, about eighty years after Aya's death, her relatives came to reclaim their "family" lands. Since no title deed could be found, the case went to court. Following the nuns' request, the court proceedings were to be held at the tomb of the saint. During the hearing, the nun who was apparently handling the case spoke in a loud voice, "Great Saint, they wish to take from us Guesmes, Nimy, Maisières, and Braine, which you gave us. Speak in favor of your daughters, and confirm the gifts you made in your life." At this point a voice broke forth, allegedly from the depths of the tomb, clearly audible to all present, declaring: "I ratify all these gifts which I made to the church." Thus through her "supernatural" intervention (this post mortem miracle), the saint confirmed the monastery's landholdings. (And appropriately enough, Aya became one of the patron saints invoked in lawsuits!)[166]

Another case in this tradition can be found in the *Translatio* of St. Edith (d. 984), patron saint of Wilton. During the reign of Canute, a certain magnate of the king by the name of Agamundus seized some land belonging to Saint Edith (i.e., the monastery of Wilton). The usurper then died suddenly (*impenitens morte*) without returning the property which he had taken. As punishment for this act, St. Edith directed her wrath toward the dead man and would not allow his soul to rest. At his wake, the corpse "awoke" and told those around him of St. Edith's anger and asked that the lands be restored to the saint. This accomplished, he was then permitted to die in peace with Edith now his protector. The *Translatio* records a similar case in which St. Edith visited her wrath on a certain Brixius who had usurped some of her monastery's property.[167]

These diverse examples, taken from the *vitae,* serve to underscore the significance for women of access to political and economic power, education, and prophecy in the pursuit of sanctity. During this early period, the intersection of public and private spheres favored the acquisition of wealth and the exercise of power by women. Also many of the activities which led to recognition of sanctity for the *mulieres sanctae* were essentially indistinguishable from those of their male contemporaries. As Eleanor McLaughlin has observed: "It was a sanctity powerful, public, practical, even administrative, and it was a power and holiness to which women were called coequally with men."[168] It is of special interest to note that at this time, when the newly organized Church needed the participation and material support of all of its members, it particularly appreciated women's active involvement and cooperation: we do not find churchmen questioning the propriety of the public roles which these powerful female figures had assumed, nor do they fear for their souls because of their close working relationships with these women. This, then, is perhaps the type of inclusive or cooperative atmosphere which was reported to have been found among the "first order" of Irish bishop saints which "did not spurn the administration or company of women . . . nor fear the wind of temptation."[169]

CHURCH REFORMS AND THE DEVELOPMENT OF EXCLUSIONARY POLICIES

Beginning in the mid-eighth and ninth centuries with the emergence of the Carolingian Empire and Church reforms, we can see in some regions of Europe a concerted attempt by the reformers at redefining authority and reorganizing society and the Church. In general, the reformers tried to reassert the Church's autonomy and power. Bishops and abbots came to assume increasing power over abbesses and women's houses. With the Church now established and organized, with its strict hierarchical ordering and its emphasis on sacramental formalism and ritual purity, the earlier practical need for women's talents and special patronage seems to have subsided. For example, many of the early female monastic communities had originally served the very important function of missionary and educational centers, as well as providing the services of a parish church. With the success of the missionary movement and the organization of parishes, these monasteries lost these indispensable roles. The Church therefore found itself in a position to attempt to enforce its gender-based restrictive policies which had been ignored or necessarily mitigated during its initial stages of development (especially during the period of the missionary movement in the north of Europe and Britain). Thus the reforms of the Carolingians (followed by those of the Cluniacs, the reforms of Gerard of Brogne, Gorze, and Richard of St. Vanne, the tenth-century English reform, and papal or Gregorian reform) introduced policies which tried to control and regularize religious activities. They worked, in general, to limit women's public involvement and their leadership activities in the Church and society through the demarcation of a "proper" feminine sphere and a delineation of female nature, abilities, rights, and responsibilities.

The reforms aimed at regularizing monasticism or restoring an earlier strictness to monastic life; they also worked to reestablish monastic foundations which had been destroyed by the Viking, Saracen, or Magyar invasions, or had fallen victim to other disorders of the age. Since an impressive percentage of the *mulieres sanctae* from this period gained access to sainthood through the cloister, these basic changes in monasticism had an indirect effect on the fluctuations of the numbers and percentages of male and female saints. We can therefore see a definite correlation between periods of Church reform, the decline in the number of new monastic foundations for women, and a drop in the number and percentage of women saints. Concurrently we can discern a substantial increase in new communities for monks, followed by a rise in the number of male saints recruited from among their founders, abbots, and monks.

Very briefly, according to the sources of the period (which are reinforced by our rough data as noted in tables 3 and 4), in the eighth century there appears to have been an overall decline in the total number of new monasteries for both men and women in Britain and France. However, what is of special significance is that along with an apparent waning in enthusiasm for monastic life in general, there occurred a sharp fluctuation in the percentages of new female communities. This decline in women's houses, in turn, seems to be indirectly reflected in a similar decline in the *mulieres sanctae,* since the cloister had been the source of *fama sanctitatis* for many women. In the first half of the eighth century, for example, France/Belgium witnesses a dramatic decline in the percentage, among new monasteries, of those established for women—from the previous 32.7 percent for the years 650–699 to 12.7 percent for the period between 700 and 749. This is the beginning of a radical decline in new foundations for women which will continue in France through the late eleventh century. This decline will, in fact, become especially exaggerated in the eleventh century, when between 1000 and 1049 only approximately 5 percent of the monasteries were established for women. For the years 1050–1099 this growing disparity became even more blatant, for during this fifty-year period, only 3.4 percent of the total number of houses were designated for women. Thus for the entire eleventh century in France, only approximately 4 percent of the new foundations were established for female religious. This low point in the foundation of new communities for women in eleventh-century France is paralleled by a similar nadir in female sanctity in which women comprised only 4 percent of the newly promoted French saints. At the same time we can also discern a substantial increase in the numbers of new orders and new communities for monks paralleled by an impressive rise in the number of male saints.

Beginning with the second half of the eighth century, Britain also witnessed a decline in the number and percentages of new monastic settlements for women. During the years 700–749, the percentage of new foundations dropped from a previous high of approximately 40 percent down to approximately 27 percent; between 750 and 799 new monasteries for women declined sharply to approximately 6 percent.[170] With the tenth-century reforms of Sts. Dunstan, Ethelwold, and Oswald, we see a strong revival in monastic life for men accompanied by a limited interest in female monasticism. Nevertheless, in contrast to the exclusionary policies of the Carolingian and Cluniac reforms, the queen of England (Queen Aelfthryth), as well as abbesses and nuns, appear to have been allowed a certain limited formal involvement in the early stages of the English reform movement. They attended the synodal council at Winchester (ca. 970) and were involved in the acceptance of the reform customary which was called the *Regularis concordia anglicae nationis monachorum sanctimonialiumque.* This reform customary, as its title denotes, recognized the roles of both monks and nuns in England. It also specifically designated King Edgar as guardian of the rule of monks and the queen as "the protectress and fearless guardian of the communities of nuns; so that he himself helping the men and his consort helping the women there should be no cause for any breath of scandal." [171]

However, despite the early formal involvement of the queen, abbesses, and nuns in the ecclesiastical revival in England, the priorities and agenda for the actual restoration and founding of new monasteries were set by Dunstan, Ethelwold, and Oswald and heavily favored male monasticism. Therefore the number of new houses for women created or reformed during this period remained relatively modest in comparison to those for men. It appears that only a few of the larger, more prominent female houses which were under royal patronage, and had suffered at the hands of the invaders or through lay usurpation, were refounded or restored for nuns. Thus it became nearly a formula for the destroyed and abandoned women's foundations to be reestablished by the reformers as houses for monks or canons. The unwritten policy of reestablishing monasteries that had formerly belonged to communities of female religious is exemplified by a 963 entry in the *Anglo-Saxon Chronicle.* Saint Ethelwold asked King Edgar "to give him *all* the monasteries which the heathen had destroyed, because he wished to restore them: and the king cheerfully granted it." According to the *Chronicle,* "the bishop [Ethelwold] went first to Ely [which had been a double community founded by St. Etheldreda], where St. Ethelthryth [Etheldreda] is buried, and had the monastery built, giving it to one of his monks. . . . He consecrated him abbot and peopled it with monks to serve God, *where formerly there had been nuns.*" [172] Hence, if we consider the actual numbers of new houses created or reformed for women, the results pale in comparison to the foundations established for women in the seventh and early eighth centuries, or in comparison to contemporary foundations for men. Knowles, for example, has attributed approximately forty new and reestablished monasteries to the half century between the reestablishment of Glastonbury in 940 and Dunstan's death in 988. Of these houses, only six or seven appear to have been principal convents of nuns. [173]

In eleventh-century Britain the number of new foundations for women declined, both in absolute numbers and relative to those for men. For the years 1000–1049, only 6.3 percent of the new monasteries were founded for women; during the years 1050–1099 the number increased, but only to approximately 10.5 percent. [174] Although the Norman Conquest encouraged and facilitated the foundation of numerous new communities for men, very few women's communities were founded in its wake.

Consequently, although the reform movements or ascetic revivals of the period, particularly those of the tenth and eleventh century, offered new choices and opportunities to men in the Church (as reflected in the multiplicity of new monastic movements and new foundations), this does not seem to have been the case for women. In fact, the founding of new monasteries for men during this period frequently appears to have occurred only at the expense of women.

Briefly, the problem of the decline in the establishment of new houses for women was based on a complex of factors including shifting preferences in patronage and church reform attitudes toward women. The increased emphasis on the mass, liturgical specialization and the intercessory value or efficacy of the prayers of monks/clerics (over and against those of aristocratic women or nuns) placed women religious at a distinct disadvantage. While women were unable to celebrate mass, they also came to be seen as primary rivals of the reformed monastic tradition in the domain of preserving *memoria*. Thus, as Patrick Geary has noted, with the Cluniac reform, monks in France were perceived as best qualified for the liturgical commemoration of, and intercession for, the dead.[175] Lay patrons viewed their endowments to the Church as essentially spiritual investments: they were cautious in placing them where they were convinced they would accrue the greatest benefits in regard to salvation and rewards in the next life. They were therefore concerned with endowing monastic foundations which would insure privileged burial space for their family, as well as responsible and competent guardians of their family's memory in liturgical *memoria*. Thus lay patrons, in general, increasingly preferred to sponsor and establish male monasteries rather than female foundations. In this context it is important to note that royal and noblewomen were also supportive of many of the values and basic priorities of the reform movements. For example, they were involved as important patrons and donors in the foundation of Cluniac monasteries and took an active role in the reforming of other communities; in Britain they displayed an impressive level of participation in the tenth-century monastic reform.[176] Thus while female patrons continued to be the major force behind the new communities established for women during the ninth through eleventh centuries, a substantial number of women during this period chose to financially support the foundation of men's monastic communities or other religious establishments. (Also, in the reform tradition, a few aristocratic women initiated the eviction of communities of nuns, only to reestablish these foundations for monks.)[177]

In addition to changing priorities of patronage and support, the ascetic revivals and reform movements of the tenth and eleventh centuries were initiated and led by churchmen who were interested almost exclusively in male monasticism. In their emphasis on celibacy, fear of the female sex, and attempts to avoid women, some of the reformers seem to have shared an extreme reluctance, if not an active disdain, for providing for women's religious needs. Moreover, this fear of female sexuality and pollution, and the encouragement of ritual purity, served as an excuse for the growing segregation of the sexes and sharpened the boundaries between them. Women's options and expectations within the Church were indeed being narrowed: they began to diverge substantially from those of their male contemporaries.

The reform councils, for example, repeatedly legislated strict enclosure for female religious—thus attempting to circumscribe the autonomy and active involvement of abbesses and nuns in the "public sphere." In this context Stephanie Hollis has argued in regard to the English reform: "Under the stricter segregation and enclosure of the English monasteries envisaged by *Regularis Concordia,* restrictions on abbesses' dealings with the world at large produced an enhancement in the role of the queen at the further expense of abbesses' autonomous rule. *Regularis Concordia,* instructing abbesses to seek assistance from no other secular but the queen, formally endowed her with the position of protective patron of the convents and Mother of the Church; to the queen, effectively, passed the role of paramount abbess of all England." [178] Strict claustration also contributed to a loss of economic independence and resulted in very real hardship and poverty for many women's communities. With a loss of autonomy came a similar loss in public influence and general visibility for the abbess and her monastery. As Suzanne Wemple has argued: "Abbesses of both types of monasteries, for Benedictines and canonesses, lost not only their freedom of movement but also their former influence. Although emperors and kings periodically summoned them, undoubtedly to discuss the disposition of monastic resources, abbesses, unlike abbots, did not participate in reforming assemblies." [179]

Jacques de Guise, in an entry of the *Annales Hanoniae* (written some five and one-half centuries after the events he purported to record), describes the attempts on the part of the Carolingian church to put into effect its new reform agenda among a group of female monastic communities. It should be noted at the outset that this late source has been the subject of some debate: it has been dismissed by some scholars as pure fiction, while others admit that it has an undeniable foundation of truth and it therefore must not be totally rejected. [180] Despite some problems, it is nevertheless worth looking at this incident in light of the reform movement, the obligation of the ecclesiastical hierarchy to disseminate its canonical decrees, as well as the response of a number of women's monasteries to these new regulations. Entitled "Concerning certain secular abbesses and certain of their colleagues," this fascinating source records the difficulties, particularly the strong resistance that Walcand, bishop of Liège, encountered from several women's communities in his attempts to enforce these unwelcomed statutes. According to the chronicle, the bishop paid a visit to the famous monastery of St. Gertrude of Nivelles, where he presented the statutes which had recently been promulgated at the Council of Aix (816). He explained the new rules and constitutions as they affected the community at Nivelles. Apparently the abbess and nuns did not take the news very well; for afterward, we are told, he "departed from there without eating; he dismissed the sisters because they were murmuring in chapter, and he was unable to quiet them." Thereafter Bishop Walcand traveled throughout his diocese and publicized the new reform regulations. Furthermore, observing the discontent in her own monastery, the abbess of Nivelles inquired of a number of other female communities of the region, including Mons, Maubeuge, and others, to see if the same "heavy provision" of the council had similarly been imposed upon them. And she found that they had all been equally affected by the new legislation.

We then learn that "these nuns in an organized fashion sent to Cologne and found many convents of nuns in accord with them—that is, unwilling to observe the statutes of the council. At length, in a concerted and organized fashion, not observing the statutes, the nuns appealed to Pope Paschal for a future council as regards encumbrances passed and levied and as regards the yoke imposed upon them." (Among the new regulations which affected the nuns was the requirement that all female religious were to follow a strict or literal observance of the Benedictine Rule.) Meanwhile, when the emperor learned that the nuns had appealed the statutes of the council, he asked Pope Paschal to confirm these acts, which he did. Later the pope wrote to Bishop Walcand and requested that he induce the nuns to at least assume the vow of chastity, if they were unwilling to adopt the Rule of St. Benedict.

In response to this, the nuns of one accord petitioned for a council to be held, within six months, at which time *they* might respond to these regulations which were being forced upon them. And thus, after the six months had expired, all the organized abbesses who were adherents of the appeal met at Nivelles. Here Bishop Walcand delivered a special sermon to them, and when it was concluded, in the presence of the duke of Louvain, the count of Mons, and other nobles, the abbesses and nuns who were adherents of the appeal replied, in one voice: "First, we declare before God and all present that we will never profess the rule of St. Benedict. Second, we propose to observe chastity, but we will in no way bind ourselves to it by vow. Third, we are ready to vow obedience to our abbesses and to vow an honest life. Fourth, if this response does not suffice, we are prepared to pursue our appeal." We then learn that the bishop attempted to remind the nuns of their necessary obedience or required subordination to the male power structure: "When Walcand heard these [declarations], he convinced the princes there assembled and under whom the nuns dwelt and held their possessions to convince the nuns that from the time they had taken up their religious lives they owed obedience to their bishops, the emperor, and consequently to the Council of Aix, and especially to the pope who had approved the council. Doda, the abbess of Mons, replied in a somewhat disorderly fashion while the rest of the nuns held their peace. Doda's response displeased the princes and Bishop Walcand." Everyone then apparently departed from this meeting without having resolved any of the issues. Bishop Walcand sent a report of these proceedings to the pope and emperor who "saw that the women were obstinately and pertinaciously determined to pursue what they had begun." Therefore, in order that they not remain without a religious rule, they sent them a short formula, or rule, without any sort of vow (except as other Christians observed), along with a few statutes and instructions. They also added that these women would be called secular religious and not nuns (*religiose seculares et non sanctimoniales appellarentur.*)

This early episode, however, concluded with the following rather telling, punitive measure directed toward these "insubordinate" women: "And as perpetual punishment for the women, [it] deposed the abbesses from many of their churches and established in their place many secular princes as abbots." The source also notes that Count Albon, "at the time of dissension in the Church of St. Waldetrude, in opposition to the emperor and the Council of Aix, procured the perpetual deposition of the abbess of the Church of St. Waldetrude."[181]

Moreover, in this context we also learn that the reform Council of Verneuil (755) had stipulated that bishops were to excommunicate female monastic communities that refused to accept the Benedictine rule. As for individual nuns who failed to conform, they were to be imprisoned and required to endure forced labor. However, as Suzanne Wemple has noted, similar punishments were not provided for recalcitrant monks who failed to adopt the Rule.[182]

This episode, which focuses on the famous Monastery of St. Gertrude of Nivelles, underscores the increasing authority of bishops and councils over abbesses as well as the concurrent loss of abbesses' autonomous control over their monasteries. And although these forceful Carolingian abbesses provided a rigorous challenge to the new regulations, and on one level won a small victory, these events also clearly demonstrate women's rather disadvantageous or restricted position in the Church during this reform period. Not allowed to actively participate or provide advice in these church councils, and having only limited influence, these abbesses and their communities suffered serious consequences when they refused to cooperate or accept the regulations which were forced upon them. They remained particularly vulnerable in the area of economic retribution. In this case, as we noted, a number of the abbesses were deposed for their involvement in this incident and then replaced by abbots.

Thus beginning with the reform movements of the Carolingian period we see in some areas an erosion of the abbess's former public role and power. For the enclosed communities, the emphasis was now placed on the abbess's "private" role within the cloister. The Church councils also stipulated the necessary separation of the sexes in monastic schools, and nuns were specifically forbidden to teach boys in their monasteries. This in turn led to a growing disparity between the levels of male and female education and the exclusion of female religious from the mainstream of education.[183] Moreover, the physical arrangement of the double monastery, with its close association of male and female religious, came under attack by the reformers. Eventually this very special experiment in monastic life, which had been extremely favorable to women's autonomy and power—particularly in rural areas—disappeared. The reform councils also strictly excluded women from sacred space, especially within many major male monastic churches (i.e., they were forbidden to enter the altar area, or approach holy tombs and relics), which again worked to their disadvantage in religious activities.[184] Thus these changes, which were strongly biased in favor of the augmentation of male authority and male positions in the Church, operated to effectively erode women's public status, influence, and power. Rather than rewarding women for their pious exercise of power and their leadership roles in the Church, the reformers now attempted to restrict women to a more privatized, invisible domestic realm.

One of the most blatant examples of this deliberate attempt to sharpen the boundaries between the sexes can be found in the following edict said to have been promulgated at the reform Council of Nantes (895), which warned: "It is astounding that certain women, against both divine and human laws, with bare-faced impudence, act in general pleas and with abandon exhibit a burning passion for public meetings, and they disrupt rather than assist, the business of the kingdom and the good of the commonweal. It is indecent and reprehensible, even among barbarians, for women to discuss the cases of men. Those who should be discussing their woolen work and weaving with the residents of the women's quarters should not usurp the authority of senators in public meetings just as if they were residents of the court." [185] It is, then, within this context that the churchmen specifically prohibited nuns from attending general councils except if called by their prince or by their bishop. [186]

Thus as an example of late-ninth century reform attitudes, this edict attempts to establish a strong dichotomy between public and private, between male and female jurisdiction and space. As dictated by "divine and human laws," men's proper roles included public meetings at court, discussion of the business of the realm, and law cases; women's proper sphere, in contrast, was confined to the "gynaecea," that is the women's quarters, where they were to be usefully employed in "women's work" and discuss issues appropriate to their sex, such as their "woolen work." And, therefore, in light of these gender-based policies, and perhaps influenced by the ideal of female enclosure, nuns, both virgins and widows, were not to venture out into the public sphere and attend general councils.

This strong condemnation of the assumption by female religious of "improper" public roles was not an isolated example; the need to control women's power and space, with perhaps an underlying fear of women usurping male prerogatives, appears to have been a major force at work in the agendas of reform. Another rather well-known ninth-century case, which underscores the reformers' need to monitor women's public roles and their attempts to silence them, recounts the story of a German woman named Theoda. In 847 Theoda was condemned by the bishop and council of Mainz for her "unofficial" prophesying. According to the *Annales of Fulda* and the Council of Mainz, a certain "pseudo-prophetissa" called Theoda, "roused with her prophecies" great crowds of people in the regions through which she traveled. She preached that the end of the world was close at hand and claimed to be privy to "the Lord's secrets" and therefore to know the exact day on which the dreaded end would arrive. Filled with fear, large crowds of men and women offered the prophetess gifts and asked her to pray for their souls *"as if she were a saint."* (This mention here of the Church's fear of "false saints" or "self-proclaimed" saints corresponds to the Carolingian reform emphasis on the need for episcopal control over the process of recognizing or the making of saints.) According to the churchmen, however, "What is more serious, [these people] turned away from church doctrines preached by clerks of holy orders to follow her as though she were a teacher sent from heaven." We learn that under Theoda's influence even monks and priests abandoned their vows. Theoda was then brought before the archbishop, Rabanus Maurus, where, after extensive questioning, she admitted that she had indeed said such things, but had only been following orders—that is, she only did what she had been ordered to do. When questioned further as to the "source" of her orders, she named "some priest." The archbishop and synod then forbade her to preach and determined that she should be punished by a public flogging. "Whereupon with shame she gave up the ministry of preaching that she had irrationally seized upon and presumed to claim for herself against the custom of the church, and perplexed, she put an end to her soothsaying."[187] Thus this episode ends rather tragically with the humiliation of this popular woman preacher, who, through her public role as prophetess—and here acting outside of the institutional framework or controlled sphere of the monastery—had dared to defy the authority of the Church.

Another notorious instance in which women's public roles and power within the Church were condemned occurred in eleventh-century pre-Gregorian-reform Italy. It concerned Abbot Guarinus of Settimo, a reformer who preached against simony and clerical concubinage. When the abbot presented his business before Bishop Hildebrand of Florence, he received his answer not from the bishop whom he had addressed but from the bishop's wife, Alberga, who sat at court beside him. Disgusted and insulted by her defiant behavior, the abbot railed against the woman: "Accursed Jezebel, are you so sunk in your sinful condition that you dare to speak before a meeting of *bonorum hominum vel clericorum?*"[188] In this incident, the abbot's rage and offended sense of propriety were directed against Alberga's pretentious intrusion, as a woman and wife of a bishop, into the realm of "good men and clerks"—that duly constituted public male sphere.

This effort to limit women's visibility and privatize their existence can be found in many of the reformers' writings of the period. St. Odo of Cluny warns that "the highest virtue in a woman is not to wish to be seen."[189] In his *vita* of Saint Adelaide, St. Odilo of Cluny praises the empress's public roles of charity toward the poor, and generosity toward the church, as well as her adoption of the virtues of humility and suffering. However, he particularly stresses the *cura domestica* as one of the basic criteria for her sanctity and as a role model for contemporary queens. Odilo also downplays the importance of her public role as miracle worker. As noted by Patrick Geary, in Odilo's characterization of Adelaide, she is "the passive, emotional supplicator. . . . he proclaims that by her tears of supplication, she did more than if she had worked miraculous cures. Her passivity is more prized than the active power of a wonder worker."[190]

Cardinal Humbert of Romans, originally a Cluniac monk from the Lorraine and an enthusiastic supporter of the reform program of Pope Gregory VII, emphasizes in his writings against simony the necessary exclusion of women from public roles. In his fear of female power within the Church, he specifically reminds the faithful that women were "permitted neither to speak in church *nor to rule over men.*" [191] In this same tradition, the twelfth-century reformer Idung of Prüfening argues for strict female claustration. He warns that members of the female sex should not appear in public. He also contends that it is inexpedient for women to have their own monastic governance because of their natural fickleness and the outside temptations which womanly weakness is not strong enough to resist. [192]

Therefore, with the various reform movements and ascetic revivals from the ninth through the eleventh centuries, we can see in some areas of Europe and Britain a distinct privileging of men in the Church, accompanied by an increased emphasis on the necessary subordination of women to male authority and a proliferation of exclusionary policies. In addition to a general decline in opportunities for women to exercise a certain autonomy and assume leadership roles in the Church, churchmen attempted to segregate female religious from the public sphere (through policies of enclosure and other means), and to restrict their activities to the domestic or private domain. Consequently, for many of these abbesses and nuns, their sphere of influence was substantially reduced as was their prestige or status.

NEW IDEALS OF FEMALE SANCTITY

Thus, with the reform ideology, new ideals and modes of behavior were presented for women. Based in part on ideas of the early patristic writers, these concepts of the *vita perfecta* denigrated women's participation in the public realm while they glorified the private role or cult of domesticity. As Suzanne Wemple has observed, these shifts began in the ninth century and brought with them a new style of female sanctity. [193] Several saints' Lives of this period, wishing to justify and promote their protagonists' careers, now singled out for praise the exceptional domestic skills of the *mulieres sanctae*. They lauded and sacralized the expertise of pious women in household management, domestic arts, and motherhood.

St. Maura of Troyes (d. ca. 861) is a good example of this new type of domestic *ancilla* saint or "holy housekeeper." Selflessly devoted to serving the bishop and cathedral of Troyes, she is described as spending her time filling the lamps of the church with oil, purchasing ecclesiastical vestments with her own money, or making an alb for the bishop-saint Prudentius after having bleached and spun the flax.[194]

The *vita* of the contemplative recluse, St. Liutberga of Wendhausen (late ninth-century), also portrays, at least in part, a domestic or professional housekeeper saint. After spending her formative years as a pious household servant (*ancilla*), overseeing her patron's household and properties, she retired to live as a recluse. We learn that she was especially "skilled in many feminine labors," (*muliebrium operum*), including the "art of weaving." In her cell she kept a charcoal burner with a vat in which to dye cloth or yarn. Here she held a weaving workshop, teaching the daughters of the nobility the arts of weaving and dyeing cloth in many colors and other similar arts. According to her *vita,* in her decision to adopt the life of a recluse, Liutberga displayed a "virile self-confidence." And it is, then, after receiving episcopal sanction, that she retired to her cell: she also preached, prophesied, and experienced visions. As her fame grew, important men and women, as well as churchmen came from distant places to ask her advice and to hear her preach.[195]

The domesticity of St. Wiborada (d. ca. 926) was also praised in her *vita.* She devoted much of her life to caring for her brother Hitto, who became a priest at St. Gall. She made his clothing and provided for all of his needs in the ministry. In addition, Wiborada worked for the monastery of St. Gall, where she proved to be especially adept at making covers for the books produced in the *scriptorium.* She also spent a good part of her life living as a recluse—immured in a cell—near the monastery of St. Gall.[196]

Perhaps the epitome of this type of domestic or *ancilla* saint was the noblewoman-saint Hunna. According to her popular local cult, Hunna's fame rested on her pious activity of washing the clothing of the poor: thus her name, "the holy washer-woman." [197]

Another aspect of this "new" type of domestic, privatized saint can be seen in the *vita* of the eleventh-century St. Godeleva/Godelieve of Gistel (d. 1070). She served as a pious example of conjugal patience, obedience, and necessary submission. Godeleva is praised by her hagiographer, Drogo, as an efficient housewife: she provided for the servants, cared for the poor, and occupied much of her time with spinning and weaving. Trapped in an abusive marriage to a nobleman by the name of Bertolf, she spent her evenings alone, in tears, begging God to bring about a change in her husband's behavior toward her. At one point, the long-suffering Godeleva escaped from her violent husband and her cruel mother-in-law and returned to her parents. They petitioned the count of Flanders and the bishop; however, the Church refused her request for a separation. Thus, in obedience to the bishop, she returned to her husband's house only to be strangled by two of Bertolf's servants. Moved by the violence of her death, Godeleva was immediately recognized as a popular saint—a martyred saint of marriage. Her *vita* glorified the privatized, passive virtues of suffering, patience, perseverence, obedience, and the essential subservience required of the wife to her husband.[198]

While the Church perhaps attempted to exercise social control through the promotion of a new female image (a domesticized, privatized saintly ideal for women), it was not entirely successful in removing women from the public sphere. England, Scotland, and certain regions of Germany, for example, still presented "new frontiers" with fresh opportunities for women to exercise a great deal of power and influence in society and the Church. In addition, the office of queenship and patronage to the Church continued to provide visibility for women and access to sainthood.

Perhaps one of the most famous women saints of this later period was Queen Margaret of Scotland (d. 1093). The roles which she assumed in the Church and society are in many ways reminiscent of those of the prominent Merovingian and Anglo-Saxon saints. As queen (*consocia*) at court, St. Margaret assumed a major public role. She exercised a great deal of influence over her husband, King Malcolm: according to her contemporary *vita*, "she had made the king himself very readily inclined to works of justice, mercy, alms, and other virtues. He learned from her also to prolong vigils of the night frequently, with prayer; he learned by her exhortation and example to pray to God with groaning of heart, and shedding of tears. . . . He was fearful of offending her in any way, a queen of such venerable life, since he perceived that Christ truly dwelt in her heart; but rather hastened in all things to obey very quickly her wishes and prudent counsellings; he too to reject the same things that she had rejected, and for love of her love to love the things that she had loved." Turgot, her biographer, notes that the queen also enhanced the royal dignity through the institution of more ceremonious service of the king and the extravagant decoration of the royal palace.[199]

The *vita* describes how the queen built a church in honor of the Trinity, "with threefold purpose of salvation; that is to say, for the redemption of the king's soul and of her own, and in order to obtain for her children prosperity in this life and the life to come. This church she decorated with various kinds of adornments. . . ." The queen was also known for her generous acts of charity to the poor both in her country and other countries as well. Occasionally she gave things which belonged to the king to the destitute; "a pious robbery which he always took altogether willingly and gladly." Moreover, she supplied ships to carry pilgrims across the sea to St. Andrews and established hostels for the pilgrims. (The names of North Queensferry and South Queensferry on the Forth still reflect this arrangement.) In addition, Queen Margaret also won praise for her work in freeing slaves and attempting to reform the practice of slavery. As noted by Turgot, "who can tell in number how many men, and how great, she restored to liberty, by payment of a price; men whom the ferocity of their enemies had led away captive from the nation of the Angles, and reduced to slavery? She had even sent secret spies everywhere throughout the provinces of the Scots, to find out which of the captives were oppressed with the harshest servitude, and treated most inhumanly; and to report to her minutely the place where and the people by whom they were oppressed: and she had compassion upon such [slaves] from her inmost heart, and hastened quickly to help them; to ransom them, and restore them to liberty." [200]

The queen was also closely involved in matters of church policy and was a supporter of the reform policies of Pope Gregory VII. Turgot recounts her active role in church councils: "For when she saw that many things were done in that nation contrary to the rule of the true faith and the holy custom of the universal church, she appointed many councils, in order by Christ's gift to bring back the wanderers, in whatever way she could, to the path of truth." He then describes an especially difficult council where the queen, along with only a few supporters, fought for three days against "the defenders of perverted custom." At this point Turgot compares the saintly queen to the "model queen-saint" Helena: as she had formerly "confuted the Jews with verdicts from the scriptures, so now did this queen also confute the erring." During this religious conflict the king "continued as her chief helper," proving to be especially useful as a language interpreter for both sides of the dispute.[201]

Another contribution to the Church and the reform movement in Scotland attributed to St. Margaret came about through her friendship with Lanfranc, archbishop of Canterbury. Lanfranc was said to have sent the queen a group of Benedictine monks from Canterbury who then initiated monastic life at her new foundation at Dunfermline.[202]

Queen Margaret also was praised for her educational achievements. According to Turgot, from her youth she began "to occupy herself in the study of divine readings, and to employ her mind upon them with delight. She was endowed with keen acuteness of intellect, to understand any matter; with much tenacity of memory, to retain it; with gracious facility of words, to express it. For (what I used to admire much in her) among the discords of law-suits, among manifold cares of state, she applied herself with wonderful zeal to divine reading; concerning which she very often discussed even minute points with the most learned men who were present. But just as none present among them was of deeper intelligence than she, so none was clearer in eloquence. And so it very often occurred that the teachers themselves went away from her much wiser than they had been when they came." Her biographer then provides us with a most illuminating comparison of the queen's erudition with the illiteracy of her husband, King Malcolm: "Thus, although ignorant of letters, he used often to handle and gaze on the books in which she had been accustomed either to pray or to read." He would then, as a special favor to the queen, have her most valued books adorned with gold and jewels.[203]

In addition to the queen's public roles and proficiency in learning, Turgot also praised her active involvement and patronage in the area of needlework. He furnishes us with a wonderful description of her special quarters: "Her chamber was never empty of these things (that is of the things that pertained to the adornment of divine service); it seemed to be a kind of workshop, so to speak, of celestial art. There were always seen copes for the cantors, chasubles, stoles, altar-cloths, and other priestly vestments, and decorations for the Church. Some were being prepared by the artist's hand: others, finished, were kept as being worthy of admiration."[204]

It should be stressed that during this period needlework or embroidery—although essentially "women's work"—was quite rightly regarded as a serious, highly valued "fine art." Women from all classes of medieval society were involved in embroidery work, and their artistic skills brought them a certain recognition in society and the Church.[205] Lisa Bitel has noted, for example, that among early Irish women the well-trained embroideress, *druinech,* "was so skilled, her talents so rare, and her product so richly valuable, that she was irreplaceable. Her artistry earned her more prestige than any queen had, according to one law."[206]

Thus, among the ranks of the *mulieres sanctae,* a number of women were singled out and praised for their impressive skills in needlework. The Irish martyrology of Oengus, for example, relates that Ercnat's sanctity was based on her role as an embroiderer and seamstress for St. Columcille/Columba of Iona. "Ercnat a virginal nun, who was cook and robe-maker to Columcille. . . . Her name, however, in truth was *Ercnat,* i.e. embroideress, for *eread* in the Old Gaelic is now *rinnaigecht* 'drawing'; for it was that virgin who was embroideress, cutter and sewer of raiment to Columcille *cum suis discipulis.*"[207]

In this tradition, the abbess-saint Eustadiola was remembered for her fine embroidery work, which she used to decorate her church. With her own hands she made holy vestments, altar cloths, and wall hangings which she embellished with embroidery and gold fringe.[208]

One of the most important and popular of all Anglo-Saxon saints, Etheldreda, founding abbess of Ely, was known for her great skill in orphrey, or gold embroidery work (see plate 8). According to the *Liber Eliensis,* she made, with her own hands, a stole and maniple which she offered to St. Cuthbert. This fine and magnificent embroidery was worked in gold and precious stones.[209] The author of the *vita* of the abbess-saints Herlinda and Renilda also glorifies the skills of these women in the making and decorating of cloth. The sisters were "carefully trained in every area of work such as is done by women's hands, in various designs and in different styles; thus they attained a high standard of excellence in spinning, weaving, designing, and embroidering interlace in gold and flowers in silk."[210]

Similarly, the empress-saint Cunegund was known for her expertise in the production of marvelous embroidery work. She was said to have made a sumptuous coronation mantle for her husband, which was then presented by Henry and Cunegund to the cathedral of Bamberg.[211] Several other female saints of this period also won recognition for their skill in embroidery work.

In general, however, the attempts of the reformers to relegate women to a privatized, domestic sphere resulted in an increasingly limited visibility for women. Despite the promotion of the feminine religious ideal of domesticity, these activities were less likely to capture the popular imagination and to inspire the enthusiastic support required for the making of saints. Greater value was still attached to the public sphere. (We do not find, for example, a parallel development of the ideal of a domestic or custodial male saint emerging at this same time; rather, men saints continued to be recruited essentially from among those active in the public spotlight—abbots and bishops.)[212] Thus, in attempting to define and circumscribe the functions and space of women, the reformers also contributed to the further restriction of their access to sainthood.

Although Church politics, beginning with the Carolingian reforms, encouraged gendered spheres and worked to shrink public boundaries for women, the effects of these efforts were further bolstered by a complex of other political, economic, and social factors of the period.

With the growth of feudal monarchies in the eleventh and twelfth centuries, governments ceased to be ruled on a personal basis but rather developed into large, impersonal institutions. Public power, which had previously been exercised by great aristocratic families through the household, was recaptured by kings who were assisted in their governance by professional bureaucrats. The loss of public power seems to have been particularly felt by queens and aristocratic women, for with the removal of the power base from the household, noblewomen witnessed the decline of much of their formal, public position of influence. The intersection of public and private spheres had encouraged and facilitated women's exercise of power: this convergence was now replaced by an increasingly rigid separation of public and domestic spheres of influence.[213]

Other important changes began to occur within the structure of the family which worked to diminish the economic independence of noblewomen in the feudal world. In general, early medieval families had bilineal or cognatic kinship networks which traced descent through both females and males. This arrangement was favorable to women and allowed them to inherit along with their brothers. With the eleventh century, however, there emerged in some areas of Europe a new lineage pattern, that of patrilineage, which discounted the importance of ties through women and inheritance by women, and favored the firstborn male.[214] Other shifts which would be detrimental to women's economic independence involved the replacement of the customary bride gift or reverse-dowry with the dowry, which was now supplied by the bride's family, as well as changes in the dower.[215] Moreover, at this same time it appears that families were attempting to keep closer surveillance over the alienation of their properties and especially to curb "extravagant" acts of patronage or generosity to the Church which might prove detrimental to the family's economic strategy. In the charters of the eleventh century, for example, we begin to see greater involvement on the part of family members in witnessing economic transactions to the Church. We also find in the *vitae* acts of extreme generosity or "pious robbery" by widows increasingly checked by male family members.[216]

Noblewomen were now frequently forced to remarry and to use their possessions to build up territorial lordships rather than piously disposing of them by establishing new religious foundations for women.[217] These economic changes in family networks and strategy worked to limit one of the important avenues by which aristocratic women could gain access to sainthood. Since sanctity was so closely tied to economics and patronage, these shifts made it increasingly difficult for noble or royal women to gain a reputation which would lead to sainthood.

Moreover, with the majority of the *mulieres sanctae* of this period recruited from the cloister, changes in monasticism had a direct effect on the making of women saints. The rather flourishing era of female sanctity (the seventh and eighth centuries) coincided with the initial popularity of monastic life for women and the enthusiastic establishment and support of family monasteries. Many of these early female communities, along with the double or affiliated monasteries, had originally served the crucial functions of missionary and educational centers, as well as parish churches. However, with the success of the missionary movement, destruction and dislocation caused by the invasions, the closing of the new frontiers and diminished opportunities for new lands, the initial momentum of the founding of family convents began to wane.[218] Furthermore, beginning with the various Church reforms, we see a preference for male power and authority, and attempts at increased episcopal control over the abbesses and their convents. The reformers' insistence on celibacy, ritual purity, along with sex-segregated spheres, fostered a heightened fear of women and female sexuality which often led to a full-blown misogyny. Many of the reformers therefore had little interest in the establishment and maintenance of women's monasteries. Reform ideas also had a profound impact on patronage which increasingly favored male monastic foundations over and against female houses.

Thus these various complex political, social, economic, and religious changes contributed to a deterioration in the formal power and economic independence that these aristocratic women had enjoyed within their families and the Church. These shifts also seemed to have contributed to a decline in women's religious prestige as reflected in the number of *mulieres sanctae*.

Nevertheless, in contrast to this later period, which witnessed a shrinking of boundaries for women, it appears that, in the early centuries of Christianization of the north of Europe and Britain, women enjoyed a certain *potentia* and, indeed, wider opportunities in the "public" realm, as confirmed by their selection to the celestial gynaeceum. In this pioneering society, when the very survival of the Church depended on the contribution and cooperation of everyone, restrictions upon the activities of the allegedly inferior sex were ignored or temporarily abated. Women with power and property were actively recruited by churchmen to aid in missionary work, to establish churches, monasteries, and centers of education, and to assume positions of leadership with very real power and authority. Their assumption of public roles within the Church apparently did not engender fears, on the part of churchmen, of female sexuality or of women usurping male prerogatives. As partners, friends, sisters, and collaborators, they partook of the rights and privileges of the newly Christianized lands and were frequently rewarded for their essential contributions through recognition of sanctity. And although this period appears as a rather flourishing or positive age in regard to female sanctity, when the Church and society acknowledged women's worth (as witnessed by the relatively high percentage of female saints for the period), the Church still failed to recognize women's equivalence fully. This failure is highlighted by the asymmetrical patterns which emerge from our broad survey of these dossiers of female and male saints.

And there were those whose desire to live chastely was so strong that they did not hesitate to deform themselves, lest they forfeit their purity which they had vowed to God, and that they might reach the bridegroom of all virgins as virgins.

Peter Abelard, Letter 7
"On the Origin of Nuns,"
PL 178:250

Great, therefore, is the privilege of purity: and if anyone who is compelled by force to relinquish it shall for that reason, contemptuous of human society, voluntarily separate himself from this life shared by all, he shall rejoice triumphantly in the celestial society among the 144,000 singing the virginal song. [Apoc. 14:1]

Aldhelm, *De virginitate,* trans.
M. Lapidge and M. Herren,
XXXI:90

At What Cost Virginity?
Sanctity and the Heroics of Virginity

In the making of women saints, the virginal life, the life of sexless perfection, was of paramount importance. Particularly for female saints, the status of *virgo intacta* was nearly a prerequisite for sainthood (see plate 9). In their pursuit of the *vita perfecta,* these saintly women were portrayed as otherworldly beings, "impatient angels"—"dead to earthly desires, breathing only heavenly affections."[1] As virgins they were seen as untouched by sexual thoughts or experiences. Thus for much of the Middle Ages the ideal state for woman, the perfect life as articulated by the Church, was that of *integritas,* total virginity, that is, uncorrupted sexual and spiritual purity. In the view of churchmen, there was only one way in which women could transcend their unfortunate sexuality and free themselves from their corporeal shackles, and this was through a life of virginity, of sexless perfection.[2]

Although within the early Church, and particularly in the monastic environment, the rigors of the chaste life were equally upheld for both sexes, an exaggerated emphasis was placed on chastity for women; that is, there was a heavily disproportionate admiration for female virginity. From the beginning, virginity was not emphasized for men in the same way as it was for women. It never dominated the total mode of perception of the male religious, nor defined the parameters for the state of masculine perfection or male sanctity as it did for women. This gender-based difference seems to have originated in the concept that women's lives, in contrast to men's, were essentially "body-centered." Women were seen as primarily carnal or bodily beings by nature, and therefore in order to lead a spiritual life they needed to deny or renounce the sexual and reproductive aspects of their being (i.e., that which specifically defined them as women) and transcend their gender.[3] For women, the preservation of virginity was the single most essential prerequisite for a life of Christian perfection; and through it they would be granted entry into heaven or the celestial gynaeceum. Therefore, the necessary responses dictated by this value system, the extremes to which individuals might be driven to preserve their virginity in hopes of salvation, or, for the would-be saint, *fama sanctitatis,* were defined in part by one's gender.

THE POLITICS OF *VIRGINITAS*

There is a great deal of continuity in the didactic works on virginity. Beginning with St. Paul's injunction on the superiority of virginity, the writings of the Church Fathers firmly implanted this concept in the mentality of the Latin West. Tertullian, Cyprian, Ambrose, Jerome, and Augustine were especially articulate in their treatment of virginity for women. In their writings they established the notion of a hierarchy of sexual perfection with distinct grades measured in terms of the degree of a person's denial of or withdrawal from sexual activity.[4] According to this scale of values, there were three separate levels or states of chastity: virgin martyrs or virgins were accorded the highest value, followed by chaste widows; married women occupied a distant third. In the writings of the Church Fathers, these three states were traditionally compared to the hundred-fold, sixty-fold, and thirty-fold fruit found in the biblical parable.[5]

Consequently, patristic writers placed the ultimate value on the denial of female sexuality and the espousal of the ideal of total virginity. In this tradition, they had nothing but the highest praise and concern for the virginity of Christian women. The virgin's body was described as a jewel, a treasure, a sacred vessel, a temple of God which was to be cherished and honored. As bride of Christ the virgin needed to be carefully guarded so as to remain "unwounded" or "untarnished" for her eternal bridegroom. According to the patristic writers, such Christian models of virginity had successfully repudiated their own female sexual identity; they had negated their unfortunate biological nature; and thus acting in a manner "forgetful of their sex" they were able to transcend the weakness and limitations inherent in their gender. It was then as sexless, gender-neutral beings that these virgins were viewed as near spiritual equals. For their rigorous repudiation of their own sexuality and espousal of virginity, they often won the highest patristic compliment: they were praised for their spiritual virility, for progressing toward perfect manhood. According to St. Jerome (ca. 341–420), through the virginal, sexless life such a one "will cease to be a woman and will be called man."[6] It is then for their heroic—that is, virile—defense of their virginal purity or chastity that these women often won recognition of sainthood and martyrdom.[7]

These patristic tracts, however, presented a dichotomized view of women. Although they showered the highest praise on virgins who denied their sex, they viewed female nature as fragile, weak, and in general, as participating in the carnal, as sexual, and thus incompatible with the spiritual world. The Church Fathers, as ascetics, and in some cases fanatical celibates, shared an uneasiness and fundamental suspicion toward women: they feared and also abhorred female sexuality. Their writings focus on the inherent dangers of woman's physical attractiveness for the male celibate. As frightening temptresses and *impedimenta,* the female sex threatened their very being and needed to be avoided at all cost.[8] Grounded in their distorted perceptions of woman, they directed their vituperative tirades against her sensual, lustful, and polluting character. The Church Fathers described the female body in abusive and disdainful terms. Although deceptively attractive, woman's body was to be shunned as an inherently ugly, repulsive receptacle. Consequently they admonish consecrated virgins to negate or destroy their physical attractiveness, and also to keep themselves enclosed, out of sight, so as not to be responsible for seducing "innocent" men, as well as causing the loss of their own chastity. Based on the dichotomized patristic view of woman, these encouragements and warnings sent a mixed as well as disconcerting message to those who espoused a life of virginity.

The writings of these Church Fathers and later churchmen emphasize the seriousness of the commitment to virginity by these brides of Christ, as well as the necessity of maintaining this privileged state. They stress the difficulties and hazards which might be encountered by those who chose to follow this profession; they also attempt to instill fear among these women. St. Jerome, in his celebrated "Letter to Eustochium," provides some of the classic admonitions and encouragements for the life of virginal perfection. In this letter he stresses the need to guard one's virginity with jealous care. A strong eschatological concern underlies his patristic admonitions. The bride of Christ must spend her earthly life balanced precariously between a continual fear of defilement and the steadfast hope of eternal life with her bridegroom, Christ. Jerome warns Eustochium of the hard road that she has chosen to follow: "I do not wish pride to come upon you by reason of your decision [to espouse virginity], but fear. If you walk laden with gold, you must beware of a robber. This mortal life is a race. Here we struggle, that elsewhere we may be crowned. No one walks without anxiety amid serpents and scorpions."[9]

St. Jerome also underscores the very real dangers involved in a virgin's leaving her protective environment and venturing outdoors: "Go not out from home, nor wish to behold the daughters of a strange country. . . . Diana went out and was ravished. I would not have you seek a bridegroom in the highways, I would not have you go about the corners of the city. . . . Your Spouse cannot be found in the broad

ways. *Narrow and strait is the way that leadeth to life. . . .* You will be
wounded, you will be stripped, and you will say, lamenting: 'The
keepers that go about the city found me, struck me, wounded me; they
took away my veil from me.'" [10]

Thus Jerome warns that if the virgin fails to walk the "straight and
narrow course" and does not endure to the end, she will not be saved,
but rather turned away from Christ's bridal chamber to feed the goats
which will be on the left hand. Again he admonishes Eustochium:
"Take care, I pray, lest sometime God may say of you: the virgin of
Israel has fallen; there is none to raise her up." And of critical importance, "although God can do all things, He cannot raise up a virgin after she has fallen. He has power, indeed, to free her from the penalty,
but *He has no power to crown one who has been corrupted.*" [11]

Jerome also skillfully utilizes negative conditioning in his vivid description of the fallen virgin or the virgin daughter / "great prostitute
who sitteth on the waters." According to Jerome, she shall "no more
be called delicate and tender. Take a millstone and grind meal, strip off
thy covering, make bare thy legs, pass over the rivers. Thy nakedness
shall be discovered and thy shame shall be seen." [12] He further elaborates on the great humiliation of the fallen virgin: "[She] shall be
stripped and her hinder parts shall be bared in her own sight. She shall
sit by the waters of solitude and putting down her pitcher shall open
her feet to everyone that passes by and shall be polluted from head to
foot. It would have been better to have submitted to marriage with a
man, to have walked on the level, than to fall into the depths of hell
while striving to attain the heights." [13]

In contrast to the negative reinforcement and shame-instilling im-
agery of fallen virgins, Jerome also provides encouragement for virgins
who might suffer in order to maintain their chastity. He cites St.
Matthew: "He that shall persevere unto the end, He says, he shall be
saved." [14] As a further source of inspiration Jerome furnishes his contemporary virgins with heroic role models, exemplary early Christian
saints and martyrs. He describes both the anguish involved in maintaining one's virginity and the joy of knowing victory, rather than
having become "slaves forever because of failure to endure a single
hour." [15] Jerome adds that no task is too difficult for the love of Christ
and the desire to always seek his embraces. He then expands in glorious detail on the rewards awaiting the undefiled virgin; the splendor of
that day when Mary, attended by her band of virgins, and Christ, her
eternal spouse, shall come to meet her. According to Jerome, the end
result is immense incredible joy, indeed well worth the perseverance
and struggle. Although utilizing masculine language, he describes the
celestial assemblage to Eustochium as follows: "Then the hundred and

forty-four thousand [virgins] shall hold their harps before the throne and in sight of the ancients and shall sing a new song: and no man will be able to say the canticle except the appointed number. These are they who were not defiled with women, for they have remained virgins. These are they who follow the Lamb whithersoever He goeth." [16]

In addition to his encomiums of virginity, Jerome briefly mentions a potential response for virgins threatened with sexual assault—namely, suicide. In his *Commentary on Jonah,* he states: "It is not man's prerogative to lay violent hands upon himself, but rather to freely receive death from others. In persecutions it is not lawful to commit suicide *except when one's chastity is jeopardized.*" [17] This position is further supported by Jerome in his *Against Jovinian.* Here he cites a number of examples from Greek and Roman history of pagan virgins who were celebrated for killing themselves in the preservation of their chastity. [18]

It is interesting that St. Ambrose (ca. 340–97) adopts this same stance on suicide in defense of chastity in his work *Concerning Virgins.* Here he responds to his sister Marcellina's concerns about the potential rape of consecrated virgins, and what in fact should be thought of those women who committed suicide rather than permit themselves to be violated. Ambrose notes the basic problem of reconciling self-martyrdom with the Scriptures which forbid a Christian to kill herself. However, through the use of *exempla* of famous virgin martyrs (specifically the virgin Pelagia and her mother and sisters, and the blessed Sotheris, who was one of Ambrose and Marcellina's relatives), Ambrose justifies the practice of suicide in the preservation of virginity. [19]

St. Augustine's *City of God* (413–26) is especially relevant to the mental conditioning of virgins in regard to the maintenance of chastity. In book 1 of this work, Augustine discusses the different appropriate responses required in the face of the present barbarian onslaughts—specifically as they had to do with the violation of Christian women. Again Augustine is very much concerned with "total virginity," *integritas,* and the interior disposition of the virgin, as well as the fact that she cannot ultimately be corrupted on a purely physical level. In offering consolation to those women within the Christian fellowship who had been sexually assaulted, Augustine assures them that "violation of chastity, without the will's consent, cannot pollute the character." He elaborates further on this dichotomy between body and soul: "In the first place, it must be firmly established that virtue, the condition of right living, holds command over the parts of the body from her throne in the mind, and that the consecrated body is the instrument of the consecrated will; and if that will continues unshaken and steadfast, whatever anyone else does with the body or to the body, provided that it cannot be avoided without committing sin, involves no blame to the sufferer." However, Augustine also stresses: "But there can be committed on another's body not only acts involving pain, but also acts involving lust. And so whenever any act of the latter kind has been committed, although it does not destroy a purity which has been maintained by the utmost resolution, still it does engender a sense of shame, because it may be believed that an act, which perhaps could not have taken place without some physical pleasure, was accompanied by a consent of the mind." [20]

In this statement Augustine, then, underscores the inevitable relationship which exists between the soul and body, and that corruption of the soul necessarily precedes corruption of the body. The fine line between "innocence" and "guilt" in the case of rape thus rested essentially within the conscience of the woman. In introducing this "pain/lust" concept Augustine suggests that in some cases it may be believed that women secretly wanted to be raped; that is, the act was actually "accompanied by a consent of the mind."

After this discussion, Augustine turns to the question of extreme solutions adopted by women in the past in response to sexual assault. He notes that some women committed suicide in order to avoid being subjected to rape; this action should be excused but not totally condoned. He reiterates that when a woman has been violated without her consent, and forced by another's sin, she has no reason to punish herself by a voluntary death; still less, he contends, before the event (in anticipation of rape), in case she should commit murder while the offense, and another's offense at that, still remains uncertain. He maintains that in these cases guilt is attached only to the rapist and not at all to the woman forcibly raped.[21]

Augustine contrasts the behavior of contemporary Christian women with that of the famous pagan heroine, Lucretia, who, unable to bear the shame and disgrace of having been raped, as well as to show her innocence, had committed suicide. He notes approvingly that when these women were raped, they did not kill themselves for another's crime; rather, they bore this crime with Christian patience and resignation. "They would not add crime to crime by committing murder on themselves in shame because the enemy had committed rape on them in lust. They have the glory of chastity within them, the testimony of their conscience. They have this in the sight of God, and they ask for nothing more. In fact there is nothing else for them to do that is right for them to do. For they will not deviate from the authority of God's law by taking unlawful steps to avoid the suspicions of men." [22]

1. Christ in Glory with the Choirs of Martyrs, Confessors, and Virgins. *King Athelstan's Psalter* (925–940)

This tenth-century miniature captures the categories and hierarchical ordering of saints as well as the gender-based disparity in the number of saints promoted during this period. The composition is dominated by a large enthroned Christ in a mandorla surrounded radially by the various choirs of saints. The top and middle registers are filled with choirs of male martyrs and male confessors, while the bottom register (located below the feet of Christ) is occupied by the choir of female saints or virgins. MS Cotton Galba A. XVIII, fol. 21. By permission of the British Library.

2. PORTRAIT OF ST. ADELHEID, ABBESS OF VILICH

This portrait of St. Adelheid is found in a thirteenth-century redaction of her *vita*. Here identified as "Adelheid, virgin," the saint is depicted with long, flowing hair and wearing an ornately decorated robe with fashionable wide sleeves. Closely resembling a Christ portrait, she holds a book in her right hand while her left hand is raised to teach or bless. MS Harl. 2800, fol. 207v. By permission of the British Library.

3. PORTRAIT OF AN AUTHOR: BAUDONIVIA WRITING THE *VITA* OF ST. RADEGUND

This marvelous late-eleventh-century miniature provides one of the earliest medieval portraits of a female author. Here the nun Baudonivia of Ste-Croix is placed within a decorative architectural framework; she is seated on a chair with a cushion and a *scabellum* or footstool beneath her feet. In her right hand she holds a stylus (used for writing on wax) with a spatula for erasing. In her left hand, leaning against her knee, are the tablets on which she writes her Life of St. Radegund. MS 250, fol. 43v. Bibliothèque Municipale, Poitiers. Giraudon/Art Resource, NY.

4. Radegund Enters Monastic Life; the Cell and Oratory of the Saint

In the upper register of this late-eleventh-century miniature from the *vita* of St. Radegund, the saint is escorted by an enthusiastic crowd of men and women into her newly founded monastery. In the lower register, at the left, St. Radegund is praying within the privacy of her cell. She is holding a book and is involved in ascetic regimens for Lent, shown by the three chains fastened tightly around her chest. Attached to the cell is the saint's oratory with its own altar. During the Middle Ages, Radegund's cell, which had been the site of many of her miracles, became a special place of veneration at Ste-Croix. MS 250, fol. 31v. Courtesy of the Bibliothèque Municipale, Poitiers. Photo Musées de Poitiers (C. Vignaud).

5. St. Etheldreda's Installation, Ely Cathedral

St. Etheldreda's installation as abbess of Ely by her bishop-friend St. Wilfrid is captured on this wonderful fourteenth-century carved corbel located on one of the pillars of the Octagon at Ely Cathedral. The abbess is shown seated on a high throne, with a special platform for her feet, and placed slightly above Wilfrid. Etheldreda wears a crown; in her right hand she holds an elaborately decorated crozier, which is presented to her by Bishop Wilfrid, and in her left hand she holds a book. Witnessing the ceremony are a number of nuns (to Etheldreda's left) and a group of clerics and monks (behind Wilfrid). Ely Cathedral. Photo by Virginia Blanton-Whetsell.

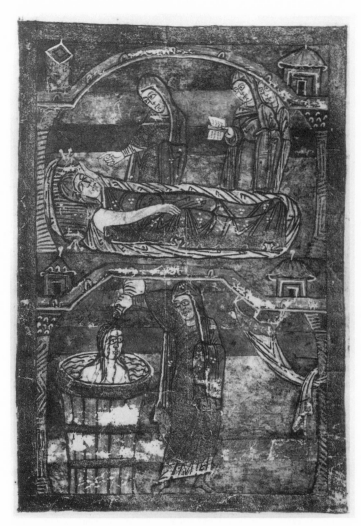

6. St. Radegund and the Miraculous Cure of the Nun Animia

In the upper register of this late-eleventh-century miniature, Animia, nun
of Ste-Croix, is shown on her deathbed. She is suffering from hydropsy,
and her stiff, swollen, outstretched arm is exposed. Standing at her bedside
are St. Radegund, who extends her hand toward the dying nun, and two
nuns who are reading final prayers. The lower register captures a dream
in which Radegund appeared to Animia and ordered her to descend nude
into a bath without water. Radegund then poured oil onto the sick nun's
head and clothed her in a new garment. After this ritual (which resembled
a mystical baptism) Animia awoke to find that she had been fully restored
to health. MS 250, fol. 39r. Courtesy of the Bibliothèque Municipale,
Poitiers. Photo by Necer.

7. The Abbess Hitda Offers a Book to St. Walburga

In this early-eleventh-century evangelistary, "Hitda abbatissa" is portrayed offering St. Walburga, first abbess of the double monastery of Heidenheim, a book. The saint is depicted standing on a decorated platform, holding in her left hand a leafy branch and with her right hand accepting the evangelistary. Although St. Walburga is shown raised above Abbess Hitda, the elongated figures are of the same height. They are placed within a wonderful monastic architectural framework. MS 1640, fol. 6r. Courtesy of the Hessische- und Hochschul-Bibliothek, Darmstadt. Foto Marburg/Art Resource, NY.

8. St. Etheldreda of Ely: "Abbess and Perpetual Virgin"

In this splendid miniature from the *Benedictional of St. Ethelwold* (963–984), St. Etheldreda, founding abbess of Ely, is depicted within a sumptuous foliate border of "Winchester" leafwork. She holds a golden book in her right hand and a flowering sprig of golden blossoms in her left hand (perhaps identifying Etheldreda as one of the Virgin Mary's "virgin flowers," as noted by Bede). Although twice married, the abbess had rejected the marriage bed and retained her virginity. She is identified with letters of gold: "St. Etheldreda abbess and perpetual virgin." St. Etheldreda was buried at Ely, and, as she was the most popular female Anglo-Saxon saint, her cult flourished there. St. Ethelwold, the Benedictine reformer who commissioned this Benedictional, refounded Etheldreda's monastery as a community for monks. MS Add. 49598, fol. 90v. By permission of the British Library. (See also Robert Deshman, *The Benedictional of Æthelwold.* Studies in Manuscript Illumination, no. 9. Princeton, 1995.)

9. Choir of Virgins

This marvelous Anglo-Saxon choir of virgins, found in the *Benedictional of St. Ethelwold* (963–984), is situated within a rich architectural framework. Here seven unidentified virgin saints are depicted with prominent gold crowns and rather unusual blue haloes. Three of the saints are shown holding books, while the figure in the center, with raised hand, appears to be teaching. Above, an angel holds a scroll. MS Add. 49598 fol. 1v. By permission of the British Library. (See also Robert Deshman, *The Benedictional of Æthelwold*. Studies in Manuscript Illumination, no. 9. Princeton, 1995.)

Engraved for Sydney's History of England.

Wale del.   *Grignion sculp.*

The ABBESS of Coldingham Monastery cutting of her nose & upper lip as an example for her Nuns to follow, to prevent being Ravished by the Danes

10. St. Ebba, Abbess of Coldingham

This dramatic eighteenth-century etching captures the heroics of St. Ebba and her nuns at Coldingham when confronted by the Viking invaders. Frozen in this horrific moment in time, St. Ebba, as abbess of her community, provides an example that was to be followed by all of her nuns. Standing before a crucifix, as bride of Christ, she dramatically brandishes a razor, preparing to disfigure herself in order to preserve her virginity. The nuns are shown reacting to her strategy with horror, shock, and fear as well as prayer. Temple Sydney, *A New and Complete History of England from the Earliest Period of Authentic Intelligence to the Present Time.* London, 1775.

11. St. Wilgefortis

This large-scale, late medieval crucifixion, found at the Cathedral of St-Etienne of Beauvais, has been identified with the popular St. Wilgefortis. In this sculptural work, the prominently bearded and mustached woman saint is shown with long, flowing, wavy hair and wearing a low-cut dress and a crown. Photo by the author.

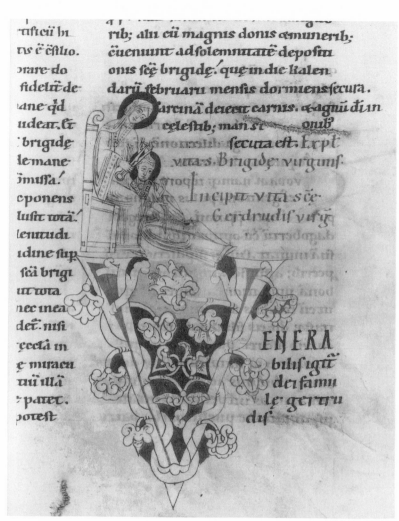

12. A Scene from the Beginning of the *Vita* of St. Gertrude of Nivelles

The tonsuring of St. Gertrude of Nivelles by her mother, St. Ida, is captured in this lovely early-twelfth-century miniature. Here St. Ida is shown seated on a chair with her daughter sitting before her. Using large shears, Ida cuts off the last tuft of Gertrude's hair. Although this illustration does not accurately depict St. Gertrude's crown-shaped tonsure as described in her *vita*, through the use of dots it shows her very close haircut. The purpose of the tonsure was to preserve Gertrude's virginity. *Passionale*. MS 1100, fol. 57. Landesbibliothek, Stuttgart. Foto Marburg/Art Resource, NY.

Thus in contrast to Ambrose and Jerome, Augustine contends that Christians were not permitted to commit suicide "to prevent themselves, and not others, from sinning for fear that their own lust might be excited by another's and that they might consent."[23]

In addition to the patristic writings on the maintenance of virginal perfection and potential responses to sexual assault, papal pronouncements and canons of Church councils dealt with these issues. Of special interest is the position taken by Pope Leo I (440–61) in a letter to the bishops of Africa. Here he maintains that the servants of God who lost the purity of chastity (*integritatem pudoris*) through the violence of the barbarians are not to be punished, but will be praiseworthy in their modesty and feeling of shame, so long as they dare not compare themselves to unpolluted virgins. For these victims of sexual assault, the body alone would be corrupted, while the spirit remained intact. Moreover, if they persevered in their chastity, it was necessary to readmit them into the bosom of the community. Again the pope states that it was unjust to blame or reprimand these women, because it was not of their own free will that they lost their chastity but by the force of the enemy.[24] It is interesting that his insistent repetition that women were not to be blamed or punished for their own victimization seems to be directed against an underlying assumption of their basic guilt and complicity in the act. The difficult, if not intolerable, position in which these violated female religious now found themselves should be underscored. They were shamed, ostracized; they no longer dared to compare themselves to virgins, nor were they to be considered as widows; and only if they "proved themselves" through rededication and perseverance in chastity would they be readmitted into the Church.

In the monastic literature of the early Middle Ages one finds repetition and elaboration of these patristic ideas on virginity. For example, the famous didactic tract, *De virginitate* by Aldhelm (d. 709), directed to Abbess Hildelith of Barking Abbey, further reinforces the patristic exhortations for the life of virginal perfection.[25] This work borrows heavily from Sts. Cyprian, Ambrose, and Jerome, and other Church Fathers, and was immensely popular up to the Norman Conquest. In this encomium, Aldhelm stresses the need for total virginity: *integritas* is "the queen of all virtues and the fruit of perpetual virginity." Citing St. Thomas the Apostle, he describes virginity as sister of the angels, " 'virginitas soror est angelorum' "; " 'virginity is victory over desires, the trophy of faith, a triumph over enemies and the surety of eternal life.' "[26] Aldhelm thus encourages his "gymnosophists" in the heroic perseverance of maintaining a pure, uncontaminated form of chastity.[27] He describes the inmates of Barking Abbey as

industrious bees who are recognized for their "peculiar chastity." He
notes that by the authority of the Scriptures, bees signify "a type of
virginity" as well as resemble the Church: that is, they reproduce
"innocent of the lascivious coupling of marriage, by means of a certain
generative condensation of a very sweet juice"; so too the Church
"fertilizes through the chaste seed of the Word the offspring who are
lawful heirs of eternity." [28] *De virginitate* is filled with specific virginal
references such as "pure," "intact," "incorrupt," "inviolable," "uncontaminated," and other terms. The poetic part of this work, the
Carmen de virginitate, presents a more aggressive or violent *virginitas*
which is shown successfully opposing and vigorously "trampling"
down the principal vices. The language utilized in this didactic poem
is equally strong and colorful when stressing the defiled filth and foul-
ness associated with the body and sins of the flesh.[29] Also, in the
patristic tradition, Aldhelm's writings describe in vivid detail the marvelous apocalyptic rewards awaiting the virgin who perseveres to the
end in a life of unblemished chastity. In this context he calls the virgins
of Barking Abbey "pearls of Christ, jewels of Paradise, participants in
the celestial homeland." [30] (See plate 21.)

Of special interest, however, to the topic of the heroics of virginity
is Aldhelm's discussion of the glory of intact virginity and the problem
of sexual assault. He cites, for example, Augustine's position on the
interior disposition or underlying guilt of the victim: "Thus the sanctity of the body is not lost provided that the sanctity of the soul remains, even if the body is overcome, just as the sanctity of the body *is*
lost if the purity of the soul is violated, even if the body is intact." [31] In
this context Aldhelm then quotes Prosper of Aquitaine's verse:

> The unimpaired mind loses nothing in a violated body,
> The wounds of the flesh do not stain it, if it's unwilling
> Nor does the unengaged will take on the guilt of the deed:
> It's a greater sin to will a crime than to suffer it;
> Thus all [sins] revert to the depths of the heart
> So that often the soul is guilty without the flesh,
> Since it alone conceives and inwardly performs with invisible
>   movements
> That which is withheld from the untouched body.[32]

Aldhelm then devotes another section of this tract to the specific
problem of the use of suicide by virgins when threatened by sexual
assault. He writes: "Great, therefore, is the privilege of purity: and if
anyone who is compelled by force to relinquish it shall for that reason, contemptuous of human society, voluntarily separate himself
from this life shared by all, he shall rejoice triumphantly in the

celestial society among the 144,000 singing the virginal song"
(Apoc. XIV.I).[33] Aldhelm cites the Greek historian Eusebius, Bishop of
Caesarea (d. 399), who tells of virgins devoted to God, "who, in order
to preserve the purity of their integrity, immersed themselves headlong
in the swift channel of the cataract—whence one of the Church Fathers [i.e., St. Jerome] says, 'It is not allowable to die by one's own
hand *except in cases where chastity is endangered*' [*in Ionam* I. 12]."
Aldhelm concludes this discussion of the problematic use of suicide
as a response to the loss of one's chastity: "Oh, matter of wonder!—
and an almost unfathomable pronouncement! When anyone forced
unwillingly to be subject to other outrageous sins—which grievously
disturb the state of the world—and, his freedom of will having been
ignored, is compelled to commit a criminal offence, if, under the pretext of avoiding sin and shunning transgression, he shall by any manner of death inflict violence on his life, he is considered, among (other)
suicides, an outcast from the society of the Church! From this one
may infer how precious to the heavenly citizens is the nobility of
chastity, which cannot by any means be destroyed or obliterated by
that which is able to make mock of the merits of the perfect and to
make void every kind of virtue."[34]

Following this discussion of the use of suicide when confronted
with the loss of virginity, Aldhelm presents as encouragement to his
contemporary nuns, a very long and impressive catalogue of female
and male virginal saints. Especially prominent are those women who
had won the "palm of virginity and triumph of martyrdom" and
therefore served as special models for the nuns of Barking Abbey.
Included among these illustrious exempla were such early Christian
saints as Cecilia, Agatha, Lucy, Eustochium, Eugenia, Agnes, Thecla,
Eulalia, and others.[35] Their shortened *vitae* emphasized the excessive
tortures, trials, and suffering endured by these women when faced
with the loss of their virginity. Their model lives were to be kept before the eyes of the nuns to underscore the reality that virginity
entailed inordinate struggle, vigorous, aggressive defense, but also,
ultimately, great rewards.

Thus within the violent context of his own age, Aldhelm, like
Jerome and Ambrose, advocates suicide as a sanctioned and "positive" means of virginal defense. He assures his contemporary readers
that those who had sacrificed their earthly, physical lives in the maintenance of virginity would receive, as brides of Christ, eternal rewards.

The popular Old English poem *Judith* (ascribed to the early tenth
century), also provided an important *exemplum* for early medieval
nuns and the defense of their virginity. According to the *Apocrypha*,
Judith, the wise and devout widow of Manasses, delivered her city of

Bethulia from the siege of the Assyrian general, Holofernes. As the chosen instrument of God, she used her great beauty to lure the general to his destruction. Through this means, Judith succeeded in beheading Holofernes and rescuing her people without compromising her chastity or honor. However, the author of the Anglo-Saxon poem refashioned the "historical," ancient Jewish widow/heroine into a bold virgin who espoused the ideals and values of the early Christian period. According to the epic, Judith's ability to maintain her chastity against the advances of Holofernes, and her heroic act of killing him were essentially predicated on her virginal purity. For virginity contained in itself extraordinary power; it was credited as the source of Judith's invulnerability.[36]

This popular poem was written during the period of the Danish invasions of England and the prefiguration of the hostile Danes by the pagan Assyrians was astutely noted in the sources of the time.[37] And indeed, the role model of Judith seems to have been especially pertinent to contemporary nuns/virgins faced with similar threats of sexual assault at the hands of the pagan Viking invaders.

In the late tenth century, Aelfric, an Anglo-Saxon abbot, appended to the poem *Judith* a moral directed to contemporary nuns. Here Aelfric emphasizes the seriousness of the commitment to consecrated virginity and stresses that becoming a *sponsa Christi* necessitated great struggle. The life of one committed to God he describes as a "martyrdom," with nuns specifically denoted as "Christ's martyrs." In order to maintain their untarnished chastity they must be involved in daily battle. Aelfric also underlines the guilt before God of those who had broken their vows of chastity; he elaborates upon the fate of lapsed virgins and their future punishments in hell. As Sr. Mary Byrne notes: "But lest the nuns to whom he is directing the moral lose confidence in their power to resist evil as Judith had resisted it, he explains to them . . . that maidenhood and purity contain in themselves very great might." [38]

Although male ecclesiastical writers virtually monopolized this didactic tradition which celebrated virginity and emphasized the need for virginal maintenance, one important early example of the *vox femina* is that of Hrotswitha of Gandersheim. A tenth-century writer within the monastic tradition, she herself interprets her name as meaning the "strong voice" of Gandersheim.[39] As a product of her age and a German canoness of the famous monastery of Gandersheim, Hrotswitha shares with her male ecclesiastical contemporaries a deep concern about the need for female virginity. Her dramatic works exalt early Christian female saints and martyrs and the defense of their chastity against pagan lechery. Attempted rape was seen as the critical test point to represent women's strength and courage as well as their virtue. Hrotswitha's plays were thus written to demonstrate women's steadfast adherence to their vows of chastity, and to inspire similar heroics among her sisters. Her writings are especially relevant for a female monastic audience and portray strong, independent, forceful virgins successfully resisting temptation and seduction. Encouraged by eschatological rewards, her heroines die glorious "happy" deaths after fearlessly preserving their virginity against the lustful sexuality of pagans.

In her preface she stresses that the greater the struggles or temptations, "the greater the merit of those who resist, especially when it is fragile woman who is victorious and strong man who is routed with confusion."[40] *The Martyrdom of Agape, Chione, and Irena* notes briefly the special dilemma of rape for those who had espoused a life of virginity. When one of the heroes of the play, Irena, is threatened by the Roman authorities with loss of her virginity through rape in a brothel, after which she would be "no longer numbered in the company of the pure," she responds with assurance (following in the orthodox, Augustinian tradition), that she is in fact not frightened by this threat because "there is no sin, unless the soul consents." And although Hrotswitha does not have her characters actually test this maxim, here we see in this short didactic response, the belief that the victim of rape is innocent and not to be blamed.[41] In another of her plays *The Resurrection of Drusiana and Callimachus,* Hrotswitha's chaste and beautiful heroine, Drusiana, is sexually harassed by a certain Callimachus. Unable to overcome his persistent attempts at seducing her, she prays to Christ to save her from this fate by allowing her to die before her chastity is violated. Her prayers are answered and she promptly dies. As M. R. Sperberg-McQueen has argued, in this case, in contrast to that of Irena, Drusiana "offers no defense of the woman whose chastity is violated against her will. Instead, her example suggests that the unchaste woman may always be indicted on two counts: losing one's chastity is a sin regardless of circumstances, and women are responsible for men's reactions to them: 'My beauty has crazed this man . . . save me / From becoming the cause of destruction / Of . . . Callimachus.'"[42]

Thus while Hrotswitha's writings in general are certainly remarkable for their championing of virginal feminism, for locating overt lustful sexuality in pagan males, and for their positive portrayals of strong, courageous, and independent women in the face of the negative images of traditional misogyny, yet I agree with Sperberg-McQueen in her assessment of the need to underscore the dual tradition or the "double-voiced discourse" that we find in these extraordinary works. We cannot dismiss the fact that as a product of her age, Hrotswitha was not unaffected by the overriding ecclesiastical patriarchal values and traditions which permeated her sources and intellectual milieu. Therefore, accompanying her ideas which celebrate the strength of women (frequently through the *topos* of weakness), we also find concepts and strategies that betray the traditional male ecclesiastical suspicion and distrust of the female body, express the fundamental fear of female beauty, and propound the need for women to obliterate or expunge all signs of their attractiveness in order to save themselves as well as those innocent men whose lives they might destroy. Furthermore, we can note in her work the patristic writers' underlying skepticism in regard to the innocence of the victims of rape. In this, Hrotswitha of Gandersheim's writings serve to reinforce male ecclesiastical control of women and their bodies.⁴³ From our "modern" vantage point there might appear to be a disturbing dissonance here between Hrotswitha's virginal feminism and her adoption of these traditions detrimental to women; however, given the perspective of the tenth-century cloister in which Hrotswitha wrote, fully immersed in the dominant male culture, this is hardly unexpected.⁴⁴ Nevertheless, what remains particularly important is Hrotswitha's refreshing defiance of much of the prevailing misogynist tradition and her characterization of strong, independent-minded *mulieres sanctae*, who continue to exercise a fascination in today's world.

Therefore these didactic works, with their extravagant praise of, and unforgiving ideological insistence on, virginal perfection, as well as the fear- and guilt-instilling mechanisms relating to the loss of virginity, formed an essential part of the female religious experience in the early medieval period. The importance of the basic patristic and ecclesiastical male ordering of female values and their control of female sexuality—with the constant repetition of these ideals and behavioral models, as well as women's accommodation to these mindsets—needs to be stressed. The use of early exemplars, especially those of virgin martyrs, played an important role in the formation of this ideology or mindset. Thus there emerges a very real concern for, or even obsession with, the perfect life which entailed the preservation of total virginity. The virgin must at all costs remain both spiritually and physically intact. However, before turning from theory to the actual practice of virginal heroics, it is necessary to mention that although the Church was especially singleminded and articulate in its establishment of virginity as the *vita perfecta* for women, this religious ideal merged with the Germanic tradition which also valued female chastity.

Very briefly, the Germanic peoples seemed to place a high value on sexual purity for women. The *Germania* of Tacitus, the Germanic law codes, and other sources all emphasize the importance assigned to chastity, along with the serious punishments exacted of women who were accused of losing their virginity or of being involved in adultery. Generally, Germanic women were made to assume a disproportionate amount of the blame and humiliation in the loss of their sexual purity. The onus of the crime was placed on the female for her perceived complicity in her loss of chastity.[45] The Germanic peoples also provided their own exempla of heroic behavior in defense of chastity. The Cimbri women, for example, were especially celebrated for banding together against the Roman conquerors to preserve their chastity and freedom. After killing their children, they are said to have hanged themselves with ropes and the reins of horses in order that their chastity would not be dishonored and they would not be subjected to the derision of the conquerors.[46]

Thus the early medieval Christian tradition of the heroics of virginity shared with pagan Germanic society a belief in the high value of sexual purity, or chastity, for women. And it appears that the newly converted Germanic women found it particularly easy to assimilate the essential Christian ideals and practices of virginity to their own values. Nevertheless, an actual commitment to put into practice these ideals would continually be tested by the violence and disorders of early medieval society.

PRACTICE: THE HEROICS OF VIRGINITY, OR *VIRGINITAS DEFORMITATE DEFENSA*

In practice, the monastic institutions of the early Middle Ages met the needs of many religious women concerned with espousing a life of virginity and accruing future heavenly rewards: and for a select few, monasteries provided the all-important career ladder to sainthood. Monasticism also afforded, for the first time, an honorable alternative to forced marriages and provided an effective escape from the very real fears and dangers of childbirth. The institution theoretically offered consecrated virgins a haven; it was compared to an ark which would shelter these women from the tempests and perils of the world. The monastery was to provide protection to its "holy fold" from the "jaws of the spiritual wolves."[47] However, the saints' Lives, chronicles, church councils, laws, charters, and letters of the period all tell us something quite different: these monasteries and their inhabitants were instead often primary targets of violence, rape, and plunder.

The monastic rule of Caesarius of Arles, written for his sister Caesaria (sixth century), responded to the special needs of women in his diocese who wanted to live the virginal life but were faced with the constant fear of becoming victims of attack. Caesarius therefore developed a model convent in his diocese situated within the protective walls of the city of Arles.[48] Also, fearing for the safety of his nuns, Caesarius instituted a policy of strict protective enclosure. He warned in his *Regula:* "If a girl, leaving her parents, desire[s] to renounce the world and enter the holy fold to escape the jaws of the spiritual wolves by the help of God, she must never, up to the time of her death, go out of the monastery, nor into the basilica, where there is a door."[49]

This need for strict claustration in response to the extreme disorders and violence of the period can also be found in the establishment of other monasteries for women. For example, the *Regula monacharum* (attributed to St. Jerome but perhaps dating to the ninth century) was concerned with problems of security for nuns and the primary need of protecting their virginity through enclosure. Here enclosure for nuns is compared to a "virgin vault" or tomb. The Rule warns: "On account of this, dearest one, let your convent become your tomb: where you will be dead and buried with Christ, until rising with Him you will appear in His glory. Finally, the thing that is most frightening to the one lying in a burial mound is the grave robber who sneaks in at night to steal precious treasure. Thieves dig this up, to steal with infinite skill the treasure that is inside. Therefore the tomb is watched over by a bishop whom God installed as the primary guardian in His vineyard. It is guarded by a resident priest who discharges his duty on the premises: so that no one enters recklessly nor tries to weaken the tomb. . . . Believe me 'there is fear for a treasure in the dead of night. From an arrow flying in daylight, from trouble walking around in shadows, from attack and the Devil at midday.' All hours should be suspect to chaste minds."[50]

There are a number of other indices which point to an uneasiness of the period and the special need for safeguarding the female religious. For example, the chronicles of the time note the violation of nuns, particularly by the royalty or nobility. Gregory of Tours in his *History of the Franks* reports devastation in the area of the Limousin by Theudebert, son of Chilperic: "He burned the churches, stole their holy vessels, killed the clergy, emptied the monasteries of monks, raped the nuns in their convents and caused devastation everywhere."[51] In a denunciatory letter directed to King Ethelbald of Mercia, Boniface and other bishops condemned the king for his sacrilege of adulterous behavior "committed in convents with holy nuns and virgins consecrated to God."[52] King Edgar (959–75) was also severely reprimanded by the Church for his abduction and violation of nuns. Perhaps the reform customary of ca. 970 provides an indirect reference to his inappropriate behavior toward female religious, as it specifically designates King Edgar as the guardian of the rule of monks and Queen Aelfthryth as "the protectress and fearless guardian of the communities of nuns; so that he himself helping the men and his consort helping the women there should be no cause for any breath of scandal."[53] Swein, brother of Harold Godwinson, was chastised for his abduction of Edgiva, abbess of Leominster, in 1046. After keeping her for a year, he was finally forced through episcopal mandate to return her to her monastery.[54]

Many chronicles, cartularies, sermons, letters, and other sources of the period also describe nuns and laywomen as victims of the violence of the invasions. An entry of the *Annales Xantenses* for the year 837 notes a Viking raid on the Frisian island of Walcheren. It specifies that many women were taken as captives. The *Annals of St-Bertin* describe a Saracen attack on Marseilles in 838: "Meanwhile fleets of Saracen pirates attacked Marseilles in Provence, carried off all the nuns, of whom there was a large number living there, as well as all the males, both clergy and laymen, laid waste the town [*urbs*] and took away with them *en masse* the treasures of Christ's churches." Or, for the year 842, the *Annals of St-Bertin* relate that the Northmen made a surprise attack at dawn on Quentovic; they "plundered it and laid it waste, capturing or massacring the inhabitants of both sexes."[55]

In a tract entitled *De coercendo et exstirpando raptu viduarum, puellarum ac sanctimonialium,* Hincmar, archbishop of Reims (d. 882), discusses the conditions of his age and the extremely serious problem of violence toward women. He notes particularly the devastating effects which the violation of nuns had on their vows of chastity and their *integritas.* This work was addressed to the king and implored his help against the brutality and disorders of the period.[56]

Another important example of the pervasive violence toward women can be found in Bishop Wulfstan's "Sermon to the English" (1014). In a striking picture of the misery, devastation, corruption, and public shame experienced by contemporary England and the Church, he includes among the especially brutal acts inflicted by the Vikings the deplorable violation of Englishwomen. "And often ten or a dozen, one after another, insult disgracefully the thegn's wife, and sometimes his daughter or near kinswoman, whilst he looks on, who considered himself brave and mighty and stout enough before that happened."[57]

Moreover, during this period law codes, canons of church councils, and penitentials continually warn of severe punishments, particularly for those who dishonor, abduct, violate, or kill women consecrated to God.[58] To provide added deterrents, the reparations established to protect female religious from violence or abduction were usually

higher than those required for the same crimes committed against
laywomen. For example, *The Lombard Laws* (713–35) warn: "He
who abducts such a woman [one who has taken the veil] shall pay
1,000 solidi as composition in order that a case involving someone
dedicated to God may exceed [the usual payment] to the amount of
100 solidi; for a composition of 900 solidi has been established in the
edict for the abduction of an unconsecrated woman." [59] *The Bavarian
Laws* (744–48) discuss the abduction of a nun from her convent. The
abductor is required to return the female religious to her monastery,
plus pay a compensation of twice that which is customarily owed by
one who steals another's betrothed. The law stipulates: "We know
that the abduction of another's betrothed is a punishable crime; how
much more punishable is a crime which usurps the betrothed of
Christ." [60] *The Laws of Alfred* (871–99) stipulate: "If anyone in lewd
fashion seizes a nun either by her clothes or her breast without her
leave, the compensation is to be double that we have established for a
lay person." [61] The repetition of these admonitions seems to point to
the very real prevalence of violence toward consecrated virgins as well
as the extreme difficulties of maintaining order and providing protection for female religious during this period.

Another index of the special need to safeguard women in the
Church is the number of female communities which were moved for
reasons of security from earlier "open sites" to protective sites *intra
muros* or within the city walls. Also, in response to the conditions of
the time, some female houses were built within castles, while others
became strongly fortified and in turn served as shelters for nuns fleeing
from local violence and especially from the invaders. [62] Some monasteries were provided with special retreats in case of attack. The very
powerful and wealthy monastery of Shaftesbury, for example, was
given an *ecclesiola* (a little church) with an adjacent manor by King
Aethelred II (1001) at Bradford-on-Avon which was to provide the
nuns and their precious relics of King Edward with a safe, impene-
trable retreat (*impenetrabile confugium*) in case they were attacked at
Shaftesbury by the Danes. According to a charter of 804, Selethryth,
abbess of the monastery of Lyminge, was given a parcel of land located in Canterbury. This was to serve as a refuge for her community
of nuns in case of Viking attack. [63]

Nevertheless, despite these attempts to provide special protection
and security for the monasteries of women, these brides of Christ continued to fall victim to attack. Many convents, along with their communities of nuns, suffered repeated devastation and violence from the
Viking, Magyar, or Saracen incursions. We have been rather well informed in regard to the invasions and their effects on the male monas-

tic establishments. Perhaps best known is the sad plight of the Lindisfarne monks whose wanderings lasted nearly a century; or the lugubrious accounts of the monks of Noirmoutier who, fleeing the invaders, ended their migrations at Tournus, more than three hundred miles from their original house.[64] However, studies of early medieval society have not similarly noted the effects of these incursions on monastic life for women. For example, how did the female monastic communities, their nuns and abbesses, meet this imminent danger? How did they cope with their very real and persistent fears, as well as the reality of rape and the loss of their virginity? How did they respond to the potential destruction and loss of their *raison d'être*, that is, their investment in *integritas*, in total virginity? Indeed, in facing this "fate worse than death," these brides of Christ had a great deal more to lose than did their contemporary male religious.

Saints' Lives, chronicles, and monastic charters of the period tell us that the basic response of most nuns to the invasions was the same as that of the monks: to flee, escape with their relics and treasures (if time allowed), but especially with their lives. In his chronicle, Sigebert de Gembloux describes the disasters provoked by the Vikings. He notes that when they were able, the "sacri ordinis in utroque sexu ministri" hid themselves and their relics from the invaders.[65] During the Viking invasions the nuns of Pavilly (in the diocese of Rouen) fled, carrying with them the relics of their founder, St. Austreberta, as well as those of their other saintly abbesses. They took refuge first at Marconne, and then at St-Omer; and finally, in the eleventh century, they established a new monastery at Montreuil-sur-Mer. Similarly, during the Viking attacks of ca. 805, the nuns of the monastery of Blangy (diocese of Thérouanne) escaped with their lives and fled to the monastery of Estrées at Strasbourg. They carried with them their greatest treasures: the bodies of their founder, St. Bertha, and her two daughters, Gertrude and Deotila.[66] According to one of the versions of the Life of St. Mildred, in the face of the Viking attacks, the community of Minster-in-Thanet fled to the monastery of Lyminge.[67] The nuns of Whitby fled from the devastations of the Danes, first to Hartlepool and then, as the invaders approached, on to the strongly fortified monastery of Tynemouth. It, too, fell to the Danes, who plundered and destroyed the church and monastic buildings. And unfortunately, all of the nuns of Whitby who had sought refuge at Tynemouth were massacred and "translated by martyrdom to Heaven."[68] We also learn that two nuns from the monastery of Jouarre escaped from the Vikings and took refuge on the lands of their father.[69] Likewise, according to the *Vita Gudilae*, the nuns of Moorsel suffered greatly from the Viking invasions and perhaps to escape from the ravages of the invaders took refuge at Chevremont.[70] Even the holy dead, in their posthumous acts, were said to attempt to escape from the savage attacks of the invaders. According to the *Vita Werburgae,* for example, the abbess-saint's body was buried at the monastery of Hanbury, where it remained in an incorrupt state. However, the *vita* claims that the holy body dissolved away by its own volition when the Vikings came, in order that it not fall into the hands of the heathen invaders.[71]

In surveying the old monastic foundations of Britain, we find that apparently few houses for men or women escaped destruction by the Danish invaders. Their litany of woe is indeed consistent. According to Knowles and Hadcock's *Medieval Religious Houses: England and Wales,* at least forty-one monasteries for women (including double houses) were destroyed by the Viking invaders. Thus, by the time of the Norman Conquest, there were only nine houses for women still in existence in Britain.[72] Some of the monastic foundations which suffered destruction at the hands of the invaders were unfortunately ill-situated. St. Sexburga's house at Minster-in-Sheppey, for example, was a favorite landing place for the Danes and probably suffered repeated devastations from the invaders.[73] Similarly the monastery of Tynemouth was frequently attacked and plundered by the Danes; in fact its history through the eighth and ninth centuries records only the series of ravages by the Vikings which occurred in 800, 832, 865, 870, and again around 876, as well as during the reign of Athelstan (924–39), and finally in the year 1008.[74]

Therefore, the sources of the early medieval period mention many houses destroyed by the invaders, with their nuns often becoming a new generation of martyr saints. Barking Abbey, for example, was destroyed in 870 by the Danes when they ravaged the eastern shores of England. According to our sources, all the nuns of this community were burned alive inside their monastery.[75] (As noted earlier, it was for the inmates of Barking Abbey that Aldhelm wrote his didactic tract entitled *De virginitate,* which encouraged the heroics of virginity.) In the same year, the famous monastery of Ely and its church were destroyed by the Danes under Inguar and Hubba. All of its nuns were also massacred during this invasion.[76] We have already noted the case of the nuns of Whitby Abbey who became martyrs at the hands of the Vikings at Tynemouth. The sources mention that St. Mildred's monastery in Thanet was plundered and burned by the Danes in 980. Again, during the invasion of 1011, the abbess of St. Mildred's was taken captive by Swein, after which the nuns dispersed.[77] Also a number of individual nuns who were victims of the invaders came to be recognized by the Church as virgin martyrs. St. Osith, a nun of the monastery of Chich (Essex), for example, became one of the first of the English virgin martyrs of this period. She is said to have been beheaded by the Danes for refusing to renounce her faith.[78] On the continent, St. Reyneld, another virgin martyr, was killed by the barbarians in 860; St. Wiborada, a recluse of St. Gall, was put to death by the Hungarian invaders in 926; and so the list continues.[79]

There are, however, a number of rather extraordinary cases of "the heroics of virginity" found in the hagiographic literature and chronicles of this period. They seem to shed some light on mental attitudes of the period as well as strategies of virginal maintenance. And while these strategems might initially seem extreme, crude, or even shocking to us today, or, perhaps for some scholars, implausibly dramatic, they should not be summarily dismissed as mere fantasy or hagiographic exaggeration. Rather, given what we know of the mental structures of the period—and the corroboration of other contemporary evidence—it seems that they reflect a certain reality and perceived value of the age.

The first case of what might be called "sacrificial self-mutilation" as a heroic response to certain sexual assault can be noted in the south of France at the monastery of St. Cyr, Marseilles. This incident is said to have occurred around the year 738 during one of the Saracen attacks on Provence.[80] According to the *Lessons of the Office of Saint Eusebia:*

> The virgin Eusebia, of distinguished piety, governed the
> monastery of nuns that the blessed Cassian founded in the
> past, in the territory of Marseilles, not far from the Church
> of St. Victor. The infidels burst into the monastery, and Eusebia
> urged the holy virgins, caring more for preserving their purity
> than their life, to cut off their noses in order to irritate by this
> bloody spectacle the rage of the barbarians and to extinguish
> their passions. With incredible zeal, she [Eusebia] and all of her
> companions accomplished this act; the barbarians massacred
> them in the number of forty, while they confessed Christ with
> an admirable constancy. Their bones, deposited in the under-
> ground Church of St. Victor, are scrupulously honored there.
> It is the tradition in their monastery, which moved within the
> walls of the city and had flourished a long time ago under
> the name of St. Sauveur, that in the past when a virgin was
> admitted to enter the novitiate or to make her vows, the priest
> recalled the martyrdom of the Abbess Eusebia and of her
> companions as a noble example of steadfastness.[81]

Perhaps the best-known case of self-disfigurement as an extreme measure of virginal defense is that of St. Ebba and her nuns of Coldingham (see plate 10). Ebba the Younger, daughter of Ethelfrith, King of Northumbria, was abbess of the monastery of Coldingham during one of the particularly active periods of the Danish invasions (ca. 870). (The monastery of Coldingham was located on an isolated site on the coast of Northern Britain (Berwickshire), overlooking the North Sea. Present-day Ebchester, St. Abb's, and St. Abb's Head take their names from St. Ebba, the first abbess of Coldingham, or perhaps from St. Ebba the Younger.) According to the earliest extant entry concerning the Danish destruction of Coldingham, found in the chronicle of Roger of Wendover, the invaders "cut the throats of both young and old who came in their way, and shamefully entreated holy matrons and virgins." [82] Roger of Wendover continues his description of the "admirable act of the holy abbess Ebba":

> The rumour of their merciless cruelty having spread throughout every kingdom, Ebba, the holy abbess of the monastery of Coldingham, fearing lest both herself and the virgins of whom she had the pastoral care and charge should lose their virgin chastity, assembled all the sisters and thus addressed them, "There have lately come into these parts most wicked pagans, destitute of all humanity, who roam through every place, sparing neither the female sex nor infantine age, destroying churches and ecclesiastics, ravishing holy women, and wasting and consuming everything in their way. If, therefore, you will follow my counsels, I have hope that through the divine mercy we shall escape the rage of the barbarians and preserve our chastity." The whole assembly of virgins having promised implicit compliance with her maternal commands, the abbess, with an heroic spirit, affording to all the holy sisters an example of chastity profitable only to themselves, but to be embraced by all succeeding virgins for ever, took a razor, and with it cut off her nose, together with her upper lip unto the teeth, presenting herself a horrible spectacle to those who stood by. Filled with admiration at this admirable deed, the whole assembly followed her maternal example, and severally did the like to themselves. When this was done, together with the morrow's dawn came those most cruel tyrants, to disgrace the holy women devoted to God, and to pillage and burn the monastery; but on beholding the abbess and all the sisters so outrageously mutilated, and stained with their own blood from the sole of their foot unto their head, they retired in haste from the place, thinking it too

long to tarry there a moment; but as they were retiring, their leaders before-mentioned ordered their wicked followers to set fire and burn the monastery, with all its buildings and its holy inmates. Which being done by these workers of iniquity, the holy abbess and all the most holy virgins with her attained the glory of martyrdom.[83]

A third incident in this heroic pattern of virginal defense concerns the famous early medieval Spanish monastery of St. Florentine, just outside Ecija. A later chronicle notes that this was a large monastery with a community of some three hundred nuns which strictly followed the rules of St. Benedict and St. Leander (Florentine's brother).[84] And according to tradition, it was during the invasions of the Saracens that the abbess and nuns of the monastery proved that they were true daughters of St. Florentine.

[Realizing] that the infidels planned to attack their monastery, the nuns feared the danger of being shamed and of losing the treasure of their virginity which they had preserved for so many years. Thus in their attempts to make themselves ugly and detestable they decided to lacerate their faces. . . . Their strategy and rather extraordinary plan turned out very well because with it they accomplished their intention: they triumphed over the Moors. For when the barbarians saw the virgins bloody and ugly, they became angry because of this. They therefore killed all of the nuns with the sword, and to the halo and crown of virginity was added that of martyrdom.[85]

In this same tradition, the twelfth-century theologian Peter the Chanter briefly describes the case of a community of nuns near Jerusalem who *se exnaseverunt* (cut off their noses) in order to prevent being raped by their pagan ravishers. We are told that the consecrated virgins adopted this strategy without knowing the consequences of their acts.[86]

Another twelfth-century case of self-mutilation as a virginal defense can be found in the well-documented Life of St. Oda of Hainault, who died in 1158. A contemporary *vita* relates in some detail Oda's heroics.[87] Despite Oda's personal dedication to virginity and Christ, her parents made arrangements for her marriage. During the wedding ceremony, Oda defiantly responded that she would not have this man, nor any other mortal man for her husband, since she had already chosen her heavenly spouse. According to her *vita*, while things remained in confusion at the church, Oda returned home. Fearing what her angered father might do to her, she withdrew to her mother's bedroom where she prayed for God's assistance. She then took the sword which was hanging at the head of the small bed and cut off her nose. Her saint's Life explains that she thus preferred to disfigure the beauty of her outward appearance, namely, to live deformed, than to marry and live in shame a worthless secular life. The author of her *vita* then mentions other holy women, who, when their own chastity had been assailed, either killed themselves with swords, drowned themselves, perished by fire, or threw themselves headlong from a precipice. Because these women chose to die heroically rather than suffer the loss of their chastity, they were revered as martyrs. Her hagiographer then argues that the virgin Oda's act of self-disfigurement for the love of Christ and the maintenance of chastity was also a major type of martyrdom. She was both virgin and martyr because virginity was not possible without martyrdom. It was then soon after this heroic defense that Oda became a nun, and ultimately was named prioress of a Premonstratensian monastery.[88]

This same heroic pattern of self-disfigurement as a strategy for the maintenance of virginity is mentioned in the Life of St. Margaret of Hungary (d. 1270). According to her saint's Life, Margaret refused a number of prominent marriage proposals including those of the duke of Poland, the king of Bohemia, and the king of Sicily. However, when she learned that the pope was dispatching a marriage arrangement for her, she expressed her strong displeasure by responding that sooner would she cut off her nose and lips and tear out her eyes than consent to marriage. Also, when it was reported that the Tartars were invading Hungary, and that among other atrocities they were known for their sexual assault of virgins, Margaret was said to have replied, "I know what I will do: I will cut off my lips [*labia mea detruncabo*] and then when they see me disfigured, they will leave me untouched [*intactam*]."[89]

In general, while the Church provided the ideological context for these desperate acts of virginal defense, the methodology of self-deformity or facial disfigurement (*se exnaseverunt*) which these early female religious utilized in their heroics of virginity was part and parcel of the Germanic tenor of the time. Mutilations, although not usually self-inflicted, were by no means unusual in this period: they were common injuries or punishments. In the Germanic law codes, repeated mention of this type of behavior is found in the treatment of criminal offenses. For example, eight chapters of the *Lombard Laws*, five chapters of *Laws of the Alamans,* and five specific laws of the *Lex Salica* and the *Lex Salica Karolina* deal with the necessary reparations for cutting off the noses and lips of members of the different classes of society.[90] However, during this period the use of facial disfigurement as a type of punishment often seems to have been gender-specific. That is, it was exacted as a chastisement directed specifically toward women who had dared to transgress the laws—especially regulations of sexual behavior. The following provision is found, for example, in the *Laws of Cnut* (1020–23): "If a woman during her husband's life-time commits adultery with another man, and it becomes known, let her afterwards become herself a public disgrace and her lawful husband is to have all that she owns, and she is to lose her nose and ears."[91] Also the *Lex Pacis Castrensis* (1158), issued by Frederick Barbarossa, has a provision in this tradition to keep prostitutes from following his armies: soldiers caught with these women were to be severely punished, while the women were to have their noses cut off (*et mulieri nasus abscidetur*).[92] Another example of this type of mutila-tion as specific punishment for women can be noted in Layamon's *Brut* (ca. 1190). Here, following one of King Arthur's banquets, a brawl ensued in which a number of knights were attacked and killed. As punishment for their behavior, Arthur specified that the instigator of the fight be buried alive in the fen, his nearest kin beheaded, and "the women that ye may find of his nearest kindred, carve ye off their noses, and let their beauty go to destruction."[93] Or Odericus Vitalis, in his *Ecclesiastical History,* describes the revenge exacted by Ralph Harenc on Eustace of Breteuil: "Ralph Harenc took Eustace's daugh-ters with the permission of the angry king and avenged his son by cru-elly putting out their eyes and cutting off the tips of their nostrils."[94]

No doubt the conviction underlying these punitive measures was that this type of chastisement would be especially devastating to a woman, as her physical attractiveness would be totally destroyed. It would make the woman an outcast, branded with the permanent reminder of her disgrace and shame. Moreover, now physically repul-sive, she would no longer be desirable to any man. Facial disfigure-ment as a punishment would therefore achieve the desired result: in transforming woman's beauty into a horrifying image it would terminate woman's adulterous involvements as well as her activities in prostitution. Thus, during this period of disorder and violence, facial disfigurements do not appear to have been uncommon as injuries or means of punishment. Although this of course did not make self-disfigurement any less extreme an act, perhaps within the context of the age and in circumstances of extreme desperation, its credibility as a strategy adopted by women themselves against sexual assault is increased.

The evidence of self-disfigurement in defense of virginity is further corroborated by a number of other early medieval hagiographic references. Several of these cases focus on young women, who, in desperation, resorted to strategies involving self-inflicted "deformities" to avoid unwanted marriages. According to the saints' Lives, these women found themselves in the very difficult situation of having consecrated their lives to virginity (sometimes privately—without the knowledge of their parents) and then being forced by their families into marriages of convenience. Thus they prayed for some kind of disfigurement or disease to make them physically "ineligible" for marriage. And, according to their *vitae*, in answer to their prayers, they became "miraculously deformed or disfigured": they were "made" blind, or became seriously ill, or contracted scrofulous tumors, or even leprosy.

In this tradition, several of the saints' Lives describe "temporary" injuries to the eyes. One of the best-known cases is that of the Irish St. Brigid. Determined to remain a virgin and to consecrate her life to the service of God, she prayed that some deformity might "save" her from an imminent marriage proposed by her parents. According to her *vita,* immediately one of her eyes "burst" in her head, thus destroying all of her beauty. She was then permitted to become a consecrated virgin, and as she knelt to receive the veil, her "lost" eye was miraculously restored.[95]

St. Burgundofara/Fara (d. ca. 645) had been consecrated to God by the missionary, St. Columbanus. When her father, however, agreed to her betrothal, Fara contracted a burning fever and her eyes became gravely affected by her crying. It was only after her father promised that he would no longer prevent her from following a life of virginity that Fara found herself completely cured. Later her father gave her lands for a double monastery (Faremoutiers-en-Brie), with St. Fara becoming its first abbess.[96]

There are also a number of interesting cases of saintly virgins who were said to become disfigured through illness in order to avoid unwanted, impending marriages. According to hagiographic tradition, the seventh-century St. Enymia dedicated herself at an early age to a life of virginity. Despite her wishes, Enymia's parents made plans for her marriage. In response to her desperate prayers to be spared this marriage and to maintain her virginity, she became a leper (*lepra ob virginitatis custodiam*). Saddened by this illness, her family rallied to her support and tried all of the available remedies to obtain a cure. Nevertheless, according to her hagiographer, all was useless since God alone could bring about the cure of an illness which he had caused. After several years during which she patiently suffered from this disease, Enymia received a vision in which she was told to go to wash in the fountain of Burle in Gevaudan. After several treatments at Burle she was cured of this disease. It was, then, at this site that Enymia decided to stay, and here, with her brother's assistance, she built a double monastery and became the first abbess of the community.[97]

The *vita* of St. Licinius, bishop of Angers (seventh century), notes a similar pattern. Against his own wishes Licinius ultimately consented to marriage. But on the eve of his wedding, Licinius's betrothed fortuitously contracted leprosy. Deeply affected by this change of events, Licinius then resolved to follow his earlier inclination of renouncing the world and entering the Church.[98]

Another seventh-century example in this tradition is that of St. Angadresima, abbess of Oroer. According to our sources, she was betrothed to a certain Ansbertus. However, for religious reasons, both wished to remain celibate and not marry. They prayed that they would be preserved from carnal love and its pleasures; and Angadresima specifically prayed that she might become disfigured (*ut speciositas illius in deformitatem verteretur*). According to the *vita* of Ansbertus, her prayers were favorably received, for her face was soon completely covered with sores and "the most foul leprosy." After a team of doctors was unable to cure her, her father began to understand the problem and asked Angadresima whether she wanted to dedicate her life to virginity. She responded that she would now become the bride of Christ, who had himself caused her leprous condition. Angadresima then went to Rouen where she received the veil; and as soon as this was accomplished, her former beauty was allegedly restored.[99]

Another example of this physiological pattern concerns St. Idaberg/ Gisla (d. ca. 770/780), who was said to have been the sister of Charlemagne. According to tradition, she had chosen a life of virginity only to be forced by her parents into an unwanted marriage. Gisla prayed for some disfigurement to make her ineligible for this union, and consequently she acquired a fever and strumas (scrofulous tumors). It was then revealed that if freed from her nuptials, she would be cured by eating a fish from the river Lys. By following this remedy, Gisla was cured and later became a nun.[100]

Perhaps one of the most telling cases in this pattern of virginal defense concerns St. Ulphia, an eighth-century virgin recluse. According to her saint's Life, Ulphia's strategy for maintaining her virginity and avoiding a forced marriage was feigned insanity. She ran here and there, her face pale with fasting. Bareheaded, with her hair untied, disheveled, and falling over her shoulders, she gave the appearance of being out of her senses. According to her *vita,* with "this contemptible deception" she was able to "disfigure her beauty" (*pulchritudine deformare*) and to ward off the "carnally panting." She was then allowed to follow a religious profession and pursue the life of a virgin recluse with the aged holy man, St. Domitius.[101]

An interesting variation of these virginal strategies of disfigurement concerns women who were said to miraculously grow noticeable facial hair, or, in its more extreme form, the popular tradition of the bearded woman saint.[102] In his *Dialogues,* Pope Gregory the Great briefly describes the events of the life of the early Italian Saint Galla (d. ca. 550). According to his account, within a year of her marriage, Galla became a widow.

> Her age and wealth invited her to a second marriage in a world
> glowing with opportunity, but she preferred a spiritual mar-
> riage with the Lord. . . . This young widow had a very passion-
> ate nature, however, and was told by her doctors that, if she did
> not marry again, she would grow a beard even though she was
> a woman. And that is what happened. But the saintly woman
> was not disturbed by this external disfigurement. She loved
> the beauty of her mystical spouse, and was not worried over
> this physical blemish, since her body was not the object of her
> heavenly spouse's love.

Thus, shortly after her husband's death, Galla joined a community of religious women located near the church of St. Peter and here she spent the remainder of her long life dedicated to "tireless prayer and generous works of charity." [103]

This sort of virginal disfigurement is also found in the more fantastic or folkloric tradition of the very popular bearded St. Wilgefortis, also called Liberata or Uncumber, as well as the legend of the Spanish virgin-saint Paula of Avila, also known as Barbata—the bearded one.

Briefly, the popular legend of Wilgefortis recounts how this young virgin was forced into an unwanted marriage by her father. She prayed for some sort of miraculous intervention that would make her so disfigured that no one would want to marry her. Her prayers were answered with the sudden growth of a beard and mustache. Undeterred by this turn of events, her father continued to push forward his plans for this marriage. However, during the ceremony, according to the story, Wilgefortis moved her veil so that her betrothed, the king of Sicily, could have a better look at his new bride. Thus, apparently on closer inspection, he immediately withdrew his marriage offer. Enraged at this change of events, Wilgefortis's father then turned his anger toward his daughter. And because of her love for the crucified Christ, he had Wilgefortis crucified (see plate 11).[104]

Similarly, the legend of St. Paula of Avila, also known as Barbata, concerns a virgin and her attempts to escape from an unwanted suitor. Seeking asylum in the church of St. Lawrence, she begged Christ to send her an affliction so that she would be disfigured and ineligible for marriage. According to the legend, Paula was soon "blessed" with a full beard.[105]

Although the heroics of Sts. Wilgefortis and Paula appear to be rather farfetched and highly improbable, medical studies might perhaps shed some light on the "miraculous appearance" of these "deformities" of facial hair and beards as described in the saints' Lives. The condition of hirsutism, for example, is characterized by women developing excess hair on the face and other locations of the body. This disorder can be caused by the use of certain drugs as well as the appearance of tumors and other medical problems related to the adrenal glands and ovaries. However, it appears that particularly during puberty, it is not uncommon for young women to develop noticeable amounts of facial and body hair, including mustaches. It is interesting to note that in many cases, after batteries of tests and examinations, doctors are still unable to find any explanation for this condition, thus the name *idiopathic hirsutism,* or "hairiness of unknown cause." It is believed that in most cases idiopathic hirsutism is caused by a slight increase in the production of the male hormone, androgen—a change which occurs for apparently no known reason.[106] These explanations might then shed some light on this rather unusual phenomenon which we have noted among our virginal saints.

A few of the *vitae* also discuss similar dilemmas which contemporary male saints faced in regard to forced or unwanted marriages. However, it appears that young men saints, having perhaps more options available to them, only infrequently were forced to resort to such extreme strategies in order to convince their parents of their intentions to avoid marriage and pursue a religious career. Nevertheless, a wonderfully creative and unique example can be found in the *vita* of the seventh-century St. Maudez, abbot of Brittany. In his youth Maudez was destined by his family to enter into marriage negotiations. However, like the female saints of this period, he, too, begged God to send him an infirmity to make him ineligible for this unwanted marriage. We learn that his prayers were quickly answered and he was forced to suffer a personal odor so intense that no one dared to approach him. Although neither the origins nor exact nature of this offensive odor are disclosed, we learn that it did in fact "save" him from any further marriage negotiations! Also, he too was fortuitously freed of this "disability" when the threat of marriage was removed.[107]

The repetition of these fascinating cases in the tradition of *virginitas deformitate defensa,* which included leprosy, strumas, temporary or hysterical blindness, insanity, and others, might initially seem extreme or merely hagiographic convention—*topoi,* stressing heroic actions or strategies of affliction which were condoned by the Church as necessary for the maintenance of chastity. There is also, however, a very strong possibility that some of these responses reflect reality or actual situations. For example, corroborative evidence can be found in the laws of the period. One law in the *Lombard Code* is especially striking for it specifically concerns women who became "disfigured" after their betrothals: "If it happens that after a girl or woman has been betrothed she becomes leprous or mad or blind in both eyes, then her betrothed husband shall receive back his property and he shall not be required to take her to wife against his will. And he shall not be guilty in this event because it did not occur on account of his neglect but on account of *her weighty sins and resulting illness.*" [108]

It is, then, interesting that both in the law and in hagiographic literature it was as a rule the young woman, rather than the man, who, perhaps as a last resort, became disfigured and thus ineligible for marriage. It seems, therefore, highly probable that some of these rather fantastic and subversive maneuvers—these strategies of affliction in defense of virginity—actually did occur and perhaps were not all that uncommon. No doubt some of the young girls who had been heavily indoctrinated in the ideals of virginity, and then suddenly forced by their families into marriages of convenience, might have had an especially strong, even hysterical aversion to the concept of matrimony and their loss of independence which was contingent on their virginal state.[109] Confronted with problems for which they saw neither hope of solution nor satisfactory escape, and limited by social structures which offered no other available recourse or appropriate means to respond to these conflicts, the assumption of a "convenient" illness or affliction provided a readily available weapon or strategy with which to cope. Moreover, the public exploitation of adversity and affliction gave them an effective vehicle by which to call attention to their problems and to manipulate their family or society: it provided a means to achieve ends which they could not readily attain directly. The strategy of affliction was, then, a realistic response, an assertive oblique tactic, or a type of "thinly disguised," indirect protest which could be used by women to their advantage. As a limited deterrent, it could be used to gain time in a traumatic situation, to achieve a viable accommodation or, in general, to forward their own demands.[110]

Thus confronted with desperate situations, the *mulieres sanctae* might show symptoms mimicking those of many illnesses; or through autosuggestion they might artificially induce disorders such as temporary or hysterical blindness, leprosy (hives or other skin diseases), strumas, insanity, and other conditions. While some of these illnesses no doubt had unknown external causes, others seem to have been largely psychogenic/psychosomatic: they originated in, or were aggravated by, the psychic or emotional processes of these young women. Frequently they appear to have been of spurious inspiration or simulated. (The fact that in nearly all of these cases the ailments quickly disappeared as soon as the crisis was over is perhaps most telling!) Nevertheless, all of these "miraculous" afflictions described in the *vitae* seem to have been ultimately diagnosed and treated by the saints' families and society as indeed real and serious.

EUNUCHS FOR THE KINGDOM OF GOD:
FEMALE TONSURE AND MALE CLOTHING

Sharing in this same mindset of *virginitas deformitate defensa,* a number of perhaps less extreme but equally compelling cases of "disfigurement" or "self-deformity" involved the deliberate tonsuring or cutting off the hair (tonsure, from the Latin *tondere*), as well as the assumption of male clothing by these holy women. By means of altering their physical appearance in a manner which defied or subverted the gender regulations and social conventions of the period, this strategy allowed these religious women to pursue the life of virginity— without being hampered by their gender. This "disguise" thus provided them with certain practical benefits; for example, a level of protection and opportunities for a greater independence and mobility which were frequently limited because of their gender. On a symbolic level this "regendering" might also be seen as a metaphor, projecting to the ultimate extreme the patristic encouragement for women to renounce their sex and become honorary males, or asexual eunuchs, when they served the Church and Christ.[111]

Briefly, for the early Christian and medieval world, long hair was the social norm for free women. It was assigned a symbolic character and served in general as an expression of woman's sexuality and gender. It was also an indicator of female moral quality. Therefore, as a formal process, hair being intentionally severed from a woman's head was invested with social significance. Depending on the circumstances under which it was done, the act assumed a variety of meanings. However, it was frequently a dramatic protest, a demonstration of a wish to be free of sex-based restrictions. As the anthropologist Raymond Firth has noted: "on the whole, deliberate shaving of the head, or close cutting of the hair, has taken on a ritual quality, intended to mark a transition from one social state to another, and in particular to imply a modification in the status or social condition of the person whose hair is so treated. At many periods women have cut their hair short to demonstrate if not an equality with men at least a repudiation of the woman's traditional sex role."[112] Thus, we can perhaps see in a number of the Lives of women saints a progression in their spiritual status (in their transition to "men" or "eunuchs of God") paralleled by their adoption of a tonsure and male clothing.

One of the most famous examples of an independent early Christian woman who cut off her hair in order to adopt a life of virginity and a religious profession was St. Paul's companion, St. Thecla. According to the apocryphal *Acts of St. Paul,* after learning about the chaste life and its rewards from the teachings of Paul, Thecla renounced both her family and her fiancé. She then became a disciple of St. Paul, telling him, "I will cut my hair round about and follow thee whithersoever thou goest." The apostle's response to her request: "The time is ill-favored and thou art comely: *beware* lest another temptation take thee, worse than the first, and thou endure it not but play the coward." And Thecla said: "Only give me the seal in Christ, and temptation shall not touch me." Thus out of fear of her "female weakness" in meeting temptation, Paul refused Thecla permission to tonsure herself and accompany him on his mission. Later we learn that after escaping from a number of tortures unharmed, Thecla baptized and tonsured herself; she also assumed male dress. Following Paul to Myra, Thecla was finally able to convince him of the seriousness of her commitment to the new faith, and he allowed her to preach.[113] It is interesting to note that a fifth-century version of the *Acts of St. Paul* defends, on pragmatic or protective grounds, Thecla's self-tonsure and her assumption of a male disguise. In this account, Thecla justifies the act of cutting off her hair and altering her appearance as a strategy to conceal her beauty. Specifically, the removal of her "beguiling" hair would permit her to avoid the looks of the over curious, while the male disguise would preserve her from torture.[114]

In the early history of monasticism there are also a number of interesting accounts which reveal the practice of the close cropping or the shaving of the heads of consecrated virgins. Palladius in his *Lausiac History* (early fifth century) reports that the nuns in the desert "had their hair closely cropped and wore cowls."[115] St. Jerome, in a fascinating letter to Sabinianus, describes this very practical usage among the desert mothers of his age:

> It is usual in the monasteries of Egypt and Syria for virgins
> and widows who have vowed themselves to God and have re-
> nounced the world and have trodden under foot its pleasures,
> to ask the mothers of their communities to cut their hair: not
> that afterwards they go about with heads uncovered in defiance
> of the apostle's command, for they wear a close-fitting cap and
> a veil. No one knows of this in any single case except the shear-

ers and the shorn, but as the practice is universal, it is almost universally known. The custom has in fact become a second nature. It is designed to save those who take no baths and whose heads and faces are strangers to all unguents, from accumulated dirt and from tiny creatures which are sometimes generated about the roots of hair.[116]

In his famous letter to Eustochium, Jerome also rails against the "false appearances" and "deceptive behavior" of contemporary women, allegedly carried out in the name of Christianity. He specifically notes women who "change their garb to male attire, cut their hair short and blush to be seen as they were born—women; they impudently lift up faces that appear those of eunuchs."[117]

St. Ambrose, in his work on lapsed virgins, specifies the religious use of female tonsure. He warns that only at the time of their penance were women to cut off their hair. Ambrose further elaborates that women's hair, through vain glory, warrants the occasion for *luxuria* or lust.[118]

The fourth-century bishop Optatus, in his writings against the behavior of the professed Donatist virgins, describes their practice of cutting off their hair and then covering their heads with veils. It is significant to note, however, that in his explanation of this practice he contends that it was apparently devised *for use against ravishers or unwanted suitors (quae contra raptores aut petitores videntur inventa).*[119]

A number of the female virgin saints of the early Middle Ages similarly adopted these practices of cutting off their hair as strategies of defense against marriage or sexual assault, or as a symbol of their new status as brides of Christ. A sixth-century case concerns the virgin saint Ermelinde (d. ca. 595) who took a vow of virginity and cut off her hair in order to dissuade her parents from pushing her into an unwanted marriage contract. Thus apparently "deformed" and physically unacceptable because of her short haircut, Ermelinde had successfully removed herself from the marriage market; she was then allowed to retire "from the world" to live the life of a hermit.[120]

Another rather famous and unique example can be found in the Life of St. Gertrude, the first abbess of Nivelles (d. ca. 658). According to her *vita,* Gertrude's mother, St. Itta/Ida, feared for the safety of her beautiful daughter's soul; specifically, that she might be carried away by violent abductors from the religious life into the pleasures of the world. She therefore seized a pair of shears and cut off the hair of the young saint in the likeness of a crown, that is, she tonsured her. According to her saint's Life, Gertrude rejoiced that she merited wearing this tonsure for Christ's sake during this brief life, and that in the future, the integrity of her body and mind might be worthy of a perpetual crown (see plate 12).[121]

Two other Merovingian cases describe female saints cutting off their hair—solely on their own initiative—in order to maintain their chastity. These two were Bilhildis and Doda: women who had been married for some time and had agreed to a separation for religious purposes. When their husbands, Sts. Faro and Arnulf, now bishops of Meaux and Metz, wanted to see their wives again, the women devised plans to erase any vestiges of their beauty or sexuality from their prior life: Bilhildis cut off all of her hair and adopted old clothing and a haircloth; Doda disfigured her face and shaved her head, therefore assuming the kind of appearance that "repulses the approaches of a man." We learn that their strategies were most successful for Sts. Faro and Arnulf were horrified at the sight of their former wives.[122]

Stories of female transvestite saints were also very popular in the medieval world, especially among monastic communities. Several of the early Christian women saints were portrayed as assuming the appearance and in some cases also the identity of male hermits or monks. A number of their lives were set in the Egyptian desert and were recorded by the desert fathers. Although there has been a great deal of important scholarship on this topic, scholars have generally dismissed the historical validity of these transvestite saints: they have treated them solely as female archetypes, popular legendary figures or *topoi*.[123] According to John Anson, these legends "are with the exception of Thecla products of a monastic culture written by monks for monks, and it is in this situation that the psychological explanation should be sought."[124] It is, however, interesting that a number of works addressed to nuns in the early Middle Ages cite as explicit *exempla* (that is, as sources of inspiration and imitation) several of these female sex-negative, or transvestite, saints. They were perceived in these tracts as especially relevant potential models for female religious.

The early Christian virgin martyr St. Eugenia appears to have been a popular figure during this period and is mentioned in a number of these works. According to her *vita*, she assumed the masculine name of Eugenius, adopted male dress, and entered a male monastery. Here, with her male disguise and "virile mind," no one suspected that she was a woman. Because of her progress in divine erudition and her holy life, Eugenia was soon elected abbot. Later she was accused by a noblewoman of adultery. In her defense before the judge, Philip, duke of Alexandria (who was her own father but did not recognize her), she argued: "So great indeed is the power of His Name that even women standing in fear of it may obtain a manly dignity; nor can a difference in sex be considered superiority in faith, when blessed Paul the Apostle, the master of all Christians, says that before God there will be no distinction between masculine and feminine, we are 'all indeed one in Christ.' Therefore, his precept I have followed with a burning heart, and from the firm trust which I have had in Christ, I have not wanted to be a woman, but preserving a spotless virginity with a total effort of the soul, I have acted consistently as a man. I have not put on a senseless pretense of respectability so that as a man I might imitate a woman, but I, a woman, have acted as a man by doing as a man, by embracing boldly a virginity which is in Christ." (In this statement, as noted by Paul Szarmach, Eugenia provides the moral explanation for her transvestism which is derived from Galatians 3.28: that male and female will be one in Christ.) [125]

Then, according to the legend, Eugenia dramatically opened her tunic to bare herself, thus proving that she was in fact a woman and could not be guilty of the charges brought against her. Later Eugenia established a monastery of virgins. On hearing of the imminent persecution of Christians, she addressed her community and described their impending martyrdom as a grape harvest where they were to sacrifice their blood as wine for the heavenly feast. She then summarized for them the attributes of virginity: "For virginity is the sign of the first virtue of being close to God, resembling the angels, the generator of life, the friend of sanctity, the way of safety, the mistress of joy, the leader of virtue, the furtherance and crown of faith, the aid and support of charity." [126] As related in her *vita,* after three failed attempts to kill her, Eugenia was finally put to death by the sword of a gladiator. This heroic *femina virilis* was then recognized as a virgin martyr of the early Church.

A number of themes found in the Life of St. Eugenia were therefore seen as particularly relevant to the encouragement and reinforcement of virginal ideals. Thus the bishop-saint Avitus of Vienne (sixth century) cites Eugenia in his poem, *De virginitate,* which was dedicated to his sister and other virgins. [127] Similarly, Fortunatus's *De virginitate,* which was addressed to Agnes, abbess of Ste-Croix, mentions a number of women saints and martyrs of the early Christian period who were to serve as models for their convent. This list includes the heroic *femina virilis* saints Thecla and Eugenia. Moreover, in a poem written after Radegund's death, in which Fortunatus describes paradise with its assembly of famous martyrs and saints, he suggests that perhaps Radegund now holds Eugenia by the hand. [128]

In praising the virginal glory of chastity in his *De virginitate,* Aldhelm discusses in some detail the Life of St. Eugenia, who went about "not like a woman, but, against the laws of nature, with her curling locks shaved off, in the short crop of the masculine sex—and she was joined with the assembly of saints and was recruited to the troops of Christ's army with the seal of her purity unbroken, and with no blemish on her chastity." [129] St. Eugenia is also included in Aelfric's *Lives of Saints*. He underscores the fact that the motivation for her disguise was the preservation of her virginity so "that she might not be betrayed." According to Aelfric:

> Well then, Eugenia, the noble woman,
> said that she had desired to keep herself secret,
> and to preserve her purity to Christ alone,
> living in virginity, unknown to man,
> and therefore at the first had assumed the robes
> of a man's garb, and had had her hair shorn.

It was then after her conversion that she dwelt in the minster or church "with a man's mind, though she were a maid." [130]

In contrast to the popularity of the early Christian transvestite *exempla* such as that of Eugenia, there is a rather fascinating account of a Merovingian female transvestite saint (perhaps flourishing ca. 5– 6th c.) found in the writings of Gregory of Tours. And although the events of this saint's life follow the general pattern of the earlier legends of transvestite saints, they may, in fact, describe an actual historical case from this period. In his *De gloria confessorum*, Gregory of Tours records the fascinating story of the Merovingian saint Papula. According to this singular account: "Papula was a committed ascetic who often demanded of her parents that she be admitted to a convent of nuns, because she was not able to serve God in the house of her parents [where she was] distracted by the concerns of this world. Her parents loved her and did not want her to be separated from them. So she cut the hair on her head, put on the clothes of a man [*totondit comam capitis sui, indutaque veste virili*], journeyed to the diocese of Tours, and enrolled herself in a community of monks." In this "disguise" she was received by the monks without suspicion. We are told that Papula led an exemplary life of fasting and praying. She also became famous for her many miracles. Gregory of Tours then notes with praise, "For Papula was like a man among men [*vir inter viros*], and no one knew of her gender." Meanwhile, her parents searched for her but were never able to find her. With the death of the abbot of this community, the monks, still ignorant of her gender, named her abbot. However, "with all her strength Papula rejected the office. Although she lived in the monastery for thirty years, no one knew what she was. But three days before she migrated from this world, she revealed her secret to the monks. When she died, she was washed by other women and buried. Through her many miracles she reveals that she is a servant of God."[131] This account furnished by Gregory of Tours is all we know of Papula and the events of her life. In looking at this biographic entry within the context of the transvestite hagiographic tradition, we can see that this story line follows closely that of the early Christian female transvestite saints. Thus it might be simply another monastic creation, devoid of historical reality; however, it is also possible that Papula, inspired by these early heroines' lives, self-consciously followed their example in order to escape from the oppressive confines of her family and to gain access to another world—that of male, monastic life. Or it might have been simply a practical response to her difficult situation. Within the cumulative context of the various virginal strategies that we have been tracing in this chapter, there does not seem to be any reason why this case should be summarily dismissed as mere romantic fantasy.

Several other *vitae* tell of women temporarily adopting male dress (rather than assuming a male identity) for essentially pragmatic or protective reasons. The rather well-known case of Christina of Mark-yate (born ca. 1096–98), although a bit late for the chronological limits of our study, is in this tradition. We learn from her *vita* that early in her life Christina made a personal vow of virginity at the church of St. Albans. Her parents, nevertheless, betrothed her against her will to a certain Burthred. Finding herself in a desperate situation, she rebelled against her parents and the bishop of Durham (who supported their position) and ran away from home. "And secretly taking masculine garb which she had got ready beforehand in order to disguise herself as a man, she went out swathed in a long cloak that reached to her heels." In nervous apprehension of her planned escape she asked herself, "Why do you respect your feminine sex? Put on manly courage and mount the horse like a man."[132] She then escaped from this proposed marriage and was ultimately allowed to spend her life as a virgin/recluse.

A number of male saints' Lives also describe cases of strong, indomitable women, who, solely on their own initiative, cut off their hair and disguised themselves as men. In these instances they adopted a male appearance in order to defy gender-based discriminatory policies and to participate in space and activities traditionally off limits to women. However, in these cases this virile behavior was not viewed favorably; rather, these women were seen as "deviant" and won swift punishment for their "deceptive" and transgressive acts. We learn, for example, that when St. Siviard was abbot of the monastery of Anisole and wrote the Life of its founder, St. Calais, a woman named Gunda attempted to enter this monastery and its church, which were strictly prohibited to women. She was interested in discovering if, after some one hundred years, St. Calais still enforced this gender-based restriction. She therefore cut off her hair and disguised herself as a man in order to enter the cloister without being noticed. She coordinated her entry with that of the monks going to Divine Office, namely, when the doors of the church were open. Gunda then went unnoticed into the oratory where St. Calais's body was located. Suddenly, according to the *vita,* she was miraculously struck down by God—she lost her sight and black blood flowed from her breast. She also let out such a horrible scream that she attracted the attention of all of those who were present in the church. When interrogated by the monks, she admitted her crime. The author then notes approvingly that this punishment had in fact a salutary effect in that it prevented other women, who might have been tempted, from trying a similar stunt.[133]

A number of other wonderful cautionary tales, describing these intrepid women disguised as men and daring to defy ecclesiastical proscriptions of sacred space, can be found during this period. The repetition of these cases in the *vitae* and chronicles of the time perhaps reflects the fact that women, dressed as men, were acting in independent, subversive ways. In challenging the basic concepts of clothing and hair as major markers of gender, they were seen as a serious threat to the order of the Church and society.[134]

Ecclesiastical and secular laws further corroborate this evidence. Many of these laws attempted to regulate women's appearances and activities and seem to underscore the fear of female usurpation of traditional male roles and prerogatives. Although recognizing the apparent pious or protective rationales behind the practice of women cutting off their hair and their adoption of male attire, this type of behavior was nevertheless viewed, particularly by churchmen, as highly inappropriate. It was not to be encouraged or tolerated by the Church or society. Already in the Synod of Gangra in Asia Minor (340–41), for example, we find canons which threatened (chapter 13) "anathema to women who dress as men, *even under the pretext of preserving more easily their virginity*"; or (chapter 17) "anathema to women who, by a similar motif, i.e., the pretext of piety or an ascetic life, cut the hair which God gave them as a memorial of obedience which they owe to their husband, and by this means abolish the precept of this obedience."[135]

The Theodosian Code (ca. 438) went so far as to ostracize women from the religious community who dared to cut off their hair: "Women who cut off their hair, contrary to divine and human laws, at the instigation and persuasion of some professed belief, shall be kept away from the doors of the churches. It shall be unlawful for them to approach the consecrated mysteries, nor shall they be granted, through any supplications, the privilege of frequenting the altars which must be venerated by all." [136]

In reiterating these warnings, the canons of medieval Church councils seem to reflect a growing concern about appropriate male and female roles and thus, in particular, the need to maintain control over the appearance, behavior, and dress of female religious. The Carolingian council of Riesbach (799–800) explicitly warned that holy nuns were not to wear male clothing, for example, male tunics or trousers (*id est rocho vel fanones*); rather they were to wear only female garments. [137] A capitulary of 844 exhorts nuns who act under the enthusiasm or inspiration of "misunderstood piety" to refrain from wearing men's clothing and cutting their hair. The capitulary then refers to the authority of the earlier Council of Gangra and its exaction of anathema for this type of inappropriate behavior. [138] An Italian collection of canons of the tenth and eleventh centuries also prohibits nuns from cutting their hair. [139] Burchard of Worms includes in his *Decretorum* the two previously cited canons from the Council of Gangra which forbid women to cut their hair and dress in a male manner. [140] The reformer Ivo of Chartres also cites the Council of Gangra and threatens anathema to any woman who for religious reasons (as she interprets them) cuts her hair, or to any female religious, who, for reasons of chastity, assumes male attire. These two proscriptive canons from Gangra are again cited by Gratian in his *Decretum*. [141]

Another rather unusual mention of female tonsure (in this case carried out under the direction of a male ecclesiastic) can be found in Florence of Worcester's *Chronicle*. In his entry for the year 1053 he notes in passing that Aed, a long-bearded Irish clerk and a man of great eminence and piety, had a large school for clerks, women, and laymen; however, "he subjected the maidens to the tonsure in the same manner as clerks, on which account he was compelled to leave Ireland." [142]

Thus taken together, the hagiographic and legal sources of this period seem to express an awareness of women involved in cross-dressing or "gender reversal." These sources also present a very real ambivalence toward this type of radical or "irregular" behavior assumed by religious women and female saints. On the one hand these acts were admired and praised in the *vitae* as highly appropriate when adopted by the individual, privileged saint in defense of her virginity. At least on a symbolic or theoretical level, as we have noted, women were continually encouraged to admire and, under certain conditions, imitate the virile or "superior" sex, to deny the carnal aspects inherent in the female nature, and to adopt the rational, spiritual attributes of man. (Perhaps one of the clearest expressions of this ideal for women can be seen in the *Gospel of Thomas,* where Simon Peter said to the disciples: "For I tell you truly, that every female who makes herself male will enter the Kingdom of Heaven.")[143] Thus, as noted by Vern Bullough, "the Christian church to a certain extent encouraged women to adopt the guise of men and live like men in order to attain the higher level of spirituality normally reserved to males." Although, Bullough adds, this was probably not the "well-thought-out intention of these church fathers," it nevertheless could have been interpreted or rationalized in this way by the women who adopted male dress and identities.[144] Or as Jocelyn Wogan-Browne has perceptively argued, hagiography frequently provided "inadvertant authorisation of female volition."[145] The Lives of women saints suggest "interesting areas of freedom within a general picture of constraint." They provide examples of heroic women who defy authority, who refuse to be accommodating, in order to achieve a greater degree of freedom in their lives. Nevertheless, these examples of heroic behavior could be problematic in regard to contemporary social practices. Women who thus transgressed social conventions and gender-based dress codes of the period (which encoded proper roles and power structures) were seen as very real threats, alarmingly disruptive of the preordained social order.[146]

Since our sources on this topic invariably represent the male perspective, and especially that of churchmen, it is rather difficult to delve into the actual motives of cross-dressing, or gender reversal, from the viewpoint of the women themselves. Were they aware of their own alleged "depraved" female nature and did they therefore, through the adoption of this male disguise, attempt to acquire a male social identity and with it a symbolic raise in social status? A reference found in a miracle of St. Hildegard of Bingen might provide some insight into the difficulties of interpretation and the perhaps multivalent meanings found in these examples. According to this account, Hildegard, the seer, encountered a young girl named Berrudis who had assumed the disguise of a schoolboy. Seeing through this dissimulation, Hildegard admonished the young girl "to convert to a better state"—here implying, as noted by Barbara Newman, that Berrudis did not have long to live. The young girl then repented and put on her feminine clothing. However, she also darkened her face "lest many men fall in love with her." She died shortly thereafter. Presumably, the miracle here lay in Hildegard's gift of foresight, though it may be more significant, Newman argues, "that she chastised the girl for renouncing her womanhood, an act that other miracle watchers would have found meritorious."[147] Thus in this case we have a striking example of a twelfth-century woman's perspective on female cross-dressing in which she strongly disapproved of this type of transgressive behavior. (We can also note in this fascinating case another virginal strategy, that of "darkening" the young woman's face.)

A reiteration of her basic disapproval of female appropriation of male dress (with, however, an important qualification), as well as her belief in preordained gendered roles and the encoding of sexual difference in clothing, can be seen in Hildegard of Bingen's *Scivias*. Here she argues that "men and women should not wear each other's clothes except in necessity." In one of her visions, God speaks to her as follows:

> A man should never put on feminine dress or a woman use
> male attire, so that their roles may remain distinct, the man dis-
> playing manly strength and the woman womanly weakness; for
> this was so ordered by Me when the human race began. Unless
> a man's life or a woman's *chastity* is in danger; in such an hour
> a man may change his dress for a woman's or a woman for a
> man's, if they do it humbly in fear of death. And when they seek
> My mercy for this deed they shall find it, because they did it
> not in boldness but in danger of their safety. But as a woman
> should not wear a man's clothes, she should also not approach
> the office of My altar, for she should not take on a masculine
> role either in her hair or in her attire.[148]

While gender reversal and the practice of cross-dressing have been popular "strategies" for women across the ages, it appears that there are certain shared similarities which have prompted these disguises. Although for some of these early medieval women there might have been some sort of symbolic notion related to status, male superiority, approval, etc., attached to their adoption of male dress or identity, nevertheless, it appears that in most cases, pragmatic considerations were of primary importance. As noted by Caroline Bynum in regard to religious women of the later Middle Ages: "My argument is basically that cross-dressing was for women primarily a practical device, whereas to men it was primarily a religious symbol. Women sometimes put on male clothes in order to escape their families, to avoid the dangers of rape and pillage, or to take on male roles such as soldier, pilgrim, or hermit. But, once freed from the world by convent walls or hermitage, by tertiary status, by the practice of continence, by mystical inspiration, or even by miraculous inedia, women spoke of their lives in female images."[149]

Although churchmen praised this elite group of holy women for their adoption of male clothing, and in some cases male identity, to further their virginal lives and religious professions, it appears that one still needed to distinguish between those deeds of the saints which should be imitated by the faithful (*imitanda*) and those which should only arouse a sense of wonderment or admiration (*admiranda*).[150] Cross-dressing and the cutting of one's hair seem to have been allocated to this second category, that of *admiranda*. These churchmen also perceived gender reversal (on anything less than a metaphoric or symbolic level, or associated with safe, dead female saints) as dangerous and frightening. Their fears are then expressed in the Church councils and laws of the period as well as in the vivid cautionary examples of women disguised as men drawn from male saints' Lives. During this period when sexual difference and social status were so highly encoded in clothing, these radical acts were considered by churchmen as outrages to the decencies of nature and as breaking the laws of God and man. They disrupted the ordered scheme, defied the prevailing notions of sexual difference, which depended on each gender maintaining its proper dress and appearance, as well as function. These women, who in their "misconstrued" religious enthusiasm dressed as men and assumed their roles, were seen as encroaching on male territory and setting a dangerous precedent for other women. This "rebellious" behavior, a defiance of male authority—acting in a manner "forgetful of their sex"—appears to have been especially threatening to churchmen during the periods of reform, when sexual difference becomes heightened and one finds a growing concern with regard to appropriate male and female roles. We can therefore see in the promulgation of church laws their attempts to regularize and control especially the behavior of female religious by forbidding them to wear male dress or to cut their hair.

OTHER STRATEGIES OF VIRGINAL DEFENSE

One of the most practical and popular strategies for avoiding forced marriages or sexual assault was that of "taking the veil." It appears that particularly during this period, many young girls and women entered convents or "took the veil" simply as a means of protection against the violence of the age, without the slightest intention of embracing monastic life. We learn, for example, that immediately after the Norman Conquest in 1066, many noble Englishwomen fled to monastic communities. As daughters and wives of Harold Godwinson's loyal supporters, they especially feared being raped by the Norman invaders. They therefore took the veil for protection and sought asylum in the English monasteries. As noted by Eadmer (d. ca. 1124) in his *History of Recent Events in England,* "Thereupon a number of women anticipating this and fearing for their own virtue betook themselves to convents of Sisters and taking the veil protected themselves in their company from such infamy." [151]

An especially fascinating case concerns one of the most famous monastic refugees from Norman violence, Matilda, daughter of Queen-Saint Margaret of Scotland. In his *History* Eadmer records Matilda's description of her "taking the veil." In response to Anselm's inquiry in regard to her status, Matilda denied that she had been dedicated as a bride of Christ, and also that she had been veiled with her own consent.

> But, that I did wear the veil, she said, I do not deny. For, when I was quite a young girl and went in fear of the rod of my Aunt Christina, whom you knew quite well, she to preserve me from the lust of the Normans which was rampant and at that time ready to assault any woman's honour, used to put a little black hood on my head and, when I threw it off, she would often make me smart with a good slapping and most horrible scolding, as well as treating me as being in disgrace. That hood I did indeed wear in her presence, chafing at it and fearful; but, as soon as I was able to escape out of her sight, I tore it off and threw it on the ground and trampled on it and in that way, although foolishly, I used to vent my rage and the hatred of it which boiled up in me. In that way, and only in that way, I was veiled, as my conscience bears witness. [152]

Matilda's case was therefore decided in her favor: although she had at one time worn the veil, she was free to dispose of her person in whatever way she decided. Cited as precedent in this case was a similar ruling by Lanfranc which dealt with a number of women, who, also in fear of being sexually assaulted by the Normans, had taken the veil for protection. [153]

This practical strategy, then, could be easily effected, especially by noblewomen who needed some sort of protection or defense from the invaders or disorders of the period. It was not as extreme as most of the strategies of disfigurement but could offer at least a modicum of protection without requiring a permanent commitment on the part of these women.

Another interesting case of virginal defense, which perhaps defies categorization, concerns the creative strategy of two early medieval Lombard women. Their very simple but highly effective response to the Avar invaders is described in Paul the Deacon's *History of the Lombards* (ca. 774). He tells us that the two noble daughters of the "abominable harlot" Romilda, who had been a traitor to the Avars, did not follow the sensual inclination of their mother. Rather, he writes approvingly:

> Striving from love of chastity not to be contaminated by the barbarians, they put the flesh of raw chickens under the band between their breasts, and this, when putrefied by the heat, gave out an evil smell. And the Avars, when they wanted to touch them, could not endure the stench that they thought was natural to them, but moved far away from them with cursing, saying that all the Langobard women had a bad smell. By this stratagem then the noble girls, escaping from the lust of the Avars, not only kept themselves chaste, but *handed down a useful example for preserving chastity if any such thing should happen to women hereafter.*[154]

This wonderful common-sense model of virginal defense is then incorporated into later works as just such a "useful example." Indeed, Christine de Pizan cites it in her *Book of the City of Ladies*. This edifying strategy is also referred to in François de Billon's work, *Le Fort inexpugnable de l'honneur du sexe Femenin* (1555).[155]

In a discussion of the special difficulties the young experienced in maintaining the virtue of chastity, Peter Damian recalls a similar exemplum of heroic virginity cited by his friend, the empress Agnes. She told of the two daughters of Berengar, king of Italy, who had been captured by Emperor Otto I after their father's defeat. As they were both beautiful and generously dowered, the king insisted that these royal women be married. However, they despised the idea of a mortal marriage; furthermore, they disdained their suitors. The more beautiful of the two adopted a strategy in which she placed meat under her clothing for a long period of time until her whole body gave off a disgusting smell. Thus when the suitors came to visit, she loosened the layers of her clothing and rejoiced at the intense odor that affected those around her. After being exposed on a daily basis to this unpleasant smell, the suitors apparently succumbed to her ruse and she was left alone. And through this strategy of the putrefaction of meat, she preserved the integrity of her inviolable body and she and her sister were allowed to spend their lives as nuns.[156]

A FURTHER LOOK AT VIRGINAL STRATEGIES
AND SACRIFICIAL MUTILATION

In this chapter we have surveyed a wide variety of fascinating heroic responses said to have been utilized by early medieval virginal saints and other religious women threatened by sexual assault or forced marriages. Although some of these strategies might appear extreme, even somewhat repulsive, or seem to be mere hagiographic *topoi,* nevertheless, when viewed collectively against a background of the violence of the time, ecclesiastical views on the superiority of virginity, and the laws of the period, these responses can perhaps be understood. In this tradition, the cases of self-mutilation (*se exnaseverunt*) are possibly the most difficult to comprehend. A closer look at the evidence found in our sources on self-mutilation might be of some assistance.

At the outset, these acts of self-disfigurement are recorded as occurring in diverse areas (northern England, northern and southern France, and Spain), and in different periods (eighth, ninth, tenth, and twelfth centuries). In addition, several of these cases contain original material and do not appear to be merely formulaic; nor do they seem to borrow directly from another tradition.

There are, however, a few difficulties which should be mentioned in regard to our hagiographic sources. Although the *vita* of blessed Oda of Hainault is written by a contemporary, and it is less likely that the events of her life are invented or distorted, some of the other primary source material on self-disfigurement as a virginal defense is not contemporary to the actual events recorded, but relies on earlier sources no longer extant. The evidence, for example, which refers to the mutilations of the nuns of St. Cyr of Marseilles and of Coldingham is relatively late. The earliest extant documentation for the events at Coldingham are two chronicles dating to the thirteenth century: the writings of Roger of Wendover (d. 1236) which were then copied by Matthew of Paris (d. 1259) in his chronicle. Although written several hundred years after the event, other information which these chroniclers recorded for this early period is accurate and is indeed corroborated by early contemporary sources. It has been suggested that perhaps the chronicle entry on the heroics of Ebba and the nuns at Coldingham was based on an older, lost source from Tynemouth.[157] The detailed description of the heroics of the nuns of St. Florentine's monastery in Spain is recounted in a sixteenth-century chronicle of the Benedictine order. This information is again based on earlier sources which are no longer extant. However, evidence for St. Cyr, Marseilles, is more problematic. What we know of the events surrounding the martyrdom is based simply on a longstanding local popular saint's cult, the relics of Eusebia and her nuns, and other indirect documentary evidence.[158]

Although the incident of self-disfigurement at Coldingham has not been treated extensively by scholars, the case of St. Cyr has traditionally been dismissed as merely an hagiographic legend. Delehaye, in his

classic study, *Les légendes hagiographiques,* discusses the role of popular imagination in the production of legend, and specifically how
pictures and statues, which are wrongly interpreted, form the starting
point for the creation of "strange" legends. He then argues in regard
to the "strange legend" of Eusebia and her virgin martyr nuns:

> An inscription now in the museum at Marseilles, refers to a
> certain Eusebia, abbess of Saint Quiricus [Cyr]: Here rests in
> peace Eusebia nun, *magna ancella Dei,* without indication that
> any cultus was accorded to this worthy woman. But her body
> had been laid in an older stone coffin, which bore the carved
> image of the dead person for whom it had originally been
> intended; it was the head and shoulders of a clean-shaven man,
> which in the course of time had become worn and damaged.
> This was enough to give birth to a legend, which related that
> St. Eusebia, abbess of a convent at Marseilles, together with
> her forty companions, cut off their noses to escape outrage
> by the Saracens.[159]

Thus in perhaps overreacting to this traditional confirmation of the
legend—based simply on an effigy with a mutilated face and severed
nose—Delehaye summarily dismisses the validity of Eusebia's existence, and the concept of self-disfigurement to avoid rape, as merely a
strange legend. Needless to say, the effigy alone does nothing to prove
or confirm the cult: one needs simply to think of all of the medieval
statuary in Europe now in this same damaged condition. Nor, however, does this effigy necessarily disprove the cult of Eusebia and her
heroics of virginity. That is, the popular tradition of Eusebia and
her martyrs did not necessarily stem simply from the mutilated sarcophagus. It seems to have been originally a popular local cult based
on a much older, well-established tradition. In the chaos and confusion following the Saracen attack, the burial of Eusebia and her forty
nuns was no doubt accomplished in haste. Their bodies were apparently brought to the church of St. Victor of Marseilles and buried in its
crypt.[160] The special marble inscription which marked Eusebia's tomb
seems to date to this early period, perhaps to the eighth century.[161]
However, the earlier sarcophagus had been originally intended for
someone else and then "borrowed" for Eusebia's burial. (The recy-
cling of sepulchers seems to have been rather common at this time.)[162]
Very briefly, in addition to the inscription and tomb, one can find
other isolated references to St. Eusebia and her martyrs in ceremonies,
charters, and an early saint's Life. This popular tradition was also
perpetuated in the local vocabulary. A very prevalent, ancient usage

designated the ruins of the later Premonstratensian monastery, which had been built on the ruins of St. Eusebia's convent, as "deis Desnarrados," "leis Desnazzados," or "leis Desnarrados," namely, the monastery of the nuns who cut off their noses.[163]

An interesting sidelight to this inquiry into the traditions surrounding Sts. Eusebia and Ebba and the heroics of virginity is the appearance in the north of France and in England of the popular saying "to cut off your nose to spite your face." The maxim "Male ulciscitur dedecus sibi illatum, qui amputat nasum suum" is found in the Latin work, *De Hierosolymitana peregrinatione acceleranda,* by Peter of Blois (archpriest of Bath, 1175–ca. 1191) and "Qui son nez cope deshonore son vis" in the Old French epic, *Garin le Loheren.* Peter of Blois notes that this phrase was already a popular proverb (*proverbium vulgare*) in the twelfth century, perhaps indicative of an earlier origin.[164] It is tempting to speculate that these traditions we have been tracing in the heroics of virginity, with the self-mutilation of nuns, might have provided the original context or occasion for this popular epigram. However, already in its twelfth-century usage there is no hint of familiarity with a female or religious origin, nor recognition of an earlier meaning or rationale which might have occasioned such a desperate course of action; rather this epigram is now found in a negative, admonitory, masculine context which underscores the senselessness or futility of an anticipated act.

Although our traditional sources do present some difficulties and do not allow us to prove historically, beyond a doubt, whether each of these cases of virginal defense actually occurred, or whether they were simply *topoi* or paradigmatic examples of saintly behavior, they still provide invaluable insight into the social values and collective consciousness of the time, particularly the deep concern about the need for female virginity. (They also shed light on the continuation of the ideal of virginity and the usefulness of these behavioral models for the later age which recorded some of these events.) However, self-mutilation as an actual defense against sexual assault can definitely be understood against the background of the period: an age obsessed with the value of sexual purity, yet filled with violent, traumatic situations for women.

We can imagine the incredible fear and the initial helplessness which must have gripped these female religious in anticipation of the invasions and certain sexual assault. Unable to flee to a place of safety, or to count on local protection, they found themselves in a totally vulnerable situation, completely dependent on their own defenses and ingenuity. In addition to the impracticality of successfully fleeing from the barbarian invaders, some of these early female monastic houses also embraced the ideal of strict, unbroken enclosure. Their uncompromising adherence to this severe policy can be seen in a few cases where, even though their monasteries were engulfed in flames and their very lives were threatened by fire, they refused to leave their cloisters.[165] This restrictive policy, then, may have entered into the decision of self-mutilation as a defense: the female religious may have preferred this strategy, along with martyrdom, to the breaking of their enclosure.

In general, these *mulieres sanctae* feared for their lives: they faced the very real possibility of being slaughtered or burned alive within their monasteries. Abbesses seemed to have occupied a particularly unenviable and frightening position during this period. They were no doubt well aware of their own special worth and position in the eyes of the invaders as potential captives or hostages. They were also responsible for the welfare of their convents. In these extremely difficult times abbesses would make the final decisions for the safety of their communities, which the nuns, in monastic obedience, would be called upon to implement.

Nevertheless, in addition to fearing for their lives, these religious women also had a "higher fear" to contend with, that "fate worse than death," namely, sexual assault. Although early medieval virgins/nuns had always lived with the very real and also imagined fear of rape, the atmosphere of the invasions, no doubt, helped to foster a protracted and exaggerated anxiety about sexual assault. The nuns could not help but be very familiar with the destructive activities of the invaders and their predictable violation of religious women and others. Tales of horror must have circulated among the houses of nuns and monks, further exacerbating their basic "normal" morbid fear of sexual assault. The level of fear that was experienced at the prospect of actual rape was probably developed and heightened by the fantasy of rape. And as might be expected, modern studies on rape victimology report that the women most traumatized by rape are religious and sheltered women.[166]

Tied to the fear of imminent physical violence was perhaps the very real fear and guilt of actually surviving the sexual assault: now living out their lives as "polluted," former brides—or perhaps even "adulteresses"?—of Christ, shamed, with all hopes for the next life extinguished. Despite the fact that patristic writings and canon law paid sympathetic lip service to the unfortunate fate of these women, on the bottom line, as we have noted, there remained a basic distrust of female sexuality and skepticism about the innocence of victims of rape. Women, even female religious, were still perceived as somehow at fault; culpable for their acquiescence or secret assent. Thus, as disgraced persons, the onus of the burden was on them. Their tolerated but extremely nebulous position—no longer virgins, yet not widows— would have been difficult, if not impossible, for them to live with.

After these various considerations, one might then ask what options were actually available to these female religious under these difficult circumstances? Suicide was a possibility. However, as we have noted, churchmen did not seem to be in total agreement in condoning suicide to avoid sexual assault. Self-mutilation, less extreme than suicide, was then a very practical methodology which would accomplish the desired end, that is, to make the brides of Christ so hideously disfigured that no man would be tempted to sexually assault them. They could also carry this protective strategy out solely by their own initiative.

The motives behind the heroics of virginity which we have been exploring in this chapter are complex but definitely understandable. The responses of the nuns at St. Cyr, Coldingham, Ecija, Jerusalem; of St. Oda and others, were all in tune with the Christian, as well as classical and Germanic, high appraisal of virginal purity. Acting within the mindset of their own age, they were simply applying to their own desperate situations the religious values and martyrdom ethics as delineated by the Church Fathers, saints' Lives, canon laws, etc., but *as they perceived and interpreted them*. Convinced that rape was a crime of passion rather than of violence, they were following to the letter the constant admonitions for female religious to obliterate their physical beauty as a basic means of virginal defense, *virginitas deformitate defensa*.[167] The eschatological implications of their actions were especially important in the adoption of their heroic responses. Conditioned that virginity was not possible without martyrdom, and with the virgin martyr models always before their eyes, some could translate this fear into a desire to meet actively the fate which they courted, that is martyrdom and sanctity. Ambitious for martyrdom, many of these women were apparently ready to suffer anything to prove their determination as brides of Christ. This methodology was in the same tradition as, for example, the self-inflicted acts of ascetic martyrdom accomplished by St. Radegund. She no doubt would have welcomed the invasions which provided that much "needed" persecutor or the opportunity for dramatic heroic actions to increase her spiritual worth through martyrdom. As Fortunatus noted in his *vita* of St. Radegund, "thus armed with courage to face suffering, since the time of persecution had passed, she prepared to make a martyr of herself."[168] Self-mutilation, as a type of martyrdom, was then also a public act which would prove to the world the seriousness of the virgins' or nuns' commitment as *sponsae Christi*. It would demonstrate beyond a doubt their innocence, namely, that they did not share the guilt as willing accomplices in the loss of their virginity. This act would thus prove to their contemporaries and those in years to come the purity of their consciences.

For the nuns, as they considered their options and planned their potential responses, timing was also of crucial importance. Forcible rape by the invaders was not something sudden or unexpected. The nuns were not caught off guard or paralyzed with fear. Rather, they had time to formulate a strategy: the invaders' violent acts could then be met with some type of aggressive, "positive" action. An alternative to fleeing, only to be inevitably raped and killed on the road or within the defenses of a castle, town, or fortified monastery; or to being raped and then killed (in this order) in their own monastery, their tactics of self-disfigurement were aimed solely at maintaining their *integritas*, their total virginity. They were not primarily concerned with saving their physical lives, rather with safeguarding at any cost their all-important spiritual lives. Right here and now they would either go to heaven as *sponsae Christi*, or be raped and then killed. In this latter case, they were convinced by the Church Fathers that they would no longer be suited for the heavenly gynaeceum; they would be turned away from Christ's bridal chamber to feed the goats "on the left hand." As St. Jerome warned, "Many tried virgins have lost their grip on the undoubted crown of chastity at the very threshold of death." He also admonished his *mulieres sanctae*, "who of the saints was crowned without a struggle? . . . Is it not better to fight for a short time . . . and afterwards to rejoice as a victor, than to be slaves forever because of failure to endure a single hour? . . . Unless you use violence, you will not take the kingdom of heaven" (see plate 13).[169]

Although, as we have noted, a number of these saints were said to care only about their "beauty," or purity, in the eyes of Christ and were unconcerned about their own physical attractiveness, others might have believed in some sort of miraculous intervention on their behalf which would include the subsequent restoration of their own mutilated features. Thus fed on the heroics of the early Christian hagiographic traditions of, for example, St. Agatha, whose severed breasts were miraculously restored; Sts. Rodena and Euphemia, whose noses and lips were cut off and then restored; Sts. Brigid, Lucy, and others, it seems very probable that the nuns might also nurture blind illusions or false hopes for their own "martyrdoms."[170] Some were probably convinced that as a sign of divine approval for their heroics, following in the tradition of the virginal saints, they too would be "protected" and have their beauty restored.

Another variable about which we are unfortunately ill-informed, but which is perhaps of significance for the heroics of virginity, is the age of the abbesses and their nuns. Our sources for Coldingham and for St. Florentine's monastery, Ecija, do not provide this information. One would expect that Blessed Oda, who disfigured herself to avoid marriage, would have been in her late teens—the normal age for females to marry at this time. Eusebia, abbess-saint, who is associated with the self-mutilations at St. Cyr, was said to have died at the age of sixty-four years.[171] We do know, however, that a number of houses in this early period were ruled by rather young abbesses, between the ages of twelve and eighteen, and their communities perhaps also had a strong composition of young members. In addition, many of the early Christian virgin saints suffered martyrdom while they were very young—often in their teens. Age, then, might very well be another important consideration in regard to the rather "extravagant" responses in this pattern of the heroics of virginity.

Fact, historical reality, or hagiographic models? Perhaps in the final analysis the distinction is not all that important. For an age which seemed to have a high cultural tolerance for this genre of moral "history," these *vitae* provided important *exempla* which were to be admired by the faithful. Also, as a new Germanic breed of virgin martyrs, these women saints of the early Middle Ages in turn provided heroes for future generations. As Matthew of Paris wrote in regard to St. Ebba's heroics: "That abbess of admirable courage, openly giving to all the sisters an example of chastity which should be profitable not only to those nuns, but which should be worthy of being followed by all succeeding virgins, and by all who should at any time exist." [172]

Although there has been a very long and persistent tradition in the heroics of virginity,[173] the concern with virginity and the need for *integritas* seem to have had a special hold on the religious collective consciousness of the medieval world. In the early Middle Ages those who had chosen this "higher life" were constantly warned that although this "privileged" status gave them special strength, it also entailed inordinate struggle: it was a "martyrdom," filled with suffering. Therefore, in fiercely defending their chastity, these strong, independent, early medieval women saints put into action the demands of their "new" religion within the context of their own Germanic milieu. The oblique aggressive strategies which they adopted were idioms of strength and defiance as well as of hopelessness and desperation. They were truly weapons of the last resort.[174] No matter what the cost, these brides of Christ were not going to be denied the meaning of their existence, nor their just rewards for perseverance in virginal perfection. After all of their years of practice, they were not about to miss the recompense of the celestial gynaeceum and the joys of singing with the 144,000 virgins the song they alone could sing![175]

For the unbelieving husband is consecrated through his wife.

1 Corinthians 7:14

As for the great benefits brought about by women regarding spiritual matters, . . . was it not Clotilda, daughter of the king of Burgundy and wife of the strong Clovis, king of France, who first brought and spread the faith of Jesus Christ to the kings and princes of France? What greater good could have been accomplished than what she did?

Christine de Pizan, *The Book of the City of Ladies,* trans. E. J. Richards, II.35.1

To Bertha, Queen of the Angli.

And we bless almighty God, who has been mercifully pleased to reserve the conversion of the nation of the Angli for your reward. For as through Helena of illustrious memory, the mother of the most pious Emperor Constantine, He kindled the hearts of the Romans into Christian faith, so we trust that He works in the nation of the Angli through the zeal of your Glory.

Pope Gregory the Great, Epistle 29
(*NPNF*)

Marriage and Domestic Proselytization

In the spiritual meritocracy outlined by the early medieval Church, virginity was awarded the highest value and marriage the lowest. Marriage was regarded by churchmen as a definite compromise (following in the tradition of St. Paul), yet it was still an honorable profession and not to be disparaged. As noted in a sermon by Caesarius of Arles: "Now, there are three professions in the holy Catholic Church: there are virgins, widows, and the married. Virgins produce the hundred-fold, widows the sixty-fold, and the married thirty-fold. One bears more, another less, but they are all kept in the heavenly barn and happily enjoy eternal bliss." [1] Thus, despite the lower status of this state of life, many of the female saints were in fact married. And it was within the context of marriage and the family that women, especially during the early Middle Ages, were able to play a crucial role within the Church and society—namely, that of "domestic proselytizers." [2] Therefore, one of the striking patterns which emerges from a study of saints' Lives during this early period is the prominent role of the *mulieres sanctae* as instruments of conversion. While most of these princesses or queens appear to have been raised in the Catholic faith, a number were early converts to the new faith. And it was then their ensuing missionary fervor, particularly within the context of the family and household, that became a major factor in their reputations for sanctity. Their primary roles as "domestic proselytizers" became nearly a formula with reference to these pious noblewomen and queens of the Germanic world. Hagiographers and chroniclers of the period were impressed by the influential and often indispensable work of these women who were frequently linked to missionary-bishops and their "official" programs of conversion. They praised their single-minded dedication to the new faith and their perseverance in proselytization. Papal and episcopal letters clearly recognized the pragmatic worth of these women: their invaluable assistance in the early stages of the conversion movement, and particularly their success in persuading their husbands and others to accept baptism. They were definitely singled out by the Church for the decisive role they played in the overall strategies of conversion. Indeed, a number of these women won recognition of sanctity for their active involvement in this area.

While a few modern historians have noted the integral part played by women in the conversion of the Germanic Kingdoms and Western Europe to Christianity, for the most part this rather important phenomenon has been frequently overlooked or treated merely in passing. Women's influence has been viewed as "unofficial," informal, or "secondary," and therefore of only marginal significance.[3] Although a neglected field of inquiry, it is of critical importance to an understanding of the complexity of the total movement of conversion and the various impulses and influences involved. This chapter will explore in some detail a few of the more prominent cases of conversion and the active participation of these *mulieres sanctae* in the ecclesiastical strategies of "domestic proselytization." The cumulative effect of these early women's activities, which encompassed the areas of France, Italy, Spain, and Britain, as well as a number of countries in Eastern Europe and Russia, is extremely powerful.

The word "conversion" has two rather distinct meanings. It can refer to a personal religious experience or "inner conversion," or to a "conscious moving from one organized religion to another," which is called an "ecclesiastical conversion."[4] This chapter is concerned essentially with "ecclesiastical conversion" and the basic shift in allegiance from paganism to a new and different religion, i.e., Christianity. In contrast to "inner conversions," "ecclesiastical conversions" are usually not sudden or precipitous acts; rather, they are frequently the result of a gradual, deliberate process. Also the new converts do not necessarily undergo the heightened emotional or spiritual experiences which are essential to inner conversions, nor does religion necessarily become a central focus of their lives. Their reasons for conversion are complex and diverse: they are often the consequence of socio-political strategies, power, economics, intellectual or psychological issues, and other motives or expediencies that have, in fact, very little to do with religious feelings.[5]

Although the medieval sources frequently depict the conversions as occurring in a relatively short period of time, Edward James has argued with regard to the conversion of Germanic kings that "there may be at least three stages in the process: first of all, intellectual acceptance of Christ's message, the 'conversion' proper; secondly, the decision to announce this publicly, to followers who may be hostile to the change; thirdly, the ceremony of baptism and membership of the community of Christians."[6] Thus the strategy of the missionaries was initially directed toward the "conversion," or its outward manifestation in baptism, of the king or ruler of each tribe or region, along with that of his family and household. It was, then, after winning over the king and this "inner circle" that the missionaries could convert en masse the entire social group which owed the king their allegiance. The end result of these conversions of expediency was usually a formalistic, superficial adherence to the new faith with frequent lapses into paganism. Full conversion, with the adoption of the new Christian lifestyle and values, was usually achieved only after many years of indoctrination.

In light of this strategy, the missionaries were clearly aware of the influence that the wife of a pagan ruler might exercise in winning her husband over to the new faith and in ultimately bringing about the conversion or baptism of their household and followers. While the kings seemed to be frequently away from the court, involved in battle and other activities, queens and aristocratic women were perhaps more accessible to the priests and missionaries. And in general, it seems that from the beginning they were more receptive to learning about the new faith. This in part may have been simply a function of the fact that the activities of these women were centered in the great hall. And although they were occupied with administrative and economic duties of the kingdom as well as their household, part of their responsibility as queen or noblewoman included welcoming guests to the court and overseeing their stay. This in itself would entail a certain amount of contact with their visitors during meals and at other times. In addition, it was their duty to organize and oversee the household: they supervised the distribution of food, clothing, charity, salaries, and gifts. These queens or noblewomen also maintained valuable networks of clientage, friendships, and extended family. As guardians of their own culture, responsible for the welfare of their *familia,* they seemed to be perhaps more open to new religious ideas and beliefs. The missionaries therefore actively cultivated the friendships of these well-connected aristocratic and royal women and clearly recognized the importance of winning over their support for the success of their mission. It was, thus, into this sphere of the royal or noble family, the household controlled by the queen or noblewoman, that the missionaries were usually welcomed; and from this center or outpost they began their local operations. In an environment which might otherwise be unwelcoming and hostile, the queen and her household could be called upon to provide the missionaries with the necessary foothold, protection, and, very importantly, moral and material support for conversion activities.[7]

The Church also realized that the queen could become a particularly invaluable ally in conversion if she espoused the new faith first, even though her husband and his followers "lagged behind" and continued in their "pagan errors." Occupying a position of great power and influence, the queen through her own example could provide the stimulus for the conversion of her household and people. And of special importance to the missionaries and churchmen was the exceptional influence which they believed the queen could exercise over her husband in his crucial decision to espouse the new faith. As wife, *consocia* or partner of the king, it was believed that she would be able to gain his attention—"get his ear"—in a way that churchmen would never be able to do. Apparently, it was also assumed that whatever the outcome of her attempts at converting her husband might be, the queen would be allowed to have her children, the future kings and queens, baptized according to her own faith. And this would then forge the first link in the process and prepare the way for the future success of the movement.

SAINT CLOTILDA

The prototype of domestic proselytization can be traced back to the early Christian world where a number of prominent women are portrayed as espousing the new faith and then dedicating themselves to the conversion of their husbands and children. One of the most famous *exampla* in this tradition is that of the empress-saint Helena (d. ca. 330) and her alleged conversion of her son, the emperor Constantine. There has been a great deal written about Constantine's conversion as well as the role assumed by Helena in these events. While a number of ancient authors did not ascribe this important religious shift to the influence of the empress, Paulinus of Nola noted that Constantine "deserved to be prince of the princes of Christ as much *through the faith of his mother Helena* as through his own,"[8] and in the Middle Ages popular tradition credited the empress-saint Helena for her primary role in the conversion of Constantine. With the spread of Christianity to the north of Europe, Helena would become an important *exemplum* or role model of domestic proselytization for other queens and noblewomen and was cited as a prototype for a number of these early medieval women saints.

Among the Germanic peoples, the royal missionary tradition began with Saint Clotilda/Clotild (d. 544), queen of the Franks and wife of Clovis.[9] Portrayed as an extremely effective domestic proselytizer, Clotilda was to become a "second Helena," the model of pious behavior for successive Catholic queens and noblewomen. Her name would be mentioned by later chroniclers and hagiographers as the prototype of their saintly protagonists, as well as a standard against which to measure their achievements. Moreover, in addition to spiritual ties and affinities, the line of female leadership involved in the conversion of many of the Germanic nations would trace its ancestry, for the most part, directly back to Clotilda.

Clotilda's activities as an emissary for the Church and domestic broker are described in some detail by Gregory of Tours in his *History of the Franks* and also in the anonymous *Liber Historiae Francorum,* written in the late seventh or early eighth century.[10] Information from these early sources was then utilized by Clotilda's hagiographer, who compiled her formal *vita* sometime between the year 814 and the end of the ninth century.[11]

Clotilda was the daughter of Chilperic, son of the king of Burgundy and his Gallo-Roman Catholic wife, Caretena. It was, then, apparently Caretena, who, in the capital at Lyons, raised her two daughters in the Catholic faith.[12] According to the *Liber Historiae Francorum,* Chilperic and his wife were killed by Gundobad, one of Chilperic's brothers. Their eldest daughter was exiled and became a nun; the younger daughter, Clotilda, was kept at home by Gundobad. "Since Clovis frequently sent legations into Burgundy, it happened that the girl, Clotild, was noticed by the legates. These legates noticed Clotild's beauty, grace, and intelligence, and told Clovis."[13] After Clovis learned of these things, he sent his legate, Aurelianus, who was on another mission to Gundobad, to ask for the hand of his niece. The author then carefully adds the important detail that "Clotild was a Christian."[14] Disguised as a poor pilgrim, the legate Aurelianus arranged to meet secretly with Clotilda and to present her with a ring inscribed with the name and image of Clovis and other betrothal gifts which she hid in King Gundobad's treasury. After this, Clotilda sent greetings to Clovis: she acknowledged his proposal, but because of her commitment to Christianity and the prohibition of "mixed marriages" (and perhaps foreseeing potential problems in gaining Gundobad's approval), she requested that it remain secret. According to the *Liber Historiae Francorum,* she said, "It is not permitted for a Christian woman to marry a pagan, therefore do not let our betrothal be known. Whatever my Lord God orders, I confess that I will do."[15]

The following year Clovis sent his legate to Gundobad to bring Clotilda back to his court for marriage. Gundobad, apparently unaware of the earlier "secret" betrothal, was taken aback. Prepared to go to war against Clovis and the Franks to avenge this affront, he was advised to ask his officers and chamberlain whether a legate of Clovis had previously brought gifts to the court in "an ingenious manner." And in checking his treasury, they indeed found the ring. Gundobad confronted Clotilda, who admitted that over the years "'small gifts of gold were brought to you by Clovis' messengers. It so happened that a little ring was placed in my hand, your little servant. I then hid it in your treasury.' He said: 'This was done innocently and without advice.' Then he grasped her angrily and handed her over to Aurelianus."[16] Clotilda was taken by Aurelianus and his followers to King Clovis and they were married in 493 in Soissons.

In this description we can note first of all the active, rather surreptitious role that Clotilda apparently assumed in arranging her own marriage and determining her future. Despite Gundobad's statement that this was done "innocently and without advice," the secrecy which Clotilda exacted in these negotiations would seem to tell us something quite different. Using this strategy, she was able to contract an advantageous marriage without obtaining her uncle's permission. Considering that Gundobad had killed her parents and exiled her sister, and continued to espouse Arianism, Clotilda was no doubt anxious to escape from his court and to start a new life. (The *Liber Historiae Francorum* and Gregory of Tours' *History,* for example, note Clotilda's unremitting hatred for her uncle, as manifested in her later attempts to have her husband and sons avenge her family's honor in a vendetta directed against Gundobad.)[17]

The sources stress the young bride's classic attributes, such as her beauty, grace, intelligence, and royal blood, as well as the fact that she was a Christian; but modern scholars have suggested that Clotilda's Catholic faith was in fact a prime consideration in Clovis's selecting her as his wife.[18] In his classic study *The Invasion of Europe by the Barbarians,* J. B. Bury, for example, writes: "If we remember that the Burgundians were largely Arian, that King Gundobad was an Arian, and Clotilda was exceptionally a Catholic, it is certainly remarkable, if it were mere chance, that Clovis's choice should have fallen on one of the Catholic exceptions." Bury believed that he was "not rash in suggesting that it was just because she was a Catholic that Clovis chose her out."[19] Although he was hesitant to personally embrace the new religion, the king appreciated the power of the Gallo-Roman Church; he no doubt realized what an enormous help Clotilda would be in winning over its confidence, as well as in negotiations with the ecclesiastics. His marriage to Clotilda, as noted by Bury, "was deliberately intended as a substitute for becoming a Christian himself, and it made clear what form of Christianity he would embrace, if he ever embraced any."[20] Moreover, from the perspective of the Church, this "mixed marriage" was clearly perceived as politically advantageous: it provided them with a proven ally who could assist them "informally" from the "inside"; one who could perhaps bring about the desired conversion of the Frankish king, his children, and his followers.

It was, then, Clotilda's commitment to Catholicism and her single-minded domestic missionary activity which would attract more public attention and praise on the part of the Church than any other aspect of her life. According to the *Liber Historiae Francorum,* the saintly queen's work began in earnest on their wedding night. At this rather propitious moment she attempted to use her conjugal influence over Clovis. In a wedding-night/honeymoon sermon, the bride is described as enumerating her special conditions of marriage. "When it was late that day, at the time when by custom the marriage was to be consummated, Clotild, moved by her accustomed prudence, confessed to God and said: 'Now is the time my lord king that you hear your servant so that you may deem to concede what I pray for before I become part of your family and pass under your lordship.' The king answered: 'Ask what you wish and I will grant it.'"[21] She asked the king first of all to believe in God the Father, in Christ, and in the Holy Spirit. He was to give up and burn his "meaningless idols which are not gods but worthless carvings" and also to restore the Christian churches that he had destroyed. He was finally asked to avenge her honor. "And remember also that I ask that you should demand the estate of my father and of my mother whom my uncle Gundobad evilly killed. Thus the Lord may avenge their blood." Clovis responded saying: "Only one thing that you have asked remains difficult and that is your request that I give up my gods and follow your God. Anything else that you ask, I will do as the opportunity arises." She answered: "I ask this above all else, that you worship the omnipotent Lord God who is in heaven."[22]

According to the sources, Clotilda continued to persevere in her attempts to convert Clovis to Christianity. With the birth of their first child, another opportunity presented itself which the queen could use to win over the king and his followers to the new religion. She was able to convince Clovis to allow her to have their son baptized in the Catholic faith. In this way the Church would be assured that the next generation of Frankish rulers would be Catholic. Clotilda no doubt also hoped that this event would have a special appeal for Clovis and would consequently influence him to adopt the new faith. Thus, according to Gregory of Tours, after the birth of their first son, Clotilda "wanted to have the baby baptized, and she kept on urging her husband to agree to this."[23] In her arguments with the king, Clotilda again stressed the worthless aspects of his gods compared to the omnipotence of her God: "'The gods whom you worship are no good,' she would say. 'They haven't even been able to help themselves, let alone others.'" But "However often the queen said this, the king came no nearer to belief." Still Clotilda persisted and prepared to baptize the infant in her own faith. The king did not attempt to stop her. "She ordered the church to be decorated with hangings and curtains, in the hope that the King, who remained stubborn in the face of argument, might be brought to the faith by ceremony." The child received baptism and was given the name Ingomer. But tragically, no sooner had he been baptized than he died while still in his white baptismal robes. With marvelous understatement Gregory of Tours describes this sad event: "Clovis was extremely angry," and he reproached Clotilda for having had the child baptized as a Christian rather than dedicating him to his pagan gods. However, according to Gregory, Clotilda, with Christian resignation, gave thanks to God for welcoming a child who was conceived in her womb into His kingdom.[24]

Clotilda's remarkable perseverance and continuing influence over Clovis are again underscored by the fact that she had their second son baptized in the Christian faith. When this child too began to ail and seemed to be following the same pattern that his older brother had, Clovis again reproached Clotilda for having him baptized in the name of Christ. According to Gregory of Tours, "Clotilda prayed to the Lord and at His command the baby recovered."[25] Thus with the baptism of this son, the first step of her conversion strategy was accomplished.

However, Clovis still remained unconvinced of the new religion. Gregory relates, "Queen Clotild continued to pray that her husband might recognize the true God and give up his idol-worship. Nothing could persuade him to accept Christianity."[26] Then during the course of a difficult war against the Alamanni, Clovis "was forced by necessity to accept what he had refused of his own free will."[27] Witnessing the annihilation of his own troops in battle, and faced with a desperate situation, the king called on his own gods for assistance. Realizing that they were powerless and had no intention of helping him, he then turned to call on Christ's assistance. According to Gregory of Tours, he raised his eyes to heaven and prayed, " 'Jesus Christ,' he said, '*you who Clotild maintains to be the Son of the living God*, you who deign to give help to those in travail and victory to those who trust in you, in faith I beg the glory of your help.' "[28] The *Liber Historiae Francorum* notes that "Aurelianus [Clovis's legate], seeing the turn of events, said to the king, '. . . believe only in the lord of heaven whom *your queen* proclaims.' "[29] Thus compelled by this extremely desperate plight in battle, Clovis called upon Clotilda's God for assistance. He then promised in return for evidence of Christ's strength and miraculous powers—specifically, victory over his enemies—that he would accept Christian baptism. According to the sources, even as he prayed, the

Alamanni turned and fled.[30] And on his return home, Clovis "told the Queen how he had won a victory by calling on the name of Christ."[31]

After this pivotal event, Gregory of Tours notes: "the Queen then ordered Saint Remi, Bishop of the town of Rheims, to be summoned in secret. She begged him to impart the word of salvation to the King."[32] (Here again Clotilda took the initiative and assumed a major role in realizing her husband's conversion.) The bishop met privately with Clovis, and soon after, the king was baptized in great ceremony. He was described by Gregory of Tours as a "new Constantine" stepping into the baptismal pool.[33] At this same time, we are told, more than three thousand of the king's army, along with two of his sisters (Albofled and Lanthechild), were baptized.[34]

In discussing Clovis's shift of allegiance from paganism to Christianity, scholars have traditionally focused on the king's "miraculous" victory in the war against the Alamanni and Suevians, which closely echoed the events surrounding the impressive, historical prototype of imperial conversion, namely, that of Constantine. Clovis's baptism, as we have noted, was also seen in larger-than-life terms: this first Christian king of the Franks was portrayed as a "new Constantine." Yet, despite the emphasis by chroniclers and scholars on the unexpected, "miraculous" element of Clovis' conversion, as well as the official institutional involvement of St. Remi, Clotilda had in fact assumed the primary role in "conditioning" her husband for this event—in making him susceptible to a Christian "solution," namely, by calling on Clotilda's God for assistance when his own gods were failing him on the battlefield. As Clovis's wife and *consocia,* or partner in ruling, as well as trusted religious adviser, Clotilda had worked unremittingly toward this goal. Through her position within the family and household, she was able to provide consistent reinforcement of Christian precepts as well as incentive for Clovis to lose faith or become disillusioned with his pagan religion. She was therefore able to provide the crucial groundwork for Clovis's official conversion. Despite her inability over the years to fully persuade him on her own to get rid of his pagan gods and accept Christianity, it was then in this "public" moment of desperation, when he was on the verge of defeat, that the king clearly acknowledged his debt to Clotilda's persistence in "domestic proselytization." It appears that he had after all been "passively" attentive to her case for Christianity over the years, but had apparently not felt the need to take a chance in making this momentous and perhaps ill-advised shift while his pagan gods continued to support him and bring him "luck." More a pragmatic than theoretical decision, the time had not been right to deny his pagan heritage. Thus in his desperate hour, when he witnessed his own gods failing him, he resorted to Clotilda's arguments which had directly attacked the impotency of his pagan gods while promoting the miraculous power of the Christian faith. In the official description of the "miracle" of conversion, the name of Clotilda appears alone as a model of faith, as perhaps a sort of interceder with Christ. It is, after all, the "Christ of Clotilda" whom Clovis invokes. It should be emphasized that at this critical moment in the history of the Church, neither St. Remi nor other members of the official church hierarchy were similarly awarded this type of prominence.[35]

Moreover, in the ninth-century redaction of the Life of St. Clotilda (based on Gregory of Tours' *History of the Franks* and the *Liber Historiae Francorum*), the author also describes the important ceremonial role that the queen assumed in Clovis's baptism. According to this *vita,* "The new Constantine came to baptism with the blessed Remigius leading the way and blessed Chrothild [Clotilda] following, the Holy Spirit governing these procedures in characteristic fashion. For it was fitting, that when the pagan king came to his baptism, holy Remigius should precede in the place of Christ Jesus and holy Chrothild [Clotilda] should follow in the place of the Church interceding with God" (see plate 14). Her hagiographer continues: "Happy Gaul, rejoice and be glad, give thanks in the Lord, take joy in the true God, for your first king chosen by the King of heaven, was drawn away from the veneration of the demons by the prayers of holy Chrothild [Clotilda] acting in the character of the Church, was converted to God by the preaching of blessed Remigius and baptized by him."[36] Clotilda's *vita* also notes that the queen continued to exercise religious influence over the king and worked toward the general conversion of her country. "*At the advice of blessed Chrothild* [Clotilda], the king undertook the destruction of pagan shrines and the erection of churches, and he enriched them abundantly with lands and privileges: he undertook generously to confer alms on the poor, to support widows and orphans in the spirit of mercy and to attend with zealous devotion to every good work."[37]

Other sources of the Middle Ages continue to acknowledge Clotilda's influential role in the conversion of Clovis and the Franks. The *vita* of the queen-saint Balthild, for example, notes the impressive legacy found among its female Frankish saints. Balthild's hagiographer compares her favorably with these royal predecessors: "Let us recall that there were in the kingdom of the Franks some noble queens, true servants of God: Clotild, first of all, wife of the first Clovis, niece of Gundobad, who through holy exhortation converted to Christianity and the catholic faith [*traxit ad christianitatem et ad fidem catholicam . . . perduxit*] her most powerful and pagan husband and with him many of the Franks."[38]

In the thirteenth-century *Speculum Historiale,* compiled by Vincent of Beauvais, Clotilda still retains a primary role in the conversion of Clovis and the Franks. This work devotes three chapters to the events leading up to and culminating in the baptism of Clovis.[39]

Christine de Pizan, in *The Book of the City of Ladies* (1405), a collection of biographies of "women worthies," dedicates a chapter to Clotilda. She writes: "As for the great benefits brought about by women regarding spiritual matters, just as I told you before, was it not Clotilda, daughter of the king of Burgundy and wife of the strong Clovis, king of France, who first brought and spread the faith of Jesus Christ to the kings and princes of France? What greater good could have been accomplished than what she did?"[40]

Even the notorious *Malleus Maleficarum* (*The Hammer of Witches*), written in 1486 by the Dominican inquisitors Heinrich Krämer and Jacob Sprenger and used to identify and condemn women as witches, includes Clotilda as one of the few positive female figures in history. In the chapter on "Why Superstition is chiefly found in Women," Krämer and Sprenger cite 1 Corinthians 7:14: " 'If a woman hath a husband that believeth not, and he be pleased to dwell with her, let her not leave him. For the unbelieving husband is sanctified by the believing wife. . . .' And all this is made clear in the New Testament concerning women and virgins and other holy women who have by faith led nations and kingdoms away from the worship of idols to the Christian religion."[41] They then cite as a source Vincent of Beauvais: "Anyone who looks at Vincent of Beauvais (*in Spe. Histor.,* XXVI.9) will find marvellous things of the conversion of Hungary by the most Christian Gilia, and of the Franks by Clotilda, the wife of Clovis."[42]

It appears then to be only in the more recent retelling and synthesizing of these events that the miraculous and the official or institutional aspects of this conversion have frequently worked to overshadow and marginalize Clotilda's primary contribution to this significant episode in history. In contrast, for the medieval world, the success of Clotilda in persuading Clovis and the Franks to accept baptism seems to have been clearly recognized and appreciated.

LOMBARD QUEENS: CLOTSINDA AND THEODOLINDA

The queens Clotsinda and Theodolinda have also been singled out by Church writers, for their roles as "royal conduits" in the Christianization of Lombardy. Bishop Nicetius of Trier, writing in 564 (some twenty years after Clotilda's death), appears to have been rather well informed in regard to the queen's role in the conversion of Clovis. In a fascinating letter written to Clotilda's granddaughter, Clotsinda, queen of the Lombards, Bishop Nicetius recognizes the strategic assistance which royal women might lend in the conversion of a king and his country.[43] Clotsinda, like Clotilda, was involved in a "mixed" or interfaith marriage; namely, that of a Catholic princess married to a non-Catholic, Arian king—in this case, Alboin, king of the Lombards. Nicetius attempts to convince Clotsinda of her conjugal duty to persuade her husband to extricate himself from the Arian heresy and espouse the Catholic doctrine. As a spiritual father he writes: "I adjure you, Lady Clotsinda, by the tremendous Day of Judgment, that you both read this letter carefully and often try to expound it to your husband." The bishop then reminds the queen of her proud religious heritage which was definitely worthy of imitation: "You have heard how your grandmother, Lady Clotilda of good memory, came into France, how she led the Lord Clovis to the Catholic law, and how, since he was a most astute man, he was unwilling to agree to it until he knew it was true." Nicetius then questions Clotsinda as to why her own husband had not yet been converted. He stresses the urgency of her mission: "I beg that you be not idle; clamour without ceasing, do not cease to sing. You have heard the saying: 'The unbelieving husband shall be saved by the faithful wife' (1 Corinthians 7:14). You know that salvation will be granted first to those who convert a sinner from his sin. Watch, keep vigil, for God is propitious to you. I pray that you so act that you both make the Lombard people strong over their enemies and allow us to rejoice at your salvation and at that of your husband."[44]

Clotsinda died at an early age before she was able to successfully carry out her assigned mission to convert the Lombard nation. This special task, however, was taken up at a later date by Theodolinda, another Christian queen who won popular recognition of sainthood (d. ca. 628?). Theodolinda was the Catholic daughter of the duke of the Bavarians. She married the Lombard king Agilulf, who, like Alboin, followed the heresy of Arianism. We are informed of her activities through the correspondence of Pope Gregory the Great and the *History of the Lombards* by Paul the Deacon.[45] The pope wrote several letters to Theodolinda in which he appealed to her directly for assistance. In this we can see the power and influence which he believed the queen was able to exercise at the court. He asked her to use her influence over her husband on behalf of the Catholics in his realm and to work toward bringing about peace. He was also convinced of the queen's usefulness and the strategic role which she could play in converting Lombardy from Arianism to Catholicism. For example, when Theodolinda gave birth to a son, Adaloaldus—who would become heir to the Lombard throne—she had him baptized in the Catholic faith. In the year 603, Pope Gregory the Great wrote to congratulate her on this event: "The letters which you sent us a little time ago . . . have made us partakers of your joy on account of our learning that by the favour of Almighty God a son has been given you, and, as is greatly to your Excellency's credit, has been received into the fellowship of the Catholic faith. Nor indeed was anything else to be supposed of your Christianity but that you would fortify him whom you have received by the gift of God with the aid of Catholic rectitude, so that our Redeemer might both acknowledge thee as His familiar servant, and also bring up prosperously in His fear a new king for the nation of the Lombards."[46] Along with this congratulatory letter, the pope also sent gifts: to Theodolinda's new son, Adaloaldus, he sent a cross said to have been made from the wood of Christ's cross and a lectionary of the Gospel in a Persian case; and to her daughter he sent three rings.[47]

In his *History of the Lombards,* Paul the Deacon also notes the strong influence of the queen in religious matters and particularly her crucial role in urging the king to renounce Arianism and adopt the Catholic faith. "By means of this queen [Theodolinda] the Church of God obtained much advantage. For the Lombards, when they were still involved in the error of heathenism, plundered all the property of the Churches. But the king, *being influenced by this queen's healthful intercession,* both held the Catholic faith, and bestowed many possessions on the Church of Christ, and restored the bishops, who were in a depressed and abject condition, to the honour of their wonted dignity."[48] As scholars have noted, the implication of this passage seems to be that through the efforts of his wife, King Agilulf became Catholic. However, a number of other contemporary sources seem to contradict this contention and indicate that the king, in fact, did not formally renounce Arianism; nevertheless, under Theodolinda's influence he exercised a certain tolerance toward her religion and seemed to offer it at least "passive support." For example, he allowed their son to be baptized with Catholic rites and he cultivated a circle of friends among the Catholic Church hierarchy. He also wanted to put an end to the Three Chapters Schism and worked for religious peace in Lombardy.[49]

Moreover, Theodolinda was an active supporter and patron of the missionary activities of St. Columbanus and his Celtic monks.

Columbanus was received with great honor at the Lombard court by
Theodolinda and Agilulf. He remained there for apparently some
months arguing against the heretical tenets of Arianism. The queen, as
throne-sharer and adviser, no doubt influenced Agilulf in providing
Columbanus with a royal gift which included the partially ruined
basilica of St. Peter and land at Bobbio. This subsequently became
Columbanus's famous monastic house of Bobbio—a missionary center of great learning and Catholic influence.[50]

CLOTILDA AND INGUND: VISIGOTHIC SPAIN

Clotilda's daughter, also named Clotilda, attempted to follow her
mother's example as a domestic proselytizer. She was sent off to Spain
with "a great dowry of expensive jewellery" to marry the king of the
Visigoths, Amalaric.[51] As the wife in a "mixed" marriage, she too
tried to convert her husband to Catholicism. She however was less
than successful in her attempts. According to the account by Gregory
of Tours, Clotilda was "very badly treated by her husband Amalaric
on account of her Catholic faith. Several times when she was on her
way to church he had dung and other filth thrown over her. Finally he
struck her with such violence that she sent to her brother a towel
stained with her own blood." [52] This plea for help moved her brother,
Childebert, to action on behalf of his "wronged" sister: it also provided
him with an excuse to set off for Spain and invade Barcelona. While
fleeing from the invaders and seeking asylum in a church, Amalaric
was killed. Gregory of Tours relates: "Childebert planned to take his
sister home with him, and at the same time to carry off a vast mass of
treasure. By some ill chance Clotild died on the journey. She was carried to Paris and buried beside her father Clovis." [53]

   In this same tradition, Gregory of Tours describes a similar attempt
at domestic proselytization which involved the Frankish princess
Ingund, daughter of King Sigebert and Brunhilda and great grand-
daughter of Clotilda. During the second half of the sixth century, the
Christians in Spain were being persecuted through the instigation of
Goiswinth, the widow of King Athanagild. Ingund was sent off to
Spain "with much pomp and circumstance" to marry the king's son,
Hermangild.[54] (He and his brother had been raised and educated
by their Catholic mother, Theodosie—while his father remained an
Arian.) [55] Although Ingund was initially received very cordially by her
Arian stepmother-in-law, Goiswinth, it soon became apparent that she
had no intention of allowing the young princess to remain a Catholic.
Through conversation, she tried to persuade her to be rebaptized into

the Arian heresy. Ingund, however, refused and reconfirmed the fact that she would never go back on her "belief in the Holy Trinity one and indivisible." According to Gregory of Tours, when the queen heard this insubordinate response, she lost her temper and became physically abusive toward Ingund. She seized her by the hair, threw her onto the ground, and kicked her until she became covered with blood. She then had the princess stripped naked and thrown into the baptismal pool. Despite all of this, Gregory of Tours adds, there remained many who witnessed Ingund's steadfast adherence to her faith.[56]

When Ingund and Hermangild left the royal court to establish their own place of residence, the Frankish princess was provided with the opportunity to begin her work as domestic proselytizer. "Ingund began to persuade her husband to give up his belief in the false Arian heresy and to accept instead the true Catholic faith. For a long time he resisted, but in the end he was persuaded by her arguments and was converted to the Catholic religion. He was anointed with the chrism and took the name John." [57] It was, then, due to the successful efforts of his wife, Ingund, that Hermangild converted. However, through his conversion to Catholicism Hermangild won the animosity of his father, who sent him into exile, imprisoned him, and ultimately had him killed. He died a martyr to his faith.[58] Ingund, who had been handed over for protection to the imperial army, died with her small son in Carthage and was buried there.[59]

Thus we see in these early medieval examples of Frankish Gaul, Italy, and Spain, the primary roles attributed to queens as emissaries for the Church. In each of these cases of "interfaith" marriage, the royal women prepared the groundwork for the missionaries to begin their work, while they used their own political power and influence to attempt to bring about the conversions of their husbands and families to the new faith. Churchmen in turn seem to have been aware of the fact that they had much to gain through these marriages where consecration of "the unbelieving husband" was expected to take place.

THE ANGLO-SAXON CONNECTION:
SAINTS BERTHA AND ETHELBERGA

The pattern of pious queens or princesses serving the Church as proselytizers, or "conduits" of conversion and Christian culture, proved to be an especially important factor in the shift from paganism to Christianity in Anglo-Saxon England. The first chapter of this missionary work, which involved the conversion of King Ethelbert of Kent, is described in the letters of Pope Gregory the Great and Bede's *History of the English Church and People.*[60] This pagan king was married to the Catholic princess, Bertha, daughter of the Frankish King Charibert and Queen Ingoberg. And although neither Bede nor Gregory the Great note this important connection, Bertha was also the great granddaughter of Clotilda and thus participated in this genealogy of royal converter saints. Bede's information about this Frankish princess is unfortunately rather limited. He states that Ethelbert had received Bertha from her parents "on condition that she should have freedom to hold and practice her faith unhindered with Bishop Liudhard, whom they had sent as her helper in the faith."[61] Thus again, as in the case of Clotilda and others, the conditions of marriage were not predicated on the king's actual acceptance of, and baptism into, the new faith; however, the queen was allowed to continue to freely practice her own faith. In the context of the arrival of the mission of St. Augustine in Kent, Bede also acknowledges the fact that the king "had already heard of the Christian religion, having a Christian wife of the Frankish royal house named Bertha."[62] (Thus Bertha had begun the process of converting her husband "at home" before the official missionaries appeared on the scene.) Bede then comments that Bertha went to pray in St. Martin's Church which was also the site where St. Augustine and his monks first preached and said Mass.[63] It was in this same church that Ethelbert would be baptized.[64]

Bede's curious silence in regard to Bertha and her primary involvement in the proselytization of the English is somewhat difficult to explain. This lacuna seems especially surprising in light of a rather crucial letter written by Pope Gregory the Great to Bertha in 601.[65] Strangely enough, this important letter is not found among Bede's documents, nor even mentioned; while its companion letter, written apparently at the same time by the pope to King Ethelbert, is quoted in full in Bede's *History.*[66]

A number of scholars have discussed the omission of this significant historical document in Bede's work. It might be explained very simply by the fact that he did not have access to, or was not familiar with, both letters; or it might be a case of accidental exclusion, or perhaps of intentional deletion, that is, for one reason or another he chose to use the letter addressed to the king while discarding the one to the queen. However, it seems that for one wishing to glorify the role of the first Christian king of England, the papal letter to the queen does not strengthen Bede's case: it does not present a particularly flattering portrait of a committed, enthusiastic king willingly adopting the new faith and assuming a leadership role in converting his kingdom. Furthermore, Bede's primary interest in exhalting Pope Gregory/Rome/

St. Peter as the major force behind the conversion of England and the formation of the English Church, rather than the Franks or the Celts, might help to explain his reticence in regard to describing Queen Bertha's initiatory role.[67]

This papal letter addressed to Queen Bertha has also caused some scholarly debate in regard to the conflicting evidence it provides for the dating as well as the sequence of events in Ethelbert's conversion. In addition, it fails to depict the king as the eager new convert described by Bede. However, in this letter Pope Gregory the Great clearly recognizes the queen's influence and the decisive role which he expected her to play in the strategy of converting Ethelbert and his followers. The pope begins his letter with praise for the queen's commitment to the Church and its mission in England. He has learned through members of Augustine's mission that the queen has provided a great deal of assistance and charity to Augustine. Gregory then focuses on the topic of pressing concern: the conversion of the English. "And we bless Almighty God, who has been mercifully pleased to reserve the conversion of the nation of the Angli for your reward. For as through Helena of illustrious memory, the mother of the most pious Emperor Constantine, He kindled the hearts of the Romans into Christian faith, so we trust that He works in the nation of the Angli through the zeal of your Glory." [68] Here the pope singles out the queen and her primary role in this process of conversion. She has been selected for this special mission and will be appropriately rewarded. He then links Bertha historically with the empress St. Helena, who, according to tradition, had exercised a crucial role in the conversion of her son, Constantine. (This model was perhaps especially relevant to a queen of Britain, for according to a confused legend, Helena was believed to be a native of the island. It is also interesting to note that in his companion letter written to Ethelbert, Gregory compares the king and his role in conversion to that of Constantine.)[69] After this very positive preamble, the pope, in a rather impatient tone, proceeds to reprimand the queen for her delay in acting and the ineffectual results of her proselytizing efforts. He writes: "And indeed you ought before now, as being truly a Christian, to have inclined the heart of our glorious son, your husband, by the good influence of your prudence, to follow, for the weal of his kingdom and of his own soul, the faith which you profess, to the end that for him, and for the conversion of the whole nation through him, fit retribution might accrue to you in the joys of heaven. For seeing, as we have said, that your Glory is both fortified by a right faith and instructed in letters, this should have been to you neither slow of accomplishment nor difficult." [70]

Gregory continues his letter by advising the queen to begin her work immediately "to make reparation with increase for what has been neglected." She was to strengthen Ethelbert's mind in the love of the Christian faith through continual urging or encouragement and solicitude for the "fullest conversion of the nation subject to him." The conversion would further enhance and verify her reputation, for her good deeds were known not only among the Romans, who prayed for her, but had spread even to the prince of Constantinople. The pope then concludes his letter, "Hence, as great joy has been caused us by the consolations of your Christianity, so also may there be joy in heaven for your perfected work. So acquit yourselves devotedly and with all your might in aid of our above named most reverent brother and fellow-bishop, [Augustine], and of the servants of God *whom we have sent to you,* in the conversion of your nation that you may both reign happily here with our glorious son your husband, and after long courses of years, may also attain the joys of the future life, which know no end." [71]

In this letter, the pope clearly acknowledges the anticipated historical agency expected of the queen (in the tradition of Clotilda), and specifically her central importance in providing the groundwork for the missionary effort in Britain. As queen, Bertha was to make a concerted effort to gain her husband's tolerance or approval of the new faith, followed by his conversion to Christianity. As a well-connected sharer of the throne, she was also to provide all possible assistance to Augustine and his missionaries. Her public and private influence and active participation were therefore viewed as crucial to the ultimate success of this mission. [72]

It is also of interest to note that in referring to the missionary group—Augustine and his servants of God—the pope specifically states, *"whom we have sent to you."* Moreover, in another letter of this same period addressed to Bertha's aunt, the Frankish Queen Brunhilda, Pope Gregory asks for her royal help, support, and protection in regard to Augustine and his missionaries as they passed through her country on their way to Britain. He informs Brunhilda "that it has reached us, that the English nation, by God's favour, *desires to become Christian,* but that the priests who are in the neighbourhood have no pastoral solicitude for them." [73] Thus in response to this request he has sent Augustine along with other servants of God to convert the English. These references perhaps suggest, as others have noted, that Bertha had actually initiated or encouraged this mission by requesting that the pope send her missionaries to aid in her work to convert the English. [74]

The cooperative missionary efforts of Queen Bertha and Augustine appear to have been successful. Pope Gregory the Great, for example, notes in a letter to the patriarch of Alexandria (598) that many of the people of England had already espoused the new faith (he mentions the somewhat exaggerated figure of ten thousand).[75] However, rather curiously, the pope fails to make specific reference in this letter to the conversion of the king. This, coupled with his letter to Bertha, seems to suggest that Ethelbert had not yet been formally converted to Christianity. At the same time, the king apparently provided a certain openness or tolerance, and at least passive support of the new faith. It is, then, in the last years of the sixth century or early seventh century that Bertha's mission of domestic proselytization would be "perfected" and Ethelbert would espouse the Catholic faith. And for her role in the conversion of the king and of the area of Kent, Bertha was recognized as a popular saint with a local cult centered around Canterbury.[76]

The tradition of royal or noblewomen as transmitters, or conduits, of the new faith was continued in England by Ethelberga, daughter of Bertha and Ethelbert of Kent and great-great granddaughter of Clotilda. Bede, writing from his northern monastery of Jarrow, was especially interested and well-informed in regard to the Christianization of Northumbria. In his *History of the English Church and People* Bede writes: "The Northumbrian people's acceptance of the Faith of Christ came about through their king's alliance with the kings of Kent by his marriage to Ethelberga, known as Tata, a daughter of King Ethelbert."[77] Edwin, king of Northumbria, had sent an embassy to Ethelberga's brother, Eadbald, king of Kent, to request the marriage of his sister. He however received a reply "that it was not permissible for a Christian maiden to be given in marriage to a heathen husband, lest the Christian Faith and Sacraments be profaned by her association with a king who was wholly ignorant of the worship of the true God."[78] Edwin then assured them that he would place no obstacles in the way of the Christian faith and would provide complete freedom for Ethelberga and her attendants, priests, and servants to practice their Christian beliefs. In his negotiations, the king also professed a willingness to accept the religion of Christ, "if, on examination, his advisers decided that it appeared more holy and acceptable to God than their own."[79] These arrangements were accepted and Ethelberga was sent north to be married to Edwin. And in accordance with the agreement, she was accompanied by her chaplain, Bishop Paulinus, who was to provide daily Mass and instruction, thus preserving her and her companions "from corruption by their association with the heathen."[80] Bede also notes that in addition to serving as her chaplain and spiritual counselor in marriage, Paulinus was determined to apply himself to the conversion of the north of England.[81]

The birth of Ethelberga's first child (as in the case of Clotilda), provided an important opportunity for the queen to use her influence in converting Edwin to Christianity. According to Bede, while the king thanked his gods for the birth of his daughter, Bishop Paulinus convinced him that it was Christ who should be thanked since he had given the queen a safe and painless delivery in response to the bishop's prayers. Impressed by Paulinus's words, the king promised that if God would grant him life and victory over his enemy, the king of the West Saxons, he would renounce his idols and become a Christian. As a pledge, Edwin gave his infant daughter to Paulinus to be consecrated in Christ. Thus on the Feast of Pentecost, the royal infant, along with twelve others of her household, became the first Northumbrians to be baptized in the Christian faith.[82] This event provides another example of group conversion within a royal household, again following the lead or precedent of the queen, rather than the king.

Despite Edwin's promises of conversion linked to his victory over the West Saxons, he followed the rather cautious pattern found among other Germanic kings and continued to procrastinate for some time. He viewed this change in religion as a very serious move and understood that it involved denying his own gods who had in the past served him well. In his *History,* Bede notes that although the king had already abandoned idol worship, he would not receive baptism without due consideration. Being a "wise and prudent man" he wanted to receive full instruction in the faith by Paulinus and to discuss this change with his counselors before adopting the new religion.[83]

Bede incorporates in his *History* a copy of a letter addressed to the king by Pope Boniface in which the pope notes the conversion of the kings of a neighboring territory (i.e., Kent), and strongly urges him to renounce idol worship and accept the true faith, especially "as we understand that your gracious Queen and true partner is already endowed with the gift of eternal life through the regeneration of Holy Baptism."[84] Of particular interest, however, is a companion letter, written by Pope Boniface to Queen Ethelberga, and this time included in Bede's work, "urging her to exert her influence to obtain the king's salvation."[85] This official letter underscores the papacy's pragmatic view of the critical assistance which the queen was believed to bring to the conversion process. He writes: "We have been greatly encouraged by God's goodness in granting you, through your own profession of faith, an opportunity to kindle a spark of the true religion in your husband; for in this way He will more swiftly inspire not only the mind of your illustrious Consort to love of Him, but the minds of your subjects as well."[86] The pope then praises the queen's religious life, noting that she showed "a shining example of good works" and worked "constantly to propagate the Christian Faith." However, Boniface had also learned that her husband "still serves abominable idols and is slow to listen to the teaching of the preachers." He then urges the queen not to avoid her conjugal duty to convert the king so that he might be added to the Christian fold. "Only in this way will you enjoy the full privileges of marriage in perfect union; for the Scripture says, 'the two shall become one flesh.' But how can it be called a true union between you, so long as he remains alienated from the daylight of your Faith by the barrier of dark and lamentable error?" Boniface then instructs her in Christian indoctrination: "My illustrious daughter, persevere in using every effort to soften his heart by teaching him the commandments of God. . . . If you do this, the witness of the Holy Spirit will most certainly be fulfilled in you, that 'the unbelieving husband shall be saved through the believing wife.'" He continues, "For this is why you have received our Lord's merciful goodness, in order that you may restore to your Redeemer with increase the fruits of faith and of the boundless blessings entrusted to you. We shall not cease from constant prayer that God will assist and guide you to accomplish this." The queen is then asked to inform the pope of her progress in converting her husband and their people as soon as a suitable messenger is available. He ends his letter with blessings from St. Peter and notes the enclosure of special gifts: "With it we send you a silver mirror, together with a gold and ivory comb, asking Your Majesty to accept these gifts with the same goodwill as that with which we send them."[87]

It was a few years later, then, in about 627, that Edwin finally accepted baptism into the Catholic faith. According to Bede, the king had been moved to accept the new religion by a vision he experienced during his exile at King Redwald's court. Paulinus learned of the details of this vision, and while Edwin again hesitated to adopt the new faith, Paulinus reminded him of his promise to become a Christian. The king called together a council of his advisers and friends, and after much deliberation they decided in favor of the new faith. Bede thus notes: "So King Edwin, with all the nobility of his kingdom and a large number of humbler folk, accepted the Faith and were washed in the cleansing waters of Baptism in the eleventh year of his reign, which was the year of our Lord 627."[88] Later, other children born to Ethelberga and Edwin were baptized in the new faith. Two, however, died while still wearing their white baptismal robes.[89] Many members of the nobility and princely rank also received baptism. (Among those baptized at this time was St. Hilda whose father was Edwin's nephew.)[90] According to Bede, "Indeed, so great was the fervour of faith and desire for baptism among the Northumbrian people that Paulinus is said to have accompanied the king and queen to the royal residence at Ad-Gefrin and remained there thirty-six days constantly occupied in instructing and baptizing."[91]

In 633 King Edwin was killed in battle and his entire army destroyed or scattered. Under the victors—Penda and Cadwalla—the countryside was ravaged; many of its inhabitants were killed, and paganism returned to Northumbria. Queen Ethelberga, her young children, and Paulinus took flight and returned to Kent. There they were received by Ethelberga's brother, Eadbald, now king of Kent. He provided his sister with a villa at Lyming, where Ethelberga built one of the first monasteries for women in Britain. Here she and her sister Edburga took the veil.[92] Both ultimately would win recognition of sainthood.

Along with the early queens of France, Italy, Spain, and England, Ethelberga then shares in this impressive female tradition of proselytization. While Bede's *History of the English Church and People* provides us with detailed information on the process involved, as Stephanie Hollis has noted, he does not focus on the queen's strategic use of political power and influence on behalf of the new faith and her active role as proselytizer. Rather he seems to relegate the queen's influence to an indirect, privatized or "behind the scenes" role.[93] Edwin's actual conversion, as described by Bede, is again part of the "miraculous tradition" and linked to a vision. However, Ethelberga and Paulinus had in fact laid the groundwork for this change and prevailed upon the king to be baptized in the new faith. Working together with her chaplain/bishop, the queen initiated the conversion of many of her subjects in the North of England. It should be noted that the first wave of converts, which included members of the royal household and others, espoused the new faith by following the example of their queen, rather than that of their pagan king. Thus in the tradition of queens as domestic brokers and emissaries for the Church, Ethelberga exercised a crucial influence over her husband's acceptance of the new faith.

Eormenhild, queen of Mercia and abbess of Ely (d. ca. 700) also played an important role in the early missionary activity. Eormenhild was the daughter of Queen Sexburga and Erconbert, king of Kent. She married Wulfhere, king of the Mercians, and is credited with winning him over to the new faith. It was, then, during their reign that Mercia was converted to Christianity.[94] Eormenhild also had two children: Coenred, who became king of Mercia, and a daughter, Werburga, who became a nun and later was named abbess of Ely. Werburga was also recognized as a saint.[95]

We learn that Eadgyth, King Athelstan's sister, married the pagan Danish king, Sihtric of Northumbria. For the love of his bride, Sihtric apparently espoused the new faith. However, when he later repudiated this Christian princess, he then lapsed into his former pagan ways. Eadgyth, having preserved her virginity, retired to the monastery of Polesworth.[96]

After the initial conversion of their peoples, Anglo-Saxon queens and noblewomen continued to exercise their religious influence over their husbands; they repeatedly reminded them of their personal commitment to the new faith and need for salvation. One example of particularly strong influence can be seen in a story told of Queen Ethelburga, wife of Ine, king of Wessex (688–726). According to William of Malmesbury, Ethelburga was unable to persuade the king to renounce the luxuries of the material world, and therefore devised a clever strategy. After spending time reveling in the splendor of their country estate, the next day, in their absence, she had it defiled with the excrement of cattle and heaps of filth; she also had a sow which had recently given birth placed in their bed. She then lured her husband back to their dwelling with promises of sex. On seeing the disgusting transformation of their royal estate, the king was astonished. Ethelburga then seized the opportunity to warn him of the transitoriness of earthly things, "And woe to those who are attached to them, for they shall be carried away by the current. Reflect, I entreat you, how wretchedly will these bodies decay, which are now pampered with luxury."[97]

The role of Queen Ethelburga is also evident in a charter of 725 in which Ine granted land to Glastonbury "with his wife Ethelburga."[98] Moreover, Ethelburga's influence can be seen in Ine's decision to abdicate the throne (after having ruled for thirty-seven years), and make a pilgrimage to Rome. According to William of Malmesbury, "Nor did his queen, the author of this noble deed, desert him, but as she had before incited him to undertake it, so, afterwards, she made it her constant care to soothe his sorrows by her conversation, to stimulate him when wavering by her example; in short, to omit nothing that could be conducive to his salvation. Thus united in mutual affection, in due time they trod the common path of mankind. This was attended, as we have heard, with singular miracles, such as God often deigns to bestow on the virtues of happy couples."[99]

Other Anglo-Saxon queens and princesses continued to use their political influence and connections to support the various interests of the Church, and in several cases they became the special lobbyists for the Roman cause. The case of the queen-saint Eanfled (d. ca. 704)

is pertinent to this tradition. After her marriage to Oswiu of
Northumbria, Eanfled continued to follow Roman practices and
brought with her to the north her own personal priest from Kent.
Thus the outcome of the Synod of Whitby (663/664), in which the Roman party was ultimately victorious over the Celtic faction, perhaps is
indicative of the queen's political power and influence over her husband.[100] We also learn that shortly after this Roman victory at
Whitby, Eanfled received from Pope Vitalian praise for her pious zeal
and good deeds, as well as a gift of a cross fashioned out of the chains
of Sts. Peter and Paul and a golden key.[101]

A similar involvement on behalf of the Church of Rome can be
noted in the strategic role adopted by Queen Margaret of Scotland
in her attempts at ammending the king's conduct and reforming the
Scottish Church. According to the *Anglo-Saxon Chronicle* Margaret
was predestined to assume a major part in the proselytization of King
Malcolm and the Scots. An entry for the year 1067 notes: ". . . for she
was destined to increase the glory of God in that land, to turn the king
aside from the path of error, to incline him together with his people
towards a better way of life, and to abolish the vices which that nation
had indulged in in the past—all of which she subsequently accomplished."[102] And although the *Chronicle* relates that she had been
married to Malcolm against her will, the king thanked God who had
given him such a wife, and he "turned toward God, and despised
every kind of impurity. As Paul the apostle, the teacher of all nations said, *Saluabitur vir infidelis per mulierem fidelem. Sic et mulier
infidelis per virum fidelem, et r[e]l[iqua]*, which in our language
means: 'Very often an unbeliever is sanctified and saved by a righteous
woman; and in like manner, a woman by a devout husband, etc.' This
aforesaid queen performed many useful works in that land to the
glory of God, and proved of great advantage to the monarchy, as was
to be expected from her ancestry."[103] Similarly Turgot, in his *vita* of
the queen, relates how she worked to reform the Scots by converting
the "defenders of perverted custom," abolishing their aberrant practices and bringing them into line with the Roman customs. Thus
through initiating many councils, "she laboured to eradicate wholly
the illegalities that had sprung up in [the Church]."[104] (See also chapter 2.) In addition, Margaret cultivated a friendship with the reformer
Lanfranc, archbishop of Canterbury, who, in response to the queen's
request sent her Godwine and two brothers from Canterbury to assist
her in her work in Scotland.[105] The evidence thus points to a very
strong role assumed by Margaret and these other early queen-saints in
the area of proselytization and reform.

OTHER CASES OF FEMALE SANCTITY
AND PROSELYTIZATION

Although they lived outside of the geographic limits of this study, there are a number of other prominent princesses and queens, who, following in the tradition of Sts. Helena, Clotilda, Bertha, Ethelberga, and others, won recognition for their early espousal of the new faith and their impressive roles in conversion. A few of these cases should be at least briefly mentioned in this survey because they suggest the widespread significance of this pattern of domestic proselytization.

The conversion of the kingdom of Bohemia, for example, can be traced to a large extent to the influence of a royal woman. St. Ludmilla was converted in about the year 879 along with her husband Boriwoi by the missionary saint Methodius. She played a primary role as protector of the new faith in Bohemia and exercised a strong influence over her grandson, Wenceslaus. Both Ludmilla and Wenceslaus were murdered and came to be recognized as martyrs and patron saints of Bohemia.[106]

The early conversion of Poland was also attributed to a royal woman, the Christian princess Dubrawa, who was married to the pagan king Miecislas. Dubrawa has been singled out for her major role in the conversion of her husband along with his people in the year 965.[107]

The activities of St. Olga (d. 969) have been described in some detail in the sources of the period, and she has been recognized for exerting an especially important influence on the early Christianization of Russia. It appears that at this time in the capital of Kiev, Christianity had already won over many new converts.[108] Thus a number of scholars believe that St. Olga was received into the Christian church in Kiev as early as 954/55 and was baptized by the priest Gregory, who then accompanied her to Constantinople. Other scholars follow the tradition recorded in the *Primary Chronicle* (compiled between ca. 1040 and 1118), which contends that Olga was formally baptized in Constantinople.[109] According to the *Chronicle,* during Olga's visit to Constantinople (in 957) she met the emperor, who found her "fair of countenance and wise as well" and "worthy to reign with him in his city." However, on hearing these words, Olga replied that "she was still a pagan, and that if he desired to baptize her, he should perform this function himself; otherwise, she was unwilling to accept baptism. The Emperor, with the assistance of the Patriarch, accordingly baptized her." After her baptism the patriarch instructed her in the faith and praised her: "Blessed art thou among the women of Rus', for thou hast loved the light, and quit the darkness. The sons of Rus' shall bless thee to the last generation of thy descendants." The *Chronicle* also notes that "at her baptism she was christened Helena, after the ancient Empress, mother of Constantine the Great." (Here again we see this important linkage between the saintly model Helena, the proselytizer/mother, and a later exemplum.) It appears that after her baptism, the emperor declared his wish to marry the Russian princess. Here Olga outwitted the emperor, for she was able to put her new faith immediately to work in reminding him of the restriction found in canon law that forbade a godfather to marry his godchild! This "technicality" therefore freed her from this unwanted marriage proposal.[110]

On her return to Kiev, Olga lived with her son, Svyatoslav. "She urged him to be baptized, but he would not listen to her suggestion, though when any man wished to be baptized, he was not hindered, but only mocked."[111] She continued to work on converting him to the new faith but met with little success. He responded to her exhortations, "How shall I alone accept another faith? My followers will laugh at that." His mother replied, "If you are converted, all your subjects will perforce follow your example."[112] But while Olga prayed day and night for her son and his people, Svyatoslav did not give up his pagan religion.

We also learn that after her visit to Constantinople, Olga asked the western emperor Otto I (ca. 959) to send a bishop to the capital city. Her messengers were well received at Otto's court and in response to her request, the emperor sent to her Bishop Adalbert, accompanied by a number of German priests.[113] In this we see Olga's involvement in another level of missionary activity as well as the attraction which the West held for the Russians.

The *Chronicle*'s entry for the year 969 tells of Olga's death and notes the fact that "Olga had given command not to hold a funeral feast for her, for she had a priest who performed the last rites over the sainted princess."[114] The chronicler then relates Olga's early espousal of the new faith. "Olga was the precursor of the Christian land, even as the day-spring precedes the sun and as the dawn precedes the day. For she shone like the moon by night, and she was radiant among the infidels like a pearl in the mire, since the people were soiled, and not yet purified of their sin by holy baptism. But she herself was cleansed by this sacred purification. . . . Thus we say to her, 'Rejoice in the Russes' knowledge of God,' for we were the first fruits of their reconciliation with him."[115]

"She was the first from Rus' to enter the Kingdom of God, and the sons of Rus' thus praise her as their leader, for since her death she has interceded with God in their behalf. . . . For all men glorify her, as they behold her lying there in the body for many years. . . . For he [the Lord] protected the sainted Olga from the devil, our adversary and our foe." [116]

Olga's baptism in the new faith and her personal pilgrimage to Constantinople would be very important in establishing Byzantine-Russian ties and in encouraging the missionary work of the Byzantine church in Russia. [117] While her son, Svyatoslav, fearing the ridicule of his followers, did not accept Christian baptism, he tolerated its presence in his kingdom and allowed the new faith to spread. It would then remain for Olga's grandson, Vladimir, to espouse the new faith and to begin the actual conversion of his people. Olga had however begun the process and was therefore given the title *ravnoapostolna* ("equal with the Apostles")—a title reserved for those saints who brought Christianity to their countries. [118]

The *Primary Chronicle* also describes in some detail Vladimir's conversion to Christianity. This account again underscores the important role which the wife, as part of a marriage-alliance/peace package, assumed in securing the ruler's acceptance of and baptism into the new faith. After having invaded the Byzantine-held land of the Crimea and taking over Cherson, Vladimir sent messengers to the emperors Basil and Constantine warning them that unless they gave him their sister for a wife, he would invade Constantinople. [119] The emperors responded that it was not proper for Christians to marry pagans; however, if he consented to be baptized, they would allow him to take their sister as his wife. Vladimir responded that he was willing to accept baptism in the new faith, as he had already given the issue some thought. [120]

Thus, when the emperors heard Vladimir's response, they rejoiced and persuaded their sister Anna to accept this marriage proposal. According to their arrangements, Vladimir was to receive baptism *before* they would send their sister to him for marriage. Vladimir, however, insisted that his baptism be delayed until the princess arrived in Russia—accompanied by her own priests—who would then baptize him. This was agreed upon, and Anna, with great reluctance, left Constantinople. Her brothers, however, reminded her of the great political and religious advantage attached to her mission: "Through your agency God turns the land of Rus' to repentance, and you will relieve Greece from the danger of grievous war. Do you not see how much harm the Russes have already brought upon the Greeks? If you do not set out, they may bring on us the same misfortunes." [121]

According to the *Chronicle*, when Anna arrived at Kherson, she found Vladimir suffering from a severe eye disease. The princess then told him that if he wanted to get rid of this disease, "he should be baptized with all speed, otherwise it could not be cured." On hearing her message, Vladimir responded: "If this proves true, then of a surety is the God of the Christians great," and he gave an order that he should be baptized. He was then baptized by the bishop of Kherson and Anna's priests; immediately afterwards, we are told, he was cured and received his sight. Many of his followers, witnessing this miracle, also accepted baptism. After his baptism, Vladimir married the princess Anna, and for her wedding gift he returned Kherson to the Greeks.[122] Moreover, according to tradition, for his new wife's sake he dismissed his five wives and eight hundred concubines! (As Dvornik has noted, this incident serves "to demonstrate what a miraculous transformation holy baptism could make in a pagan soul.")[123]

Vladimir then turned his attention to his new religion: he founded a church and set up statues in Kherson; in Kiev he had idols publicly "humiliated" and destroyed. He ordered that all of his people accept baptism in a mass ceremony in the Dnieper River. Vladimir founded churches, assigned priests, and invited "the people to accept baptism in all the cities and towns." It is interesting to note that according to the *Chronicle*, Vladimir was seen as "the new Constantine of mighty Rome, who baptized himself and his subjects; for the Prince of Rus' imitated the acts of Constantine himself."[124]

Thus we see in this account another important and especially well-documented case in this pattern of queens serving as brokers of the new faith. For through her marriage to Vladimir, Anna assisted in hastening the conversion of the Russ to Christianity. It is also important to note that in the deliberations of whether to accept the Greek faith, the Russ used historical precedent as one of their arguments: that is, the fact that this tradition had been adopted by Vladimir's grandmother, Olga, "who was wiser than all other men."[125] In addition, Anna no doubt played an important role in furthering the development of Byzantine-Russian ties. Moreover, it is interesting to note that Anna's cousin, the empress Theophano, widow of Otto II, sent an embassy from Rome to Anna and Vladimir. She had them bring, especially for Anna, a number of saints' relics along with a few words of consolation.[126] Anna died ca. 1011 and was recognized as a popular saint among the Russ.[127]

In this same tradition, the queen of Hungary won recognition for the important role she played as an instrument of conversion. In the second half of the tenth century, King Geysa (Geza) and his wife, Sarloth, were baptized in the Christian faith. According to one of the accounts, while her husband remained a nominal Christian, Sarloth, struck by the mysteries of the new faith, became a fervent believer. She attempted to follow a life of Christian perfection with a fervor worthy of the saints. During her pregnancy she was said to have had a vision in which St. Stephen assured her that the infant she carried would complete the work that she and her husband had begun, namely, that he would rid the country of paganism and convert their people to Christianity. Subsequently, the child received at baptism the name of Stephen.[128]

Later, King Stephen and his wife, Gisela (sister of Henry, duke of Bavaria, the emperor-saint Henry II), would actually implement the conversion of Hungary. Vincent of Beauvais, in his *Speculum Historiale*, relates that in the early eleventh century the Hungarians were converted to Christianity through the efforts of a woman. He tells us that these people, who were given over to idolatry, were converted to the faith by Gisela, sister of the emperor, who had married the king of Hungary. And it was through her perseverance that she led the king and all of the people of Hungary to desire to be baptized in the new faith.[129]

In this rather impressive catalogue of early women, beginning with St. Helena or St. Clotilda, we see the major role these royal princesses and queens assumed in the introduction of Christianity. From the beginning, they were valued by the Church as special emissaries, strategic agents in this movement. Chroniclers, hagiographers, popes, and other churchmen of the period frequently acknowledged their contributions in providing the much needed openings for the expansion of Catholicism and described in some detail their personal involvement in the missionary activity.

MOTHERS OF SAINTS AS PROSELYTIZERS

One of the striking patterns which emerges from a general study of the early *vitae*, and one which parallels that of queens as domestic proselytizers, is the role of saints' mothers as principal converters of their families. The fathers, in contrast, are frequently shown as pagan—either ultimately converted by their wives, or remaining obstinate in their old religion and attempting to hinder the process of conversion within the family. In a few cases, these mothers of saints would themselves win recognition of sainthood through their successful role in domestic proselytization.

A famous early example in this tradition is that of St. Monica and Patricius, the parents of St. Augustine. In his *Confessions* Augustine discusses his delayed baptism and notes: "Even at that age I already believed in you, and so did my mother and the whole household *except for my father.* But, in my heart, he did not gain the better of my mother's piety and prevent me from believing in Christ just because he still disbelieved himself. For she did all that she could to see that you, my God, should be a Father to me rather than he."[130]

A number of Lives of saints also provide indirect information relating to domestic conversion among the nobility. According to tradition, the sixth-century saints Medard (bishop of Noyon) and Godard/Gildard (archbishop of Rouen) were the twin sons of the pagan nobleman, Nectard, and his Catholic Gallo-Roman wife, Protagie. (Appropriately enough, "Protagie"—following the Greek etymology—means "first saint.")[131] We learn that one of the first results of this marriage was Nectard's conversion to Catholicism. Apparently unable to resist the powerful arguments of Protagie, Nectard was made to renounce the cult of idols and to worship the sovereign God of Christianity. And it is, then, in this context that St. Paul's formula is again cited: "Salvabitur vir infidelis per mulierem fidelem." ("For the unbelieving man will be saved through his believing wife.")[132]

The ninth-century confessor saint Rupert (diocese of Mainz) was also born of parents of a "mixed marriage." His mother, Bertha, was a Catholic princess from the Lorraine and was married to a pagan duke named Robolaus. Rupert was only three years old when his father was killed in combat fighting against a Christian army. Bertha spent the remainder of her life devoted to the education of her son and charitable works.[133] One can find many more examples among the saints' Lives of mothers successfully converting their children to Christianity.[134] (See also chapter 5.)

WOMEN AS CONVERTERS IN PIERRE DUBOIS'S *RECOVERY OF THE HOLY LAND*

Continued recognition of the strategic role that women might play as domestic brokers or emissaries for the Church can be found in a fascinating tract, *De recuperatione terrae sanctae* (Recovery of the Holy Land), written by Pierre Dubois in 1309.[135]

In this work, Dubois outlines an interesting utopian scheme for the education of a select group of young women and men. The purpose of this intensive training program was to produce students who would be competent to work as missionaries in the Orient, who would then be able to successfully occupy or control the Holy Land.[136] According to this plan, girls were to receive instruction in "medicine and surgery with other subjects prerequisite to these." Dubois explains: "These girls, thus trained and knowing how to write, namely the noble and other more prudent ones, suited in body and form, will be adopted as daughters and granddaughters of the greater chiefs of these regions, the Holy Land and others near it, so that they may conveniently be given as wives to the greater princes, clergy and other wealthy Orientals." [137] He notes that "it will be expedient that those girls whom it is intended to marry with those who do not hold the articles of our faith as the Roman church holds, teaches, and observes, be taught to carry with them briefly and plainly written all the articles so that they may understand them sufficiently." [138] Dubois also comments that it would be advantageous if the eastern prelates and clergy, who still insisted on being married, had learned wives who believed in the Roman Catholic sacraments so that they could properly influence their husbands and children in the faith.[139] These women would then procure many girls from this educational foundation "to marry their sons and other great men of the county; they also would have chaplains celebrating and chanting by the Roman ritual, and gradually would draw the inhabitants of those places to the Roman ritual." [140]

Dubois then notes the special attraction these women missionaries would have for pagan women "whom they helped by their practice of medicine and surgery, especially in their secret infirmities and needs. It could hardly help but be the case that they, nobler and richer than other matrons and everywhere having knowledge of medicine and surgery and experimental science would attract matrons who required their counsels, who admired their prudence and proficiency, and who loved them on these accounts—would attract these strongly to communicating with them, delighting and agreeing in the same articles of faith and sacraments." [141]

Thus, in his tract Dubois acknowledges the particular importance of women, who, through marriage to the "unconverted," would gradually win these great men of the East over to Catholicism. He emphasizes the primary need of education for these women missionaries: they were to know the tenets of the faith as well as have knowledge of medicine, which would help them to win new converts to the faith. He stresses the special attraction that these female missionaries—through their medical assistance—would exercise over non-Christian women in the Holy Land. Although apparently never implemented, the ideas put forth in this utopian work are intriguing and follow in the tradition that sees women as emissaries of the Catholic Church and appreciates their special role as domestic proselytizers.[142]

Looking, then, at these various sources, we can see the impressive role that women were expected to play, or actually assumed, in the area of domestic proselytization. During the period of transition from paganism to Christianity women were encouraged to use their special influence to bring about the baptism/conversion of their husbands and children to Christianity. It was within the approved context of the family and household—this admixture of the private and public—that these women were to set about their proselytizing mission.

The new faith obviously held a special attraction for these early medieval women. Unfortunately, our sources do not provide us with any detail, similar to that relating to their husbands, on the complex of reasons or motivations behind their original espousal of the new faith. Although in pursuing their missionary work they suffered certain gender-based liabilities—for example, they were denied entry into the priesthood and thus were unable to baptize their new converts, and they were officially unable to preach in public—still they were allowed and encouraged to assume initiatory roles in the conversion of Europe.[143]

The impressive early medieval "chain of queens,"[144] beginning with Saint Clotilda, vividly shows the primary roles these women assumed as domestic proselytizers. However, while the sources of the time provide us with details of the conversionary tactics utilized by these Catholic queens and the necessary perseverance required before they ultimately achieved their "goals," the actual "conversion" of the king is often described in "miraculous" or epic terms, occurring in a single momentous event—e.g., a battle, or a particular vision, and thus outside of the queen's purview. The king's conversion is also shown as a very deliberate, carefully considered or calculated, "rational" act, often carried out in concurrence with his male advisers. The exchanging of his pagan gods for Christ occurred only after a long period of internal struggle and self-conscious deliberation, only after he became convinced of the impotence of his old gods and the superiority of the new faith. Thus this all-important act of delayed conversion, rather than being attributed directly to the queen's public or political power, or to her "private/informal" influence or conjugal/"female" arguments, is described instead within a more cosmic and perhaps more "impressive" public context, that of the miraculous; or it is seen as the result of (male) episcopal, papal, or institutional influence. And although some of the sources throughout the Middle Ages continued to acknowledge and emphasize the crucial role these women played in early proselytization, frequently in later histories this part of the historical or hagiographical memory unfortunately became dimmed or forgotten. In the reshaping of these events, or in "abridged" versions, these conversions came to be seen as the result of exclusively masculine or institutional influences. Nevertheless, for the medieval world, many of these enterprising women were clearly singled out and appreciated by the Church and society for their roles as key agents in the vanguard of the early missionary movement: and for their notable successes, a few won recognition of sainthood. As Christine de Pizan has rather astutely argued in her *Book of the City of Ladies,* with regard to St. Clotilda's successful role as proselytizer, "What greater good could have been accomplished than what she did?" [145]

Woe to those that are with child and that give suck.

Matt. 24:19, Mark 13:17

Yet woman will be saved through bearing children, if she continues in faith and love and holiness with modesty.

Paul, 1 Timothy 2:15

As long as woman is for birth and children, she is different from man as body is from soul. But when she wishes to serve Christ more than the world, then she will cease to be a woman and will be called man.

Jerome, *Commentary on the Epistle to the Ephesians,* Lib. III, cap. V, no. 658, PL 26:533

For a mother is a venerable treasure, a mother is a goodly treasure, the mother of saints and bishops and righteous men, an increase of the kingdom of Heaven, a propagation on earth.

Cáin Adamnáin (The Law of Adamnan) trans. K. Meyer, no. 4, p. 5

"Golden Wombs": Motherhood and Sanctity

Motherhood seemed to hold a special fascination for the hagiographers of this period. As biological and spiritual sons and daughters, the medieval authors of sacred biographies appear to have been rather well-informed on many aspects of this topic. They provide us with idealized or stereotypic depictions of saintly mothers as well as intriguing incidental details concerning motherhood which are not found in any of the other sources of the period. This chapter will survey a number of aspects of motherhood as presented in the *vitae*. It will focus on women saints who were "also mothers"—women who were remembered for their roles as biological mothers but whose major claim to sainthood was perhaps based on "second careers" in monasticism as "spiritual mothers"; mothers of saints who won recognition of sanctity through their influential roles as mothers or through the fame of their children; and mothers who are mentioned in the *vitae* but are not recognized by any local or official cult, as well as surrogate mothers. This chapter will also explore a variety of other topics treated by the hagiographers including pregnancy, childbirth, naming of infants, care and nursing of infants, preference for male offspring, abortion, infanticide, abandonment, mortality of children, and "good" and "bad" mothers.

THEORIES OF MOTHERHOOD

Over time the Church has had a great deal to say about motherhood. Beginning with the Old and New Testaments, and followed by the Church Fathers and monastic writers, we have been provided with a wide spectrum of frequently ambivalent and contradictory opinions and beliefs regarding motherhood. These early writers furnished a mixed tradition in regard to the value and role of motherhood: it was regarded as a "sacred calling," beneficial and empowering for women; at the same time, in comparison to virginity, it was seen as a definite compromise, and as such it was physically and spiritually harmful. It was viewed as an unnecessary encumbrance or frustration which thwarted women's dedication to a life of spiritual perfection.[1]

Against a background of eschatological fear and expectation, a number of the early Church Fathers wrote disparagingly of motherhood. In their extravagant praise of virginity, many of these writers perhaps unintentionally discredited or condemned motherhood. A few of the early Church Fathers went so far as to single out and warn pregnant women, and those who had given birth, of their essential spiritual ineligibility for a coveted spot in the celestial gynaeceum. Tertullian, for example, in his preoccupation with personal salvation and the imminent end of the world, underscored the burdensomeness of having children and the danger they constituted to the faith. He asked, "Why did our Lord prophesy, Woe to those that are with child and that give suck, if he did not mean that on the day of our great exodus children will be a handicap to those who bear them?"[2] He condemned the irresponsible behavior of those who married and continued to have children right up to the end of time; especially those with "swollen breasts, nauseating wombs and whimpering infants."[3] According to Tertullian, women who had given birth had the unwelcome distinction of being denied entry into the kingdom of heaven. He contended that it would be only the childless, the widows, those with "none of the heaving baggage of marriage in their wombs or at their breasts" who would be able to serve Christ at his Second Coming.[4]

Similarly the Rule of Leander of Seville, in praising virginity, recalled the ultimate burdens of marriage and motherhood. Leander noted that "A virgin may marry, but she who does not is numbered among the angels. 'For at the resurrection they shall neither marry nor be given in marriage, but shall be as angels of God.' . . . One may, indeed, bear sons, but those who have scorned such necessities hear Christ saying: 'Blessed are the barren that never bore, and breasts that never nursed.' On the other hand, there it is said to married women: 'Woe to those that are with child, and nurse in those days.'" In comparing the states of virginity and marriage, Leander warned, that "a nun preserves the integrity of the virginity with which she was born, a married woman is corrupted by giving birth." And in the tradition of the Church Fathers, he admitted that God instituted marriage, "but it was in order that virginity might spring therefrom, that by increasing the number of virgins, married women might gain in offspring what they had lost in marriage."[5]

Caesarius of Arles also noted the spiritual rewards which would accrue to those who remained childless: "No one should be sad or grieve over his lack of children when he sees so many priests, monks, or religious persevere in God's service to the end of their lives without

earthly children. They will receive a greater crown and more glory because they have willed to be physically barren. . . . Those who practice
physical sterility should observe fruitfulness in souls, and those who
cannot have earthly sons should endeavor to beget spiritual ones."[6]

The writings of St. Jerome are particularly rich in regard to his
perceptions of motherhood. In his emphasis on virginity, he stressed
the need for women to reject their corporeal shackles, their female
reproductive nature, and in this context we find his infamous admonition: "As long as woman is for birth and children, she is different from
man as body is from soul. But when she wishes to serve Christ more
than the world, then she will cease to be a woman and will be called
man."[7] In a number of his didactic works Jerome disparaged pregnancy and motherhood. Following in the eschatological tradition of
Tertullian, he, too, cited the biblical warning: "Woe to those who are
with child, or have infants at the breast on that day."[8] Moreover he
described in some detail the various "humiliations of nature, a womb
teeming for nine months, nauseation, the birth of the child, blood,
swaddling clothes . . . the rough crib, the wailing of the infant." He
asked, why would anyone want "prattling infants," "brats . . . crawl-
ing upon his breast and soiling his neck with nastiness."[9] Or, in further elaborating upon what he perceived to be some of the more
annoying or disgusting aspects of motherhood, he wrote: "She carried
you long, and she nursed you for many months; her gentle love bore
with the peevish ways of your infancy. She washed your soiled napkins
[diapers] and often dirtied her hands with their nastiness. She sat
by your bed when you were ill and was patient with your sickness,
even as she had before endured the sickness of maternity which you
caused."[10]

Jerome also condoned or even praised the abandonment of children
and the distractions of family life by holy women in order to dedicate
themselves to a "higher purpose"—a life of spiritual perfection. In his
celebrated letter to console Eustochium on the death of her mother,
Paula, Jerome recounts in some detail this "model" mother's dramatic
abandonment of her children and her departure from Rome for the
deserts of Egypt. He notes that "disregarding her house, her children,
her servants, her property, and in a word everything connected with
the world" she was eager to go on her own "alone and unaccompa-
nied" to the desert. When the winter was over and the sea open,

> she went down to Portus accompanied by her brother, her kins-
> folk and above all her own children eager by their demonstra-
> tions of affection to overcome their loving mother. At last the
> sails were set and the strokes of the rowers carried the vessel

into the deep. On the shore the little Toxotius [her son]
stretched forth his hands in entreaty, while Rufina [her daugh-
ter], now grown up, with silent sobs besought her mother to
wait till she should be married. But still Paula's eyes were dry
as she turned them heavenwards; and *she overcame her love for*
her children by her love for God. She knew herself no more as
a mother, that she might approve herself a handmaid of Christ.
Yet her heart was rent within her, and she wrestled with her
grief, as though she were being forcibly separated from parts
of herself. The greatness of the affection she had to overcome
made all admire her victory the more. Among the cruel hardships which attend prisoners of war in the hands of their enemies, there is none severer than the separation of parents from
their children. Though it is against the laws of nature, she
endured this trial with unabated faith; nay more she sought
it with a joyful heart: and overcoming her love for her children
by her greater love for God, she concentrated herself quietly
upon Eustochium alone, the partner alike of her vows and
of her voyage. Meantime the vessel ploughed onwards and all
her fellow-passengers looked back to the shore. But she turned
away her eyes that she might not see what she could not behold
without agony. No mother, it must be confessed, ever loved
her children so dearly. Before setting out she gave them all that
she had, disinheriting herself upon earth that she might find
an inheritance in heaven.[11]

Therefore, Paula, acting "against the laws of nature," acting in a manner "forgetful of her sex," denied motherhood: "she no longer knew
the mother" (*nesciebat matrem, ut Christi probaret ancillam*) and for
a "greater love" she became a servant of Christ. In choosing to abandon her children, Paula was portrayed as simply following Christ's
counsel: "Whoever loves father or mother more than me is not worthy
of me; and whoever loves son or daughter more than me is not worthy
of me; and whoever does not take up the cross and follow me is not
worthy of me" (Matthew 10:37–38). This single-minded dedication
to the religious life—at the expense of renouncing maternal obligations—thus won praise from St. Jerome and would become a religious
role model for mothers (new Paulas) in the following centuries.

In addition to the spiritual liabilities of motherhood, early medieval writers also stressed the immediate, "this-worldly" horrors—the
physical dangers and the very real hardships and disappointments
of motherhood. In Fortunatus's poem, *De virginitate,* addressed to
Agnes, abbess of the Monastery of Ste-Croix at Poitiers, we find a

careful and extraordinarily moving description of the immense pain and grief associated with childbirth. "Happy Virgin! . . . She does not weigh down sluggish limbs with an imprisoned embryo; she is not depressed and worn out by its awkward weight. . . . When the belly swells from its wound and sensual dropsy grows, the woman's exhausted health hangs by a hair. The raised skin is so distent and misshapen that even though the mother may be happy with her burden, she becomes ashamed. . . . How describe the tears shed at the moment when the muscles relax to release the prisoner and procure relief for the viscera? A way is forced violently through the passage and a being, perhaps lifeless, brought to life. The mother painfully turns her dull glance toward him. What does she see? An infant stretched motionless . . . So that she no longer deserves to be called either mother or virgin." [12] Although Fortunatus's intention in this work was to extol or promote the virginal life, he provides a very realistic depiction of the grief and tragedy which frequently attended childbirth.

Similarly Leander of Seville noted in his Rule for nuns the misfortunes of marriage: "The first dangers of marriage are these: the corruption of the flesh, the disgust caused by the corruption, the weight of the womb when pregnant, the pangs of birth that often bring one to the threshold of death, wherein both the function and the fruit of marriage perish, as the mother and her offspring are both lost and all that nuptial pomp is brought to naught by the finality of death." [13]

Another aspect of the Church's theory and policy toward female sexuality and motherhood can be seen in its fear of the pollution of menstrual blood and of the unclean blood associated with childbirth, as well as its discriminatory burial policies and practices.[14] As medieval women approached childbirth, they were encouraged by the Church to take communion, both for their own spiritual welfare— since there was a high incidence of death in childbirth—and because of the policy that from the time of their labor to their "churching," or required purification, they "would bear the double stigma of unclean blood and the "filth of sin" (*sordes peccati*) without the consolations of the church." [15]

Fear of female pollution associated with motherhood was also reflected in the burial policies of the period. It was apparently common practice to refuse to allow the bodies of women who had died in childbirth a funeral procession or entry into the church. This policy was based on the fear that the pavement of the church would be polluted by the women's blood.[16] Special cemeteries were designated for exiles and women who died in childbirth; infants were buried in yet another cemetery. Other arrangements specified that pregnant corpses be buried outside of the consecrated churchyard.[17]

In contrast to these general theories of the Church which disparaged motherhood, stressing its various spiritual and physical liabilities, another popular current—a tradition which praised and idealized
motherhood—can also be found among the ecclesiastical writers of
the period. Thus, in the writings of some of these same Church Fathers
we can also find "positive" statements about mothers and motherhood. St. Jerome, for example, cites St. Paul's famous maxim: "Yet
woman will be saved through bearing children, if she continues in
faith and love and holiness with modesty." [18] Among his personal
acquaintances Jerome showed respect and admiration for a number of
noblewomen who were mothers. In one of his letters, for example, he
praised the mother of his friends as their "close associate in holy life,"/
"companion in the practice of sanctity." He then provided this wonderful description of her celebrated motherhood: "but she has one advantage over you in that she is the mother of such sons as yourselves.
Truly *her womb may be called golden.*" [19]

While the patristic and Merovingian writers in general stressed the
perfection of virginity over the state of marriage and motherhood,
beginning in the ninth century with the Carolingian period we can
find several ecclesiastical works which celebrate women for their roles
as wife and mother. As noted by Suzanne Wemple, Haimo of Auxerre
contended that married women pleased God as much as those who
remained permanently chaste, for by bearing children and educating
them in faith and religion, women were leading a good life and carrying out the work of God. [20] Also in this tradition is a sequence written
by the court poet Notker (ninth century) which was intended to be
sung on the feasts of holy women. In this work Notker recognized a
broadened base of female sanctity, for in addition to praising virgins,
widows, and even reformed prostitutes, he also included mothers. He
noted specifically: "And married women now bearing sons who please
God . . . Women who spur on their sons bravely to conquer all your
tortures." [21]

A similar appreciation and praise for mothers and motherhood
can be found in the ninth-century Irish Law of Adomnan/Adamnan.
Here the seventh-century abbot-saint Adomnan was said to have freed
women/mothers from bondage and advocated their special protection
for the sake of his own mother and for Mary, the mother of Christ.
The special value he placed upon mothers and motherhood is described in the Law of Adomnan: "For a mother is a venerable treasure,
a mother is a goodly treasure, the mother of saints and bishops and
righteous men, an increase of the kingdom of Heaven, a propagation
on earth." [22]

Moreover, it is during this same period that the cult of the Virgin gained prominence: the figure of the Virgin Mary as mother became increasingly popular and contributed to the idealization of motherhood.[23] A growing devotion to the Virgin can be found in Carolingian, Anglo-Saxon and Irish society. Marian feasts, offices and prayers to the Virgin multiplied; details of the Virgin's life proliferated. A wealth of images of the Virgin as mother were captured in the art works and literature of the period. Ivory carvings, reliefs in stone and wood, altar frontals, manuscript illuminations, textiles, etc., depicted the virgin mother seated in majesty with the Christ child on her lap. Also dating to this period can be found a number of early images of the *virgo lactans* or the Virgin nursing Christ.[24] Furthermore, already in the Carolingian period the Virgin was particularly venerated at Chartres. The famous Virgin's tunic, said to have been worn at the moment of the annunciation when the Word was conceived, was sent by the Byzantine emperor to Charlemagne. Charlemagne placed this precious relic in the church of his palace of Aix-la-Chapelle. In 876 the tunic was transferred to Chartres by Charles the Bald. With this holy relic in its possession, the cathedral of Notre-Dame of Chartres became the major center of the cult of the Virgin in the North of France.[25]

As Mary Clayton has convincingly argued in her work *The Cult of the Virgin Mary in Anglo-Saxon England,* this cult was also well developed in pre-Conquest England. Although Carolingian influence was important for the Anglo-Saxon cult, evidence of its popularity can be found as early as the late seventh through first decades of the ninth century in Anglia, Northumbria, and Mercia. Promoted by the monastic reform movement, the cult of the Virgin also flourished during the second half of the tenth through the eleventh century in the south of England. Moreover, a number of Anglo-Saxon authors, including Aldhelm and Bede, focused on the Virgin Mary in their writings. Many Anglo-Saxon churches and especially female monasteries were dedicated to the Virgin; in addition, a number of her alleged relics, including fragments of her sepulchre, as well as her clothing, hair, milk, etc., were venerated in their churches during this early period.[26]

Also, beginning with the Carolingian era, and corresponding to the development of the cult of the Virgin, we can note a growing idealization of motherhood—a pattern in maternal values—in the Lives of saints. While comparatively few women were elevated to sainthood during this period, a number of those who were, were mothers. While the *vitae* still promoted the preferred status of virginity, followed by that of chaste widowhood and chaste spiritual marriage,[27] they now also stressed the dignity of marriage and motherhood. In some of these Lives the young women are described as clearly preferring the virginal life; nevertheless, they found it necessary to acquiesce to their parents' wishes for them to marry. This was viewed as an act of Christian obedience, resignation, and charity. Also a number of the *vitae* note that it was God who singled these women out for a maternal role and that it was then only through divine selection and inspiration that they became mothers.

In surveying the general formation of mental attitudes and values during this period, it should also be noted that in the pagan Germanic world there was clearly a considerable respect for motherhood and the family.[28] Among the Germanic peoples the family was highly valued, and there was a practical appreciation of women, particularly in their childbearing years. This "pro-motherhood" value system is reflected, for example, in the Germanic law codes, which attempted to protect women and especially to deter violent acts against them and their future offspring. Therefore, we find in these early law codes rather extraordinary provisions in the form of extremely favorable wergelds or reparations exacted for killing or causing physical harm to women. The Salic code, for example, stipulated triple wergeld during a woman's childbearing years—that is, it required a penalty three times that exacted for harming or killing a male of her same free status; during pregnancy, the woman's wergeld was four times that of a man.[29] As David Herlihy has argued, this high valuation of women in the Germanic period seems to reflect a very real demographic imbalance in which there was a scarcity of women; thus the special need to protect this invaluable resource.[30]

It is, then, fascinating to contrast the practical Germanic value system, in which women of childbearing age and during pregnancy received the highest value (as reflected in the wergeld), with the soteriologically based value system established by the Church Fathers, where the biologically infertile/spiritually fecund—namely virgins and chaste widows—were allotted the highest measures (fruits of a hundredfold and sixtyfold). However, in the making of popular saints during this period, a synthesis of the Christian and Germanic value systems and modes of social perception seems to have occurred. And while the status of virginity still retained the highest value and praise, many of the prominent patrons, founders of monasteries, and abbesses of the early medieval church were, in fact, mothers. Motherhood was therefore accorded a certain worth and dignity by the Church and society, as evidenced by the attention paid to motherhood in the *vitae* and the selection of these women as saints.

Si ignoras te o pulchra int[er]
mulieres, egredere y abi p[er]
uestigia gregum tuar[um] & pasce
hedos tuos. Qui h[a]ec ut c[on]loq[ui]
tur. Quo habet h[a]ec infelix p[er]
gredi uel qui sunt hedi. Vir-
ginem sua[m] sponsa[m] et[er]nis deo
sponsa[m] dicatam sp[iritu]s s[an]c[tu]s alloq[ui]t[ur]
que int[er] mulieres pulchra p[re]
bet. quia pudicicie sig[n]aculo p[re]
ceus exornat. T Quid hortat[ur]
P Ut donu[m] quod divina[m] aci
p[er] agnoscat. & quia sit p[ro]fessa
milicia[m] intelligat. Milicia e[st]
uita hominis sup[er] terram. Qui
amat inquit d[omi]n[u]s patrem a
matre[m] sup[er] me non e[st] me dig[nus].
& qui non accipit cruce[m] & s[e]-
quit[ur] me n[on] e[st] me dignus. It[em]
xp[istu]s passus est p[ro] nobis ex[em]pl[um]
p[re]figendo ut sequa[m] uestig[ia]
eius. Virgo xp[ist]i que h[a]ec igno-
rat. & quid sue p[ro]fessioni con-
uenia[t] aut dissimulat aut no[n]
curat. que int[er] ad sufferent[es]
temptationu[m] non p[ro] p[ar]t[e] sicu[t]
s[cri]ptu[m] est. fili accedens ad s[er]
uitute[m] d[e]i sta in timore & p[re]p[ara]
anima[m] tua[m] ad temptatione[m]
egredit[ur] a sponsi sui familiaritate que eius passioni uolu[n]-
tarie noluit p[ar]ticipare. Qui
enim d[omi]no suo pugnante fuga l[a]-
b[itur]. quo amore caluerit int[er]
ignauia testat[ur]. Quid ig[itur] restat

13. THE LADDER OF VIRTUE, *SPECULUM VIRGINUM*

This lively mid-twelfth-century representation of a popular iconographic
theme, "the Mirror of the Virgin," portrays the testing of seven heroic
virgins, who are shown scaling the ladder of virtue and seeking eternal
rewards from Christ. They are depicted fighting off the dragon of
wickedness or monster of hell with their spears topped with crucifixes,
and escaping from the violence of a fierce pagan (shown as an Ethiopian
with swords). One of the virgins pulls the pagan's hair and stomps on his
shoulder. This iconography is also associated with St. Perpetua's dreams
of facing the ordeal of the ladder and defeating the Ethiopian, as well as
Christ's victory over the Ethiopian and the dragon in the harrowing of
hell. (See Dronke, *The Medieval Lyric*, pp. 41–44.) MS Arundel 44,
fol. 93v. By permission of the British Library.

14. The Baptism of Clovis

This fine tenth-century French ivory book cover is thought to be the earliest representation of a popular iconographic theme. Divided into three registers, it portrays episodes from the Life of St. Remi. The bottom register focuses on the ceremony of the baptism of Clovis. Situated within the abbreviated architectural framework of a church and surrounded by churchmen, the bearded king is portrayed naked from the waist up in a close-fitting baptismal font. Above Clovis's head is shown the dove carrying the holy ampulla in its beak. Situated on the far left is a prominently crowned (but not haloed) female figure who can be recognized as Queen Clotilda. Courtesy of the Musée de Picardie, Amiens. Giraudon/Art Resource, NY.

15. St. Notburga with Her Nonaplets

This lovely fifteenth-century gothic carving in wood depicts the popular
St. Notburga with her iconographic attributes—her nonaplets. Notburga
is shown here as a serene young mother holding on her lap, within the
deep folds of her gown, her carefully arranged miniature children.
Although the depictions of the children are abbreviated, each appears as
a unique individual with a distinct expression and different hairstyle.
Schwaben, ca. 1420. Photo by Mireille Madou.

16. Sts. Benedict and Scholastica

In this eleventh-century miniature, the saintly siblings Benedict and Scholastica are shown seated across from each other at a table. In response to her brother's refusal to stay the night and talk with her, Scholastica is portrayed deep in prayer with her folded hands placed on the table and her head resting on them. Benedict expresses his surprise at the miracle of the storm, which was performed in answer to Scholastica's prayers and kept Benedict from leaving—thus causing him to disobey his own rule. At the right, St. Benedict is shown looking up toward the sky, where he witnesses his sister's soul (represented as a dove) entering heaven. MS Vat. lat. 1202, fol. 72v. Foto Biblioteca Vaticana.

Soror mea Floren
tina accipe codicem
Quem tibi compo
sui feliciter
amen

17. St. Isidore Presenting His Book to His Sister Florentine

An example of the special affection expressed between saintly siblings is captured in this illustration (ca. 800), which depicts Florentine with her younger brother Isidore, bishop of Seville. Seated on a high chair or the bishop's throne, Isidore is formally depicted presenting Florentine with his book *De fide catholica . . . contra Iudaeos*. Isidore notes in the dedication to this work that he had written this book for his sister Florentine: "Soror mea Florentina accipe codicem quem tibi composui feliciter, amen." MS lat. 13396, fol. 1. Courtesy of the Bibliothèque Nationale de France, Paris. Giraudon/Art Resource, NY.

Beccelm ꝼr
mandara Gutht
pegt.

Pega ſoꝛoꝛ Gutlaci.

18. St. Pega Receiving Her Brother's Last Instructions

In this fine twelfth-century line drawing from the *vita* of St. Guthlac, St. Pega is
shown receiving her brother Guthlac's last instructions from his disciple Beccelm.
Pega is depicted with her right hand on her cheek and her head bent in sorrow,
clearly overcome with grief on learning the news of her brother's death. Beccelm
helps Pega into a boat, which would take her to Croyland to attend to Guthlac's
burial. The tonsured figure behind Pega is probably the anchorite Ecgberht, while
seated in the stern of the boat is a boatman with a paddle. The plume and glasses
on this figure appear to be later additions. The Guthlac Roll. MS Harley Roll Y.6,
plate XV. By permission of the British Library. (See also *The Guthlac Roll*, intro. by
George Warner. The Roxburghe Club. Oxford, 1928.)

19. St. Pega and Beccelm Lay Guthlac's Body in a Tomb

This lovely twelfth-century roundel, from the *vita* of St. Guthlac, depicts the
translation of St. Guthlac. In an elaborate architectural framework, St. Pega and
Beccelm lower St. Guthlac's tightly wrapped body into a richly carved sarcophagus,
which was placed above the ground. Pega's immense sorrow is remarkably portrayed
in her grief-stricken face. Between St. Pega and Beccelm is a priest in a chasuble,
swinging the censer over the body and holding a book. Behind the priest is another
tonsured figure. Rays of light, emanating from a cloud, fall upon the body of St.
Guthlac. The Guthlac Roll. MS Harley Roll Y.6, plate XVI. By permission of the
British Library. (See also *The Guthlac Roll*, intro. by George Warner. The Roxburghe
Club. Oxford, 1928.)

20. St. Cuthbert and Abbess Aelffled

This striking early-twelfth-century outline drawing in red, from Bede's *Life of St. Cuthbert*, portrays St. Cuthbert's meeting with St. Aelffled, abbess of Whitby, on the island of Coquet. Here Cuthbert, holding his bishop's crozier, is shown seated with the abbess on a long, decorated bench. As indicated by their expressive hands, they are involved in conversation. In response to Aelffled's questions, Cuthbert prophesies the death of her brother Ecgfrith in battle. On the left is a diminutive figure shown leaning out from a tower and surveying the empty margin of the manuscript. MS 165, p. 72. University College, Oxford. Courtesy of the Masters and Fellows of University College, Oxford.

21. St. Aldhelm and the Nuns of Barking Abbey

In this finely drawn late-tenth-century illustration, Bishop Aldhelm is shown presenting his tract *De virginitate* to Hildelith, abbess of Barking Abbey, and eight of the nuns of her community. The nun at the right is also depicted holding a book. In the dedication to this work, Aldhelm singles out Hildelith, "teacher of the regular discipline and of the monastic way of life," and nine nuns: Justina, Cuthburg, Osburg, Algith, Scholastica, Hidburg, Berngith, Eulalia, and Thecla. MS 200 (part II), fol. 68v. Lambeth Palace Library, London. Courtesy of the Archbishop of Canterbury and the Trustees of Lambeth Palace Library.

22. The Attempted *Furta Sacra* of the Relics of St. Attala

The legend surrounding the attempted *furta sacra* of the relics of St. Attala, abbess of the monastery of St. Etienne in Strasbourg, has been captured in this fascinating sixteenth-century German etching. Here the priest, sent by Werentrude, abbess of Hohenbourg, to procure a relic of her friend Attala, is shown alone in the monastery's church at the saint's coffin—caught in the act of attempting to cut off St. Attala's left arm. At the right looms a large figure of St. Attala, who observes this sacrilege and holds in her hand the severed limb. Holzschnitt von Leonhard Beck 1517, in Simon Laschitzer, *Die Heiligen aus der Sipp-, Mag- und Schwägerschaft des Kaisers Maximilian I.* (Tafel II.) Reproduced in Medard Barth, "Die Legende und Verehrung der hl. Attala." *Archiv für Elsässische Kirchengeschichte* 2 (1927): 105.

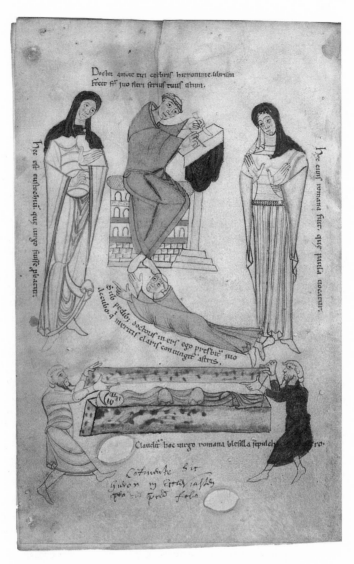

23. Sts. Jerome, Paula, and Eustochium and the Death of
St. Blaesilla

This early-twelfth-century French miniature is found in St. Jerome's
Commentarius in Ecclesiasten, which was dedicated to Sts. Paula and
Eustochium. It captures the tragedy surrounding St. Blaesilla's untimely
death. In the center, St. Jerome is shown seated at his writing desk; lying
prostrate at his feet is the patron of the manuscript, the priest Ivo. On
either side are depicted the elongated mourning figures of St. Paula, on
the right, and St. Eustochium, on the left. Paula and Eustochium's grief is
focused on St. Blaesilla (Paula's daughter and Eustochium's sister), who
died as a result of extreme fasting and is shown here in her coffin. MS It.
13350. Courtesy of the Bibliothèque Nationale de France, Paris.

24. "St. Radegund at the table with the king, praying in her oratory, and prostrate on the floor"

This late-eleventh-century manuscript illumination portrays several episodes from the Life of the queen-saint Radegund. In the upper register, Radegund is shown at court living as a nun manqué. At royal banquets, while those around her feasted, she fasted and retired to her oratory to pray. In the lower register, Radegund is depicted leaving the royal bed to lie prostrate in prayer on the cold floor near the latrine, thus proving that "she was more Christ's partner than her husband's companion." Because of this ascetic behavior it was said that "the king had married a nun rather than a queen." MS 250, fol. 24r. Courtesy of the Bibliothèque Municipale, Poitiers. Photo Giraudon/Art Resource, NY.

PROFILES OF SAINTLY MOTHERS

Of the popular women saints of the period under consideration in this study, approximately 25–30 percent were specifically said to be mothers. Of the three officially canonized women saints, only one was a mother.[31] Moreover, as might be expected, the greatest number of women saints who were also recognized as mothers can be found in the period of the proliferation of female saints—the seventh and eighth centuries. A collective study of these Lives is therefore especially useful in our exploration of early medieval motherhood.

In general, the *vitae* were particularly interested in the parentage of saints and their genealogies. Hagiographers frequently attempted to prove the special worthiness of their protagonists and to predict their future greatness by tracing their lineage back to their royal or noble ancestors. The vast majority of saints of this period are therefore described as born of noble or royal parents. Nevertheless, while the *vitae* often provide us with the names of both parents of a saint, there are many cases where only the name of the saint's mother is given, and the father's name remains unknown. Also, during this early period, the Lives describe entire families of saints, where the mother, father, and their children were all recognized locally as popular saints. This is particularly true for a number of royal Anglo-Saxon, Belgian, and northern French families of the seventh and eighth centuries. However, in a significant number of cases, only the mother and a few of her children were designated saints (with the *vitae* noting the mother's primary role, through the "piety of her milk," of transmitting her sanctity to her sons or daughters). The fathers, on the other hand, frequently assume a negative role or remain shadowy figures at best.

Although interested in motherhood and the details surrounding these saintly mothers, the *vitae* provide incomplete information as to the ages of these women at marriage and first conception. A number of the Lives mention early marriages: for example, the empress Adelaide's first marriage at approximately sixteen, her second at twenty, and Queen Mathilda's at fourteen years of age. St. Hildegard (wife of Charlemagne) was also married at an early age, since she died at the age of twenty-five with the birth of her ninth child; and St. Godeleva was eighteen years old at marriage. However, a few *vitae* note a later age for first marriage: for example, Margaret of Scotland married at twenty-four years of age.[32]

It appears that, in general, these women had their children in close succession shortly after marriage. A number of these saintly mothers, following the tradition of Genesis 1:28, "Be fruitful and multiply," had large families, with many having four, six, or even more, children. The following is a mere sampling of such cases: according to their *vitae,* St. Bertha of Blangy had five daughters (two recognized as saints); Salaberga had five children (all designated as saints); Waldetrude had four children (all saints); Rictrude had four children (all recognized as saints); Ida had three children (two daughters designated as saints); Amelberga had four children (all recognized as saints); Gerlinde and Adalbert (brother of St. Odilia) had five daughters; Hildegard and Charlemagne had nine children; St. Oda and Luidolf had twelve children (two recognized as saints); Queen Mathilda had five children (one designated as a saint); Queen Adelaide had six children (including St. Mathilda, abbess of Quedlinburg); Sts. Regina and Adalbert (niece of Pepin) had ten daughters, all of whom became nuns in their family house and were recognized as local saints! Ethelburga had four children (one daughter was recognized as a saint); Domne Eafe had three daughters (Sts. Mildrith, Mildberg, and Milgith) and one son, who died in childhood; Hereswitha (wife of King Anna) had four daughters (all recognized as saints); Margaret of Scotland had eight children (including St. David); etc. (A few Lives, perhaps in the tradition of hagiographic exaggeration, note extremely large families; for example, St. Patrick's sister was said to have had seventeen sons and five daughters.)[33]

Based on our incomplete data collected from the saints' Lives, it appears that these women had an average of approximately three or four children each. This includes a number of mother saints who became widows at an early age and had only one or two children. In this tradition, for example, we see St. Bilhild who was already a widow with a child at eighteen years of age, or St. Eustadiola who was widowed at twenty years of age with one son.[34] Other women, after having given birth to one or two children, adopted a chaste life within marriage or separated from their husbands in order to pursue a life of chastity: they therefore cut short their childbearing years with their families left "uncompleted." Another important pattern that can be discerned among several of the saintly mothers is that of delayed pregnancies. In these cases the women remained for many years apparently infertile or convinced of their inability to have children, and then, only much later in life, did they conceive their "special child." (This aspect will be discussed in more detail later in this chapter.)

A number of Lives also record multiple births. There are several cases of twins: for example, the Merovingian St. Protagie was the mother of twin Sts. Medard and Godard, and St. Hildegard (wife of Charlemagne) gave birth to twins.[35] However, on a more fantastic level—in the exaggerated hagiographic tradition—a number of these saintly mothers were said to have given birth to several infants at the same time. St. Notburga (9th c.), according to legend, gave birth to nine infants at one time (see plate 15). She and her maid then quickly christened the children, with only one dying before they could baptize it.[36] According to tradition, St. Lutrude was one of seven daughters born in one day; St. Wilgefortis was said to have been one of seven (or nine) children born at the same time.[37] St. Achachildis (11th c.) was said to have had five children at one time. And according to her *vita*, after this, she and her husband took a vow of celibacy! (This is perhaps an excellent example of children bringing on birth control.)[38]

The *vitae* also note the rather frequent deaths of these women during childbirth or from postpartum complications. In these cases the infant was then raised by a father, stepmother, grandmother, or foster mother, or by the monks or nuns of a monastery. Other sources note a high rate of infant mortality among these saintly families.

COITUS SACER: PREGNANCY AND THE MIRACULOUS

In their discussions of the conception and birth of saintly offspring, hagiographers frequently underscored the special circumstances or miraculous elements involved. This was done to set apart these "uncommon" infants, to establish from the outset the concept of divine election of these saintly children. Thus, in attempting to distance their protagonists from ordinary conceptions which entailed "sinful coupling"—lust and pollution—their explanations turned to the use of metaphor or the device of a vision.[39] These hagiographers incorporated some rather fantastic or folkloric elements in their "creation myths." Their legends of *coitus sacer* tend to accentuate the supernatural or the miraculous, and they frequently describe conceptions coinciding with the appearance of a bright light, "extra-vaginal" conceptions, paternity not attributed to a human male, miraculous erections, and conceptions among those convinced of their infertility or those substantially advanced in years. This emphasis seems to have been especially prevalent among Lives of monastic saints or Lives written or shaped by monastic reformers.

A number of early Irish saints' Lives, following in the tradition of the bright light motif, relate the occurrence of fiery manifestations during intercourse. Some saints are described as having actually been conceived of fire.[40] Several Irish and English saints' Lives describe a vision of a flame of fire, star, or a moon falling into the mother's mouth at the time of conception.[41]

The mother of the Irish St. Finan of Kinnity was said to have seen a vision of a red-gold fish entering her mouth at the time of conception.

In another version of this story, however, St. Finan is said to have been conceived through intercourse which took place between a "red-gold salmon" and his mother while she was bathing in Loch Lein.[42] Another Irish source notes the wonderful case of the conception of St. Colman. Here the cleric Comgall of Bangor gave writing ink to a barren woman, who, after drinking it, conceived a son called Colman of the ink of Cuilenn.[43] The miraculous impregnation of the Irish St. Baithin's mother, Creda, was said to have occurred while she was at the well washing her hands. According to the legend, a robber who intended to steal from the church was hiding in a thorn tree over the well. When he saw Creda he desired her and his semen fell on a spring of cress. Creda ate the cress and in this way Baithin was conceived.[44] The purpose of these miraculous descriptions of conception was then not to glorify the mother-to-be but to further enhance the purity of the future saint through their specific emphasis on the extra-vaginal aspect of conception as well as the denial of paternity to a human male.

A rather detailed and fascinating description of the conception of a tenth-century saint can be found in the Life of St. Gerald of Aurillac, written by St. Odo of Cluny. According to this *vita*, Gerald's father "was so careful to conduct himself chastely in his marriage, that he frequently slept alone far from the marriage bed, as though for a time giving himself to prayer according to the word of the Apostle [I Cor. vii. 5]." During his sleep one night, Gerald's father was warned that he should know his wife because he would beget a son. His son was to be called Gerald and he would become a man of great virtue. When he awoke from his dream "he was full of joy at the vision." Odo continues his explanation of Gerald's miraculous conception: "Having fallen asleep again it seemed to him that a rod grew up from the big toe of his right foot, which gradually grew into a great tree, which burst into leaf and spread itself at all sides. Then seeming to call workmen he ordered props in the form of forks or poles to be put underneath it. And even when it grew very great, he felt no weight on his toe." Odo then concludes with the following observation: "In truth visions of dreams are not always vain. And if faith is to be put in sleep, it seems that this vision agrees in its result with future events. He knew his wife, who conceived a son as the vision foretold." And finally, no doubt aware of this rather far-fetched account and of pushing the credulity of his audience perhaps a bit too far, Odo adds: "The dream may perhaps be doubted, but the mark of virtue evidently followed."[45]

A good number of *vitae,* following in the biblical tradition of, for example, Sarah and Abraham (Gen. 18:11 f.) and Elizabeth and Zachariah (Luke I: 5 f.), describe the parents of the saint as advanced in years, sterile and unfruitful. And it is then through sacrifice and prayer that these couples were able to miraculously conceive long after the normal age of childbearing. In his Life of St. Columbanus, Jonas of Bobbio notes the childlessness of Duke Waldelen and his wife, Flavia (who would become the future parents of St. Donatus). He explains that their delayed parenthood occurred "in order that, as Juvencus says of Zachariah and Elizabeth, 'the gift might be more welcome to those who had already given up hope.'"[46] The long period of hopelessness and waiting, followed by a miraculous pregnancy, also served to further emphasize how special the future saint was. We therefore find in the *vitae* many cases of couples, advanced in age, desperately wanting to have children; they prayed and fasted, they sought out confessors and bishops, other holy men or women, or they visited the tombs of saints who specialized in gynecological problems, to ask for their assistance in conceiving a child. Thus fortified by these intercessory prayers, they were provided with hope and assurance that they would soon be granted their wish: they would conceive and give birth to their much-desired offspring.

The Life of St. Odo of Cluny, written by John of Salerno, notes that Odo's father was "accustomed to celebrate the vigils of the saints throughout the night." Thus one Christmas eve, while he was celebrating the watch in tears and prayers, he decided to ask God in the name of the Virgin birth to give him a son. "And by the insistency of his prayers he merited that his wife should bear him one, though past the age when that might be expected." And according to Odo, "My father often related that in no other way had my nativity been brought about."[47]

The contemporary *vita* of St. Benno II (eleventh century) relates that Benno's parents had waited many years for a child. They then made a special pilgrimage to Rome and brought with them a votive offering of a little doll made of silver. As was the custom in the Roman world, these votives were small pledges or offerings (frequently miniatures representing the desired result of the request—an infant, a limb, or an eye to be cured, etc.) which were then left behind by the pilgrims at the pilgrimage site. Along with the votive offering, Benno's parents made a vow that if God answered their prayers and provided them with a son, they would dedicate him to the Church. And according to the *vita,* their prayers were answered and this promise was ultimately carried out.[48] The tradition surrounding the aged and ostensibly barren parents of the early Welsh Saint Samson relates a similar procedure. Amon, the father of the future saint, was told to give a silver rod which was of his wife's height as a type of votive offering. The parents also promised the hoped-for child to the priesthood. And in this way, we are told, this much-wanted conception occurred.[49]

The *vita* of St. Salaberga also describes the difficulty that she and her husband, St. Baso, encountered in conceiving an infant. "But although they enjoyed these good works by the Lord's favor and they were living an active Christian life, still they were sterile. Salaberga, most Christian lady, disturbed [to be] deprived of so many favors [*privilegiis*] and recollecting the faith of the holy women Anne and Elizabeth, who after prayers and night vigils in the Lord's temple and two years' childlessness were favored with the birth of two holy children, sought out the basilica of Blessed Remigius the Bishop, who had shed renown on the city of Rheims and the land of Compiègne by his holy virtues and miracles, and there in night-vigil and prayer she vowed that if children were divinely granted her, she would devote herself to the Lord." We learn that she returned home without delay, and "what she had in faith and solicitude begged of the Lord was granted her." And according to this tradition, Salaberga ultimately gave birth to five children—three daughters and two sons.[50]

The Life of St. Leoba also relates this pattern of delayed motherhood. As noted by her hagiographer, "But as [Leoba's father and mother] were barren, they remained together for a long time without children. After many years had passed and the onset of old age had deprived them of all hope of offspring, her mother had a dream in which she saw herself bearing in her bosom a church bell, which on being drawn out with her hand rang merrily." When she awoke, she related her dream to her old nurse who interpreted it as follows: "We shall yet see a daughter from your womb and it is your duty to consecrate her straightway to God. . . . Shortly after the woman had made this vow she conceived and bore a daughter, whom she called Thrutgeba, surnamed Leoba because she was beloved."[51]

Thus a good number of the saints of this period can perhaps be best described as "miracle babies"; that is, in the biblical tradition of Abraham and Sarah, Zachariah and Elizabeth, these future saints were born of parents convinced of their infertility and advanced in years, who had given up all hope for a child.[52]

It is also in this general context that certain saints came to be viewed as fertility specialists and were thus invoked by the faithful to assist in conception. Infertility then, as now, seems to have been a major concern. Historical demographers estimate that between 10 and perhaps 20 percent of married couples in premodern societies did not have children. Moreover, during this early period the onus of infertility seems to have been invariably born by the woman: it was seen as a "female problem" and a curse from God.[53] Therefore we find in the *vitae* many references to the efficacy of saints in bringing about miraculous fertility and conception. It appears that the faithful invoked a group of "generic" male saints who have been classified as "phallic saints"; these included Sts. Phallier, Genitour, Greluchon, and René (Reins), and others.[54] Many other local male and female saints also were recognized for their special efficacy in the area of female fertility. The Merovingian saint, Leonard de Noblac, hermit and abbot (d. ca. 560) was known for assisting in the fecundity of sterile women. The "bolt" or "lock" of St. Leonard was said to bring about this miracle.[55] According to a later tradition, St. Gertrude of Nivelles was said to have left her cloak to her monastery and it became a highly prized relic which was hung around the shoulders of those who wanted to become pregnant.[56] Pilgrims frequented the holy well of the Welsh St. Winifred to ask her special assistance in dissolving "obstructions causing barrenness."[57] St. Richarde of Andlau was also regarded as an important patron saint of infertile women. According to tradition, those who wanted to become pregnant would go to her church of Andlau and sit astride the carved stone bear which was located in the crypt.[58] A similar tradition developed around the cult of St. Lucy of Sampigny, where over the centuries barren women would climb up Mont Ste-Lucie and on entering the grotto, they would sit in her seat carved in the rock, in the hope that the saint would send them children.[59] The popular St. Verena was also known to assist couples in their problems with infertility: during the ninth and tenth centuries several German dukes and their wives made pilgrimages to her cult center at Zurzach in order to secure offspring.[60] Infertile women invoked St. Wilgefortes (or Uncumber) and at least in the later years, they hung votive wombs beneath her statues.[61]

From the repetition of these miracles, infertility appears to have been a prevalent problem during this period. Therefore, saints were sought out and frequently invoked as gynecological specialists or fertility experts.

Although many of the *vitae* describe the conceptions of saints in miraculous or metaphoric terms, a few saints seem to have been conceived as the result of violence or rape. And while the hagiographers admit that these women were victims of sexual assault, this explanation also helped to confirm the moral purity, the innocence of the mother (and infant) by denying her "complicity" in the "act." According to Rhigyfarch's Life of St. David, for example, the conception of St. David was the result of a rape. While passing through Dyfed, King Sanctus met "a maiden called Nonita, exceedingly beautiful, a modest virgin. Her the king, inflamed with desire, violated, who, neither before nor after this occasion had any intercourse with any man, but continued in chastity of mind and body, leading a most faithful life; for from this very time of her conceiving, she lived on bread and water only."[62]

The birth of the Scottish St. Kentigern (d. ca. 603) is also in this tradition. Kentigern's mother, Thaney, was said to have been of royal birth. According to the two twelfth-century Lives of the saint, Thaney was devoted to the Virgin Mother: she constantly meditated on the "maternal blessedness" of the Virgin Mary and prayed that she might imitate Mary in conception and in birth. The *vitae* emphasize, however, that what she wished could not be granted and that she conceived in another manner. She was apparently raped by Owein, an unsuccessful suitor, who was disguised as a woman. After the sexual assault, Owein reassured Thaney by saying: "Weep not, my sister, for I have not known thee as a man is used to know a virgin. Am I not a woman like thyself?" Therefore, in her innocence, Thaney remained unsure of whether she had been raped. Later, when interrogated by her father about her pregnancy, she claimed she was innocent of having had intercourse with a man and refused to reveal the name of the person who had violated her. The result of this rather unusual incident, which underscored the innocence and chastity of the mother, was the birth of a special infant, St. Kentigern. According to the hagiographers, their attempts at explaining the extraordinary circumstances surrounding this conception were aimed in part at the "foolish" people who lived in the diocese of St. Kentigern and believed that he was conceived and born of a virgin.[63]

The confused tradition surrounding the conception of St. Edith also relates that it occurred against her mother's will. In this episode, the Anglo-Saxon king, Edgar, carried off the nun Wilfrida, or induced her to leave the Monastery of Wilton. According to one source, as soon as Wilfrida was able to escape from the king, she returned to her cell at Wilton, and there in the monastery she gave birth to Edith. Another tradition, however, says that only after Edith's birth did Wilfrida retire with her baby to Wilton. Wilfrida was later selected as abbess of Wilton; and her daughter, Edith, took vows and became a nun. Both mother and daughter came to be recognized as popular saints.[64]

Following their accounts of conception, many of the *vitae* describe the mothers of saints, who, while pregnant with their special offspring, received visions foretelling the future greatness of their children. Although a few of the fathers shared in these apparitions, they were primarily aimed at the mothers of saints. A number of these visions used light motifs—fire, gold, and bright colors. And again, the Irish hagiographers provide us with some of the most fascinating and creative examples in this genre.

The mother of St. Brendan was visited by a vision which foretold her son's future greatness. "Now the mother of Brendan saw a vision before he was born. (It seemed to her) that her bosom was full of pure gold, and that her paps shone like snow. When she told this vision to Bishop Erc, he said that a wondrous birth would be born to her, who would be full of the grace of the Holy Ghost, meaning Brendan." [65]

Bede also records a similar vision in his discussion of the life of St. Hilda of Whitby. He notes that Hilda's mother had a dream that "she discovered a most valuable jewel under her garments; and as she looked closely, it emitted such a brilliant light that all Britain was lit by its splendour. This dream was fulfilled in her daughter, whose life afforded a shining example not only to herself but to all who wished to live a good life." [66]

The Life of St. Findian of Clonard notes that after Telach's vision of her future son, her husband reconfirmed their infant's special piety and proposed that they refrain from sexual intercourse during Telach's pregnancy. The hagiographer then relates that "Telach herself used not to eat rich meats, but only mild herbs and light victuals, until that gifted offspring was born." [67]

Wulfstan of Winchester notes in his Life of St. Aethelwold: "So his fortunate mother, while pregnant with him, saw at dead of night a dream that was an unerring indication of the future." In her dream she saw a banner whose top seemed to touch heaven as well as "an eagle of gold, leaping from her mouth and flying away. It was wonderfully large, and in its flight it shaded all the buildings in the city of Winchester with the gilded wings that carried it along." When she awoke, unable to interpret her dream, she went to "a servant of Christ called Aethelthryth, a woman ripe in years and experience, and the nurse of the virgins dedicated to God at Winchester. To her she told the full story of what had been shown her in her vision by night. Aethelthryth, being a sensible and sharp woman, and one to whom God at times revealed knowledge of the future, had many predictions to make of the child who was to be born; and the outcome showed their truth." [68]

A number of Lives, in the tradition of the miraculous, also note unborn saints "speaking" or "communicating" from their mothers' wombs. Perhaps one of the most famous examples can be found in the dream of St. Aleth, mother of St. Bernard of Clairvaux, in which she saw in her womb a little white dog that barked. This was interpreted to mean that her future son would be a great preacher against the infidel. [69]

In their descriptions of the conceptions of saints and the pregnancy of these holy mothers, hagiographers frequently resorted to visions and metaphors. Such marvelous explanations provided further evidence of the saint's special nature and thus early "participation" in the divine and miraculous.

SAINTLY BIRTHS

The *vitae* are especially rich in their descriptions of labor and childbirth as experienced by these holy mothers. Although the miraculous again plays an important role for the hagiographer, there are many incidental details included in the Lives which add to our knowledge about medieval childbirth.

While most of the Lives stressed the pain and extreme hazards of childbirth, a few of the *vitae* note that these special mothers of saintly infants were spared the pangs of labor. Since pain in childbirth was associated with Eve and sin, these women were exempt from this punishment. For example, "at the time of Coemgen's birth no pains of labour nor pangs of childbearing came to his mother, as to other women, for innocent, faithful, righteous was the offspring that she bore." The birth of St. Leon, archbishop of Rouen (d. ca. 900), was also said to have occurred without his mother suffering the ordinary pains of childbirth.[70]

However, many of the *vitae,* in a somewhat more "realistic" bent (but still within the framework of the miraculous), stress the excruciating pain that the mothers suffered in the birthing process. The legend of St. Nonna, the mother of St. David, for example, notes that "the mother, in her travail, had near her a certain stone, on which she leaned with her hands when hard pressed by her pains; whereby the marks of her hands, as though impressed on wax, have identified that stone for those who have gazed upon it: it broke in half in sympathy with the mother in her agony."[71] Eithne, the mother of St. Maedoc of Ferns, was said to have held a webstress's slay (an instrument made out of hard, dry hazel-wood used in weaving to beat up the weft) during labor and her infant's birth. Afterward, at the time that the *vita* was redacted, this piece of wood was said to have produced leaves and flowers and to still be standing as "a fresh unaging tree." And according to the Life, "The learned men of the district say with reference to this hazel, that when earth from it over which nine Masses have been said is inserted between prisoners and their chains (lit. irons), they thereupon escape forthwith."[72] (It is interesting to perhaps see in this later miraculous attribution to the hazel of its opening of chains and freeing prisoners a reflection of its original use in the hands of Eithne during her "time of travail" and the unbinding or freeing of the saintly infant from its prison in the womb.)

The description of the birth of St. Aed is particularly interesting. It had been revealed to the saint's mother, through the prophecy of the bishop, that if the birth of her unborn infant was delayed until the following morning, he would be endowed with greatness in both heaven and earth. After hearing this, the mother returned home and then, as might be expected, she went into labor. Determined to hold off the imminent birth, she resolved that unless the child came out through her sides ("nisi per latera mea venerit, non egredietur ex utero meo") it would not be born until the next day. Thus in a heroic attempt to forestall the birth (and thereby assuring her son's future greatness) she was said to have sat on a stone and there she remained suffering in labor until morning when the infant was finally "allowed" to emerge. According to the hagiographer, the stone became indented in the birthing process by the infant's head being driven down into it, and, up to the time of the redaction of the *vita,* water from the hollow of this special stone was used to cure the sick.[73]

In prolonged and extremely difficult labors, women urgently called upon their patron saints for their much needed expertise and assurance. The life-threatening complications and dangers of pregnancy and childbirth were simple realities which all of these women had to face. For many, no doubt, the fear of death by hemorrhage or puerperal fever or permanent paralysis caused by the trauma of birth or crude surgery, as well as the possibility of stillbirths, must have been overwhelming. Although women would usually be accompanied and assisted by other women or midwives in the delivery of their infants, difficult labors, lasting from a few days to several weeks, were apparently not uncommon.[74]

A whole battery of saints were, then, looked to as "gynecological specialists." It is interesting to note, however, that while the activity surrounding childbirth itself was considered very much a woman's preserve (i.e., usually only women served as midwives and attended those in labor), the patron saints invoked at this difficult time were both male and female, with perhaps a predominance of women saints. Included among the early Christian saints who were called upon by pregnant women for a safe delivery were Sts. Honorine de Graville or de Conflans, Felicity of Carthage, Eulalia, Margaret of Antioch, and Foi.[75] (A number of these virgin saints had suffered violent death and martyrdom and thus were probably viewed as especially appropriate patrons for women in labor. Honorine and Foi were also patron saints of prisoners. Here again we see perhaps the relationship between the saint's ability to break chains or to free prisoners and childbirth with the safe delivery of the infant from the womb.)

According to the *vitae,* girdles or belts associated with saints became objects of special devotion for women in labor. The girdles of Sts. Foi,

Margaret of Antioch, Brigid, Beuve, Ghislain, and others were believed to be especially efficacious in helping to relieve women's pains
during labor and to bring about a safe delivery.[76] In this tradition,
Hildegard of Bingen's *vita* describes how three women were assisted in
their difficult labors by placing several strands of the saint's hair on
their bare skin.[77]

However, it appears that beginning in the twelfth century, St. Margaret of Antioch became especially popular as the patron saint par
excellence of women in childbirth. According to tradition, on refusing
to give up her virginity, St. Margaret was imprisoned by the Roman
prefect Olibrius. While in prison she was attacked and, in some versions of the story, swallowed by a dragon. Nevertheless, she was able
to free herself and emerged unharmed from the dragon's belly by making the sign of the cross. Margaret was then subjected to various other
tortures which failed to harm her; finally Olibrius had her beheaded.
Shortly before her death, Margaret prayed to God that the memory of
her escape from the belly of the dragon might provide help to those
suffering the pains of childbirth. Thus any woman in labor, who called
upon St. Margaret for assistance, would be preserved from danger and
her child would have a safe delivery.[78]

While it appears that the cult of St. Margaret was well developed,
at least in late Anglo-Saxon England, the widespread belief in her role
as patron saint of childbirth seems to date to the period after the Norman Conquest—to the twelfth or thirteenth century. In this context,
Matthew of Paris's chronicle entry for the year 1240 notes that on the
second of October "Queen Eleanor, brought the king a daughter, who
received the name of Margaret, which was the name of her aunt, the
queen of the French, and also *because in the pains of childbirth the
queen had invoked St. Margaret.*"[79]

It was believed, at least during the later Middle Ages, that one
could obtain the saint's assistance by offering special prayers to St.
Margaret, by having the Life of St. Margaret read aloud to the woman
in labor; or by placing the manuscript or book of the Life of St. Margaret on the woman's stomach; or the most efficacious method entailed actually touching St. Margaret's girdle or belt which was believed to be the saint's most precious relic or amulet.[80] Moreover, we
learn that pregnant women gave St. Margaret candles whose length
was determined by the circumference of their girths during pregnancy.
And finally, after childbirth, they would offer the saint, as ex-votos,
the umbilical cords of their infants.[81]

Also during the later Middle Ages, the Virgin Mary and St. Anne
were extremely popular interceders invoked by women for assistance
during childbirth. In the fifteenth century, for example, pilgrims, on

their visit to Chartres, bought lead badges made in the shape of a miniature robe of the virgin which were used to bring relief to women in childbirth. Women's chemises, or shifts, which had touched the Virgin's reliquary were also used to help women endure the pains of childbirth.[82]

A number of local saints who flourished between the sixth century and the end of the eleventh century also won recognition for their successful interventions in childbirth. According to tradition, St. Leonard de Noblac had obtained through his prayers the safe delivery of Queen Clotilda. He was also involved in the freeing of prisoners. Thus women in childbirth prayed for his intercession during difficult labors.[83] The Life of the Irish Saint Gerald, abbot of Mayo, notes that this saint was born with a stone in his right hand, and this stone therefore had miraculous qualities which proved to be especially beneficial to women in labor. They believed that they would receive special protection by drinking water that had come in contact with this sacred stone.[84] St. Opportune, abbess of Montreuil (8th c.), was also invoked by women to ease their difficult deliveries.[85] We learn that St. Leon, archbishop of Rouen, was recognized for his concern for women in labor. As noted in his Life, his mother had allegedly given birth without suffering the ordinary pains of childbirth, and therefore, shortly before his death, he asked God to grant that women who prayed to him during their pregnancy would be safe from all difficulties and harm.[86] Many other *vitae* note the special role which saints assumed during childbirth.

A number of *vitae* describe prolonged labor and in utero death of the fetus. The Life of St. Molua, for example, relates that a certain woman had carried a dead fetus in her uterus for three years. Unable to rid herself of this overwhelming burden by the use of any means or medicine, she was afflicted with great sorrow. One day as she was walking she met the young St. Molua and recognizing his sanctity, she begged him to bless her uterus. After his blessing she was cured and the next night freed of this fetus.[87]

A number of *vitae* and their miracles also document the use of caesarean sections. The Life of St. Melania the Elder (d. 410), for example, tells of a woman whose infant had died in utero. A surgeon had been called in to extricate the fetus and to save the woman from certain death. However, as the surgeon was performing a caesarean section, St. Melania, along with her group of virgins, arrived to offer their assistance. Melania then took over, and using her special girdle, she tied it around the desperate woman's girth. And we learn that through this saint's intercession, the fetus was delivered and the woman's life was saved.[88]

In her study *Not of Woman Born: Representations of Caesarean Birth in Medieval and Renaissance Culture,* Renate Blumenfeld-Kosinski has noted several fascinating cases involving the intercession of early medieval saints. According to the account of the miracles of the bishop St. Paul of Merida (7th c.), a noblewoman of Merida had become ill, as her child had died in her womb. In desperation the woman's husband approached the bishop (who was also a *medicus*) for help. Initially the holy man refused to treat the woman on the basis of propriety and potential scandal: "wicked men will throw this matter up to me." [89] Later relenting, he spent a day in prayer in the church of the virgin St. Eulalia (who was also a patron saint of childbirth), after which he "laid his hands on the sick woman in the name of the Lord, and, trusting in God, very carefully made a very small incision with a sharp scalpel and withdrew in sections, member by member, the already corrupt body of the infant. The woman, already almost dead and only half-alive, he at once restored safely to her husband with the help of God and *bade her henceforth not to know her husband:* for at whatever time she should know the embraces of her husband worse perils would come upon her. Nevertheless they fell at his feet and thanked him and promised to observe in detail everything the man of God had commanded." [90] This case is remarkable, as Blumenfeld-Kosinski has pointed out, in that the "miraculous" deliverance was executed by the extreme skill of a bishop physician (working of course with divine support). Also, the holy man's marital counseling appears extremely enlightened, for he was clearly concerned with the woman's health risks and interests.[91]

The account of the miracles of the eighth-century missionary bishop St. Vulframmus also describes in some detail this saint's intervention in a difficult childbirth and the need to resort to a caesarean section for delivery. "After insistent prayers [to Saint Vulframmus] her belly was swelling up from the pectoral bone to the navel when—wonderful to tell—it divided itself across the middle like a field newly plowed. Her cries made people flock around and look at her without modesty. After some consultation they opened her belly further and pulled the flesh and bones of the putrid child out of the half-dead woman's body. When this was done, the woman again prayed to the saintly patron who had delivered and completely healed her." [92] In this miracle we see another example of the intervention of a male saint in childbirth, although in this case accomplished from a distance, through prayer.[93]

In sum, while a number of *vitae*—in highlighting the saintliness of these mothers—noted that they were spared the pangs of labor during childbirth, others describe prolonged labors and extremely difficult deliveries. The Lives and miracle stories also relate the desperation which many women experienced during childbirth and the important roles attributed to saints as specialists in gynecological problems and obstetrics. Thus, from the variety of evidence found in the *vitae* it appears that in the very frightening and dangerous process of giving birth, saints as miracle workers were urgently called upon. This is one of the major areas of medieval life in which saints were seen to be especially beneficial and assumed prominent, indispensable roles. They provided comfort, sympathy, and assurances to the mothers and fathers in their time of desperation; and through the success stories found in their collected miracles, they offered much needed hope and support when none other was forthcoming.

MIRACLES OF THE NEWBORN AND THE NAMING OF SAINTS

After the drama of birth, the *vitae* frequently describe miracles surrounding the newborn infant. Many of these miracles, again, were seen as portents of the saint's future greatness.

In a wonderful description found in his *Life of the Fathers*, Gregory of Tours explains how St. Nicetius, from the moment of his birth, was seen to be predestined for the clergy. "As soon as he had been born one could see that his head was completely deprived of hair, as is often the case with the newly born, but that there was a ring of down all around his head, so that one would have thought from that ring that he had been granted clerical tonsure. Because of that, his parents brought him up with great care."[94]

The *vita* of St. Bruno (later Pope Leo IX; d. 1054), notes that when he was born his body was covered with little red crosses. This remarkable prodigy was then regarded as a sign of his future sanctity.[95]

The Life of the Irish St. Fechin of Fore mentions that every sign of sanctity surrounded him: "for his birth was a marvel and his infancy was marvellous. For when his parents used to go asleep, they would put him between their breasts, and when they awoke they would find him on the bare floor, with his hands stretched out in the form of the cross!"[96] (These details are of special interest as they indicate the practice of infants sleeping with their parents. It is this habit which was believed to be responsible for the deaths of infants caused by parents "laying over" and suffocating their small children while sleeping. In this case, little Fechin was perhaps routinely edged out of bed.)

In addition to describing miracles associated with the saint's infancy, a few of the *vitae* provide information related to the process of naming the newborn. It appears from the Lives that close family members—the parents or grandparents—shared in this decision, although in a number of cases the mother of the child seemed to exercise a decisive influence. Bishops or priests involved in the infant's baptism sometimes assumed a role in the naming of the child, and, beginning in the tenth century, godparents or sponsors also exerted an influence on the selection of names, in some cases bestowing their own names on the infant.[97]

The Life of St. Wulfstan, bishop of Worcester, is an extraordinary source in regard to the naming process. The author notes: "The boy was given the name Wulfstan, made up from the first part of his mother's name [Wulfgifu] and the second of his father's [Aethelstan]. It was an auspicious omen that the child in happy expectation should adopt elements from the name of both parents, as if to transfer to himself the holiness of both, and for all I know incomparably to exceed them, for surely their memory would have completely vanished had it not been raised up to a mirror by their son's conspicuous holiness of spirit."[98] In this same self-conscious tradition, St. Hilda of Whitby's sister was named Hereswid which was a combination of her father's name, Hereric, and her mother's name, Breguswid.[99]

A rather blatant case of the mother's determining her infant's name concerns St. Corbinianus (d. ca. 725), who was initially baptized with his father's name, Waldigiso. However, soon after his baptism, his father died, and the mother changed his name to Corbinianus, the masculine form of her own name.[100] St. Firmin and his wife Aula had a son named Aulus who was thus named for his mother; and St. Serein was named after his mother, Serena.[101] The Irish saint, MacNisse, took his name from his mother, Ness.[102] The *vita* of the missionary bishop St. Amand (d. ca. 674) states that Amand's mother was named Amantia and thus he was named after her.[103] Fechin of Fore also was named by his mother. When he was a child he happened to gnaw on a bone in front of his mother who then called him her "little wee raven" or Inde Fechin.[104] The *vita* of St. Salaberga notes that Salaberga named her first daughter "Saretrude after her grandmother." The Life also relates that she named her second daughter Ebana, and her third daughter "she called Anstrude at baptism."[105] As noted in the Life of Leoba, the saint's mother, Aebba, "bore a daughter, whom *she called* Thrutgeba, surnamed Leoba, because she was beloved, for this is what Leoba means."[106] According to our sources, the name of St. Hubert, monk of Bretigny (d. ca. 714), was apparently selected by the saint's mother, although his godfather was also called St. Hubert.[107] Or we learn that in the naming of St. Arnoul, bishop of Soissons (d. 1087), Arnoul d'Oudenarde was the infant's godfather and he insisted on giving the child his name. However, the saint's mother, Pamèle, held that she had received a vision in which it was revealed to her to name her future son Christopher. She therefore adopted this name for him.

Despite this, he officially assumed the name Arnoul, although he was frequently identified by the matronymic—as he was called Arnoul de Pamèle.[108] Perhaps one of the most extraordinary examples of this tradition is that of St. Margaret of Scotland, who seems to have controlled the naming of all of her eight children, since none was given a Scottish name. And for her first four sons she adopted the names from the genealogy of the West Saxon kings.[109]

In contrast to this pattern, which underscores the primary involvement of mothers in the naming of their children, a few of the *vitae* tell of fathers assuming this function. The Life of St. Willibrord, for example, notes that "when he was born a second time at the sacred baptismal font his father gave him the name of Willibrord."[110]

The general custom of naming infants after specific saints seems to date to the later Middle Ages, although it was not uncommon for nuns and female saints, from the period of the sixth through the eleventh century, to bear the names of early women saints such as Agnes, Agatha, Alena, Thecla, Eulalia, or Scholastica.[111]

THE CARE AND NURSING OF SAINTLY INFANTS

A number of the Lives are particularly informative about the special care which these future saints received as infants. A rather fascinating case can be found in the Life of an eleventh-century saint, Adelviva (mother of St. Poppo), which notes that she gave birth to a premature, high-risk infant. According to the hagiographer, this baby was born early, "in the seventh month of his gestation. . . . Thus his parents were at a loss in the circumstances of their despair for his life and were in anxiety and fear for his untimely and delicate young life, especially since they loved him tenderly as their first-born and were they to lose him they had little hope of having another child like him."[112] The hagiographer continues, "then, by the plan of the Almighty, as I believe, it occurred to a certain matron—his grandmother, as a matter of fact—with wise care to keep him warm in the softest [*suavissima*] of wool until such time as he was strong enough to take his first baby steps. It thus came about that, as the little boy emerged from the dangers of premature birth, his parents experienced exultant joy."[113] In this interesting case we see an awareness of the special provisions or adaptations which were necessary to keep premature infants alive.

Ekkehard IV of St. Gall (980–1060) describes the caesarian birth and clever care of one of the brothers of the monastery who was called Purchard or "the Unborn." According to Ekkehard, a certain noblewoman by the name of Wendigart came under the influence of the recluse St. Wiborada of St. Gall. The source relates that after conceiving, Wendigart "paid a votive pilgrimage with her husband to her beloved St. Gall and to the anchoresses; there she pledged herself, if she bore a male child, to devote him as a monk to St. Gall; and thence they went home." Ekkehard continues: "Her time drew near; she fell into a sore sickness before her time, and died a fortnight before the expected birth. The child was cut from her corpse and wrapped in the fat of a new-born pig, until his skin should grow; and, since he promised well, they baptized him and called him Purchard." [114]

Several Lives discuss in some detail the nursing of these saintly infants. A number of *vitae* underscore a belief that the milk of the saint's mother was uniquely pure (a reflection of her moral character) and that it contained within it certain miraculous qualities. For example, the blind monk who foretold the birth of St. Remi received his sight by having his eyes washed in the milk of St. Cilinia (St. Remi's mother). [115] The tradition surrounding St. Lambert, martyred bishop of Maestricht (d. ca. 708), recounts how shortly before his birth, the blind daughter of a nobleman was forewarned by an angel to go to find Herisplendis, the mother of the future saint, and to offer her services as the wet-nurse. Miraculously provided with milk, this young woman then used it to wash her eyes and immediately recovered her sight. It is on this special "virginal milk" that St. Lambert was suckled in his infancy. [116]

Although, as noted by Mary McLaughlin, the maternal ideal of nursing one's own child seems to have become popular only in the late eleventh and twelfth centuries and is perhaps related to the proliferation of the Cult of the Virgin and the *Virgo lactans* or the nursing mother of Christ, there are a number of early medieval sources which emphasize the positive role of mothers nursing their own infants. Archbishop Wulfad of Bourges, for example, recommended that women of his diocese breast feed their own infants rather than resort to the use of wet-nurses. [117] There are also several examples in the *vitae* of mothers choosing to nurse their own infants. This personal commitment to their saintly infants, according to the Lives, rested on a belief that their child was special and they were therefore obligated to personally devote themselves to his or her care. They also seem to have been convinced that their milk possessed certain desirable qualities that could affect the moral or spiritual character of the infant, and thus through nursing they would be able to pass on to their children their own piety and spiritual purity. Moreover, it appears from the *vitae* that this commitment on the part of noblewomen, to nurse their own infants, was viewed as especially important in regard to their male offspring. The mother of St. Loup, archbishop of Sens (7th c.), for example, had a divine revelation that the child she was carrying would one day be a great "light of the church." This, according to the *vita,* obliged her to nurse the infant herself—which was apparently against the custom of women of her rank—in order to have him nourished on the "piety of her milk."[118] The mother of St. Bruno (Pope Leo IX, 11th c.) also was said to have received a vision of her son's future sanctity and greatness, which subsequently convinced her of her duty to nurse him herself.[119] Robert, abbot of Chaise Dieu (11th c.) was given successively to two bad or evil wet-nurses and he refused to take their milk. We learn, however, that he apparently drank freely from his mother's breast.[120] (Although no doubt written to show the young saint's early discernment of purity and rejection of "evil," this case may also point to problems surrounding disfunctional wet-nurses—problems of getting milk in, producing enough milk to satisfy the infant, etc.) The Blessed Ida of Boulogne (d. ca. 1113) was recognized for nursing all three of her children; the Life of St. Bernard of Clairvaux also relates that Aleth, Bernard's mother, was committed to nursing her own children.[121]

A number of the Lives also provide information on the saintly infants' nursing schedules, which were interpreted as an early adherence to programs of fasting or abstinence. This motif can be found in the early legends associated with Nicholas of Myra (a fourth-century saint), whose first Latin *vita* was translated from the Greek in ca. 880. St. Nicholas's fasting was said to have begun while he was still in the cradle: on Wednesdays and Fridays the little saint allegedly refused nourishment from his nurse's breasts, except in the evening, when he sucked vigorously.[122] Various versions of this theme can be found in a number of other *vitae* of this period. The *vita* of St. Coemgen relates that "moreover, it is to be reckoned as a marvel, that while he was at his mother's breasts, he would only suck them once on Fridays and other fast-days, and that at evening."[123] According to the legend of St. Procule (11th or 12th c.), from the beginning she was predestined for sanctity, as witnessed by her eating habits: every Tuesday and Thursday she nursed from her mother only once at night.[124] Or the later Life of the fifth-century St. Candid notes that as an infant he totally rejected his mother's right breast; however, if she had eaten a delicious meal, he then also refused to drink from her left breast.[125]

Other *vitae,* in their discussions of the "miraculous" aspect of nursing, are bit more imaginative and clearly strain one's credulity. The case of St. Gwen the White (the sixth-century mother of St. Guenole of Brittany) is especially interesting, as it appears to embody early folkloric traditions or traces of nature worship. According to this legend, St. Gwen was apparently already the mother of two young sons when she gave birth to a third. Thus, as shown by the hagiographer and later artistic depictions, in order to aid her in nursing her third infant, she was fortuitously provided with a third breast! She then became appropriately known as "Gwen of the Three Paps" or in Latin, "Alba Trimammis." Sharing in this same tradition is the mother of several early Irish saints who was called "Derinnell cetharchichech" or "of the four paps."[126] It should be noted that during this period at least some women apparently nursed their children for several years. For example, one of the miracles related by Gregory of Tours in his *Glory of the Confessors* focuses on a little boy "about three years old, who still sucked his mother's breasts." The child was afflicted by a fever and had become so weak "that he was unable to take her breast or any other food."[127] (Thus it would no doubt have been particularly convenient for these women with several small children to be miraculously provided with an additional breast or two!)

Also in this tradition of hagiographic fantasy we find a wonderful legend surrounding the birth and nursing of the Irish St. Finntan. According to this source, one of the queens of the king of Leinster fled to the holy man, Findchua, for protection. On the journey she went into labor and gave birth to a son. Since women were forbidden to come to Findchua's church, the boy was taken from her to the holy man to be baptized and was given the name Finntan. However, we learn that "the boy is reared by Findchua, who gives him his right breast, and milk grew therein, and his mother is warned to go into her own country." The hagiographer also assures the reader "that boy throve as he would not have thriven with his own mother if he had had nine wet-nurses under him."[128] Thus, since no women were allowed within the monastic precinct, Findchua was said to have been miraculously provided with the necessary "equipment" which more than satisfied his charge!

The Life of the Irish St. Colman Ela notes that as a result of an incestuous relationship Columba's sister gave birth to twin sons. While admitting that he preferred that the infants die, Columba came to Colman Ela for advice. The holy man then told Columba to give the infants to him to nourish and foster, "For I have two paps such as no saint ever had before, a pap with milk, and a pap with honey, and these I will give to them (to suck)."[129]

In a similar vein is the remarkable story surrounding the infancy of the Irish St. Berach. According to the *vita*, Berach's uncle (his mother's brother), named Fregius, adopted him at a very early age. And while it was usual for the mother to offer her breast to her infant, in this case we are told, St. Fregius adapted himself to the situation and nursed St. Berach with his own right earlobe. Or as noted by the *vita:* "When the baby had been baptized, his mother attempted to keep him with her to nurse him tenderly with her own milk rather than that of an unrelated wet-nurse. But the holy man of God did not permit this: 'You should know, my dearest sister,' he said, 'that you will no longer carry the burden of care for this boy. He will stay with me in the name of Christ. For God, who made him from nothing, is able to bring about his perfect physical development without being served his mother's milk.' " The hagiographer then assures us: "And in fact that is what happened. He was accustomed, indeed, while he was being reared with diligent care by the man of God, to suck St. Fregius's right earlobe as from his mother's breast. And thus it happened that at the behest of him who was able to bring honey from the rock, the boy grew from the touch of the man of God's earlobe as if he enjoyed the full abundance of his mother's milk." [130]

A final example in this miraculous tradition surrounding the nursing of a future saint can be found in the Life of St. Odilia (d. ca. 720). This miracle relates that at the time of the death of Odilia's nurse, the saint was "not unmindful of the great pains her nurse had taken in raising her and she gave orders for the ground to be prepared for the burial. With her own hand she saw to the burial." We then learn that after about eighty years, the grave that Odilia's nurse occupied was emptied in order to accommodate another body. The hagiographer notes that the nurse's body had essentially decomposed, "but her right breast alone was discovered to be whole and as incorrupt as if at that same moment it had been removed from her body." The author then explains: "This fact was taken as proof of the holy virgin's fostering care [almitatem], because her keen-witted nurse, realizing that something of heaven was in Odilia, had offered her milk only from her right breast and through the whole period of lactation had kept it shrouded in a linen covering." [131]

The vitae also note that saints were frequently called upon to assist mothers and wet nurses who experienced difficulties in nursing their infants. Problems in this area relating to "getting milk in," "drying up," or mastitis could be extremely serious and could mean the difference between life and death for many of these infants. St. Agatha, appropriately enough, became the patron saint of wet nurses and nursing mothers, as well as those who suffered from abscesses or cancer of the breast. Agatha's expertise was allegedly due to the special torture which she was said to have suffered as a virgin martyr which included having her breasts cut off. [132] Women with breast problems might also invoke a "generic saint" such as St. Mafmert or Mammes, who was said to have adopted this specialty because of his name. [133] St. Gilles was also recognized as a popular saint for nursing mothers. According to legend, he had asked God to preserve from harm the doe that had miraculously nursed him as an infant. [134]

One of the miracles attributed to St. Savin (hermit and missionary of Lavedan, 8th c.) describes this saint's special assistance to nursing mothers. According to the *vita*, a poor mother named Gaudentia was in despair since her "dried up" breasts refused to provide the necessary nourishment for her small infant. After having exhausted every possible means available to her through nature, in desperation she turned to God and St. Savin. Accompanied by her husband, she made a pilgrimage to see St. Savin. There, with tears in her eyes, she presented her sickly infant to the holy hermit. Savin, moved by compassion, prayed, and according to the *vita,* soon God restored to the mother what for so long nature itself had refused. And from this time on, Gaudentia's breasts provided an abundant supply of milk to nourish her infant.[135]

PREFERENCE FOR MALE OFFSPRING

In addition to information on conception, childbirth, and the nursing of infants, a number of the *vitae* also indicate a definite societal preference for male offspring. Again, through indirect or incidental information, these sources provide fascinating insights in regard to attitudes prevalent during this period.

Several Germanic law codes, as we have noted, clearly show a high valuation and special protection of women as childbearers and of female offspring. For example, according to the *Laws of the Alamanni,* if someone caused a pregnant woman to abort her fetus, and if the sex of the fetus could be determined, the party responsible was required to pay twelve solidi if it was male and twenty-four if it was female. Thus the punishment for an act causing the loss of a female fetus was twice that required for the destruction of a male fetus.[136] However, as Emily Coleman has suggested in her study of "Infanticide in the Early Middle Ages," this "consistent care" of females as seen in the Alamannic Code might be "at least partially due to the precariousness of a girl's life as well as her sexual value as an adult." [137]

During this period, daughters were definitely valued by their families, particularly as players of major roles in the formation of marriage alliances and extended connections, as childbearers, and as abbesses of family monasteries, interceders for their families' souls, etc. Nevertheless, these women usually left their families and natal households to take up residence on the property of their husbands or within monasteries. In addition to leaving home and depriving their families of their presence and contributions through work, they also expected to receive a portion of the family inheritance. They then brought with them (either into marriage or monastic life) a dowry of some sort, thus further depleting the family's holdings. Therefore, if a couple had a number of daughters (a "surplus" in this area), they might well be looked upon as unnecessarily expensive drains on the family's limited resources. In comparative terms, daughters were perhaps viewed as not providing the same long-term investment or return to the parents and family as was expected from sons. The major "interest" in the investment in daughters seemed to accrue to their future husbands and the families they married into, rather than to their own biological family.[138] Thus in practical terms, the family's future financial and protective benefits seemed to favor sons rather than daughters.

In a few cases, as described in the sources, preference for male offspring or a male heir was specifically related to royal succession and the necessary continuity of power. This expectation consequently placed royal wives under extreme pressure to provide a child of the "required" male sex. The Life of St. Eloi is remarkably informative in regard to this problem. The hagiographer specifically notes that Queen Balthild, the wife of Clovis II, was very much aware of the pressing need for a male heir to the throne. During her pregnancy "the queen, fearing that she would give birth to a daughter and that by this the kingdom would succumb," realized that without a male heir, Neustria and Burgundy would be reunited to Austrasia under Sigebert III.[139] According to our sources, through her prayers as well as her close friendship with Eloi, bishop of Noyon, Balthild found consolation and support. St. Eloi kept the queen's spirits up as he cheerfully conversed with her, complimenting her on her imminent motherhood and on the son to whom she was going to give birth. He promised that he would be the godfather of the royal child and that he would be called Clothar. Eloi's prophecy of a male heir made Balthild extremely happy and she saw this as heaven's answer to her prayers as well as divine recompense for all of her charity and good works.[140] And in 652, as had been foretold, Balthild gave birth to a son, and Eloi baptized the infant and named him Clothar.

Perhaps one of the most fascinating examples of this preference or need for a male heir can be found in the Life of the Irish St. Abban where the sex of the infant is miraculously changed from female to male. According to this marvelous legend: "Now the king was old at this time, and he had no heir except a daughter whom his wife bore that very night. And he requested Abban to baptize her. And he perceived the sadness of the king at having no heir. 'If God pleases,' said Abban, 'thou shalt have an heir.' 'Nay,' said the king, 'that is impossible for me owing to my age.' Abban took the infant in his hands, and prayed earnestly to God that the king might have an heir; *and the girl that he immersed in the font he took out as a boy,* and laid it in the king's bosom. 'Here is thy son,' said he. And the king was exceeding glad, and so were the people of the country, at these miracles." [141]

Another interesting version of a miraculous "sex change" brought about by a saint can be found in the Life of St. Gerald, abbot of Lismore. According to this story, the king's only child, a daughter, had died. Having no heir to the throne, the king gathered together his counselors and told them, "let none of us reveal my daughter's death to these stranger saints; but let us say that mine only son is dead." And he added, "Unless they raise up to me a son instead of that daughter, I will cast them all into prison." The king then called St. Gerald and his companions to the royal court in order to bring his "son" back to life. He promised them that if they succeeded, they would be able to establish in his country a well-endowed abbey; however, if they failed, they would be forced into slavery or driven out of the kingdom. Thus, in response to the king's request, St. Gerald prayed over the corpse of the dead girl and asked God to transform her into a male child. After making the sign of the cross, he poured water into the girl's mouth from the miraculous stone, which he always carried with him. And, as related by the *vita,* to the amazement of all present, a royal male child arose from the bier. [142]

This preference or perceived need for male heirs can, then, be seen in these rather fascinating examples described in the *vitae.* It is perhaps unnecessary to point out that we do not find a similar concern among these parents with the need to produce daughters, nor any miracles involving regendering, or infant sex changes from male to female. Furthermore, in practice this preference for male progeny could be more explicitly harmful to female offspring; that is, it appears that in some cases, in their exercise of control over the size and sexual composition of their families, these early medieval parents were involved in active or passive infanticide of females. [143]

ABORTION, INFANTICIDE, AND ABANDONMENT

In general, the *vitae* usually portray mothers of saints as patient, pious, holy women: as exemplars of maternal behavior. A close study of some of these Lives, however, reveals perhaps a less conventional or less idealistic side of some of these women who, overburdened with children, are depicted instead as weak, exhausted, and depressed. In desperation they resort to self-induced abortions, or are faced with difficult decisions of complicity in infanticide, exposure, or the abandonment of their own infants.

Many of the sources of the period, including canons of church councils, penitentials, letters, sermons, and saints' Lives and miracles, provide references to the practice of abortion, infanticide, and the abandonment of infants. Strong warnings and penalties for these types of behavior among the faithful are especially found in the collections of penitentials and canons.[144] In several of his sermons, Caesarius of Arles provides us with a rather remarkable exposé of women's use of self-induced abortion and infanticide. For instance, he warns his audience that those "women whom God wants to bear more children should not take medicines to prevent their conception . . . [they] should take care of all that are conceived, or give them to someone else to rear. As many as they kill after they are already conceived or born, before the tribunal of the eternal Judge they will be held guilty of so many murders." Caesarius then adds that those women who attempt "to kill the children within them by evil medicines" and who die as a result of this, are guilty of three crimes: suicide, spiritual adultery, and murder of their unborn infant. By "taking impious drugs to prevent conception" they are negating the nature which God wanted to be fruitful. "Let them not doubt that they have committed as many murders as the number of the children they might have begotten."[145] In his "Homily to the Catechumens" he warns that it is a very grave sin "if a woman catechumen has ever taken diabolical potions for purposes of abortion and has killed her children when they were either still in the womb or already born."[146] In another sermon, he asks if it is not the devil exercising his deceits when he persuades women "after they have had two or three children, to kill either any more or those already born, by taking an abortion draught? . . . By an impious, murderous practice women take poisonous draughts to transmit incomplete life and premature death to their children through their generative organs. . . . However, if there is not yet found a tiny infant that could be killed within the womb of its mother, it is no less true that even the natural power [of generation] within the woman is destroyed." Caesarius then concludes that if women do not want to have any more children, they should settle this with their husbands: have them agree to an end of childbearing by adopting a life of chastity.[147] In these accounts we then see perhaps an indirect index to women's rather widespread use of abortion during this early period. With very limited options of birth control, they resorted to self-induced abortions in their attempts to limit the size of their families. However, as Caesarius noted, sometimes these abortions had the end result of killing the mother and the fetus, or permanently destroying women's reproductive organs.

In this same tradition we find a fascinating, detailed account of an attempted abortion related by Fortunatus in his Life of St. Germain (bishop of Paris, d. 576): "His mother, in that she had conceived

Germain a short time after her other son, was moved by a feminine shame and wanted to extinguish the infant Germain before birth. She procured the draught to cause the abortion but it did no harm. She took to sleeping on her stomach to suffocate Germain with her weight since she did him no harm with the poison. The mother was in battle with her baby; her baby was fighting back from the womb: it was a battle between mother and womb. The mother was wounded but the baby was not hurt: the 'bundle' fought lest the mother become a murderess [*parricida*]. And so it happened that, kept safe, he came forth unharmed and rendered his mother innocent. From this it was possible to foretell the future in that Germain practiced virtue before his birth." [148] According to the *vita,* these attacks against the child apparently did not stop with his birth; Germain's mother continued to mistreat him. This strange aversion toward her young son was said to have been prompted by the fear of having her house too heavily burdened with children. [149]

The saints' Lives also note several examples of recourse to infanticide. The Life of St. Berach (d. ca. 600) describes a period of great scarcity in Ireland. A certain man named Laegachan, having no provisions on his island, went out to look for food "and left his wife, who was pregnant, on the island with a single woman in her company; and he told her, if she should bear a child after his departure, to kill it, as they had no means of rearing it." According to the *vita,* "the woman bore a male child afterwards, and the woman who was with her asked her what was to be done with the boy. And she said: 'Kill it.' The other woman said: 'It is better to take it to the clerk of the church here to the west to be baptized, and let his service be offered to him in return for his maintenance.'" Following this plan, the infant was brought to Berach who baptized it, giving it the name of Ineirge, and "its service in life and death, and the service of its seed and offspring till doom was offered to Berach in return for its nurture." Berach then said that the infant should be returned to its mother and "assistance of food and means will come to them." This was done and, as the saint had foretold, the women were soon furnished with food in the form of a giant salmon. Thus with this source of nourishment the breasts of the mother were immediately filled with milk and the child was spared. [150]

This episode deals with the grave effects of famine and the inability of mothers to produce milk to feed their infants. Because of the extreme scarcity of food at the time, there was a basic assumption that the infant would be killed. Moreover, in this instance the gender of the infant was not a consideration; their only concern was with another mouth to feed. Apparently the only alternative to infanticide in this dire situation was that of deeding the child in perpetuity to the Church or monastery in exchange for its support.

Perhaps one of the best-known cases of attempted infanticide described in a *vita* can be found in the Life of St. Liudger (d. 809). In this source the hagiographer discusses the birth of the saint's mother. When Liudger's mother, Liafburg, was born, she "had a pagan grandmother, the mother, that is, of her father, who renounced altogether the Christian faith. This woman, whose name is unmentionable, became enraged that [her daughter-in-law] gave birth only to daughters, and did not produce a living son. She sent *lictores* who were to seize the then delivered girl from the breast of the mother, and kill her, before she took milk. For this was the custom of the pagans: if they wished to kill a son or daughter, they did so before they took material food." [151] However, when the servants took the baby out to drown her in a tub of water, she struggled for her life—clinging with her tiny fingers to the rim of the container. Fortunately, a neighbor woman, hearing the cries, rescued the infant from the arms of the servant. She then placed a little honey on the baby's lips, so that they would no longer be permitted to kill the infant. Also, with the help of a nursing horn, she gave the baby milk. The mother, learning of the fate of her newborn infant, secretly continued to support her. And it was then, only after the grandmother's death, that the child was returned to her home. [152]

This incident is especially revealing in its details about infanticide in the early Middle Ages. It gives a clear account of gender-based liability and female-selective infanticide. It also notes the pagan practice that required the infant to be killed before it had received any nourishment. Moreover, it was customary, among the Germanic peoples, that the father held the ultimate authority over whether the newborn would be allowed to live. This case, however, underscores the immense power a mother-in-law could wield, for she alone seems to have made the decision that the newborn infant be killed.

The Life of St. Odilia, first abbess of Hohenbourg, is also of interest for it recounts another attempted infanticide. According to this *vita*, for many years Odilia's parents, the duke and duchess of Alsace, had been unable to conceive a child. Finally, in answer to their prayers, the Duchess Berswinde became pregnant. They desperately hoped for a son; however, much to their disappointment the duchess gave birth to a daughter, Odilia, who, in addition to being the wrong gender, was blind. According to the *vita*, Duke Ethico, apparently ashamed of his newborn, and interpreting her blindness as divine punishment for his own sins, privately ordered the infant to be killed or at least abandoned and allowed to die. Publicly it was proclaimed that his wife had given birth to a dead infant. Berswinde then handed the child over to a servant who had just given birth to a son. Thus, instead of carrying out the orders to do away with the infant, she took in Odilia and nursed her as her own. A year later, the child was given to a relative in the convent of Beaume where she was said to be baptized and named by Everard, abbot of Eberheim-Münster. And with her baptism, she was said to have miraculously regained her sight. Later Odilia, with the help of her father, founded the monastery of Hohenbourg which became a famous community for women.[153]

The details of Peter Damian's infancy and early rejection (or perhaps an attempt at "passive" infanticide) by his mother are rather well known. We learn from his *vita* that at the moment of his birth his mother was "worn out by childbearing."[154] In addition, she had been severely chastised by an adolescent son for having added yet another mouth to feed to their already overcrowded household as well as another heir to share the family's fortune. Therefore, in her despair she rejected her newborn infant, refusing to nurse him or even to "hold or touch him with her own hands."[155] When the frail, half-frozen infant grew dark with hunger and cold, nearly dying of "maternal neglect," he was rescued by a priest's wife or servant. This woman then reproached the mother for her "unnatural" maternal behavior. She particularly warned her that if she did not turn her attention toward caring for her newborn, she would be guilty of the "dreadful sin of infanticide."[156] Apparently shaken out of her postpartum depression or moved from thoughts of infanticide, Peter Damian's mother then accepted her infant and nursed him; he recovered and flourished under her care.

Other sources of the period also casually mention the use of infanticide in regard to blind or physically deformed children. Gregory of Tours, in his collection of miracles of St. Martin, describes a severely deformed male who was "more a monster than a being imitating the human form." When the mother was asked how she could have given birth to such an infant, she confessed while crying that he had been conceived on a Sunday night (which was one of the nights on which the Church forbade couples to have sexual relations). However, Gregory then notes, "not daring to kill him, as mothers were accustomed to do [in regard to severely deformed infants], she raised him just as if he had been a healthy boy."[157]

According to tradition, the Irish St. Fillan, the son of St. Kentigerna, was born physically disfigured: he had the appearance of having a large stone in his mouth. His father therefore ordered that as a "monster" the infant should be killed, that is, thrown into the nearby lake. His mother, St. Kentigerna, with tears, commended him

to divine pity. According to the story, the infant was miraculously rescued from the bottom of the lake by St. Ibar and was then baptized by
the saint.[158]

One of the Lives of St. Brigid notes that a woman with her child,
who had been born deformed—"table-faced" or "flat faced" as well
as blind—came to seek the saint's assistance. She told Brigid that her
husband wanted to kill the infant. Brigid then bathed the child's face
in water and, as related by the *vita,* its physical deformity and blindness were miraculously cured.[159]

Other sources indicate that families also resorted to the selling of
their children. The seventh-century *Penitential of Theodore,* for example, asserts that a father "driven by necessity" has the power to sell
his son into slavery. And this action can be performed "without sin"
on the part of the father.[160] In this context it is interesting to recall that
several of the saints of this period, at least according to tradition, had
been sold by their relatives or parents. St. Balthild, for example, was
said to have been an English slave bought from her parents or perhaps
stolen by slave merchants, and then sold to the mayor of the Palace
of Neustria.[161] St. Brigid was allegedly threatened with being sold by
her father because he was displeased with her profligate behavior in
bestowing his wealth on the poor.[162]

The *vitae* also provide cases of abandoned infants and the role that
the Church assumed in either providing care or serving as a clearing-
house for the adoption of these children. The Life of the Irish St. Cum-
mine notes that he was born of an incestuous relationship: "On his
own daughter Fiachna begot him through drunkenness: for the girl
used to sleep with her mother." The father then interrogated his
daughter to determine who was the father of the child. After learning
that he was the infant's father, he ordered that the child be killed.
However, when the infant was born, he was brought to Cell Ite "and
there he was left on the top of a cross in a little basket (cuimin): hence
he was called Cuimmin, and there he was nursed and taught." [163]

Another Irish anecdote concerns Comgall and the naming of Molua,
son of *ochae.* When Comgall and his monks were traveling they heard
the cry of an infant who had been abandoned in the rushes. One of the
monks, on kicking the rushes, saw the baby, whom he picked up and
brought to his "armpit." When asked by Comgall what he had found
and what he had done with it, he responded that he had found a baby:
"I gave my kick to it . . . and I have brought it in my armpit. This shall
be its name," said Comgall, "My-kick son of Armpit" (*Mac ochae;*
i.e., son of armpit). After this he was fostered by Comgall.[164]

The ninth-century Life of the hermit priest St. Goar, in describing
a test of the saint's chastity, relates in some detail the practice of

abandoning children at the church. "For it was then the custom at Trier that when a woman bore a child whose parents did not wish to be known, or whom they [she?] could not afford to rear because of poverty, she would expose the newborn infant in a certain marble basin designated for this . . . and when the exposed child was found, there would be someone who, moved by pity, would take him and rear him. If, as sometimes happens, the wardens or *matricularii* of the church took the child, they would ask among the people if someone wished to bring him up and have him for his or her own, and when someone would come forward for this, the abandoned child would be taken to the bishop, and by his authority the right to bring up and retain the infant would be assigned to the person who had accepted him from the *matricularii*." [165]

A number of Lives also indicate that the saints' mothers died in childbirth or shortly thereafter, and consequently the abandoned infants were raised by the monks or nuns of a local monastery. The Life of St. Paschase Radbert, abbot of Corbie (d. 865), records that he was abandoned without resources at the death of his mother (which occurred either at his birth or while he was still an infant). Ordinarily the infant would have died; however, according to the customs of the time, he was left on the parvis of the Monastery of Notre-Dame de Soissons. Here, on finding the abandoned child, the nuns of the community hurried out and brought the orphan into their convent. They took it upon themselves to provide for all of his needs, and later they entrusted his education to the monks of St. Pierre. At the age of twenty-two he retired to the abbey of Corbie. There he was welcomed by Adelard, abbot and brother of Theodrade, who had been abbess and Paschase's benefactor at Notre-Dame de Soissons. Later in life he recalled the great kindness of the abbess and nuns at Soissons and dedicated many of his works to his "adoptive mothers." [166]

There have been a number of studies on the abandonment of children and infanticide in the Middle Ages. [167] Saints' Lives, with their interest in demography and human (as well as divine) intervention in infant mortality, seem to further corroborate the conclusions of a number of these investigations; namely, they provide evidence of the practice of abandonment of infants, as well as the use of infanticide, and in some cases female-selective infanticide, during this period. John Boswell has produced numerous cases which indicate that at least some of the infants who were abandoned or "marked" for infanticide were in fact rescued by the "kindness of strangers." Thus through the Church or through the institution of fosterage, they were provided with "artificial or constructed families" which assumed the role of the biological family. [168] However, by the very nature of our sources, we generally hear only about the "success stories" (those who were rescued and grew up to be famous individuals) and not much about the others who were abandoned or killed or who died because no one made an extraordinary effort to keep them alive.

Although it is difficult, if not impossible, to determine the extent of the use of "active"/"positive" or "passive"/"negative" infanticide during this period, it appears to have been used by people of all classes, the rich as well as the poor, and it involved a wide variety of motives. However, there seems to be clear evidence, such as that recorded in the Life of St. Liudger, that infanticide was in some cases gender-based, namely, they practiced female-selective infanticide. Apparently, despite the high regard for female children and the exceptional protection accorded to women in their childbearing years, as expressed in the Germanic law codes, this special attention might reflect in part the actual "precariousness of a girl's life," as Emily Coleman has suggested.[169] Thus under certain conditions, such as a "surplus" of daughters, and in light of limited inheritance and dynastic strategies, there remained a preference for male offspring, and in some situations female infants were then singled out for infanticide.[170] (Further corroboration of this tradition can be found in an early twelfth-century source of the missionary bishop St. Otto of Bamberg. In his warning directed to the pagan Pomeranians, the bishop specifically attacked their heathen practice of female infanticide as unnatural.)[171] Nevertheless, although we do have evidence of female-selective, "passive" and "active" infanticide, the actual cases of attempted infanticide mentioned in the saints' Lives and their miracles provide a definite mix of female and male infants.

It appears from the examples in the *vitae* that parents resorted to infanticide in order to rid their family of an "excess" of children, children with severe birth defects, or children begotten of incestuous relationships. Infanticide was also used to avoid the shame of scandal, for example, among communities of nuns.[172] Moreover, it appears that especially during times of great scarcity and famine, and as a measure of desperation, families had recourse to this practice. During these periods, infanticide and abandonment were by no means gender specific: male and female infants would be killed or allowed to die through exposure, nonfeeding, and other means. It is, then, in this context that the Church provided reduced penalties for destitute mothers who killed their children. According to the *Penitential of Theodore,* for example, "if a mother slays her child, if she commits homicide, she shall do penance for fifteen years"; however, "if a poor woman slays her child, she shall do penance for seven years." Thus the punishment was reduced by more than half if the mother involved was indigent.[173] Similarly an eighth-century collection of penitentials seems to be especially forgiving: it warns that "a woman who exposes her unwanted child because she has been raped by an enemy or is unable to nourish and sustain [him] is not to be blamed, but she should nevertheless do penance for three weeks."[174] Therefore the punishments for infanticide suggested by the penitentials seem to show a certain awareness or understanding of the dire situations that some of these poor women faced.

MOTHERHOOD, SERIOUS ILLNESSES, AND THE MORTALITY OF CHILDREN

Following this brief look at abortion, abandonment, and infanticide, it is perhaps important to also examine hagiographic perceptions of mothers who experienced the loss of a child. Although it is difficult to generalize or to attempt to ascertain the mothers' feelings in cases of infanticide, from hints found in the *vitae* many of these women seemed to have been extremely reluctant to turn over their newborns to be abandoned, exposed, or killed. In many of these cases, as part of a family strategy or as a general practice (e.g., in regard to infants with severe birth defects), these women probably had little choice in the matter. Nevertheless, in a few cases, these mothers seem to have been secretly involved in strategies or negotiations with servants and others who would then spare their infants' lives and provide care for them until other arrangements could be made.

A number of casual references in the *vitae* note the incredible grief and trauma which mothers suffered at the death of their infants. As might be expected, with the very high infant mortality rate of the period, many families suffered the loss of at least one child and our sources frequently mention these untimely deaths. For example, St. Hildegard (wife of Charlemagne) had nine children and lost three at a very early age; seven of the twenty children of the blessed Agnes of Germany died in infancy; St. Domane lost all three of her children at an early age; St. Monegund lost her two daughters when they were very young; and so on.[175]

Some scholars have therefore contended that the frequent loss of children bred a feeling of careless indifference or a certain "callousness" toward one's offspring during this period. Parents could not allow themselves to become too attached or invest too much of themselves in children who would be regarded as likely to be lost.[176] This theory, however, as others have argued, seems to underestimate the very real love and affection of medieval parents for their offspring. It fails to take into consideration the many expressions of strong emotional attachment between parents and children that can be found in the sources; rather, it seems to reflect, at least in part, a partristic ideal, a behavioral convention or formula fostered by the Church.

The grief-filled occasions of the loss of a child therefore provided the hagiographers with an opportunity to expound on the transitoriness of life and the rewards of heaven; they also allowed Church writers to attempt to loosen the earthly bonds between mother, or parent, and child—to urge parents to distance their emotional attachments and to encourage "spiritual selfishness" in order to dedicate oneself completely to God and the Church. Thus Jerome in his letter to Paula on the tragic death of her daughter, Blaesilla, offers sympathy and attempts to moderate her grief. He warns her, however, that "too great affection towards one's children is disaffection towards God. Abraham gladly prepares to slay his only son, do you complain if one child out of several has received her crown." [177] Therefore, according to St. Jerome and other ecclesiastical writers, those mothers who accepted their children's deaths without excessive grief and with proper resignation were to serve as role models of Christian perfection. In this tradition Gregory of Tours, for example, provides us with Clotilda's alleged response to the death of her firstborn infant son shortly after his baptism: "'I give thanks to Almighty God,' replied Clotild, 'the creator of all things, who has not found me completely unworthy, for He has deigned to welcome to His kingdom a child conceived in my womb. I am not at all cast down in my mind because of what has happened, for I know that my child, who was called away from this world in his white baptismal robes will be nurtured in the sight of God.'" [178]

The early tenth-century Life of St. Rictrude (d. ca. 688) relates that Rictrude, founder of the monastery of Marchiennes, entered the convent along with her three daughters. There Adalsendis, her youngest daughter, died on Christmas Day. The *vita* then describes in some detail how Rictrude acting in a manner "forgetful of her sex," suppressed her personal or maternal emotions, moderated her grief, and dutifully followed proper monastic comportment at this difficult time. According to the *vita*: "And what did good Rictrude, strong and long-suffering in adversity, do then? With her mind running in two contrary directions, did she rejoice or did she mourn? While the whole world listened to the angel intoning: 'Behold, I bring you good tidings of great joy which shall be to all people,' she had her dead daughter before her eyes. But did she give in to the natural sorrow of her condition? *The strength of the manly mind within her overcame her womanly feelings.* Sorrow for her daughter's death was not suffered to dominate her nor sadness allowed to enter where the birth of Life was celebrated. Let me absolve myself briefly of the worthy memory: the due office of burial was completed according to the custom of the faithful, but the custom of mourning her loved one was set aside. Then in sequence the solemnities of the first, second and third days were celebrated. Then, on the forth succeeding day, when Holy Church recalls the massacre of the Innocents slaughtered by Herod for Christ and the misery of their bereft mothers, prudent Rictrude knew how she should spend the time. For there is a time for all things under heaven: a time for joy and yet a time for tears. She did not mourn during the explication of the mystery where honor is shown to the holy martyrs in praise of God; for then ceremonial devotions are tendered, not tears." She then told the nuns that now, " 'for myself, I will follow the example of those ladies, the mothers of the most holy innocent children—so like my own little innocent—for whom much mourning and wailing is heard today. For now, it is permissible to mourn this one snatched too soon to death.' And she asked a friend for a private place to mourn so that her grief might be satisfied as is compatible with nature." [179]

In contrast to these official models of controlled behavior and moderated grief, we can see perhaps a more realistic response of bereaved parents portrayed in a number of *vitae,* miracles, and other sources of the period. In these accounts, mothers neither resigned themselves nor took consolation in the death of their children; rather, they showed great love and emotional attachment to their young and continually expressed their deep anguish and grief at their children's death. Ronald Finucane, in his work *Miracles and Pilgrims: Popular Beliefs in Medieval England,* notes the case of a woman who, after the death of her newborn infant, fled to the forest and lived like a crazed beast.[180] Finucane also observes that children's accidents brought about temporary insanity in some of these medieval parents. "One woman collapsed and nearly lost her mind when she learned that her son had fallen into a ditch and drowned, while another, deranged with grief, kept the body of her child for five days and refused to allow burial. Accidents claimed many more children than adults, and the violent grief of the mothers and fathers so often noted in the miracles reminds us that medieval parents were as capable of feeling anguish as modern." [181] (In this context it is interesting to note that a number of saints' Lives condemned mothers who had lost their children for their excessive displays of grief.) [182]

An especially moving case concerning the loss of children and its effect on an early medieval mother-saint can be found in the life of the sixth-century blessed Monegund, recorded by Gregory of Tours. "She had been married according to her parents' wishes, and had two daughters, which brought her a profound joy, so that she used to say 'God has made me fertile so that two daughters might be born to me.'" Gregory continues: "But the bitterness of this world soon dissipated this earthly joy, for both were brought to their death by a light fever. From that time the mother was desolate; mourning and lamenting for the death of her children she did not stop weeping, day and night, and neither her husband nor her friends nor any of her relations could console her." We learn that after some time she "came to herself." Removing her mourning clothes, and having "nothing more to do with her husband," Monegund retired to live in a cell as an anchorite. She devoted herself entirely to God and spent her time in prayer, fasting, and vigils. She also performed many miraculous cures.[183]

These examples and others in this pattern seem to reaffirm the strong love and affection of medieval parents for their offspring. Moreover, the proliferation in the *vitae* of special miracles which were enacted on behalf of children also reflects this high valuation of children. Many of the miracle stories focus on desperate parents who invoked the saints to bring about the miraculous cures of their sick or injured children, or to resuscitate them and bring them back to life. These medieval parents, like parents of today, would go to any extreme to see their ailing children restored to health. And while these strong emotional attachments and feelings of anguish for their offspring might initially appear highly incongruent with family strategies of abandonment, the selling of one's children, or infanticide—which, as we have seen, were all practiced during this same period—these behavioral modes are not necessarily incompatible. In many cases, these measures seem to have been acts of desperation or of last resort; they were drastic steps that parents were forced to take and, in some cases, they were no doubt viewed as the only way to save one's children or one's own life. For example, as Boswell has noted, the sale of one's children or their abandonment at a church might have provided the best hope for a child's survival.[184] In this subsistence economy, during periods of extreme shortage and cycles of famine, infanticide can be seen as essentially a pragmatic measure, adopted to increase the chances of survival of the other members of the family. It might also have been viewed as a type of mercy killing since with no immediate prospect of food, malnourished mothers would not be able to produce enough milk to keep their infants alive for any length of time. Infanticide, under these dire conditions, was an act of desperation (not an expression of callousness toward one's children); and it would not necessarily preclude parents' great love for and attachment to their children.

Nevertheless, infanticide, unrelated to famine and extreme poverty, and as practiced by the aristocracy—especially female-selective infanticide (e.g., as noted in the Life of St. Liudger and perhaps that of Odilia)—is in many ways more difficult for us to see in a sympathetic way or to attempt to explain in light of the exigencies of the age. It reflects quite a different set of values and family strategy, with a definite preference for male offspring.

MATERNAL INFLUENCES ON SAINTLY
OFFSPRING: "GOOD MOTHERS"

In many of the *vitae,* mothers are depicted as looming large in the lives of their sons and daughters. They are shown as exercising an immense amount of influence and control over their saintly offspring throughout their lives. Frequently their piety, religiosity, and active encouragement of their children to follow careers in the Church are contrasted strongly with the passive or "negative" behavior of their husbands. For in many of the *vitae,* the fathers assume a rather marginal role in the raising of their children, or they are presented as attempting to hinder or obstruct plans for their children to enter religious professions.

In their desire to see that their infants were nourished on the "milk of the Catholic faith," mothers of saints were concerned with the early dedication of their offspring to the Church. As we have noted in our study of domestic proselytization, one of the primary functions of mothers within the Church was to secure the baptism of their infants in the Catholic faith.

Many of the mothers described in the *vitae* were celebrated for their role in the Christian education and spiritual direction of their young children. (This important function appears to have been reserved for the mother of the family rather than for the father). A good number of these women were mothers of bishops, abbots, and priests and were singled out for the formative role they exercised, particularly in the education of their sons.

Ausentia, the mother of St. Avitus/Avite, bishop of Vienne (d. 518), was praised for her role in educating her four children. She was seen as a model for Christian mothers, and the education which she provided for her children prepared them for their saintly lives and careers in the Church.[185] St. Clarus, abbot of St. Marcellus at Vienne (d. ca. 660) lost his father while he was still an infant and was raised by his pious mother. She apparently took special pains in her son's education and in his early formation of Christian virtues and pious practices. According to the *vita,* she often took him to the churches of the holy martyrs in Vienne; here she passed many hours in prayer before the tombs of the saints. Clarus apparently became so accustomed to this exercise that even as young as he was, he soon became a "man" of prayer and brought about miracles.[186] St. Rictrude and her husband, the blessed Adalbald (7th c.), were the parents of four children, all of whom came to be recognized as popular saints. The credit for their sanctity, after God, was attributed to their mother, St. Rictrude. For, according to the *vita,* it was specifically through her influence—her lessons, tears, prayers, fasts, charity, and almsgiving—that they were raised to become saints.[187]

St. Eugenie d'Obernai, abbess of Hohenbourg (d. 735) received her early religious training and dedication to the Church from her mother. According to the *vita,* each morning the pious duchess, Gerlinde, took her daughter into the castle's chapel and there, prostrate before an image of Christ and Mary, she consecrated her daughter to their service and entreated them to instill in her all of the Christian virtues. Gerlinde occupied herself with teaching her daughter to hear the language of piety and to see only the most edifying things. We are told that she was so successful in her training program that she soon found it necessary to moderate the religious fervor of her young daughter.[188]

The Life of the empress St. Adelaide notes her single-minded focus on the raising of her son, Otto. After she had given birth to two young princes who both died very young, Otto was born. He was scarcely two months old when Adelaide carried him into the chapel and offered him to Christ, begging him to shed his grace on her infant. Moreover, she considered the education of her young son as her primary duty. While he read his studies, she stayed in the same room with him, adding her own ideas to the lessons of the masters. She provided him with encouragement and praise when he needed it. She also taught him about poverty and deprivation, frequently taking him with her on her rounds to visit the poor, in order to make him more aware of and sensitive to their miserable condition in life. We also learn that she seized all occasions to inspire in him the fear of God and hatred of sin, as well as the duties of a Christian and a prince.[189]

According to the Life of St. Bruno (Pope Leo IX), Bruno's mother, Heilvige, took charge of his early education. In order for him to learn the psalms, she purchased a beautiful psalter written in gold letters which she placed in the hands of her young son.[190]

The Life of St. Margaret of Scotland notes that she was very much involved in the education and disciplining of her children—especially that of her sons. According to her *vita,* "she gave no less care to her sons than to herself, so that they should be brought up with every attention, and instructed as far as possible in honourable ways. And because she knew that it is written, 'he who spares the rod hates his son,' she had directed the steward of the household to restrain them himself with threats and whippings whenever they erred in infantile naughtiness, as is young children's way." According to Turgot, it was "through this scrupulous care of their mother, as children they excelled in uprightness of manners many who were more advanced in age." [191] He also notes that "she took great pains bringing her sons very often before her, to teach them, as far as their age could understand of Christ and of Christ's faith, and to exhort them always to fear him." [192]

References to the active involvement of mothers in their children's upbringing and lives proliferate in the *vitae*. According to the Church, it was a mother's duty to inculcate within her children proper morals and values and to educate them in the Christian faith. This was to be accomplished through example and formal study. Therefore a number of saints' Lives of this period, in underscoring the importance of a mother's influence, stressed her obligation not to abandon her children in order to adopt a second career in the Church; instead, she was encouraged to delay her own career plans or to take her young children along with her when she entered monastic life.[193]

In a number of instances, these exemplary mothers did not begin their second careers alone, but brought with them their young daughters and, in a few cases, their young sons. Within the confines of the monastic community, aided by the other nuns, they continued their role as mother. In this tradition we find St. Rictrude and her three daughters who retired to the family monasteries at Marchiennes and Hamage; and her contemporary, St. Bertha, abbess and founder of Blangy, in Artois, whose two daughters also received the veil in their mother's monastery.[194] St. Ida, founder of the family monastery of Nivelles, entered the community with her young daughter, Gertrude, with whom she shared her rule as abbess.[195] St. Salaberga was joined in the family monastery that she had founded in Laon by her daughter, Anstrude, when she was twelve years of age.[196] There are also a few cases denoted in the saints' Lives of mothers who brought their young sons with them into the convent. One example is that of St. Bertha (9th c.) who retired with her young son Rupert to the monastery of Bingen, where she dedicated herself to providing him with a Christian education. Later Bertha and Rupert founded a monastery and hospice for the poor.[197] The Life of St. Stephen, abbot of Obazine, mentions that he was brought up by his mother in a monastery of women. And when he was past the age of five years (beyond which no males were apparently permitted to dwell there), he was removed from the women's quarters and sent to the male section of the monastery.[198]

Thus one of the prominent patterns of saintly motherhood that emerges from the *vitae* is the extremely formative role these women played in the lives of their children: as a compelling, persistent presence, they were responsible for the baptism of their children in the Catholic faith; they encouraged them to lead lives of moral virtue and to enter professions within the Church; and they dedicated themselves to their education through books as well as by example.

THE CHARACTERIZATION OF BAD MOTHERS IN THE *VITAE*

Saints' Lives also have their share of "evil" or "bad" mothers. These women are often depicted as nonmaternal, as inordinately severe and regularly abusive toward their children. These figures provide a strong contrast to the "ideal" maternal images so prevalent in the *vitae*, while their "bad" behavior also serves to accentuate the "saintliness" of their own children. As noted by Mary McLauglin, the "bad mother" and her consistently malicious role served to test the future saint's heroic virtue: she tested the mettle, or the patience and "charity," of the young, aspiring saint.[199]

A number of the saints' Lives furnish rather clear incidents of child abuse, which range from hitting and severe beatings to attempted poisoning or even the alleged murder of children. The *vita* of St. Genovefa notes an instance in which the young saint insisted on attending church with her mother, Geroncia. Irritated by her daughter's obstinate behavior, Geroncia hit Genovefa sharply, and soon thereafter, according to the *vita,* the mother became blind. She remained in this state for some twenty-one months and, relates the hagiographer, it was only through a miracle performed by her daughter that she was cured.[200] Thus in this story, in response to her abusive behavior toward her saintly daughter, the mother became the object of divine punishment.

A particularly interesting case of possible child abuse among saintly mothers and their daughters can be found in a Life of St. Eusebia, abbess of Hamay (7th c.). According to this account, the young Eusebia had been adopted by her great-grandmother, Gertrude, abbess of Hamay, and appointed as her successor. Although only twelve years of age at the time of her great-grandmother's death, Eusebia accepted the position and became abbess of Hamay. Eusebia's mother, St. Rictrude, abbess of the neighboring community of Marchiennes, objected to Eusebia's rule on grounds of her youth, and ordered her to come to Marchiennes. The teenaged Eusebia refused, and her mother therefore had to obtain a special "restraining order" from the king, which forced her to come to Marchiennes. Thus with great sorrow,

Eusebia and her small group of nuns went to Marchiennes. They brought along with them the body of Eusebia's great-grandmother, St. Gertrude, and other holy relics. Eusebia, however, continued to defy her mother by returning each night to her old monastery in order to celebrate the vigils and offices of the hours in her church. Learning of this disobedient behavior, Rictrude forbade Eusebia to leave Marchiennes, but Eusebia persisted, and the battle of the wills continued. Rictrude then turned to force. She called in her son (the future St. Maurontus) to whip his sister, which he was said to have accomplished with such excessive strength and brutality that, according to the *vita*, he nearly killed her. During the beating, Eusebia was held by a man whose sword hilt jabbed her painfully in the side, causing her from then on to spit blood. And although she recovered from this rather fierce beating and lived for many more years, Eusebia's wounds apparently never fully healed. It is, however, interesting to note that after all of these attempts to reduce Eusebia to an obedient, submissive daughter and to dissuade her by force from returning to Hamay, Rictrude, in consultation with the bishops and abbots of the area, ultimately relented and allowed Eusebia and her nuns to return to her monastery of Hamay where she ruled as a successful abbess for many years.[201]

After describing these events, the hagiographer then attempted to answer various accusations directed against this family of saints. The detractors contended that those involved in this type of unseemly behavior, namely, "a mother who attacked her innocent daughter for wanting to serve God; a daughter who detested her own mother and fled her as an enemy; a son who, with his mother's consent, branded his sister like a fugitive taken away in secret, or like a condemned thief whipped her so viciously that she nearly died," did not deserve sainthood. The hagiographer therefore attempted to defend the "holy mother Rictrude" saying that she did not persecute her innocent daughter; rather, Eusebia was too young and needed to be under her supervision "in order to achieve greater perfection by more powerful exhortations and examples." Furthermore, Eusebia, as a bride of Christ, "did not spurn or despise her blessed mother for she knew that her Spouse commanded: 'Honor thy father and thy mother that thy days may be long upon the land.'" Still "she wished only to delight in Him and show no other love, not even affection for her mother, lest it should detract from her love's immoderate fervor." The author also argued that Maurontus's behavior did not come "from hate or cruelty but rather from fraternal charity for her insolence and disobedience . . . knowing the Scripture: 'He that spareth the rod, hateth his son.'" Thus, according to the *vita*, Rictrude and Maurontus, although perhaps mistaken in their human judgment, corrected the holy virgin, Eusebia, for at that time they were unaware of the divine grace that was in her.[202]

Perhaps one of the most blatant and well-documented cases of child abuse found in a *vita* concerns St. Christina of Markyate (12th c.). The hostility in this case centered on the parents' wish for Christina to marry and her obstinate refusal to comply. According to the *vita:* "at the instigation of the devil, [Beatrix, the mother] loosed all her fury on her own daughter, neglecting no sort of wicked artifice which might in her opinion, destroy her integrity. . . . she persecuted her with unheard-of cruelty, sometimes openly, at other times secretly." The account continues its documentation of these attacks: "There was one time when on impulse she took her out from a banquet and, out of sight of the guests, pulled her hair out and beat her until she was weary of it. Then she brought her back, lacerated as she was, into the presence of the revellers as an object of derision, leaving on her back such weals from the blows as could never be removed as long as she lived."[203]

A number of mothers of saints, who were singled out for their cruel behavior, were stepmothers and conform to the "wicked stepmother" stereotype. According to the Life of St. Brigid, for example, her jealous stepmother mistreated the young saint by forcing her to work at various heavy tasks which were thought to be inappropriate or beneath her. According to one of her *vitae,* after hearing stories of Brigid's fame and virtues, Brigid's stepmother grew increasingly perverse: her "jealously grew into a hatred and the whole poison of her malice spewed forth against the innocent Brigid." She loaded Brigid "with the dishonor and drudgery of servile work, and she therefore conspired to crush Brigid under the weight of the task or the shame of the humiliation by imposing such jobs as cooking, baking, herding swine, sheepherding, reaping, weaving, and one more degrading thing after another both at home and abroad."[204]

The popular legend of the virgin St. Lufthildis (9th c.) notes that she suffered much from the persecutions of her "cruel" stepmother. She was severely beaten for failing to keep the wild geese out of her father's fields. The young saint's stepmother was apparently particularly provoked by Lufthildis's profligate behavior: she is accused of wasting their food and their bread through her generosity to the poor.[205]

The stepmother of St. Wilfrid was also remembered for her cruelty toward her young son. Eddius Stephanus in his Life of Wilfrid comments briefly on this treatment: "When he was fourteen he decided to leave his father's estates to seek the Kingdom of Heaven, for his stepmother was harsh and cruel. His own mother was dead."[206]

Perhaps the most exaggerated case in this tradition of "wicked step-mothers" concerns the legend surrounding Elfrida, the stepmother of Edward the Martyr (d. 979). Edward's mother, Ethelfleda, died soon after his birth. As a youth he ruled for about three years under the guidance of St. Dunstan and was then murdered. The earliest account attributes this murder to Ethelred's retainers. However, about one hundred years after the event (and apparently without any good evidence), Elfrida, Edward's stepmother, is accused of perpetrating this act.[207] Thus, according to William of Malmesbury's account, the young king was murdered by his stepmother, Elfrida. He notes that Elfrida was anxious to advance her own son Egelred, only seven years of age, so that she might govern the land. "The woman, however, *with a stepmother's hatred,* began to meditate a subtle stratagem, in order that not even the title of king might be wanting to her child, and to lay a treacherous snare for her son-in-law [stepson]." And after he had been murdered, Elfrida was said to have been seized by remorse for this heinous crime. She therefore adopted the monastic life and built the monasteries of Amesbury and Wherwell.[208]

There are also a number of cases of "evil" mothers-in-law portrayed in our sources. We have already noted the abusive behavior of the Spanish queen, Goiswinth, toward her daughter-in-law, Ingund.[209] Perhaps one of the most wicked mothers-in-law depicted in the *vitae* is found in the Life of the saint and martyr Godeleva (d. ca. 1070). The hagiographer, Drogo, notes at the outset that "all mothers-in-law hate their daughters-in-law. They long for their sons to get married, but when they do they soon grow jealous of them and their wives."[210] We also learn that from the start this woman particularly disliked her daughter-in-law because of her appearance: i.e., her dark hair and eyebrows. Out of jealousy and hatred she persecuted Godeleva: she took all of her jewels and precious objects, imprisoned her, and tried to starve her with a sparse regimen of bread and water. Ultimately, as we have noted, Godeleva was strangled by two of her husband's servants and came to be regarded as a patron saint of marriage.[211]

The grandmother of St. Germain is also described as an "evil" or "wicked" woman. According to the *vita,* not only did the little saint suffer abuse from his mother, but while still a young child his grandmother tried to poison him. Favoring another of her grandsons, she did not want Germain to have a share in the family inheritance. She therefore sent a servant with two bottles, one of wine and the other of poison, to carry out her plan. However, according to the saint's Life, through divine intervention her evil plans were foiled: the other grandson received the poison and the future saint was spared.[212]

A number of mothers and stepmothers are, then, portrayed in the *vitae* in a rather unflattering and negative light. Although perhaps in some cases their responses were not totally "unprovoked" by their precocious offspring, these women were seen as self-consciously cruel and unrelentingly abusive toward their children. As such, their "unmaternal" behavior served as an initial test or trial which these young saints had to patiently endure or overcome in the early stages of their lives.

SPIRITUAL MOTHERHOOD AND FOSTERAGE

The *vitae* and chronicles of the time also provide many references to "voluntary" motherhood in an inclusive or generic sense. Abbesses were viewed as "mothers" of their monastic communities, or queens were seen as "mothers" by members of their court and the people of their kingdom. They were called "mother of all" or "mother of all poor," or within the monastic community: *mater congregationis, mater familias, mater monasterii, mater spiritualis,* etc. Bede provides a number of examples of these "all inclusive" mothers: he notes one abbess who was "mother not only to her vast community but mother to all who know her—so great is her devotion and solicitude." He describes other abbesses as a "virgin mother of many virgins vowed to God," or as "mother and instructress of women devoted to God," or a "careful" or "watchful mother," or "the mother and nurse of consecrated women."[213]

Baudonivia tells us that St. Radegund loved her community so much "that she forgot her family." She told her nuns: "I have chosen you for daughters, you are my light, my life, my repose, and all my happiness, you are my new plantation [*novella plantatio*]."[214] "The Letter of the Seven Bishops," which was sent to Radegund when she established her convent in Poitiers, notes that the nuns "leave their families and choose you as their mother in God's grace, if not by nature." In his description of Radegund's funeral, Gregory of Tours relates that near the saint's coffin crowded a group of about two hundred nuns, who in their grief cried: "Holy mother, to whom will you leave us orphans? To whom do you entrust us who have been abandoned? We have left our parents, our possessions, and our homeland, and we have followed you. What will you leave us except perpetual tears and endless grief? . . . Alas for us, who have been abandoned by our holy mother! Happy were those who migrated from this world while you were alive!"[215]

The *vita* of St. Balthild describes this queen-saint as an "inclusive" mother—particularly while she remained at court: she was for "the great men of the realm mother . . . she appeared to be the *optima nutrix* [the best foster mother] of the young and adolescents, and she attracted the affections of all." We also learn that she took it upon herself to be guardian of the orphans and of the wards of her kingdom. Through her role in amending the head tax, Balthild attempted to stop families oppressed by extreme poverty from wishing for the death of their children.[216]

According to Hrotswitha of Gandersheim, St. Oda, in response to a vision of her mother, was moved to establish the monastery of Gandersheim. The family convent was then ruled by three of St. Oda's daughters. As foundress and mother of twelve children, Oda spent her final years at Gandersheim, where she applied her experience as a mother to her new role of "mother of souls" and foster mother: "As the sweet love of a foreseeing mother at one time restrains her daughters from wrongdoing through fear, and at another time persuades them to do good through friendly advice, so this saintly woman instructed her dear foster daughters."[217]

The Ottonian queen-saint Mathilda was also celebrated in her *vitae* as a loving mother who in public and private dispensed her maternal affection. She was the mother of five children as well as an extensive spiritual family which included the poor, pilgrims, widows, orphans, and especially nuns of the monasteries she established: *sanctimoniales semper dilexit materno amore* ("she always loved her nuns with a maternal love"). As noted by Corbet in his *Les Saints ottoniens,* she was characterized in the *Vita Mahthildis antiquior* fifteen times as *mater,* ten times as *regina,* three times as *genitrix,* and five times each as *beata, sancta, sanctissima.* Thus the special emphasis on the queen as mother can be seen in the prevalent use of the qualifying terms *mater* and *genitrix* found in the *vitae.*[218]

The Life of St. Adelheid, abbess of Vilich, also underscores her role as mother to her own monastic community as well as to her extended spiritual family. Her notable maternal charity and affection or *officium matris* is reinforced by the abundant use of *mater* in her *vita:* this saintly abbess is designated as "mother" twenty times in her Life.[219] Bertha, the author of the *vita,* also provides a number of wonderful personal details relating to Adelheid's role as mother of the monastery. She writes: "and remembering the precepts of the holy father, St. Benedict, through her deeds, she acquired the name and status of a mother who gave to those in need without thought of recompense. In the winter when, after early matins, they went back to their dormitories, Adelheid herself checked the girls' beds and rubbed their feet with her loving hands until they were warm again. Contrary to the Rule, she did not leave the care of sick sisters to other prudent and careful sisters but she herself attended to them every day without interference. She would humbly kneel before the bed of each sister and gently holding their heads up in her hands, she would lovingly give them food and drink and tears would fall down her noble cheeks as if she herself had borne them from her womb." Bertha also notes that "Adelheid aided and strengthened the institutions of religious ceremonies and the schools of divine service which were always the most important responsibilities of her office. Adelheid would visit them frequently and ask questions on grammar and when she received a correct answer, she would reward the pupil quickly with a maternal kiss, filled as she was with spiritual joy at the prospect of further advances." With the death of Adelheid's sister, Bertrada, Adelheid was asked to rule over Bertrada's convent in Cologne in addition to her own house at Vilich. According to her hagiographer, it always pained Adelheid to be away from her community at Vilich: "But if the daughters were granted the return of their mother, they cried for such joy as if they had seen God himself. Like the hen which gathers her chicks under her wings, thus did Adelheid draw them all to her in wondrous love and kindness." Adelheid's great generosity as a mother abbess is also emphasized in the *vita*: "at one time, almost the whole world was afflicted by a bitter famine and great masses of the starving came from everywhere, to partake of her generosity, as from the breast of a mother" (see plate 2).[220]

Unusually touching is the description of the queen-saint Margaret of Scotland and the important maternal role that she assumed in her kingdom. According to her *vita*, she was called "the kindest mother" to the poor, orphans, and widows. In describing the queen's daily schedule, Turgot relates: "She caused to be brought in to her in the first hour of the day nine baby orphans, destitute of all support: she had ordered the softer foods, in which the age of babyhood delights, to be prepared for them each day; and when they were brought she deigned to place them on her knees; to make their little drinks for them, and to put food into their mouths with the spoons that she used herself. Thus the queen who was honoured by the whole population filled for Christ's sake the part of a servant and a kindest mother."[221]

Indeed, one of the most prominent areas of motherhood described in the *vitae* is that of surrogate or foster mothers. These women are frequently designated in the saints' Lives by the term *nutrix* (nurse), or *matertera* (second mother). The use of fosterage, or the rearing of young children outside of the household into which they were born, seems to have been a rather common arrangement during this period. Although fosterage occurred within aristocratic circles in secular society, many of these relationships were also concentrated within the monastic milieu. The monastic community served as a type of "extended" or "artificial" *familia* and played an especially important role in the nurturing and education of these "foster children"—a number of whom won recognition of sainthood.

The *vitae* furnish a wealth of detailed information on specific adoptive or fosterage relationships. Some of these cases seemed to consist of formal adoptions; others entailed rather informal arrangements between the biological parents and the adoptive or spiritual parent: in both of these arrangements the biological parents retained legal authority over their children. Other arrangements seem to have been based on oblation, that is, the donation (Latin, *oblatio,* "offering") of a child as a permanent gift to a monastery.[222] In some cases we learn that the foster parent was a relative of the child. The special relationship of maternal uncles and maternal aunts, as well as other matrilineal ties, often seemed to play an important role in the assigning of foster parents.[223] In other cases the grandmother or even great-grandmother of the child or perhaps a friend of the family would assume the role of foster mother. It appears that some of these foster mothers also served as sponsors at the child's baptism. In some situations the child went to live with the foster parent from an early age, and in others the foster parent seems to have had a role similar to a benevolent godparent, and the child stayed at home with his or her biological parents.

The Irish saints' Lives are extraordinarily rich in information on this special aspect of motherhood. It appears from a number of *vitae* that St. Ita, abbess of Killeedy, was foster mother *par excellence* to a number of famous male saints.[224] The *vita* of St. Brendan, for example, notes that this virgin Ita "brought up from infancy many of the saints of Ireland."[225] The Life also discusses the important role that Ita played throughout Brendan's life as his own foster mother. After the young saint's baptism, his biological family nurtured him for a year. "At the end of the year Bishop Erc took him to his foster-mother, Ita, and he was with her [five] years. And the nun loved him exceedingly, because she saw the attendance of angels above him, and the grace of the Holy Spirit evidently abiding on him. And Brendan was always smiling at the nun whenever he saw her. So one day Ita asked him 'What is it that pleases thee, O holy child?' said she. He answered: 'Thou,' said he, 'I see thee talking to me continually, and numberless other virgins like thee, nurturing me in turn.' But these were really angels in the forms of virgins. After this, at the end of his five years, Brendan studied with Bishop Erc; and to Ita the time seemed long without him."[226]

Throughout Brendan's life he maintained close contact with Abbess Ita and Bishop Erc, his foster father. He particularly valued Ita's advice and judgment. At one point, after having studied the Old and New Testaments, Brendan wanted to "write out and learn the rule of the saints of Ireland." He therefore went to consult his foster mother,

Ita, who concurred with his plans.[227] On two other occasions Brendan sought out Ita for advice. And according to the *vita,* she told him that he would only succeed in finding the country he was searching for by building timber boats. She also advised him to cross the sea: "'A foreign land is seeking thee,' said she, 'that thou mayest rule and instruct the souls of men there; and now depart.'"[228] We can see in this case the very prominent role attributed to Ita as foster mother. Except for the early mention of Brendan's biological parents, they do not appear to assume any substantial role in his life. The close, affectionate relationship which developed in the early years between Ita and Brendan was followed by a mutual admiration and respect as they grew older. We can note that Brendan continued to value his foster mother's advice, and according to tradition, it was through Ita's suggestion that he embarked on his famous voyage.

Another of Ita's renowned foster children was St. Mochoemog. Mochoemog was Ita's nephew, the son of her sister, Nessa. It was through Ita's prayers that her sister, who was believed to be barren, was finally blessed with a son, Mochoemog. Ita then ordered her sister to bring her son to her "for it is fitting that I should nourish him." Mochoemog was said to have spent some twenty years under his aunt's tutelage before going to Bangor to continue his studies. His *vita* also mentions Ita many times and underscores the great influence she exercised over his life.[229]

Perhaps the ultimate role in this tradition of surrogate motherhood can be seen in a legend where Ita asked God that she become the foster mother of Christ. She was then said to have been given the Christ child to nurse and foster in her little hermitage.[230]

The importance of fosterage can also be seen in the life of Colman, son of Darine. Colman's biological mother was Sanct. She had a sister named Darine who was childless while Sanct had many children. Thus shortly after Colman's birth, Darine asked for the infant and he was given to her to be raised as her foster child. It is interesting to note that he was then called Colman, son of Darine; that is, he is primarily identified with his foster mother.[231]

The Life of Maedoc of Ferns provides a wonderful description of the foster mother of St. Maedoc. "The child was nurtured zealously and affectionately by Ua Dubthaig (O-Duffey) and his other fosterers, more carefully indeed than any other child, and was kept from everything unlawful by reason of the abundant shining and enlightment of the Holy Spirit in him. And his nurturers, that is his foster-mother and nurses, as is the way of loving and affectionate foster-mothers, openly gave him through love and affection an eke-name, calling him habitually 'my little Aed' (mo Aed oc), so that the name Maedoc stuck to him as a surname to the exclusion of other names."[232]

The *vitae* of St. Cuthbert also note the saint's special relationship with his foster mother, Kenswith. In describing an episode in which Cuthbert saved this woman's house from fire, the anonymous Life relates, "At the same time the holy man of God was invited by a certain woman called Kenswith, who is still alive, a nun and widow who had brought him up from his eighth year until manhood, when he entered the service of God. For this reason he called her mother and often visited her."[233]

The Life of St. Brigid recounts her role as foster mother within the monastic community at Kildare. We learn that Tighernach, who would become bishop of Clones, was one of her fosterlings. Brigid had been Tighernach's sponsor and held him at the baptismal font; during his early years he was under her care as well. For his entire life he remained devoted to Brigid and when he established a church in Cornwall, he dedicated a chapel to St. Brigid.[234]

One of the most moving examples of fosterage, and the deep love and friendship which could evolve in this relationship, concerns Brigid and her young fosterling, Darlugdach, who was committed to Brigid when she was a small child.[235] (See chapter 7 for details on this friendship.)

The Life of St. Balthild relates a similar case of a close fosterage relationship. According to the *vita,* the queen-saint loved her sisters with pious affection, as her own daughters, and obeyed their abbess, Bertilla, as a mother. She had with her in the monastery of Chelles a young girl of seven years of age named Radegund. She had received her as her godchild on the day of her baptism. (It has been suggested that this young girl might have been a captive who had been freed by Balthild.) She came to be very fond of her spiritual daughter, and as she neared the end of her life, not wanting the tomb to separate her from her young companion, she prayed that her young charge not survive her. And thus, according to her *vita,* the child died shortly before Balthild and they were then buried together in the same tomb.[236]

The special relationship cultivated between St. Radegund and Abbess Agnes should also be noted. In her "Letter of Foundation" Radegund describes the maternal affection she felt for Agnes, whom she loved and brought up "as if she were my daughter from her childhood onwards."[237] Fortunatus also records this close relationship and explains that Agnes, this "daughter of Radegund" was not born of her uterus but of *gratia* or love.[238]

Another variation of the fosterage relationship can be found in the ninth-century Life of St. Liutberga. Liutberga, as a young girl, was hired to manage the household of the noblewoman, Gisla. Within a short time she endeared herself to Gisla, and became invaluable through providing her with advice, as well as taking care of the cooking, nursing, etc. When on her deathbed, Gisla made provisions for her own children and included among her daughters the *delicta* Liutberga, Gisla explained that she had promised to adopt her as a daughter.[239]

The contemporary Life of the tenth-century recluse of St. Gall, St. Wiborada, also recounts a strong fosterage/mother-daughter relationship. According to this *vita,* Wiborada volunteered to take into her cell the daughter of a local noble family. This young girl, whose name was Rachildis, had been afflicted by various ailments and was believed to suffer from, among other things, an incurable skin disease. Thus in the name of Christian love and charity, Wiborada embraced the young girl and adopted her as her spiritual daughter. In obedience to God, she promised to look after Rachildis's soul and body for the remainder of her life. According to the *vita,* through her prayers and special care, the young girl was restored to perfect health. Because of her affection for Wiborada, Rachildis, however, continued to serve her, and after some time she too adopted the life of a recluse. The two lived together in Wiborada's cell until Wiborada's death at the hands of the Hungarian invaders in about 926.[240]

Thus we have seen that surrogate motherhood or the fosterage relationship was apparently a rather common arrangement during this period. It was a way of distributing or sharing the riches of the family in the form of its children. For the most part, this practice (as described by our sources) seems to have provided the children with a caring environment as well as educational and career opportunities. It also appears to have been a very positive arrangement for religious women, the abbesses and nuns who had dedicated themselves to a life of religion—for it allowed them to "adopt" and raise children as their own; to cultivate strong bonds and affectionate ties with the young; and to have a close family relationship within the context of the larger monastic community. Many of the *vitae* note the great love, affection, and strong emotional attachments which developed through these relationships. Moreover, these spiritual foster mothers did not have the disadvantages of single mothers, or widows, for they would receive help and support in the rearing of their children from the other members of the convent. In this arrangement they were able to be "mothers" without having to submit to unwanted forced marriages, lose their virginity, or subject themselves to the extreme dangers of pregnancy and childbirth. For some of these women, especially female religious, fosterage appears to have been a way to have it all.

At the same time, one might wonder how this arrangement affected the biological mothers. What was their reaction to "giving up" their own children to fosterage? Were they able to see their children frequently and continue to maintain a close relationship? In this same context it also appears that many of these women who sent their children out to surrogate mothers, received in exchange other children (especially nieces and nephews) for whom they became foster mothers. This arrangement can be seen especially among mothers who entered monastic life and then adopted other young women as their fosterlings.[241]

This chapter has attempted to survey a variety of topics related to motherhood and sanctity. The *vitae* are an extraordinarily rich source for the study of medieval motherhood, and this exploration has only begun to scratch the surface. Saints' Lives present us not only with idealized visions and maternal stereotypes, but also with everyday details on motherhood which are not found in any other sources of the period. The collections of miracles also provide a great deal of fascinating information about motherhood. In addition, these sources underscore the important roles saints assumed in the lives of medieval women. As trusted authorities, they were relied on for their miraculous assistance in all areas related to motherhood: conception, labor, childbirth, nursing, and the care of sick or injured children. Saints provided a certain expertise in medicine, as well as strength and assurance in times of distress when no other sources of support were available. Many of these miracle stories are incredibly touching and, again, seem to reflect a high valuation of children and a great deal of love and affection as well as overwhelming grief felt by these early medieval mothers and fathers for their children. They again serve to remind us that these parents shared many of the same strong feelings and concerns of today's parents.

It is important to reemphasize that for the Church there remained throughout this period a dichotomized view of women and motherhood. These ambivalent attitudes seem to have become stronger and more exaggerated with the reform movements of the eleventh and twelfth centuries—with the proliferation of the Cult of the Virgin and the concurrent idealization of motherhood based on the model of the Blessed Virgin Mary.[242] Despite this idealization of maternal qualities, it appears that there was not an improvement in the position of mothers during this period—or as Caroline Bynum has shown, "there was no mystique of motherhood."[243] It should be underscored that the very same churchmen who elevated and worshipped the motherhood of the Blessed Virgin, and also pushed the ideal of maternal selflessness, glorification of private domestic life, idealization of the maternal nursing role, and so on, at the same time frequently disparaged and denigrated real, biological mothers. In their attempts to follow a severely rigid ascetic life with its emphasis on celibacy and ritual purity, in some cases they even exhibited a blatant hostility or fear toward their own mothers for their unfortunate female nature.[244]

Throughout this period women invariably had to try harder to win recognition of sainthood. While the most promising or likely way for a female to become a saint was through the denial of her sexuality and the espousal of virginity, another approved profession was that of motherhood. It is interesting to note that the majority of mothers who were recognized as saints, however, did not achieve recognition of sanctity simply through their "golden wombs" or their roles as mothers. In only a few cases was their sainthood directly predicated on their relationship to their famous offspring (invariably a male saint), and these "mother saints" usually had only very limited or local cults.[245] Instead, these saintly mothers often achieved the added visibility necessary for recognition of sanctity through their public roles as inclusive or "generic mothers," as abbesses of monastic foundations. That is, in many cases they combined biological motherhood with a delayed, second career in monasticism. Their visibility for sainthood included their roles as mothers, bolstered by their new or second family, the nuns and monks of their monastery: the biological mothers now became the spiritual mothers of these communities— *mater congregationis, mater monasterii, mater spiritualis*. The practical expertise they had acquired in managing their households, in nurturing and educating their own children, was easily transferred to the monastic environment where this experience was highly valued. And within their monasteries these "former mothers," in many cases now abbesses and foster mothers, were again designated "mother."

The Church and society offered men a wider choice of careers which might lead to sanctity; women's opportunities were clearly more limited. As we have noted elsewhere, they therefore found themselves much more dependent on the framework of their families for recognition and fame. And although St. Paul held that "woman will be saved through bearing children, if she continues in faith and love and holiness with modesty," this in itself did not provide women with any special advantage; it did not help to move them closer in their quest for *fama sanctitatis*. As noted by Anneke B. Mulder-Bakker, some women were recognized as saints "despite rather than because of their children."[246] In the making of saints and the clear preference for virginity and chastity, one no doubt questioned how a woman who produced children like any "ordinary" woman could be considered holy. Indeed, for many would-be women saints, this obvious "concession to the flesh," with its undeniable or visible result—children—worked to their distinct disadvantage.[247] Although valued, on its own this essentially private role of motherhood did not easily extend to public recognition; nor did it often warrant consideration for full membership in the celestial gynaeceum.

Entrusted with the affairs of this convent, she always bore herself in a manner worthy of her brother the bishop, upright of life and constantly planning for the neeeds of her community, as heavenly miracles attest.

Bede, *A History of the English
Church and People,* trans.
L. Sherley-Price, IV, 6:218

After my spirit has left this poor body, go to my sister Pega and tell her that I have in this life avoided her presence so that in eternity we may see one another in the presence of our Father amid eternal joys. Tell her also to place my body in the coffin and wrap it in the cloth which Ecgburh sent me.

Felix's Life of Saint Guthlac,
trans. B. Colgrave, L:155–56

Sorores Sanctae and Their Saintly Siblings: Terrestrial and Celestial Bonds

Although opportunities which led to the recognition of female sanctity were for the most part directly dependent on the family during the period discussed in this book, according to ecclesiastical theory the *vita perfecta* involved a certain hostility toward one's family and its demands. It required an essential renunciation or abandonment of family ties and affection. The severity of this renunciatory ideal is emphasized in the Scriptures, which warn: "If any one comes to me and does not hate his own father and mother and wife and children and brothers and sisters, yes, and even his own life, he cannot be my disciple."[1] And "every one who has left houses or brothers or sisters or father or mother or children or lands, for my name's sake, will receive a hundredfold, and inherit eternal life."[2] Similarly, monastic rules stressed that in the search for divine love, monks and nuns were to distance themselves from familial obligations and human affections.[3] In the same tradition, early medieval hagiography frequently articulated that the perfect life, as practiced by the saints, was accomplished only at the expense of renunciation of familial bonds. The *vitae,* for example, in their descriptions of the early proclivity of children toward saintly behavior, note that they not only fled the company of those outside of the family, but even avoided too frequent conversations with their own "relatives, household members, brothers, and sisters."[4] Yet in actual practice, and in the attitudes, values, and indirect evidence found in the *vitae,* the family, and within it especially the sibling relationship, played one of the most crucial roles in both the lives and the actual making of these early medieval saints.

As we have noted in previous chapters, for this period recognition of sanctity or celestial prominence had an essentially "this-worldly" or terrestrial base. With the locus of power situated within the family, the status of sainthood was predicated on the landed wealth and irregular powers of the family. Saints were therefore recruited from a very narrow and elite sector of society, that of the wealthy and powerful nobility or royalty. Particularly during the Frankish, Anglo-Saxon, and

Ottonian periods, sacred prestige and sanctity became concentrated within small groups of the aristocracy, with those selected as saints often interrelated, as if there were some sort of "holy gene pool."

However, in the Lives of the saints the most significant and enduring family relationship providing women with access to the *vita perfecta* or to recognition of sanctity, was that of siblings—brothers and sisters, sisters and sisters. Usually close contemporaries, siblings identified with each other for a longer period of time than with other family members such as their parents or husbands and wives.[5] As siblings, they had a common stake in the family enterprise. They shared many of the same interests and important events in their lives. The *mulieres sanctae* were also frequently identified in the sources by their sororal status, that is, they were recognized as the sister of a certain bishop, king, abbot, hermit, abbess, or saint. The exceptionally close ties, the deep bonds established between these siblings often precluded and outlasted other friendships, marriages, and, according to the *vitae,* even death.

The Lives of saints are a unique source in the portrayal of familial relationships and sentiments—and particularly the cultural valuation of sibling bonds across the centuries. They provide us with examples of sisters sharing in, or publicly reflected in, their brothers' political or religious prestige. In eulogizing their brothers, for example, the *vitae* shed light on the glory or *fama sanctitatis* of the sisters. Moreover, brothers or sisters frequently assumed a crucial role in establishing and promoting the cults of their siblings. In a number of cases they were involved in the translations of their saintly brothers' or sisters' bodies, or commissioned the redactions of their *vitae.*

This chapter will explore the cultural emphasis on the *soror fraterque* and the *soror sororque* relationship as described in the *vitae* of the period. It will look at some of the very real and practical functions which these ties fulfilled—the mutual obligations owed to one another as well as the support and opportunities these relationships afforded women. It will also examine some of the social and ecclesiastical ideals surrounding this bond, and particularly the changing expectations in regard to proper deportment in sibling relationships.

COOPERATIVE VENTURES IN MONASTICISM

It is perhaps not surprising that within the early monastic milieu (essentially that of family monasteries) we find impressive evidence of the significance of sibling ties and the development of unusually strong sibling relationships. As generous patrons of the monastic movement, or as founding abbesses, abbots, and bishops, these brothers and sisters frequently gained recognition of sanctity.

The strong tradition within monasticism of brother-sister saintly dyads can be traced back to Egypt and the origins of cenobitic or monastic life. The Life of Pachomius, for example, notes that Pachomius (d. 346) set up a monastery for his sister at some distance from his own monastery for brothers. And here she "followed the monastic regimen eagerly." "Pachomius also wrote down the rules of the brothers' monastery and sent them to the sisters . . . that they might proceed to govern themselves by them." [6]

We also find in the writings of the Latin Church Fathers letters of direction and advice addressed by churchmen to their sisters who had espoused a life of virginity. St. Ambrose's tract on virginity and Augustine's famous letter to his sister providing regulations for monastic life are especially well known.[7] In an interesting tract in praise of virginity written by St. Avitus, bishop of Vienne (d. ca. 525), for his sister Fuscina, Avitus expressed his great admiration for his sister. In fact, he attributed his own conversion to a religious life and the *vita perfecta* to her special influence.[8]

Perhaps the most famous of these early medieval monastic brother-sister dyads was that of St. Benedict of Nursia and his sister, St. Scholastica, who was said to have lived as a nun at nearby Plombariaola. (More will be said about this important sibling relationship later in this chapter.)[9]

In this tradition, St. Caesarius, bishop of Arles, wrote a detailed Rule for his sister, St. Caesaria, and her community of nuns. Caesarius also endowed and built Caesaria's monastery in Arles, and served along with his sister as spiritual advisor to the convent. According to his *vita,* Caesarius formulated the idea "that the church of Arles should be adorned and the city protected not only with countless troops of clergy but also by choirs of virgins." He therefore began building a monastery for his sister, which was then destroyed by the Franks and Burgundians as they besieged the city: "its beams and upper rooms were ripped apart and overturned by savage barbarians. . . . Meanwhile, Caesarius [rebuilt] in particular the monastery that he had begun to prepare for his sister, according to its original rule and with cloister for [the protection of] virginity [512]. . . . He built it for the companions and sisters on the side of the church. He recalled from a monastery in Marseille his venerable sister Caesaria whom he had sent there to learn what she would teach, and to be a pupil before becoming a teacher. He then set her up with two or three companions in the dwellings that he had prepared. Great numbers of virgins arrived there in throngs. By renouncing their property and parents they spurned the frail and deceptive blossoms of mortal existence and sought the lap of Caesarius, their father, and Caesaria, their mother." In 524 Caesarius built a basilica, which also provided a place of burial for the nuns of Caesaria's convent. "Not long after this his sister, holy Caesaria [the Elder], mother of the monastery, passed on to the rewards of Christ. He buried her among the sisters he had buried there before, between the altar and his episcopal throne, next to the grave he had prepared for himself." [10]

Donatus (d. 624), educated at the Monastery of Luxeuil and bishop of Besançon, also wrote a Rule for his mother and sister's monastery of Jussa. Donatus's sister, Siruda, would become second abbess of this new foundation.[11] And in Spain St. Leander, bishop of Seville (d. 596), wrote a treatise on *The Training of Nuns and the Contempt of the World*, directed to his sister, Florentine, who was entering monastic life as a nun at St. Maria de Valle, at Ecija.[12] The pervasiveness of this pattern, which we see beginning in the deserts of Egypt with Pachomius and his sister, suggests that in addition to the historical reality of these brother-sister relationships, these familial dyads also can serve as an important metaphor for gender inclusion within monastic life. They encapsulate the monastic ideal of gender symmetry.[13]

It was, however, during the conversion of the north of Europe to Christianity that perhaps one of the most remarkable chapters in sibling ties and monasticism appears. As outposts of missionary activity and centers of education, the early monasteries were essentially family houses. A number of these important foundations were located in the countryside, and as double monasteries or affiliated houses their communites consisted of both monks and nuns. While the monasteries utilized family properties and resources, family members managed to maintain control and continue to receive material benefits from their estates through assuming the position of abbess or abbot over their communities. These monasteries also provided burial privileges as well as spiritual insurance for the founding family and major patrons through the preservation of their *memoria* in the liturgy and intercessory prayers of the community's nuns and monks. Therefore, among the noble and royal families of especially the seventh and eighth centuries in England and the north of France/Belgium, many brothers and sisters worked together in the establishment of these early monasteries.[14]

The brothers, through their positions of power—as abbots and bishops, or princes of the region—assisted their sisters in their new foundations in the role of spiritual and legal advisors and through donations, the acquisition of important relics and immunities, etc. Their presence also seemed to help safeguard their family's or the community's assets from usurpation. Moreover, these sibling relationships appear to have provided additional opportunities for these women's assertive behavior, visibility, and access to major networks of power; and perhaps helped to further enhance their power and prestige as founding abbesses of their new communities.

During this formative period we find an impressive number of examples of prominent brother-sister, sister-sister saints involved in the founding and subsequent rule of family monasteries. We are informed in detail about some of these cases, while others are simply mentioned in the *vitae,* chronicles, or cartularies of the period. One rather well-known case concerns the double monastery of Faremoutiers, founded by St. Burgundofara/Fara on a family estate. Among the first monks of the abbey was Fara's brother, St. Cagnoald, who came from the monastery of Luxeuil to assist her at Faremoutiers. Another brother, St. Burgundofaro, was originally a member of the king's court and married to a young noblewoman. After visiting his sister, Fara, however, he was so impressed by her holy life that he decided to "put away" his wife and take religious orders. He then became bishop of Meaux and continuously supported Fara and her monastic community with advice and comfort.[15]

During this same period, Jouarre became a double monastery under Bishop Burgundofaro. St. Theodechilde was named the first abbess of Jouarre, and she was assisted by her brother, St. Agilbert (the future bishop of Paris), who then installed a group of monks at Jouarre and constructed two buildings for the community. Later St. Agilbert built the famous crypt of Jouarre, which is still extant and contains the magnificent tombs of the first abbesses as well as his own cenotaph.[16]

A number of sources from Anglo-Saxon England also underscore the important relationship between brothers and sisters in the founding of monasteries. Charters and wills of the period, for example, are especially illuminating in this regard. A grant by Nothhelm, king of the South Saxons, to his sister Nothgyth, dated to ca. 692, describes a donation of land at Lidsey and other places for the establishment of a monastery: "I, Nothhelm, king of the South Saxons, for the relief of my soul, knowing that whatever I devote from my own possessions to the members of Christ will benefit me in the future, will gladly give to you, my sister Nothgyth, some portion of land for the founding of a monastery on it and the building of a church which may be devoted to the divine praises and honouring of the saints; namely 38 hides in the places which are named: in Lidsey and Aldingbourne 12, in Genstedesgate 10, in Mundham 11, on the east bank 2, on the west 3; that you may hold and possess it, with all things belonging to it, fields, woods, meadows, pastures." [17]

In his *History of the English Church and People,* the Venerable Bede recorded several prominent monastic brother-sister relationships. He noted that before Earconwald/Erkenwald became bishop, he "had built two well-known monasteries, one for himself and the other for his sister Ethelburga.... The convent where his sister was to rule as mother and instructress of women devoted to God was at a place called (Barking).... Entrusted with the affairs of this convent, she always bore herself in a manner worthy of her brother the bishop, upright of life and constantly planning for the needs of her community, as heavenly miracles attest." [18] In the miracles of St. Erkenwald we see a continuation of this sibling bond beyond the grave. In the account of one miracle, a crippled nun of Barking Abbey prayed daily at St. Ethelburga's tomb for a cure for her disability. One night the saint appeared to the nun and told her that the time of her healing drew near. She, however, asked the faithful virgin: "Only remember to call continually to my brother Erkenwald and ask him to intercede for you; for with his merits to help you, you will be restored to health." And the next day during lauds, while the nun succumbed to sleep in a shady corner near the tomb of St. Ethelburga, the holy bishop Erkenwald was said to have appeared to her and she was restored to full health. In this cooperative miracle effected by Ethelburga and Erkenwald we can see the continuity of this sibling bond.[19] Likewise, Goscelin began his *vita Ethelburgae* (1087) by describing in some length the *fama sanctitatis* of her brother. He thus incorporated in his Life of Ethelburga Erkenwald's preconquest *vita* which explained, as Gordon Whatley has shown, "how Ethelburga's sanctity was first aroused by that of her brother; second, it casts some glory upon the sister by eulogizing the brother." [20]

Bede also noted the venerable abbess Ethelhild and her brother Abbot Aldwin who both ruled over nearby monasteries in the province of Lindsey. The bishopric of Lindsey was also in the family: it was held by Ethelwin, the brother of Ethelhild and Aldwin.[21]

The *vitae,* chronicles, and other sources of the period mention briefly many other houses which were founded as cooperative ventures between brothers and sisters. The impressive catalogue of saintly dyads includes, among others: the brother saints Romanus and Lupicinus (5th c.) who founded the monastery of Leuconum (St. Lupicin) for men and installed their sister nearby in the monastery of Balma, La Balme;[22] St. Finnian of Clonary, bishop (d. ca. 549), built a monastery for his two sisters and his mother;[23] St. Balderic/Baudri (Montfaucon, 7th c.) founded for his sister, St. Bova/Beuve,

the monastery of St-Pierre de Reims;[24] Modoald, archbishop of Trier
(d. ca. 640), established the community of St. Symphorien (on the Mo-
selle), which he placed under the governance of his sister, St. Severa;[25]
St. Adile, abbess (d. ca. 650) sister(?) of St. Bavo, patron of Gand, established a monastery in Brabant to serve as a missionary center;[26]
St. Annemond/Chamand, archbishop of Lyon (d. ca. 657), established
the monastery of St. Pierre where his two sisters Petronilla and Lucy
took the veil;[27] Adalsind, abbess of Dorniaticum, and her nuns joined
Adalsind's brother (Abbot Waldelen) and his community of monks at
Bèze in 657, and through this merger established a double monastery
at Bèze.[28] St. Ebba was the sister of St. Oswald, King of Northumbria,
and half-sister of Oswy. Especially through the pious donations of
Oswy, Ebba was able to establish the monastery of Ebbchester on
the Derwent, followed by the double foundation of Coldingham.[29]
St. Meneleus, hermit (d. ca. 700), built cells and an oratory near his
hermitage for his mother, Docula, and his sister, Bocula, as well as for
his fiancée, Sensa! It was perhaps this cluster of buildings that became
the monastery of Lisseul.[30] St. Rupert, a missionary in Bavaria, built
the monastery of Nonnberg for his sister (or perhaps his niece) Erentrude (d. ca. 718?), who became its first abbess;[31] St. Gerald of Mayo
(d. 732) was said to have founded a convent which he placed under his
sister, St. Segretia;[32] St. Chrodegang, bishop of Séez (d. ca. 770), gave
his sister, St. Opportuna, the veil. She became abbess of Montreuil
and remained closely attached to her brother.[33] St. Ludger, bishop of
Münster (d. ca. 809), was also involved in missionary work and near
the church of Nottuln he built a house for his sister, Gerburge, who
became a nun.[34] St. William of Gellone built a monastery for men
at Gellone, and in the vicinity he established a convent for women
in which his sisters became nuns;[35] St. Raoul, archbishop of Bourges
(d. ca. 866), established his sister Immenana as abbess of the new
monastery of St. Gênes at Sarrazac;[36] and, finally, perhaps one of the
best-known cases is that of St. Hugh, abbot of Cluny (d. 1109), who
founded the monastery of Marcigny where his sister became the first
prioress.[37] It is also interesting to note in this context that a number
of these cases of brother-sister saints will be used on another level
to account for traditional bonds or special relations which existed
among their monasteries. These legends would help to explain the origins of ties of institutional affiliation or dependence in the communities founded by siblings; they would emphasize the customary links,
obligations, privileges, and in general, the close contact maintained
between their houses. This rather impressive yet incomplete listing,
then, serves to underscore the prominence of these brother-sister relationships in the spread of monasticism.[38]

It appears that in a few cases these brother and sister saints ruled together over the double monasteries or "affiliated houses" which they established. In about 670, for example, a double monastery was founded at Hasnon. And according to the administrative arrangements, the men of the community were governed by John and the women were placed under the rule of his sister, Eulalia.[39] We learn that in compliance with the request of his mother, St. Rictrude, St. Maurontus, abbot of Breuil, agreed to serve as abbot of the double community of Marchiennes, where his sister, St. Clotsendis, ruled as abbess.[40] An especially interesting case concerns St. Walburga, the sister of Sts. Willibald and Wynnebald. She apparently ruled with her brother Wynnebald over the newly established double monastery of Heidenheim. According to tradition, after her brother's death, Walburga was appointed abbess over both houses by her brother, Willibald, who had become bishop of Eichstatt. It seems that Walburga occupied this position as ruler over monks and nuns until her death in ca. 780, and in the following centuries the monastery continued to be identified with Walburga's name.[41] Sts. Renilda and Herlinda (8th c.) were the founders and joint abbesses of the monastery of Eyck. According to their *vita,* the sisters established their monastery on family lands. After the death of Herlinda, Renilda then ruled alone as abbess for many years.[42]

The *vitae* and chronicles of the period also recount that the office of abbess was frequently kept within the family and passed from one sister to another. St. Sexburga, queen of Kent, for example, established a monastery at Sheppey where she assumed the position of abbess. Later, however, she left her community at Sheppey in order to go to Ely and place herself under the rule of her sister, St. Etheldreda. (Sexburga's daughter, Ermenilda, then succeeded her as abbess of Sheppey.) On Etheldreda's death in 679, Sexburga then assumed the position of abbess of Ely. Sexburga's daughter Ermenilda became the next abbess of Ely and she, in turn, was succeeded by her famous daughter, Werburga, who had been trained by Etheldreda. Here we see this rather remarkable continuity of influence concentrated in the family of the founder at Ely.[43] The monastery of Gandersheim was established by Duke Liudulf and his wife, Oda. Their daughter, Hathumoda, who had been raised by her grandmother at the monastery of Herford, became the first abbess of Gandersheim. She was the eldest of five sisters, all of whom apparently lived together as part of the religious *familia* at Gandersheim. Hathumoda was succeeded as abbess by her sister, Blessed Gerberga; after Gerberga, the youngest sister, Christina, assumed the position of abbess.[44] The monastery of Vilich had been established by the parents of St. Adelheid, Megengoz and

Gerberga. Adelheid became its first abbess, while at the same time her sister, Bertrade, was abbess of the nearby community of Santa Maria in Cologne. On Bertrade's death, the bishop asked Adelheid to replace her sister, and therefore for the last years of her life she governed both houses, that of Vilich and Santa Maria in Cologne.[45]

Another important aspect of the sibling relationship in monasticism was the special bond established between aunt and niece. As noted in the last chapter, it was rather common for abbesses to assume the role of surrogate mother or *matertera* for their siblings' daughters, and in turn these young women (nieces of the abbess) frequently acquired the position of abbess. For example, the case of St. Odilia, the founding abbess of Hohenbourg, is especially notable. At Hohenbourg, Odilia ruled over some 130 nuns, and included in this number were three daughters of her brother, Adelard. All three of these women subsequently became abbesses of major foundations: Eugenia succeeded Odilia as abbess of Hohenbourg, Attala became abbess of St. Etienne, Strasbourg, and Gundelind was named abbess of Nidermünster; similarly, each of them won recognition of sanctity.[46]

Within the context of the family monastery we find many examples of female religious who exercised a great deal of influence over the lives of their brothers and sisters. We learn, for instance, that with the help of her sister, the early Irish saint Fanchea (d. ca. 500) built a monastery at Rosairthir on the banks of Lough Erne. As abbess of this new foundation she also influenced her brother, St. Enna/Enda. When he wanted to marry one of the young nuns under her care in the convent, Fanchea worked to convert Enda and convinced him to adopt the life of a monk. He then spent some time at her new monastery, where under her direction he dug trenches and did manual labor. After Enda had established his own community at Cell Aine, he again followed his sister's advice and went abroad to continue his studies at the famous monastery of St. Ninian in Scotland. Later, after returning to Ireland and establishing several foundations, he consulted Fanchea and again, acting on her advice, went on to Aran. Or as Lisal Bitel has pointed out, "according to the vita of Saint Énna, he might never have become a saint if not for his sister, Fáenche, who preached to him about damnation until she made him cry. Under Fáenche's guidance, Énna gave up a perfectly good kingdom to become a monk, a recluse, and a famous saint."[47]

St. Waldetrude also had a strong influence over her younger sister, St. Aldegund. According to our sources, after separating from her husband, Waldetrude had a cell and chapel built for herself at Castrilocus (Mons); soon thereafter she was joined by several women who placed themselves under her direction. Waldetrude however worried about leaving her sister behind for fear that she might be caught by the "jaws of this world" and turn away from a pious life. She therefore wrote letters to her mother asking her to send her younger sister, Aldegund, to visit her. Aldegund apparently spent some time with Waldetrude and consequently decided to accept the veil and become a nun.[48]

The Life of St. Thierry I, abbot of St-Hubert (d. ca. 1087) also notes the role of *matertera* assumed by the saint's sister, Ansoalde, who was a nun at the monastery of Maubeuge. According to the *vita,* Thierry was placed for some time under his sister's care at Maubeuge, where she taught him his letters and the psalter. According to the *vita,* at the age of ten Thierry became an oblate at the monastery of Lobbes.[49]

Siblings were often called upon to provide various kinds of support and assistance. According to the legend surrounding St. Paul Aurelian, bishop of Léon (d. ca. 573), the saint's sister had adopted a religious life with a few other nuns in Cornwall. Once when he visited her, she asked him to stay for some time and begged him for his help. She told him that the site on which they lived was too narrow and, moreover, too close to their "tiresome relatives." She then implored him to pray so that the sea would retreat into a stationary bed and the land would be extended. St. Paul and his sister placed two rows of stones along the low-water mark and then knelt down on the shore to pray, and, according to tradition, the sea immediately receded to leave behind an extended area of dry land which could be used by the nuns. The legend also notes that the stones miraculously became great pillars, which served as an embankment to keep out the sea.[50]

Another case of brotherly assistance concerns St. Findian of Clonard. When he went to visit the Cell Rignaige, which had been established for Findian's sisters and his mother, he found the nuns in rather dire straits: they lacked a water supply. Findian then used his special powers to find them a well which would satisfy their needs.[51]

The *vitae* are, then, especially rich in describing the significant role of sibling ties within the early development of monastic life, as we find a number of prominent brother-sister and sister-sister saints associated with this movement.

PARTNERSHIPS IN TRAVEL AND MISSIONARY ACTIVITIES

Another area in which the sibling relationship proved to be especially beneficial during this early period was that of travel. Many of the *vitae* and other sources frequently portray brothers and sisters as traveling companions. The great popularity of travel, and particularly of embarking on pilgrimages, is brought out clearly in the sources of the time. Many laywomen as well as nuns apparently took to the road to travel to Rome.[52] In light of the great dangers and difficulties involved in travel at the time, these trips were frequently cooperative ventures or group travel. A number of *vitae*, then, describe in some detail saintly brothers and sisters who chose to travel together, providing each other with a measure of safety, or protection, as well as companionship.

According to our sources, Sts. Valerie and Pollene (d. ca. 640) were sisters of St. Liephard, bishop of Canterbury, whom they accompanied on a pilgrimage to Rome.[53] We learn that as teenagers, St. Dominica (d. ca. 710), her brother Indract, and nine companions left Ireland to make a pilgrimage to Rome. En route, they established an oratory near Plymouth where Dominica remained while the others went on to Rome. After their return from Rome, Dominica joined the group and they went to visit Glastonbury. However, they were soon killed for the treasures which they carried; and according to tradition, they were buried at Glastonbury where miracles occurred near their tombs.[54] According to legend, a certain St. Brigid and her twin sister, St. Maura, were of Irish royalty. Their mother died in childbirth, and on the death of their father the two sisters, along with their brother, Hispadiu, went off on a pilgrimage to Rome. In Rome they paid visits to all of the holy shrines and sites. Afterwards they settled in the area of Beauvais. Here Brigid and Maura were killed by robbers. (Later their remains were translated by St. Balthild to her monastery of Chelles.)[55] Sts. Alfrida, Sabina, and Edith (virgin martyrs, d. ca. 819) were daughters of Kenulf, king of Mercia. According to tradition, they decided to make a pilgrimage to Rome and, in so doing, they also avoided being forced into unwanted marriages by their parents. After crossing the sea, they traveled to Mardick and then on to Cassel where they stayed for several days in a monastery. However, they were said to have been murdered soon after by assassins who had been sent after them by the knights they had refused to marry.[56] According to the Life of St. Wiborada, recluse-martyr of St. Gall (d. ca. 926), Wiborada and her brother, Hitto, also made a pilgrimage to Rome.[57] There are a number of other examples of these saintly siblings making pilgrimages together during this early period.

Several *vitae* note brothers and sisters traveling together with the intent to relocate in another country in which they then planned to adopt a religious life. According to an Irish legend, St. Cathan left Ireland with his sister, Ertha, to lead an eremitic life in Scotland.[58] St. Fiacre (d. ca. 670) and his sister, St. Syre (who was said to have become blind in order to avoid an unwanted marriage), left Ireland and traveled together to France. There Fiacre was given land by St. Faro, bishop of Meaux, where he established a small community of monks:

Syre entered the monastery of Faremoutiers, which was under the rule of St. Burgundofara (Faro's sister). Through a revelation, Fiacre learned that his sister would recover her sight through the intervention of St. Savinien, martyr of Troyes. He therefore brought Syre to Troyes and there, by means of prayer and divine inspiration, she was said to have discovered the tomb of St. Savinien, which had been lost following the disruptions of the barbarian invasions. And here she then recovered her sight. St. Syre decided to build a cell and chapel near her benefactor's tomb, where she spent her days and nights in prayer and good works in the company of a group of virgins who had traveled with her from Ireland.[59]

Among the missionaries to the north of Europe, there appear to have been several cooperative ventures which involved brothers and sisters. For example, a Lombard group which was selected by Pope Martin I to assist St. Amand in his proselytizing activities, included at least two women: one of these was St. Vinciana, the sister of St. Amand and of St. Lomdoald, the leader of the group. They left Rome around 633 to do missionary work in Belgium, and Vinciana was said to have assisted them greatly in their efforts of conversion.[60] A small Irish missionary group which worked to convert the Picts at the beginning of the eighth century was comprised of abbot saint Comgan, his sister, St. Kentigerna, along with her three sons, and a number of missionaries.[61] The missionaries who followed St. Boniface from England to Germany also included a very famous brother-sister team: that of the abbess St. Walburga and her brothers Sts. Willibald and Wynnebald.[62]

LOVE AND AFFECTION AMONG SIBLINGS

The *vitae* are also extraordinarily rich in wonderful insights into the emotional aspects of the saints' lives. There are many descriptions of strong attachments—mutual love and affection—among saintly siblings. In the Life of St. Brendan, for example, the hagiographer introduces the saint's sister, Briga "whom he warmly loved" (*intime diligebat*). At times the face of his sister took on "the appearance of the splendid moon," or, "Brig . . . his sister, was with him there, and great was his love for her, for he saw the attendance of angels above her."[63] The Irish St. Cainnech found "immense joy" in visiting his sister Columba. During his visits she carefully ministered to him and also had a small boy named Brachtanus who was her *alumpnus* (fosterchild). The child had a great deal of love for Cainnech, and Cainnech returned this affection.[64]

Perhaps one of the most famous examples of affection and love within the saintly sibling relationship concerns Sts. Scholastica (d. ca. 543) and Benedict (d. ca. 550). Their final visit before Scholastica's death is described in Gregory the Great's *Dialogues* and is accompanied by a miracle attributed to Scholastica (see plate 16). There has been some scholarly debate about this saintly pair and about whether Scholastica was in fact a "real" historical figure or a fictional creation serving an allegorical function. However, as Paul Meyvaert has argued, to deny Scholastica's historical existence because "we are doubtful about the miracle she worked in *Dialogues* 2.33 is to neglect other historical data."[65] He then cites as historical evidence: the *Dialogues* which note that Benedict and Scholastica were buried close to each other in the oratory of St. John the Baptist; sources pertaining to the discovery of contiguous tombs under the altar erected by Abbot Desiderius (11th c.) at Monte Cassino; the reexamination of these tombs in the fifteenth century; and finally, archaeological excavations in the 1940s after the destruction of the church at Monte Cassino.[66] Although Scholastica's existence appears to be supported by historical evidence, and, for that matter, should not be subjected to any more or less scrutiny than that of her brother, Benedict, it should also be mentioned that in the formulation of the spiritual dimension of monasticism it was perhaps necessary to incorporate the ideal of gender symmetry, and thus a feminine principle. Therefore Benedict, as the "father of monasticism," was seen as needing to have a feminizing aspect (here in the form of a famous saintly sister) associated with him.[67]

According to the legend recorded in the *Dialogues*, "His sister Scholastica, who had been consecrated to God in early childhood, used to visit with him once a year. On these occasions he would go down to meet her in a house belonging to the monastery a short distance from the entrance. For this particular visit he joined her there with a few of his disciples and they spent the whole day singing God's praises and conversing about the spiritual life. When darkness was setting in, they took their meal together and continued their conversation at table until it was quite late. Then the holy nun said to him, 'Please do not leave me tonight, brother. Let us keep on talking about the joys of heaven till morning.' 'What are you saying, sister?' he replied. 'You know I cannot stay away from the monastery.'" However, Scholastica prayed and her prayers were immediately answered: although the sky had been clear and cloudless, as she prayed a severe thunderstorm blew in that kept Benedict from leaving and caused him to disobey his own rule. "They spent the entire night together and both of them derived great profit from the holy thoughts they exchanged about the interior life." Gregory the Great then comments on this case where St. Benedict did not receive what he desired while his sister did, noting: "Surely it is no more than right that her influence was greater than his, since hers was the greater love." Scholastica then returned to her monastery the next morning, which according to legend was located at Plombariaola, approximately five miles south of Monte Cassino. And she died three days later.[68]

A similar affection between siblings can be found in the relationship of Leander of Seville (d. 600) and Florentine (see plate 17). In his work on *The Training of Nuns,* Leander of Seville refers a number of times to his sister, Florentine, using terms of endearment. He calls her, for example, "dearly beloved sister," "sister whom I love," "my comfort and solace," "shelter in Christ . . . security," as well as the "better part of our body." [69]

Other incidents of spiritual affection and love between siblings are captured in the *vitae.* The Lives of St. Bova and her brother, St. Balderic, tell how Balderic, abbot of Montfaucon, sometimes left his monastery to visit his sister, St. Bova, abbess of the monastery of St. Pierre at Reims. Here they would spend time together discussing the business of their monasteries. Balderic provided Bova with advice, and they encouraged each other in virtue.[70] The case of St. Hiltrude (d. ca. 785) and her brother, Guntard, abbot of Liessies, is also of interest. Since childhood, Hiltrude shared her religious sentiments with her brother, and it was through his encouragement that she defied her parents and escaped marriage. Later Hiltrude received the veil and retired to a small cell adjoining the monastery of Liessies which was under her brother's rule. Here St. Hiltrude was frequently seen with her brother. According to the *vita,* they were like "another Jerome and Eustochium" or "another Scholastica and Benedict"; they spent their time conversing on heavenly matters, stimulating each other with the love of God, and yearning for eternal blessedness. For seventeen years these two saintly siblings met, during which time they rivaled each other in their pursuit of the *vita perfecta* and, according to the hagiographer, "she was an example not only for the feminine sex, but for the masculine as well" (*exemplum facta non solum femineo sexui, sed et masculino*).[71]

Among the correspondence found in the Boniface collection are three very moving and passionate letters written by the nun Berthgyth to her brother Balthard (second half of the eighth century).[72] Berthgyth and her mother Cynehild (Cynehild was the aunt of St. Lul, one of Boniface's major followers) had left their home in England to join the missionary movement in Thuringia. After the death of her mother, Berthgyth felt isolated and extremely lonely in her adopted country.

Thus in her correspondence with her brother, her only living relative, she describes the constant grief, anguish, and desolation she experienced in his absence. She therefore begs him to visit her. "Do you not know for sure that among all the living there is none whom I set higher than your love? Look, I can't suggest all this to you by letter. Already I feel certain you don't care about me, who am naught." [73] In a second letter she continues to emphasize her loneliness and longing to see him: "My soul is weary of my life, languishing for our fraternal love . . . There are many congregations of waters between me and you—still let us be one in love, for true love is never broken by severance of place." [74] Here we see the belief that love between siblings is not limited by space—although separated by an insurmountable distance, it still remains strong. [75] Berthgyth again begs her brother to come to visit her, or to ask her to return so that she might see him before she dies. Her hope is that they will be together in heaven. Her third letter, in response to her brother's letter and gifts, again stresses her longing to see Balthard one last time: "And now, my brother, I adjure and beseech you to take away the sorrow from my soul, for it hurts me deeply. For I tell you, even though it were only the space of a single day and you then went home again, the Lord inclining your will, nonetheless the sorrow will then recede from my soul and the pain from my heart. But if it displeased you to fulfil my petition, then I call God to witness, that in me our love would never grow destitute." [76] Thus even if Balthard would not come to visit her, Berthgyth admits that she would continue to love him.

Another brief reference to special affection between siblings can be found in a letter from Abbess Ecgburg to Boniface. Here confiding in Boniface and asking for his support and consolation, she writes: "For since cruel and bitter death has taken from me one whom I loved beyond all others, my own brother Oshere, I have cherished you in my affection above almost all other men." [77]

References to love and affection displayed between sister saints (the soror sororque) are perhaps more difficult to find because of the nature of our sources. However, in Abbess Ecgburg's letter to Boniface we can find a moving example of this strong identification with and affection between siblings. Ecgburg notes that coinciding with her brother's death, she also lost her sister, Wethburga, who departed on a pilgrimage to Rome. This painful separation affected her deeply. "And when at the same time my dearest sister Wethburga vanished from my sight—a new wound and a new grief; she with whom I had grown up, whom I adored and who was nursed at the same mother's breast— Christ be my witness, everywhere was grief and terror and the dread of death. Gladly would I have died if it had so pleased God from whom no secrets are hid, or if slow-coming death had not deceived me." She then continues, "But what shall I say now? It was not bitter death but a still more bitter and unexpected separation that divided us one from the other, leaving her, as I think, the happier and me the unhappy one to go on, like something cast aside, in my earthly service, while she, whom, as you know, I loved so tenderly, is reported to be in a Roman cell as a recluse. But the love of Christ, which grew and flourished in her breast, is stronger than all bonds, and 'perfect love castest out fear.'"[78]

Another incident of female friendship is described in the *vita* of Hathumoda. The contemporary redactor of the Life notes that one day when Hathumoda lay on her couch, her sister Gerberga, who was *maxime familiaris* to her, sat with her on the couch. And there Hathumoda had a secret vision which she then described or shared with her sister.[79] Shared interests and intimacy between sisters can also be found in the Lives of Sts. Aldegund and Waldetrude. As related by the hagiographer: "Now Waldetrude had vowed that, once her sister Aldegund had taken the veil, she would give her care of the sisters living there. Unquestionably the Holy Spirit was at work that they should be of one mind in serving God and live in common habitation in this world. Steel is sharpened on steel, as it is written, and so one is sharpened by a friend's attention. They shone like two splendid lamps, offering the other sisters guidance to the eternal light of Our Lord Jesus Christ which they deserved to achieve with them." The *vitae* describe Aldegund and Waldetrude spending time together, speaking about love and the behavior of the women who had gathered about them and followed their teaching and example.[80] We also learn that when they were abbesses of separate houses, Aldegund frequently came from her monastery to visit Waldetrude where they were involved in discussions of the heavenly homeland.[81] We can therefore find in the *vitae* and other sources of the period an important pattern of special affection and friendship cultivated by these saintly siblings.

CONFLICTS AND DIFFICULTIES SURROUNDING THE *SOROR FRATERQUE* RELATIONSHIP

However, despite the many depictions of strong partnerships, and genuine love and affection between siblings, the *vitae* also portray another side of these relationships which was perhaps more in tune with the scriptural warning of renunciation, abandonment, or even necessary "hatred" of family members, brothers, and sisters. In some cases this took the form of conflict or a certain level of competition between these "saintly" brothers and sisters. Moreover, in a few Lives the brothers assume the function of moral guardian, and in this role they display an unsympathetic and uncompromisingly cruel side in their actions toward their sisters. In apparently attempting to underscore their sisters' need to reform their lives, and perhaps to make moral examples of them, a number of these brother saints are shown resorting to rather drastic measures.[82]

The tradition surrounding the Irish St. Attracta/Tarahata and her brother, St. Conallus (5th or 6th c.) is perhaps particularly revealing in regard to aspects of conflict as well as competition between siblings.[83] According to her *vita* (redacted in the eleventh or twelfth century), St. Attracta was of royal Irish descent, and in order to avoid marriage she fled from her family and established a church and monastery in the area. On one of her trips into the countryside she came across an especially lovely site where her brother, St. Conallus, had founded a church. Attracta then sent him a message to inquire if she might also build in this area. After receiving her inquiry, he was apparently forewarned (through prophecies) of Attracta's bright future and of her predestined fame and miracles. No doubt aware of the possible conflicts this might cause in regard to his own interests, and not wanting the additional competition for donations and offerings of the faithful of the area, he decided not to allow her to build in his territory. He sent a message to his sister in which he begged her, in the name of God, not to build on his land. When Attracta received her brother's response, she was infuriated. Nevertheless she replied, "Since you ask me in the name of God, I cannot refuse. And since you order me to leave your lands, I obey your decree." In her anger, however, she added her own special curse, "But that Conallus may feel how bitter is my sentence, I pray that no corn may ever grow on his estate, and that no father and son together may ever serve there. I foretell that a sound of bells will come into your dwelling, which will diminish the offerings you receive from the people, or deprive you of them altogether."[84] And according to the legend, as Attracta had predicted, these things did in fact happen—soon another monastery was built on this land and it usurped all of the donations which had previously supported St. Conallus and his church.[85]

We can see in this interesting episode, on the one hand perhaps a practical realization on the part of Conallus that in light of the limited base of economic support it was unwise to concentrate too many religious foundations in the same vicinity. This type of behavior was, however, viewed by hagiographers as uncharitable, and it did not win praise in the *vitae*. We can perhaps also see here a certain competition between siblings, for Conallus was aware of his sister's future success and this clearly bothered him and influenced his decision.

Furthermore, there was an apparent lack of brotherly support, for rather than working out a cooperative plan, where he and Attracta might share the land, profits, and governance over two churches or communities (perhaps a double or "affiliated" community), he refused to entertain any other project on his land, even that of his sister. Attracta is shown in this episode as a very strong-willed, determined woman, and while she reluctantly acquiesced to Conallus's request, she successfully vented her anger on her brother. And again, in the hagiographic tradition, he apparently paid later for this "error" in judgment.

Other *vitae,* while they might provide moving examples of mutual devotion and affective ties, also present saintly brothers who were painfully aware of the clear and present dangers inherent in these associations and thus the moral necessity of maintaining a strictly circumscribed relationship with their sisters. This relationship required deference to certain cultural demands, a reserve or a distancing, or even the total avoidance of their sisters. Similarly, verbal communications between brothers and sisters necessitated a degree of restraint. In general, churchmen were concerned about how their close *soror fraterque* relationships might appear to others in the "outside" world, especially to their detractors; they feared they might be misconstrued and provide an opportunity for scandal. Some seemed to be particularly aware of the apparent societal repugnance toward mature brothers and sisters living in the same dwelling and eating together. Vowed to lives of strict and uncompromising chastity, some of these brothers cultivated an exaggerated suspicion and fear of female sexuality; and in this mindset it seemed difficult for them to accommodate their feelings for their sisters. Therefore they never allowed themselves to forget that even their own flesh and blood—their own sisters—were also members of that same pernicious gender as Eve.

A number of the Lives, especially those of the male eremitic and monastic saints, underscore this basic distrust and fear of women—including their own mothers and sisters. In this tradition, they emphasized the need to distance themselves from all women and to establish certain spatial regulations and boundaries. The *vita* of St. Pachomius notes, for example, that when his sister came to see him, "he sent the brother who was gate-keeper of the monastery to tell her, 'you have indeed heard about me that I am alive. Do not grieve because you have not seen me.'" [86] He then suggested that if she wanted to share in his holy way of life, the brothers of his community would construct a monastery for her and for the other women who would join her. This monastery was thus established in a village "at some distance from that of the brothers." [87] Pachomius appointed Peter, a brother who was advanced in years, to visit the nuns: he preached to them, and it was through him that Pachomius sent them the monastic rule of the brothers' community so that they might govern themselves. The *vita* also recounts, "If anyone of the brothers who had not attained perfection yet wished to visit a woman related to him, Pachomius through his house manager would send him to the aged Peter. Thus a report was made to the mother of the monastery. It was in the presence of another reverend sister that the visit to the relative would take place in strict propriety and oblivion to kinship of flesh. . . . The hope and remembrance of future eternal blessings was sufficient to them." [88]

In Possidius's Life of St. Augustine of Hippo he writes approvingly that "no woman ever lived or stayed within Augustine's household, *not even his own widowed sister*, although she had long served God and lived as superior of His handmaids until the day of her death. He also refused his brother's daughters who were also serving God, although they were considered exceptions to this law by the councils of bishops. However, Augustine used to say that, even if no evil suspicion could arise from the fact that his sister and nieces lived with him, they could not exist without other servants and women being with them, and that still others would enter from outside to visit them. From these, in turn, a stumbling block or scandal might arise for the weak. . . . For this reason, then, Augustine stated that women should never live in the same house with God's servants, even the most chaste, lest by such an example some scandal or stumbling block be placed before the weak." [89]

While warning monks of the need to flee from all women and bishops, Cassian (d. ca. 435) notes his own inability to avoid his sister. Thus, following in the tradition that was already well-established among the desert fathers, he observes: "Wherefore this is an old maxim of the Fathers that is still current,—though I cannot produce it without shame on my own part, *since I could not avoid my own sister*, nor escape the hands of the bishop,—viz., that a monk ought by all means to fly from women and bishops. For neither of them will allow him who has once been joined in close intercourse any longer to care for the quiet of his cell, or to continue with pure eyes in divine contemplation through his insight into holy things." [90]

The Life of St. Romanus (d. ca. 460) records the foundation of an affiliated house for nuns (La Balme) near St. Romanus's own monastery. Here his sister became the *mater* or abbess of this community of virgins. According to the *vita*, when a mother had a son at the nearby monastery, or a sister had a brother there, neither of them knew, by sight or by hearsay, if the other was still alive—each considered the other as already entombed or buried. They feared that the sweetness of family memories would little by little break down, through a sort of weakening, the bonds of the religious profession.[91]

The example of the Irish St. Fanchea and her brother, St. Enda, is especially informative in regard to the perceived need for strict segregation of the sexes, including brothers and sisters. As we have noted, St. Fanchea played a major role in her brother's life and is credited with his conversion to religion and his decision to undertake monastic vows. Later, she, along with three of her nuns, were said to have made a pilgrimage to Rome to visit her brother, who had gained great fame as abbot of his monastery, Latinum. According to the *vita,* it was secretly revealed to Enda that his sister and the holy nuns from Ireland were coming to visit him and he therefore prepared his monks for Fanchea's arrival. Thus when she arrived and asked to see Enda, she was given a message that she would have to choose between two options: that of receiving his greetings without seeing him, or seeing him without greetings (*silicet aut salutacionem sine visitacione eius haberet, aut vero visitacionem sine salutacione*). She chose the salutation without being able to see her brother. This, we learn, was accomplished by hanging a curtain across the room from behind which St. Enda spoke to her. (*Extendit igitur vir Dei tentorium in solo monasterii, et cum velamine alloqui cepit sororem sic.*)[92]

The case of the famous Anglo-Saxon brother-sister saints Pega (d. ca. 716) and Guthlac (d. 714) is also in this tradition. They lived the eremitic life in the fen country, with Guthlac residing on the island of Croyland (or Crowland) and Pega occupying another island some four leagues away.[93] According to a contemporary *vita,* during their lifetime Guthlac denied himself his sister's company for ascetic reasons, so that he might enjoy her company later, in heaven.[94] However, in a poem composed by Henry of Avranches in the thirteenth century (after Peter of Blois and perhaps reflecting the misogynisim of the reform period), the origins of this necessary segregation of domiciles is explained. According to this later source, at the beginning of Guthlac's career as a hermit Pega shared the island of Croyland with her brother. However, at one point, the devil cleverly assumed his sister's appearance and tempted Guthlac to take food before sunset, which was strictly against his vow. Guthlac soon detected the origin of this ruse, and in order to prevent further attacks of this nature, he was said to have commanded Pega to leave the island, and he never saw her again.[95]

The general concern with female sexuality and the need for strict separation of the sexes, even between close blood relations, can also be found in the legislation of Church councils as well as the penitentials of the period. From approximately the fifth through the ninth century, the canons of the councils contain a progression of increasingly detailed and strict spatial restrictions aimed at the secular clergy and the women who assisted them. Initially the canons specify that the only women approved for this function would be the priest's mother, sister, aunt, or niece. However, with the growing concern and need to curtail clerical sex, as well as to avoid the suspicion and scandal that might surround cohabitation, the laws became self-consciously more restrictive: at first they specify the necessary segregation of beds, then separate rooms, and finally, the canons stipulate that no females whatsoever (not even one's own close relative—i.e., mother, sister, aunt, or niece) were to be found living under the same roof with a churchman.[96]

Underlying these increasingly severe restrictions was apparently a growing concern with incest between brothers and sisters.[97] One canon, for example, specifies that these regulations were required because of clerks sinning with even their own sisters; another cites the scandalous acts of priests who impregnated their own sisters; or another notes that there have been reports of dreadful incest.[98] One of the specific categories of sexual transgression or unnatural sexual relations designated in the penitentials and canon law of the period was that of incest between brothers and sisters. In the notorious Carolingian divorce case initiated by King Lothar II (855–69), we see, for example, the prominent use of accusations of incest between brother and sister. In his desperate attempts to dissolve his marriage to Queen Theutberga, Lothar accused his wife of having sexual relations with her brother, Hubert, who was a cleric.[99]

Thus, it appears that particularly beginning with the Carolingian reforms and continuing with the later monastic and papal reforms, we can see an increased fear of incestuous relationships, especially between siblings, reflected in the literature of the period. It is then perhaps in this context of a growing concern by the reformers of the Church with maintaining proper appearances in regard to any member of the opposite sex—including one's own sister—and the potential for accusations of incest, that the following *vitae* should be read. Serving as exempla for the faithful, these Lives might contain the following encoded message: if the most saintly of siblings could find themselves accused of this type of behavior, ordinary churchmen, priests and monks, as well as laymen, must be even more cautious in the exercise of their brother-sister relationships. In the hagiographic tradition, the ruinous accusations of incest and scandalous behavior might also be seen as simply another test or trial that these siblings would be subjected to as candidates for sanctity.

The two Lives of St. Wiborada are especially illuminating in their

depiction of a close brother-sister bond as well as the particular difficulties inherent in this relationship. The first Life of St. Wiborada was
written by Hartmann, a monk of St. Gall, about thirty years after
Wiborada's martyrdom (d. 926).[100] Based on firsthand evidence, it is
filled with a great deal of fascinating information which appears to be
quite reliable. It portrays the strong bonding, friendship, and devotion
between Wiborada and her brother, Hitto, which can be found among
many of our saints. Dedicated from an early age to a religious life at
home, Wiborada was overjoyed when her brother decided to become
a priest. She made his clothing, his linens, and the equipment that he
needed for the priesthood. While he studied theology at St. Gall, she
continued to care for him as well as to work for the monastery's scriptorium by making covers for their books. Later Wiborada and Hitto
turned their home into a hospital and working together, in this cooperative venture, they cared for the sick and provided food for the
poor of the area.[101]

At this time, the *vita* notes, Wiborada learned Latin and the psalms
from her brother so that she could say the office with him and even
serve him in the choir and at the altar. According to the *vita:* "And
since in saying his divine office he would be spending time with the
book of psalms, [our] virgin put even more pressure on him in her discussions with him about everything good, to instruct her too in the
word. He promised that he would comply with her wishes and made a
fervent start in instructing her, but gradually his interest cooled, and
he finally fell off altogether. Then one night he was chided in a vision
and commanded to maintain a fast until he should instruct his sister in
the fiftieth psalm. He had instructed her in the prior psalms and the
fiftieth alone remained. There was no more to be said, he rose up in
the night, sought out his sister, told her about the vision and that he
was ready to give her instruction. And thus he became an insistent
teacher, whereas before he had reneged in his teaching. In this way her
brother schooled her at different times in fifty psalms."[102] The author,
Hartmann, then notes: "On Sunday at the beginning of Lent when the
aforementioned priest was ready to celebrate Mass and complained
that he was without a server, [our] blessed virgin consoled him saying:
'Take heart in the Lord's help and He himself will be with you in your
need.' He took the virgin at her word and proceeded to begin his spiritual duty. And with that she began right off to deal with the psalmody
with such a command of all the learning that was entailed in the singing
*that she seemed in no way inferior to [no less than] a priest [nequa-
quam inferior esse videretur Sacerdote]*. . . . The priest and the whole
congregation that were present, when they heard these things, ascribed
them to God's power and glorified Him in their great amazement."[103]

This brother-sister team also made a pilgrimage together to Rome, where they visited the tombs of the holy apostles and martyrs. It was apparently during this time that Wiborada convinced Hitto to become a monk at St. Gall. Hartmann notes how Wiborada had already renounced the world and its possessions and therefore admonished her brother of the transitoriness of life. According to the *vita*, she warned Hitto: "You who know the Sacred Scriptures surely require no instruction from bungling me about the need for sober wisdom and vigilance for the coming of the Bridegroom's return, but I do admonish you in this one respect, for the time is at hand. . . . Upon this admonition of his sister, the brother's heart was changed," and after this he "bent himself to the sweet yoke of the regular life in the monastery of Saint Gall." [104]

After Hitto's "conversion" and entrance into the monastery, Wiborada returned to their home and, on her own, attempted to live a saintly life of austerity and extreme mortification—fasting and spending her nights in prayer. However, according to a second *vita* (written in about 1062 by Hepidannus, a monk of St. Gall), at this time one of Wiborada's servants began spreading a malicious rumor: "The unjust avenger of the image of God . . . stirred up one of Wiborada's maids against her so that she would assert that Wiborada arose secretly every night, not in order to pray, but in order rather to carry on shameless activities that she would blush to carry on in the daylight but that she could carry on with greater security under the cover of darkness. . . . But on top of these things people had to keep still about whether or not Wiborada was free from incest with her brother." These rumors, begun by the maidservant and repeated by others, then came to the attention of Salamon, the bishop of Constance. As a result, "the spouse of Christ stood before the bishop as if she were an adulteress. She who was guilty of none, stood accused of multiple adulteries. She who was her brother's guide in undertaking chastity, was defamed as her brother's mistress (*diffamatur fratris esse concubina, fraternae castitatis consiliaria*")."[105]

The hagiographer continues: "Wiborada denied the accusations of the faithless maidservant, but people in their ignorance of the truth gave equal credence to both. The bishop, however, wanted to put an end to the uncertain accusations and set up a day for Wiborada to appear under oath before the confused public and respond to the accusations." He encouraged Wiborada to "take heart" in her action and mentioned several historical precedents of those who had suffered similar tribulations; for example, Jesus who was accused of not being a prophet "because of the harlot's touch"; or Susanna who was defamed by two elders only to be vindicated. The *vita* then describes the trial: "A large crowd gathered with the bishop on the appointed day, and Almighty God vindicated Wiborada's innocence so clearly to all, that by reason of the incredible joy the ceremonial thanks to Him redoubled both because He had preserved her innocence and because He had freed [unshod] her of the infamy with which she had been maligned."[106]

After the trial, saying she wanted to get away from her accusers, Wiborada left her old estate and went to live in a cell near St. Gall. She ultimately had herself formally immured in a cell attached to the Church of St. Magnus which was served by her brother, Hitto. Wiborada died a martyr at the hands of the Hungarian invaders in ca. 926, after warning her brother and the other priests of St. Magnus to take refuge inside the walls of St. Gall.[107]

The two *vitae* of St. Wiborada, separated by some one hundred years, are, then, unusually rich in detail about the *frater-sororque* relationship. They provide fascinating information about shared lives, opportunities, and the extremely important roles and visibility sisters could assume through this relationship. The episode in which Wiborada assists her brother at Mass is of particular interest. Here, through her special training, she was able to "transcend her sex" for "she seemed in no way inferior to" or "no less than a priest." While providing details in regard to shared or nearly inseparable lives and strong bonds of affection, these sources (particularly the second *vita*) also convey an uneasiness, an underlying fear of female sexuality and potential scandal; they transmit a certain base suspicion and repugnance which seemed to surround these close relationships; particularly onerous were the perceived problems associated with the cohabitation of mature brothers and sisters.

The extant Latin Life of St. Cerona, redacted sometime between 1050 and 1150, is also of interest in regard to special difficulties surrounding the brother-sister relationship. Although borrowing from other Lives, this *vita* allegedly reconstructs the events of the much earlier Life of Cerona and her brother, Suffranus, who were said to have lived at the end of the fifth century. According to the legend, Cerona and her brother were born into a royal, pagan family near Béziers. Together they fled their home to go to Bordeaux, where they were educated by a priest. Here they decided to live together and dedicate their lives to religion: Cerona took the veil and Suffranus became a priest.[108] However, while in Bordeaux, they became the object of malicious gossip and attacks. According to the *vita,* "certain inhabitants of that place seeing the holiness of these people and their equally holy way of life began to slander them with malicious talk." They accused Cerona and Suffranus of declaring that they were brother and sister in order to "covertly carry on the amusements they wished." Their accusers also asserted that they had left their homeland in order "that they might with greater license give themselves over to their own amusements."[109] When Cerona and Suffranus got wind of these rumors, they discussed what would be the best course of action: "to remain, on the one hand, in their own little place and quietly put up with the biting complaints of their slanderers, or to give up their property and yield to the unholy gossips. . . . At this point Suffranus affectionately addressed his sister: 'Stay here, dear sister, and I will go off to wherever Almighty God desires.' His sister replied: 'No, dear brother, for I can no longer abide in this place, since the common madness accuses me of much greater wrongdoing than you. You stay here and I will go into exile.'"[110]

The hagiographer then notes Suffranus's astonishment at his sister's proposition: "I am amazed you utter such words. Do you forget yourself and your frailty? Aren't you aware of your frailty as a woman? If the stronger sex and masculine strength . . . often suffers disaster in the pursuit of virtue and with the greatest difficulty is able, sure-footed, to avoid the pitfalls of the ancient enemy, however will the weaker [sex], the sex more prone to falling, be able without anyone's support to go off into exile and not suffer harm." Moreover, Suffranus warned Cerona of the threat of falling "before the sudden wild passion of savage men . . . evil men corrupted by their wicked love of the flesh [who] will forthwith snatch you up and, God forbid, subject you to unspeakable desires."[111]

When Cerona heard these things, she replied: "Why, brother, do you try to divert me from my intent by saying these things? Why do you seem *of little faith,* mistrusting the power of the Most High?" (She then cites several examples where faith overcame danger, e.g., Daniel in the lion's den.) "It behooves us to enter the heavenly kingdom through many tribulations, because we know that 'no man will receive a crown who has not contended lawfully.' But know this, I have decided to travel to that part of Gaul that lies across the Liger."[112] Thus, through her forceful argument, Cerona convinced her brother to accept her plan and allow her to leave.

The hagiographer then describes in moving terms their separation; "When their loving dispute was thus at an end, they rushed into a mutual embrace, wetting each other with their tears, pouring forth long heartrending prayers, according to apostolic precept 'giving place to wrath'; and making their final farewell, they said: 'May we be found worthy to meet again in the kingdom of heaven.' And thus at length they parted." According to tradition, Cerona then went on to Normandy (Mortagne) where she lived as a hermit and worked to convert the region. A group of women gathered around her and she established for them a monastery with two chapels. Suffranus also left Bordeaux and went to Rome; here he visited the tombs of the Apostles and martyrs and died as a saint.[113]

The Life of St. Cerona, then, provides another interesting look at the brother-sister relationship. Although it perhaps tells us more about the period of the hagiographer, that is, the eleventh or twelfth century, and its ideals of spirituality, gender relations, and so forth, than of the early Middle Ages, it does portray the importance of close bonding of siblings and the formation of an affectionate as well as useful partnership. As behavioral models, Cerona and Suffranus follow the scriptural message to the letter; for they renounce or abandon their parents and their country, and then, finally, separate from one another and go into exile.[114] The *vita*, however, also seems to depict a certain equality in Cerona's relationship with her brother. For example, despite the fact that Cerona was reminded that she belonged to the *sexus fragilis* (perhaps a formulaic usage underscoring a certain strength in this weakness?), we also find in the *vita* mention of "equal agreement" and "equal conversation," as well as Cerona's convincing victory in their argument about who should take the initiative and leave Bordeaux.[115] In addition, the Life provides an example of an intrepid woman who went off, "on her own," into exile—an activity, which in most *vitae*, remained the prerogative of the male saint.

Moreover, the *vita* provides insight into a very real difficulty in sibling relationships: medieval society's suspicions concerning cohabitation. While on the one hand, Church and society seemed to require that women should not be "out on their own," but should somehow remain under the tutelage or protection of a male (father, husband, brother, bishop, priest, etc.), on the other hand, by its very nature this relationship could easily become suspect. In this case, Cerona and Suffranus were accused of pretending to be brother and sister in order to conceal an improper sexual relationship, whereas in other cases, saintly siblings were confronted with allegations of incest. And finally, in these accusations of sexual impropriety and incest, the special guilt was invariably attached to women. As in the previous cases, and as Cerona is said in her *vita* to have observed, *she* (Cerona) was accused of much greater wrongdoing than her brother—thus, women seemed to bear the primary onus of these attacks.

It is interesting that both of these Lives which underscore the problems of incest are hagiographic products of the eleventh century. Again, while allegedly portraying the behavior of saints of an earlier age, these later redactions instead often reflect the ideals, moral concerns, and propaganda of the author and the period in which they were written.[116]

DEATH AND PROMISES OF CELESTIAL REUNIONS

It was only with the realization of impending death that some of these male siblings finally felt free to see their sisters and express the affection which they had withheld for ascetic purposes during their lifetime. A primary focus of many of the *vitae* is on the saint's final hours and deathbed scene: this was an especially important moment to be shared with one's closest relatives and friends. Therefore, sisters and brothers often assumed a crucial role in the events surrounding the death of their saintly siblings: they were designated to carry out special instructions for burial; they remembered each other in prayers, or with property and personal gifts in their wills; they frequently expressed a final wish that they be buried together, and promised each other that they would meet again in the celestial realm. Many of the Lives also describe the profound sorrow and grief expressed at the death of a sister or brother.

In a number of *vitae* siblings were singled out to be the recipients of special visions either foretelling the death of their brothers or sisters or describing their arrival in heaven. According to the Life of St. Benedict, three days after his memorable visit with Scholastica, "as he stood in his room looking up toward the sky, he beheld his sister's soul leaving her body and entering the heavenly court in the form of a dove. Overjoyed at her eternal glory, he gave thanks to God in hymns of praise. Then, after informing his brethren of her death, he sent some of them to bring her body to the abbey and bury it in the tomb he had prepared for himself. The bodies of these two were now to share a common resting place, just as in life their souls had always been one in God." [117]

The Life of St. Waldetrude describes Waldetrude's contemplation of the heavenly city and how she and her sister, Aldegund, "would be treated in the divine examination." It was "divinely revealed to her that she and her sister, the blessed Aldegund, would inhabit one mansion and equal beatitude in the kingdom of God for reward of their labors. So, each in her own way, [that is, one as a married woman and mother, the other as a virgin] they would arrive at that mansion." [118] The Life of St. Aldegund then notes that St. Waldetrude received a vision five days before her sister's death, in which she saw the Virgin Mary, Peter and Paul, and many other saints leading Aldegund into the celestial kingdom.[119]

Other *vitae* specifically mention saints dying in the presence of their brothers or sisters. One of the Lives of St. Brendan, for example, describes Brendan's deathbed surrounded by the monks of his monastery and his beloved sister, Briga, abbess of Annaghdown (Galway). As he lay dying, Briga provided him comfort and asked: "Of what are you afraid, Father?" He responded, "I am afraid if I go forth alone, if the road be dark. I fear to come into a place I do not know, to see face to face the King, to hear the sentence of the Judge." Brendan then gave the kiss of peace to his monks and his final request was to his sister, Briga: "Remember me to my friends, and tell them to keep from unkind words, even be they true. For such are children of hell." [120]

According to the Life of St. Romanus, in his old age and worn out by bodily weakness, this hero of Christ went to his sister whom he had placed at the head of the monastery of La Balme. Assured of his departure from this life by Christ, he wanted to say his final farewell to her. Romanus was then laid low by a violent illness and died there. The holy man chose to be buried in the church of his sister's monastery of La Balme and around his tomb many miracles occurred. [121]

During one of St. Balderic's visits to his sister, St. Bova, at her monastery of St-Pierre de Reims, he became ill. He died in her convent with his sister and niece in attendance. The *vita* describes the immense desolation experienced by Bova at his death. He was then buried in her church of St-Pierre, although later his body was transferred to his monastery of Montfaucon. [122] Erentrude, abbess of Nonnberg (d. 718?) and the sister or niece of St. Rupert, was summoned one day by Rupert, who revealed to her that his death was imminent. He therefore asked her to pray for his soul. On hearing this, Erentrude begged him to ask God that she be allowed to die first, since she had followed him on this mission and was alone in a foreign country. He told her that it was a sin to encroach on providence, so she then asked that she at least be able to follow him without delay. Rupert agreed and consented to pray for her request. According to the account, they spoke together for a long time of heaven—shedding tears of joy—and finally they said their farewells. Rupert died and shortly thereafter, as Erentrude prayed for his soul, Rupert appeared to her in a vision and told her to come to join him in heaven. And as related by the *vita,* soon after this she became ill and died. [123] St. Ludger, bishop of Münster (d. 809), was said to have died in the presence of his sister, Abbess Gerburge, and his disciples. This special bond between siblings can be found in William of Malmesbury's Life of St. Wulfstan (d. 1095). In the saint's final illness, Wulfstan became convinced of his own approaching death when he learned that his only sister had died. He said, "The plough's furrow reached me just now, and the brother will follow the sister within a few days." [124] There are many other examples which can be found in this tradition.

Several of the saints had to deal with the violent and tragic deaths of their siblings. St. Radegund's letter to her cousin Hamalafred, entitled "The Fall of Thuringia," depicts the intense grief, suffering, and guilt which she experienced when her young brother was murdered on the orders of her husband, King Clothar. In her lament, Radegund painfully relates that she was denied the consolation of sharing her brother's last moments of life and was not allowed to weep over his corpse or attend his funeral.[125]

> The Youth was struck down while in his first downy beard,
> Nor did I, his absent sister, attend the dire funeral.
> I lost him and could not even close his pious eyes
> Nor lie across the corpse in final farewell,
> My hot tears could not warm his freezing bowels.
> I placed no kiss upon the dying flesh,
> No embrace in my misery. I could not hang weeping on his neck
> Nor sighing, warm the unlucky corpse in my bosom.
> Life was denied: how should I snatch the fleeting breath
> From the mouth of the brother to the sister?
> I might have sent the fringes I made while he lived to his bier.
> Couldn't my love at least adorn the lifeless shell?
> Brother, I salute you, and stand accused of this impiety:
> You only died because of me and I gave you no sepulchre.
> . . .
> He bore my joy away with him to the land of the shades.[126]

The Life of St. Anstrude, abbess of the monastery of St. John of Laon (d. before 709), also describes in some detail the intense guilt, grief, and desolation which the saint experienced at the murder of her brother, Baldwin. According to the *vita*, "because fraternal love knows no bounds," Anstrude began to weep, saying: "Now may those who have brothers in the flesh be mindful of mercy and have compassion on my sorrowful fears. Let them not condemn my weeping but be moved to pity by my cries while I mourn my brother bitterly. He alone remained to me and this day I have lost him." In speaking to her community of nuns who mourned her brother's death, she reminded them of how much he had loved them all and how he had tried to provide for their well-being. She then asked that "despite my own pain at the loss of my brother . . . you will remember his soul in your prayers so his cruelly slaughtered soul may possess the joy of Paradise." Anstrude found comfort in the support of her sisters, and the *vita* notes that in her grief "she presented a reasonably calm and manly face," and her strength was "more of the manly than the feminine kind." However, when she saw her brother's bier, she said: "Now, now you come back to me dearest brother. Yesterday you were alive, today slaughtered. Yesterday, I sent you out unhurt; today I receive you back for burial.

Brother, brother, best loved of my soul! Why was your life torn away by such unworthy men when you were so young?" [127]

The Life of St. Opportuna (abbess of Montreuil, d. late 8th c.), recounts the tragic death of her brother, St. Chrodegang, bishop of Séez. After visiting his sister, Chrodegang was murdered in the village of Nonant. Opportuna had his body brought to her monastery and deposited with great honor in one of the crypts of her abbey church. Almost immediately a cult developed and pilgrims flocked to his tomb. However, Opportuna was so distraught by her brother's death that, according to her *vita*, she asked God to reunite her with him. Shortly thereafter, feeling her wish fulfilled, she called her nuns together to announce her own impending death. On the twelfth day, after suffering from a fever, she died. She was then buried in her monastery church alongside of her brother. [128]

A few of the Lives tell of saints arriving shortly after their siblings' deaths and miraculously resuscitating them. The *vita* of St. Munnu/Fintanus (d. ca. 635) relates that Munnu's sister, Conchinna, had recently died. When Munnu arrived at his family's church, unaware that there had been a death in the family, he saw a new grave. According to the Life, through the spirit of prophecy, he knew that this was the tomb of his sister. His mother then told him that Conchinna had died and begged him to resuscitate her. He prayed through the night at the new grave of his sister and according to the legend, the tomb opened and his sister emerged from it fully cured. [129]

The *vita* of St. Guthlac is an extraordinary source in regard to the importance of the *soror fraterque* relationship at the time of death. Written sometime between 730 and 740, by a monk named Felix, it provides us with some wonderful details. St. Pega, Guthlac's sister, is introduced in the *vita* only at the very end of the saint's life, in book 50 of fifty-three books. Her major role is therefore in the context of Guthlac's death and burial. According to the *vita*, shortly before his death Guthlac was questioned by his brother monk, Beccel, as to whom the hermit saint spoke with each morning and evening, and Guthlac replied that it was an angel sent by the Lord. Beccel, however, was to tell no one of this except for his sister, Pega, and Ecgberht, the anchorite. [130] Guthlac's dying words, which were entrusted to Beccel, also concerned his sister: "After my spirit has left this poor body, go to my sister Pega and tell her that I have in this life avoided her presence so that in eternity we may see one another in the presence of our Father amid eternal joys. Tell her also to place my body in the coffin and wrap it in the cloth which Ecgburh sent me." [131]

On Guthlac's death, Beccel went to find Pega and "told her in order all her brother's commands" (see plate 18). The *vita* then proceeds to

describe in moving detail the immense grief which Pega felt on learning of her brother's death: "When she heard them she fell down in a
headlong fall, and as she lay upon the ground she withered away to
the very marrow by the mighty affliction of her grief; her tongue was
silent, her lips were mute, and she lost all life and strength, just as if
she were dead. After an interval she aroused herself as though from
sleep and, heaving deep sighs from the very bottom of her heart, she
gave thanks for the Almighty's judgement." Pega then arrived on
the island of Croyland the following day. According to Felix, Pega assumed the primary role in her brother's burial: "The handmaiden of
God spent three days of commending the spirit of her brother to
heaven with divine praises, and on the third day in accordance with
his command she buried his blessed limbs in his oratory, covering
them with earth." [132]

Less than a year after Guthlac's death and before the translation of
his body, according to the *vita,* a blind man from the province of
Wissa had learned of Guthlac's holiness and came to Croyland to seek
a cure. When he and his friends arrived on the island, they immediately sought out Pega. "She, recognizing his undoubting hope and fervent faith, allowed him to be led into the oratory in which the body of
the blessed Guthlac lay. She also took a piece of glutinous salt which
had previously been consecrated by St Guthlac and, grating it lightly,
let the scrapings fall into consecrated water. She made this water drip,
drop by drop, under the blind man's eyelids and, marvellous to relate, at the first touch of the first drop, the clouds of blindness were
scattered and the light returned, pouring into his eyes." [133] We thus see
Pega's essential presence at her brother's tomb or healing cult site and
her assistance in his miracles.

Twelve months after Guthlac's burial, Pega arranged for the translation of her brother's body (see plate 19). This event in turn helped to
call attention to the holy dead and to advertize or promote Guthlac's
cult as a saint. As noted in the *vita,* "God put it into the heart of his
sister to place her brother's body in another sepulchre. So, having
gathered together the brethren and the priests, as well as other ecclesiastical ranks, they opened the sepulchre on the anniversary of his
death, and found his body whole as if it were still alive, and the joints
of his limbs flexible and much more like those of a sleeping than a
dead man. Moreover all his garments in which he had been wrapped
were not only undefiled but shone with all their former newness and
original brightness." Those who were present "stood trembling and
amazed"; they could scarcely speak or look on this miracle. "When
Pega, the handmaiden of Christ, saw this, she was stirred with spiritual joy, and again wrapped the sacred body with veneration and

divine praises in the cloth which the anchorite Ecgberht had sent him . . . however, she did not hide the coffin in the ground, but placed it instead in a certain monument; and now, built around it, we behold wonderful structures and ornamentations put up by King Aethelbald in honour of the divine power. . . ." [134]

Ingulf's *Chronicle of the Abbey of Croyland* sheds further light on this brother-sister relationship. "Saint Pega . . . shortly after the close of the first year from his death, leaving there, in the hands of Abbot Kenulph, the scourge of Saint Bartholomew and the Psalter of her brother, together with some other relics, returned by boat to her cell, which lay to the west, at a distance of four leagues from the oratory of her said brother. Having lived there two years and three months in tearful lamentations, she travelled, suffering greatly from cold and hunger, to the threshold of the Apostles Peter and Paul." [135] Ingulf then describes her entry into Rome in the hagiographic or miraculous tradition, for it was said to have caused "all the bells to ring for the space of one hour." And, after showing the people "the merits of her sanctity" and devoting herself entirely to the service of God, Pega died in Rome in about 716. [136]

Bede records in some detail the role of St. Sexburga in the translation of the body of her sister, St. Etheldreda. Sexburga had succeeded Etheldreda as abbess of Ely. According to Bede, "Sixteen years after Etheldreda's burial, this abbess decided to have her bones exhumed, placed in a new coffin, and transferred into the church." [137] Here again we see the use of the sibling's translation of a saint as an opportunity to focus attention on the holy dead and further promote her cult. The ritual provided an appropriate occasion to "stage" a drama, surrounded by an atmosphere filled with an expectant hope of the miraculous. As Bede reports, Sexburga also sent out several brothers to look for an appropriate stone with which to make a new coffin. They found a white marble sarcophagus near the city walls of Grantchester, which they brought back to the convent. [138] In the preparations for the translation, Sexburga again played a major role. "When her [Etheldreda's] bones were to be taken up out of the grave so many years later, a pavilion was raised over it, and the whole community stood around it chanting, the brothers on one side, and the sisters on the other. The abbess herself, [i.e., Sexburga, sister of Etheldreda] with a few others, went in to take up and wash the bones, when we suddenly heard her cry out in a loud voice, 'Glory to the Name of the Lord!' " [139] Shortly after this they called in the physician Cynifrid and showed him that the incision that he had made before the saint's death had miraculously healed, and there remained only a faint scar. All of the linen cloths in which the body had been wrapped also appeared fresh and new. Afterwards the nuns washed the saint's body and dressed it in new clothing. They carried it into the church and placed it in the special tomb which had been discovered by the monks. "This same sarcophagus was found to fit the virgin's body in a marvellous way, as though it had been especially made for her, and the special place cut out for the head exactly fitted the measurements of her own." [140] (After Sexburga's death in 699, according to her wishes, she was buried in the church next to the tomb of her sister, Etheldreda.) [141]

A number of other saints were also involved in the translations of their saintly siblings. St. Walburga, for example, is noted as attending the translation of the body of her brother, St. Wynnebald, to Eichstatt in 776. After her own death in 779, she was buried first at her double monastery of Heidenheim and was later interred beside her brother in the church of the Holy Cross. [142]

Siblings played another important role in the promotion of their brothers or sisters to sainthood through the commissioning or writing of their *vitae*. The short Life of St. Maura (d. ca. 850) written by her friend, Bishop Prudentius of Troyes, specifically notes that the author was approached by Maura's brother to write something about his sister's life. "You insist, beloved sons, importunately [and] opportunely that, in place of my sermon, which I usually offer you on feast days, I not only say something about the glorious life and the precious death of our sister Maura, but that I leave something written as well that will be of value to those who come after us. To this end her brother Eutropius, your bishop, who was more closely related in the spirit than in the flesh, has earnestly entreated me on your part." [143]

Other brothers and sisters made special requests of their saintly siblings to intercede for their souls and, serving as their representatives, make the necessary reparations for them at the Last Judgment. Leander of Seville, for example, in his *Training of Nuns and the Contempt of the World,* made such a request to his sister, Florentine. Convinced that her virginal chastity and her recompense as bride of Christ could be used to further his own salvation, he asked for her special assistance. In this work, which was directed to Florentine as she entered monastic life, Leander exhorted her to behold in her mind's eye the virginal procession accompanying Mary, "follow those bands, join them with eager heart. Hasten there, hurry there. . . . Realize that your brother's heart desires your safe journey, realize that your brother's most fervent desire is that you should be with Christ." [144] Leander then confessed his special attachment to his sister as well as his critical need for her intervention for the salvation of his

soul. He admitted that she was in fact "the better part of our body . . .
my shelter in Christ . . . my security . . . my most sacred offering,
through which I doubt not that I shall be purified of the uncleanness of
my sins. If you are acceptable to God, if you shall lie with Christ upon
the chaste couch, if you shall cling to the embrace of Christ with the
most fragrant odor of virginity, surely, when you recall your brother's
sins, you will obtain the indulgence which you request for that brother's guilt. . . . Held thus in the Bridegroom's embraces, you may ask
and obtain pardon for me. Your love in Christ shall be my indulgence,
and however little hope of forgiveness I have, if the sister whom I love
shall be married to Christ, and, if in that terrible and dreadful judgment when there is a weighing of deeds, acts, and omissions, and I,
woe is me, am forced to give an account of my own services, you will be
my comfort and my solace, then, the punishment that is due me for my
errors may possibly be relieved by the intercession of your chastity."[145]

In conclusion, during much of the period 500–1100 the biological
family played a primary role in the making of saints. In the lives of the
mulieres sanctae the sibling bond appears to have been the most significant and enduring of the relationships in which strong attachments
were formed. It often precluded or outlasted other kin relationships,
friendships, and marriages, and it even transcended death. Stories of
these special bonds are plentiful in the *vitae,* beginning with the early
Irish, Merovingian, and Anglo-Saxon saints' Lives up through those of
the eleventh century. In a number of cases these sibling relationships
proved to be crucial in the actual formation and promotion of the
cults of saintly siblings.

Although our sources are perhaps not as revealing as one would
like in regard to the *soror sororque* relationship, they do note the existence of a great many sister saints. They tell of the strong ties which
were maintained between many of these early medieval women, and
the practical as well as emotional support which they provided for one
another throughout their lives. Sisters' sharing of their concerns, their
professions, and their lives in general, seem to have been particularly
impressive within the monastic setting.

The *soror fraterque* tie is especially evident in the *vitae* of this
period. On a practical level, the brother-sister bond appears to have
been in many cases an especially positive and complementary relationship. Although there were a number of *frater fraterque* saints, it
seems—at least from what is expressed in the *vitae*—that the relationship between brothers and sisters was more openly affectionate and
much closer than that between brother saints. In this tradition a number of Lives emphasize the special devotion and profound love be-

tween saintly brothers and sisters. For the sisters, the *soror fraterque* relationship appears to have been particularly important in providing them with opportunities for an active role in the Church—with increased access to the *vita perfecta*. During the period of the conversion of the north of Europe to Christianity and the great proliferation of family monasteries, this relationship among siblings became especially prominent, with a great many of these brother-sister teams winning popular recognition of sanctity. While these sisters wielded considerable influence over their brothers, and in a number of cases were credited with bringing about their "conversions," the prestige or fame of their male siblings also frequently afforded these exceptional women public notice and distinction. Moreover, in many of the *vitae* we can see a remarkable level of respect and devotion between siblings as well as a certain equality in these relationships.

On the other hand, a few *vitae* stress the special "liabilities" of the brother-sister relationship. In these we find a certain fear, distrust, or abhorrence of the female sex, which dictated a policy of distancing oneself, or even avoidance of one's own sister. It is of interest to note that in a number of cases it is the later versions of these Lives that evince this fear of a close relationship with one's sister, recount problems of incest, and so forth. They perhaps reflect the base suspicions and misogynism of the reform movements of the time of the redaction of the *vita,* rather than the conditions of the actual period during which the saint lived.

Despite whatever difficulties there were, it seems that, on the whole, the affective ties between these saintly siblings remained strong and positive. And although one continues to find important examples of saintly siblings after the eleventh century, the pattern no longer seems as significant then as it had been during this early period when entire families won popular recognition of sainthood. This is due in part, as André Vauchez has noted, to the substitution of the artificial family for the biological family in the making of saints,[146] as well as to the other shifts that we have noted, such as various church reforms (with their underlying misogynism, reaffirmation of hierarchical authority, and centrality of the sacraments), changes from popular sanctity to formal canonization procedures, changes in education, shifts in family strategies and inheritance practices, etc. And with these changes— which were, to a large degree, adverse to an appreciation of women and unfavorably disposed to their active participation in the public sphere—opportunities for common family goals, patronage, and shared aspirations and lives among siblings, both within society and in the Church, were unfortunately diminished.

Farewell for evermore, my dearly beloved lady and sister; farewell, most precious half of my soul.

Rudolf, *The Life of St. Leoba*, trans.
C. H. Talbot, p. 224

Everyone who is unequal to his own task and distrusts his own judgment seeks a faithful friend upon whose counsel he can rely and in whom he can have such confidence that he will lay open to him every secret of his heart. As is said: "what is sweeter than to have some one with whom you can talk of everything as with yourself?" . . . Long have we sought, and now we believe that we have found in you the friend whom we have wished, prayed, and hoped for. . . . "A friend is long to seek, hard to find, and difficult to keep."

Letter from the Abbess Eangyth
and Bugga to Boniface, trans.
E. Emerton, VI [14]: 38

You, who, because of your dignity, are a mother to me and [who]are my sister by the privilege of friendship, you to whom I pay homage involving [all] my heart, faith, and piety, you whom I love with a divine, entirely spiritual affection devoid of the guilty complicity of the flesh and senses . . .

Poem 6, Fortunatus to Agnes, *MGH,*
AA, 4, VI: 260

Gender Relationships and Circles of Friendship among the Mulieres Sanctae

Scholars have traditionally perceived "real" or "true" friendship as a singularly male experience. With few exceptions the myths about devoted friends, societal models of friendship, or treatises on friendship have been about men and for men.[1] Aristotle in his discussion of friendship between unequals even held that women, by their very nature, were incapable of being true friends.[2] In their studies, historians, anthropologists, sociologists, philosophers, and others have either failed to observe female friendships and cross-sex friendships, or have treated them as merely a peripheral part of the social system. Scholars have generally seen women as totally subsumed by their families with little need or time for the cultivation of external bonds or friendships.[3]

Only recently has the historical significance of friendship for women been recognized.[4] Thus, for the Middle Ages, and particularly the early medieval period, in general the significance of female friendships (cross-sex or especially same-sex) has not received the kind of attention it warrants. For example, Gerhart Ladner has observed: "Medieval friendship, at least before the later Middle Ages, was essentially a monastic and male phenomenon. . . . The sources tell us surprisingly little about friendships between nuns and other women. . . . Perhaps, in the Middle Ages, Christians rarely did fathom the friendship of which women are capable and it remains questionable to what extent this situation has changed even today."[5]

However, contrary to this generally held view, which has tended to minimize the importance of cross-sex and same-sex friendships for women, bonds of friendship seem to have played an extraordinarily significant role in the lives of medieval women and men. Our sources, in fact, are extremely rich in indications of the prominence of these relationships for this early period. This chapter will explore a few aspects of the theory and practice of friendship, and the cultural importance of friendship for women as reflected in the Lives of saints. It will survey shifts in the cultivation and valuation of cross-sex and same-sex friendships. It will also explore the apparent conflict between the requirements of monastic community and the desire for personal friendship; and, as in the case of sibling relationships, it will look at the cultural demands of deference, the rules of contact, and in some cases, the necessary avoidance of members of the opposite sex. This focus on friendship thus provides another indirect index of modes of social perception in regard to gender relationships, attitudes toward women, as well as women's experiences.

Friendship is perhaps somewhat difficult to define, for there are many kinds of relationships in which the term "friend" may be applied. Friendship has been characterized by sociologists as "extra kin" in theory, meaning it can exist with any person other than a member of one's kinship group.[6] This is not to say that kinship cannot involve friendship; in fact, as we noted in the last chapter, many of the sibling relationships were characterized by very strong emotional bonds and deep affection—that is, true friendship. However, kinship and friendship as social roles are seen as mutually exclusive. Friendship refers to relationships that are entered voluntarily and are socially recognized as such by the friends and also by others. The concept of friendship also frequently implies a basic symmetry or balance—an assumption of a mutuality or equality on both sides.[7]

With the majority of women saints for this early period recruited from the cloister, it is not surprising that the monastic community, as a type of surrogate family, also provided an environment especially conducive to the cultivation of strong friendships. A milieu where people worked together and shared mutual experiences, ideals, and goals, the monastery produced an impressive number of male and female friendships.

GENDER RELATIONSHIPS: FEMALE TEMPTATION AND SAINTLY STRATEGIES

The Church, in theory, encouraged and valued love and friendship among the faithful. Tracts, sermons, and letters written by churchmen discuss the different types of love and friendship: they describe the useful and necessary steps in the cultivation of perfect love and charity. Friendship was seen as a form of love (*caritas*): it was a means to attain spiritual perfection. In his work *Friendship and Community: The Monastic Experience 350–1250*, Brian McGuire describes friendship according to the definition provided by Gregory the Great and Isidore of Seville, in which a friend is the *custos animi* or guardian of one's soul.[8] Friendship (*amicitia*) was thus to be spiritual and not concerned with the this-worldly or physical aspects of the relationship. At the same time, cross-sex or same-sex friendships were frequently viewed by churchmen as problematic and potentially dangerous. Hence within the tradition there was an awareness of the need to maintain a balanced or "disciplined" friendship as well as of the dangers of either loving too much or too little.[9] Moreover, there seems to have been some agreement among ancient scholars and churchmen that it was virtually impossible for women to enter into and maintain "pure" friendships with members of the opposite sex. Rosemary Rader has noted in her work *Breaking Boundaries: Male/ Female Friendships in Early Christian Communities* that the prevailing opinion found in the writings of Plato, Aristotle, Cicero, and Augustine stresses that by nature friendship could not exist between members of the opposite sex.[10] Biblical examples of cross-sex relationships further reinforced these beliefs in women's incompatibility to form heterosexual friendships: the stories of Adam and Eve, David and Bathsheba, Samson and Delilah, Judith and Holofernes all clearly illustrate the potential dangers lurking in these relationships.[11]

In general, based on the Church's fear of and hostility toward sexuality, close friendships provided a potential source of tension for churchmen and women during this period. They posed a serious threat to celibacy; furthermore, they afforded an opportunity for scandal. Thus the growing emphasis on virginity and celibacy, and the need to prevent occasions for temptation and suspicion of improper behavior ruled against the easy formation, or public display, of cross-sex friendships among churchmen and women. In this tradition Gregory the Great underscored the basic tensions and problematic nature of cross-sex relationships in his warning that men should love women as if they were sisters, but they must also flee from them as if they were one's enemies.[12]

Monastic rules were especially articulate in their provisions to avoid the fostering of close friendships. Caesarius of Arles, for example, warns: "no one shall have a secret intimacy or companionship of any kind with religious or lay persons, either men or women, nor should a woman and a man be allowed to speak together alone for more than a moment."[13] In his "Letter to Nuns" Caesarius devotes an entire section to admonishing the nuns of his monastery to flee disordered or "irregular" and "shameful intimacy" with men. He then provides a long catalogue of evils which can result from this pernicious familiarity.[14] In the Abbess Cesaria of Arles's letter to Radegund and Richilde, Cesaria warns, "Know most certainly that a woman who does not avoid a familiar relationship with men will rapidly destroy either herself or another."[15] Church councils and penitentials of the early Middle Ages issued strong warnings against the establishment of any type of close relationship between male and female religious. As was the case for siblings, proper living arrangements for churchmen and women were clearly defined so as to carefully regulate or to avoid altogether any opportunities for the "co-mingling" of the sexes. The early *subintroductae* arrangement, the chaste household of a clergyman and virgin, was perceived by the Church as potentially scandalous and was strongly discouraged. The double or mixed-sex monastery also came to be looked upon with suspicion.[16] Bede's famous cautionary tale of the alleged debauchery found at the double monastery of Coldingham underscored the potential dangers of "co-educational" institutions.[17] Church councils stipulated that convents of nuns must not be established in the neighborhood of monasteries of monks, as much because of the ruses of the devil as the rumors that would result from this.[18] Penitentials provided appropriate penances for fornication committed among churchmen and -women. For example, the eighth-century Penitentials of Bede and of Egbert require a seven-year penance for a monk accused of having intercourse with a nun.[19]

The changes involved in the perception or valuation of cross-sex relationships can perhaps be seen in an Irish "catalogue" which dates to the period of the ninth or tenth century. According to this source (which was discussed briefly in chapter 2), the saints of the Irish Church were divided into three orders or classes. The first order of saints, *sanctissima,* made up of bishops (432–544), "rejected not the services and society of women," or, according to another version, "they excluded not laymen and women from their churches." And also of importance for gender relationships, they did not "fear the wind of temptation." In contrast, the saints of the second order, *sanctior* (representing the more rigid monastic system of the period 544–98) "fled the companionship and administration of women and even excluded them from their monasteries," while the third class, *sanctus* (of the following four decades) "retired to solitary places and despised all earthly things."[20]

In some cases the extravagant institutional emphasis on celibacy and the prerequisite need for female avoidance among churchmen reflected a basic fear of women and female sexuality. Behind this mindset of suspicion toward women we see the practices of the desert fathers, the early eremitic and monastic saints, with their heroic acts of fleeing women and all temptation. The incidents of their lives captured in the *vitae* continued to exercise a strong influence on the religious mentality of the period. These wonderfully creative Lives provided fair warning to all men of what they perceived to be woman's essentially sexual and disruptive nature; they underscored the clear and present dangers inherent in these relationships and stressed the necessary caution required when associating with any member of the opposite sex.

As we have noted, hagiographers attempted to portray their protagonists as "impatient angels"—"dead to earthly desires." At the same time, the male hermits or monastic saints were frequently depicted as very much "alive" and susceptible to various "temptations of the flesh." Thus in the heroic tradition they are shown successfully repelling these dreaded seductions, particularly those involving women. Many of the *vitae*, while expressing a basic contempt for the human condition in general, also demonstrated a hatred of the body, and a concern for, or obsession with, celibacy. In part motivated by fear of their own weakness and susceptibility to female seduction, these holy men are shown fleeing to the "desert"—the wilderness of the hermit or the cloister of the monk—to shield themselves from their struggles with women and sexuality.[21] In these saints' Lives, woman is portrayed as the handmaid of the devil, or, for the Irish, man's "guardian devil." The Irish reform attitude with its fear of female sexuality can be seen in an anecdote about Máel-ruain, founder of Tallaght and head of a community of ascetics, and the holy woman, Samthann, who was foundress of the monastery of Clonbroney (d. 739). According to the story, Samthann sent a message with an itinerant pedlar to Máel-ruain telling the holy man that he was her favorite among the clerics. She also wanted to know if he received "womankind to his confession" and if he would accept her "soul-friendship." After some time the holy man responded that he would seek counsel from her. When the pedlar told Samthann this, she pushed her brooch pin deep into her cheek and with difficulty squeezed out a droplet of yellow liquid. St. Samthann then provided the following warning: "So long as there is this much juice in his body, let him [Máel-ruain] bestow no friendship nor confidence upon womankind."[22]

Thus, as the source of perpetual temptation, no woman was to be trusted. The mere sight, touch, or sound of a woman was thought to be potent enough to provoke concupiscent thoughts or, worse, instant fornication. Some of the early Celtic male saints, as portrayed by their hagiographers, seemed to possess an especially pronounced fear of female temptation, lustful thoughts, and fornication. For example, in this tradition they are shown fleeing after hearing the mere sound of a cow or sheep because of the close association of cattle with women. A *vita* of an early Irish holy man notes: "In this place I will not go, for where sheep, therein a woman; where a woman, therein sin; where sin, therein the devil, and where the devil, therein hell."[23] These *vitae* then focus at some length on the would-be saints' heroic struggles with female temptation and the persistent demon of fornication. The wide range of strategies which these holy men adopted included fleeing from women, defining restrictive boundaries to keep women at a safe distance, mortification of the flesh, actively courting temptation (with the intent to extinguish lust), and praying for some sort of miraculous intervention to stave off their problems with concupiscence and women.

Some of the *vitae* portray blatant examples of female temptation with the intent to dissuade these holy men from their profession. During the period of conversion to Christianity, for example, pagans were frequently described as employing a clever sexual strategy, that is, the use of "lewd and lascivious women" as a type of "secret weapon" to disturb the peace of churchmen. In the Life of St. David, written by Rhigyfarch (d. 1099) several centuries after the saint's death, a pagan man named Baia tried to rid his land of these unwelcome churchmen; however, after his abortive attempt his wife assumed command. According to the *vita*, this woman, "afire with a jealous spite, called her maids and said: 'Go where the monks can see you, and with bodies bare, play games and use lewd words.' The maids obey, they play immodest games, imitating sexual intercourse and displaying love's seductive embraces [*impudicos exercent ludos, concubitus simulant, blandos amoris nexus ostendunt*]. The minds of some of the monks they entice away to lust, the minds of others they irritate. The monks endeavour to abandon the place." Despite these brazen attempts, the hagiographer assures us that St. David remained steadfast and encouraged the ascetic resolve of his disciples. Soon their problems disappeared: Baia was killed and his wife became mad. Thus St. David and his monks remained at this place and they established a successful monastery which became St. David's (Dyfed), South Wales.[24]

The Celtic saint Columbanus, abbot of Luxeuil and Bobbio (d. 615), was apparently also confronted by temptations of the flesh. According to his biographer, Jonas, the devil aroused within Columbanus lust for certain *lascivae puellae*, "especially of those whose fine figure and superficial beauty are wont to enkindle mad desires in the minds of wretched men." Strongly tempted to yield to their undisguised wishes, he consulted a wise woman who lived as a hermit. She advised him to flee the fleshy world and free himself from these women, since he could not associate with the female sex without sin.[25]

Strategies of avoidance or flight were not always easily executed. Many of the hermit saints, in the tradition of St. Symeon the Stylite, were known for their strict policies of refusing to see any woman or forbidding women to step foot on their property. Some had established boundaries such as marking stones and barriers near their hermitages and churches, which were intended to keep women away. As a further deterrent, cautionary stories circulated of fierce vengeance wrought by the offended saint on the "brazen" women who tried to overstep these boundaries. These offenders were even threatened with excommunication for their attempts to enter buildings which were strictly off limits to women.

The tradition surrounding St. Calais/Carilefus, first abbot of Anisole, in Maine (d. ca. 540?), is of special interest. According to his *vita,* which was redacted by St. Siviard, abbot of the monastery of Anisole, approximately a century after the founding of the monastery, Queen Ultragotha (wife of King Childebert) wanted for some time to visit the holy abbot. She sent him an envoy to beg him to come to see her at her palace at Matovall. Calais responded that if he could assist the queen in any way, he would offer prayers for her; but she knew that as long as he lived he would never see the face of a woman and no woman would be allowed to enter into the monastery that he had founded. According to the *vita,* although the queen resented having her request denied and was displeased at not being able to see the holy man, she apparently admired his wisdom and feared that she might have disturbed him.[26]

Siviard also mentions that this "rule" initiated by St. Calais (which excluded women from the cloister and church) was still inviolably observed at his monastery some one hundred years after the holy man's death. As proof of this uninterupted tradition, he cites a case of a contemporary woman named Gunda who, wanting to test this policy, entered the cloister and church disguised as a man. As she approached the saint's tomb, she was struck down by God. This divine chastisement was then seen by the hagiographer to have a salutary effect as it inhibited others from attempting a similar stunt. (See chapter 3, above.)[27] (The possible influence of St. Calais's misogynist policy on the posthumous cult of St. Cuthbert at Durham will be discussed later in this chapter.)

In this same tradition we learn that the hermit St. Goeznou (6th c.) had such a deep fear of women that he set up a huge stone as a marker beyond which no female was to tread—under penalty of death. And according to his *vita,* a woman was said to have pushed another past this barrier—just to test this policy—whereupon the assailant fell dead, while the woman who had reluctantly transgressed, remained unharmed.[28] Other examples include the case of a woman who attempted to enter St. Goulven's oratory, who in turn was said to have been struck blind by the saint; or female trespassers of St. Fiacre's chapel who allegedly went mad on the spot.[29] According to tradition, when Queen-St. Margaret of Scotland attempted to enter the church of St. Lawrence with her offerings in 1091, she encountered similar difficulties; she was suddenly smitten and repelled, for this church was also off limits to all members of the female sex. Fortunately, after this transgression, the sources relate, St. Margaret was restored to health by the prayers of the clergy and she was able to give her donations to the Church.[30] Other cautionary stories featuring these strategies of female avoidance, as well as the necessary distancing or segregation of the sexes, proliferated in the sources of the period.

It appears, however, that at least a few churchmen were aware of the special problems that these policies might cause for women. A wonderful example which might reflect a certain sensitivity concerning exclusionary space can be found in Gregory of Tours' *Life of the Fathers*.[31] Here he relates a discussion which was said to have occurred between the brother abbot-saints, Lupicinus and Romanus, who were advanced in age and making preparations for their burial. Romanus said to his brother, "I do not want to have my tomb in a monastery, which women are forbidden to enter. As you know, the Lord has given me the grace of bringing cures, although I am unworthy and do not deserve it, and many have been snatched from various illnesses by the imposition of my hands and the power of the Lord's cross. Thus many people will gather at my tomb when I leave the light of this life. That is why I ask to rest far from the monastery."[32] For that reason, when Romanus died he was buried ten miles from his monastery, and here a great church was built, with large crowds coming each day to receive miraculous cures at the tomb of the holy man.[33] In this rather unusual case, Romanus is sympathetically portrayed as recognizing the special hardship which these discriminatory policies caused for women, and therefore chose to be buried not in his own monastery, which would have forbidden female entry, but rather at the church of his sister's convent at La Balme, a site which would accommodate female as well as male pilgrims. This marvelous description of how the saint chose La Balme as his final resting place and cult center, then, perhaps shows a certain enlightenment toward gender relations and women's religious needs which could be found among a few of these early holy men. It also provides an indication of the wide range of ecclesiastical views concerning the regulation of contact with women, as well as the negotiation of sacred space, that can be found during this period. Nevertheless, the predominant or official monastic policy emphasized the basic need to establish exclusionary practices based on gender.

Thus, following in the celibate tradition of the fear of female temptation and the necessary avoidance of women, we can find an impressive number of male saints who adopted more physical and painful strategies which focused on the mortification of the flesh. They committed themselves to rigorous programs of fasting or sleep deprivation in order to "deaden" their bodies and minds to temptation. Some experienced painfully realistic visions which rid them of sexual urges; others resorted to more extreme or dramatic means of mortification, inflicting on themselves sharp physical pain to "counteract" or temporarily distract them from their concupiscent thoughts.

In his *Dialogues,* Gregory the Great recounts the story of a man named Equitius, who, because of his great holiness, had been made abbot over many monasteries in the province of Valeria. Nevertheless, as a young man he had suffered greatly from violent temptations of the flesh. As told by Gregory: "One night while he was earnestly begging God for aid in this matter, he saw himself made a eunuch while an angel stood by. Through this vision he realized that all disturbances of the flesh had been taken away, and from that time on he was a complete stranger to temptations of this kind as though his body were no longer subject to the tendencies of human nature." Gregory also points out that "relying on this virtue" the holy man assumed the guidance of a number of communities of women. However, no doubt fearing the "natural" seductiveness of women and their threat to men's ascetic profession, as well as convinced that his acts should be admired but not imitated, "he warned his disciples to be distrustful of themselves and not to be too eager to follow his example, for they would be the cause of their own downfall in trying to do what God had not given them the power to do." [34]

One of the most famous episodes in this tradition of extreme mortification of the flesh can be found in Gregory the Great's *vita* of St. Benedict of Nursia. According to this Life, while Benedict lived hidden in a small cave at Subiaco, temptation arrived in the form of a blackbird. "The moment it left, he was seized with an unusually violent temptation. The evil spirit recalled to his mind a woman he had once seen, and before he realized it his emotions were carrying him away. Almost overcome in the struggle, he was on the point of abandoning the lonely wilderness when suddenly with the help of God's grace he came to himself. Just then he noticed a thick patch of nettles and briars next to him. Throwing his garment aside, he flung himself naked into the sharp thorns and stinging nettles. There he rolled and tossed until his whole body was in pain and covered with blood. Yet once he had conquered pleasure through suffering, his torn and bleeding skin served to drain off the poison of temptation from his body. Before long the pain that was burning his whole body had put out the fires of evil in his heart." Gregory thus concludes, it was "by exchanging these two fires" that Benedict triumphed over sin so completely that he never experienced another temptation of this type.[35]

The Life of the reformer St. Wulfstan, bishop of Worcester (d. 1095), relates a similar cure adopted by this holy man when confronted by sexual temptation. According to his *vita,* on one occasion a local girl "with the accompaniment of a harp began to dance in front of him with lewd gestures and shameless movement such as might gratify the eyes of a lover. And he, whom neither words nor touches had weakened, now panted with desire, completely reduced by her disarming gestures." However, we are told that Wulfstan "immediately came to his senses" and "bursting with tears, fled away into some rough undergrowth and prickly scrub." He remained in these "prickly scrubs" for some time and when he emerged, he was cured. And "from that time on no marvelous figure excited either his mind or eye; nor was the peace of his sleep disturbed by wet dreams."[36]

Other eremitic or monastic saints were said to mortify their flesh by adopting the ordeal of lying on burning coals or applying burning firebrands to their skin.[37] In contrast, some of the Celtic saints regularly practiced ascetic immersions in icy water during the night in order to suppress sexual desire. Giraldus Cambrensis, for example, relates that the early Welsh saint Dogmael (5–6th c.) regularly plunged himself into the river near his hermitage: this rite was done specifically *"ad domandam libidinem."*[38] One of the legends of St. David of Wales relates a similar practice: "Also he sought cold water at some distance, where by remaining long therein, and becoming frozen, he might subdue the heat of the flesh."[39] The *vita* of the sixth-century St. Kentigern, bishop of Glasgow, notes how this saint immersed himself in icy water "because the law of sin, which wars within the *membris pudendis,* thus was weakened, and the fire of desire having ceased and extinguished, in order that no corruptness of wanton flesh might pollute or soil the lily of his chastity in waking or even in sleeping." This Life also claims that following his "cold-water treatment," Kentigern enjoyed absolute immunity from temptation even by the most beautiful women.[40] The early Life of St. Wandrille notes that when this saint was tempted by the devil during the night, he would get up and plunge himself into the river. And there in the middle of winter, he recited the complete psalter in the midst of the ice floe, dipping down into the water at the end of each psalm.[41] The reformer Saint Peter Damian, cardinal bishop of Ostia, was said to plunge his body in icy waters when attacked by temptations of the flesh during the night, and he remained immersed in the water until he obtained the relief he sought.[42] A popular episode in the Life of St. Bernard of Clairvaux notes this same method of extinguishing temptation and lust. As related in this account, when Bernard realized that he was deriving an inordinate amount of pleasure from looking at a woman, as well as entertaining concupiscent thoughts, he threw himself into a pool of icy water.[43]

In contrast to this whole assemblage of popular exempla of holy men fleeing sexual temptation or adopting strategies of self-mortification, a few cases describe male saints deliberately courting female temptation with the intent to "deaden their flesh." These examples involve the rather dangerous "trials of chastity" or "ordeals of the flesh"—experiments which essentially involved male ascetics chastely sharing their beds with virgins. In these heroic tests of endurance, the male saints attempted to prove their miraculous asceticism or self-control by actively seeking out attractive virginal women and confronting sexual temptation. Among the saints who were said to have "excelled" in these heroic trials of chastity were the Celtic saint Scothin/Scuthin (a disciple of St. David) and the Anglo-Saxon saint Aldhelm, as well as Robert of Arbrissel (d. 1117).[44]

While these hagiographic accounts focused on the heroics and the moral strength of the holy men when faced with "incredible temptations of the flesh," these stories also provided a negative image of women: their end result was to dehumanize them. In exaggerating gender differences, they emphasized the deleterious aspects of the female nature. Woman was seen as a sex object and was viewed as solely responsible for these unwanted trials or afflictions. With the temptress being frequently the only female figure in these *vitae,* woman became synonymous with sinful flesh, sexual distraction, perpetual temptation, and *luxuria* or lust.[45] The power and pervasiveness of the sexual dimension in cross-sex relationships thus became one of the underlying messages of these *vitae:* women were a serious threat and were to be avoided at all cost.

Moreover, in practical terms these holy men did not need a female presence in their lives; all of their spiritual, religious, and material needs could be satisfied "in house," that is, without recourse to women. In fact, some were convinced that they were much better off without the threat of potential sexual tension associated with "womankind." In order to live a holy and chaste life, men needed to flee from the presence of women; to practice mortification of the flesh, or pray for a miraculous release from female temptation. Thus, in this genre of saints' Lives, any type of cross-sex relationship was perceived as extremely dangerous, as evidenced by the extremes to which these holy men were driven in order to maintain their chastity. These popular models of rather skewed gender relations therefore present a negative message in regard to women: they attempt to discourage the easy

association of men with women or the fostering of friendships between men and women—particularly for those within the Church
who were committed to a life of chastity.

In contrast to these male Lives, the contemporary *vitae* of women
saints seem to capture a somewhat different perspective which in turn
might have reflected and also influenced women's perceptions of cross-
sex friendships. While many of the male Lives focus on the basic intrusion of sex in such relationships, the women saints seem to be more
positive, open, and appreciative of these potential bonds of friendship.
Some even seem to reflect a sense of humor in regard to the impractical and obsessive practices adopted by their male colleagues; in fact, in
a few cases, they make the phobic holy men and their conduct toward
women appear rather ridiculous! In this tradition is the wonderful
anecdote which was attributed to the early desert mothers: "A monk
ran into a party of handmaids of the Lord on a certain journey. Seeing
them he left the road and gave them a wide berth. But the Abbess said
to him: If you were a perfect monk, you would not even have looked
close enough to see that we were women." [46]

Although it is difficult to generalize because of the nature of our
sources (including the fact that the majority of the Lives were written
by male ecclesiastics), it appears that the *vitae* of the *mulieres sanctae*
in our study do not exhibit a similar level of obsession or fear of all
males (even churchmen) as potential objects of sexual distraction; nor
do they disclose a subsequent need to avoid or flee from men at all
costs. The lives of these women saints, at least as officially portrayed
by their hagiographers, appear to be more balanced, or perhaps the
women were simply more practical or enlightened in regard to gender
relationships in the Church and society. [47]

In one of the Lives of St. Brigid we can see a definite wit or a wonderful sense of humor on the part of these nuns (at the expense of
the anchorite's vow to shun all women). According to the *vita*, Brigid
spent some time with her followers living near the sea, and "not far
from them there lived a certain anchorite who shunned the sight of
women, wholly and completely given to God." One day when the anchorite set out to travel to a certain island, he came upon Brigid near
the place. "His companions therefore said: 'Let us go to St. Brigid for
her blessing.' He replied: 'Don't you know my vow that I do not wish
to look upon any woman?' So they rose up from the chairs upon
which they had been sitting while saying these things, and they forgot
all their baggage on the way, and came an entire day's journey." Later
that evening, when they stopped at a hospice, they remembered their
baggage and said, "So, we have lost our baggage because we didn't go

over to Brigid for her to bless us and because of this wrongdoing we will fast tonight." In the meantime, Brigid had ordered her nuns to go and bring to their house the baggage of these holy men which had been left near them on the road so that it would not be lost. The next morning, the anchorite and his followers were then obliged to go back to Brigid where they found their baggage safely stored in her house. They then spent three days and nights with Brigid and her nuns "in praise of God and in preaching the word." [48] Underlying this episode there seems to be a certain awareness of the practical need for cooperation between the sexes. The message appears to be that the holy man had been humbled and was shown that he could no longer afford to despise or ignore women.

Later we learn that when this same anchorite attempted to move to another island, he experienced a major problem. Here he found that a certain peasant, along with his wife and children, had already claimed this land as their property. According to the hagiographer, "The anchorite avoided the sight of the woman and asked the peasant to leave the island, but was unsuccessful in his request." Unable to resolve this problem with the man and his family, "the anchorite then sent for St. Brigid." And it was ultimately through her intervention that the woman, her husband, and her children were removed from the island and the anchorite could settle there in peace. This episode again seems to bring out the fact that the anchorite, despite his rather impractical vow and his public protestations of avoiding all women, in the end could not get along without their help. [49]

A profoundly moving example of a holy woman's assertiveness and an early feminist argument against these gender-based exclusionary policies can be found in the Life of the Irish St. Senan (d. 544). [50] According to this later *vita*, the holy woman Canair lived in a hermitage on her own property in the south of Ireland. One night as she prayed she saw a vision of a high tower of fire rising up to heaven from all of the churches of Ireland, but the most impressive came from the Cell of Inis Cathaig (Scattery Island). Anticipating her own imminent death, Canair thus got into her boat and headed to Inis Cathaig. Senan, the abbot of the church at Inis Cathaig, alerted of her arrival, went to the harbor to meet her. The *vita* then captures this remarkable discussion which was said to have occurred between the two saints. Canair was greeted by Senan who immediately told her that she would have to leave Inis Cathaig and go to another island to the east and stay with her sister. Canair responded that she had not come for that, but rather to stay with Senan on this island. However, Senan remarked that women were not allowed on this island.

Canair then argued, "How can you say that? Christ is no worse than you. Christ came to redeem women no less than to redeem men. No less did He suffer for the sake of women than for the sake of men. Women have served and cared for Christ and His Apostles. No less than men do women enter the heavenly kingdom. Why, then should you not allow women on your island?"

"You are stubborn," said Senan.

"What then," said Canair, "shall I get what I ask for, a place for my side on this island and the sacrament?"

"A place of resurrection," said Senan, "will be given you here on the brink of the wave, but I fear that the sea will carry off your remains."

"God will grant me," said Canair, "that the spot where I shall lie will not be the first that the sea will bear away."

"You have my permission, then," said Senan, "to come to shore."

For thus had she been while they were conversing, standing upon the wave, with her staff under her bosom, as if she were on land. Then Canair came on shore, and the Sacrament was administered to her, and she straightway went to heaven.

This episode is an especially interesting example of the gender-based barriers established by churchmen to keep women at a safe distance or to hold them at bay. They caused women a great deal of hardship in their attempts to pursue a religious life. Although the woman in this case was known for her virginity and holy life, and was apparently old and about to die, nevertheless this condition did not assure her preferential treatment: she was still, after all, a female and, as long as she drew breath, she had the potential for sexual distraction. However, as related in this episode, Canair refused to be put off. In questioning the legitimacy of this exclusionary policy, she cited as rather strong historical precedent for her case Christ's positive attitude toward women, women's roles in assisting Christ and his Apostles, and finally, women's equal entry into heaven. Apparently convinced or embarrassed by Canair's argument, and perhaps unable to deny a dying woman the Sacraments and proper burial, Senan finally relented. Canair was therefore allowed to receive the Sacraments and to be buried in this "sacred" male space, albeit on the edge or "the brink of the wave"!

Although there are a few examples in the *vitae* that attempt to show the *mulieres sanctae* as displaying a certain deference or circumscribed behavior when in the presence of men,[51] their appreciation of cross-sex relationships seems to have differed from that of the male ascetics. On the one hand, this apparent difference in emphasis may be due in part to the fact that in the practice of their religious life and pursuit of holiness, these women saints simply could not get along without men. Their lives required a male presence. They were dependent on priests, confessors, abbots and bishops, as well as male *advocati,* procurators, workmen, and others. These women did not have the same luxury that male saints had of being able to completely close out of their lives members of the opposite sex. Therefore we see in these Lives a clear appreciation of the practical need for cooperative ventures, a recognition of the necessary interaction and the benefits of women and men working together within the context of the religious community.

This difference in emphasis might also be explained by the fact that the *vitae* were mainly the work of churchmen who no doubt frequently saw their female protagonists from a protective and deferential distance, as essentially asexual virgins or widows. Thus in their descriptions of the activities of these women, who were in some cases their biological, foster, or spiritual mothers, or their sisters and saintly associates, they perhaps assumed that these special women (in contrast to ordinary women, i.e., daughters of Eve, temptresses, etc.) remained unaffected by sexual temptation, lust, and sex. From their perspective, these types of sexual concerns or distractions did not enter the minds of these female saints. When the hagiographers do treat women saints and sex, the women are frequently seen as victims of male lust—placed in dire situations (not of their causing), where their virginity or chastity is forcefully threatened by sexual assault. It is in these desperate circumstances that they are forced to resort to various heroic strategies of virginity or to die as virgin martyrs. (See chapter 3.)

Thus we can see in the *vitae* different patterns of attitudes toward gender relationships and the valuation of cross-sex relationships. Many of the early Lives dealing with male eremitic or monastic saints presented cautionary examples for those attempting to live as "impatient angels"; they were deeply concerned with sexual temptation and strategies for avoiding women and concupiscent thoughts. These didactic works appear on the whole rather negative in regard to gender relationships. In contrast, many of the women saints, as depicted in the *vitae,* seemed to be more "balanced," or on a more even keel; the *mulieres sanctae* appeared to accept and appreciate the need for a male presence in their lives and encouraged the cultivation of spiritual friendships with men.

MULIERES SANCTAE AND CROSS-SEX FRIENDSHIPS

Despite the various efforts on the part of churchmen to discourage cross-sex friendships, in the early fervor of the Church and its missionary activities these gender-based prohibitions seem to have been temporarily disregarded. During this period in which the Church was newly established, weak, and rather loosely structured, there were increased opportunities for men and women to work together and to share their vocations, religious commitments, and experiences. It was, in other words, an ideal atmosphere in which to foster friendships. Moreover, the early monastic milieu (with its double or affiliated monasteries as centers of missionary activity) has provided particularly impressive evidence of many strong friendships and emotional ties among the saints. Such relationships appear to have been rather common during this early period: they were sought after and accepted.

These saintly friendships were manifested in a variety of ways. According to the *vitae,* bonds of friendship were maintained through visits or correspondence. Friends frequently exchanged handmade gifts and small tokens of affection as well as requests and promises of prayers. They sought out and offered advice and consolation. However, friendship became especially important during times of physical separation, dislocation, or periods of great difficulty or disaster. During these times friends would freely call upon one another for assistance; they listened to each other's problems, they bonded together and offered support. In illness, these holy friends cared for one another, and they assumed a special role in the important events surrounding a friend's death and burial. It is also through friendships that memories of the future saint were kept alive and the reputation for sanctity came to be recognized. As friends of the holy dead, they witnessed special miracles, lobbied for the establishment of cults, and wrote or commissioned the writing of *vitae.* The Lives of the saints are, then, especially rich in their descriptions of these early friendships.

At the outset there were a number of prominent "historical" precedents for these holy alliances. These exempla include the relationship of Christ with Martha and Mary; the Virgin Mary and St. John; Sts. Paul and Phoebe, or Sts. Paul and Thecla; and St. Jerome and his famous circle of women friends—Sts. Paula, Marcella, Asella, Blaesilla, Eustochium, etc.[52] These models were not lost on hagiographers and other ecclesiastical writers of the medieval period, who cited them as historical evidence for cross-sex friendships. For example, Bishop Azecho of Worms, in a rather remarkable letter written in the second quarter of the eleventh-century to an abbess or nun of an unnamed community, discusses spiritual love or friendship between women and men. Unlike some who held that one must flee familiar acquaintance and conversation with women, he argued that there was no reason that men and women should not be involved in close friendships. In his defense of chaste, spiritual friendships established by those brothers and sisters "cohabiting in God," he specifically cited as precedent Mary, the mother of Christ, and her friendship with St. John, and St. Jerome's friendship with Sts. Paula and Eustochium.[53] However, it is of interest to note that although Jerome and his celebrated friendships with Paula, Eustochium, and other aristocratic women of Rome are in subsequent centuries singled out as a model of *amicitia,* or spiritual friendship, during his own lifetime these close relationships came to be looked upon with suspicion and caused serious scandal in the Roman Church. It appears that it was especially Jerome's close friendship with Paula which brought about the damaging insinuations about his moral conduct and was the cause of the bitter scandal. As noted by J. N. D. Kelly in his work, *Jerome: His Life, Writings, and Controversies,* "His only crime, he declares, was his sex, and this only became a crime when the story got around that she [Paula] was planning to accompany him to Jerusalem." There was an official inquiry by the Church into Jerome's allegedly improper behavior. A judgment was passed and although he was apparently acquitted of the charges of impropriety, an agreement was reached that he would depart from Rome immediately.[54]

It is, then, during the formative years of monasticism that there emerges an impressive number of holy alliances or close friendships between prominent churchmen and churchwomen who will be recognized as saints.

Among the early Irish *vitae,* for example, we find frequent mention of affection and friendship between women and men saints. St. Brigid, for instance, was described as cultivating a wide network of friends. According to legend, she maintained close ties with a number of bishops, including Erc of Slane, Mel of Armagh, Ailbe of Emly, as well as with St. Patrick. She was also described as a friend of Sts. Brendan, Findian, and Ibar of Begery. These churchmen provided her with advice and material and spiritual assistance at various times. The scholar Gildas was said to have made a bell which he sent to St. Brigid.[55] On her deathbed, Brigid was attended by a former student and friend, St. Nindid Pure-hand. According to Brigid's *vita,* as she lay dying, Nindid Pure-hand came from Rome. "The reason why he was called Nindid Pure-hand was that he never put his hand to his side, when Brigit repeated a paternoster with him. And he gave communion and sacrifice to Brigit, who sent her spirit to heaven."[56]

Ita, a contemporary of Brigid, also cultivated an impressive circle of friends. St. Cumine, bishop of Clonfert, the abbot-saint Coemgen, St. Luchtigern, and St. Susrean were included among this group.[57] She was especially close to St. Erc, bishop of Slane, who was her principal adviser and friend. Ita also shared fosterage of St. Brendan with Erc.[58] The Life of St. Ita notes that as St. Coemgen of Glendalough lay dying he specifically asked for her to come to him. He then begged Ita to minister to him as no one else would do. On his death she was to place her hand over his mouth and close it. And she did this as directed.[59]

The Lives of the Merovingian saints are also extraordinarily rich in their descriptions of cross-sex friendships. One rather interesting mention of a long-distance expression of friendship can be found in the Life of St. Genovefa. Here it is noted that St. Symeon the Stylite (who was notorious for his avoidance of all women) "made eager inquiries about Genovefa from merchants going back and forth and asked them to greet her and convey his veneration for her; they also say that he earnestly desired her to remember him in her prayers."[60]

One of the most famous spiritual alliances of the *custos animi* or "guardian of one's soul" pattern is that of St. Radegund and Agnes with Fortunatus. While residing at Radegund's monastery, Fortunatus handled the former queen's correspondence, he provided her with advice, and served as her almoner. He shared conversations, meals, special foods, and flowers with both Radegund and Agnes.[61] Fortunatus also recognized their learning and intelligence and specifically asked for their assistance in writing the Life of St. Martin of Tours.[62] Ultimately, using his talents as an author and his position as bishop of Poitiers, he would write Radegund's saint's Life and work to promote her cult. In his poetry, Fortunatus affectionately called Radegund his "mother" and Agnes his "sister."[63] At one point, apparently having to defend himself from suspicions surrounding his close friendship with Agnes, he noted that he did not feel for Agnes any sentiment which he was not able to demonstrate toward his sister, Tatiana. In this text addressed to Agnes he argues: "You, who, because of your dignity, are a mother to me and [who] are my sister by the privilege of friendship, you to whom I pay homage involving [all] my heart, faith and piety, whom I love with divine, entirely spiritual affection, devoid of the guilty complicity of the flesh and senses, I call to witness Christ, the Apostles Peter and Paul, Saint Mary and her pious companions that I have never looked at you with any other eye and with any other sentiments than if you had been my sister Tatiana, if our mother Radegund had carried us both in her chaste flanks, and if her holy breasts had nourished us with their milk. I fear, alas! for I see the danger in it, that the least insinuations of evil tongues repress the demonstration of my feelings. However, I am resolved to live with you as I have done up to now, if you are willing to continue our friendship."[64] Fortunatus also wrote a number of poems which he offered to Radegund and Agnes as a small token of his friendship. In one of his poems he recounts: "With my own hands I have composed this small gift to you and my lady, the sweet and gentle Radegund, in recognition of our friendship, although it is very feeble, second-rate, and of a poor execution. These little things become great by affection and love. If you think as much, you will see that the small gifts of those who love with constancy possess a charm greater than the others."[65] In one of his letters he sends Radegund and Agnes prayers for their safekeeping through the night under the care of angels. Similarly, he provides Agnes with a crucifix to protect her.[66] In several of his letters he describes the acute loneliness and desolation he experiences being away from Radegund and Agnes.[67] An indication of his great love and affection for Agnes and Radegund was his suggested project of establishing a single tomb for the three of them which would insure that he never be separated from his friends.[68]

Outside the monastery, Radegund cultivated a wide network of friends. Included among this group, which consisted mainly of bishops and abbots, was Avitus of Clermont, whom she thanks in her correspondence for his presents and to whom she commends her friendship; she was also a friend of Aredius of Limoges, Felix of Nantes, Domitianus of Angers, Martin of Braga, and Gregory of Tours, among others.[69] According to Baudonivia, Radegund maintained a close friendship with the hermit St. John of Chinon. Through her "trusted nun, Fridovigia, whom she kept at her side, and Fridovigia's trusted men," she sent the holy man an expensive adornment cast in gold and encrusted with gemstones and pearls, worth one thousand gold solidi. In return for this gift she asked John to pray for her and to "send her a garment of hair cloth with which she might refine her body through penance. He sent her a hair cloth from which she made an outer and inner garment, and he informed her that if he should by the Holy Spirit become aware of that business that she feared [i.e., that the king wanted to have her back as his wife], he would send word." And this he did; however, he assured her "that God would not permit it [and] that the king would suffer God's punishment before he would have her in marriage."[70]

An especially intimate and moving spiritual friendship developed between Radegund and St. Junien, founder and abbot of the monastery of Maire. Conforming to their shared love of austerity and rigorous ascetic exercises, they exchanged a number of presents and requests for mutual prayers. While Radegund furnished Junien with necessary clothing, he fashioned for her some special instruments of penance: a hair shirt made of goat hair and an iron chain which Radegund wore tightly around her waist as a belt. They also were said to have promised each other that as soon as one of them felt death approaching, the other would be warned by a messenger so that the survivor could pray for the soul of the departed friend. According to Junien's *vita*, while the saint lay dying, he sent word to Radegund of his imminent death; however, his messenger and that of Radegund met half way on the road as both saints died appropriately on the very same day—August 13, 587.[71]

A final example of Radegund's important network of friends can be found in Gregory of Tours' *Glory of the Confessors*. Following the saint's death, Gregory describes the extreme sorrow and grief he experienced during his guided tour of Radegund's sacred cell: "I returned to the convent [after the funeral], and the abbess and the virgins led me to the particular spots where St Radegund had been accustomed to read or to pray. The abbess was weeping and said: 'Behold, we are entering her cell, but we do not find the mother who is lost! Behold the mat on which she bent her knees, wept, and prayed for the mercy of omnipotent God, but we do not see her! Behold the book in which she read, but her voice that was seasoned with a spiritual sharpness does not strike our ears! Behold the spindles on which she used to weave during the long fasts and while weeping copiously, but the beloved fingers of her holiness are not to be seen!' As they said this, they wept again and sighed, and even the internal organs of those weeping were dissolved in tears because of the emotion. Such grief overwhelmed my breast that I would not have stopped weeping if I did not realize that the blessed Radegund had departed from her convent in body but not in power, and that she had been taken from the world and placed in heaven."[72]

The *vitae* of Queen-St. Balthild and of St. Eloi also describe the mutual affection demonstrated between these two saints. As we have noted, during Balthild's first pregnancy, St. Eloi acted as the queen's confidant. He provided her with much-needed support in his assurances that she would bear a son. A gifted artisan and goldsmith, Eloi made a special toy for her unborn child and served as the infant's godfather.[73] Balthild and Eloi also worked together on their favorite charity, the buying and freeing of slaves. We learn that the queen was devastated when she heard of St. Eloi's death. According to the *vita* of St. Eloi, she arrived at Noyon the day after he died. Already a great crowd pressed around the holy man's body. Overcome by grief, Balthild cried and kissed the dead bishop's face, after which a miracle was said to have occurred in reward for her piety: blood flowed from the nostrils of the dead saint. This in turn provided the faithful with precious relics—for they dabbed pieces of linen in the holy man's blood. Balthild had hoped to have Eloi's body appropriately buried in her monastery of Chelles, which she had recently restored and enlarged. However, the Parisians, as well as the people of Noyon, had similar claims on the saint's body. As recorded, the choice of burial place was dictated by the saint himself through a miracle: the body was said to become too heavy to move and thus had to be buried in Noyon.[74] Also, according to the Life of St. Eloi, Balthild received a posthumous warning from Eloi, and, following his advice, she sold her precious jewels and gold ornaments—using the money to provide alms for the poor and to pay for the elaborate decoration of Eloi's tomb.[75]

Another impressive Merovingian friendship was that of the abbess St. Waldetrude with the hermit St. Gislenus/Ghislain (late seventh century). As related by our sources, Gislenus initially served as spiritual adviser to Waldetrude and her husband, Mauger. He encouraged Waldetrude to adopt a religious life and assisted her by offering her a cell at Castrilocus (present-day Mons) located some four miles from his own hermitage on the river Haina (modern Saint Ghislain), in which she could follow the eremitic life. According to the *vitae*, up to the end of his life Gislenus would meet with St. Waldetrude to converse about spiritual things and matters related to their respective monasteries. And when the infirmities of old age made it too difficult to travel easily between the two monasteries, Gislenus had a little oratory built in honor of the martyr saint Quentin which was part way between the two houses at a place called Quaregnon. And it was here that they would meet.[76] We learn that Waldetrude's sister, St. Aldegund, abbess of Maubeuge, also cultivated a close friendship with St. Gislenus. According to our sources, Gislenus and Aldegund entered into an agreement that the monastery of Maubeuge and Gislenus's monastery of Celle would support one another in all of their needs. They also agreed to build a bridge over which the faithful might pass in order to pray at the monastery of Celle.[77] In addition Aldegund and St. Humbert, abbot of Marolles, shared a close friendship. As related in the sources, this holy man seldom left his monastery except to visit and give consolation to the abbess St. Aldegund. They shared a great deal of affection based on their charity and prayers.[78] Moreover we learn that Aldegund was bound in a "friendship of spiritual intimacy" to the bishop-saint Amand. One night she received a vision of her friend, St. Amand, who appeared to her crowned by God in heaven and surrounded by a great company of souls. In one redaction of Aldegund's *vita*, the saint saw herself among this large troop of souls.

When she asked Gislenus the meaning of this vision, he told her that it forecasted her own imminent death.[79]

The *vitae* and chronicles of the Anglo-Saxon period are also rich in examples of close male-female spiritual friendships. An early saintly friendship of the north of England was that of St. Hilda, abbess of Whitby, and Aidan, bishop of Lindisfarne. According to Bede, Hilda was recalled to Northumbria by St. Aidan, who had discovered her worth; and he therefore gave her a small piece of property on the River Wear, at which place she established a small monastic community. Afterward she was made abbess of Hartlepool. According to Bede, Bishop Aidan and all the religious men "who knew her and admired her innate wisdom and love of God's service, often used to visit her, to express their affection and offer thoughtful guidance."[80]

Several prominent abbess-saints play an important role in St. Cuthbert's network of friends. Although he is shown as strongly desiring to lead a life of solitary meditation, in his pastoral role he frequently found himself traveling around his bishopric. St. Aelffled, abbess of Whitby, was one of his special friends. While installed as a hermit on an island near Lindisfarne, Cuthbert left his retreat at the request of Aelffled. Their meeting took place on Coquet Island, at which time she urged him to accept a bishopric which King Egfrid wanted to bestow upon him; she also questioned him on how long her brother would live and who would be his heir (see plate 20). They met a second time at Ovington where, during a feast, he had a vision which he then shared with Aelffled.[81] Bede's Life of Cuthbert describes another incident relating to their special friendship. According to the *vita*: Aelffled "always had a great affection for the man of God. . . . At that time . . . she had been stricken by a grievous sickness and long afflicted, and seemed almost to have reached the point of death." After having recovered somewhat from her sickness, Aelffled found that she could no longer stand or walk. According to Cuthbert's Life: "One day amid the afflictions of her sad thoughts, the blessed and quiet life of the most revered father Cuthbert came into her mind and she said: 'Would that I had something belonging to my Cuthbert! I know well and believingly trust in God that I should speedily be healed.' Not long afterwards there came one who brought her a linen girdle which he had sent. She greatly rejoiced at the gift and, realizing that her desire had been made known to the holy man by heavenly means, she girded herself with it, and in the morning she was able forthwith to stand erect, and on the third day was entirely restored to health."[82] It also appears that in 698, eleven years after Cuthbert's death, Aelffled was present and assisted at the translation of Cuthbert's body to a new shrine at Lindisfarne. According to an inventory of the church at Durham, one of the cloths which was removed from Cuthbert's body during the translation of the saint's relics to the new Norman cathedral in 1104 is listed as "a linen cloth of double texture which had enveloped the body of St. Cuthbert in his grave; Elfled the abbess had wrapped him up in it." [83]

Cuthbert cultivated the friendship of a number of other abbesses during his lifetime. On one occasion he visited Abbess Ebba of Coldingham. "She sent to the man of God asking that he would deign to visit her and her monastery for the sake of exhorting them. Nor could he deny the loving request of the handmaiden of God. So he came to the place and remained there some days and opened up to them all the path of righteousness about which he preached, as much by his deeds as by his words." [84] On another occasion he stayed at the monastery of Abbess Verca, where he was "magnificently received." During this visit he also allegedly performed a miracle of changing water to wine. [85] It is from this same saintly friend that Cuthbert received a special linen cloth which he saved to be used as his winding sheet. According to his final wishes he noted: "I was unwilling to wear the cloth while alive but, out of affection for the abbess Verca, a woman beloved of God, who sent it to me, I have taken care to keep it to wrap my body in." [86] We also learn that St. Etheldreda, abbess of Ely, who was extremely skilled in gold embroidery work, sent Cuthbert a gift of a stole and maniple magnificently embroidered with gold and jewels. [87]

Bede also describes the holy alliance fostered between St. Etheldreda and Bishop Wilfrid (see plate 5). According to Bede, "the king (her husband) knew that there was no man for whom she had a higher regard" or, "she loved no man more than Wilfrith." After receiving encouragement from Wilfrid, she left her husband and entered the monastery of Coldingham. Here Wilfrid gave her the veil and the clothing of a nun. [88] After he had been banished from Northumbria, Wilfrid visited Etheldreda at her new monastery of Ely where he is said to have planned the buildings and assisted her in the construction. He also installed Etheldreda as abbess of Ely, ca. 670. During one of his trips to Rome, he obtained from the pope a special charter of privileges for Etheldreda's new foundation. [89] Moreover, we also learn that Etheldreda bestowed on Wilfrid extensive property at Hexham and here he built an impressive church dedicated to St. Andrew. [90]

Saint Ebba, abbess of Coldingham, was also a close friend of Bishop Wilfrid. She proved to be a staunch supporter of the bishop during his rather stormy career. According to Eddius Stephanus's Life of Wilfrid, Abbess Ebba (King Oswy's sister) "was a very wise and holy woman." [91] On one occasion, as the king and his queen were traveling through their lands, they stopped at the monastery of Coldingham.

Here the queen became seriously ill—according to Eddius Stephanus she was "possessed by a devil during the night and, as in the case of Pilate's wife, the attacks were so severe that she was hardly expected to last till day." As morning arrived, the abbess came to the queen and saw that she was dying. She then went to her brother, the king, and with tears in her eyes told him that the cause of his wife's grave affliction was their ill treatment of Wilfrid. "Indeed she rounded on him." She then blamed her brother for removing her friend Wilfrid from his see and placing him in prison. Ebba then warned Oswy, "Listen, my son, to your mother's advice. Loosen his bonds. Restore the relics your queen has taken from his neck and carried round from city to city like the ark of the Lord to her own doom. Send a messenger with them now. The best plan would be to reinstate him as bishop, but if you cannot bring yourself to do this, then at least let him and his friends leave the kingdom and go where they will. Do this and, as I see it, you will live and your queen will recover. Disobey and, as God is my witness, you shall not escape punishment.'" Stephanus then notes the successful outcome of Ebba's strong argument: "The king obeyed the holy matron, freed our bishop, and let him depart with his relics and all his friends. And the queen recovered."[92]

Aelffled, abbess of Whitby, also assumed an important role as Wilfrid's friend and prominent supporter. Theodore, archbishop of Canterbury, wrote to Aelffled and asked her to back Wilfrid after he was recalled from exile by King Aldfrith. Again according to Eddius Stephanus, Aelffled was a witness to King Aldfrith's dying statement which requested a reconciliation with Wilfrid and that he be restored to his see. Later Wilfrid's case was settled at the Synod of Nidd and "Abbess Aelffled, the best of advisers and a constant source of strength to the whole province, was with them." She was called upon and spoke strongly in defense of Wilfrid. At the end of the synod, after some discussion, the archbishop gave his advice and "Abbess Aelffled gave them hers." They all agreed to make peace with Wilfrid, and Ripon and Hexham were returned to him along with all of their revenues.[93]

Our sources also note Aelffled's special friendship with St. Trumwin. After working among the Picts, the missionary-bishop St. Trumwin retired to Aelffled's monastery at Whitby, where he spent his last years. Aelffled found him to be extremely helpful in the administration of the monastery and a great comfort in her own life. Trumwin also chose to be buried at Whitby.[94]

One of the most prominent saintly dyads of the early eighth century was that of Hildelith, second abbess of Barking Abbey and Aldhelm, bishop of Sherborne (d. 709). Aldhelm appears to have been a frequent

guest at the double foundation at Barking, where he shared his scholarly interests with Hildelith and her nuns. He dedicated his prose treatise *De virginitate* to Hildelith and a number of her nuns (see plate 21).
In the opening passages of this work, he thanks the nuns of Barking
for the letters which they had sent him and praises their eloquence and
intellectual sophistication. He writes: "To the most reverend virgins of
Christ, (who are) to be venerated with every affection of devoted
brotherhood, and to be celebrated not only for the distinction of
(their) corporeal chastity, which is (the achievement) of many, but also
to be glorified on account of (their) spiritual purity, which is (the
achievement) of few: Hildelith, teacher of the regular discipline and
of the monastic way of life; and likewise Justina and Cuthburg; and
Osburg too, related (to me) by family bonds of kinship; Aldgith
and Scholastica, Hidburg and Berngith, Eulalia and Thecla—(to all
these nuns) unitedly ornamenting the Church through the renown of
their sanctity, Aldhelm, dilatory worshipper of Christ and humble servant of the Church, (sends his) best wishes for perpetual prosperity." [95]
Aldhelm concludes his tract by asking them to continue to stimulate
him with their letters. He also begs these "soldiers of Christ," as a
reward for his *De virginitate,* to intercede for him through their
prayers, and at the same time he would pray for them. He then writes:
"Farewell, you flowers of the Church, monastic sisters, scholarly
pupils, pearls of Christ, jewels of Paradise, and participants in the
celestial homeland! Amen." [96]

Furthermore, among Aldhelm's official correspondence is found a
letter written to the nun, Sigegyth, which again captures the churchman's concern and affection for a friend. He writes "To Sister Sigegyth,
most beloved and most loving and venerable to me for the sincere
emotion of (her) charity." Later he says, "I greet you earnestly, O Sigegyth, from the deepest chamber of my heart," and asks her to continue
to occupy herself with meditation on the Scriptures. He concludes his
letter, "Farewell, ten times, nay a hundred times and a thousand times
beloved, and may God cause you to fare well." [97]

The Life of Saint Guthlac provides another example of these early
bonds of spiritual friendship. Although Guthlac adhered to a strict ascetic and eremitic life, he apparently still cultivated "long-distance"
friendships with women. According to his hagiographer, Felix, Guthlac
received his tonsure at the double monastery of Repton which was
then under the abbess Aelfthryth, and for two years he was instructed
in letters, psalms, canticles, prayers, Holy Scriptures, and monastic
discipline at Repton. Afterward he retired to the "desert," i.e., the
wilderness of the fens, to adopt a solitary life.[98] "On another occasion, some time after, the most reverend maiden Ecgburh, abbess of

the virgins and brides of Christ and daughter of King Aldwulf, sent to Guthlac, that venerable man of high merit, a leaden coffin with a linen cloth folded up in it, and asked that the man of God might be wrapped therein after his death; she invoked him by the terrible and awful name of the heavenly king, with arms outstretched in the form of the cross of our Lord and with palms extended in token of humble prayer, that the man of God would receive the gift for this said purpose." Felix continues: "She instructed another faithful brother that he should make this sign in Guthlac's presence, and sent him with this humble request."[99] (Ecgburh apparently thought this dramatic measure was necessary in order to make Guthlac accept her gift.)

The tradition of male-female spiritual friendship appears to have been especially strong in the Anglo-Saxon missionary movement in Germany. We are particularly well-informed about the important network of friends fostered by St. Boniface, due to the vast collection of his correspondence which has survived. It is interesting to note that a good number of these letters were addressed to female religious or were written by nuns and abbesses to Boniface.[100]

The special bond of friendship between Boniface and Leoba (who were also distant relatives) is rather well-known. In an early letter to Boniface (written soon after 732), Leoba requested his prayers for her parents. As an only child, she said she would like to regard Boniface as her "brother." Moreover, she noted that she sent him a little gift so that he would not forget her, "but rather be knit more closely to me in the bond of true affection." In this letter she also asked him to correct the style of her writing and assist her with her poetry.[101]

Later Leoba, along with a number of nuns from her monastery of Wimborne, joined Boniface's mission in Germany. Here she became a highly successful abbess, and according to Leoba's *vita* Boniface held her "in great affection."[102] It was also because of his great affection for Leoba that she was given the special privilege of entering and praying in Boniface's monastic church of Fulda, which was otherwise strictly off limits to women.[103] Before he departed for his fatal mission to Frisia, Boniface called Leoba to him and exhorted her to remain in Germany to continue her missionary work. At this time, "he commended her to Lull and to the senior monks of the monastery who were present, admonishing them to care for her with reverence and respect and reaffirming his wish that after his death her bones should be placed next to his in the tomb, so that they who had served God during their lifetime with equal sincerity and zeal should await together the day of resurrection. . . . After these words he gave her his cowl and begged and pleaded with her not to leave her adopted land."[104]

Leoba also cultivated a wide circle of friends in Germany. In her role as abbess, she assumed the responsibility of overseeing several monasteries, which required her to travel about the countryside visiting her daughter houses. According to her *vita*, "the princes loved her, the nobles received her, the bishops welcomed her with joy." [105]

Through extensive correspondence, Boniface also maintained an active and close friendship with a number of other Anglo-Saxon abbesses and nuns who remained in Britain.

In a letter asking for Boniface's advice in regard to a proposed pilgrimage to Rome, Bugga and her mother, Eangyth, enumerate all of the miseries and grievances which they were experiencing in their monastery. They then underscore the importance of a good friend or kindred soul who would listen to their problems and offer advice. "Everyone who is unequal to his own task and distrusts his own judgment seeks a faithful friend upon whose counsel he can rely and in whom he can have such confidence that he will lay open to him every secret of his heart. As is said: 'What is sweeter than to have some one with whom you can talk of everything as with yourself?' Therefore, on account of all those miseries which we have recounted at too great length, we are compelled to seek a faithful friend, such a one in whom we can confide better than in ourselves, who will consider our pain and sorrow and want, will sympathize with us, console and sustain us by his eloquence, and uplift us by his most wholesome discourse. Long have we sought, and now we believe that we have found in you the friend whom we have wished, prayed, and hoped for." They end their letter to Boniface with "Farewell, brother in the spirit, most loyal, beloved with pure and sincere affection, and may you be strong and prosper in our beloved Lord." And they then borrow the wonderful phrase from St. Jerome, "A friend is long to seek, hard to find, and difficult to keep." [106]

In another letter, which congratulates Boniface on his success in Frisia, Bugga expresses her intense feelings for him. "Therefore I am the more confident that no change of earthly conditions can turn me away from the sheltering care of your affection. The power of love grows warm within me, as I perceive that through the support of your prayers I have reached the haven of a certain peace." [107] Bugga then makes several requests: she asks Boniface to intercede for her with God, to offer Masses for the soul of her relative, and to send her some select passages of Holy Scripture. In addition, she notes that she would send him as soon as possible a copy of the *Sufferings of the Martyrs*, which he had requested. And finally, she ends her letter in a rather apologetic tone, noting that she is sending him fifty *solidi* and an altar cloth, "the best I can possibly do. Little as it is, it is sent with great affection." She signs it: "Farewell in this world and in love unfeigned." [108]

In another letter, Boniface provides Abbess Bugga with advice regarding her proposed pilgrimage to Rome. He calls her "my very dear sister—nay mother and most sweet lady," and says, "rest assured that the long-tried friendship between us shall never be found wanting." [109] And we learn that during her visit to Rome, Bugga finally met up with Boniface whom she had not seen for many years. They then toured the holy city together, making frequent visits to the shrines of the Holy Apostles. At this time she confided in him all of the problems she was experiencing with her monastery and was "strengthened by the blessing" of his prayers. [110]

Among Boniface's correspondence is also found a letter of consolation directed to Abbess Bugga. He prefaces his letter, "in sympathy with your misfortunes and mindful of your kindnesses to me and of our ancient friendship, I am sending you a brotherly letter of comfort and exhortation." [111]

Boniface maintained a close friendship with the Anglo-Saxon abbess St. Ecgburg. In a letter to Boniface, Ecgburg notes her deep love for the holy man: "As I acknowledge the bonds of your affection for me, my very inmost soul is filled with a sweetness as of honey. And though, for a while, having but just gained sight of you, I am deprived of your bodily presence, yet I ever clasp your neck in a sisterly embrace." She then confides that since having lost her beloved brother "I have cherished you in my affection above almost all other men. Not to waste further words: not a day nor a night goes by without some remembrance of your instruction." Although she admits (in humility) that she is far behind her brother in learning and beneath him in character, "yet in my regard for your affection I am his equal." She then asks for his friendship and support in this time of despair and grief. She also requests a "little remembrance, perhaps a holy relic or at least a few written words, that so I may always have you with me." [112]

In this collection we also find Boniface's correspondence with Eadburga, abbess of Minster-in-Thanet. In one of his letters he addresses her "in the bond of spiritual love and with a holy and virginal kiss of affection." Boniface thanks her in another letter for the books which she sent him, calling her "his beloved sister . . . to whom he has long since been bound by the ties of spiritual propinquity . . . [who] has consoled with spiritual light by the gift of sacred books an exile in Germany." [113] In another letter he mentions "all the kindnesses you have shown me, the solace of books and the comfort of the garments with which you have relieved my distress," and closes with the request

that Eadburga send him a copy of the Epistles of St. Peter in letters of
gold. He was also sending her, by the priest Eoban, the materials for
copying this work.[114]

Moreover, we can find in this extraordinary collection of correspondence of the Anglo-Saxon missionaries other letters to religious
women in Britain. Lul, Denehard, and Burchard, for example, in their
letter to Abbess Cuniburg express their affection for this holy woman,
whom they held "in the innermost chamber" of their hearts. They
reveal their high esteem for her by confiding "that if any one of us
should happen to visit Britain we should not prefer the obedience and
government of any man to subjection under your good will; for we
place the greatest confidence of our hearts in you." They then ask
Cuniburg and her community to pray for them and their mission.
Accompanying their letter were some precious gifts which included
frankincense, pepper, and cinnamon—"a very small present, but
given out of heartfelt affection. We pray you not to think of the size of
the gift but to remember the loving spirit."[115] In another letter, addressed to Eadburga, Lul begs the abbess to pray for him and through
her strength to fortify him at this difficult time. He also notes that he
is sending her some small presents, "a silver style and some pieces of
storax and cinnamon; so that you may know from these poor gifts
how pleasing to me are the presents which have come with your greetings." Lul adds, if Eadburga should have need of anything, "be assured, by that love which binds us in a spiritual kinship, that my
weakness will strive with all its powers to fulfil it. Meanwhile I ask
that you may not refuse to send me a letter."[116]

In a letter addressed to an unnamed abbess and a nun, Lul recalls
his pilgrimage to Rome and his subsequent illness and loneliness. He
recounts how for five months during his illness he was cared for with
great "loving kindness. This mercy, as I am aware, you showed me in
my infirmity and sickness, obeying the precepts of the Lord, and hoping for the eternal reward; and to this day you have displayed towards
me as towards a brother this same unwearying affection in consideration of the divine love." His letter continues with the promise that
when he finds proper writing material, he will celebrate in verse "the
spiritual bond of your loving kinship with us." Lul then asks them not
to show this work to anyone without his consent or to betray its authorship, "but rather be ever mindful of the plighted troth and intimacy found between us by the firm link of our hands." He concludes
with the request that they "lighten the burden" of his toil with their
prayers.[117]

It is, then, within the context of these early missionary movements
that cross-sex friendships seem to have been particularly valued and

strong. Churchmen involved in missionary work in Germany, for example, needed the special support of female religious—friends and relatives from their homeland in Britain. They therefore maintained a lively correspondence with a number of women from Anglo-Saxon monastic communities. And in their extant letters we can see special requests for prayers, letters, books, vestments, and so forth. Their letters also reveal the impressive dynamics of friendship: they show a deep affection, a remarkable admiration and respect for one another. Moreover, the female religious who were part of the missionary group in Germany formed, along with the male missionaries, a type of surrogate family. Dislocated and working together in their "adopted" homeland, they needed one another and valued each other's support and friendship. Thus the missionary venture seemed to provide an atmosphere which was particularly conducive to the formation of circles of cross-sex friendships.

The *vitae* provide a number of other important examples of cross-sex friendship within the framework of early monastic life. The contemporary Life of St. Hathumoda, abbess of Gandersheim, written by the monk Agius, notes that Hathumoda was apparently slow in forming friendships, but to those she befriended, she was said to remain a fast friend throughout her life.[118] Agius was also an intimate friend or perhaps even a close relative of St. Hathumoda, and during the abbess's final illness he spent a great deal of time with her. A particularly moving testimony of this special affection can be found in Agius's elegy. Written in the form of a dialogue, it was intended to comfort the nuns of Gandersheim on the death of their beloved abbess. Agius writes: "Believe me, you are not alone in this grief, I too am oppressed by it, I too am suffering, and I cannot sufficiently express to you how much I also have lost in her. You know full well how great was her love for me, and how she cherished me while she lived. You know how anxious she was to see me when she fell ill, with what gladness she received me, and how she spoke to me on her deathbed. The words she spoke at the last were truly elevating, and ever and anon she uttered my name." [119]

We can also find a number of examples of cross-sex friendship among the tenth-century Anglo-Saxon churchmen and religious women. While the churchmen of this period seemed to demonstrate a definite male preference in their priorities for religious reform, and therefore focused their efforts on the re-establishment and rebuilding of monasteries for men, the sources of the period continue to mention their professional interaction and personal friendship with women.[120] The *vita* of the great reformer, St. Dunstan, tells of his special relationship with a holy woman named Elgiva.[121] She was apparently a close relative of King Athelstan, and having learned of Dunstan's fame, she decided to move to Glastonbury where she could benefit from the holy man's personal instruction and attention. She therefore had a house built close to the monastery of Glastonbury in which she lived for several years. Here she practiced on her own an exemplary religious life. Also, with Dunstan's consent, Elgiva constructed a chapel which was dedicated to the Virgin Mary. Canons were appointed to serve the chapel and she supported them generously. When Elgiva became ill, Dunstan visited her and encouraged her to endure her suffering with patience. They discussed her final wishes in regard to the disposal of her estate: her possessions were to be distributed to the poor and her property was to be sold with the proceeds going to the Church. The two friends remained together talking late into the night and, according to the *vita,* they were said to have witnessed a miracle. On the following day, Dunstan returned to perform final rites, and he also oversaw Elgiva's burial in her own church.

Dunstan was also a close friend of St. Edith, nun of Wilton. With immense sadness he foretold her death and assisted in her burial. According to a later version of her *vita,* during the dedication of the oratory which St. Edith had built in honor of St. Denis, while Dunstan was at Mass it was revealed to him that she would die within a short period of time. He immediately burst into tears and wept bitterly. When asked why he wept so, he sighed deeply and responded that "this starry gem shall soon be taken from us into the Saints' country, for this wicked world is not worthy to enjoy the presence of so clear a light." Thus Dunstan assisted Edith "unto her last gasp" and buried her in her church of St. Denis. We also learn that after some years St. Edith was said to have appeared to St. Dunstan and provided him with instructions for her translation.[122]

The *vita* of St. Dunstan mentions another female acquaintance, a noblewoman named Aethelwynn, who "called him to her on one occasion with a friendly request to design her a stole for the divine service, with divers figures, which she could afterwards diversify and adorn with gold and gems. When he came to her for this work, he usually brought with him his cythera, which in the native language we call 'harp,' that he might at times delight himself and the hearts of his listeners in it." The *vita* then describes a marvelous event which occurred one day when he and Aethelwynn returned with her workwomen to their embroidery work. At that time his harp, while still hanging on the wall, was said to have played on its own the hymn " 'Let the souls of the saints who followed the steps of Christ rejoice in the heavens; and because they shed their blood for his love, they shall reign with Christ for ever.' And when they heard it, he and the aforesaid woman and all her workwomen were terrified, and completely forgetting the work in their hands, gazed at one another in astonishment, marveling greatly what new warning that miraculous act might prefigure." [123] This fascinating and unique reference shows, in addition to the cross-sex friendship, the process involved in early embroidery work. Here Dunstan, who was apparently also an artist of some renown, was called upon to "draw" the design which the embroiderer would then use as the basic pattern for her work.

Another Anglo-Saxon reformer of this period, St. Ethelwold, bishop of Winchester, also cultivated a circle of female friendships within the Church. We learn that he especially admired Abbess St. Merwinna of Romsey. Apparently, to escape the demands and pressures of his position as bishop, he visited her monastery and found peace there. Furthermore, Ethelwold consulted with Merwinna and kept her current on the news of the outside world. His special relationship with Merwinna and her monastery can perhaps be seen in the following incident: Ethelwold was said to have received from St. Dunstan an important relic—some sacred hair of the Virgin Mary. He then shared three of these precious hairs with Merwinna and Romsey Abbey.[124]

The *vita* of St. Adelheid, abbess of Vilich, notes the great respect, admiration, and love which Heribert, the archbishop of Cologne, held for her. "According to the judgement of the archbishop, no one in the whole order was her equal in wisdom, piety and sanctity. For that reason the venerable high priest held her in such high esteem that he always followed her advice in spiritual matters. Between these two was such a wonderful love and God-willed trust that in all good deeds they seemed to be of one mind. That is why, without doubt, they are now united in heaven in the same eternal home." [125]

We are particularly well informed of the exceptional friendship and affection found in the relationship of Queen-St. Margaret of Scotland and her personal confessor, Turgot. For it was Turgot, the prior of the monastery of Durham and overseer of the queen's church in Dunfermline, who was chosen by the saint's children to write Margaret's *vita*. He notes that he was entrusted with this job "because you [i.e., the children] had heard that, by reason of my great friendship with her, I was in great part familiar with her secret thoughts." [126] Turgot, then, provides us with many personal insights into their special relationship. In praising the queen's intelligence and her wonderful zeal in "divine reading," he observes that "she had in fact great religious greed for holy volumes, and *her intimate friendship and friendly intimacy with me compelled me to exert myself very much in procuring them for her.*" [127] When she focused her thoughts on the final judgment, she frequently asked Turgot "not to hesitate to rebuke her in private, and point out to her whatever I received to be blameworthy either in her words or her deeds. When I did this more rarely and less warmly than she wished, she was harsh with me; she told me that I was sleeping, and as it were neglecting her." [128] Turgot also describes their private conversations. "For she deigned to speak to me most intimately, and to expose her secret thoughts; not because there was anything good in me, but because she thought that there was." [129] When she spoke of salvation and eternal life, Turgot notes that he was so affected "that by her emotion my mind was moved to weeping." [130] For some time the queen was apparently aware of her own impending death and, as Turgot recounts, "she therefore spoke to me privately, and began to relate her life to me in order; and to pour out rivers of tears at every word . . . while she wept, I wept also; weeping long, we were meanwhile silent; because we could utter no words, for the rising sobs. . . . And while I listened to the words of the holy Spirit spoken with her tongue, and gazed through her words upon her conscience, *I counted myself unworthy of so great favour of her friendship.*" [131] Her final request to Turgot was for him to remember her soul in Masses and prayers, and to take charge of her children—to love and teach them. "Again, bursting into tears at these words, I promised diligently to do what she had asked." [132]

We also learn that St. Margaret maintained a close friendship with her priest (who remains unnamed in the *vita*). According to Turgot, "she had loved him more intimately than the rest, because of his simplicity, innocence, and chastity." [133] He was "inseparably present in the last hours of the queen's life" and he commended her soul to Christ. After the queen's death the special devotion of this priest can be seen in the fact that he then "gave himself up to the perpetual service of Christ for the sake of her soul," and offered himself "as a sacrifice for her" at St. Cuthbert's tomb. [134] The Life of St. Margaret is, then, a remarkably rich source concerning the importance of cross-sex friendships during this period. Turgot's recollections of the deep affection he felt for the queen and her great fondness for him are especially moving. The great love and sacrifice demonstrated by her priest are also impressive.

Another rather poignant example of spiritual friendship can be found in a famous letter sent ca. 1082 by Goscelin of St. Bertin to the holy woman Eve of Wilton Abbey (d. ca. 1125). Goscelin, a Flemish monk and professional hagiographer of English saints, was a friend of Eve's parents. During his years as a chaplain at Wilton Abbey, Goscelin became acquainted with Eve, who was a nun at the monastery; moreover, in his role as her spiritual mentor, they developed a close friendship. Around the year 1080, after Goscelin had left Wilton,

Eve suddenly departed from the abbey and went to Angers, where, along with a number of other hermits and hermitesses, she adopted the life of an *inclusa* or enclosed one. Goscelin's response to her move, which had been done without consulting him, came in the form of a long, impassioned letter entitled the *Liber confortatorius*.[135] In this work we can see Goscelin's deep affection as well as a certain possessiveness for his spiritual daughter, who, at this time, was twenty-five years of age while he was approximately forty-five to fifty years old. The letter, which ultimately attempts to console and exhort Eve, also betrays his overriding feelings of regret, desolation, and betrayal. Inconsolable and unable to come to terms with losing her, he reminisces about the times they had shared and their intimate friendship at Wilton. He also discusses in some detail the topic of the separation of loved ones. Goscelin begins his letter to Eve, "Oh dearest light of my soul." As Sharon Elkins has noted: "He reminded Eve of their affection [*dilectio*] and perpetual love [*caritas*] when they were together at Wilton. 'I spoke to you, I was exhorted by you, I was consoled by you.' Together they had 'panted' for the love of Christ. Writing in an attempt to be 'present with an inseparable soul' even during this 'torment of separation,' Goscelin poured out his feelings for Eve."[136]

Later in the letter, despite his own suffering and strong feelings of betrayal and abandonment, Goscelin realizes that Eve's leaving behind her native land and everyone she loved also caused her much grief. Furthermore, this heroic act was a type of martyrdom which she had undertaken for the love of Christ and for the hope of heavenly rewards; for there was no greater sorrow for Eve "than separation from friends and loved ones."[137] In trying to console her, he notes that the sweetness of friendship has never lasted for a long time. He then examines their own loss within the historical context of others who had been separated from their loved ones. He includes among his examples of classic friendships: David and Jonathan, the Apostles, St. John and the Virgin Mary, Peter and Paul, Sabinus and his sister Sabina, and the pagan Orestes and his friend. He then describes the enduring friendship of the seventh-century abbesses Modesta of Trier and Gertrude of Nivelles. Although separated by a long distance from her cherished friend, Gertrude appeared in a vision to Modesta and told her of her (Gertrude's) death.[138] (This case will be discussed later in this chapter.) After citing a number of other examples of saints who appeared in spirit to their faithful, he argues that those friends who confide in God will remain inseparable. In this context Goscelin admits that he often thought about St. Edith of Wilton and felt she was present. He also concedes that Eve was no less saintly.[139] Thus through his exhortations, Goscelin hoped to encourage Eve's love and patience; and he especially wanted her never to forget him. And although physically absent, he was still present—in the inseparable presence of the soul. Goscelin allows that he continued to suffer on her account; he never stopped thinking about her.[140]

Goscelin concludes his letter to Eve with a description of the end of the world, the last judgment, and heaven. In his portrayal of the final assembly and the patron saints with their special ties to their faithful, he notes that one will find St. Denis with the people of Gaul and Paris, St. Martin with those of Tours, St. Hilary with those of Poitiers, St. Augustine with those of England, St. Bertin with those of Sithiu, and Edith with the nuns of Wilton.[141] According to Goscelin, Eve, along with the holy dead, would be able to move at will, freely from heaven to earth, and she could thus visit Wilton and her ancient cell. In highlighting Wilton Abbey and its community of saints or special friends, he notes that one would find at the abbey, Queen Edith, Christ, the Virgin Mary, angels, apostles, martyrs, kings, and a crowd of virgins; namely, Thecla, Agnes, Cecilia, Argive, Catherine, and the entire family of Wilton.[142]

It is then in heaven that they would be rewarded for all of their sufferings and here friendship would assume a primary role; for in heaven friends would once more be reunited, never again to be separated.[143] It would also be in heaven that Goscelin would finally be reunited in eternal joy with his beloved daughter, Eve—the "dearest light of his soul"—although he notes that he would be placed far from her.[144]

Although we have this wonderfully detailed account of a late eleventh-century spiritual friendship, it provides us with only Goscelin's perspective: we therefore remain uninformed about Eve's thoughts and feelings in regard to this spiritual-emotional relationship.[145] However, it is of interest to note that despite Goscelin's concern for Eve's great suffering because of the separation from her sisters at Wilton, friends, and family, she is reported to have cultivated another intimate cross-sex friendship while living as an *inclusa* in France. According to the poet Hilary, Eve lived for a long time in Saint-Eutrope "with Hervey as her companion."[146] Hervey was a monk from Vendôme and, like Eve, he had left his monastery to become a hermit. As friends, they helped and inspired one another in a "perfect and irreproachable partnership." Also, in his role as a priest, Hervey celebrated mass for Eve. As Sharon Elkins has pointed out: "In case anyone might be suspicious of such a friendship, Hilary explained, 'This love [*dilectio*] was not in the world but in Christ.' Hilary praised 'the wondrous love [*amor*] of such a man and such a woman and pleasing companionship [*societas*]' that nourished their piety and was free of anxiety. . . .

When she died in her late sixties, Hervey was left 'dejected with a great desolation.'"[147]

This notable case of Eve of Wilton then provides another example of intimate friendships which flourished between religious women and churchmen during this period. The sources underscore the ardent love and great affection experienced by these soul-mates. It was, however, as an *inclusa* that this type of close friendship was especially sought after and valued; for, in providing the ascetic male presence and the necessary priestly functions, it allowed Eve and other women to follow their vocation as hermitess.[148] Thus the special milieu, the shared spaces, and the material and religious requirements of the enclosed life seem to have encouraged friendships between male and female hermits during this period and in the following centuries.

A few final examples of late eleventh-century networks of cross-sex friendship should also be mentioned briefly. Despite his public stance as a fierce defender of celibacy and a strict reformer, it appears that Peter Damian cultivated several close friendships with noblewomen—these included Countess Blanche of Milan, Countess Guilla, Duchess Beatrice of Tuscany, and especially the empress Agnes.[149] Among his correspondence is found a letter addressed to the young Countess Guilla in which he admits his underlying fear of female sexuality and the fundamental tension in regard to male-female relationships: "It is safer for me to converse in writing with young women in whose presence I am apprehensive. Certainly I, who am already an old man, can licitly and securely look upon the face of an old woman, lined with wrinkles, whose features are moist with rheum from her watering eyes; but like boys from a fire, I guard my eyes at the sight of more beautiful and attractive faces. My heart is indeed unhappy, for a hundred readings of the Gospel mysteries do not suffice to retain them, whereas the recollection of beauty, seen but once, never leaves my memory."[150]

The reform pope, Gregory VII, also cultivated a circle of female friendships: he was a close friend of Mathilda, countess of Tuscany (one of his most staunch supporters), as well as of Empress Beatrice.[151] In fact, in his correspondence the pope suggested that Mathilda, and her mother Beatrice, accompany him on a crusade to the Holy Land. He hoped that this shared experience would bind them together in a friendship which would last throughout eternity.[152]

Although we can find notable cases of close spiritual friendships among the holy elite throughout the Middle Ages, it appears that many of the prominent examples, particularly involving abbesses and abbots, are again concentrated in the north of Europe and England, and date to the early years of Christianization. They reflect the atmosphere of the early medieval church and monasticism, which was particularly rich in opportunities for women and which valued their participation. In this pioneering environment, gender differences seem to have been minimized; women were not viewed primarily as females, but as fellow citizens in the celestial homeland, partners, dear "sisters" and friends, who were indispensable members of the Christian workforce. Religious women had the opportunity to labor alongside of men: they shared in the hardships, responsibilities, and advantages of the period. For those involved in the missionary movement—far removed from their homelands and families—their success and their very survival depended on both the practical and moral support of their co-workers as well as of their friends back home. In the early enthusiasm of the movement, lending their skill and energy, these *mulieres sanctae* commanded respect as effective participants in the Church and were frequently acknowledged and rewarded for their efforts with lasting affection and friendship.

It was, then, along with the family that these special friendships worked to bolster women's roles in the Church. Through such friendships one could gain access to the Church hierarchy and a wide network of acquaintances; in this way women could cultivate important connections outside of the family sphere of influence. In some cases the public achievements of prominent holy men conferred special benefits on their female friends, helping them to gain positions of leadership and even recognition of sanctity. Sometimes these friendships provided opportunities for religious women to be publicly reflected in and to share in their male friends' prestige. Moreover, in a number of cases these male friends worked to preserve the memory and reputation of their special friends and to validate their existence, either by writing their *vitae,* or commissioning these Lives. They also used their influence to formulate and promote their public cults.

REFORMERS AND SHIFTS IN THE PERCEPTION
OF CROSS-SEX FRIENDSHIPS

Beginning with the ninth century, the visibility and importance of cross-sex holy alliances among saints seems to have diminished— particularly in France and Belgium. Furthermore, it appears that many of the cases of friendship noted in the *vitae* of the ninth through eleventh centuries were now no longer monastic—between abbesses and abbots—but rather friendships of noblewomen, queens, and empresses (still living "in the world") with great abbots, bishops, priests, confessors, etc. The visibility of these *mulieres sanctae* now appears to be based on their positions of political prominence, their generous donations to male foundations (Cluny, for instance), as well as their patronage of Church reform.[153]

With the success of the missionary movements in the north of Europe and the constricting of the religious frontiers, the initial need and opportunities, as well as the enthusiasm, for women co-workers in the Church seems to have waned. With the invasions and the wholesale destruction of monastic foundations for women and men, along with the Carolingian, Cluniac, Gregorian, and other reform movements, the cultural valuation of women in monasticism and in religion in general seems to have deteriorated. In this new atmosphere of reform, with its emphasis on regularization of ecclesiastical life, clerical celibacy, ritual purity, and sacramental formalism, as well as its hardening of hierarchical structures, the Church appears to have looked upon these relationships with increasing suspicion and discouraged the cultivation of cross-sex friendships. Whereas previously these holy bonds had been highly esteemed and even encouraged, beginning with the Carolingian reforms an atmosphere of renewed distrust and suspicion of women and female sexuality seems to have emerged. One can see a basic shift from the earlier perception of woman as sister and partner, to an exaggerated fear or abhorrence of woman as female, as a sexual being or "sister of perdition." This was manifested, for example, in the provisions of the reform councils against the institution of the double monastery, regulations requiring separate domiciles for priests and their female relatives, requirements for priests to "put away" their wives, policies of strict enclosure specifically for female religious, exclusionary policies of sacred space, gender-specific policies in education, and so forth. We also find during this same period a growing concern on the part of the Church with problems of incest as well as adultery.[154]

The friendship of the empress-saint Richarde (d. ca. 909) with the very influential and powerful Liutward, bishop of Vercelli, archchancellor and archchaplain of the court, perhaps provides an example of the difficulties surrounding cross-sex relationships in this increasingly suspicious atmosphere. Against a background of a power struggle and a search for grounds for divorce, many rumors and accusations were directed toward Liutward, including that of adultery with the empress. According to the chronicle of Regino of Prüm, Liutward crossed the line of proper behavior with the queen: "he became involved with the secrets of the queen with more familiarity than was necessary."[155] He was therefore removed from the court and sent back to his bishopric of Vercelli. Before a court proceeding, the empress proclaimed her innocence, swearing that she had never had sexual relations with her husband or with any other man and thus glorified her virginity. As a religious woman she was also prepared to prove her innocence by either a duel or by walking on burning coals. The king refused the use of trial by ordeal; however, this declaration served his purpose and provided grounds for their separation.[156] This incident, along with several others in this pattern, also serves to underscore the general distrust and suspicion toward female sexuality and the difficulties inherent in cross-sex relationships.

One of the most fascinating and striking examples of this shift in the cultural valuation of cross-sex friendships—and in attitudes toward women in general—can be found in the manipulation or posthumous "use" of St. Cuthbert by the post-Conquest reform movement in Britain. These changes began in 1083 with the introduction of reformed Benedictine monks at Durham. At this time William of St. Calais, who had previously been a monk at the monastery of St. Carileph (St. Calais) in Maine, was named bishop of Durham.[157] According to the chronicler Symeon of Durham, while at the monastery of St. Calais, William "was regarded as one who was especially remarkable above all his fellows for his love and devotion towards the monastic order, and thus he was gradually promoted until he attained higher offices." He was finally elected abbot of the monastery of St. Calais. As related by Symeon, among the qualities which brought him to the attention of William the Conqueror (who was seeking a reform bishop for Durham) was the fact that he was "so remarkable for good conduct that he had no equal amongst his contemporaries in this respect." He was also "chaste in his body."[158] Thus this newly elected monk-bishop of Durham became an ardent reformer. One of his first duties was to "clean house"; in order to implement the new reform emphasis on celibacy and ritual purity, he found it necessary to replace the married secular canons of Durham with monks from the recently refounded foundations at Wearmouth and Jarrow.[159] As was the case for many changes in the Middle Ages, the new was frequently ushered in under the guise of the old or venerated traditions of the past. The reform propaganda consciously made its new policy appear as if it was in fact an old tradition at Durham which had only temporarily fallen into disuse with its community of married clergy. Therefore, the "revival" of this policy and the changes which it mandated were then presented or advertised as having the enthusiastic support of its original architect, St. Cuthbert. In this context, Rosalind Hill has suggested that while the married priests and their families caused no concern for the Church during the tenth and up to the latter part of the eleventh centuries, with the late eleventh century their lifestyle appeared rather scandalous and outdated in light of the standards of the reform church.[160] With the introduction of reform by an "outsider,"

Bishop William of St. Calais, and the rather unpopular ousting of the clergy, their wives, and their children, there was naturally a great deal of resentment felt. As Hill argues, the monks must have been conscious of this local resentment toward them (as "newcomers") and thus turned to the patron St. Cuthbert himself. In their adoption of a reform propaganda which publicized an image of Cuthbert as a fierce defender of celibacy, as well as a misogynist, they worked to discredit their married predecessors, the secular canons, and in so doing they bolstered their own reform position in this hostile milieu.[161]

In this context it is interesting to stress the new bishop's direct connections with the early misogynist St. Calais, who, as we have noted, maintained a well-known policy of prohibiting women from entering his hermitage and monastery. No doubt conditioned by this traditional fear of women and the strict policy of female avoidance at the monastery of St. Calais, it seems highly probable that Bishop William was personally involved in introducing this new precedent into his reform program at Durham—i.e., an intense misogynism with the requisite need to control and severely limit women's access to the church.[162] Thus it appears that with this shift brought about by the new reform policy, the famous seventh-century St. Cuthbert, the patron saint of Durham, was conveniently "remade" to share in the long-lived misogynistic tradition of St. Calais. "Refashioned" to respond to the present needs of the monastery, he was provided with a "posthumous" hatred of females. And this was then used to provide "historical" justification for the reform policy of celibacy and the exclusion of women from his churches.[163]

According to Symeon of Durham, writing in the twelfth century, Cuthbert, their patron saint, had in fact been an avowed misogynist all of his life, and even from the tomb he continued to vent his anger against members of the female sex. On account of the scandalous behavior of the nuns at the double monastery of Coldingham, during his lifetime Cuthbert was said to have prohibited women from entering the church at his monastery on Lindisfarne Island. Moreover, because of his great abhorrence of women, Symeon contended, "It is a well-known fact that into scarce one of the churches which the blessed confessor illustrated with the presence of his body . . . has permission to enter been granted to a woman. . . . This custom is so diligently observed, even unto the present day, that it is unlawful for women to set foot even within the cemeteries of those churches in which his body obtained a temporary resting-place, unless, indeed, compelled to do so by the approach of an enemy or the dread of fire."[164]

Also in the name of St. Cuthbert's alleged aversion toward women, a line of local blue frosterly marble was placed in the second bay of the nave of Durham cathedral. This line can still be seen today, stretching across the pavement from north to south—approximately one foot wide, with a cross at its center. And beyond this "holy barrier" women were forbidden to pass. As related in the later *Rites of Durham*, if by chance any woman dared to cross this line into the nave of the church, she would be taken straightaway and punished for some days.[165]

This same popular misogynist reform tradition—which underscored the necessary avoidance of women—can also be seen in the interpretation of events surrounding the building of the Lady Chapel at Durham in the first part of the twelfth century. During the construction of the chapel (which originally was to be located at the far east end of the church, behind St. Cuthbert's shrine), the foundations and lower walls began to shrink and crack. According to a later source, this basic structural problem was attributed by churchmen to Cuthbert's great hatred of women. They believed that the saint was simply objecting, in his own very "subtle" way, to having a chapel of the Virgin (which would in fact attract hordes of women) built so uncomfortably close to his tomb.[166] Thus, contrary to the traditional spatial arrangement which placed the Lady Chapel at the east end of the church, the Lady Chapel at Durham came to be situated in a rather unusual location: it was built outside the west wall of the cathedral, thus keeping women as far away as possible from the sacred east end of the church and the feretory or shrine of the holy St. Cuthbert.[167]

Therefore, conveniently ignoring the information pertaining to the historical Cuthbert found in his two well-known *vitae*—which, as we have noted, told of his great affection and high esteem for several saintly abbesses, as well as his befriending his foster mother, Kenswith, etc.—these monastic reformers through their revisionist history essentially manipulated St. Cuthbert to fit their own antifeminist reform agenda. Or as noted by Joan Nicholson, "Cuthbert's sanctity was never threatened by the women with whom he was so friendly; the misogynist seems to have emerged after some three hundred years of posthumous reflection."[168]

On a practical level this tradition of female avoidance associated with Cuthbert could then be used to keep female temptation at a safe distance; this strict policy would assist the reform abbot and his new monastic inmates at Durham in the difficult task of maintaining their program of celibacy and ritual purity. Furthermore, this gender-based policy was no doubt aimed at setting this reformed monastery apart from other religious communities, and making it appear all the more attractive or holy because of its moral rigor and exclusivity.

Cuthbert's alleged abhorrence of women and his "well-known" practice of female avoidance could thus be used to justify the exclusion of women from the east end of the church and St. Cuthbert's tomb, and their containment in the far west end of the church. Moreover, based on the "ancient tradition" associated with the patron saint, Cuthbert, all women were said to be prohibited from entering any of the churches, or even the burial grounds of those churches, with which Cuthbert had been associated. To further reinforce this concept, the reformers circulated stern warnings that those "brazen" women who dared to test or violate these "sacred" proscriptions were liable to severe punishment meted out by the angry saint himself from the depths of his tomb. In fact, Symeon of Durham and later sources describe in some detail the marvelously gruesome punishments inflicted on a number of "imprudent" women who dared to violate these "sacred" proscriptions.[169] These cautionary examples, Symeon notes, were then meant to serve as strong deterrents to future female transgressors. (Not surprisingly, these wonderful stories closely resemble those told in regard to St. Calais's strong misogynistic practices and his severe punishment of disrespectful or shameless women who challenged his "sacred space.")[170]

Quite clearly the new reform ideal—intrinsic to the "revisionist image" of Cuthbert—portrayed a holy man radically different from the one described by his near contemporaries. In posthumously refashioning Cuthbert as a blatant antifeminist and in denying his holy alliances with women, the reformers attempted to expunge and rewrite part of a very important and positive chapter in the history of gender relations in the Church: one of very special friendships between holy women and men. We are particularly fortunate in the case of Cuthbert to have still extant the two earlier *vitae* which record the saint's affection and notable friendships with women; for without the benefit of these sources—to serve as a check—we, too, might have succumbed to believing Symeon's "revisionist history" which places Cuthbert strongly in the misogynistic tradition along with St. Calais and others.[171] In this context—in light of the copying, rewriting, revising, and updating of the *vitae,* especially during periods of reform—one wonders how many other positive traditions of cross-sex friendships suffered a similar fate.

SAME-SEX FRIENDSHIPS AMONG THE *MULIERES SANCTAE*

While the *vitae* and other sources provide many marvelous examples of cross-sex friendships between holy men and the *mulieres sanctae,* same-sex friendships for women seem at first glance to have been ignored. This frustrating silence perhaps reflects in part the nature of our sources, accidents of their survival, and the fact that the majority of the *vitae* were written by men. Therefore the details surrounding women's friendships (which were often private in nature in comparison to cross-sex friendships) were no doubt frequently overlooked, unknown, or simply not recorded. This invisibility might also be attributed to the generally held notion which has tended to minimize the importance of friendships for women, and particularly that of same-sex friendships.

However, in contrast to this common assumption which has generally overlooked the importance of cross-sex and especially same-sex friendships for women, bonds of friendship seem in fact to have played a remarkably important role in the lives of these early medieval women. It appears that women routinely established deeply felt emotional ties with other women, and that these "sororal" relationships in turn formed an essential aspect of medieval society. As might be expected, it is often as extensions of family relationships and particularly within the confines of female monastic communities that the cultivation of friendships among women seemed to flourish.

As noted in the discussion of cross-sex friendships, while in theory the Church encouraged and valued the cultivation of perfect love and friendship as a means to spiritual perfection; nevertheless, in practice, the fostering of close same-sex friendships was frequently viewed by churchmen as problematic and potentially dangerous. Although much of the literature of the period focuses on male issues, and specifically the need for celibate churchmen to avoid cross-sex or homosexual friendships, same-sex friendships among women were also a matter of some concern. The fears and suspicions aroused by the numerous opportunities to foster intimate female friendships or "particular friendships" were especially articulated by churchmen concerned with the monastic milieu. For it was the sexually segregated all-female world of the convent which made intense bonds of friendship among women (spiritual and sexual) an essential part of their lives.

PRESCRIPTIVE LITERATURE

A variety of monastic regulations call our attention to the basic conflict between the requirement of community and the desire for personal friendship. The early monastic rules for women emphasized the need to avoid the cultivation of close or intimate ties of friendship. On one level, the special bond between two friends could create problems within the monastery since, ideally, friendship was to embrace the entire community.[172] Thus abbesses were especially discouraged from entering into close friendships because of the dreaded threat to the community of favoritism and divisive factions. The Rule of Donatus, for example, warned that the abbess "must make no distinction of persons in the monastery and not love one more than another, unless one may excel in good actions or obedience."[173] The *Regula mona-charum* attributed to St. Jerome, but perhaps dating to the ninth century, advises that the abbess is not to single out friends or relatives because this would excite envy in others. Her affection or love was not to be carnal, which is frequently harmful, but she should cherish her nuns in holy ways. She was to love them all as daughters with equal charity and spiritual affection.[174]

Moreover, of perhaps greater importance was the need to minimize or remove any opportunity for moral suspicion or potential scandal concerning the monastic community. A number of these prescriptive policies or prohibitions therefore seem to reflect this much deeper fear of the formation of lesbian relationships among female religious. In his famous letter of direction to his sister, Augustine stresses the need for kindness and love in her religious community. He then specifically warns her: "The love between you, however, ought not to be earthly (or carnal) but spiritual, for the things which shameless women do even to other women in low jokes and games are to be avoided not only by widows and chaste handmaids of Christ, living under a holy rule of life, but also entirely by married women and maidens destined for marriage."[175] In this same context, The Rule of Caesarius of Arles warns that "no one shall have a secret intimacy or companionship of any kind with religious or lay persons, either men or *women*."[176] The Rule of Aurelian, bishop of Arles (546–55), notes that a sister who is so bold as to hold the hand of a sister is to be chastised.[177] Similarly, the Rule of Donatus of Besançon stipulates that "it is forbidden for anyone to take the hand of another for affection, whether they are standing or walking around or sitting together. She who does so will be corrected with twelve blows. And anyone who is called [the endearment] 'little girl' [*juvencula*] or who calls one another 'little girl,' forty blows if they so transgress."[178]

We can find in monastic *regulae* other precautionary measures aimed at avoiding temptation among nuns. In general, detailed regulations of active and passive enclosure attempted to provide some control over the fostering of improper friendships with laywomen from outside of the convent. The Rules of Caesarius and Aurelian of Arles specifically prohibit the clandestine exchange of letters, messages, or gifts. Caesarius notes, however, that special arrangements could be made to accommodate anyone "out of love for her relatives, or because of an acquaintance with someone, should she wish to send blessed bread." [179] Other regulations stress the idea of moral or spiritual safety in numbers. Augustine, in his letter to his sister, advises that "if they go to the baths or wherever they have to go, let there be not less than three. The one who is under the necessity of going somewhere shall not go with the companions of her choice, but with those whom the Superior shall ordain." [180] The Rule of Leander of Seville warns that "a nun alone shall not speak with another nun alone." He further adds: "Do not become accustomed to speaking to one nun and avoiding others . . . That is no longer a good thing which a nun speaks to another in private, as she keeps looking around so as not to be seen by others. 'Everyone who does evil,' says the Lord, 'hates the light'. . . . Therefore, let your conscience be innocent, your conversation free from blame. Do not delight in hearing or thinking what should be disdained, much less in speaking or doing such." [181]

It is, however, in their prescriptive literature concerning dormitory regulations that the churchmen's fear of the formation of inappropriate relationships of an intimate nature can especially be noted. Proper sleeping arrangements were clearly defined so as to minimize, among other things, opportunities for the fostering of lesbian relationships. Caesarius of Arles advises, for example, that "no one may be permitted to choose a separate room, nor to have a cell or a chest, or anything of this nature, which can be locked for private use, but all shall occupy one room with separate beds." [182] In rather telling detail the Rule of Donatus notes that "each [nun] should sleep in a separate bed. . . . If possible all should sleep in one place, [but] if the large numbers do not permit this, they should then sleep by tens and twenties with the elders who have charge of them." He further specifies that "lights should burn in each chamber until daybreak." The nuns "should sleep clothed, with their girdles bound about them." He then specifically warns that "they should not have the younger sisters with them in bed but be joined by elders or groups." [183]

The Rule of Waldabert of Luxeuil (629–670) also attempted to discourage the formation of intimate relations among nuns. In a rather detailed section entitled "In What Manner They Ought to Sleep in the Dormitory," Waldabert warns that they must take special care for fear that "through a lapse in their maternal solicitude, foolishness should seize their captive limbs." He advises that the nuns sleep in beds two by two, with one of the pair always a "senior" nun whose moral scruples were above suspicion. He writes: "Hence we therefore decree that, except for the sick and the aged, they sleep two by two [binae et binae] in their cots; in such a way, however, that they do not carry on conversation, nor that they look at one another, that is, face to face—rather, that they lie down one after the other to take their rest, lest the ancient enemy, who with an eager countenance [*ore*] longs to injure souls, should score some deception in his striving, *and stir up carnal desires through their conversation.* So let it be that one of the sisters, whose religious spirit is above question, always act as senior [religious]. It is moreover our considered judgment that young religious should never sleep together *lest they should be caught up in some sin of passion* [*aestu delicto*] through the opposition of the flesh. All, if possible, should be situated in a single dormitory, except those oppressed by sickness or old age, or condemned for a fault, or of novitiate status who should be kept apart in a private room. All should sleep clothed and girded. In the dormitory room a light should burn throughout the night." [184] The Rule also notes in its discussion of the "qualifications of the prioress" that "on every Saturday, after the prayer at nones, the senior prioresses as well as the junior visit the beds of all the sisters and investigate their negligence, whether anything illicit may be found or anything kept without permission. And then after compline, they visit all the beds with lamps to uncover any sensual awakening or cooling from prayer." [185]

The canons of Church councils further emphasized this moral concern with the fostering of "particular friendships" among female religious. The reform council of Aix (816), for example, described the need for the correction of nuns who perpetrated "shameful" or "indecent" acts in their dorters or dormitories. It again specified that all nuns should sleep in the dormitory; they should sleep alone in single beds while a lamp burned throughout the night. [186]

Penitential literature also provides specific prescriptive information on lesbian relationships among female religious as well as among laywomen. Details of practice along with the comparative penances required for these sexual "improprieties" can be found in a number of the penitentials. Pierre Payer has noted in his study, *Sex and the Penitentials: The Development of a Sexual Code, 550–1150,* those works which deal specifically with lesbian relationships. [187] While penances for women varied somewhat, in general they were less than those recommended for men involved in homosexual acts. The early Anglo-Saxon Penitential of Theodore (668–690), for example, prescribes that "if a woman practices vice with a woman, she shall do penance for three years"; however, "a male who commits fornication with a male shall do penance for ten years." [188] In the penitential ascribed to Bede we see perhaps more equality in the punishments stipulated for "fornication": male sodomites were to receive a four-year penance while a woman who fornicates with a woman, three years. [189] It also warned that homosexual behavior among monks, or fornication involving a monk and a nun, incurred a seven-year penance.[190] However, it is interesting to note that this same penitential singles out nuns who fornicate with nuns *per machinam*, that is, using a special instrument or artificial phallus. These women religious were to receive a heavier sentence than women who fornicate with women; this act *per machinam* required a seven-year penance.[191] The increased punishment for this offense was no doubt partially attributable to the fact that those involved were nuns; in addition, as Ann Matter has noted, their lesbian activity *per machinam* was perceived as especially threatening as they were involved in "male posturing" or "appropriating recognized male sexual roles."[192] In this same tradition Hincmar of Reims, in his work on the divorce of Lothar and Theutberga, notes that women "are reported to use certain instruments [*quasdam machinas*] of diabolical operation to excite desire."[193] Burchard of Worms in his *Decretum* discusses in greater detail these "mechanical devices" in the form of the male sex organ, with dimensions being calculated to give women pleasure. (Burchard also warns against lesbianism among nuns as well as laywomen.)[194] Lesbian relationships are noted in the early twelfth century by St. Anselm in his commentary on Romans 1:26: "Thus women changed their natural use into that which is against nature, because the women themselves committed shameful deeds with women."[195] In his explication of Paul's reference to women's acts against nature, Peter Abelard also observed, "Against nature, that is, against the order of nature, which created women's genitals for the use of men, and conversely, and not so women could cohabit with women."[196]

The early twelfth-century *vita* of St. Godeleva (martyr d. 1070) in praising the saint's model behavior mentions that younger women were particularly vulnerable to feelings of desire, against which there was no defense. The hagiographer then notes briefly that it was through homosexuality that these lustful desires were usually satisfied.[197]

Thus these various prescriptive and exegetical sources taken together seem to undermine a general perception that medieval churchmen were unaware of the importance of the wide range of friendships and relations of intimacy—from the purely "spiritual" to the overtly sexual—found among religious women during this early period. The potential for intimate same-sex friendships was not ignored: the Church was definitely well aware that women were emotionally and physically attracted to one another, and this "temptation" was apparently taken seriously. Clearly, some of these churchmen seem to have been acquainted with the practices involved in lesbian relationships.

And within the context of their rather limited overall interest in female religious and women in the Church, they appeared to have shown a surprisingly active awareness and concern for this area of female experience.

TESTIMONIES OF SAME-SEX FRIENDSHIPS

While the prescriptive literature can provide an indirect index of friendships and especially intimate relationships among women, our other sources for the period are somewhat more frustrating in their silences. For this early period our sources are unfortunately not as detailed or descriptive as, for example, those of the twelfth or thirteenth century. We do not have such moving testimonies of strong attachments between women as witnessed by the letter written by Hildegard of Bingen to her beloved friend, Richardis; or the passionate friendships noted in two letters exchanged by female religious at Tegernsee.[198] Nor do we have the remarkable reminiscences of female friendship provided, for example, by the four women servants of the popular St. Elizabeth of Thuringia (d. 1234).[199]

The very nature of our sources for this early period, with few exceptions written by men, along with the frequently private nature of female friendship, make this limited body of information extremely frustrating and very difficult to get at. While the impressive cross-sex friendships of a number of these women can be traced in some detail in their exchange of letters with churchmen, it would appear that much of their correspondence with other women is unfortunately no longer extant. Some of this correspondence no doubt was lost during the invasions with the destruction of many of the women's houses. Furthermore, the subsequent reconstitution of these female communities as male monasteries disrupted the continuity of literary and historical traditions. Thus, due to the nature of the selection process— the preservation and copying of letters, and in general, the accidents of transmission—there seems to have been a notable loss of women's correspondence for this early period.[200] Nevertheless, the lack of explicit literary references to female friendship is no proof of its nonexistence or unimportance within society. It is interesting in this context to mention a rather well-known prohibition, found among Charlemagne's *Capitula* of 789, which stipulated that abbesses and the nuns of their communities were forbidden to write or to send out from their convents *winileodas*, or vernacular women's "songs for a lover."[201] This prohibition in itself seems to point to a certain literary tradition found among these early nuns. (It might also serve as an indirect index of the formation of close friendships of these religious women with women or men outside of the cloister. Churchmen viewed these activities as inappropriate and problematic, and therefore attempted to check them.) Despite the general paucity of extant source material on same-sex friendships, a collective study of saints' Lives, supplemented by information gathered from chronicles, can provide us with a number of small yet vivid incidents which help to illuminate these important bonds of friendship among women of this early period.[202]

The majority of extant examples of same-sex friendship from the early Middle Ages originate in the monastic milieu. In a number of cases these bonds are found within those of spiritual guardianship—the surrogate mother-daughter or the mentor-student relationship—and involve a rather wide discrepancy in age. One of the Lives of St. Brigid notes the deep affection and friendship which the saint cultivated with her young fosterling, Darlugdach. Darlugdach had apparently been committed to Brigid when she was a small child. As she entered adolescence we learn that she failed to keep custody of her eyes and saw a man with whom she fell in love. She thus came to dislike the constraints of the convent and decided to leave. According to the *vita,* on the night of her planned escape, she slept, as usual, in the same bed with Brigid (*in lectulo cum S. Brigida*). Torn between her love for her foster-mother, Brigid, and the lure of freedom from the convent, she prayed to God to strengthen her resolve to stay within the safe confines of the monastery. She then pushed her bare feet close to the red coals on the hearth until she could bear the pain no longer and then returned to bed. In the morning Brigid awoke and saw the scorched flesh on Darlugdach's feet. She then told her that she had been awake during her fosterling's struggle, but she chose not to interfere so that Darlugdach would work out her problems by herself. And since she had conquered this temptation, she no longer needed to fear it.[203] This anecdote, then, portrays the strong bonds of affection and intimacy obviously felt by these two women. Their special relationship can also be noted at the time of Brigid's death. When Brigid was on her deathbed, Darlugdach clung to her, and with tears she begged her foster mother to let her die with her. Brigid assured Darlugdach that she would follow her soon; and according to tradition, on the next anniversary of Brigid's death, her spiritual daughter contracted a fever and died.[204]

The eleventh-century *vita* of the Irish saint Moninne also describes a holy friendship between the abbess-saints Moninne and Ita.[205] According to the hagiographer, Ita sent a generous gift of a book to Moninne. It was carried between the two monasteries by a girl, who, on her way to Moninne's hermitage, fell off a wooden bridge and disappeared in a deep river. Three days later, Saints Ita and Moninne met at the river to look for the girl. In tears they prayed together for her return. Moninne summoned the girl three times and finally, after the girl responded from the depths of the river, she was returned to safety. Moninne then signed her with the cross and "handed her to Ita and said: Here is the girl." In this moving scene, as Lisa Bitel has pointed out, we find a depiction of "women saints working miracles together as a friendly team." [206]

As we have previously noted, the Frankish queen-saint Radegund cultivated a broad network of both male and female friends. In her Letter of Foundation, she describes her special affection for Agnes, whom she had designated as abbess of her new monastery in Poitiers. According to Radegund, Agnes "became like a sister to me"; she also calls her "my sister in God." She notes that she loved her and brought her up "as if she were my daughter from her childhood onwards." [207] In a poem Fortunatus describes Radegund's special celebration of Agnes' birthday. He explains that this "daughter of Radegund" was not born of her uterus, but of *gratia* or love. He also happily notes in another work the reconciliation of Radegund with Agnes after apparently a period of disagreement. [208] One of the characteristics of Radegund's doting attachment to Agnes, which is similar to that of Brigid and Darlugdach, is its resemblance to a mother-daughter bond or that of fosterage with a view to furthering the fosterling's ecclesiastical career.

The *vita* of the queen-saint Balthild is also informative in regard to female friendship within the monastic community. The author of Balthild's Life notes the queen's special fondness for Bertilla of Chelles. Balthild had specifically chosen Bertilla to become abbess of her newly refounded house at Chelles. And according to her *vita,* "the abbess always welcomed the requests of her royal companion, for they were, like the apostles, *one in heart and soul and they loved each other tenderly in Christ.*" Balthild's concern for her friend can be noted on her deathbed. Aware of her own imminent death, Balthild did not wish to alert abbess Bertilla who was herself very ill, for fear that her friend might die of grief. [209] While an inmate at the monastery of Chelles, Balthild also cultivated a particularly close fosterage relationship with a young girl named Radegund, who was her godchild. (See chapter 5.) Balthild was adverse to the idea of being separated from her young companion in death, and her prayers were apparently answered: Radegund died shortly before the holy queen, and the two were then buried together. [210]

The *vita* of St. Bertha, founding abbess of Blangy (d. ca. 725), tells of the strong friendship of Bertha with Rictrude, who was abbess of the monastery of Marchiennes. Their monasteries were approximately thirty miles apart and they frequently visited one another. During one of these visits, as these close friends sat talking together at Marchiennes, they are said to have heard a loud crash coming from the direction of Bertha's monastery at Blangy. It was learned that this was the collapse of Bertha's newly constructed church. Rictrude then tried to console her friend and she encouraged Bertha to rebuild her church on another site. In response to Bertha's request, the community of Marchiennes strictly observed a three-day fast and offered prayers for the success of the abbess's plans to rebuild. According to Bertha's *vita,* on the third day it was revealed to one of the workmen in a dream where the new foundations of the church should be located.[211]

However, one of the best descriptions during this early period of networks of female friendship can be found in the *vita* of St. Leoba (d. 779). As we have noted, along with a great influx of English clerics, monks, and nuns, Leoba left her monastery of Wimborne and traveled to Germany to assist Boniface in his missionary activity. A female relative of Leoba, Thecla, accompanied her and was made abbess of Kitzingen and perhaps Ochsenfurt.[212] In Germany this colony of Anglo-Saxon compatriots continued to work together in establishing monasteries for women or double communities, which became local centers of education and conversion. Leoba maintained contact with her various friends and their foundations through frequent visits. According to Leoba's *vita:* "Her deepest concern was the work she had set on foot. She visited the various convents of nuns and, like a mistress of novices, stimulated them to vie with one another in reaching perfection."[213]

Moreover, outside of this group of abbesses and nuns, Leoba developed a particularly close spiritual friendship with the queen-saint Hildegard, the wife of Charlemagne. Leoba's *vita* describes this relationship of *custos animi* or "guardian of one's soul" in some detail: "Queen Hiltigard [Hildegard] revered her with a chaste affection and loved her as her own soul. She would have liked to remain continually at her side so that she might progress in the spiritual life and profit by her words and example."[214] Their final meeting (shortly before Leoba's and Hildegard's deaths) is described in rather moving terms: "Queen Hiltigard sent a message to her begging her to come and visit her, if it were not too difficult, because she longed to see her before she passed from this life. And although Leoba was not at all pleased [she was old, ill, and did not want to leave her cell], she agreed to go for the sake of their long-standing friendship. Accordingly, she went and was received by the queen with her usual warm welcome. But as soon as Leoba heard the reason for the invitation she asked permission to return home. And when the queen importuned her to stay a few days longer she refused; but, embracing her friend rather more affectionately than usual, she kissed her on the mouth, the forehead and the eyes and took leave of her with these words: 'Farewell forever more, my dearly beloved lady and sister; farewell, most precious half of my soul. May Christ our Creator and Redeemer grant that we shall meet again without shame [*sine confusione*] on the day of judgment. Never more on this earth shall we enjoy each other's presence.'"[215] Thus despite the queen's announcement of her impending death and her wish for Leoba to stay with her, Leoba refused to remain at court. And as noted by Stephanie Hollis, "Recognizing that the death of one to whom she is so closely bound in the spirit spells her own end, Leoba returns to her anchorage, immediately sickens, and dies a few days later."[216]

In this fascinating description we can see a very close spiritual friendship, a soul union between the queen and Leoba. While noting that Hildegard loved Leoba "as her own soul" and Leoba regarded the queen as the "most precious half of her soul," the hagiographer, however, explained that their friendship was indeed pure or spiritual, and that their emotional enthusiasm was maintained within proper bounds, by his use of the terms "chaste affection" and perhaps by his reference to the fact that they would meet again "without shame" on the day of judgment. Moreover, the *vita* stresses the idea that true friendship endures separation, and that the bonds of spiritualized friendship would last forever—that is, Leoba and Hildegard had taken each other as friends for life and beyond. Thus their friendship would not be severed with death, but would transcend mortal life—or as Leoba promises, they would meet once again on the judgment day. And it is, then, with their future reunion in heaven, that all of their love would be made perfect.

In contrast to this idealized depiction of spiritual friendship, Hollis has pointed out the importance of the polemical intentions underlying this relationship. As in the hagiographic portrayals of bishops as soul-friends of kings, here the concern was in fostering closer ties between the throne and Church: in this case, the special interest in showing the queen as protective patron of Leoba's monastery.[217] Janet Nelson has also suggested in regard to the queen's wish for Leoba to prolong her stay at the court, that it is possible Hildegard knew Leoba was dying and therefore wanted control over her relics.[218] However, neither the queen nor Leoba's own community at Bischofsheim was able to claim the relics of their holy friend; for Leoba was buried, as planned, in Boniface's monastery of Fulda. Although it is interesting to note, as

Rudof points out in Leoba's *vita,* that on Leoba's death the seniors of Fulda "remembered what St. Boniface had said, namely, that it was his last wish that her remains should be placed next to his bones. But because they were afraid to open the tomb of the blessed martyr, they discussed the matter and decided to bury her on the north side of the altar which the martyr St. Boniface himself had erected and consecrated in honour of our Saviour and the twelve Apostles." [219]

It is, then, in the events and miracles surrounding a saint's death that friendship took on a special importance. Frequently death was structured around female rituals with close friends assuming major roles at this time. It is therefore not surprising that within this context we can find a number of vivid incidents of friendship. The *vita* of Queen-Saint Mathilda (d. 968), for example, portrays the great fondness that the queen felt for her former chamber-woman, Richburge, who as confidante had been told all of her secrets. Mathilda had selected Richburge as abbess of her new foundation of Nordhausen. On the queen's last visit to Nordhausen, Richburge foretold Mathilda's imminent death and begged her to choose her convent as her burial place. However, Mathilda went on to Quedlinburg to die with the intent to be buried in the family mausoleum next to her husband. Nevertheless, as the day of her death approached, Mathilda called on Abbess Richburge. The abbess then assisted the queen in her final moments, calling her "mistress, most dear to me." Mathilda consoled her in her desolation and provided her with emotional support to carry on after the queen's death.[220]

In a number of cases of close female friendship we have noted that in their final requests these *mulieres sanctae* begged that they not be allowed to die alone but rather in the company of their dearest friends. We have seen this pattern, for example, with St. Brigid and Darlugdach, or St. Balthild and Radegund. In his *Dialogues,* Gregory the Great notes the case of St. Galla. On her deathbed Galla experienced a vision of St. Peter who told her that her sins had been forgiven and that she was to come with him. "But because of her very great love for one of the nuns of the convent, Galla added immediately, 'I beg you to let Sister Benedicta come with me.' He was unwilling to grant this request, but allowed another sister to accompany her. 'Sister Benedicta,' he explained, 'will follow you in thirty days.'" [221] According to Pope Gregory, this ended their conversation, and Galla then told her abbess everything that had happened. Galla died three days later accompanied by the nun who had been mentioned by St. Peter. "And the sister for whom Galla had especially asked followed in thirty days." Gregory then notes that this episode was still one of the memorable events of this convent. And the younger sisters of the community, who had heard this story told, now related it themselves as if they had personally witnessed the miracle.[222]

Another index of the deep affection which these women felt for one another can be found in several of the *vitae* where friends were singled out to be recipients of special visionary experiences foretelling another's death. In the Life of St. Gertrude of Nivelles, for example, we learn that Gertrude was bound together in a close spiritual friendship with Modesta, abbess of Trier. According to the redactor of the Life, although physically separated by many miles, and unable to see each other, they remained soul mates: they always assumed an emotional centrality in each other's life. As recorded in Gertrude's *vita*, "she [Modesta] had been consecrated from infancy to God and was likewise bound closely up in an intimately holy friendship with St. Gertrude. Although they were physically separated by a great distance and because of many miles of earth and intervening space were unable to gaze upon each other with their bodily eyes, nevertheless they were ever close [*presentes*] in spirit and heartfelt love, since they carried on an equal discipline of service and served the Lord in sincerity of heart and without guile." The hagiographer continues: "The story I want to tell and narrate for your remembrance took place after a long period of time. One day the aforementioned servant of God, Modesta, was in her monastery and went to chapel to pray, and knelt in prayer before the altar of the Blessed Virgin Mary. At the end of her prayers, as she was arising, she looked about her on all sides and suddenly she looked up and beheld St. Gertrude standing on the right side of the altar in the same condition and outward appearance in which she [i.e., St. Gertrude] had been fashioned. [St. Gertrude] then said to her: 'Sister Modesta, hold this vision as something certain, and without a doubt [*ambiguitate*] know that I have today at this hour been relieved of the dwelling of this flesh. I am Gertrude, whom you loved much.' With these words Gertrude disappeared from Modesta's sight even as she beheld her. Modesta was thinking silently to herself: 'Now why should this great vision take place?' And on that day she made no mention of the vision to anyone."[223] On the following day, however, Clodulfus, bishop of Metz, came to Modesta's monastery. And after questioning him about Gertrude's appearance, she understood that what she had seen was true. She then related this miraculous vision of Gertrude's apparition and death to Clodulfus, who confirmed the day and hour of Gertrude's death and verified that everything was as Modesta had told him.[224]

Bede records two similar incidents connected with the death of St. Hilda of Whitby. He tells us that Hilda's death was revealed in a vision to a devout nun named Begu at Hilda's convent of Hackness, some thirteen miles from Whitby.[225] Bede notes that "it is said that Hilda's death was revealed also on the same night in a vision to one of the sisters in the actual monastery where the servant of God passed away. This sister, who loved her dearly, saw her soul ascend to heaven in the company of angels, and immediately awoke the servants of Christ with her and told them to pray for her soul."[226]

With the death of a saint, the circles of female friends and relatives frequently experienced a special need to possess some remembrance or personal keepsake of the holy woman's life. On the death of the ninth-century St. Maura of Troyes, for example, the saint's aunt and two female cousins seized her haircloth vest [cilicium] and divided it into four parts, with the women keeping three of these as relics and the local bishop preserving the fourth part.[227] The vita of St. Gertrude of Nivelles notes that the saint's sister, Begga, received for her new monastery part of the bed on which Gertrude had died.[228]

In some cases, however, this need for a remembrance or relic of one's holy friend could take a rather bizarre turn. Such was the case of the popular eighth-century abbess-saint Attala of Strasbourg. According to a later legend, Werentrude, abbess of Hohenbourg, had been a special friend of Attala when they had lived together at the convent of Hohenbourg. The redactor of the legend notes that Werentrude, hearing of Attala's death and hoping for her own well-being and future salvation, desperately desired either the right or left hand of her friend or some other portion of her relics. She therefore employed a priest to go to Attala's monastery of St. Etienne in Strasbourg, under cover of darkness, in order to cut off the hand of the saint and steal the relic (see plate 22). Unfortunately, his covert attempts were foiled, as his rather blatant theft was discovered. And the saint's hand, which the priest had apparently severed, was then enclosed separately in a crystal reliquary and preserved in Attala's church of St. Etienne.[229]

These various pieces of indirect evidence, when taken together, serve to build up a picture of the significance which same-sex female friendships assumed for this early period. As noted, churchmen were definitely aware that women were in fact attracted to one another and expressed deep affection for each other, and that female friendship was to be taken seriously. They were alive to the benefits and value of spiritual friendships between women and they describe in the vitae many moving examples of soul mates and of true and deeply felt affection among these religious women. However, at the same time, these ecclesiastical writers were clearly convinced of the need to maintain a balanced or disciplined friendship: they were aware of the problems involved in the formation of "particular friendships," especially

within the sexually segregated monastic community. Thus their prescriptive literature recognized the inherent dangers which "irregular"
and "shameful intimacy" held for the spiritual life.

It is, then, the shared, all-female world of the monastic community
which was extraordinarily important for the cultivation of personal
bonds of friendship. And it is interesting to note the variety of inter-
personal relationships that are described in the *vitae:* friendships between equals (between abbesses, abbesses and nuns, abbesses and
queens), as well as those between women of unequal status and of
disparate ages (that is, those friendships based on the fosterage or
noble-servant relationship). We can also find a wide range of intimate
relationships—from purely "spiritual" friendships to those which appear to have been perhaps more overtly physical or sexual.

Thus these circles of special friends, female and male, as *custos
animi* and surrogate family, supported and helped one another to lead
meaningful and "independent" lives outside of the strictures of the
family. The majority of friendships noted in the *vitae* were between
celibates who had renounced or "neutralized" their sex, thus allowing
for these holy alliances. Frequently dislocated, lonely, and far away
from home, these people formed friendships that became an especially
important and necessary part of their lives. They worked closely together as "sisters" and "brothers" sharing common aspirations and
goals within their religious communities. Through visits or correspondence they maintained their extensive network of friends. In their
exchange of gifts they pledged to remember one another; their gifts
served as tokens of affection or reaffirmations of their friendships.
Although physically separated from one another, they still maintained
a close emotional or spiritual bond. Friends assumed a special role
in the important events and rituals surrounding death. In their belief
or hope that friendship transcended death, they frequently received
visions or posthumous visits from their beloved friends; and they often
chose to be buried next to each other to await the final judgment
together.

As previously noted, in many cases these circles of friends were
also crucial in helping to formulate and spread the *fama sanctitatis* of
their holy friends. They collected their relics, validated their miracles,
provided a collective memory of their lives, commissioned the redaction of their *vitae,* or arranged for the translation of their relics.
Saints' Lives, then, provide wonderful clues to these little-explored but
vital circles of female and male friendships. They provide unique details concerning friendship and support found within the cloister.
They also show—as, for example, in the case of St. Cuthbert—how
sometimes these positive traditions of friendship have been denied or

manipulated to serve new misogynist reform agendas. Despite the dearth of source material, it appears that it was not uncommon for women to routinely form deeply felt emotional ties with other women and with men. Many seemed to recognize the true importance of friendship within their lives, indeed, valuing their friends as "the most precious half of their soul."

The time came when she must relinquish the carnal habitation and, fully ninety years of age, migrate to the celestial kingdom.

Life of Eustadiola, Widow of Bourges
(*SWDA*, 7:110)

Hildilid . . . ruled the convent with great energy until extreme old age, promoting observance of the regular discipline and making provision for the needs of the Community.

Bede, *A History of the English Church and People*, trans. L. Sherley-Price, IV, 10:222

Moreover, after some years, when on account of excessive fasting and keeping of vigils, this small human body became grievously burdened with much sickness, she learned through divine revelation that her passing from the world was drawing nigh.

Vita Sanctae Geretrudis Nivialensis, MGH, SRM, II, 6:459

ℒongevity, 𝒟eath, and 𝒮anctity: 𝒜 𝒟emographic 𝒮urvey of the 𝒞elestial 𝒢ynaeceum

Life in the Middle Ages has been traditionally viewed in Hobbesian terms as being nasty, brutish, and short. With its high infant and child mortality rate, life expectancy at birth was extremely low. On the average, the medieval person might live to about thirty years of age. In this milieu, one became an adult and assumed adult responsibilities and rights much earlier in life than in our society today; for example, laws provided for early marriages; secular and ecclesiastical power was often entrusted to, or thrust upon, the very young. However, as J. C. Russell has noted in his classic work *Late Ancient and Medieval Population*: "The average length of life was about thirty years, but if one could survive the first thirty years he had a fair expectation of life. Some, indeed, lived to a great old age."[1]

One of the fascinating patterns which emerges from a collective study of medieval saints' lives is the rather extraordinary longevity of the members of the celestial kingdom. It appears that among the rank and file of the blessed, rather more than might be expected passed into old age. One frequently finds among the "heavenly dossiers" abbesses, abbots, and bishops who served their communities or dioceses for forty or more years and died as octogenarians or even nonagenarians.

In the actual recognition and "making" of saints, longevity or time seems to have been a disproportionately important factor. That is, in order to achieve positions of leadership, influence, power, and a visibility which provided access to *fama sanctitatis,* one needed time: the longer the lifetime, the greater one's chances to be in the public eye or to be noticed, and thus to make an impression on one's peer group and community. In his work *Altruistic Love: A Study of American "Good Neighbors" and Christian Saints,* Pitirim Sorokin argues: "Among the most important conditions of eminent leadership and creative genius [categories from which saints are recruited] are a long life and vigorous health. Most leaders and successful creators have needed time to realize their potentials for this requires long training, experience, and an opportunity (sometimes occurring only late in life) to grow, to develop fully, and to realize itself."[2] He then concludes: "For this reason, many would-be creators who die early do not have the chance to realize their talent. The bulk of those who do realize their potentialities do so because they live long and have all the time necessary for turning their potential genius into actuality. Hence the supernormal longevity of men of genius and real leaders, including our saints."[3] Thus, a long active life generally worked to enhance the chances of a would-be saint to gain a greater visibility in society and to accumulate a more impressive spiritual dossier.

AVAILABLE DATA ON SANCTITY AND LONGEVITY

The Lives of saints provide a rich and unique source of information on the life spans of the spiritual elite. Through a collective examination of the *vitae* we can obtain rough data on the membership of the celestial gynaeceum, including general age distribution among saints, life duration and the influence of gender, as well as the adoption of various holy lifestyles and ascetic practices which had implications for the longevity of saints.

At the outset, however, it is necessary to note that saints' Lives and chronicles present a number of difficulties as we attempt to calculate the longevity of the holy dead. It appears that many authors of medieval saints' Lives were little interested in exact dates or figures, or perhaps they did not have this information available to them. Although they frequently devoted what might seem to be an inordinate portion of the *vita* to detailed descriptions of the holy person's death and the miraculous circumstances surrounding it, they often failed to provide any precise information on the age of the saint or specific details on the physiological cause of death. Concerned essentially with dramatizing the last hours of the saint's earthly existence and his or her heroic death, as well as promoting the cult of the saint, the *vita* often furnished only the day and year of the saint's death and neglected to mention the date of birth (if this fact was indeed known at the time). Moreover, a few of the Lives which do include information on the age of the saint utilize *topoi* or the tradition of hagiographic exaggeration. In attributing a life span of a hundred or more years to their protagonists, they seem to be adopting the epic bent of the Old Testament in which Methuselah, for example, is described as having lived 969 years or Jacob 147 years.[4] The redactors of the *vitae* might also have been influenced by the tradition in which St. Paul is said to have died at 120 years of age, or St. Jerome's assertion that St. Anthony died at 113.[5] Thus, within the hagiographic perceptual mode, extreme longevity could be viewed as simply part of the tradition of the holy

TABLE 5 Ages of Saints at Death, 500–1099

AGES	MEN	WOMEN	MARTYRS	NON-MARTYRS	TOTAL
11–20	1	1	0	2	2
21–30	9	2	3	8	11
31–40	13	2	3	12	15
41–50	21	3	4	20	24
51–60	35	6	3	38	41
61–70	64	6	1	69	70
71–80	44	6	1	49	50
81–90	32	1	1	32	33
91–100	9	0	0	9	9
Total	228	27	16	239	255

life; it further substantiated the supernatural aspects or miraculous characteristics of the saint's extraordinary existence.

Nevertheless, many of the authors of saints' Lives or chroniclers of the period were apparently not interested in distorting the length of the saint's life span for hagiographic effect and appear to provide reliable demographic data. Bede, for example, in his *History of the English Church and People,* notes that Abbess Hilda "a most religious servant of Christ, after an earthly life devoted to the work of heaven passed away to receive the reward of a heavenly life on the seventeenth of November at the age of sixty-six. Her life on earth fell into two equal parts: for she spent thirty-three years most nobly in secular occupations, and dedicated the ensuing thirty-three even more nobly to our Lord in the monastic life."[6]

In the collection of saints catalogued in the *Bibliotheca Sanctorum* for the six-hundred-year period (ca. 500–1100), and limited to the countries under consideration in this study, approximately 255 entries provide specific demographic information on the holy dead. That is, we know the life duration of only approximately 12 percent of the male saints and 8 percent of the female saints for this period; therefore, a rather large percentage of the total celestial population remains unaccounted for in this survey. Clearly, in light of this small cohort of female saints, our limited data does not lend itself to any unqualified generalizations in regard to longevity among the *mulieres sanctae*. The results of our rough "statistics" on life duration therefore remain approximate at best, and provide only a hint in regard to the much larger picture of sanctity and longevity.

Table 5 summarizes the rather rough statistics regarding the ages of saints at death as provided by the *Bibliotheca Sanctorum*. In general, we can see an impressive number of both male and female saints who

TABLE 6 Longevity of Male and Female Saints, 500–1099

SEX	NUMBER OF INDIVIDUALS	AVERAGE AGE AT DEATH
Female	27	57.6
Male	228	65.1

TABLE 7 Ecclesiastical Saints, 500–1099

POSITION	NUMBER	MARTYRS	NON-MARTYRS	AVERAGE AGE AT DEATH
Abbess/nun	18	0	18	56.5
Bishop	102	3	99	63.8
Abbot/monk	89	5	84	70.1

had very long life spans. Approximately 70 percent of the women saints for whom complete data is provided died after the age of 50; almost half (48 percent) died after the age of 60, while approximately one-quarter of these female saints died after reaching 70 years of age. The longevity statistics for male saints appear to be even more impressive, especially when one considers the number of martyrs found among this group. Approximately 80 percent of the male saints died after 50 years of age and 65 percent died after 60 years. However, what is especially noteworthy is that almost 40 percent of the men saints had a life span of more than 70 years, while approximately 18 percent died after 80 years—and included among this number were several nonagenarians and centenarians.

Data on the comparative longevity of male and female saints is collected in table 6. The average age at death for both sexes does not appear to be highly differentiated. In general, from these limited statistics, male saints appear to have outlived female saints by approximately seven years.

Comparative data on the longevity of ecclesiastical saints (that is, those saints who had officially taken vows and entered the Church as nuns, abbesses, abbots, monks, and bishops is presented in table 7.

From the available data, it is interesting to note that female religious appear to have had a shorter life span than either bishops or abbots and monks. One might perhaps expect some sort of symmetry or equality in longevity between abbesses and nuns and abbots and monks; however, based on our limited sample, the longevity of abbots and monks surpassed that of their female counterparts by some thirteen years.

Table 8 summarizes the comparative longevity of male and female saints drawn from the laity. (The majority of these saints were kings, queens, and members of the upper aristocracy.)

According to this very limited sampling—which indirectly reflects the small number of lay saints at this time—the average age of death of female lay saints was approximately 60 years, while the life span of male lay saints was some seventeen years shorter than that of their female cohorts. This rather wide gender-based discrepancy in longevity can be explained in part by the number of male saints whose lives were cut short by martyrdom, for the average age at death of the male martyr lay saint was approximately 34 years. Moreover, it is interesting to note that the average age of death for the male, non-martyr, lay saint was only about 49 years, i.e., some eleven years shorter than that of the female lay saint.

Table 9 provides the comparative results of collected data on the longevity of female saints recruited from among the laity and from the cloister.

From this limited sampling, we can again see a rather long life span for this group of elite women saints. Moreover, the *mulieres sanctae* drawn from the laity seemed to have a slight edge over their saintly sisters of the cloister. The average age at death for laywomen was approximately 60 years, while that of female religious was about 56½ years.

The conclusions which can be drawn from this sampling of saints are again rather limited and tentative and must be used with caution. They only indirectly reflect a select group of individuals with apparently a rather greater life span than might be expected from among their "non-haloed" contemporaries.

TABLE 8 Lay Saints, 500–1099

SEX	MARTYRS	NON-MARTYRS	AVERAGE AGE AT DEATH
Female	0	9	59.9
Male	5	8	43.2

TABLE 9 Longevity of Female Saints, 500–1099

CATEGORY	NUMBER OF INDIVIDUALS	AVERAGE AGE AT DEATH
Female Religious	18	56.5
Laywomen	9	59.9

In contrast to these limited statistics of the holy dead, studies on life expectancies in medieval society in general underscore a significantly shorter life span for women. J. C. Russell, for example, has argued that more men died between the ages of 40 and 60 than between 20 and 40, while the reverse was true of women.[7] In his study "Life Expectancies for Women," David Herlihy has found that while females dominated the ranks of children in the surveys of two peasant communities of the late eighth and early ninth centuries, as the population aged, females lost their numerical preponderance. The shifts in the sex ratio prevailed against females from approximately age 15 years onwards, implying that women were dying sooner than their male contemporaries.[8] In her examination of the age at death of the royal women of the Carolingian dynasty, Suzanne Wemple has also found a shorter life expectancy for these women. Although in early childhood the mortality rate for Carolingian males was higher than that for females, Wemple notes that "the ratio was reversed in the early teens. . . . A higher mortality rate also prevailed for women between the ages of fifteen and thirty-nine, with 31 percent of the men as opposed to 48 percent of the women dying. Only 39 percent of the women lived to age forty and beyond, compared to 57 percent of the men. The highest proportion of male mortality occurred between the ages of forty and fifty-four, and of female mortality between the ages of twenty-five and thirty-nine. Clearly the disparity between the two mortality rates had some connection with women's biological function."[9] It is interesting to note that in contrast to these general findings, Karl Leyser's study of the life expectancies of the Saxon nobility and royalty points to a longer life span for many of these women. He argues: "In collecting materials for the history of the leading kins in the tenth and early eleventh centuries, it would be difficult and rather purblind not to notice the surprising number of matrons who outlived their husbands, sometimes by several decades and sometimes more than one, their brothers and even their sons."[10] Leyser then cites numerous and rather widespread examples taken from the Saxon ruling class and nobility to support his contention of women's better chances for survival.[11]

Thus on one level, as we have noted, there was a close relationship between a long life span—which encouraged a long, illustrious career in the cloister or at court—and the subsequent elevation to sainthood. In general, a short life span followed by an "ordinary" death (i.e., not martyrdom) normally would not provide the candidate with the necessary prerequisites for *fama sanctitatis*. This in part helps to explain the rather impressive longevity of these early women saints. Therefore, among the female lay saints for this period, the average life span was approximately 60 years in comparison to the 36 years for Charlemagne's female descendants.[12] Many of these *mulieres sanctae* had also been married and had given birth to numerous children. As noted by Wemple, "It is not altogether possible to draw a direct correlation between the mortality rate of women and their childbearing function. No royal descendant, wife, or concubine is known to have died during childbirth. It would be equally wrong to assume that a woman who bore many children would die sooner than one who had none."[13] (In this context we find, for example, St. Hildegard, wife of Charlemagne, who after giving birth to her ninth child, died in 783 at the early age of twenty-five years or, on the other extreme, Oda, the mother of St. Hathumoda, who after having had twelve children was said to have died at the age of 107 or 109.)[14]

It also appears, at least from our limited sampling of saints, that these noble and royal laywomen who were elevated to sainthood seem to have been less prone to becoming victims of violence or martyrdom than were their husbands and brothers. Although it is possible that this was more a function of "styles" of sanctity among male nobility than an indirect reflection of the reality of this time, more than one-third of the male saints recruited from among kings, dukes, etc., were martyrs, while none of their female lay cohorts (i.e., those for whom we possess full data on longevity) met with violent deaths.

MONASTIC LIFE AND FEMALE LONGEVITY

The majority of these early female saints were, however, recruited from the monastic milieu. What then were some of the conditions of this lifestyle which might have contributed to the increased life expectancies of the *mulieres sanctae?*

At the outset, entry into monastic life required a certain screening process in the form of a probationary period which tested the health and stamina of its recruits. For example, the Rule of Caesarius of Arles required that the entrant, "who, by the inspiration of God undertakes religious life shall not be allowed immediately to assume the religious garb, until beforehand her will has been proved by many trials."[15] The Rule of Donatus of Besançon also stresses that those who wish to enter the community "should not be allowed to assume the religious habit until her resolve has already been proved in many tests." They must demonstrate their perseverance and "bear difficulties and injuries"; they are also warned that "the road to God is hard and narrow."[16] The Benedictine Rule stipulates: "Let the newcomer not be granted an easy entrance. . . . Test the spirits to see whether they are from God. Let the novice be told all the hard and rugged ways by which the journey to God is made." [17]

It seems that, at least in theory, in discerning vocations monastic communities therefore attempted to discourage the weak and physically unfit, and encouraged only those candidates who were capable of fulfilling the obligations required of religious life. This assumed a certain level of health, strength, and stamina. Thus we find in the canons evidence that at least some monasteries refused to accept young women who were either ill or in poor physical condition.[18] It appears that those in poor physical or psychological health, or those who were weak and unable to live up to the harsh monastic expectations during their trial period, were discouraged from taking monastic vows. Aside from the large dowries which they might provide to the monastery (indeed, no doubt a serious consideration or incentive), acceptance of weak and sickly women as novices would not be to the advantage of the community in the long run; it would require a proliferation of personal exemptions which would adversely affect monastic regularity of observance, obedience, and policies of nondifferentiation, as well as the general morale of the community.[19] Therefore, the procedure of admittance was aimed at selecting women who were in reasonable health and would not be a burden to the community.

The regularity of monastic life and virtues practiced within the cloister also had the potential to encourage or favor a long life. The monastic schedule, for example, was to be divided between physical labor and religious duties: regular hours were assigned for meals, rest, and sleep. Moderation was to be practiced in all things; excesses in general were to be avoided.

The hygienic level of some of the wealthier monasteries and the medical attention given to their nuns perhaps also helped to increase the longevity of their inmates.[20] For example, monastic rules made special provisions for nuns who were ill: they were given additional opportunities for baths for the sake of their health. In Augustine's famous letter to the nuns of his sister's monastery, he writes: "The washing of the body, also, and the use of baths is not to be too frequent, but may be allowed at the usual interval of time, that is, once a month. In the case of illness, however, where there is urgent need of bathing the body, let it not be postponed too long, but let it be done without objection for medical reasons. If the patient herself objects, she must do what health requires to be done at the bidding of the Superior." [21] The Rule of Caesarius of Arles stipulates: "By no means let baths be denied those whose infirmity demands it, and let them be taken without murmuring on the advice of the doctor, so that even if she who is ill does not wish to bathe, at the command of an elder religious that is to be done which is necessary for her health. If, however, bathing is not required because of some infirmity, assent should not be given to an eager desire." [22] The Rule of Donatus of Besançon specifies that "daily baths, which are only reluctantly conceded to the young, need to be allowed to the sick for health's sake." [23] In this context, the Life of Radegund describes how the saint cured a sick nun by having her bathe in hot water for two hours (for a similar miracle, see plate 6). [24]

Monastic rules also focus on the special attention which was to be shown to the sick and elderly. Six chapters of the Rule of Caesarius of Arles deal with the care of the infirm. The old and sick were to be provided with their own storerooms and kitchen, as well as special sleeping quarters which were separate from the community. All those in authority and the infirmarians were to be responsible before God for the devoted care of the sick. The sick were to be treated in such a way that they might convalesce quickly. [25] Caesarius also recommends that older nuns should not be required to keep to the rigor of the monastic rule in regard to food—they could eat before regular hours and be given special foods, including meat. He suggests a special diet be provided for the ill: "Fowls are to be brought forth only for the sick; they are never to be served in community. No flesh meat is ever to be taken at all for nourishment; if, by chance, someone should be gravely ill, she may take it by the order and permission of the abbess." [26] The Rule of Donatus of Besançon also stipulates that the abbess may prescribe meat for the desperately ill. [27]

Moreover, the monastery was to provide a favorable milieu for growing old; it was to afford a caring environment which would help to allay the increasing difficulties and fears associated with old age. According to the monastic rules, elder religious were to be shown special consideration and respect by the younger nuns. [28] The elderly nuns were also expected to continue to contribute to the variety of religious tasks of the community; for example, older nuns were responsible for training new candidates of the community, they assigned work to the nuns, etc. [29] Frequently they participated in monastic routines on reduced levels until their deaths. In many cases abbesses occupied their positions of leadership until their deaths and we therefore find an impressive number of abbesses continuing to wield power well into their seventies and eighties. Thus the older inmates of the convent were able to maintain a useful role and an active involvement in the community. This framework provided for a continuation of strong social bonds among its members. These factors of community—of a surrogate family—no doubt helped to foster increased life expectancies among its members.

Another perhaps rather elusive area which might also have contributed to the longevity of these monastic saints concerns the realm of mental attitudes. As noted by their biographers, many of these saints seemed to possess a certain spiritual stamina and an inner peace provided by their extreme religiosity. Their "conversion" to a life of religion or monastic life, and hope for entrance to heaven and membership in the choir of 144,000 virgins which this "sacrifice" promised, seemed to provide at least some of the female religious with an assurance, a contentment, and a sense of tranquillity within their lives. As Sorokin has noted: "The profound peace of mind which most of these saints acquired was one of the conditions which could easily counterbalance poor food, clothing, unhealthy environment and self-mortification. Most of them knew well that peace of mind is one of the most important—sometimes the most important—of the conditions for health and longevity."[30]

EARLY MONASTIC DIETS

While monastic rules attempted to maintain a regulated and balanced regimen within the female communities, many of the early women saints in fact won fame and recognition for their dramatic acts of self-mortification and practices of heroic fasting which they carried out within the confines of their monasteries. These "immoderate" acts, which in many cases proved in the long run to be extremely dangerous to their health, were viewed by their contemporaries as positive expressions of female piety and indeed worthy of imitation. The authors of saints' Lives were consequently interested in the details surrounding the diets of their protagonists. In describing their avid pursuit of the *vita perfecta,* hagiographers often praised their abstemious behavior in regard to food and drink, and especially commended their remarkable adherence to a strict or heroic regimen of fasting.

In general, the regular diets of medieval women (without the added issue of fasting) seem to have been sorely deficient. In a study "Female Longevity and Diet in the Middle Ages," Vern Bullough and Cameron Campbell evaluate the short supply of protein and iron in the early medieval diet with its specific effect on female life expectancy.[31] Since women during menstrual age require at least twice as much iron as men, and during pregnancy and lactation approximately three times that of men, they conclude that, in general, by the age of twenty-three, early medieval women would be severely anemic, even if one discounted pregnancy. While anemia in itself is seldom a primary cause of death, the authors argue that it increases the risk in relation to other bodily stress or crisis. For example, with anemia, moderate blood loss, or pulmonary diseases such as pneumonia, bronchitis, and emphysema can become especially dangerous health threats. Bullough and Cameron point out that "probably the leading anemia-related death for women in the early medieval period was childbirth, and this alone would be enough to explain the predominance of men over women in the early medieval population."[32]

A variety of sources of this early period provide information on diet and specifically the daily food rations required for female religious. Although in most cases their diets were somewhat better than those of the peasants (e.g., with more supplementary sources of protein), their intake was similarly heavily dependent on grains and breads, because of their insistence on avoiding meat. According to the calculations of Michel Rouche, the daily rations for a nun of Notre-Dame of Soissons in 858 consisted of the following: 1.440 kg. of bread, 1.380 l. of wine, 70 g. of cheese, 133 g. of dry vegetables, 16 g. of salt, .60 g. of honey. This provided a total of some 4,727 calories. Although this specified allotment of food was less than one-quarter or one-fifth of that designated for monks, it was nevertheless excessive in caloric intake—exceeding the daily requirement for women by over two thousand calories! As Rouche has noted, while these rations were of enormous quantity, with the high amount of bread making up for the lack of meat, they were also gravely deficient in quality—totally lacking in vitamins A, D, E, K, and C.[33]

However, it is important to emphasize, as the Carolingian *De Institutione Sanctimonialium* warned, that in some of the poor monasteries rations will be less copious, while on feast days provisions will be better.[34] This observation appears to have been especially pertinent to some of the smaller, poorly endowed female houses, or larger popular communities in which the number of nuns began to exceed their resources: situations in which the nuns therefore found themselves reduced to very real poverty.

Letters, charters, canons of Church councils, and other sources refer to the poverty and special difficulties that many of these women's monastic communities experienced in providing the necessary sustenance for their inmates. The Life of St. Brigid, for example, while praising the saint's great generosity and openhandedness, notes a number of incidents in which the community appears to have experienced real difficulties in regard to the procurement of food.[35] The *vita* of the Irish saint Moninne (d. ca. 517) describes how the nuns under her care were so closely confined that one season they had no fresh water. The Life also relates that during certain periods St. Moninne's own monastery found itself so short of food that its inmates were in danger of starvation. Moreover, near Moninne's monastery was a very

small women's house that was extremely poor: its existence was totally dependent on the saint's handouts or charity.[36] In his description
of the notorious revolt of the nuns of the monastery of Ste-Croix,
Gregory of Tours notes that one of the complaints which the nuns
leveled against their abbess concerned provisions of food. According
to the text of the judgment in which these grievances were answered
by the abbess: "As to the poor food about which they complained, she
denied that they had ever gone short, especially if one considered what
hard times these were."[37] (The qualification found in this last phrase
is perhaps especially telling.) The Life of St. Gudula relates that after
the destruction of the monastery of Moorsel by the Vikings and the
return of the nuns, the community experienced the usurpation of its
properties and immense poverty. Only with great difficulty were six
nuns able to find enough bread and water for their sustenance.[38] In
fact the poverty of Moorsel was so extreme that St. Berlinde left the
monastery and returned to live in her village of Meerbeke.[39] The correspondence of Abbess Eangyth with Boniface (ca. 719–722) again
underscores the immense misery and misfortune which some of these
communities experienced. She writes: "We are further oppressed by
poverty and lack of temporal goods, by the meagerness of the produce
of our fields and the exactions of the king based upon the accusations
of those who envy us."[40] The ninth-century community of Jouarre is
similarly described as destitute, living under the weight of misery and
weakened by hunger.[41]

Several of the canons of the Carolingian reform councils were specifically concerned with the poverty of female communities. They
prescribe that the abbess, bishop, or king be called upon to provide
subsidies so that the nuns may obtain the sustenance (specifically food
and drink), necessary for their way of life, and for the continued practice of strict enclosure and the maintenance of their chastity.[42]

Many of the miracles found in the *vitae,* and particularly those
performed by abbess-saints, directly concern the low food supplies
of their monastic communities.[43] Faced with empty cellars and casks,
and the extremely difficult and unenviable responsibility of providing for the needs of their own houses, as well as the required hospitality for visitors and charity for the poor, these saints were said to
have miraculously restored or multiplied their monasteries' supplies
of wine, milk, grain, fish, salt, and so forth. Although reminiscent of
biblical miracles such as the multiplication of the loaves and fishes,
these rather commonplace "miracles of plenty" found in the saints'
Lives no doubt indirectly reflect the very real problems of depleted
food supplies, famine, hunger, and in a few instances starvation,

which some of these communities and those who were dependent upon them were forced to endure.

REGIMENS OF FASTING AMONG THE *MULIERES SANCTAE*

Moreover, in addition to the basic dietary deficiencies of the period, and isolated episodes of food shortages, severe famine, and even starvation, many of the *mulieres sanctae* also voluntarily adopted strict regimens of fasting which were frequently accompanied by the keeping of vigils and sleep deprivation. Pious self-mortification through fasting, or the refusal to eat, was a culturally acceptable form of asceticism for women and men during this period, and it was frequently taken as a sign of holiness. Thus one of the particularly strong expressions of female piety or popular metaphors of sanctity was abstinence or rejection of food.

Over the past decade a number of fascinating studies have explored female piety and practices of fasting and eucharistic devotion in the high and late Middle Ages. Of special import are the works by Caroline Bynum, Rudolf Bell, Donald Weinstein, Richard Kieckhefer, and André Vauchez.[44] In general these studies have viewed heroic fasting as essentially a characteristic of female piety of the thirteenth through fifteenth centuries. During this later period, fasting and the miraculous abstinence from food, along with the cultivation of illness, provided the central theme or primary visibility for sanctity for many of the *mulieres sanctae*. It is interesting to note that while there are definitely some basic differences in perception, as well as the extent and degree of these practices of female piety from the early to late Middle Ages, this phenomenon of pious self-mortification through fasting and the cultivation of illness also proved to be extremely important in the making of female saints from approximately 500 to 1100. Nevertheless, in contrast to the female saints of the high and late Middle Ages whose recognition of holiness often centered on heroic fasting, for most of the *mulieres sanctae* of this early period fasting appears to have been only one among several pious themes in their lives which qualified them for sainthood. It was listed by their biographers in a catalogue of behavioral models of saintly conduct. And for the most part, this component of their sanctity appears to have been only moderately emphasized in their *vitae*. In a number of cases, however, this behavior was presented as a formative element in the saint's life: it was perceived as a cause or the effect of spiritual development, a response to a crisis, or the condition for visions and especially for miracle-working.[45]

In general, the Church expected each Christian to adhere to some level of the ascetic practice of fasting. In its strictest sense, the term *jejunium,* or a fast, designated the abstinence or voluntary refusal of all food, sometimes even water, during a given period of time. However, the ordinary practice of fasting frequently took the form of *monophagia,* that is, eating only one time per day, usually late in the day after vespers and the celebration of Mass and communion. Another level of fasting consisted of the restriction of certain foods and was called *xerophagia,* meaning the eating of dry food: it required abstaining from substantial or tasty foods and adopting an abstemious diet of dry food consisting of bread, salt, and water—sometimes accompanied by fruit and vegetables.⁴⁶

From the beginning, the Church attempted to regulate the practice of fasting and to establish specific times, days, and periods during which religious fasts were to be observed. In general, the faithful were expected to fast before receiving the eucharist. The Church set aside Mondays and Wednesdays, and in certain areas Saturdays, as special fast days. The most important period of fasting was that of the forty days of Lent. Outside of those fasts which were liturgically fixed to certain dates, extraordinary fasts were also imposed by bishops, princes, and local holy men and women in response to special circumstances. Preparation for baptism, ordination, and the consecration of a bishop required a period of fasting. In some areas fasts were observed to prepare for the construction of churches and monasteries. Ritual fasting was utilized by saints in the working of miracles—for example, in resolving problems of female infertility. Moreover, during times of disaster, pestilence, fire, famine, and invasion a general fast would frequently be called with the intent to appease the anger of God and obtain divine assistance. Fasting was also one of the most important penances imposed on sinners to obtain remission of their sins.⁴⁷

There remained, however, a great deal of variety among the faithful in the actual practice of fasting. Those aspiring to the *vita perfecta* were frequently dissatisfied with the rigor of the basic fasting schedule prescribed by the Church. They therefore supplemented these regulated ecclesiastical practices by multiplying the days which they devoted to self-mortification through fasting.

Beginning with the patristic writers, we can find a special interest in and articulation of the theory and practice of fasting. And while fasting was recommended for everyone who wished to pursue the holy life, a slightly different emphasis seems to have been placed upon this ascetic ideal as well as on the benefits derived from this practice for religious women and men.⁴⁸ Since the locus of sin for the female sex was identified with the body, sex, excess, and indulgence, women bore the special burden in regard to food and fasting. They therefore felt a particular need to negate their natural female proclivity toward sexuality and sin through heroic regimens of fasting.

In their writings, the Church Fathers strongly recommended fasting to those who wished to pursue the *vita perfecta*. In his mid-fourth-century tract *De virginitate,* Pseudo-Athanasius of Alexandria, for example, contended that to fast was to live the life of angels. He argued: "Fasting . . . cures disease, dries up the bodily humors, puts demons to flight, gets rid of impure thoughts, makes the mind clearer and the heart purer, the body sanctified, and raises man to the throne of God."[49] The patristic writers believed that there was a close connection between fasting and chastity: abstinence, or food deprivation, was necessary to "control the flesh." St. Augustine, for example, advised female religious to "subdue your flesh by fasting and abstinence from food and drink as far as your health allows."[50] Patristic writers believed that voluntary self-starvation would bring about the suppression of sexual appetites along with other bodily urges such as taking pleasure in eating and sleeping. They contended that enjoyment of food and sleep was closely identified with the sins of lust, gluttony, and sloth. Thus perhaps conditioned to be suspicious and frightened of their own bodies and to abhor their physical desires, pious women could use the avoidance of food as a means to destroy bodily needs and to punish and purify their bodies. Extreme or heroic fasting, by obliterating any feeling of sexual desire, pain, fatigue, or hunger, allowed them to have a certain power and control over their bodies and lives, and—for a few—to become active agents in determining their own sanctity.[51]

The writings of St. Jerome are particularly instructive and influential in regard to the ideal of fasting for pious women and its role in the maintenance of virginity. In his letter to console Eustochium on the loss of her mother, Jerome provides a description of Paula's austerities. He notes her incessant desire "to depart and to be with Christ." "As often too as she was troubled with bodily weakness [brought on by incredible abstinence and by redoubled fastings], she would be heard to say: 'I keep under my body and bring it into subjection.'"[52] Later he writes: "Her self-restraint was so great as to be almost immoderate; and her fasts and labours were so severe as almost to weaken her constitution."[53] In his well-known Letter 22, Jerome advises Eustochium to seek as companions women "thin from fasting, of pallid countenance." He admonishes Eustochium that the preservation of her chastity required abstinence from wine and luxurious foods.[54] He warns that "the mind when sated grows sluggish, and watered ground puts forth thorns of lust."[55] Thus Jerome ties concupiscence or lust to rich diets, wines, and luxurious foods. Mortification of the body through food deprivation conquered lust: for through fasting, according to Jerome, "the moisture of lust has been cooked out." [56]

In his instructions to Laeta on how she should bring up her daughter, Jerome provides the following advice on fasting: "Let her meals always leave her hungry and able on the moment to begin reading or chanting." However, Jerome also stresses the need for moderation in fasting: "I strongly disapprove—especially for those of tender years— of long and immoderate fasts in which week is added to week and even oil and apples are forbidden as food. . . . If perpetual fasting is allowed, it must be so regulated that those who have a long journey before them may hold out all through. . . . By vigils and fasts she mortifies her body and brings it into subjection. By a cold chastity she seeks to put out the flame of lust and to quench the hot desires of youth." [57]

In his letter to Marcella, Jerome describes the model behavior of Marcella's sister, Asella. As a consecrated virgin, Asella had lived a life of the most rigorous asceticism. According to Jerome, since the age of twelve, "shut up in her narrow cell she roamed through paradise. *Fasting was her recreation and hunger her refreshment.* If she took food it was not from love of eating, but because of bodily exhaustion; and the bread and salt and cold water to which she restricted herself sharpened her appetite more than they appeased it. . . . All the year round she observed a continual fast remaining without food for two or three days at a time; but when Lent came . . . [she] fasted well-nigh from week's end to week's end with 'a cheerful countenance.'" [58]

It is perhaps not surprising that St. Jerome's overzealous advocacy of these ascetic practices among his small group of female disciples in Rome seems to have been the cause of strong accusations directed against him. Particularly the untimely death of Blaesilla, daughter of Paula, provoked an outcry against his pious regimens. In Jerome's letter of condolence to Paula, he praised Blaesilla's abstinence in fasting: "Her steps tottered with weakness, her face was pale and quivering, her slender neck scarcely upheld her head." [59] He then noted with difficulty: "When you [Paula] were carried fainting out of the funeral procession, whispers such as these were audible in the crowd. 'Is not this what we have often said. She weeps for her daughter, *killed with fasting.* She wanted her to marry again, that she might have grandchildren. How long must we refrain from driving these detestable monks out of Rome? Why do we not stone them or hurl them into the Tiber? They have misled this unhappy lady'" (see plate 23). [60]

These extravagant regimens of fasting, recommended by the Church Fathers, and the heroic measures of abstinence found among the early female saints, would then serve as models of behavior for religious and laywomen for centuries to come. However, the ascetic ideal of fasting became an especially important ingredient in the development of female monastic life. According to the *vita* of St. Caesarius of Arles, for example, vigils and fasting were among the primary occupations of his brides of Christ.[61] The Rule of Caesarius of Arles provided specific directions for fasting: it indicated the designated seasons and days, and supplied detailed regulations for the amount of food and drink. He specified that "from Pentecost until the first of September—in this period choose how you ought to fast; that is, as the mother of the monastery sees the strength or possibility, she shall endeavor to make regulations. From the first of September to the first of November there should be fasting on Monday, Wednesday, and Friday; from the first of November to Christmas, except on feast days and Saturdays, there should be fasting every day. Before Epiphany there should be fasting for seven days. From Epiphany to the week before Lent there should be fasting on Monday, Wednesday, and Friday." [62] (It is interesting to note that in Caesarius's Rule there is no mention of the Lenten fast.) The one meal which was served on fast days was called the *refectio*. Caesarius warns that this meal was not to be increased greatly and that the younger sisters were not to receive a larger meal for their *refectio*. However, despite the strictness required by his fasting schedule, Caesarius made provisions in his Rule for those of more "delicate constitution" or who suffered from gastrointestinal troubles and found this regimen too difficult to follow.[63] Similarly, the Rule of Donatus warned that conventual life for women required a perpetual fast. This Rule also provided a schedule for fasting, similar to that of Caesarius, with special provisions for those "sisters [who] need to be more carefully nourished or if any suffer frequently from stomach ailments and cannot abstain like the rest or fast without great suffering." [64] (Perhaps as an indication of the difficulties inherent in maintaining these strict programs of fasting, both of these rules forbid their religious inmates to hide anything to eat or drink near their beds.) [65]

The ascetic practice of fasting was then very much an integral part of the religious life of the period. As an ideal of female piety, it was also adopted by laywomen who as nuns manqué followed a somewhat modified monastic regimen outside of the cloister. Therefore chronicles, saints' Lives, letters, canons of councils, and other sources of the period provide us with many fascinating accounts of holy women and their fasting practices.

We find among the Irish *mulieres sanctae* a number of examples in which pious fasting was used to achieve higher spiritual perfection. The Irish St. Ita, for example, was well known for her love of severe fasting. She was said to have fought against and conquered the demons in her cell by fasting for three days and three nights. One incident described in her *vita* notes that she went without food for some four days. She was then said to have been warned by an angel to moderate her behavior: "Without a measure [of food] you weaken your body with fasting, and therefore you are not able to do anything." The Life however maintains that "a bride of Christ would not wish to ease up on her burden." Thus this difficult situation was handled in a miraculous way, that is, Ita was said to have received her sustenance from heaven each morning.[66] The *vita* of St. Moninne also notes this holy woman's penchant for fasting. On one occasion, Moninne was involved in an extended fast, apparently unaware that the nuns under her care were starving and understandably upset with her pious excesses and neglect. It was a churchman who happened to be passing by who brought this critical situation to Moninne's attention; she then had to perform a miracle in which the necessary nourishment was supplied to her charges.[67]

One of the most famous female saints known for her pious fasting and austere diet was the early Merovingian saint Genovefa. From the age of fifteen years, when she received the veil from the bishop of Paris, to that of fifty, she was said to have followed an extremely abstemious diet. Frequently eating only twice a week—on Sundays and Thursdays—she kept to a sparse diet consisting of barley bread with a few beans. At the age of fifty, in obedience to her priests and in order to sustain her body which had been destroyed by such rigorous fasting, she consented to add to her diet a small amount of milk and fish. However, according to her *vita,* she never ate any meat or drank wine.[68]

The Frankish saint Monegund (d. 570) lived as a recluse after the death of her two daughters, eating only bread which was made from a coarse barley meal mixed with water which had been strained carefully through ashes. Her sparse meals were separated by long periods of fasting. On one occasion, when she was abandoned by the woman who was responsible for supplying her food, Monegund remained for some five days without receiving her required allowance of food and water. During this time, she prayed that "He Who fed the people with manna from Heaven and produced water from a rock for their thirst would deign to indulge her with similar food that her exhausted little body might be comforted for a little while. And immediately after her prayer, snow fell from heaven and covered the ground." She was thus able to reach outside of her window and collect some snow which allowed her to make her customary loaves of bread. This sustained her until her next supply of food arrived some five days later.[69]

One of the most famous Merovingian saints who won special notoriety for her excessive mortifications and fasting was the queen-saint Radegund. Her dietary habits and heroic fasting are described in some detail by her friend and biographer, Fortunatus, in his *vita* and poetry. While still queen and residing at the court, Radegund deceived those around her who were feasting at the royal banquets, by substituting for herself a special menu consisting of beans and vegetables (see plate 24). Moreover, while the king was absent from the court, the saintly queen carried on long fasts.[70] After leaving the royal court but prior to entering monastic life, we learn that Radegund lived on barley bread, vegetables, herbs, and water mixed with honey or perry.[71] In her later life within the monastery of Ste-Croix, her practice of austerities, abstinence, and fasting became even more exaggerated. During Lent she followed a dietary regimen of barley or rye bread, vegetables, and herbs. She refused to eat any meat, fish, eggs, or fruit. Only on feast days and Sundays did she allow herself to eat the fruit which Fortunatus sent her. Her liquid intake was also limited to water sweetened with honey or perry. However, as Fortunatus noted, the amount of water that she allowed herself was so restricted that it did not quench her thirst. In fact, the first Lent which Radegund spent enclosed within her private cell, she permitted herself only a few drops of water per day: the end result was that she could hardly participate in the chanting of psalms because her throat was too dry. The following Lents Radegund eased up slightly on her austerities: she permitted herself to eat a few leaves of mallow and roots, served without oil or salt, two days a week instead of only on Sundays.[72]

It is interesting to note that—as in the case of St. Genovefa—Radegund's contemporaries became seriously concerned about her health. Apparently witnessing a noticeable deterioration in her physical condition, Fortunatus and Abbess Agnes attempted to dissuade her from her severe austerities. They tried to convince Radegund to eat more food and drink wine for the sake of her health. In their arguments for moderation, they referred to the authority of St. Paul who had counseled Timothy to take care of his stomach.[73] Similarly, Abbess Caesaria the Younger of Arles warned Radegund in a letter: "I have learned that you are fasting to excess. Act reasonably in all things. . . . For if, because of this excess, you begin to be ill afterward—which does not please God—it will be necessary for you to try to obtain some delicate [or refined] food and to take food outside of meal times, and you will no longer rule these Benedictas [or sisters]. Listen to what Christ said in the Gospel: 'It is not that which enters by the mouth which defiles the man'; and the Apostle 'That our form of worship should be reasonable.' . . . Act in everything, domina, as you find it written in the rule that you have demanded . . . You are 'a model for the faithful' [*forma fidelium*], since 'she who will practice and teach, that one will be called great in the kingdom of heaven.'"[74] Their practical advice to Radegund, however, went unheeded, even when the saint experienced periods of intense exhaustion.

The contemporary Life of St. Gertrude of Nivelles relates that through her austerities and mortifications she had treated her body so severely that by the time the saint was thirty she was worn out by fasting and want of sleep: "Moreover, after some years, when on account of excessive fasting and keeping of vigils, this small human body became grievously burdened with much sickness, she learned through divine revelation that her passing from the world was drawing nigh."[75] Gertrude therefore resigned as abbess of her foundation of Nivelles, passing the position on to her niece who was only twenty years of age. According to her *vita,* the saint spent the last three years of her life suffering from her self-inflicted ascetic regime; moreover, throughout all of this she continued to wear under her clothing a rough haircloth vest. Thus wasted by her austerities, St. Gertrude died at the early age of thirty-three.[76]

The author of the *vita* of St. Berlinde of Meerbeke notes that she ate only twice a week. Her meager diet consisted of whole meal bread and a small amount of fresh water. Only on Sundays and feast days did she allow herself to eat vegetables, dairy products, and fish.[77]

St. Opportuna, abbess of Montreuil, was also remembered for her austerities and especially her regimen of fasting. According to her *vita,* she frequently abstained from all food during the day, eating only a small amount after vespers. Her diet consisted of barley bread and on Sundays she added a small portion of fish. On Wednesdays and Fridays she ate nothing at all. When one of her nuns asked her why she allowed her body to waste away through such frequent fasting, Opportuna was said to have answered her with the following argument: Adam was ejected from paradise for eating the forbidden fruit. We therefore must be reconciled or make amends for that through fasting; we should neither eat meat nor drink wine.[78]

St. Maura of Troyes adopted the life of virginity while living at home: she also followed a regimen of great austerity in her diet. Restricting herself to only bread and water, she fasted every Wednesday and Friday. Maura died at the early age of twenty-three.[79]

The recluse saint Liutberga also won praise for her abstinence in eating. Her meager diet consisted of bread with salt and herbs. Sundays and feast days she ate a small helping of vegetables and fish; infrequently she had strawberries and wild fruit. According to her *vita,* in order to fulfill her vow, Liutberga adopted such oppressive austerities in her abstinence from food and drink that her body wasted away: she became extremely weak and thin. In addition, her complexion changed and she grew increasingly pale; her skin clung to her bones, giving her an emaciated appearance. When asked what infirmity she had, Liutberga responded that she did not have any particular illness, rather her condition was connected to her fasting and vigils. These practices then brought about the progressive weakening or infirmity of her body.[80]

In his Life of Queen Margaret of Scotland, Turgot describes in some detail the royal saint's austere practices in eating. After she had served dinner to twenty-four poor persons, he tells us that "she used to refresh her own little body also. But because she did not (as the apostle says) 'make provision for the flesh, in its desires,' she had in this refection barely enough to satisfy the necessities of life. She ate merely in order to preserve life, not to yield to pleasure. The light and moderate repast provoked hunger instead of satisfying it. She seemed to taste food rather than to consume it. Gather from this, I ask you, the extent and manner of her continence in fasting, when such was her abstinence in feasting." Turgot also notes, "And although she passed her whole life in great continence, yet in these days, the forty before Easter and the forty before Christmas, she used to afflict herself with incredible abstinence. Because of the excessive rigour of her fasting, she suffered acutest pain in her stomach to the end of her days." The end result of her excessive austerities, according to her biographer, was a self-inflicted illness: "But what shall I say of her fasting; except that by excessive abstinence she brought on the molestation of a very serious disease?"[81]

It is interesting to note that in all of the *vitae* that I have surveyed, there are very few references to overweight or obese women. The Life of St. Bruno/Pope Leo IX (d. 1054), however, describes the saint's mother, Heilvige, as extremely overweight. Despite her fasting and austerities, the woman was scarcely able to move and had to be transported in a little wagon from place to place. We learn that her obesity caused her a great deal of difficulty and was especially troublesome in regard to her modesty. She therefore prayed that before her death her body might waste away so that one woman would be able to shroud her and place her in her tomb. According to our sources, her prayers were answered, and before Heilvige died she lost the required weight.[82]

This sampling of a few early female saints and their fasting practices, then, underscores the popularity and prevalence of this culturally approved form of piety among women. Because of the lack of detailed information found in many of the *vitae*, it is difficult to know the full extent of these ascetic exercises. However, in at least a few of

these cases, one can see clear behavioral patterns of excessive or heroic fasting. The obsession of these holy women with food and regimens of spiritually inspired self-starvation frequently began when they
were impressionable adolescents. In their pursuit of rigorous austerity and spiritual perfection, inspired by the models of Christ and
female saints, as well as by their mothers, abbesses, and other female
religious, these women voluntarily starved themselves to the point
at which their lives were at risk. Some, through the moderation of
their fasting practices, succeeded in prolonging their lives; others,
as we have noted, died in a state of inanition or exhausted by their
austerities.[83]

In considering the effects of these ascetic programs of self-starvation,
it is necessary to re-emphasize the fact that these regimens were carried out in conjunction with the already sorely deficient diets of the
period. Moreover, the physical problems associated with excessive
fasting were no doubt further compounded by other practices, such as
bloodletting. Like fasting, this custom appears to have been utilized
for purposes of health, as well as to "control the flesh" and rid the
body of its lustful tendencies. During this early period, within the monastic milieu, great importance was apparently attached to the practice of bloodletting or bleeding. Bloodletting usually occurred four
times a year and was a simple procedure performed in the monastery
by a nun or monk.[84] Among the miracles of St. John of Beverley
(bishop of Hexham and York) for example, Bede tells of a young nun
of the monastery of Wetadun who was seriously ill and had been bled
in the arm. Subsequently it appears that she suffered complications
due to the procedure: she was seized by intense pain, the arm which
had been bled became so swollen that "it could hardly be encircled
with two hands," and she was unable to bend it. When the bishop
came to visit the convent, the abbess told him about this nun, who
was especially dear to her and now appeared to be dying. He then
inquired as to when she had been bled. Learning that it had been carried out on the fourth day of the moon, he said that this was a very
dangerous time to bleed someone, as the light of the moon and the
pull of the tide was increasing. The bishop then visited the girl: he said
a prayer over her and gave her his blessing. Soon the pain disappeared
from her body and the swelling subsided.[85] A Carolingian capitulary
of 789 also briefly notes the practice of bloodletting for female religious in its description of the nuns' pallor due to the loss of blood.[86]
This practice, then, in conjunction with severely deficient diets and
exercises of extreme fasting, would have clear implications for the
health and longevity of women religious.

VIGILS AND SLEEP DEPRIVATION

The general physical weakness which these regimens of pious fasting and extraordinary austerities promoted among some of these holy women was further aggravated by voluntary practices of keeping vigils and sleep deprivation. In theory as well as practice, fasting and vigils were intimately related: usually one fasted while keeping a vigil. Also one of the side effects of fasting seems to be the suppression of the feeling of fatigue. Fasting provided its practitioners with a certain restless energy; in some cases it seems to have led to a state of hyper-activity, euphoria, or ecstasy. It also appears to have produced a mental condition or psychological disposition especially receptive to visions.[87] It is during these long periods of fasting and vigils that the *mulieres sanctae* were said to have experienced visions of Christ or other sainted members of the heavenly kingdom. The practice of voluntary sleep deprivation was thus another culturally approved type of self-mortification. It was recommended to those who wished to lead the *vita perfecta*.

St. Jerome, in his description of St. Paula's model behavior, notes that "she mourned and fasted, she was squalid with dirt, her eyes were dim from weeping. For whole nights she would pray to the Lord for mercy, and often the rising sun found her still at her prayers." In his advice to Eustochium, Jerome also recommends frequent night vigils for women who wished to pursue the perfect life. He writes: "Be the grasshopper of the night. Wash your bed and water your couch every night with your tears. Keep awake and become like a lonely sparrow."[88]

In this tradition, saints' Lives frequently mention the long, heroic vigils maintained by the *mulieres sanctae*. As part of their practice of corporal self-mortification, they permitted themselves only a minimal amount of sleep. They spent long hours, day and night, in prayer and vigils before the holy altars. One of the long-term side effects of this ascetic practice of kneeling in prayer and vigils was, according to St. Jerome, "holy knees hardened like those of a camel."[89] Gregory the Great recalls that when the body of his saintly aunt, Tarsilla, "was washed in preparation for burial, her elbows and knees were found covered with a thick skin like that of a camel. Thus, in death, her body gave witness to the many hours she had spent in pious prayer."[90]

Together with her extraordinary regimen of fasting, St. Radegund was known for her self-mortification through vigils and sleep deprivation (see plate 24). While at court she was said to leave the royal bed on the pretense of the need to "relieve nature." She would then, however, spend a good part of the night in prayer, prostrated on the freezing floor by the privy. Covered only by a haircloth, the chill penetrated her body through and through. According to Fortunatus, all of her flesh was prematurely dead (*tota carne praemortua*); her mind intent on paradise, she did not pay attention to the torments of her body. She wanted to mortify her flesh in order to be worthy of Christ.[91] Radegund's practice of sleep deprivation became even more exaggerated at the monastery of Ste-Croix. According to Baudonivia, the saintly queen spent her nights reading and allowed herself only an hour for sleep.[92] In addition, Radegund devised her bed as an instrument of torture (*lectulum vero poenalem sibi construxit*). She refused to allow herself soft or comfortable coverings, or any linen, but rather haircloth and ashes were used to punish or conquer her body.[93]

The *vita* of St. Rusticula, abbess of Arles, relates that "she also practiced fasting and vigils, wearing a hair shirt and eating every third day in fulfillment of the Apostle's instruction: 'In fasting and vigils and many labors . . .' While the other sisters were asleep, Rusticula spent the entire night in the church at her psalms, hymns, and prayers. With abundant tears she prayed to the Lord for her flock or for the whole world."[94]

In Bede's description of the austerities of St. Etheldreda, he notes that "she always remained at prayer in the church from the hour of Matins until dawn unless prevented by serious illness."[95]

St. Berlinde of Meerbeke was particularly well known for her practices of self-mortification in regard to sleep. She chose to sleep on the bare ground, and according to her *vita,* she used a stone for a pillow. (The stone pillow motif is perhaps a hagiographic *topos* based on Genesis 28, where Jacob is described as having slept with his head on a stone.) Berlinde was also said to wear a haircloth which completely covered her body.[96]

The recluse St. Wiborada of St. Gall was noted for inflicting punishment on her body through vigils and fasts. She customarily allowed herself only a very limited amount of sleep. According to her contemporary hagiographer, after resting for a short period of time Wiborada would get up and then spend the remainder of the night in prayer. Although she had a proper bed with expensive coverings in her cell, she never used it; rather, she slept on the ground, covered with a simple haircloth. She was also said to have chosen a stone for a pillow.[97]

In addition to the rather prevalent expressions of female piety found in the practice of fasting and vigils, there are a few extraordinary cases of bodily self-mortification found in the sources of the period. In comparison to the late Middle Ages, when self-inflicted torture seems to have been a fairly common expression of female sanctity, these examples of extreme self-mortification appear to have been rather unusual and limited during this early period of "practical sanctity." There is one particularly popular case, that of St. Radegund, which is of special interest to this topic. In his *vita* of St. Radegund, Fortunatus provides detailed information on his protagonist's bodily self-punishment and destruction. He writes: "One time she had brought to her three [circles] or bracelets of iron which she wore during Lent around her neck and arms; she also took three chains which she pulled tightly, so that her delicate skin came up and covered the hard metal, and after Lent she was no longer able to remove this belt since her skin enveloped it. In order to disengage the iron chain, it was necessary to make an incision all around in the back and chest; there was a heavy loss of blood and her weakened body seemed to be at death's door."[98] "Another time," according to Fortunatus, "she had a brass plate made into the monogram of Christ, then enclosing herself in her cell, she made it red-hot in the fire and pressed it so deeply to two places on her body that the skin was destroyed." Fortunatus continues: "But like a clever torturer, she contemplated going still further: during one Lent she had brought to her a brass pot filled with glowing coals; when all of the sisters had retired, subduing the trembling of fear which raced through her limbs, she summoned up her courage to confront the suffering, and since the time of persecution had passed, she made ready to make a martyr of herself. Then . . . wishing that her body was also overtaken by this fire, she brought it in contact with the incandescent pot: her burning flesh crackled, her burnt-up skin disappeared and left large gaping wounds, as far as the effect of the fire had penetrated. The saint was silent, trying to conceal her wounds; but the spent blood betrayed by its odor that which she forced herself not to say."[99] (For the bracelets of iron, see plate 24.)

It is interesting to note that while many episodes from the Life of St. Radegund served as models of behavior for other saints (and their hagiographers) and were reproduced in their *vitae*, her rather extreme acts of self-torture or mortification seem to have inspired admiration but were not similarly imitated during this period.

BODILY MORTIFICATION AND THE RECLUSIVE LIFESTYLE

A number of the *mulieres sanctae* carried out their acts of self-mortification away from the watchful, moderating eyes of their superiors, that is, in the privacy of their cells. (This was the case, as we have noted, for St. Radegund, who, during Lent, enclosed herself in a special cell within her convent at Poitiers where she put into practice her program of extreme austerities.) In general, the life of the hermitess or *inclusa* (enclosed one) allowed the ascetic practitioner a certain degree of independence in her pursuit of the *vita perfecta,* and particularly in the multiplication of her austerities. Moreover, the adoption of the solitary life and permanent confinement within a very small space provided yet another component of self-mortification, and it was viewed as a means to move one closer in the quest for holiness. Along with fasting, vigils, and the practice of other austerities, the restricted, frequently unhealthy living space of the cell (with problems concerning the procurement of food and water, dampness, the lack of exercise and fresh air, sanitation, etc.) appeared to further compromise the health of some of these holy women. Although accommodations of hermitesses seemed to vary considerably, some chose to live their lives in narrow cells, or cells with dimensions so cramped that they would be unable to either stand up or to lie down full length to sleep. These cells were often contiguous to, or adjoining, a church in a city or village, or they might be dependent on a rural or urban monastery. The cell would frequently have a small window opening onto the apse of a church which allowed the *inclusa* to participate in communion from her enclosure. In a few cases, the holy woman lived as a hermit in an isolated cell in the countryside. The recluse would then remain confined, enclosed in her cell, often until her death.[100]

Gregory of Tours mentions several of these holy women in his writings, including Georgia, the female hermit who lived near Clermont, and St. Monegund, who lived as a recluse at Chartres and later at Tours.[101] Particularly beginning in the eighth century, a number of other saints' Lives attest to the popularity of this ascetic lifestyle for women. We learn, for example, that St. Hiltrude (8th c.) followed an austere life for some seventeen years in a cell adjoining the monastery of Liessies.[102] St. Bertha, abbess and founder of Blangy (d. ca. 725), spent the last years of her life in a cell she had built onto the monastery's church. According to her *vita,* it had a small window located near the altar through which she could participate in the Mass and receive communion. And each day her two daughters and some sixty nuns of her community came to her for special instruction.[103]

A number of sources, however, note *inclusae* who made still greater commitments to their lives of self-mortification and spiritual perfection by choosing to be permanently enclosed or immured in their cells. In his *History of the Franks,* Gregory of Tours provides us with a fascinating case of self-immolation or immurement at St. Radegund's monastery of Ste-Croix. He notes that a certain woman of the convent had been deeply moved by a vision. Then "a few days later she asked the abbess to prepare a cell and to shut her up there for ever. The abbess wasted no time in doing so." The bishop of Tours then describes in some detail the procedure of being immured or walled up in a cell. "All the other nuns assembled, with their lamps lighted. They sang psalms together and then their sister was taken in a procession to the spot, the blessed Radegund leading her by the hand. They all bade her farewell and she gave to each the kiss of peace. Then she was enclosed in her cell and the door through which she had entered was bricked up. There she now passes her days in prayers and holy reading." [104]

The *vita* of St. Liutberga also describes how she had a small cell prepared for her self-enclosure. The bishop, accompanied by a number of priests, came to bless it with a benediction and sprinkle it with holy water. She received instruction and was forbidden to leave the cell. The bishop then sealed the cell by placing an obstacle before it. And it was then within this space that Liutberga continued to practice her life of austerities. [105]

For several years St. Wiborada lived in a cell near the Church of St. George, not far from the monastery of St. Gall. Because of her reputation for sanctity and asceticism she was besieged by crowds of people who came to ask her advice, to beg for food, or to provide her with donations. Wiborada therefore decided to escape from the distractions of the world by becoming formally immured in a cell located beside the church of St. Magnus, near St. Gall. (Wiborada's brother, Hitto, was a priest of this church.) Thus the saint's friend, the bishop of Constance, was called upon to bless her new cell and provide the solemn religious ceremony of enclosure. Wiborada then lived as an *inclusa*, enclosed within her cell, for some thirty-four years: for part of this period she shared her cell with a young woman named Rachild, whom she had cured of a serious disease. In 926 the Hungarian invaders attacked the area. Refusing to leave her cell or to allow Rachild to go without her, Wiborada was killed by the invaders when they broke into her cell in their search for treasure. Rachild remained unharmed and lived as an anchoress for another twenty-one years. [106]

With the late eleventh century, the eremitic life became increasingly popular in France and Italy. Inspired by this Continental movement, the holy woman Eve of Wilton (ca. 1058–1127) moved from Wilton Abbey to Saint-Laurent de Tertre in Angers, and later to Saint-Eutrope, where she espoused the life of the *inclusa*. [107] (Apparently, while she was still living at Wilton, Eve had withdrawn from her community to occupy a cell where she followed a life of strict asceticism.) According to her friend Goscelin's *Liber confortatorius*, Eve was enclosed in a very small eight-foot cell in Angers: her only communication with the outside world was a tiny window. Here she became famous as a holy woman and won praise for her regimen of fasting, prayers, and renunciation of secular things. When Eve began her life as a hermitess in France she was approximately twenty-five years old: she was in her late sixties when she died.

Thus, in their quest for the *vita perfecta,* a number of holy women adopted the life of the hermitess or enclosed one which allowed them to seek the challenges of "the desert." In limiting their access to the world, or in removing themselves from the demands of secular society, they were able to concentrate on intensifying their austerities and acts of self-mortification. For some of these women, the life of the *inclusa* did not seem to be detrimental to their health and longevity; in fact, it might have encouraged a longer life span. For others, however, the rather extreme programs of fasting, vigils, and self-mortification that they followed within the privacy of their cells clearly had a deleterious effect on their health.

"IN ORDER THAT HER STRENGTH MIGHT BE MADE PERFECT IN WEAKNESS"

In addition to the practice of self-mortification and heroic austerities, we find among many of the *mulieres sanctae* the metaphor of patient suffering or the endurance of a prolonged illness. This was seen as a further test of the holy woman's spiritual stamina. It was viewed as a sign of holiness or a gift bestowed by God on his chosen few: through sickness, prolonged suffering, and intense pain their strength was said to be perfected. For many of these women this experience provided a final arena for the heroics of sanctity.

The ninth-century *Martyrology of Oengus* notes that St. Ita "succoured many grievous diseases: she loved many severe fastings." It also describes one of the more memorable afflictions suffered by one of the women saints. According to the *Martyrology,* with the help of God, Ita was said to have patiently endured "a stag-beetle as big as a lap-dog a-sucking her [which] destroyed the whole of one of her sides." Apparently she kept her condition to herself since no one knew of her special ailment.[108]

In his description of Hilda of Whitby's last years, Bede writes: "When Hilda had ruled this monastery for many years, it pleased the Author of our salvation to try her holy soul by a long sickness, in order that, as with the Apostle, *her strength might be made perfect in weakness.* She was attacked by a burning fever that racked her continually for six years; but during this time she never ceased to give thanks to her Maker or to instruct the flock committed to her, both privately and publicly. . . . In the seventh year of her illness the pain passed into her innermost parts, and her last day came."[109] Bede also notes in describing the vision of the nun Tortgyth: "In order that her strength might be 'made perfect in weakness' as the Apostle says, she was suddenly attacked by a serious disease. Under the good providence of our Redeemer, this caused her great distress for nine years, in order that any traces of sin that remained among her virtues through ignorance or neglect might be burned away in the fires of prolonged suffering."[110]

The *vitae* of St. Aldegund, founding abbess of Maubeuge, also describe her final days during which she suffered from cancer. One of her hagiographers notes that Aldegund had cancer in her left breast which tormented her exceedingly up to end of her life. Following the lesson of Job's endurance of his afflictions, as well as the example of a number of saints, she supported her suffering with patience and with gladness accepted it as a divine gift.[111]

Turgot further underscores this belief of "virtue perfected in weakness" in his Life of St. Margaret of Scotland. While noting the acutely painful illness brought on by the "incredible abstinence" of the saintly queen, he observes: "And because she knew that it is written, 'Whom the Lord loves he reproves; and he scourges every son whom he receives,' she gladly accepted with patience and rendering of thanks her bodily suffering, as the scourging of her gentlest Father. . . . Thus . . . labouring under constant infirmities, so that according to the apostle's words, 'virtue was perfected in infirmity': she rose from virtue to virtue . . . and burned with full desire in her thirst for heavenly things."[112]

The expression of female sanctity through the adoption of extreme austerities, and the cultivation of bodily suffering and illness accompanied by a "holy patience" is then prevalent in many of the saints' Lives of the period. And while we can find parallel modes of behavior among the male hermit saints of the period, fasting, self-mortification, and the cultivation of illness were not common metaphors of sanctity for the majority of abbot- and bishop-saints. However, as Caroline Bynum has shown in her study *Holy Feast and Holy Fast,* this expression of piety will become an even more significant component, a central aspect of female sainthood, in the late Middle Ages.

MOTIVATIONS OF THE *MULIERES SANCTAE*

The Lives of the *mulieres sanctae* of the early medieval period are therefore especially informative in regard to the role of self-mortification and the active cultivation of illness and suffering in the pursuit of spiritual perfection. The adoption of these culturally acceptable forms of asceticism was based on a complex mixture of religious and personal motives. As we have noted, many of the *vitae* emphasized theological or religious principles as the primary motivation behind these actions. Very briefly, these ascetic practices with their self-inflicted suffering and illness were viewed as having a redemptive value. Through self-punishment and suffering these pious women believed that they could bring about their own personal salvation as well as that of others. For these brides of Christ, their own self-mortification and suffering fused with the agonies of the crucifixion of Christ.[113] One of the fundamental messages of the New Testament was "if any man would come after me, let him deny himself and take up his cross and follow me" (Mark 8:34). Thus in attempting to pursue the *vita perfecta,* one was expected to imitate Christ by adopting a life of self-abnegation, mortification, persecution, and suffering. In this context, a strong preoccupation, or in some cases an obsession, with the agonies of Christ and his crucifixion can be found among a number of these early women saints. The period of Lent required a special redoubling of austerities and practices of self-mortification to be deemed worthy of Christ. In this context, St. Radegund seemed to have been particularly moved by the sufferings of Christ and expressed her intense devotion to the passion and crucifixion by branding herself with Christ's monogram during her Lenten exercises of self-mortification. The desire on the part of these saintly women for direct contact with Christ, for the opportunity to share in his agonies of death and to be ultimately worthy of his attention, can also be seen in Radegund's passion for relics and specifically her aggressive and relentless campaign to procure a fragment of Christ's instrument of torture, the Holy Cross, for her monastery at Poitiers.[114]

In their attempts to actively seek opportunities to suffer physical pain in order to be more worthy of Christ, and to approximate or imitate his sufferings on the cross, a number of these women were said to yearn for the earlier age of persecution and for their own martyrdom. Thus we can find in the *vitae* references to the ideal of martyrdom and various attempts on the part of the *mulieres santae* to recreate the milieu of martyrdom or persecution on a personal level in order to resemble the martyrs. In describing Radegund's practices of self-torture, Fortunatus notes clearly how during one Lenten period she had to summon up her courage to confront the suffering, and "since the time of persecution had passed, she made ready to make a martyr of herself."[115] The *vita* of St. Bertilla, abbess of Chelles, notes that she was ambitious for martyrdom, but as the persecutions were not forthcoming, she brought on her own martyrdom through excessive austerities and self-mortification—especially the practice of unabated fasting and vigils. "For when she had reached an advanced age, she drove her weary and senescent members to spiritual service. She did not follow the common custom and modify her life in old age or seek for better diet. As she had begun, she went on ever more strongly never taking enough of anything but barely sustaining her aged body, lest she might weaken from within. She indulged in a modicum of food and drink to force her weakening limbs into their nightly vigils." [116] According to St. Opportuna's *vita,* this saint's austerities were also seen as a type of martyrdom. The hagiographer argues that there are two kinds of martyrs: one secret or concealed and the other public. The readers are then assured that those who in private suffer daily "the cross of Christ," through renouncing the delights of the flesh, the world, and the devil, would also win a crown of martyrdom.[117]

It is, however, in this whole area of subjugating the flesh, in controlling one's body, that these practices of self-mortification were particularly relevant to female piety. Conditioned in part by patristic writers and other churchmen to have a low or negative opinion of their own bodies and female sexuality in general, as well as a belief in their own "natural" weakness or vulnerability to sin, many of the *mulieres sanctae* apparently felt that they needed to redouble their efforts to prove their worthiness to Christ. Through their ascetic practices of self-starvation, sleep deprivation, the wearing of haircloths, the avoidance of baths, and so forth, these pious women attempted to control their "unavoidable sexuality" by destroying their bodily needs and ridding themselves of the fearful sensations of lust or gluttony.

An interesting anecdote, which stresses the male celibate or monastic suspicion of female sexuality, the belief in women's greater tendency toward lust, and the subsequent need for women to discipline their bodies through the reduction of their allotment of food, can be found in the Irish ascetic reform traditions of the Monastery of Tallaght (late 8th and 9th c.). Here it is noted that "Molaise of Daimnis had a sister named Copar. Now desire lay heavy upon the girl, *for it is a third part as strong again in women as in men.*" In attempting to rid his sister of her preoccupation with lust, Molaise reduced her food allotment for one year. After Copar had completed her first year on the restricted diet, she came to her brother and "confessed that her desire still persisted." At this time Molaise was busy sewing: he therefore took his needle and thrust it three times into his sister's palm and three streams of blood flowed from her hand. It was no wonder, he observed, that it was hard for the body that had these strong currents of blood to contain itself. Molaise again reduced Copar's rations, but after a year had passed her desire had still not subsided. He therefore thrust the needle into her hand three times and three streams of blood flowed from it. And for a third time he restricted her annual food allotment. When at the end of that time, however, he thrust the needle into her hand, "not a drop of blood came out of her." He then told his sister that she should keep on this ration until her death.[118] This episode captures the ascetic reformers' view of women's lustful nature, which is described here as being a full one-third stronger than that of men. Moreover, since it required three attempts to adjust Copar's diet, the incident emphasizes the need for the adoption of extreme measures in food restriction to successfully rid women of desire or lust.

It is interesting that one of the ascetically beneficial side effects of heroic fasting was amenorrhea, or the absence or suppression of menstruation. Thus the ascetic practices of self-mortification and relentless fasting would provide these holy women with still another level of purification; for in suppressing menstruation, they further rid themselves of their "inherently polluting nature." This freedom from menstruation also allowed women to transcend their alleged sexual disabilites; to become "forgetful of their sex" and enter the ranks of honorary males. St. Jerome, for example, noted specifically in regard to post-menopausal women, "She who is no longer subject to the anxieties and pain of childbirth, she who has ceased to be a married woman with the cessation of the function of the menstrual blood, is freed from the curse of God."[119] Albertus Magnus, writing in the thirteenth century, observed the specific relationship between fasting and the practice of austerities with the cessation of menstruation among holy women. He commented that their health was apparently not compromised as a consequence of these practices.[120] Although our *vitae* are silent on this aspect of women's lives, some of the *mulieres sanctae* were no doubt also aware of the causal relationship between their exaggerated practices of self-mortification and at least the temporary stoppage of menstruation. This additional "benefit" could then have been one of the desired side effects which they actively sought in their pious exercise of austerities.

Fasting, heightened austerities, and practices of self-mortification were also used in a more personal and self-serving way by these *mulieres sanctae*. They appear in our sources as a type of oblique strategy adopted by some of these women to gain control over otherwise extremely difficult or even hopelessly impossible situations. As we have noted in our exploration of the heroics of virginity (chapter 3), these practices were frequently espoused by young women, especially during their adolescence, and were skillfully employed as an effective weapon against their parents or other authority figures. According to the *vitae*, such tactics seem to have been particularly efficient as deterrents to forced or unwanted marriages. Through the adoption of excessive fasting and vigils, a number of these young women were able to "disfigure their beauty" and encourage or bring about the onset of various diseases and "deformities"—thus becoming ineligible for marriage. Therefore, confronted with problems for which they saw neither hope of solution nor satisfactory escape, and limited by social structures which offered no other available or appropriate means of response, they turned to self-starvation, mortification, and other culturally approved practices of austerity. These provided a weapon with which to cope and a way to exercise control over their social environment. The public exploitation of their suffering and the afflictions brought about by fasting and the cultivation of illnesses gave these women an effective vehicle to manipulate their family or society. This strategy provided them with a means to achieve ends which they could not otherwise readily attain.[121]

For some, the use of fasting and other exaggerated austerities was only a temporary or short-term strategy. After the young women had attracted public attention—sympathy for their cause—and had made their statement or achieved their immediate ends, they returned to their accustomed way of life. They resumed their regular meals and sleeping practices. Others, however, in their early enthusiasm and strenuous pursuit of the *vita perfecta,* continued to follow strict regimens of fasting, sleep deprivation, and other austerities.

Although it is difficult to prove conclusively from our sources, it would appear, in general, that various combinations of these ascetic practices of self-mortification, such as excessive fasting, sleep deprivation, enclosure in a cell, and the wearing of haircloths, would have had an adverse effect on the health as well as longevity of these early female saints. In fact, according to the literature of the period, one of the specific purposes behind the adoption of these rigorous austerities was to hasten or encourage premature death among these "impatient angels" or holy women. For example, as noted by Aldhelm: "every day they (the virgins) eagerly long to depart from the prison of the body, transported from the adversity of this world; and *through the chariness of their abstemiousness they bring it about that they hasten as quickly as possible to the celestial homeland of Paradise."* [122] In this context our sources provide indirect evidence of the success of a number of the *mulieres sanctae* in actually achieving a shortened life span through consciously undermining their own health with their heroic exercises of self-mortification.

As mentioned, the author of the Life of St. Gertrude of Nivelles observed that by the time the saint was thirty she was worn out by fasting and want of sleep, and she died at the age of thirty-three.[123] St. Arthelais, a sixth-century Italian saint, who dedicated herself to prayer and fasted daily, except for Sundays, was said to have died of a fever at the age of sixteen.[124] St. Eusebia, second abbess of Hamay, assumed the leadership of her community at twelve years of age. According to some authors she died at the age of twenty-three; others claim she lived a decade or so longer.[125] St. Maura of Troyes practiced the virginal life at home and was known for her austerities and assistance to the Church. According to her contemporary Life she was said to have died at the age of twenty-three.[126] Hathumoda, the first abbess of Gandersheim, entered monasticism as a young child and followed a life of severe austerity. She died at the age of thirty-four. (It is interesting to note that in our sources, St. Hathumoda's mother, who had given birth to twelve children, is said to have lived to be 107 or 109.)[127] Edith, abbess of Wilton, who spent her entire life in the cloister, died at the early age of twenty-two or twenty-three years.[128] Other *vitae* note saints whose lives were significantly shortened as a result of their self-inflicted austerities, although these sources do not provide us with specific information as to their ages at death.

However, in contrast to this catalogue of saints who died at a rather early age, there are a number of *mulieres sanctae* who won reputations for their abstemious behavior and exercises of self-mortification and yet managed to live remarkably long lives. It is interesting to note that St. Jerome observed this rather amazing phenomenon in his description of the virgin Asella and her life of extreme austerities which began at the early age of twelve. He writes: "What would perhaps be incredible, were it not that 'with God all things are possible,' is that she lived this life until her fiftieth year without weakening her digestion or bringing on herself the pain of colic."[129] In this context, recent scientific studies on aging have argued that the "secret elixir" for longevity consists of fasting or caloric restriction and sexual abstinence: "eating very little food, maybe to the point you would say was starving. And postponing sex or avoiding it altogether." They maintain that "having less access to food resets the mechanism so that the body can get by with less energy"; also, with this ascetic program a major shift occurs "from a growth and reproduction strategy to a survival strategy."[130] Thus this "modern formula," which some scientists believe has the potential to slow the aging process and increase life spans possibly past 150 years, in fact closely resembles the *vita perfecta* or the lifestyle adopted by many of the early medieval saints. Therefore, it appears that perhaps for some of these women saints, the regimen of rigorous fasting and other austerities, sexual abstinence, and/or the adoption of the eremitic life did not undermine their health or substantially shorten their lives, as they had hoped; rather, these practices seem to have had a somewhat beneficial effect on their health and actually encouraged longevity. (In this context we find many male hermit saints who lived to be octogenarians and nonagenarians, with a few living beyond one hundred years.) Although in some cases we might not know the exact age at death of some of our *mulieres sanctae*, according to contemporary observations they were perceived as advanced in years or "old." For example, St. Genovefa, who was known for her extremely austere diet, was believed to have been approximately eighty years of age when she died.[131] Despite all of her austerities, St. Radegund was in her sixties at the time of her death.[132] St. Eustadiola, who practiced an ascetic life and did not eat meat for some seventy years, died at ninety years of age.[133] St. Balda, abbess of Jouarre, died at one hundred years of age, and St. Bertilla, abbess of Chelles, governed her community for some forty-six years.[134] St. Rusticula died at approximately seventy-seven years of age.[135] St. Pharailde, virgin and patron of Gand, spent her life macerating her body through the practice of extreme fasting and vigils. She was said to have died at the ripe old age of ninety.[136] The *vita* of St. Leoba describes her as "an old woman . . . decrepit through age." [137] Or, despite her "incredible abstinence," St. Margaret of Scotland lived to be forty-seven years old.[138]

We therefore find in this limited survey of the celestial gynaeceum an admixture of the old and young. The rather impressive average life span of male and female saints (57.6 years for females and 65.1 for males) does not by any stretch of the imagination reflect the average longevity of their non-haloed contemporaries. For as we have noted, sanctity was in part a function of longevity—it was based on one's visibility and reputation and therefore, in general, the longer one lived, the better one's chances were for the magnification of one's virtues and recognition of sainthood. However, it is interesting to speculate on the discrepancy in ages between male and female saints. Although our statistics are rough and limited, female saints in general seemed to die approximately seven and one-half years before their male contemporaries, with abbesses or nuns dying some fourteen years before their brothers in the cloisters. This discrepancy in longevity between male and female monastic saints is a particularly fascinating problem, for one might expect a certain equivalency or symmetry in the life expectancies between these closely related groups.

One explanation for this disparity might rest in the different gender-based expressions of the cultural ideals of holiness and sainthood. As we have noted, although both male and female saints were expected to follow a life of austerity which included fasting, vigils, and other exercises of self-mortification, at least the expression of this ideal seems to have been much more common, as well as more exaggerated, among the female saints. Moreover, since females have substantially higher dietary requirements of iron, calcium, etc. than males, the results of these regimens of fasting, compounded in some cases by their already sorely deficient diets, would seem likely to be much more detrimental to women than to men. Having fewer options for an active participation within the hierarchy of the Church (and being influenced, as well, by the cultural emphasis on the locus of sin within the female body), these women perhaps chose to focus more of their energy on their holy regimens of fasting and self-mortification than did their male cohorts. Because this practice did not depend on external resources or position, but rather simply on the pious commitment of their own minds and bodies, it was a readily available means or instrument of piety. They could carry out their austerities privately and independently, with a minimum of exterior interference. Thus as we have noted, through what appears to have been long periods of excessive fasting and extreme asceticism, some of these pious women cultivated illness and early death. The cumulative effect of these practices, however, seems to have been especially damaging to those who entered monastic life as very young children. Frequently embracing with excessive enthusiasm a program of self-mortification at the age of twelve or thirteen, by their mid-twenties or early thirties a number of these women appear to have been completely worn out or wasted by their austerities. In their weakened conditions, also perhaps suffering from anemia, they would then have been at especially high risk of pneumonia, bronchitis, tuberculosis, emphysema, and other diseases. In this context it is interesting to note that in a significant number of cases there appears to be a rather notable difference in age at death between, for example, daughters who entered monastic life at an early age and immediately adopted a strict regimen of austerities, and their mothers, who as founders of the community had espoused religion as a "second career" and followed a more sensible or moderate path.

It is also possible that this apparent gender-based discrepancy in longevity between abbesses and abbots, nuns and monks, could be related to the very real poverty and food shortages which some of these women's monasteries seem to have experienced during this early period. And as we have noted, in a number of these cases these problems were further exacerbated by the ideals of charity and hospitality, and the profligate behavior of their saintly abbesses. Furthermore, there was a general belief that women religious required substantially less food than their brothers in the monasteries: this assumption was reflected, for example, in the daily rations for the nuns.[139]

Another potential explanation for the disparity in age between abbot and abbess saints might be based on a difference in the cultural perception or valuation of older people, predicated on gender, during this period. It is possible (as is perhaps the case in more modern ages) that there was a greater societal appreciation attached to older men than to women. For example, the experience, wisdom, and holiness of the aged abbot or bishop might have made him appear particularly attractive or venerable and thus worthy of election to sainthood; while the stereotypic image of the aged abbess might not have had a similar appeal to the faithful or to her community. Thus, perhaps based on this difference in social peception, we might find fewer elderly women singled out as saints in comparison to their male cohorts. A number of saints' Lives and other sources of the period, however, appear to undermine this possibility. Rather than disparaging older women, they seem to value the impressive wisdom and experience of abbesses in their later years and respect their dispensing of advice. They praise the continued involvement of these older women in political negotiations, their patronage to the Church, as well as their cultivation of alliances and friendships.[140] Thus it appears from our sources that longevity was clearly valued in the selection of both male and female saints: it was seen as providing yet another sign of the extraordinary or miraculous character of the saint's holy life.

On the whole, the *mulieres sanctae* could look forward to a longer life span than could their "nonhaloed" sisters. Although by no means do we find octogenarians and nonagenarians monopolizing the membership of the celestial city, it does have something of the appearance of a gerontocracy. Indeed, despite the efforts of some of these "impatient angels" to shorten their life spans through the practice of rigorous fasting, severe asceticism, and self-mortification, considerably more than one might expect seemed to enjoy an extraordinary longevity.

The Celestial Gynaeceum

When studying Women's History, it is tempting to look for a "golden age," or "bon vieux temps," when there was a certain symmetry in men's and women's experience or when women enjoyed a "rough and ready equality" with men.[1] As noted by Olwen Hufton, after apparently failing to "find" or "locate" this elusive age in either the modern industrial world or early modern European society, scholars have begun to look to the Middle Ages.[2] However, as Judith Bennett has argued persuasively in her study *Women in the Medieval English Countryside: Gender and Household in Brigstock before the Plague,* in spite of "this appealing image of a golden age" or favorable judgments about the status of medieval women, in reality a "bon vieux temps" cannot to be found in the medieval countryside.[3]

In my assessment of women's status in early medieval society and the Church—based on the popular selection of women saints—I have not been immune to the temptation of singling out a few of these early centuries as a "relative golden age." Motivated essentially by pragmatic considerations, the early medieval period seemed to encourage more fluid or flexible roles for the sexes, a certain symmetry in male and female experience, and an atmosphere in which the distinctions of gender were somewhat blurred. The route to fame for these early would-be saints was closely tied to the weak, fledgling churches of the period and to the strong position of royal and aristocratic women within the family. Such women therefore assumed primary roles as generous patrons and founding abbesses of early monasteries and churches in the recently converted regions of the north of Europe.[4] From our rough statistics on women saints, as well as those related to the founding of women's monasteries, the seventh and eighth centuries in France and Anglo-Saxon England and the first half of the tenth century in England and Germany, then, emerge as rather positive or inclusive eras. They provided new and expanded opportunities for noblewomen, as well as a genuine appreciation of their contributions to society and the Church. Nevertheless, this rather favorable judgment needs to be qualified.

At the outset it is necessary to reiterate that this route to fame or recognition was open only to women of extraordinary power, privilege, and wealth—essentially aristocratic and royal women. Therefore, there is a strong class bias in the sources as well as in the acceptable routes by which a person could achieve the visibility which might lead to sanctity during this early period. (In contrast, with the later Middle Ages one witnesses a growing democratization of sanctity, with many of the saints drawn from the urban middle class.)

Moreover, if we focus solely on women saints and their access to *fama sanctitatis*—without making any comparisons to male saints— these rough statistics indicate a relatively bright era in these early centuries of the Church. These figures appear perhaps especially impressive in comparison to the "nadirs" experienced during this six-hundred-year period by the *mulieres sanctae,* occurring, in part, as a result of the various reform movements which curtailed opportunities for women and denied them avenues of recognition through the Church. However, what is of primary importance is that, when compared to the "norm" for male saints, none of these so-called golden ages appears to have been remarkably bright or promising for women. Thus, in assessing these rough statistics in a comparative manner based on gender, an average of approximately 15 percent women saints—with a comprehensive high for one fifty-year period of only 23.5 percent—is not overly impressive. These figures do not suggest— by any stretch of the imagination—a symmetry or an egalitarianism among the members of the celestial city or the earthly religious community. For throughout this entire period, there was, in effect, an essential difference in access to power, positions of leadership in the ecclesiastical hierarchy, and the concomitant opportunities for recognition and sanctity in the Church, based on gender. Thus from ca. 500 to ca. 1100 there was a definite gender-based asymmetry in the selection of saints, which became more exaggerated during certain eras than during others. In sum, throughout this entire period women were noticeably underrepresented in their membership in the celestial city.

On one level the disproportionate numbers of male and female saints are not surprising or unexpected. Despite religious claims of a spiritual egalitarianism in "life beyond the grave," there was a definite tendency to organize the celestial realm according to the customs and values of earthly society. Membership in the heavenly kingdom, and specifically the celestial gynaeceum, reflected the values of the hierarchically ordered and gender-based religious and secular society of the

Middle Ages. Celestial prominence clearly had a "this-worldly" or terrestrial base. Therefore, in order for women to establish impressive
credentials—to build up their spiritual dossiers and achieve a visibility
which could lead to recognition of sanctity—it was necessary for them
to be provided with opportunities or roles in society which would lend
them this prominence, recognition, and power. There also had to be
a certain tolerance toward women; a favorable atmosphere which
encouraged, appreciated, and valued women's active participation in
society and the Church. And as we have noted, certain periods and
geographic regions seem to have been more forthcoming than others
in the encouragement of women's causes and potential, and the subsequent making of women saints. However, throughout this whole period women were denied many of the opportunities available to men,
and thus invariably it was much more difficult for women than for
men to enter the ranks of the spiritual elite in the celestial hierarchy.

Although underrepresented numerically, these *mulieres sanctae*
seem to have played a disproportionately important role in the lives of
women in the medieval world. While the clientele of saints was not
gender-specific—that is, women and men appealed to both female and
male saints—women saints seemed to be especially dedicated to serving the needs of "their" nuns as well as those of local women. As
noted by Barbara Newman, they provided women with "a trusted authority of their own sex," who had their special interests in mind, and
who understood and sympathized with their problems or illnesses,
many of which were gender-based.[5]

We therefore find in a number of our sources this special concern of
the *mulieres sanctae* for the welfare of women. In St. Radegund's "Letter of Foundation," for example, she expressed her need to assist other
members of her sex: "I asked myself, with all the ardour of which I am
capable, how I could best forward the cause of other women, and
how, if our Lord so willed, my own personal desires might be of advantage to my sisters. Here in the town of Poitiers I founded a convent
for nuns."[6] In this letter Radegund also asked that she be buried in the
new church which she had begun to build in honor of the Blessed
Mary "with the nuns of my own community all around me."[7] The
continuity of her powerful patronage and great concern for her foundation of Ste-Croix can be seen in Gregory of Tours's description of
her death and funeral in which he noted that he would not have stopped
weeping if he had not realized "that the blessed Radegund had
departed from her convent *in body but not in power*, and that she had
been taken from the world and placed in heaven."[8] Thus, because she
was a special friend of God and now an inhabitant of both worlds, her
body and relics would provide continued access for her community

and the faithful of the region to sacred power. As noted by Thomas Head, "They [relics] were literally 'pledges' (*pignora* in Latin) of the continued presence and patronage of the saint."[9] Thus in Radegund's *vitae*, as well as in those of a number of other female saints, we find a major emphasis on the saint's special affection toward, concern for, and sympathetic treatment of, women, both in the acts she accomplished while still alive, and in her posthumous miracles. For example, out of a total of some twenty miracles described in Radegund's *vitae*, fourteen concern female principals.[10] The special attraction of Radegund and her *virtus* (power, efficacy) in regard to women can be noted in the following incident related by Baudonivia. On the eve of the feast of St. Hilary, the abbot and monks of Radegund's basilica were keeping vigil at the church of St. Hilary in Poitiers. However, their offices were disturbed throughout the night by the loud cries of a number of people possessed by demons. Among these were two women, one of whom roared so violently that the whole basilica shook. When the abbot and his monks returned to Radegund's basilica to complete the office, these two women accompanied them. After they reached the church they prayed that Radegund would spare them, and before the night was over both were freed of their possession. While Baudonivia notes that Sts. Radegund and Hilary were equal in grace and in virtue, this particular example shows that through Radegund's special intercessory power these women had been restored to health, while they had not received a similar cure by St. Hilary at his own feast.[11] Belief in St. Radegund's special concern for members of her own sex and her attraction as an interceder for women has continued to recent times. As noted by René Aigrain, in 1871 the women of Poitiers addressed themselves to their patron saint in order to ward off or avert a Prussian invasion of the city. They dedicated a Mass each Easter Monday in recognition of the fulfillment of their prayers. During World War I Radegund was looked to as the "Mère de la patrie," and crowds of pilgrims came to her tomb to pray for their country.[12]

Other *vitae* of women saints stress the special concern the *mulieres sanctae* expressed for members of their own sex, especially in their bestowing of miraculous cures. As we have noted, of the twenty healing miracles which took place at the tomb of St. Anstrude, abbess of the monastery of St. John of Laon, all concerned women, with eleven of the beneficiaries nuns.[13] The recipients of miracles attributed to St. Austreberta of the monastery of Pavilly included twenty-one women and four men.[14] One of the miracles described in the Life of St. Austreberta relates how she rescued a woman who had thrown herself into a river to preserve herself from rape. Thus this virgin saint appears to have been a special patron saint of victims of sexual assault. Another of Austreberta's miracles describes how she cured a woman (who had formerly been the saint's friend) of breast cancer.[15] Other *mulieres sanctae* also specialized in female health problems such as infertility, childbirth and difficult labors, breast problems, excessive or prolonged menstrual flow, crippling arthritis of the hands, blindness of women, and female possession by demons.

The *vita* of St. Wiborada notes this saint's particular relevance for a female constituency. "When it is spoken in German her name sings out 'Counsel of Women.' . . . Praise-worthy, I say is the name of Blessed Wiborada, because with Martha in carrying on the active life and with Mary the contemplative, to all those men and women who are living pious lives, she has shown forth in herself the counsel of achieving perfection in both choices." [16]

Women saints were, then, intended to provide *exempla*, models of "women worthies," for the "admiration," "wonderment," edification, and emulation of the faithful (*forma fidelium*). One of the purposes of saints' Lives was to "provoke" or "shock" women and men into reforming their lives and adopting certain approved behavioral modes.[17] As didactic literature, the *vitae* reflect the changing attitudes, the moral values, and the ideals of the male-ordered Church and society. The *vitae* frequently provided cultural symbols of gendered images. Many of the exempla of women saints were, then, imprinted or inscribed with the ecclesiastical or patriarchal morality of the period. In some cases the *mulieres sanctae* were "regendered": they assumed, for example, a masculine appearance or disguise. Living as monks or hermits they approached the ideal of the "manly" life. It was, however, as virgins and other heroic women, who were seen as honorary males, that they were praised for their virile strength and behavior—for acting in a manner that was "forgetful of their sex." (It seems in retrospect that this strong, independent behavior was especially attractive and nonthreatening to churchmen when it was attributed to women of the "distant" past, of the early Christian Church—safe/dead female saints rather than contemporary female religious.)

While the Church attempted to promote rather restrictive models of saints as virgins and mothers, these cultural symbols did not have a fixed or intrinsic meaning, but instead they embodied "multivalent meanings." [18] They could therefore be used or "read" in a variety of ways by their female audiences. Also underlying many of the *vitae* was the rather subtle message or understanding of the necessary distinction between *admiranda* and *imitanda* of saints' acts. This distinction was particularly relevant in regard to extreme or extravagant modes of female behavior which might have been encouraged under certain specific circumstances but were generally viewed as transgressing the boundaries of permissible diversity.[19] Thus in some cases the "alternate reading" or adaptation of the saints' extraordinary behavior to one's own special circumstances was not at all that which had been originally intended by the male redactors. These saints' Lives could then be appropriated by women for their own purposes and refashioned as positive models or vehicles of empowerment.[20] In their obvious lack of control over these pious symbols and their meanings, and their unsuccessful attempts to eliminate these "alternate readings," churchmen warned women of the dangers inherent in their independent interpretations or adaptations of the Lives of the *mulieres sanctae*. They also frequently reproved them for their misunderstood piety or misconstrued religious enthusiasm.

On the other hand, if we look at the "underside" or subplots of many of the *vitae* of male saints, we can find women purposefully funneled into extreme behaviors. This was a means of understanding them as the dangerous "other" who must be marginalized and contained. Thus a recurrent theme in the *vitae* was the denunciation of women through the portrayal of negative role models. These notorious female figures who made their appearance in male saints' lives (in contrast to those who won the approval of the church hierarchy and were celebrated for their saintly behavior) also self-consciously defined their own lives and realities, but in an unconventional, "morally corrupt" manner, according to the hagiographers. Many of these exempla are described in highly unfavorable, rather frightening terms, particularly in the *vitae* of male hermit or monastic saints. These women were seen (from the celibate male perspective) as exercising profoundly invasive and disturbing roles. Also acting in a manner "forgetful of their sex," but now relegated to the margins or fringes of society or outside of the law, these females had the audacity to challenge the patriarchal order of the Church. They were viewed as extremely threatening and deviant in their behavior, introducing disorder and sexual distraction. Women, for example, who cut off their hair and adopted male dress were seen as committing outrages to the decencies of nature and breaking the laws of God and man. They disrupted the ordered scheme; they defied the prevailing notions of sexual difference (which was highly encoded in clothing and hairstyle). Their defiance of male authority appears to have been particularly threatening to churchmen during periods of reform, when sexual difference became heightened, to the accompaniment of a growing concern with maintaining proper male and female roles. These women were, then, frequently portrayed as "testing" unpopular male policies which were often exclusionary to women—for example, defying proscriptions of sacred space or assuming priestly roles in dispensing the eucharist. They were seen as encroaching on male territory, threatening male power, and they set a decidedly dangerous precedent for other women. Described as aggressive, brazen, shameless, impudent, and deviant, these daring women were invariably chastised, according to the *vitae,* for their improper or scandalous behavior by horrible punishments meted out by the "wronged" or angered male saints. These stories, then, provided cautionary examples with the intent to deter other women who might be tempted to adopt similar strategies of defiance. They also warned churchmen in particular of the pernicious nature of women as *impedimenta,* or threats to celibacy and salvation. Churchmen must remain forever alert to these destructive tendencies viewed as innate to members of the opposite sex.

Recognition of sanctity, as we have noted, was frequently predicated on extreme or extravagant behavior. In order to be noticed, to win recognition or *fama sanctitatis,* one needed to act in a fashion "out of the ordinary," which sometimes approached, even stretched or transcended, the limits of "socially acceptable" behavior. Thus, within the context of the cultural relativity of sanctity, extravagant acts, accomplished under certain circumstances, might be viewed as most praiseworthy, holy, or saintly, while under other conditions or at other times (for example, during periods of reform when the Church became increasingly powerful and less tolerant, and attempted to curtail women's roles), the same or similar behavior might be condemned as aberrant. Therefore it seems that at times, only a fine line separated the holy from the abhorrent in the acts of these notably intrepid, independent-minded women, who, through the aggressive, self-conscious adoption of certain modes of behavior, might either be elevated to sainthood or denounced for their injudicious, ill-advised, or "deviant" acts.

In this collective study we have looked at the lives of over two thousand female and male saints. And using this information we have attempted to explore a few of the different ways in which women were able to gain status in society and win popular recognition of sainthood. Within this context we have examined how the patriarchal sexual ideologies, as articulated by the Church, affected women's lives. At the same time we have also looked at how these uncommon women self-consciously defined or articulated their own lives or realities in relation to the changing ideologies, values, and social conditions of the period.

The *vitae* of saints, then, offer us an extraordinary glimpse of the past. For our period, which is often frustratingly silent about women, the *vitae* are remarkable for their particularly strong interest in women's lives and experiences—for the wealth of information they provide in regard to this elite membership of the celestial gynaeceum. For some aspects of medieval life, the *vitae* provide us with marvelous details not found in any other sources of the period. They are especially rich for their insights into the private lives of medieval women and men, affective ties within the family, friendship, and the collective psychology or mentalities of the period.

The *vitae* are like a medieval *speculum*, or condensing lens, reflecting or magnifying (not without flaws or distortions) some of the ideals and values, as well as the "realities" or practices, of the age. However, we need to be continually alert to the limitations and problems of our sources—to recognize both the literary character and the strong propaganda component of the *vitae*. We also need to be reminded that our sources are only indirect indexes of the period; we cannot move automatically from the realm of the ideal, from theoretical or prescriptive literature, to actual practice or historical experience. The realities or common experiences of ordinary women's lives do not necessarily conform to what we might expect from a reading of the *vitae*.[21]

The collective use of saints' Lives over the *longue durée* (i.e., a six-hundred-year period) provides us with enough information to study a number of patterns of change over these early centuries. We can note shifts in beliefs, attitudes, ideals, and contexts. In some cases the Lives themselves are adapted, refashioned, or "renegotiated" over time to serve the special interests and changing needs of the churches or monasteries which "possessed" the saints' relics. Information described in the *vitae* can frequently be corroborated or strengthened by evidence from other sources of the period, such as chronicles, canons of church councils, penitentials, letters, archaeological evidence, etc. And within this broader context seemingly incredible episodes, or what previously had been dismissed as unbelievable *topoi*, now become more readily understood.

Many of our saints' Lives were originally written some one thousand to fifteen hundred years ago. They reflect the ideals of this early society as well as the special needs, occasions, interests, and challenges of the communities responsible for redacting and "refashioning" the *vitae*. This tradition of sanctity has been extremely long-lived. The continued usefulness and durability of the early medieval Lives and female *exempla*, as well as their timeless quality in regard to capturing the imagination of the faithful, can be seen in the repeated copying and the preservation of these *vitae* over the centuries. These Lives were also translated into the vernacular and into verse. In some cases they have survived in multiple copies. Many of the Lives, in shortened forms, came to be incorporated in popular anthologies, for example, Aldhelm's *De virginitate* (ca. 675–709/710), Christine de Pizan's *Book of the City of Ladies* (1404), or *The Lives of Women Saints of Our Contrie of England* (ca. 1610–1615).[22] The especially dramatic events of the saints' lives have also been vividly captured in various major art forms across the centuries—in manuscript illumination, painting, sculpture, embroidery, tapestry, stained glass, and so forth.

The long-lived interest in saints and their lives, the tradition of the making of saints, the search for the "reputation for holiness" and saintly miracles, all these have continued, very little changed, into our modern world. In fact, within the past decade or so there has been a resurgence of interest in this whole area of popular religion and church history. There has been a proliferation of scholarly and popular books which focus on individual saints, local cults of saints and relics, the concept of sainthood (within Catholicism and in the world religions), the psychology of sanctity (e.g., "holy anorexia"), and canonization and the making of saints, as well as new translations of saints' Lives and collections or catalogues of saints.

Moreover, despite an extremely crowded Roman Catholic calendar in which each day is "shared" by several saints, new candidates for sainthood continue to be nominated and processed, and record numbers of new saints are being "made." During the papacy of John Paul II, the Vatican's saint-making machinery—i.e, the Congregation for the Causes of Saints (which prepares official biographies for the candidates for sainthood), the panel of nine theologians, and the cardinals of the Congregation (who pass judgment on the merits of the case)—have been extraordinarily busy. According to Kenneth L. Woodward's study *Making Saints,* Pope John Paul II has already "made" more saints than all of his twentieth-century predecessors combined. During his first ten years in office, he was responsible for promoting 23 canonizations and 123 beatifications. These base figures, however, include a number of group causes, for example, 118 Vietnamese martyrs who were canonized as a single unit. Thus up to 1989, the pope had directed a total of more than 254 individual canonizations and 305 beatifications.[23] These numbers, furthermore, continue to grow at a rapid rate, and as of January, 1995, this total had increased to 268 canonizations and 606 beatifications.[24] Apparently behind this sharp increase in the making of saints rests the hope that heroic virtues and devout role models can be used to strengthen or reinforce the Catholic faith. The pope has been criticized for the large number of new saints he has made and the speed of their promotion, as well as the quality of some of the newly elected members of the celestial hierarchy. Journalists have referred to the Vatican as the "saint-machine," or the "saint factory," as the Italian newspapers call it; and a *Los Angeles Times* article described this flurry of activity as "a holy rampage, a beatific binge."[25] The pope's enthusiasm for the making of saints underscores the continuing importance of this early institution to the Vatican and the Church. However, in comparison to the informal early medieval process of popular recognition of sanctity, this procedure has become heavily formalized, bureaucratic, patriarchal, and frequently politically charged and prohibitively expensive. In determining the reputation of the would-be saint, the authorities check the spiritual dossier and look for heroic virtues, particularly martyrdom, virginity, selfless lives of charity, care for the indigent, extraordinary suffering, etc.; they also attempt to further verify the candidate's sanctity through the "authentication" of posthumous miracles. Martyrdom or one posthumous miracle is required for beatification (i.e., declaration of the title "blessed," a type of local, less than full recognition of sanctity, and sometimes a first step toward canonization); two miracles are required for canonization, in which case the saint is honored and invoked by the universal Catholic church.[26]

In light of the long tradition of sainthood and the making of saints, it is interesting to keep a close watch over this process, and to continue our "nimbus count" according to gender. How many of the new candidates, for example, are women? Are they members of the laity or are they women religious? What kinds of virtues or roles provided them with a visibility for sainthood: the safe, conventional, negative virtues of patience, subservience, long-suffering acts, or more independent, public, aggressive, positive contributions and virtues? For example, among those beatified in 1994, who were to serve as "rallying symbols" for the Church and role models for women, there are a number of laywomen; they include an Italian mother, abandoned by her husband but praised for keeping her family together, and an Italian pediatrician who died after refusing to have an operation which might have saved her own life but would have killed her unborn child.[27]

Another issue to consider when examining the making of contemporary saints and proofs for sanctity is how many of the female (as compared to the male) candidates will be judged as falling a little short of "exceptional holiness" or as weak on "major miracles" and therefore will have to settle for beatification, and how many will actually win full recognition of sanctity and be canonized?[28] A certain continuity can be found, for example, in the inequitable evaluation of miracles based on gender: those performed by women saints, that is "female miracles," in general, have been viewed by churchmen as less impressive or inferior to "male miracles." This basic difference was already expressed in early Ireland, where, as Lisa Bitel has noted,

St. Ailbe (d. ca. 541) was said to have been told by an angel that miracles of women saints were in fact *minima miracula* in comparison to those of male saints.[29]

Thus, despite all of these years, sanctity and the models of saintly behavior (in many cases based on early Christian and medieval exempla of martyrdom) are still thriving. Although the original context has long since disappeared, the heroics of virginity, for example, continue to exert a certain powerful influence in modern times. And while women in the twentieth century have perhaps not followed the models of the medieval virgin martyrs to the letter, there is a fascinating resemblance in some of their responses when they are faced with similar threats of sexual assault. In *Against Our Will: Men, Women and Rape*, Susan Brownmiller notes, for example, that during World War II, thousands of women were raped by the invading armies and, as a result, there emerged another generation of virgin martyrs. According to Brownmiller, "Some women of Berlin committed suicide, either in fear of rape or in shame after the act." A suicide poem appeared in an American Jewish magazine in 1943, "supposedly the last testament from ninety-three girls of the Beth Jakob Seminary in Krakow who took their own lives after being informed that the Nazis intended to turn their seminary into a brothel." Other instances of calculated avoidance of sexual assault bear an uncanny resemblance to that of the medieval saints: "Some avoided assault by making themselves appear diseased or as unattractive as possible with the aid of coal dust, iodine and bandages." One woman avoided being raped by claiming that she had tuberculosis.[30] It is unnerving to note that despite the more than one thousand years which separate these responses, there remains an essential sameness in some of the "successful" defenses against sexual assault. We can also see, in this continuity in strategies, the negative forms that female self-assertion could assume when constrained and determined by patriarchal sexual ideology.[31] (Moreover, these examples continue to promote the basic belief that rape is a crime of passion and lust rather than an act of violence against women.)

It should be mentioned that one of the most popular twentieth-century female saints is St. Maria Goretti. She was a poor, young Italian girl, who, in 1902, at approximately twelve years of age, died a violent death while attempting to resist sexual assault. Beatified by Pope Pius XII in 1947, three years later she was canonized by the same pope in the piazza of St. Peter's before the largest crowd ever assembled for a canonization. In his address on the beatification of Maria Goretti in 1947, the pope resorted to historical or hagiographic precedent and presented the saint as a "new St. Agnes." Moreover, he took this opportunity to "call down woe on the corrupters of chastity in press and theatre and cinema and fashion-studio." [32]

It is interesting to note that as recently as the 1960s, in some American Catholic high schools for girls, the life and martyrdom of Maria Goretti was utilized with the intention of instilling fear and values and molding appropriate behavior. Each year, before the prom, these high school girls would be subjected to a tape which recorded in high drama the details of the attempted rape, the saint's successful defense of her virginity, and her martyrdom. These students were also provided with a popular comic-book version of this story. This exemplum of the virgin martyr Maria Goretti was then used on a popular practical level to warn these high school students not to wear "seductive" dresses to the prom—i.e., to avoid the popular spaghetti-strapped formals, to say nothing of low-cut or strapless dresses! On a deeper level, it attempted to instill or exacerbate a fear in these young girls in regard to their sexuality and especially their virginity; it also showed them the necessary extremes which might be required in the "dangerous" association with members of the opposite sex. However, the underlying message was that surviving rape was not a desirable thing: clearly, the admirable route was to die in defending one's virginity. [33]

In a similar tradition, I was told about an incident which occurred in the 1950s in a New York Catholic grade school. At this time, when an imminent attack or takeover by the Russians was feared, these grade school girls were apparently warned that among the atrocities that would be committed by the new-age "barbarian" invaders would be to attack the schools and rape the young female students. They were therefore provided by their nuns with the very "useful" example of disfiguring their faces by scratching or lacerating them with their fingernails. [34] And one of my colleagues related to me that during the 1960s, at Queen of Martyrs Catholic School in Buffalo, New York, she and her classmates were also told by nuns to disfigure their faces in the event that the Russians invaded. To accomplish this they were to use pencils or other school supplies from their pencil cases. [35] By resorting to these strategies (again straight out of the medieval tradition of turning violence upon themselves, of *virginitas deformitate defensa*), these young girls would be able to protect their virginity and avoid being raped.

These "modern" cases thus stress the incredibly long and persistent tradition of the ideal of *integritas* and the heroics of virginity. These strategies of virginal defense as negative, destructive forms of self-assertion, turning violence upon themselves—acts of desperation and strength, worthy of our admiration as well as abhorrence—bear a disturbing resemblance to those adopted by our early medieval saints. These extravagant acts of women saints as "transgressors"—to be admired, to inspire us, if not to be actually imitated—were, as noted by Elizabeth Petroff, "both attractive and repellent, pointlessly mad and unshakeably sane at the same time." [36] In providing exempla for future generations of women, the medieval hagiographers or chroniclers no doubt realized that the commitment to put into practice the ideals of heroic virginity would continually be tested by the recurring disorders and violence of society. It is, then, in this context that Matthew of Paris described the "useful" example provided by St. Ebba and her nuns of Coldingham. In singling out St. Ebba, he praised her as "that abbess of admirable courage, openly giving to all the sisters an example of chastity which should be profitable not only to those nuns, but which would be worthy of being followed by all succeeding virgins, and by all who should at any time exist." [37]

Abbreviations

AASS	*Acta Sanctorum.* Ed. Joannes Bollandus et al. Nov. ed. J. Carnandet et al. 64 vols. Paris, 1863–present.
AASS B	*Acta Sanctorum Belgii Selecta.* 6 vols. Ed. Jos. Ghesquierus. Brussels, 1783–94.
AASS OSB	*Acta sanctorum ordinis S. Benedicti.* 9 vols. Ed. L. d'Achéry and J. Mabillon. Paris, 1668–1701.
AB	*Analecta Bollandiana.* Société des Bollandistes, Brussels. 1882–present.
ACW	*Ancient Christian Writers.* Westminster, Md., 1946–present.
BHL	*Bibliotheca hagiographica latina: Antiquae et mediae aetatis.* 2 vols. Brussels, 1898–1901. Supplement, 1911.
BS	*Bibliotheca Sanctorum.* 12 vols. Rome, 1961–69.
Butler	Alan Butler. *Butler's Lives of the Saints.* 4 vols. Ed. and rev. Herbert Thurston and Donald Attwater. New York, 1956.
DACL	*Dictionnaire d'archéologie chrétienne et de liturgie.* 15 vols. Ed. Fernand Cabrol and Henri Leclerq. Paris, 1907–53.
DHGE	*Dictionnaire d'histoire et de géographie ecclésiastiques.* 17 vols. Ed. Alfred Baudrillart et al. Paris, 1912–present.
Dict. Sp.	*Dictionnaire de Spiritualité.* Ed. M. Viller et al. 1937–present.
DSW	Agnes B. C. Dunbar. *A Dictionary of Saintly Women.* 2 vols. London, 1904–5.
FC	*Fathers of the Church.* Washington, D.C.
MGH	*Monumenta Germaniae Historica.* Ed. G. H. Pertz et al. Berlin, Hannover, and Leipzig, 1826–present.
MGH AA	*MGH, Auctores antiquissimi.*

MGH EPP	*MGH, Epistolae.*
MGH LEG I–IV	*MGH, Legum.* Sections I–IV.
MGH SRM	*MGH, Scriptores rerum merovingicarum.*
MGH SS	*MGH, Scriptores.*
NPNF	*A Select Library of Nicene and Post-Nicene Fathers of the Christian Church.*
ODS	*The Oxford Dictionary of Saints.* Ed. David Hugh Farmer. Oxford, 1982.
PB	*Les Petits Bollandistes vies des saints.* 7th ed. 14 vols. Ed. Paul Guérin. Paris, 1876.
PL	*Patrologiae cursus completus, Series latina.* 221 vols. Ed. J.-P. Migne. Paris, 1844–64.
SC	*Sources Chrétiennes.* Paris, 1943–present.
SWDA	*Sainted Women of the Dark Ages.* Ed. and trans. Jo Ann McNamara and John E. Halborg with E. Gordon Whatley. Durham and London, 1992.
VSB	*Vies des saints et des bienheureux. Les RR. PP. Bénédictins de Paris.* 13 vols. Paris, 1935–59.

𝒩otes

INTRODUCTION

1. Jerome, "Letter CVIII," *St. Jerome's Letters and Works, NPNF,* 2d series, vol. 6 (New York, 1893), ch. 14, p. 202 (emphasis mine); "CVIII. Epitaphium Sanctae Paulae," in *Saint Jérôme, Lettres (Collection des Universités de France),* ed. and trans. Jérôme Labourt (Paris, 1955), vol. 5, ch. 14, p. 176. The Life of Melania the Younger also notes that when she visited "the Cells" of Nitria, "the fathers of the most holy men there received the saint as if she were a man. The truth, she had been detached from the female nature and had acquired a masculine disposition, or rather, a heavenly one." Elizabeth A. Clark, trans., *The Life of Melania the Younger: Studies in Women and Religion,* vol. 14 (New York and Toronto, 1984), pp. 53–54.

2. Gregory of Tours, *Life of the Fathers,* Translated Texts for Historians, Latin Series I, trans. Edward James (Liverpool, 1985), ch. 19, p. 124. Palladius also notes the special strength of women in his *Lausiac History:* "I must also commemorate in this book the courageous women ['manly women'] to whom God granted struggles equal to those of men, so that no one could plead as an excuse that women are too weak to practice virtue successfully" (Palladius, *The Lausiac History,* trans. Robert J. Meyer. [*ACW* 34] [Westminster, 1965], ch. 41, p. 117). A number of other saints' Lives of this early period emphasize that these women transcended the weakness of their sex and acted in a virile manner rather than as women. See, for example, the *vita* of St. Austreberta, which notes: "She thought her time for martyrdom had come. Proving that the heart in her breast was in no way feminine but virile, she drew the finely woven veil she wore on her head smoothly about her throat, extended her hands and bowed her head to expose her neck to the blow. And, as they tell it, he [Amalbert] stood astounded and immobile, admiring such fortitude in a woman as he had never seen in a man" (*SWDA,* p. 313). For this topic of the virile woman in early Christianity, see also Kerstin Aspegren's *The Male Woman: A Feminine Ideal in the Early Church,* Acta Universitatis Upsaliensis, Upsala Women's Studies: A. Women in Religion, 4, ed. René Kieffer (Uppsala, 1990); and for the central and late Middle Ages, see Barbara Newman's fascinating study, *From Virile Woman to WomanChrist: Studies in Medieval Religion and Literature* (Philadelphia, 1995).

3. Leander of Seville, *The Training of Nuns*, in vol. 1 of *The Iberian Fathers*, FC 62, trans. Claude W. Barlow, (Washington, D.C., 1969), p. 192.

4. See Richard Kieckhefer, *Unquiet Souls: Fourteenth-Century Saints and Their Religious Milieu* (Chicago and London, 1984), pp. 12–14. Here Kieckhefer makes the important distinction between *imitanda* and *admiranda*— "the imitable deeds of the saint and those which should arouse a sense of wonder."

5. Charlton T. Lewis and Charles Short, *A Latin Dictionary* (Oxford, 1879, 1980), p. 1625.

6. J. F. Niermeyer, *Mediae Latinitatis Lexicon Minus* (Leiden, 1957), fascicule 10, p. 937.

7. Thomas Head, *Hagiography and the Cult of Saints: The Diocese of Orleans, 800–1200,* Cambridge Studies in Medieval Life and Thought (Cambridge and New York, 1990), p. 10.

8. Hippolyte Delehaye, *Sanctus: Essai sur le culte de saints dans l'antiquité* (Brussels, 1927), p. 235.

9. John M. Mecklin, *The Passing of the Saint: A Study of a Cultural Type* (Chicago, 1940), p. 17.

10. Ibid., pp. 5–7, 17. In this tradition S. Bonnet provides the following definition: the saint is "a response to the spiritual needs of a generation. He is moreover a man who is the eminent representation of the ideas which Christians of a given time have developed of sanctity." S. Bonnet, *Saint-Rouin, histoire de l'ermitage et du pèlerinage* (Paris, 1956), p. 75, cited by André Vauchez, *La Sainteté en occident aux derniers siècles du moyen âge: d'après les procès de canonisation et les documents hagiographiques,* (Rome, 1981), p. 8.

11. Petroff, *Body and Soul*, p. 161.

12. Eric Waldram Kemp, *Canonization and Authority in the Western Church* (London, 1948), p. 35; Vauchez, *La Sainteté en occident*, pp. 13–67.

13. Kemp, pp. 29, 36–39, 169; Vauchez, pp. 13–24. See the Council of Mainz (813), ch. 51. "Ne corpora Sanctorum transferantur de loco ad locum. Deinceps vero corpora Sanctorum de loco ad locum nullus praesumat transferre, sine consilio Principis, vel Episcoporum, & sanctae Synodi licentia." Jacques Sirmond, ed., *Concilia Antiqua Galliae* (Paris, 1629, reprint Scientia Verlay Aalen, 1970), 2:286.

14. Kemp, *Canonization and Authority*, pp. 52, 55.

15. See Vauchez, *La Sainteté en occident*, especially pp. 39–120; Pierre Delooz, *Sociologie et canonisations, Collection scientifique de la faculté de droit de l'Université de Liège* (Liège and The Hague, 1969), pp. 23–40; Kemp, *Canonization and Authority*, pp. 82–150.

16. Kemp, *Canonization and Authority*, pp. 82–106; Delooz, *Sociologie et canonisations*, pp. 23–40.

17. See Delooz, p. 257.

18. For example, in his study *L'Idéal de sainteté dans l'Aquitaine carolingienne*, Joseph-Claude Poulin notes that in Aquitaine all of the saints who merited a biography in the Carolingian period were in fact men (pp. 42–43).

19. Galatians 3:28.

20. René Metz, "Le Statut de la femme en droit canonique médiéval," in *Recueils de la société Jean Bodin pour l'histoire comparative des institutions* (Brussels, 1962), 12, pt. 2:61.

21. See Jo Ann McNamara and Suzanne Wemple, "The Power of Women through the Family in Medieval Europe: 500–1100," in *Clio's Consciousness Raised: New Perspectives on the History of Women,* ed. M. Hartman and L. W. Banner (New York, 1974), pp. 103–18; Suzanne Fonay Wemple, *Women in Frankish Society: Marriage and the Cloister, 500 to 900* (Philadelphia, 1981), especially pp. 27–74; David Herlihy, *Medieval Households* (Cambridge, Mass., and London, 1985), pp. 29–78.

22. See Herlihy, *Medieval Households,* pp. 82–98.

23. While there has been a great deal of interest in women saints in the later Middle Ages, until recently there have been relatively few studies which have focused on the *mulieres sanctae* of the early Middle Ages. See especially Suzanne Wemple's classic study *Women in Frankish Society;* Patrick Corbet, *Les saints ottoniens, Sainteté dynastique, sainteté royale et sainteté féminine autour de l'an Mil,* Beihefte der Francia 15 (Sigmaringen, Jan Thorbecke Verlag, 1986); Robert Folz, *Les Saintes reines du moyen âge en occident (VIe–XIIIe siècles),* Subsidia Hagiographica, no. 76 (Brussels, 1992); and Stephanie Hollis, *Anglo-Saxon Women and the Church: Sharing a Common Fate* (Woodbridge, Suffolk, and Rochester, N.Y., 1992). See also Jo Ann McNamara and John E. Halborg, trans., with E. Gordon Whatley, *Sainted Women of the Dark Ages (SWDA)* (Duke University Press, 1992); and Joyce E. Salisbury, *Church Fathers, Independent Virgins* (London and New York, 1991). There have been a number of important monographs on saints in general (without a special focus on female saints) which also examine the early medieval period. For a discussion of recent works on saints during this period, see notes 28 and 29 below.

24. See especially R. I. Moore's fascinating monograph, *The Formation of a Persecuting Society: Power and Deviance in Western Europe, 950–1250* (London and New York, 1987). In this study he notes many of the same societal changes which I have found in regard to women saints and "deviants." I would like to thank Lee Patterson for recommending this work to me. See also R. W. Southern's classic study, *The Making of the Middle Ages* (New Haven and London, 1953), which focuses on this formative period and the important changes in society and mentalities—the silent revolution—that occurred in Western Europe from the late tenth to the early thirteenth century.

25. *BHL* 2:1025. A typical entry, for example, contains the following information: "Radegundis regina Francorum, 587.—Aug. 13. 1. *Vita Auct. Fortunato.*—" followed by a listing of all of the known editions of that *vita;* "2. *Vita Auct. Baudonivia Moniali.*—" again followed by the various editions in the *AASS, MGH, PL,* etc., as well as a number of secondary works on the saint.

26. See also David Herlihy's comments and calculations in regard to the *Bibliotheca Hagiographica Latina antiquae et mediae aetatis* in his study, "Did Women Have a Renaissance?: A Reconsideration," *Medaevalia et Humanistica: Studies in Medieval and Renaissance Culture,* new ser., no. 13

(1985): 1–22. Also see Schulenburg, "Sexism and the Celestial Gynaeceum—from 500–1200," *Journal of Medieval History* 4 (1978): 117–33.

27. See Schulenburg, "Women's Monastic Communities, 500–1100: Patterns of Expansion and Decline," *Signs: Journal of Women in Culture and Society* 14/2 (1989): 261–92. At this writing the computer-assisted project, "Women's Religious Life and Communities," originally coordinated by Suzanne Wemple, Mary Martin McLaughlin, and Heath Dillard, remains incomplete. The finished study will be of tremendous importance for medievalists working in the areas of women saints (abbesses, patrons, etc.), and women's monastic life.

28. Beginning in the mid-1960s—with the rising interest in social history, the history of mentalities, and popular religion and the burgeoning of interdisciplinary and cultural studies and the history of women—hagiography became part of a growing body of historical scholarship. Frantisek Graus, in his *Volk, Herrscher und Heiliger im Reich der Merowinger: Studien zur Hagiographie der Merowingerzeit* (Prague, 1965), emphasized the collective use of saints' Lives for the study of society, attitudes, values, and the political history of the Merovingian period. He also noted that "the legends are certainly not 'historical works' in the nineteenth-century sense; they are rather 'literature' and, more particularly, propaganda literature" (p. 39). Also in the 1960s, Pierre Delooz produced several significant sociological studies of canonization in which a collective, statistical approach was applied to hagiographic material. His work includes "Pour une étude sociologique de la sainteté canonisée dans l'Eglise catholique" (1962) and a major study, *Sociologie et canonisations* (1969). Peter Brown's work on saints and society, especially his classic study "The Rise and Function of the Holy Man in Late Antiquity" (1971), as well as *The Cult of the Saints: Its Rise and Function in Latin Christianity* (1981) and *Society and the Holy in Late Antiquity* (1981), have been extremely influential for scholars working in hagiography and history. In addition to bringing a new sympathy and imagination to the study of saints, his work has also contributed greatly to legitimizing the subject. As Patrick Geary notes, "by placing at the very center of late antique life figures whom political and social historians had long dismissed as 'marginal,' by connecting their 'religious' meaning to issues recognizable to the most secular twentieth-century intellectual, Brown not only invented 'the world of late antiquity' as a fashionable area of research and inspired studies of holy men around the world, but made hagiography respectable to the generation of historians trained in the traditions of the social sciences" (*Living with the Dead*, p. 13).

In the 1980s we see a veritable explosion of literature on saints. These studies have furnished introductions to hagiography and its literature; explored the ideals of sanctity, cults, and miracles of saints against a background of the social and cultural history of the period; and provided important new critical studies and translations of medieval saints' Lives. The following represents only a few of the recent titles, with an emphasis on works in English: Elizabeth Alvilda Petroff, *Consolation of the Blessed: Women Saints in Medieval Tuscany* (1979), *Medieval Women's Visionary Literature* (1986), and *Body and Soul: Essays on Medieval Women and Mysticism* (1994); André

Vauchez, *La sainteté en Occident aux derniers siècles du Moyen Age d'après les procès de canonisation et les documents hagiographiques* (1981); E. Patlagean and P. Riché, eds., *Hagiographie, cultures et sociétés, IVe–XIIe siècles* (1981); Donald Weinstein and Rudolph Bell, *Saints and Society: The Two Worlds of Western Christendom 1000–1700* (1982); Michael Goodich, *Vita Perfecta: The Idea of Sainthood in the Thirteenth Century* (1982) and *Violence and Miracle in the Fourteenth Century: Private Grief and Public Salvation* (1995); David Rollason, *The Mildrith Legend: A Study in Early Medieval Hagiography in England* (1982) and *Saints and Relics in Anglo-Saxon England* (1989); Stephen Wilson, *Saints and Their Cults: Studies in Religious Sociology, Folklore and History* (1983), with an annotated bibliography of some 1,300 entries; Richard Kieckhefer, *Unquiet Souls: Fourteenth-Century Saints and Their Religious Milieu* (1984); Richard Kieckhefer and George D. Bond, eds., *Sainthood: Its Manifestations in World Religions* (1988); Robert Folz, *Les saints rois du moyen âge en Occident (VIe–XIIIe siècles)* (1984) and *Les saintes reines du moyen âge en Occident (VIe–XIIIe siècles)* (1992); Rudolph Bell, *Holy Anorexia* (1985); Patrick Corbet, *Les saints ottoniens, sainteté royale et sainteté féminine autour de l'an Mil* (1986); Elissa R. Henken, *Traditions of Welsh Saints* (1987) and *The Welsh Saints: A Study in Patterned Lives* (1991); Caroline Walker Bynum, *Holy Feast and Holy Fast: The Religious Significance of Food to Medieval Women* (1987); Susan J. Ridyard, *The Royal Saints of Anglo-Saxon England: A Study of West Saxon and East Anglian Cults* (1988); Thomas J. Heffernan, *Sacred Biography: Saints and Their Biographers in the Middle Ages* (1988); Thomas Head, *Hagiography and the Cult of Saints: The Diocese of Orleans, 800–1200* (1990); Mary Clayton, *The Cult of the Virgin Mary in Anglo-Saxon England* (1990); Kathleen Ashley and Pamela Sheingorn, eds., *Interpreting Cultural Symbols: Saint Anne in Late Medieval Society* (1990); Sharon Farmer, *Communities of Saint Martin: Legend and Ritual in Medieval Tours* (1991); Joyce E. Salisbury, *Church Fathers, Independent Virgins* (1991); Renate Blumenfeld-Kosinski and Timea Szell, eds., *Images of Sainthood in Medieval Europe* (1991); *The Lady as Saint: A Collection of French Hagiographic Romances of the Thirteenth Century*, trans. with a commentary by Brigitte Cazelles (1991); *Les fonctions des saints dans le monde occidental, IIIe–XIIIe siecle* (1991); Richard Sharpe, *Medieval Irish Saints' Lives: An Introduction to Vitae Sanctorum Hiberniae* (1991); *Sainted Women of the Dark Ages*, trans. with introductions by Jo Ann McNamara and John E. Halborg with E. Gordon Whatley (1992); Aviad Kleinberg, *Prophets in Their Own Country* (1992); Osbern Bokenbam, *The Legends of Holy Women*, trans. with an introduction by Sheila Delany (1992); Raymond Van Dam, *Saints and Their Miracles in Late Antique Gaul* (1993); Jacobus de Voragine, *The Golden Legend: Readings on the Saints*, trans. with an introduction by William Granger Ryan (1993); Patrick Geary, *Living with the Dead in the Middle Ages* (1994); Barbara Abou-El-Haj, *The Medieval Cult of Saints: Formations and Transformations* (1994); Anneke B. Mulder-Bakker, ed., *Sanctity and Motherhood: Essays on Holy Mothers in the Middle Ages* (1994); Thomas F. X. Noble and Thomas Head, eds., *Soldiers of Christ: Saints and Saints' Lives from Late Antiquity* *and the Early Middle Ages* (1995); *The Book of Sainte Foy,* trans. with an introduction by Pamela Sheingorn (1995); *Virgin Lives and Holy Deaths: Two Exemplary Biographies for Anglo-Norman Women,* trans. with introductions by Jocelyn Wogan-Browne and Glyn S. Burgess (1996).

A number of new translations of early medieval saints' Lives have been published by Liverpool University Press, and the Peregrina Publishing Company also has an impressive collection of translations of medieval women saints' Lives in the *Matrologia Latina* and *Matrologia Graeca* series. Dumbarton Oaks has initiated an important series of translated Lives of Byzantine saints, of which the initial volume is *Holy Women of Byzantium: Ten Saints' Lives in English Translation,* ed. and trans. Alice-Mary Talbot (1996).

Other indices of the popularity of the field are the growing number of conferences focusing on medieval saints, their cults and relics, and sessions on these topics at the major medieval conferences. New journals devoted to the study of medieval hagiography have also been established—for example, *Hagiographica: Journal of Hagiography and Biography of Società internazionale per lo studio del Medio Evo latino* (Brepols); *Litterae Hagiologicae* (Brepols); and *Sanctorum* (also on the Internet). However, the *Analecta Bollandiana, revue critique d'hagiographie,* established by the Bollandists in 1882, remains the official journal in the field, providing translations, critical studies, and notices and reviews of new work in hagiography. The Société des Bollandistes (Brussels) has initiated two on-line services: *Hagiomail,* a scholarly mailing list dedicated to issues of Christian hagiography and the cult of saints, and a site on the World Wide Web that provides useful information on the Bollandists' recent publications, hagiographic organizations, conferences, and reference works. It is located on the server of the Bibliothèque Royale Albert I in Brussels at the following address: <http://www.kbr.be/~socboll>. The Hagiography Society's 1996 *Annual Directory of Researchers in Medieval Hagiography and Related Fields* lists more than four hundred active members, along with their special areas of interest, and includes an extensive bibliography. The directory notes new initiatives and major collaborative projects such as the development of indexes of saints' Lives, data bases of saints and their miracles, new editions of texts, and dictionaries of saints. (For information on the Hagiography Society's *News Letter* and *Directory,* contact Sherry L. Reames, Department of English, University of Wisconsin-Madison).

In his essay, "Saints, Scholars, and Society: The Elusive Goal," Patrick Geary has provided a perceptive discussion of this resurgence of interest in saints among social historians and has proposed new directions for research (*Living with the Dead,* pp. 9–29). See also Pamela Sheingorn's review essay "The Saints in Medieval Culture: Recent Scholarship," *Envoi: A Review Journal of Medieval Literature* 2, no. 1 (1990): 1–29.

29. The major studies in English published since the 1970s in the field of women in medieval religion and society, in addition to those listed in note 28, include, for the early medieval period, Karl J. Leyser, *Rule and Conflict in an Early Medieval Society, Ottonian Saxony* (1979); Suzanne Fonay Wemple, *Women in Frankish Society: Marriage and the Cloister, 500 to 900* (1981); Jo Ann McNamara, *The Ordeal of Community, The Rule of Donatus of Be-*

sançon, and the Rule of a Certain Father to the Virgins, trans. with John Halborg (1993), and *Sisters in Arms: Catholic Nuns through Two Millennia* (1996); Stephanie Hollis, *Anglo-Saxon Women and the Church: Sharing a Common Fate* (1992); Lisa M. Bitel, *Land of Women: Tales of Sex and Gender from Early Ireland* (1996). For the central and late Middle Ages, see Caroline Walker Bynum, *Jesus as Mother: Studies in the Spirituality of the High Middle Ages* (1982) and *Fragmentation and Redemption: Essays on Gender and the Human Body in Medieval Religion* (1992); Barbara Newman, *Sister of Wisdom: St. Hildegard's Theology of the Feminine* and *From Virile Woman to WomanChrist: Studies in Medieval Religion and Literature* (1995); Ann K. Warren, *Anchorites and Their Patrons in Medieval England* (1985); Sharon K. Elkins, *Holy Women of Twelfth-Century England* (1988); Penelope D. Johnson, *Equal in Monastic Profession: Religious Women in Medieval France* (1991); Sally Thompson, *Women Religious: The Founding of English Nunneries after the Norman Conquest* (1991); Dyan Elliott, *Spiritual Marriage: Sexual Abstinence in Medieval Wedlock* (1993); Roberta Gilchrist, *Gender and Material Culture: The Archaeology of Religious Women* (1994) and *Contemplation and Action: The Other Monasticism* (1995). Among important collections of essays are John A. Nichols and Lillian Thomas Shank, eds., *Distant Echoes: Medieval Religious Women I* (1984) and *Peace Weavers: Medieval Religious Women II* (1987); Lynda L. Coon, Katherine J. Haldane, and Elisabeth W. Sommer, eds., *That Gentle Strength: Historical Perspectives on Women in Christianity* (1990). For a bibliographic overview, see Margaret Schaus and Susan Mosher Stuard, "Citizens of No Mean City: Medieval Women's History," *Choice*, December 1992, pp. 583–95. See also the *Medieval Feminist Newsletter* and its reviews of research and bibliographies, and especially the *Medieval Feminist Index (MFI): Scholarship on Women, Sexuality, and Gender* on the Web at <http://www.haverford.edu/library/reference/mschaus/mfi/mfi.html>.

CHAPTER ONE

1. Paul Fouracre, "Merovingian History and Merovingian Hagiography," *Past and Present* (1990): 3.

2. Hippolyte Delehaye, *Les Légendes hagiographiques*, 2d ed. (Brussels, 1906), p. 2; see also pp. 1–13, 79–102. English translation, Donald Attwater, *The Legends of the Saints* (New York, 1962); see pp. 3–11, 55–68; see also Attwater's preface, p. xviii.

3. Kathleen Hughes, *Early Christian Ireland*, p. 219. See also Susan J. Ridyard, *The Royal Saints of Anglo-Saxon England: A Study of West Saxon and East Anglian Cults*, Cambridge Studies in Medieval Life and Thought (Cambridge and New York, 1988), pp 8–16.

4. D. W. Rollason, *The Mildrith Legend: A Study in Early Medieval Hagiography in England*, p. 69.

5. Gregory of Tours, *History of the Franks*, trans. Lewis Thorpe (Harmondsworth, 1974), pp. 164, 168, 305, 356–58, 365, 420, 479–81, 526–31, 533, 535–38, 571–72; Gregory of Tours, *Glory of the Confessors*, Translated

Texts for Historians, Latin Series 4, trans. Raymond Van Dam (Liverpool, 1988), pp. 105–8; Fortunatus, *De vita Sanctae Radegundis liber I*, *MGH SRM* 2: 364–77; Baudonivia, *De vita Sanctae Radegundis liber II*, *MGH SRM* 2: 377–95; for an English translation of the two Lives of Radegund and "The Thuringian War," see *SWDA*, pp. 65–105. Over the years there have been many important studies dealing with St. Radegund and her monastery of Ste-Croix. A few of these works include René Aigrain's *Sainte Radegonde (vers 520–587); Les Saints*, 2d ed. (Paris, 1918); *La riche personnalité de Sainte Radegonde*, Conférences et homélies prononcées à Poitiers à l'occasion du XIVᵉ Centenaire de sa mort (587–1987) (Poitiers, 1988); Labande-Mailfert, Y., and R. Favreau, et al., *Histoire de l'Abbaye Sainte-Croix de Poitiers: Quatorze siècles de vie monastique*, Mémoires de la Société des Antiquaires de l'Ouest, 4ᵐᵉ série, vol. XIX (1986–1987); Emile Ginot, "Le manuscrit de Sainte Radegonde de Poitiers et ses peintures du XIᵉ siècle," *Bulletin de la Société Française de Reproduction de Manuscrits à Peintures: Années 1914–1920* (Paris, 1920); Magdalena Elizabeth Carrasco, "Spirituality in Context: The Romanesque Illustrated Life of St. Radegund of Poitiers (Poitiers, Bibl. Mun., MS 250)," *The Art Bulletin* (September 1990) LXXII, no. 3: 414–35.

6. Turgot, *Life of Queen Margaret*, in *Early Sources of Scottish History: A.D. 500–1286*, trans. Alan Orr Anderson (Edinburgh and London, 1922), pp. 59–88; *ODS*, pp. 262–63; Derek Baker, "'A Nursery of Saints': St Margaret of Scotland Reconsidered," in *Medieval Women*, pp. 119–41. For a discussion of the two Lives of St. Margaret—a long and a short *vita*, see Lois L. Huneycutt, "The Idea of a Perfect Princess: The *Life of St. Margaret* in the Reign of Matilda II (1100–1118)," in *Anglo-Norman Studies*, vol. 12, *Proceedings of the Battle Conference*, 1989, ed. Marjorie Chibnall (Woodbridge, 1990), pp. 81–84; see also Alan J. Wilson, *St Margaret Queen of Scotland* (Edinburgh, 1993).

7. Turgot, *Life of Queen Margaret*, p. 68.

8. See Baker, "'A Nursery of Saints.'"

9. Throughout the *vita* we can see her special concern for Benedictine monasticism and the rule, the organization of her life as a nun manqué, etc.; see also Turgot, *Life of Queen Margaret*, pp. 82–86; Baker, "'A Nursery of Saints.'"

10. Delooz, *Sociologie et canonisations*, pp. 5–25.

11. Head, *Hagiography and the Cult of Saints*, p. 16.

12. Delehaye, *Les Légendes hagiographiques*, p. 2.

13. Simone Roisin, *L'Hagiographie cistercienne dans le diocèse de Liège au XIIIᵉ siècle* (Louvain, 1947), p. 274; John M. Mecklin, *The Passing of the Saint: A Study of a Cultural Type* (Chicago, 1940), pp. 62–63.

14. *SWDA*, p. 222; *Vita Sanctae Geretrudis*, *MGH SRM* 2:453.

15. "Minus licet periti scholastica, sed magis studere volumus patere aedificationi plurimorum" (Prologue, *Vita Domnae Balthildis Reginae*, ch. 1, in *MGH SRM* 2:482, col. A). *SWDA*, p. 268.

16. *SWDA*, p. 1; Hucbald of Saint-Amand, *Vita S. Aldegundis virginis*, *AASS*, Jan. III (Jan. 30), p. 662.

17. *SWDA*, p. 255; *Vita S. Waldetrudis*, *AASS*, April I (April 9), pp. 829–33.

18. "The Life of St. Leoba by Rudolf, monk of Fulda," in *The Anglo-Saxon Missionaries in Germany*, trans. and edited by C. H. Talbot (New York, 1954), p. 205.

19. Odilo of Cluny, *Vita Sanctae Adalheidis Imperatricis*, in *Bibliotheca Cluniacensis*, edited by Martinus Marrier and Andreas Quercetanus (Brussels and Paris, 1915), pp. 354–69; Corbet, *Les Saints ottoniens*, pp. 81–110, especially p. 108.

20. Turgot, *Life of Queen Margaret*, p. 59.

21. Huneycutt, "The Idea of the Perfect Princess."

22. Ibid., p. 91.

23. See, for example, Graus, *Volk, Herrscher und Heiliger im Reich der Merowinger*; Friedrich Prinz, *Frühes Mönchtum im Frankenreich: Kultur und Gesellschaft in Gallien, den Rheinlanden und Bayern am Beispiel der monastischen Entwicklung (4. bis 8. Jahrhundert)* (Munich and Vienna, 1965), especially the following chapters: "Die Selbstheiligung des frankischen Adels in der Hagiographie," pp. 489–93; "Heiligenvita—Adel—Eigenkloster," pp. 493–95; "Ein neues hagiographisches Leitbild," pp. 496–501; "Kult und adeliges Heiligengrab," pp. 502–3. See also Maria Stoeckle, *Studien über Ideale in Frauenviten des VII.–X. Jahrhunderts* (Munich, 1957), especially pp. 87–103.; de Gaiffier, *Etudes critiques*, pp. 463–68; Wilson, *Saints and Their Cults*, pp. 33–34; Poulin, *L'Idéal de sainteté dans l'Aquitaine carolingienne*, p. 126.

24. Head, *Hagiography and the Cult of Saints*, pp. 1–19; Farmer, *Communities of Saint Martin*.

25. Corbet, *Les Saints ottoniens*, pp. 120, 200–203.

26. See Benedicta Ward, *Miracles and the Medieval Mind*; Wilson, *Saints and Their Cults*, pp. 26–31; Roisin, *L'Hagiographie cistercienne*, p. 77.

27. Murray, *Reason and Society*, pp. 386–93.

28. Roisin, *L'Hagiographie cistercienne*, p. 126.

29. Christine Fell, "Hild, Abbess of Streonæshalch," in *Hagiography and Medieval Literature: A Symposium*, ed. Hans Bekker-Nielsen et al. (Odense, 1981) pp. 93–95. Fell notes church dedications to St. Hilda (dating to the pre- or post-Conquest period): Yorkshire, 9; Cumberland, 1; Northumberland, 1; Durham, 2.

30. Van der Essen, *Etude critique et littéraire sur les "vitae" des saints mérovingiens de l'ancienne Belgique* (Louvain and Paris, 1907), pp. 309–11. The author of the *vita Berlindis* also writes: "Non enim immerito haec virgo ab illis debet honorari quibus et ipsa in hac vita consanguinitate vel familiaritate coniucta fuit, vel qui ex eius parentela genealogiam ducant, vel qui eius atque maiorum illius famulatui obnoxii, obsequiis eius deservierunt. Indigena namque istius loci atque domina fuit." *AASS Belg.*, 5:625, cited by Van der Essen, p. 311.

31. Rollason, *Saints and Relics in Anglo-Saxon England*, pp. 86–87.

32. Poulin, *L'Idéal de sainteté dans l'Aquitaine carolingienne*, pp. 120–21.

33. Aldhelm, *De virginitate* in *Aldhelm: The Prose Works*, trans. Michael Lapidge and Michael Herren (Totowa, 1979), pp. 14, 51, 59.

34. Fortunatus, *De vita Sanctae Radegundis liber I*, ch. 24, *MGH SRM* 2:372; ch. 7, p. 367; ch. 30, p. 374; ch. 23, p. 372.

35. Here the pious exercise of washing the feet of the nuns and visitors imitates the ministry of Christ to his disciples. Ibid., ch. 23, p. 372; ch. 24, p. 372.

36. Ibid., ch. 23, p. 372.

37. Baudonivia, *De vita Sanctae Radegundis liber II*, ch. 12, *MGH SRM* 2:385–86. In contrast to this, the miracles of Austreberta portray the saint taking the side of a young servant who had been denied admission to her monastery by the abbess. After having expelled the servant from the community, the abbess became seriously ill. This was seen as punishment inflicted by St. Austreberta for the abbess's improper behavior toward the poor woman. The abbess repented and was cured; she agreed to allow the girl to be received into the congregation. *SWDA*, pp. 319–20.

38. See Ridyard, *The Royal Saints of Anglo-Saxon England*, p. 87.

39. Ibid., p. 99. For the concept of *humilitas* among the Ottonian saints, see also Corbet, *Les Saints ottoniens*, pp. 96–99, 174–76.

40. Kieckhefer, *Unquiet Souls*, p. 14.

41. Aldhelm: *De virginitate*, in *Aldhelm: The Prose Works*, trans. Lapidge and Herren, p. 119.

42. *Vita Sanctae Geretrudis*, *MGH SRM* 2:453; or *Vita Aldegundis prima*, ch. 18, in *AASS Belg.*, vol. 4. See also Van der Essen, *Etude critique*, p. 221; however, he notes the stereotypic character of this formula in hagiographic literature and suggests that we should not attach too much importance to these statements.

43. Ridyard, *The Royal Saints of Anglo-Saxon England*, pp. 8–16.

44. Head, *Hagiography and the Cult of Saints*, pp. 20–57; "enterprising textual editors," p. 44.

45. McNamara, "A Legacy of Miracles," p. 37.

46. Corbet, *Les Saints ottoniens*, pp. 120–21, 153, 156–174.

47. Rollason, *The Mildrith Legend*, pp. 60–61.

48. Ibid., p. 61.

49. Julia M. H. Smith, "The Problem of Female Sanctity in Carolingian Europe c. 780–920," *Past and Present* 146 (Feb. 1995): 9; see also Poulin, *L'Idéal de sainteté dans l'Aquitaine carolingienne*. Poulin notes "D'abord, tous les saints aquitains ayant mérité une biographie à l'époque carolingienne sont des hommes. . . . Par opposition à ce qui s'est passé dans d'autres régions de l'Empire carolingien, les auteurs ecclésiastiques d'Aquitaine n'ont pas été inspirés par la promotion d'un idéal de sainteté féminine . . . ou d'un centre de pèlerinage au reliques d'une sainte" (pp. 42–43).

50. De Gaiffier, *Etudes critiques*, p. 424.

51. *Vita Sanctae Geretrudis*, p. 453; also *SWDA*, p. 223.

52. Van der Essen, *Etude critique*, pp. 221–23; *Vita de S. Aldegunde*, *AASS, Ian. III* (Jan. 30), ch. 2, pp. 651–52; see also *SWDA*, pp. 235–36.

53. *SWDA*, pp. 304, 306.

54. De Gaiffier, *Etudes critiques d'hagiographie*, p. 425.

55. Hucbald, prologue to the *Vitae Rictrudis sanctimonialis Marchianensis*, MGH SRM 6:91–94; AASS Belg. 4:488–503; *Vita Aldegundis, abbatissae Malbodiensis*, MGH SRM 6:79–90, AASS Belg., 4:315–24. See also Van der Essen, *Etude critique*, pp. 225–28, 260–65; de Gaiffier, *Etudes critiques*, pp. 426–27, discusses the prestige of professional hagiographers "à la mode."

56. De Gaiffier, *Etudes critiques*, p. 425.

57. Delehaye, *Les Légendes hagiographiques*, p. 69.

58. The authorship of the *Life of Saint Willibald* (d. ca. 786) and the *Life of Saint Wynnebald* (d. ca. 761) has been attributed to a nun of the Monastery of Heidenheim (*BHL* 2:1288, 1297). Also, the *Passion* in meter of St. Gengulfus or Gangolfus (d. ca. 760) was written by Hrotswitha of Gandersheim (ibid., 1:498). (Among the writings of the twelfth-century St. Hildegard of Bingen are the *Life of Saint Rupert* [ninth century] and the *Life of Saint Disibodus* [seventh century], ibid., 2:1071, 1:333]).

59. See Hrotswitha of Gandersheim, *Gesta Ottonis* and *Primordia coenobii Gandeshemensis*, ed. K. Strecker, *Hrotsvithae opera*, Bibl. Teubner (Leipzig, 1906); Paul von Winterfels, ed., *Hrotsvithae opera* (Berlin, 1902); or Helena Homeyer, ed., *Hrotsvithae opera* (Munich, 1970). See also Corbet, *Les Saints ottoniens*, especially pp. 111–19.

60. See for St. Cecile, Abbess of Remirement, AASS, Aug. II (August 12), p. 732, and VSB 8 (August): 207; for St. Gebetrude, Abbess of Remirement, AASS, Nov. III (November 7), pp. 409–13, and VSB 11 (November): 211; for Leutwithe, Abbess of Auchy, in note on St. Silvin, PB, 2 (Feb. 17): 560.

61. Roisin also notes this pattern in *L'Hagiographie cistercienne*, p. 10.

62. See, for example, the letters of St. Jerome found in *St. Jerome: Letters and Select Works*, NPNF, 2d series,vol. 6. Letter 23, to Marcella, consoles her for the loss of a friend, Lea, and praises Lea's holy behavior, pp. 341–42; Letter 24, to Marcella, describes the model behavior of the virgin Asella, pp. 42–43; Letters 38 and 39, to Marcella and Paula, praise Blaesilla's saintly austerities, pp. 47–54; Letter 66, to Pammachius, praises the life and virtues of his deceased wife, Paulina, pp. 134–40. Letter 108 to Eustochium was written to console her on her mother, Paula's, death; it is a long and very interesting panegyric describing the events of Paula's saintly life, pp. 195–212. Letter 127, to Principia, provides a saint's life of the holywoman, Marcella, pp. 136–48; Letter 130 to Demetrias, summarizes this woman's exemplary life in Rome and Africa, pp. 260–72. See also Palladius, *The Lausiac History*, trans. Robert T. Meyer (Westminster, Maryland, and London, 1965). This work, written in the early fifth century (419–20), is one of the most important sources for the history of early monasticism in Egypt, Palestine, Syria, and Asia Minor. In this book Palladius devotes a great deal of attention to the lives of women and their pursuit of spiritual perfection. See also Gregory the Great, *The Dialogues*, FC, vol. 39, bk. 4, ch. 14, pp. 205–7 (Galla); bk. 4, ch. 16, pp. 208–10 (Romula); bk. 4, ch. 17, pp. 210–11 (Tarsilla); bk. 4, ch. 18, pp. 211–12 (Musa).

63. Odilo of Cluny, *Vita Sanctae Adalheidis Imperatricis*, p. 354. See also Corbet, *Les Saints ottoniens*, pp. 84–85.

64. Roisin, *L'Hagiographie cistercienne*, p. 124.

65. Hollis, *Anglo-Saxon Women and the Church*, pp. 274, 250. Hollis also notes, for example, in regard to St. Hilda/Hild: "Hild is a prototype for abbesses in an age of enclosed monasticism, whose Lives, written by their female communities, generally held so little interest for the world beyond their monasteries that they failed to gain sufficient currency to ensure their preservation; unless the relics chanced to pass into the possession of monks—then a cleric like Goscelin would be employed to mould them closer to the Roman virgins and deck them in all the colours of his rhetoric." *Anglo-Saxon Women and the Church*, p. 250.

66. See André Wilmart, ed., "La Légende de Sainte Edithe en prose et vers par le moine Goscelin," *AB* 56 (1938): 5–101, 265–307; D. W. Rollason, *The Mildrith Legend*; M. Esposito, ed., "La Vie de Sainte Vulfhilde par Goscelin de Cantorbery," *AB* 32 (1913): 10–26. See also Susan Millinger, "Humility and Power: Anglo-Saxon Nuns in Anglo-Norman Hagiography," in *Distant Echoes*, pp. 115–29.

67. Talbot, *The Anglo-Saxon Missionaries in Germany*, p. 152.

68. See Janet Nelson, "Queens as Jezebels: The Careers of Brunhild and Balthild in Merovingian History," in *Medieval Women* (*Studies in Church History; Subsidia* I), ed. Derek Baker (Oxford, 1978), p. 46, n. 83; Rosamond McKitterick, "Nuns' Scriptoria in England and Francia in the Eighth Century," *Francia* 19, no. 1 (1992): 1–35; Rosamond McKitterick, "Frauen und Schriftlichkeit im Frühmittelalter," in Hans-Werner Goetz, ed., *Weiblicher Lebensgestaltung im frühen Mittelalter* (Cologne, 1991), pp. 99–105; and Wemple, *Women in Frankish Society*, pp. 179–88.

69. Corbet, *Les Saints ottoniens*, pp. 120, 153.

70. Richard Sharpe, *Medieval Irish Saints' Lives: An Introduction to Vitae Sanctorum Hiberniae* (Oxford, 1991), pp. 19–20.

71. *Aelfric's Lives of Saints*, ed. W. W. Skeat (The Early English Text Society; London, 1881), 2 vols.

72. De Gaiffier, *Etudes critiques d'hagiographie*, p. 476.

73. Rollason, *Saints and Relics in Anglo-Saxon England*, p. 86; see also Julia M. H. Smith, "Oral and Written: Saints, Miracles, and Relics in Brittany, c. 850–1250," *Speculum* 65 (1990): 319. Smith also notes Hincmar of Rheims and the different purposes he proposed for various versions of his *Vita Remigii*. He marked the specific sections of the Life which were to be used as lections for the *populus* and which sections were to be reserved for the *illuminati* (n. 40, p. 319).

74. See, for example, De Gaiffier's discussion of prologues, *Etudes critiques d'hagiographie*, pp. 431–37, 499–502.

75. Rudolf, *The Life of St. Leoba*, trans. Talbot, p. 206; Goodich, *Vita Perfecta*, p. 63.

76. Ridyard, *The Royal Saints of Anglo-Saxon England*, p. 12.

77. Rudolf, *The Life of St. Leoba*, trans. Talbot, pp. 205–6. See also Hollis's comments on Rudolf's *Life of Leoba*, *Anglo-Saxon Women and the Church*, pp. 271–300.

78. "A clericis et sanctimonialibus congregationis Deo dilectae famulae beatae Rictrudis rogitatus apponere novum ad conscribendum gesta ipsius naatorumque eius calamum, diu multumque renisus sum, vel quia meam quantulamcumque scientiolam tantae imparem materiei noveram, vel quia, tanto transacto tempore, nulla certae relationis de his scripta videram vel audieram, veritus, ne forte dubia pro certis vel falsa pro veris assererem. Cumque renitenti mihi quaedam historiarum exemplaria suis ostenderent concordantia dictis, de cetero illis, quorum non contemnendae videbantur personae, mihi fidem facientibus, quod haec quae referebant eadem olim tradita litteris fuerint, sed insectatione Northmannicae depopulationis deperierint." Hucbald, *Vitae Rictrudis sanctimonialis Marchianensis, Prologus, MGH SRM* 6:93–94. See also *SWDA,* p. 198.

79. Hughes, *Early Christian Ireland,* p. 234.

80. Fell, "Hild, Abbess of Streonæshalch," p. 87.

81. Ridyard, *The Royal Saints of Anglo-Saxon England,* p. 59. Ridyard argues that the hagiographer's explanation of how his ignorance came about is perhaps rather suspect.

82. St. Rotrude, *VSB* 6 (June): 353.

83. *Mater Spiritualis: The Life of Adelheid of Vilich,* trans. Madelyn Bergen Dick. Peregrina Translations Series, 19 (Toronto, 1994), pp. 17–18; Bertha, *Vita Adelheidis Abbatissae Vilicensis,* ch. 2, in *MGH, SS* 15:756.

84. Odilo of Cluny, *Vita Sanctae Adalheidis Imperatricis,* p. 353.

85. See for example, Peter Dronke, *Women Writers of the Middle Ages: A Critical Study of Texts from Perpetua (203) to Marguerite Porete (1310)* (Cambridge, 1984), p. 66. Here he comments on the *topos* of feminine weakness in the writings of the "strong voice of Gandersheim," Hrotswitha of Gandersheim.

86. Huneberc of Heidenheim, *The Hodoeporicon of St. Willibald,* trans. Talbot, in *The Anglo-Saxon Missionaries in Germany,* p. 153 (emphasis mine). This same type of "apology" or submissive *topos* can then be found in several of the prefaces of the tenth-century works of Hrotswitha of Gandersheim. For example, in one of her prefaces she writes: "To think that you, who have been nurtured in the most profound philosophical studies and have attained knowledge in perfection, should have deigned to approve the humble work of an obscure woman! You have, however, not praised me but the Giver of the grace which works in me, by sending me your paternal congratulations and admitting that I possess some little knowledge of those arts the subtleties of which exceed the grasp of my woman's mind." She also hopes that through her work "the Creator of genius may be the more honoured since it is generally believed that a woman's intelligence is slower." In Hrotswitha's preface to her poetical works she states (as Dronke notes, "with tongue in cheek"): "Although prosody may seem a hard and difficult art for a woman to master, I, without any assistance but that given by the merciful grace of Heaven (in which I have trusted, rather than in my own strength), have attempted in this book to sing in dactyls." In a preface written to Gerberg, Hrotswitha describes the special vulnerability of her situation as an author: "At present I am

defenceless at every point, because I am not supported by any authority. I also fear I shall be accused of temerity in presuming to describe in my humble un-cultured way matters which ought to be set forth with all the ceremony of great learning. Yet if my work is examined by those who know how to weigh things fairly, I shall be more easily pardoned on account of my sex and my in-ferior knowledge, especially as I did not undertake it of my own will but at your command." *The Plays of Roswitha,* trans. Christopher St. John (New York, 1966), pp. xxviii–xxx, xxxii–xxxiii, xxxv. See also, Dronke, pp. 65–66.

87. *SWDA,* pp. 306–7.

88. *Mater Spiritualis: The Life of Adelheid of Vilich,* trans. Dick, p. 18.

89. Head, *Hagiography and the Cult of Saints,* p. 17.

90. Gregory of Tours, *Life of the Fathers,* trans. Edward James (Translated Texts for Historians, Latin Series 1) ch. 19, p. 124.

91. Fortunatus, *De vita sanctae Radegundis liber I,* ch. 1, p. 364 (emphasis mine).

92. Aviad M. Kleinberg, "Proving Sanctity: Selection and Authentication of Saints in the Later Middle Ages," *Viator* 20 (1989): 183.

93. See, for example, "Biographies spirituelles: moyen âge," in *Dict. Sp.,* vol. 1:1646–1656.

94. An interesting example of the uncomfortable presence of *detractores* and the use of miracles as evidence of sanctity, can be found in the "Virtues of St. Gertrude of Nivelles." One of the nuns of Nivelles was confronted by the blatant skepticism of a noblewoman named Adula who openly voiced her doubts in regard to the efficacy of this female saint. The nun tried to defend her patron saint with promises of St. Gertrude's posthumous intervention on her feast day. Then only through the working of a personal miracle on the an-niversary of the saint at Nivelles (the restoring to life of the son of the skeptic after he had drowned in the convent's well) did the woman become convinced of St. Gertrude's supernatural powers. *De virtutibus Sanctae Geretrudis,* ch. 11, *MGH SRM* 2:469–71. See also Jo Ann McNamara's comments in "A Legacy of Miracles," p. 50, and *SWDA,* pp. 233–34. A number of Lives of women saints, however, emphasize the fact that miracles were unimportant compared to the good deeds and virtues cultivated by the holy woman. The Life of St. Margaret of Scotland argues: "Let others admire in others the signs of miracles; I esteem much more in Margaret the works of mercy. Signs are common to the good and to the bad; but works of true piety and love are pe-culiar to the good. The former sometimes show sanctity; the later constitute sanctity. Let us, I repeat, more worthily admire in Margaret the deeds that made her holy, than the miracles, if she had done any; since they could only show her holiness to men. Let us more worthily hold her in awe, because through her devotion to justice, piety, mercy, and love, we contemplate in her, rather than miracles, the deeds of the ancient fathers." Turgot, *Life of Queen Margaret,* p. 80.

95. Rollason, *Saints and Relics in Anglo-Saxon England,* p. 34.

96. Eric W. Kemp, *Canonization and Authority in the Western Church* (London, 1948), pp. 29, 38–39.

97. Fortunatus, *De vita Sanctae Radegundis liber I*, pp. 364–377. See also *SWDA*, pp. 70–86.

98. Baudonivia, *De vita Sanctae Radegundis liber II*, pp. 377–95. See also Louise Coudanne, "Baudonivia, moniale de Sainte-Croix et biographe de sainte Radegonde," *Etudes mérovingiennes* (Poitiers, 1953), pp. 45–51, and Sabine Gäbe, "Radegundis: Sancta, Regina, Ancilla: Zum Heiligkeitsideal der Radegundisviten von Fortunat und Baudonivia," *Francia* 16/1 (1989): 1–30. See also *SWDA*, pp. 86–105.

99. Baudonivia, *De vita Sanctae Radegundis liber II*, p. 378, see also Isabel Moreira, "Provisatrix optima: St. Radegund of Poitiers' Relic Petitions to the East," *Journal of Medieval History* 19 (1993):305.

100. For a discussion of the relationship between these *vitae*, see the important works by Jacques Fontaine, "Hagiographie et Politique de Sulpice Sévère à Venance Fortunat," *Revue d'Histoire de l'Eglise de France*, vol. 62, no. 168 (1975), especially pp. 114–15, and Sabine Gäbe, "Radegundis: Sancta, Regina, Ancilla."

101. Coudanne, "Baudonovia, moniale de Sainte-Croix," pp. 47–48.

102. Baudonivia, *De vita Sanctae Radegundis liber II*, pp. 377–78.

103. René Aigrain, *Sainte Radegonde*, pp. vii–ix.

104. René Aigrain, *L'Hagiographie* (Paris, 1953), pp. 302, 161.

105. Etienne Delaruelle, "Sainte Radegonde, son type de sainteté et la chrétienté de son temps," in *Etudes mérovingiennes* (Poitiers, 1953), p. 69.

106. Graus, *Volk, Herrscher und Heiliger im Reich der Merowinger*, pp. 409–11.

107. Fontaine, "Hagiographie et politique," especially pp. 136–37.

108. Ibid., p. 132.

109. Baudonivia, *De vita Sanctae Radegundis liber II*, ch. 16, p. 388; "Quod fecit illa in orientali patria, hoc fecit beata Radegundis in Gallia." Fontaine, "Hagiographie et politique," p. 135. See also Isabel Moreira's interesting study, "Provisatrix optima: St. Radegund of Poitiers' Relic Petitions to the East."

110. Baudonivia, *De vita Sanctae Radegundis liber II*, ch. 16, p. 388. See also Wemple, *Women in Frankish Society*, pp. 184–85.

111. Baudonivia, *De vita Sanctae Radegundis liber II*, ch. 16, p. 388.

112. Fontaine, "Hagiographie et politique," p. 132.

113. Ibid., pp. 137–39. In her interesting study, Sabine Gäbe also notes that the two *vitae* are tied to the specific historical context of their authors. Fortunatus's *vita*, on the one hand, stresses the saintly virtues of Radegund; particularly her rigorous asceticism and humility. In his rather obvious omissions, Fortunatus defends the interests of the bishop of Poitiers and the Church as far as its management of the monastery was concerned. Baudonivia's "Klostervita," on the other hand, describes Radegund as charismatic miracle-worker and royal founder of the monastery, as well as exemplary nun. She also underscores the close ties between Ste-Croix and the king and the continuing royal relationship maintained by Radegund. These royal ties provided a protective element and a tradition important for the stability of the

monastery which was especially threatened at the time of Baudonivia's redaction of the *vita*.

114. Wemple, *Women in Frankish Society*, p. 183.

115. Ibid., p. 184.

116. Christine de Pizan, *The Book of the City of Ladies*, trans. Earl Jeffrey Richards (New York, 1982).

117. Barbara Newmann, "Review of Caroline Walker Bynum's *Holy Feast and Holy Fast*," *Envoi: A Review Journal of Medieval Literature* 2, no. 1 (spring 1990):53; Pamela Sheingorn, "Saints in Medieval Culture: Recent Scholarship," *Envoi: A Review Journal of Medieval Literature* 2, no. 1 (spring 1990):1–29; Kleinberg, *Prophets in Their Own Country*, pp. 50–70; Patrick Geary, *Living with the Dead in the Middle Ages* (Ithaca and London, 1994), p. 24 (citing Max Manitius's description of Otloh's *Vita S. Altonis*).

118. E. C. Babut. *Saint Martin de Tours* (Paris, 1912), pp. 108–9 cited by Jacques Fontaine. See also Jacques Fontaine for a discussion of this early hypercritical attitude toward saints' lives, "Sulpice Sévère, Vie de Saint Martin," *SC* 33 (Paris, 1967) 1:173–74.

119. Ferdinand Lot, *The End of the Ancient World and the Beginnings of the Middle Ages*, trans. P. Leon and M. Leon (New York, 1961), pp. 162–63; Ferdinand Lot, *Mélanges d'histoire bretonne VIᵉ–XIᵉ siècles* (Paris, 1907), p. 97, cited by Wilson, *Saints and Their Cults*, p. 1.

120. T. Wright, "On Saints' Lives and Miracles," in *Essays on Archaeological Subjects* (London, 1861), 1:227, cited by Ridyard, *The Royal Saints of Anglo-Saxon England*, p. 11.

121. Hubert Silvestre, "Le Problème des faux au Moyen Age (A propos d'un livre récent de M. Saxer)," *Moyen Age*, 66:351–70.

122. Marc Bloch, *The Historian's Craft*, trans. Peter Putnam (New York, 1953), p. 63.

123. Stephen Wilson, *Saints and Their Cults: Studies in Religious Sociology, Folklore and History* (Cambridge, 1983), p. 1; Geary, *Living with the Dead in the Middle Ages*, pp. 9–10.

124. See, for example, Roisin, *L'Hagiographie cistercienne*, p. 209. Also, for a general overview of the problems in working with early saints' Lives, see "Biographies spirituelles: moyen âge," *Dict. Sp.*, 1:1646–79. For an excellent discussion of the historical value of saints' Lives and the use of new methodologies and analyses, see Jacques Fontaine, *Sulpice Sévère, Vie de Saint Martin*, pp. 171–210; B. de Gaiffier, "Mentalité de l'hagiographe médiéval d'après quelques travaux récents," *Analecta Bollandiana* 86 (1968): 391–99, and de Gaiffier, "Hagiographie et historiographie," in *La Storiografia Alto-medievale* (*Settimane di studio del centro italiano di studi sull'alto medioevo* 17) (Spoleto, 1970), pt. 1, pp. 139–66; Weinstein and Bell, *Saints and Society*, pp. 1–18; Van der Essen, *Etude critique*, pp. ix–xi; and Schmitt, "Note critique: la fabrique des saints." See also the recent studies on saints and their cults by Corbet, Ridyard, Head, Rollason, and Farmer.

125. Kleinberg, *Prophets in Their Own Country*, p. 50.

126. Bloch, *The Historian's Craft*, pp. 60–63.

127. See, for example, Jo Ann McNamara and Suzanne Wemple, "The

Power of Women through the Family in Medieval Europe: 500–1100," in *Clio's Consciousness Raised: New Perspectives on the History of Women,* ed. Mary Hartman and Lois W. Banner (New York, 1974), pp. 103–18; Suzanne Wemple, *Women in Frankish Society,* pp. 27–123; K. J. Leyser, *Rule and Conflict in an Early Medieval Society, Ottonian Saxony* (London, 1979), pp. 49–73; David Herlihy, *Medieval Households* (Cambridge, Mass., and London, 1985), pp. 29–111. See also Laurent Theis, "Saints sans famille? Quelques remarques sur la famille dans le monde franc à travers les sources hagiographiques," *Revue Historique* 255 (1976): 3–20; André Vauchez, "'Beata Stirps': Sainteté et lignage en occident," in *Famille et parenté dans l'occident médiéval* (Actes du colloque de Paris, 6–8 juin, 1974), Collection de l'école française de Rome, 30, communications et débats par Georges Duby et Jacques Le Goff (Rome, 1977), pp. 397–406.

128. See, for example, Roisin, *L'Hagiographie cistercienne,* p. 277.

129. For a discussion of the phenomenon of religious women fasting, see the fascinating studies by Caroline Bynum (*Holy Feast and Holy Fast*) and Rudolph M. Bell, *Holy Anorexia.*

130. On this topic see Charles Doherty, "Some Aspects of Hagiography as a Source for Economic History," *Peritia: Journal of the Medieval Academy of Ireland,* 1 (1982): 300–328.

131. See Benedicta Ward, *Miracles and the Medieval Mind: Theory, Record, and Event, 1000–1215* (Philadelphia, 1982); Pierre-André Sigal, *L'Homme et le miracle dans la France médiévale (XIᵉ–XIIᵉ siècle)* (Paris, 1985); Ronald C. Finucane, *Miracles and Pilgrims: Popular Beliefs in Medieval England* (Totowa, 1977); Jo Ann McNamara, "A Legacy of Miracles"; Martin Heinzelmann, "Une source de base de la litterature hagiographique latine: le recueil de miracles," in *Hagiographie, cultures et sociétés IVᵉ–XIIᵉ siècles,* pp. 235–57; Michel Rouche, "Miracles, maladies et psychologie de la foi à l'époque carolingienne en Francie," ibid., pp. 319–38.

132. Kieckhefer, *Unquiet Souls,* pp. 3–20.

133. For a thoughtful discussion of the problem of sacred image and social reality see *Immaculate and Powerful: The Female in Sacred Image and Social Reality* (The Harvard Women's Studies in Religion Series), ed Clarissa W. Atkinson, Constance H. Buchanan, and Margaret R. Miles (Boston, 1985), pp. 1–14.

134. Mecklin, *The Passing of the Saint,* pp. 62–63.

135. Jocelyn Wogan-Browne, "Queens, Virgins, and Mothers: Hagiographic Representations of the Abbess and Her Powers in Twelfth- and Thirteenth-Century Britain," in *Cosmos 7: Women and Sovereignty,* ed. Louise Olga Fradenburg (Edinburgh, 1992), p. 15.

136. Jocelyn Wogan-Browne, "'Clerc u lai, muïne u dame': Women and Anglo-Norman Hagiography in the Twelfth and Thirteenth Centuries," in *Women and Literature in Britain, 1150–1500,* ed. Carol M. Meale (Cambridge, 1993), pp. 64–65.

137. Atkinson et al., *Immaculate and Powerful,* especially pp. 5, 139, 164.

138. William of Malmesbury, *The History of the Kings of England,* p. 29, n. 5.

139. Fortunatus, *De vita Sanctae Radegundis liber I*, ch. 2, pp. 365–66; ch. 26, p. 373.

140. *Vita Sadalbergae abbatissae Laudunensis*, ch. 25, in *MGH SRM* 5:64.

141. Jocelyn Wogan-Browne, "Saints' Lives and the Female Reader," *Forum for Modern Language Studies* 27, no. 4 (1991): 320.

142. *Joan of Arc: Fact, Legend, and Literature*, ed. Wilfred T. Jewkes and Jerome B. Landfield (New York, Chicago, San Francisco, Atlanta, 1964), pp. 28, 34; Marina Warner, *Joan of Arc: The Image of Female Heroism* (New York, 1981), pp. 130–37; Anne Llewellyn Barstow, *Joan of Arc: Heretic, Mystic, Shaman*: Studies in Women and Religion, vol. 17 (Lewiston, Queenston, Lampeter, 1986), pp. 26–29, 58–59. Barstow notes that it was at St. Catherine's shrine at Fierbois that Joan was miraculously furnished with the sword that she carried in her victories. According to legend, Charles Martel had left his sword at this site after his famous victory over the Saracens.

143. Dorothy Day, *The Long Loneliness* (New York, 1952), p. 25.

144. Kay Hogan, "Of Saints and Other Things," in *Catholic Girls*, ed. Amber Coverdale Sumrall and Patrice Vecchione (New York and London, 1992), pp. 60–61.

145. Kathryn Harrison, "Saint Catherine of Siena: Catherine Means Pure," in *A Tremor of Bliss: Contemporary Writers on the Saints*, ed. Paul Elic (New York, San Diego, London, 1994), pp. 32–33.

146. For the difficulties inherent in attempting this type of study, see Geary, *Living with the Dead in the Middle Ages*, pp. 18–29; see also Paul Fouracre, "Merovingian History and Merovingian Hagiography," *Past and Present* 127 (May 1990): 3–38.

CHAPTER TWO

1. *Vita Sadalbergae Abbatissae Laudunensis*, ch. 8, *MGH SRM* 5:54. See also Wemple, *Women in Frankish Society*, pp. 158–59; *SWDA*, p. 183.

2. *Incipit Catalogus Sanctorum Hiberniae secundum diversa tempora*, trans. James H. Todd, in *St. Patrick Apostle of Ireland: A Memoir of His Life and Mission* (Dublin, 1864), pp. 88–89; See also Haddan and Stubbs, *Councils and Ecclesiastical Documents relating to Great Britain and Ireland*, 2:292–94; Hughes, *The Church in Early Irish Society*, pp. 69–79. Carolus Plummer, *Vitae sanctorum hiberniae* (Oxford, 1910), vol. 1, p. cxxi; John Ryan, *Irish Monasticism: Origins and Early Development* (Dublin and Cork, 1931), pp. 97, 261, and 305.

3. André Vauchez, *La Sainteté en occident aux derniers siècles du moyen âge d'après les proces de canonisation et les documents hagiographiques* (Rome, 1981), p. 20.

4. For a study of this topic see Robert Folz, *Les Saints rois du moyen âge en Occident (VIᵉ–XIIIᵉ siècles)*, Subsidia Hagiographica no. 68 (Brussels, 1984).

5. See especially McNamara and Wemple, "The Power of Women," pp. 103–15; Nelson, "Queens as Jezebels: The Careers of Brunhild and Balthild

in Merovingian History," in *Medieval Women*, ed. Derek Baker (Oxford, 1978), pp. 75–77; Wemple, *Women in Frankish Society*, pp. 9–123; Pauline Stafford, *Queens, Concubines, and Dowagers: The King's Wife in the Early Middle Ages* (Athens, Ga., 1983).

6. M. Z. Rosaldo, "The Use and Abuse of Anthropology: Reflections on Feminism and Cross-cultural Understanding," *Signs* 5/3 (1980): 397.

7. M. Z. Rosaldo and Louise Lamphere, eds., *Woman, Culture and Society* (Stanford, 1974), pp. 18–87.

8. Mary Erler and Maryanne Kowaleski, eds., *Women and Power in the Middle Ages* (Athens and London, 1988), p. 3.

9. For a discussion of some of the issues involved in utilizing the public/private construct, see Rayna Rapp, "Review Essay: Anthropology," *Signs* 4/3 (1979): 479–513; Joan Kelly, *Women, History and Theory: The Essays of Joan Kelly* (Chicago, 1984), pp. 1–18, 51–64; Sherry Ortner and Harriet Whitehead, eds., *Sexual Meanings: The Cultural Construction of Gender and Sexuality* (Cambridge and New York, 1981); L. Imray and Audrey Middleton, "Public and Private: Marking the Boundaries," in *The Public and the Private*, ed. E. Gamarnikow et al. (London, 1983), pp. 12–27; Carol P. MacCormack and Marilyn Strathern, eds., *Nature, Culture and Gender* (Cambridge and New York, 1980); and Judith M. Bennett, *Women in the Medieval English Countryside: Gender and Household in Brigstock Before the Plague* (New York and Oxford, 1987), esp. pp. 6–9, 18–47.

10. Erler and Kowaleski, eds., *Women and Power in the Middle Ages*, p. 4.

11. See especially Jo Ann McNamara and Suzanne F. Wemple, "The Power of Women through the Family in Medieval Europe: 500–1100," in *Clio's Consciousness Raised: New Perspectives on the History of Women*, ed. Mary Hartman and Lois W. Banner (New York, 1974), pp. 103–18; Suzanne F. Wemple, "Sanctity and Power: The Dual Pursuit of Early Medieval Women," in *Becoming Visible: Women in European History*, 2d ed., ed. R. Bridenthal, C. Koonz, and S. Stuard (Boston, 1987), pp. 130–51; Susan Mosher Stuard, *Women in Medieval Society* (Philadelphia, 1976), pp. 1–12. For the strong public role assumed by women in the Merovingian period, see Nelson, "Queens as Jezebels," pp. 31–77.

12. Jane Tibbetts Schulenburg, "Sexism and the Celestial Gynaeceum— from 500–1200," *Journal of Medieval History* 4 (1978): 117–33.

13. The most complete modern compilation of saints can be found in the *Bibliotheca Sanctorum*, Istituto Giovanni XXIII della Pontificia Università Lateranense (Rome, 1961–70), 12 vols.

14. For another interpretation of the statistics on female saints, one which incorporates both early and late medieval saints, see David Herlihy, "Did Women Have a Renaissance? A Reconsideration," *Medievalia et Humanistica: Studies in Medieval and Renaissance Culture*, n.s., no. 13 (1985): 1–22.

15. Many difficulties surround our attempts at identifying the "primary" geographic locations of the holy dead and defining the *loca sanctorum*. In some cases, saints might appear to "belong" at the same time to a number of localities or even several countries. They might claim, for example, one region

by birth, another in which they spent the major portion of their life, another made famous by their death and burial, and perhaps still another area which celebrated their translation and cult. Therefore, studies of the geographic distribution of saints might focus on any one of these criteria, as well as on the proliferation of various sites associated with the saint's cult. Moreover, while many of the saints' *vitae* are careful to record the saint's place of origin, a number of hagiographers do not provide this information. Rather, they are especially interested in preserving details of the place of the saint's death and the site of the initial cult. The *vita* then celebrated the anniversary of the holy dead and the cult that originated at the saint's tomb. As Delehaye has noted in regard to identifying the *loca sanctorum,* the true country or city of the holy dead is where the saints chose to leave their mortal remains. This was usually the site where the saint was first honored. Therefore, because of the special attention given in our sources to details surrounding the saint's death and burial, with particular reference to "place," the criteria used in this chapter to determine the geographic distribution of saints will be based on the location/ country of the saint's death and burial. See especially Hippolytus Delehaye, "Loca sanctorum," *Analecta Bollandiana* 68 (1930): 43–64.

16. See *The Fontana Economic History of Europe: The Middle Ages,* ed. Carlo M. Cipolla (Glasgow, 1972), pp. 25–41; Delooz, *Sociologie et canonisations,* pp. 176–77.

17. For general studies on place-names in France, see A. Longnon, *Les noms de lieux de la France* (Paris, 1920–29); A. Dauzat, *Les noms de lieux* (Paris, 1928); A. Vincent, *Toponymie de la France* (Brussels, 1937); G. Lavergne, *Les noms de lieux d'origine écclésiastique,* in V. Carrière, *Introduction aux études d'histoire écclésiastique locale* (Paris, 1934). See also *"On the Resting-Places of the Saints": Die Heiligen Englands,* ed. F. Liebermann (Hanover, 1889); Frank Stenton, "The Historical Bearing of Place-Name Studies: The Place of Women in Anglo-Saxon Society," *Transactions of the Royal Historical Society,* 4th series, 25 (1943): 1–13; Christine Fell, *Women in Anglo-Saxon England,* esp. pp. 98–100.

18. Delehaye, "Loca sanctorum," pp. 44, 50.

19. Charles Higounet, in his study "Les saints mérovingiens d'Aquitaine dans la toponymie," in *Etudes Mérovingiennes,* pp. 157–67 has provided an excellent regional study of the adoption of Merovingian saints' names. In this article he traces, for example, the impressive spread of the name of St. Radegund, which was attributed to various sites associated with her life or travel: Saint Radegonde (Som); three Sainte-Radegondes in Neustria; Sainte-Radegonde near Tours; Sainte-Radegonde-des-Pommiers; Sainte-Radegonde-des-Villiers; the ancient chapels of Sainte-Radegonde de Derce, Mierebeau, and Marconnay. Near Poitiers the countryside is filled with various reminiscences of the saint: the village of Sainte-Radegonde, the "footprint" of Sainte-Radegonde at Verrières, the priory of Sainte-Radegonde de Tartifame at Ingrande, the priory of Sainte-Radegonde de Troussaye at Ceaux. In addition, various sites along pilgrimage routes carry the saint's name: Sainte-Radegonde of Berry (Cher) appears later; Sainte-Radegonde near Saintes; Sainte-Radegonde-de-Baignes; Sainte-Radegonde (Gir) and Sainte-

Radegonde in Perigord (Higounet, pp. 163–64). An index of the popularity of the saint and the spread of his/her cult can also be seen in church dedications. For this important topic, see for example, F. Bond, *Dedications and Patron Saints of English Churches* (London, 1914); F. E. Arnold-Forster, *Studies in Church Dedications; or, England's Patron Saints* (London, 1899); Alison Binns, *Dedications of Monastic Houses in England and Wales, 1066–1216* (Woodbridge, 1989).

20. See especially Nelson, "Queens as Jezebels," pp. 33–77; Stafford, *Queens, Concubines, and Dowagers,* pp. 60–174; Wemple, "Sanctity and Power," pp. 130–51; Wemple, *Women in Frankish Society,* especially pp. 27–50, 63–70, 97–98.

21. For an introduction to domestic proselytization, see Godefroy Kurth, *Sainte Clotilde* (Paris, 1905), pp. 1–19.

22. Gregory of Tours, *History of the Franks,* bk. 2, chs. 29–31, pp. 141–45; Kurth, *Sainte Clotilde,* pp. 50–64.

23. See Marion Facinger, "A Study of Medieval Queenship: Capetian France 987–1237," *Studies in Medieval and Renaissance History* 5 (1968): 3–48; Stafford, *Queens, Concubines, and Dowagers,* pp. 99–174.

24. Gregory of Tours, *History of the Franks,* bk. 3, ch. 18, p. 182. Clotilda's *vita* also catalogues her great generosity to the Church: "In the suburbs of the castle of Laon, she built a church in honor of Saint Peter where she established a clerical congregation. She expanded the church of Saint Peter within the walls of the city of Reims and enriched it with lands and ecclesiastical ornaments. . . . From its foundations, she rebuilt that monastery of wonderous magnitude which was built in the time of Saint Denis in the suburbs of Rouen near the walls and dedicated to the twelve apostles by that same apostolic man, . . . There she collected no modest congregation of clerks for the service of God" (*SWDA,* pp. 48–49).

25. Fortunatus, *De Vita Sanctae Radegundis liber I,* ch. 3, *MGH SRM* 2:366; *SWDA,* p. 72.

26. Ibid., ch. 13, p. 369; *SWDA,* pp. 75–76.

27. Ibid, ch. 13, p. 369; ch. 14, p. 369; and ch. 3, p. 366; *SWDA,* pp. 72, 75–76.

28. Gregory of Tours, *History of the Franks,* bk. 9, ch. 41, p. 535.

29. *Vita S. Balthildis Reginae,* ch. 4, *MGH SRM* 2:485–87; ch. 7, 2:489; *SWDA,* pp. 270–72.

30. Ibid., ch. 7, 2:489–91; ch. 8, 2:491–93; ch. 9, 2:494; *SWDA,* pp. 271–73.

31. Ibid, ch. 9, 2:493; *SWDA,* p. 273.

32. See also Ian Wood, *The Merovingian Kingdoms 450–751* (London and New York, 1994), pp. 198–99. Like Brunhild, Balthild was accused by her detractors of having been involved in the murder of many leading churchmen of the period. See especially Janet Nelson, "Queens as Jezebels."

33. *Vita S. Balthildis Regina,* ch. 7, *MGH SRM* 2:489–91; ch. 8, 491–93; ch. 15, 501–2; *SWDA,* pp. 271–72, 276.

34. Folz, *Les Saintes reines,* pp. 46–55. Folz has also noted that the queen-saint Richarde borrowed some books from the famous library of St. Gall.

According to the oldest inventory of manuscripts of the monastery, certain works contain the notation "Rickard habet" (p. 160).

35. Ibid., pp. 58, 60–61. See also Corbet, *Les Saints ottoniens,* pp. 32–40, 120–235.

36. Odilo of Cluny, *Vita Sanctae Adalheidis Imperatricis* in *Bibliotheca Cluniacensis,* ed. Martinus Marrier and Andreas Quercetanus (Brussels and Paris, 1915), pp. 357–58, 360.

37. Corbet, *Les Saints ottoniens,* p. 108.

38. Folz, *Les Saintes reines,* pp. 82–93, *DSW,* 1:211.

39. Leyser, *Rule and Conflict in an Early Medieval Society,* p. 72.

40. Ibid.; Geary, *Phantoms of Remembrance,* p. 61.

41. Geary, pp. 52–80; Corbet, pp. 140–42, 148–51, 171–73; Leyser, p. 72.

42. Jo Ann McNamara, "A Legacy of Miracles," *Women of the Medieval World* (Oxford, 1985), p. 45.

43. For women as "peace-weavers" or "peace pledges" in Anglo-Saxon society, see, for example, Jane Chance, *Woman as Hero in Old English Literature* (Syracuse, 1986), pp. 1–11; Christine Fell, *Women in Anglo-Saxon England* (Oxford, 1984), pp. 37–38.

44. See the sources cited in the preceding note; Janemarie Luecke, "The Unique Experience of Anglo-Saxon Nuns," in *Peace Weavers,* vol. 2 of *Medieval Religious Women,* ed. John A. Nichols and Lillian Thomas Shank (Kalamazoo, Mich., 1987), pp. 56–59. Also see ch. 4 on domestic proselytization and ch. 5 on motherhood and sanctity.

45. Baudonivia, *De vita Sanctae Radegundis liber II,* ch. 10, *MGH SRM* 2:384–85; ch. 16, 2:388; *SWDA,* pp. 93, 96–99.

46. Gregory the Great, Epistle IX, 43, cited by Thomas Hodgkin, *Italy and Her Invaders, 376–814* (New York, 1880–89, 1967), 5:420.

47. *Vita S. Balthildis Reginae,* ch. 5, *MGH SRM* 2:487–88; *SWDA,* pp. 270–71.

48. Corbet, *Les Saints ottoniens,* pp. 91–92.

49. *SWDA,* p. 28; Heinzelmann and Poulin, *Les Vies anciennes de sainte Geneviève de Paris,* pp. 97–98.

50. Fortunatus, *De Vita Sanctae Radegundis liber I,* ch. 11; *MGH SRM* 2:368; ch. 38, p. 374; *SWDA,* pp. 74, 85. In this same tradition, the early Christian martyr, St. Foi, patron saint of Conques, was especially known for her many miracles which involved the freeing of captives and especially those imprisoned by the Saracens. Many of those who had been miraculously freed by the saint then brought to her church at Conques, as a thank offering, their iron chains, fetters, or "bracelets"—symbols of their captivity. A representation of this can be seen on the marvelous romanesque portal of St. Foi of Conques where handcuffs and chains are depicted hanging above the patron saint's altar. Inside the church one can still see large grills which were said to have been fashioned of the chains that were brought to the saint by the freed prisoners. For the miracles of St. Foi concerning the freeing of prisoners, see Pamela Sheingorn, *The Book of Sainte Foy,* especially, 1.31, pp. 102–3; 1.32, pp. 103–4; 2.6, pp. 128–29; 3.15, pp. 164–65; 4.4, pp. 185–86;

4.5, pp. 186–87; 4.6, pp. 187–89; 4.7, pp. 189–91; 4.8, pp. 191–96; 4.9, pp. 196–97; A.2, pp. 234–36; A.3, pp. 237–39; L.1, pp. 242–44; L.2, pp. 244–46.

51. *Vita S. Waldedrudis, Analectes hist. eccl. Belgique*, vol. 4 (1867), p. 229. See also L. Van Der Essen, *Etude critique et littéraire sur les Vitae des saints mérovingiens de l'ancienne Belgique* (Louvain, 1907), pp. 231–40; *SWDA*, p. 262.

52. *Vita S. Balthildis Reginae*, ch. 2, MGH SRM 2:483; *SWDA*, pp. 268–69.

53. Ibid., ch. 6, 2:488; ch. 9, 2:494 (emphasis mine); *SWDA*, pp. 271, 273.

54. See J. Campbell, "Elements in the Background to the Life of St Cuthbert and his Early Cult," in *St Cuthbert: His Cult and His Community to AD 1200*, ed. Gerald Bonner, David Rollason and Clare Stancliffe (Woodbridge, 1989), p. 11. For the topic of women and monastic life, see Penelope D. Johnson's important study, *Equal in Monastic Profession: Religious Women in Medieval France* (Chicago, 1991).

55. *Vita Sadalbergae abbatissae Laudunensis*, ch. 8, MGH SRM 5:54; *SWDA*, p. 183.

56. Rudolf, *The Life of St. Leoba*, p. 221.

57. Jane Tibbetts Schulenburg, "Women's Monastic Communities, 500–1100: Patterns of Expansion and Decline," *Signs* 14/2 (winter 1989): 261–92.

58. Leyser, *Rule and Conflict*, pp. 63–73.

59. Ibid. Also, as Kathleen Hughes has noted with regard to the development of women's monastic communities in early Christian Ireland, some aristocratic women established religious houses on their family lands with, it seems, the intention that their foundations would endure for only the length of their own lifetimes. These small "family houses" attracted female relatives and friends of the founder, as well as a few women from the local area. Thus, when the founder died (and the life interest in the property she had inherited was terminated), the community was dispersed: its members joined other houses or returned to secular life, and the land reverted to the founder's family. Hughes, *Early Christian Ireland: An Introduction to the Sources* (Ithaca, 1972), pp. 234–35.

60. See also Stafford, *Queens, Concubines, and Dowagers*, pp. 175–90; Wemple, *Women in Frankish Society*, pp. 158–65.

61. Ridyard, *The Royal Saints of Anglo-Saxon England*, p. 102.

62. Ibid.

63. Ibid., pp. 96–139, 176–210, 234–52.

64. *Vita S. Balthildis Reginae*, ch. 12, MGH SRM 2:498; *SWDA*, pp. 274–75.

65. Leyser, *Rule and Conflict*, pp. 49–62; Wemple, *Women in Frankish Society*, pp. 47–49; Stafford, *Queens, Concubines, and Dowagers*, pp. 171–82.

66. Hucbald, *Vita S. Rictrudis, AASS, Mai. III*, May 12, p. 83; *AASS B* 4:488–503; *SWDA*, pp. 205–7.

67. Leyser, *Rule and Conflict*, pp. 49–62; Wemple, *Women in Frankish Society*, pp. 47–49; Stafford, *Queens, Concubines, and Dowagers*, pp. 171–82.

68. Baudonivia, *De vita Sanctae Radegundis liber II*, ch. 5, *MGH SRM* 2:381; *SWDA*, p. 89.

69. Gregory of Tours, *Liber in gloria confessorum*, ch. 104, in *MGH SRM* 1:814.

70. *AASS, Oct. II*, October 4 (St. Aurea), p. 477; David Knowles and R. Neville Hadcock, *Medieval Religious Houses: England and Wales* (London, 1971), p. 261; Rollason, *The Mildrith Legend*, pp. 76, 78; Rudolf, *The Life of St. Leoba*, p. 210; *DSW* 2:241; *SWDA*, p. 188.

71. See, for example, W. Braunfels, *Monasteries of Western Europe: The Architecture of the Orders* (London, 1972); Edward James, "Archaeology and the Merovingian Monastery," in *Columbanus and Merovingian Monasticism*, ed. H. B. Clarke and Mary Brennan, BAR International Ser. 113 (1981): 33–55; M. Vieillard-Troiekouroff, *Les monuments religieux de la Gaule d'après les œuvres de Grégoire de Tours* (Paris, 1976); J. Mertens, "Recherches archéologiques dans l'abbaye mérovingienne de Nivelles," *Archaeologia belgica*, 61 (*Miscell. archaeol. in honorem J. Breuer*, 1962); C. Heitz, "Saint-Pierre-aux Nonnains," *Archeologia* 56 (1973): 15–23; Marquise de Geneviève Aliette de Rohan-Chabot Maillé, *Les Cryptes de Jouarre* (Paris, 1971); C. Peers and C. A. Ralegh Radford, "The Saxon Monastery of Whitby," *Archaeologia* 89 (1943): 27–88; F. S. Scott, "The Hildithryth Stone and the Other Hartlepool Name-Stones," *Archaeologia Aeliana*, 4th ser., 24 (1956): 196–212; Jean Hubert, "L'Eremitisme et archéologie," *L'Eremetismo in occidente nei secoli XI et XII* (Milan, Univ. Catt. del Sacro Cuore, Contributi, Ser. 3, Var. 4; Studi Medioevali; Misc. 4; Milan, 1965), pp. 462–90.

72. De Rohan-Chabot Maillé, *Les Cryptes de Jouarre*, p. 26.

73. *AASS, Sept. VI* (September 22), p. 527.

74. *De virtutibus Sanctae Geretrudis*, ch. 10, *MGH SRM* 2:469; de Rohan-Chabot Maillé, *Les Cryptes de Jouarre*, p. 41; *DSW* 1:111–12.

75. *SWDA*, p. 314.

76. *Vita S. Bertae abbatissae Blangiacensis, AASS, Iul. II*, July 4, ch. 1, pp. 50–51; *AASS B* 6:562–69. The poetic works of Aldhelm describe the church of St. Mary built by Bugga: "The renowned daughter of King Centwine built this church: it was erected through the excellent effort of Bugga. . . . [she] built [this] new church with its lofty structure, in which holy altars gleam in twelve-fold dedication; moreover she dedicates the apse to the Virgin. . . . The church glows within with gentle light on occasions when the sun shines through the glass windows, diffusing its clear light throughout the rectangular church." *Aldhelm: The Poetic Works*, trans. Michael Lapidge and James L. Rosier (Cambridge, 1985), pp. 47–49.

77. See, for example, the primary role attributed to St. Genovefa in the building of St. Denis in Paris (Heinzelmann and Poulin, *Les Vies anciennes de sainte Geneviéve de Paris*, pp. 95–96; *SWDA*, pp. 25–26).

78. M. J. Swanton, "A Fragmentary Life of St. Mildred and Other Kentish Royal Saints," *Archaeologia Cantiana: Being Contributions to the History and Archaeology of Kent* 91 (1975): 23; also cited by Fell in *Women in Anglo-Saxon England*, p. 120.

79. *AASS, Feb. I,* February 2, p. 306.

80. *Vita Rusticulae sive Marciae abbatissae Arelatensis,* ch. 8, *MGH SRM* 4:343; *SWDA,* pp. 126–27.

81. *AASS, Iul. II,* July 8, p. 626.

82. *AASS, Mar. III,* March 22, p. 385.

83. See Hrotswitha, *Carmen de Primordiis Coenobii Gandersheim, PL* 137:1141–42. The Life of the Irish saint Samthann notes how her monastery's first oratory was constructed of wood. Later, when the buildings of the convent were enlarged, it was necessary to move the oratory. The *vita* also describes how, after Samthann's death, the prioress, Nathea, traveled to Connacht to procure pine timber for her building project. After several days of trying to find a sufficient supply of timber, without any success, the prioress was visited in her sleep by Samthann. The saint told her where she would find suitable pine trees for building. St. Samthann also appeared in a vision to the man who owned the timber. She then struck him with her bachall and convinced him to give the wood to the nuns as well as to transport it to their monastery. Plummer, *Vitae Sanctorum Hiberniae,* 2:254–55; see also Daphne D. C. Pochin Mould, *The Irish Saints* (Dublin and London, 1964), p. 283.

84. Frank Barlow, ed., *The Life of King Edward Who Rests at Westminster, Attributed to a Monk of St. Bertin* (London, Edinburgh, 1962), pp. 46–47.

85. *AASS, Iun. II* (June 8), p. 132; *SWDA,* p. 108. Aldhelm also provides a detailed description of the decoration of Bugga's church: "The new church has many ornaments: a golden cloth glistens with its twisted threads and forms a beautiful covering for the sacred altar. And a golden chalice covered with jewels gleams so that it seems to reflect the heavens with their bright stars; and there is a large paten made from silver. . . . Here glistens the metal of the Cross made from burnished gold and adorned at the same time with silver and jewels. Here too a thurible embossed on all sides hangs suspended from on high, having vaporous openings from which the Sabaean frankincense emits ambrosia when the priests are asked to perform mass." Lapidge and Rosier, *Aldhelm: The Poetic Works,* p. 49.

86. *AASS, Aug. VI* (August 31), p. 686.

87. *AASS, Mai. I* (May 1), p. 117.

88. See Patrick J. Geary, *Furta Sacra: Thefts of Relics in the Central Middle Ages;* Finucane, *Miracles and Pilgrims;* Sigal, *L'Homme et le Miracle;* Sumption, *Pilgrimage: An Image of Mediaeval Religion.*

89. Brown, *Society and the Holy,* pp. 240–41.

90. Paulinus of Nola, *The Letters of St. Paulinus of Nola: Ancient Christian Writers,* trans. P. G. Walsh (Westminster and London, 1967), Letter 31: "To Severus," 2:125–33. Paulinus also notes that a piece of the holy cross was brought to him from Jerusalem by the holy Melania as a gift of the holy bishop John (p. 125); *DSW* 1:371. See also Jan Willem Drijvers, *Helena Augusta: The Mother of Constantine the Great and the Legend of Her Finding of the True Cross* (Leiden, 1992).

91. Baudonivia, *De vita sanctae Radegundis liber II,* ch. 13, *MGH SRM* 2:386, ch. 14, pp. 386–87; *SWDA,* pp. 94–96. See especially the studies by

Moreira, "Provisatrix optima: St. Radegund of Poitiers' relic petitions to the East," and Brian Brennan, "St. Radegund and the Early Development of Her Cult at Poitiers," *Journal of Religious History* 13 (1985): 340–54.

92. Baudonivia, *De vita sanctae Radegundis liber II*, ch. 16, *MGH SRM* 2:387–89; *SWDA*, pp. 96–99; McNamara, "A Legacy of Miracles," p. 47.

93. *Vita S. Reineldis virg. mart.*, *AASS, Iul. IV*, July 16, ch. 7, p. 177.

94. Rollason, *The Mildrith Legend*, pp. 36, 76, 78, 98, 127–28; St. Mildred, *AASS, Iul. III*, July 13, pp. 490–93; see also *The Lives of Women Saints of Our Contrie of England, c. 1610–1615*, ed. C. Horstmann (London, 1886), pp. 63–66.

95. *Vita Sanctae Hathumodae*, *PL* 137:1171.

96. *DSW* 1:4.

97. Ibid., 1:413.

98. See Geary, *Furta Sacra*.

99. Gregory of Tours, *Libri miraculorum* vol. 1 (Paris, 1857), bk. 1, ch. 14, pp. 45–49 (and note no. 1, p. 45); *AASS, Iun. VII*, June 25, pp. 63–67.

100. *The Lives of Women Saints of Our Contrie of England*, ed. C. Horstmann, pp. 59–60; *AASS*, Feb. I, Feb. 3, pp. 391–94; C. J. Stranks, *St. Etheldreda, Queen and Abbess*, p. 26.

101. De Rohan-Chabot Maillé, *Les Cryptes de Jouarre*, pp. 82–83.

102. Geary, *Furta Sacra*, pp. 111–12, 115.

103. See, for example, McNamara, "A Legacy of Miracles," especially pp. 40–47.

104. *Life of St. Brigit*, in *Anecdota Oxoniensia: Lives of Saints from The Book of Lismore*, trans. Whitley Stokes (Oxford, 1890), p. 195 (emphasis mine).

105. See also McNamara, "A Legacy of Miracles," pp. 40–47.

106. Fortunatus, *De vita Sanctae Radegundis liber I*, ch. 17, *MGH SRM* 2:370, ch. 19, 2:370–71; *SWDA*, pp. 77–79.

107. *DSW* 2:115; Georges J. Uhry, *Le Mont-Sainte-Odile au moyen âge*, (Strasbourg, 1967), p. 20; James F. Kenney, *The Sources for the Early History of Ireland: Ecclesiastical, An Introduction and Guide* (Shannon, 1968), p. 519, no. 323.

108. Rudolf, *The Life of St. Leoba*, trans. Talbot, p. 216.

109. Joan Morris notes this in her study, *The Lady Was a Bishop* (New York and London, 1973), pp. 130–31. For the Moissac Sacramentary, see Morris, p. 173, citing E. Martène, *De antiquis ecclesiae ritibus* (Venice, 1736), vol. 2, p. 425.

110. Cited by Ryan, *Irish Monasticism*, p. 180 (emphasis mine).

111. Todd, *St. Patrick*, pp. 11–22.

112. Ryan, *Irish Monasticism*, p. 181.

113. Edward C. Sellner, "Brigit of Kildare, Golden Sparkling Flame: A Study in the Limnality of Women's Spiritual Power," *Vox Benedictina* 8, no. 2 (winter 1991): 287; Bitel, *Land of Women*, p. 192.

114. Ryan, *Irish Monasticism*, p. 183; Sellner, "Brigit of Kildare," pp. 285–88. See also, K. Meyer, ed., *Tertia Vita*, in *Anecdota Oxoniensia* (Oxford, 1885), part 4.

115. Bitel, *Land of Women*, p. 192.

116. Wemple, *Women in Frankish Society*, pp. 149–74. We find, for example, St. Fara, abbess of Faremoutiers, described as frequently hearing confessions from her nuns. On St. Fara, see Jonas, *Vita Columbani abbatis discipulorumque eius liber II, MGH SRM* 4:130–41. See also the Rule of Donatus which required that senior and junior nuns were to confess daily at any convenient hour. "Nothing shall be hidden from the spiritual mother because this is ordered by the holy fathers that confession should be given before meals or before going to bed or whenever it will be convenient because with confession penitence frees us from death." *The Rule of St. Donatus of Besançon*, trans. Jo Ann McNamara and John E. Halborg, ch. 23, p. 47; see also Hollis, *Anglo-Saxon Women in the Church*, pp. 134–35.

117. *Vita Bertilae, MGH SRM*, 6:105, ch. 5; *SWDA*, p. 285. Bede, *A History of the English Church and People*, bk. 4, ch. 6, p. 218.

118. *Life of St. Brigit*, in *Anecdota Oxoniensia: Lives of Saints from The Book of Lismore*, ed. Stokes, p. 191.

119. Charles Joseph Hefele and H. Leclercq, *Histoire des Conciles*, 3/1 (Paris, 1909), p. 539; Arthur West Haddan and William Stubbs, *Councils and Ecclesiastical Documents Relating to Great Britain and Ireland* (Oxford, 1871 [1964]), vol. 3, pp. 238–40.

120. Eddius Stephanus, "Life of St. Wilfrid," in *Lives of the Saints*, trans. J. F. Webb (Harmondsworth, 1965), ch. 59–60, pp. 195–8.

121. *Two Lives of St. Cuthbert*, trans. Bertram Colgrave (New York, 1969), ch. 24, p. 236.

122. See especially Rosamond McKitterick's important study, "Nuns' Scriptoria in England and Francia in the Eighth Century," *Francia*, 19, no. 1 (1992): 1–35; Wemple, *Women in Frankish Society*, pp. 175–88.

123. Ryan, *Irish Monasticism*, p. 139.

124. *Caesarius of Arles: Life, Testament, Letters*, trans. William E. Klingshirn (Liverpool, 1994), bk. 1, no. 58, p. 39.

125. Fortunatus, *Opera Poetica, Carminum liber VIII*, poem 1, *MGH AA* 4:179–80.

126. Baudonivia, *De vita Sanctae Radegundis liber II*, ch. 9, *MGH SRM* 2:384; *SWDA*, pp. 91–92.

127. Gregory of Tours: *Glory of the Confessors*, trans. van Dam, no. 104, pp. 107–8; *MGH SRM* 1:816. Listed in the inventory of relics of Ste-Croix and still extant today is a small piece known as the saint's reading desk, made of wood and decorated with carvings. According to Yvonne Labande-Mailfert this "pupitre de sainte Radegonde" is actually a head rest (*Histoire de l'Abbaye Sainte-Croix*, pp. 74–75).

128. *Vita Rusticulae sive Marciae abbatissae Arelatensis*, ch. 6, *MGH* 4:342; *SWDA*, p. 126.

129. *Vita Sanctae Geretrudis*, ch. 3, *MGH SRM* 2:458; ch. 2, 2:457; *SWDA*, pp. 224–25.

130. S. Aurea, *AASS, Oct. II*, October 4, pp. 475–76: *BHL* 1:129.

131. *Vita Anstrudis abbatissae Laudunensis*, ch. 1, *MGH SRM* 6:66–67;

see also David Herlihy, *Opera Muliebria: Women and Work in Medieval Europe* (New York, 1990), p. 41; *SWDA*, pp. 291–92.

132. *Vita Bertilae abbatissae Calensis*, ch. 6, *MGH SRM* 6:106. Translation from *SWDA*, p. 286.

133. Bede, *A History of the English Church and People*, bk. 3, ch. 8, pp. 153–55, and ch. 23, p. 246.

134. Rollason, *The Mildrith Legend*, pp. 11, 76, 78, 85, 98, 120. St. Mildred, *AASS, Iul. III*, July 13, pp. 490–93 (see also Horstmann, *The Lives of Women Saints of Our Contrie of England*, pp. 63–65).

135. Bede, *A History of the English Church and People*, bk. 3, ch. 8, pp. 153–55; ibid., bk. 4, ch. 23, p. 246.

136. *Hildelitha, abb. Berecingensis, AASS, Mar. III*, March 24, pp. 482–85, and *BHL* 2:587; Aldhelm, *De laudibus virginitatis, PL* 89:103–6, or *Aldhelm: The Prose Works*, trans. Michael Lapidge and Michael Herren, pp. 59–63.

137. Bede, *A History of the English Church and People*, bk. 4, ch. 23, pp. 246–47.

138. Ibid., bk. 4, ch. 23, p. 247 (emphasis mine).

139. Ibid.; see also Hollis's perceptive study of Bede and "Rewriting Female Lives" in *Anglo-Saxon Women and the Church*, pp. 243–70.

140. *Two Lives of Saint Cuthbert*, trans. Colgrave, ch. 24, p. 234.

141. Rudolf, *The Life of St. Leoba*, trans. Talbot, pp. 211–12, 214.

142. Ibid., pp. 214–215.

143. *Vita de sanctis virginibus Herlinde et Reinula seu Renilde abbatissis Masaci in Belgio, AASS, Mar. III*, March 22, ch. 1, pp. 384–86.

144. Agius, *Vita Sanctae Hathumodae, Appendix ad Opera Hrotsvithae, PL* 137:1171, ch. 1; 1173–74, ch. 3.

145. *Vitae sanctorum Hiberniae ex codice olim salmanticensi nunc brusellensi*, ed. W. W. Heist (Subsidia Hagiographica 28; Brussels, 1966), p. 84. Cited by Herlihy, *Opera Muliebria*, pp. 30, 45 n. 22.

146. See, for example, Fortunatus, *De vita Sanctae Radegundis liber I*, ch. 29, *MGH SRM* 2:373–74; *SWDA*, p. 82.

147. *Vita S. Balthildis Reginae*, ch. 11 *MGH SRM* 2:497; *SWDA*, p. 274.

148. St. Milburga, *AASS, Feb. III*, February 23, pp. 395–96; *BHL* 2:869; *DSW* 2:92.

149. Rudolf, *Life of St. Leoba*, pp. 220–21.

150. *De miraculis Sanctae Waldburgis*, bk. 1, ch. 3, *MGH SS* 15, pt. 1, p. 540. See also Horstmann, *The Lives of Women Saints of Our Contrie of England*, p. 84; *DSW* 2:297–98.

151. See Schulenburg, "Saints, Gender and the Production of Miracles in Medieval Europe," paper presented at the Ninth Berkshire Conference on the History of Women, Vassar College, June 13, 1993.

152. See, for example, Elisabeth Schüssler Fiorenza, "Word, Spirit and Power: Women in Early Christian Communities," in *Women of Spirit: Female Leadership in the Jewish and Christian Traditions*, ed. Rosemary Ruether and Eleanor McLaughlin (New York, 1979), pp. 39–44.

153. Tacitus, *The Agricola and the Germania*, trans. H. Mattingly (Harmondsworth, 1948, 1970), p. 108; *The Histories*, trans. W. Hamilton Fyfe (Oxford, 1912), vol. 2, p. 171. Tacitus also describes the special power of Veleda. A deputation was sent to her: "They were not, however allowed to approach and speak to Veleda or even to see her, but were kept at a distance to inspire in them the greater awe. She herself lived at the top of a high tower, and one of her relatives was appointed to carry all the questions and answers like a mediator between god and man" (p. 176).

154. Bede, *A History of the English Church and People*, bk. 4, ch. 19, p. 239.

155. Baudonivia, *De vita Sanctae Radegundis liber II*, ch. 20, *MGH SRM* 2:391; *SWDA*, pp. 101; see also Wemple, *Women in Frankish Society*, p. 186.

156. *Vita S. Balthildis Reginae*, ch. 13, *MGH SRM* 2:498–99; *SWDA*, p. 275. See also, for the visions of St. Gertrude, *De virtutibus Sanctae Geretrudis*, ch. 2, in *MGH SRM* 2:465–66; *SWDA*, pp. 229–30.

157. *Vita Aldegundis*, ch. 18, in *MGH SRM* 6:88. See also Wemple, *Women in Frankish Society*, pp. 185–87, and Wemple, "Female Spirituality and Mysticism in Frankish Monasteries: Radegund, Balthild and Aldegund," in *Peace Weavers: Medieval Religious Women II*, ed. John A. Nichols and Lillian Thomas Shank (Kalamazoo, Mich., 1987), pp. 39–53; Barbara Abou-El-Haj, *The Medieval Cult of Saints: Formations and Transformations* (Cambridge, 1994), pp. 114–15, figs. 195–96; *SWDA*, pp. 235–54.

158. *AASS, Ian. III*, January 30, ch. 6, p. 660; Wemple, *Women in Frankish Society*, p. 186.

159. Wemple, "Female Spirituality and Mysticism," pp. 47–48.

160. There has been a great deal of interesting literature in this area, especially for the late Middle Ages; see, for example, Elizabeth Alvilda Petroff, ed., *Medieval Women's Visionary Literature* (New York and Oxford, 1986); Clarissa W. Atkinson, *Mystic and Pilgrim: The Book and the World of Margery Kempe* (Ithaca and London, 1983); Richard Kieckhefer, *Unquiet Souls: Fourteenth-Century Saints and Their Religious Milieu* (Chicago, 1984).

161. *SWDA*, pp. 23–24; Heinzelmann and Poulin, *Les vies anciennes de Sainte Geneviève de Paris*, pp. 32, 59.

162. *Vita S. Godeberthae, AASS, Apr. II*, April 11, pp. 33–34.

163. Rudolf, *Life of St. Leoba*, pp. 218–20.

164. *SWDA*, p. 263.

165. Benedicta Ward, *Miracles and the Medieval Mind*, especially pp. 3–32, 166–91.

166. *AASS, Apr. II* (April 9), pp. 575–78; *DSW* 1:97. See also J. Warichez, *L'Abbaye de Lobbes depuis les origines jusqu'en 1200* (Louvain, 1909), pp. 5–6, 16–17, 178; *Dictionnaire d'histoire et de géographie ecclésiastiques*, ed. Alfred Baudrillart, et al. (Paris, 1931), vol. 5, pp. 1259–60.

167. Goscelin, *La Légende de Ste. Edith*, ed. Wilmart, ch. 12, pp. 278–80. See also Susan Millinger, "Humility and Power: Anglo-Saxon Nuns in Anglo-Norman Hagiography," in *Distant Echoes: Medieval Religious Women I*, ed. John A. Nichols and Lillian Thomas Shank (Kalamazoo, 1984), pp. 115–29.

168. Eleanor McLaughlin, "Women, Power and the Pursuit of Holiness in Medieval Christianity," in Ruether and McLaughlin, *Women of Spirit: Female Leadership in the Jewish and Christian Traditions,* p. 107.

169. Todd, *St. Patrick,* pp. 88–89; Haddan and Stubbs, *Councils and Ecclesiastical Documents,* 2:292–94.

170. See Schulenburg, "Women's Monastic Communities," especially p. 268. The number of new foundations and the percentages of houses for women in the first half of the eighth century would no doubt have been greater if one considered the missionary efforts of the Englishwomen in Germany during this time. Under the auspices of the missionary-saints Boniface and Leoba, a number of English nuns were recruited to spread the new faith in Germany. There they established several religious communities for women, or double houses, which became centers of missionary activity and education.

171. Saint Aethelwold, *Regularis Concordia: The Monastic Agreement of the Monks and Nuns of the English Nation,* ed. Thomas Symons (London, 1953), pp. 1–2.

172. *The Anglo-Saxon Chronicle,* trans. and ed. G. N. Garmonsway (London and New York, 1972), p. 115 (emphasis mine). Following is a partial listing of famous early houses for women or double monasteries ruled by abbesses that were destroyed or abandoned during the invasions, only to be restored as exclusively male settlements. In Britain: Whitby, Coventry, Gloucester, Folkestone, Leominster, Minster-in-Thanet, St. Milburga of Wenloch, Tynemouth, St. Frideswide, Oxford, Repton, Bath, Carlisle, Exeter, Berkeley, Wimborne, Winchcombe, and Chichester. In France and Belgium: Vézelay, les Andelys, Auchy, Blangy, St-Pierre-le-Pullier in Poitiers and Bourges, St-Vincent de Laon, Marchiennes, Alden-Eyck, Mouzon, St. Enimie, Tuffé, and St. Trinité de Fecamp. See Schulenburg, "Women's Monastic Communities," p. 281.

173. David Knowles, *Christian Monasticism* (New York, 1969), p. 54.

174. Immediately after the Norman Conquest in 1066, many noble Englishwomen joined monastic communities. As daughters and wives of Harold Godwinson's loyal supporters, they were particularly afraid of being raped by the Norman invaders. They therefore took the veil for protection and sought asylum in the English monasteries. As noted by Eadmer (d. ca. 1124) in his *History of Recent Events in England,* "Thereupon a number of women anticipating this and fearing for their own virtue betook themselves to convents of Sisters and taking the veil protected themselves in their company from such infamy." Geoffrey Bosanquet, trans., *Eadmer's History of Recent Events in England: Historia Novorum in Anglia* (London, 1964), p. 129. (See also chapter 3 below) On the neglect of female monaticism by the Normans, see Elkins, *Holy Women of Twelfth-Century England,* pp. 1–2, 13–18.

175. Geary, *Phantoms of Remembrance,* pp. 51–80. As Geary has noted, in contrast to women in France, aristocratic women in the empire continued to exercise direct roles in liturgical *memoria.*

176. Schulenburg, "Women's Monastic Communities," pp. 285–90; Marc A. Meyer, "Women and the Tenth-Century English Monastic Reform," *Revue Bénédictine* 87 (1977): 34–61. In this article, Meyer underscores the impor-

tance of the generosity of royal and noblewomen to the monastic revival of the period; Geary, *Phantoms of Remembrance*, p. 69.

177. Schulenburg, "Women's Monastic Communities," p. 288.

178. Hollis, *Anglo-Saxon Women in the Church*, p. 298; see Schulenburg, "Strict Active Enclosure and Its Effects on the Female Monastic Experience (ca. 500–1100)," in *Distant Echoes*, pp. 51–86.

179. Wemple, *Women in Frankish Society*, p. 169.

180. Jacobus de Guisia, *Annales Hanoniae*, bk. 13, ch. 37, in *MGH SS* 30, pt. 1., pp. 162–63. For a detailed discussion of this source, see J. J. Hoebanx, *L'Abbaye de Nivelles des Origines au XIVe siècle*, Mémoires de l'Académie Royale de Belgique, vol. 46, fasc. 4 (Brussels, 1952), pp. 171–79.

181. De Guisia, *Annales Hanoniae*, pp. 162–63.

182. Wemple, *Women in Frankish Society*, p. 166.

183. Ibid., p. 188.

184. See Schulenburg, "Women and Sacred Space: Symbol and Practice," paper presented at the Seventh Berkshire Conference on the History of Women, Wellesley College, June 21, 1987. I am currently working on a book which focuses on gender-based proscriptions of sacred space. It examines the placement and displacement of women within the Church and is particularly concerned with the configurations of monastic space.

185. Council of Nantes, 895, canon 19. *Acta Conciliorum*, ed. Harduin (Paris, 1714), 6, p. 461, cited by McNamara and Wemple, "The Power of Women," p. 112. In this tradition see also the Penitential of Silos, ca. 800, no. XI (107): "A woman, however learned and holy, shall not presume to teach men in a meeting." McNeill and Gamer, *Medieval Handbooks of Penance*, p. 289.

186. It is also important to note the context of this decree, for it appears to have been aimed especially at behavioral problems associated with nuns of the period and the need for the Church to curtail their public roles. As stated in the canon: "Cum Apostolus dicat: Mulieres in Ecclesia taceant, non enim permittitur eis loqui: turpe est enim mulieri loqui in Ecclesia, mirum videtur, quod quaedam mulierculae, contra diuinas humanasque leges attrita fronte impudenter agentes, placita generalia & publicos conuentus indefinenter adeant, & negotia regni, vtilitatesque reipublicae magis perturbent, quam disponant: cum indecens sit, & etiam inter barbaras gentes reprehensibile, mulieres virorum causas discutere: & quae de lanisiciis suis, & operibus textilibus, & muliebribus, inter genitiarias suas residentes, debuerant disputare, in conuentu publico, ac si in curia residentes, senatoriam sibi vfurpant auctoritatem. Quae ignominiosa praesumptio fautoribus magis imputanda videtur, quam feminis. Vnde, quia diuinae leges, vt supra monstratum est, hoc contradicunt, & humanae nihilominus id ipsum prohibent, vt feminae nihil aliud prosequantur in publico, quam suam causam: ait enim lex Theodosiana; Nulla ratione feminae amplius quam suas causas agendi habeant potestatem, nec alicuius causam a se nouerint prosequendam. *Idcirco ex auctoritate canonica interdicimus, vt nulla sanctimonialis virgo, vel vidua, conuentus generales adeat, nisi a principe fuerit euocata, aut ab Episcopo suo: nisi forte propriae necessitatis ratio impulerit, & hoc ipsum cum licentia Episcopi sui.*"

(Italics mine). Jacques Sirmond, ed., *Concilia Antiqua Galliae* (Paris, 1629, 1970 reprint), vol. 3, Concilium Namnetense, ch. 19, pp. 606–7.

187. *Annales Fuldenses* for the year 847, *MGH SS* 1:365; Hefele and Leclercq, *Historie des conciles*, vol. 4, pt. 1, pp. 135–36 (emphasis mine). This fascinating case is translated and discussed by Wemple in *Women in Frankish Society*, pp. 144–45. See also Aron Gurevich, *Medieval Popular Culture: Problems of Belief and Perception* (Cambridge Studies in Oral and Literate Culture, 14), trans. by Janos M. Bak and Paul A. Hollingsworth (Cambridge and New York), pp. 68–69.

188. *Vita S. Iohannis Gualberti Anonyma*, ch. 2, in *MGH SS* 30, pt. 2: 1105. See also the fascinating study by R. I. Moore in which he discusses this case: "Family, Community, and Cult on the Eve of the Gregorian Reform," in *Transactions of the Royal Historical Society*, 5th ser., vol. 30 (London, 1980), p. 68.

189. Odo of Cluny, *Collationum, Bibliotheca Cluniacensis*, ed. Martinus Marrier and Andreas Quercetanus (Brussels, 1915), bk. 2, p. 192.

190. Corbet, *Les Saints ottoniens*, pp. 107–8; Geary, *Phantoms of Remembrance*, p. 70; Odilo of Cluny, *Vita Sanctae Adalheidis*, pp. 353–61.

191. *Liber iii adversus simoniacos*, bk. 3, ch. 12, in *MGH, Libelli de Lite*, 1:212 (emphasis mine).

192. Idung of Prüfening, in *Cistercians and Cluniacs: The Case for Citeaux* (Cistercian Fathers Series, 33), trans. J. Leahey and G. Perigo (Kalamazoo, 1977), pp. 175–76.

193. Wemple, *Women in Frankish Society*, p. 171; see also Johnson, *Equal in Monastic Profession*, pp. 248–66.

194. *AASS, Sept. VI* (Sept. 21), p. 276.

195. *MGH SS* 4:158–64; Wemple, *Women in Frankish Society*, pp. 100, 145, 171, 173–74; Smith, "The Problem of Female Sanctity in Carolingion Europe," pp. 14, 18–25.

196. *MGH SS* 4:452, ch. 6.

197. *DSW* 1:397. See also a note on St. Hunna in the *Analecta Bollandiana*, 66 (1948):343–45. There was also a legend that grew up around the popular German St. Guntild, patron saint of Eichstatt and Suffersheim, in which this noblewoman was forced to work as a servant doing domestic and farm labor. She came to be known as the "cow-maid," the patron saint of cattle whose milk jug was never empty. See *DSW* 1:357–58; also Michael Goodich, "*Ancilla Dei*: The Servant as Saint in the Late Middle Ages," in Kirshner and Wemple, *Women of the Medieval World*, p. 121.

198. For the Lives of St. Godeleva, see *AASS, Iul. II*, July 6, pp. 404–14. See also Renée Nip, "Godelieve of Gistel and Ida of Boulogne," in *Sanctity and Motherhood: Essays on Holy Mothers in the Middle Ages*, ed. Anneke B. Mulder-Bakker (New York and London 1995), pp. 191–223. Georges Duby, *The Knight, the Lady, and the Priest: The Making of Modern Marriage in Medieval France*, trans. by Barbara Bray (Harmondsworth, 1983), pp. 130–35.

199. Turgot, *Life of Queen Margaret*, in *Early Sources of Scottish History:*

A.D. 500 to 1286, trans. Alan Orr Anderson (Edinburgh, 1922), ch. 6, pp. 67–68; ch. 7, p. 68.

200. Ibid., ch. 4, pp. 64–65; ch. 9, pp. 75–77; note 1, p. 77.

201. Ibid., ch. 8, p. 70.

202. This activity is, however, not mentioned by Turgot in his Life of St. Margaret. See, for example, Huneycutt, "The Idea of the Perfect Princess," p. 88; *The Letters of Lanfranc Archbishop of Canterbury,* ed. and trans. Helen Clover and Margaret Gibson (Oxford, 1979), letter 50, p. 160–63. This letter discusses negotiations between Margaret and Lanfranc in which Lanfranc was to become her spiritual adviser and Christ Church was to establish a daughter-house in Dunfermline. See also Derek Baker, "Nursery of Saints," p. 128.

203. Turgot, *Life of Queen Margaret,* ch. 6, pp. 67–68.

204. Ibid., ch. 4, p. 65.

205. On women's dominant role in medieval embroidery, see the classic study by A. G. I. Christie, *English Medieval Embroidery* (Oxford, 1938); Kay Staniland, *Medieval Craftsmen: Embroiderers* (Toronto and Buffalo, 1991); Donald King, *Opus Anglicanum: English Medieval Embroidery,* Arts Council Exhibition Catalogue, Victoria & Albert Museum (London, 1963); Marguerite Calberg, "Tissus et broderies attribués aux Saintes Harlinde et Relinde," *Bulletin de la Société Royale d'Archéologie de Bruxelles* (October, 1951): 1–26; Mildred Budny and Dominic Tweddle, "The Maaseik Embroideries," *Anglo-Saxon England,* ed. Peter Clemoes (Cambridge and London, 1984), 13:65–96; M. Schuette and S. Muller-Christensen, *The Art of Embroidery* (London, 1964); S. A. Brown, *The Bayeux Tapestry* (Woodbridge, 1988); David Wilson, *The Bayeux Tapestry* (London, 1985); and Rozsika Parker, *The Subversive Stitch: Embroidery and the Making of the Feminine* (London, 1984), especially pp. 40–70.

206. Bitel, *Land of Women,* p. 128.

207. Stokes, *Martyrology of Oengus,* p. 43; see also Bitel, *Land of Women,* p. 128.

208. Eustadiola, *AASS, Iun. II,* June 8, p. 132; *SWDA,* p. 108

209. *Liber Eliensis,* Camden 3d Series, ed. E. O. Blake (London, 1962), 92: 24. Etheldreda "stolam videlicet et manipulum similis materie ex auro et lapidibus pretiosis propriis, ut fertur, manibus docta auritexture ingenio fecit . . . ," *Liber Eliensis,* p. 24. See also *AASS, Iun. V,* June 23, p. 430; Budny and Tweddle, "The Maaseik Embroideries," p. 90. The Church also warned that female religious were not to devote too much attention to embroidery. The English Council of Cloveshoe (747) stipulated that nuns should "devote more time to reading books and to chanting psalms than to weaving and decorating (*plectendis*) clothes with various colors in unprofitable richness" (*Councils and Ecclesiastical Documents relating to Great Britain and Ireland,* eds. Arthur West Haddan and William Stubbs [Oxford, 1871], 3:369); Eckenstein, *Woman under Monasticism,* p. 226; Wemple, *Women in Frankish Society,* pp. 176–77.

210. Herlinda and Renilda, *AASS, Mar. III,* March 22, p. 385; See Budny and Tweddle, "The Maaseik Embroideries."

211. *DSW*, 1:211.

212. It is, however, interesting to note the ninth-century *vita* of St. Severus (d. 4th c.) which describes how Severus lived at home with his wife and daughter and "with them to earn his bread, [he] performed women's labors. For he was accustomed to stitch and weave wool, after the manner of women, and hence he was popularly called lanarius." *AASS, Feb. I* (Feb. 1), p. 88, cited by Herlihy, *Opera Muliebria*, p. 34.

213. See Wemple, *Women in Frankish Society*, especially pp. 194–97; McNamara and Wemple, "The Power of Women," pp. 113–15; Susan Stuard, ed., *Women in Medieval Society* (Philadelphia, 1976), pp. 9–11;

214. David Herlihy, *Medieval Households* (Cambridge, Mass., and London, 1985), especially pp. 6–7, 32–35, 51–52, 82–83, 97, 132, 136–38.

215. Diane Own Hughes, "From Brideprice to Dowry in Mediterranean Europe," *Journal of Family History* 3 (1978): 385–411; Wemple, *Women in Frankish Society*, pp. 12–14, 31–35, 44–45, 207; Herlihy, *Medieval Households*, pp. 35, 38, 49–52, 73–74, 77, 82–87, 95, 98–100; Susan Stuard, "The Dominion of Gender: Women's Fortunes in the High Middle Ages," in *Becoming Visible*, 2d ed., pp. 152–72.

216. As noted by Georges Duby, in the period prior to the year 1000 it was rare to see the charters' principals seeking out their relatives' approval for land transactions: sales, donations, usufruct grants, and so forth were all done independently and generally without consent. If there was any type of approval, it was given by a husband or other immediate relative. However, after the year 1000, the alienation of an allod became increasingly a family affair. One's immediate family, in addition to brothers and sisters, were all present to give their permission in the charters. It was then viewed as an effective safeguard to prevent unrestrained behavior on the part of one's relatives which might result in the complete alienation of a landed estate. See Georges Duby, *La société aux XIe et XIIe siècles dans la région mâconnaise* (Paris, 1953), p. 272. As noted by Duby, "et l'on voit fréquemment l'ardente recherche du salut détruire en un jour par un dépouillement brutal, le résultat de toute une vie de patientes acquisitions" (p. 87); see also Duby, *The Knight, The Lady and the Priest*, pp. 90–104. This tendency can also be seen, for example, among the charters which record donations to the Monastery of Savigny in the Lyonnais. See Schulenburg, "Savigny in the Lyonnais ca. 825–1138: An Analysis of a Rural Society" (diss., University of Wisconsin-Madison, 1969), pp. 49ff. We can also find a few examples among the *vitae* in which women saints were killed by apparently frustrated family members in an attempt to protect their family fortunes from the continued "pious robberies" carried out by these holy women. See also Corbet, *Les Saints ottoniens*, pp. 149–50, in regard to the royal family's fear of the collapse of their landed properties and wealth and their resistance to the profligate behavior of St. Mathilda.

217. Leyser, *Rule and Conflict*, pp. 71, 202. It should be noted, however, that these women still could play important indirect roles by influencing their families on where to place donations. Geary, *Phantoms of Remembrance*, pp. 51–80.

218. Leyser, *Rule and Conflict*, pp. 49–62.

CHAPTER THREE

1. William of Malmesbury, *The History of the Kings of England,* vol. 3, pt. 1 of *The Church Historians of England,* trans. J. Sharpe, rev. by J. Stevenson (London, 1854), p. 29, n. 5.

2. There is a great deal of literature on the subject of virginity in the Middle Ages. See, for example, John Bugge, *Virginitas: An Essay in the History of a Medieval Ideal* (The Hague, 1975); Peter Brown, *The Body and Society: Men, Women, and Sexual Renunciation in Early Christianity* (New York, 1988); Joyce Salisbury, *Church Fathers, Independent Virgins* (London and New York, 1991); Demetrius Dumm, *The Theological Basis of Virginity According to St. Jerome* (Latrobe, Penn., 1961); R. R. Ruether, ed., *Religion and Sexism: Images of Woman in the Jewish and Christian Traditions* (New York, 1974), pp. 150–83; Jo Ann McNamara, "Sexual Equality and the Cult of Virginity in Early Christian Thought," *Feminist Studies* 3, no. 3/4 (spring/summer 1976): 145–58, and *A New Song: Celibate Women of the First Three Christian Centuries* in *Women and History,* nos. 6 and 7 (summer/fall 1983).

3. See for example, Joyce E. Salisbury's study, *Church Fathers, Independent Virgins,* and Carolly Erickson, *The Medieval Vision: Essays in History and Perception* (New York, 1976), pp. 189–95.

4. See Peter Brown, *The Body and Society,* p. 359.

5. This scale of values can be found in a number of the writings of the early Church Fathers as well as in Aldhelm's *De virginitate* in *Aldhelm: The Prose Works,* ed. and trans. Michael Lapidge and Michael Herren (Totowa, 1979), p. 55. See also *Caesarius of Arles, Sermons, FC,* trans. Sr. Mary Magdeleine Mueller (New York, 1956), vol. 1, no. 6, p. 43.

6. St. Jerome wrote "as long as woman is for birth and children, she is different from man as body is from soul. But when she wishes to serve Christ more than the world, she will cease to be a woman and will be called man." St. Jerome, *Commentarius in Epistolam ad Ephesios,* III, v (658) in *PL* 26: 533, cited by Vern Bullough, *Sexual Variance in Society and History* (Chicago, 1976), p. 365. According to St. Ambrose, "She who does not believe is a woman and should be designated by the name of her sex, whereas she who believes progresses to perfect manhood, to the measure of the adulthood of Christ. She then dispenses with the name of her sex, the seductiveness of youth, the garrulousness of old age." *Expositio Evangelii secundum Lucam libri X,* 161 (1539), *PL* 15:1844; cited by Bullough, p. 365.

7. Elizabeth A. Clark, *The Life of Melania the Younger,* Studies in Women and Religion, vol. 14 (New York and Toronto, 1984), p. 54; Rosemary Rader, *Breaking Boundaries: Male/Female Friendship in Early Christian Communities* (New York, 1983), pp. 86–87; Arthur L. Fisher, "Women and Gender in Palladius' *Lausiac History,*" *Studia Monastica* 33 (1991): 49; Aspegren, *The Male Woman: A Feminine Ideal in the Early Church;* Ruether, *Religion and Sexism,* pp. 150–83; McNamara, "Sexual Equality," pp. 152–54; Salisbury, *Church Fathers, Independent Virgins;* Bugge, *Virginitas.*

8. Fisher "Women and Gender in Palladius' *Lausiac History,*" p. 24.

9. *The Letters of St. Jerome: Ancient Christian Writers,* trans. Charles Christopher Mierow (Westminster, Md., 1963) vol. 1, Letter 22, p. 135.

10. Ibid., p. 158 (emphasis mine).

11. Ibid., p. 138 (emphasis mine).

12. Ibid., citing Isa. 47:1 ff.

13. Ibid., pp. 138–39.

14. Ibid., p. 156, citing Matt. 10:22 and 24:13.

15. Ibid., p. 177.

16. Ibid., pp. 178–79.

17. St. Jerome, *Commentariorum in Jonam Prophetam liber unus, PL* 25: 1129 (emphasis mine): "Unde et in persecutionibus non licet propria perire manu, absque eo ubi castitas periclitatur." On this topic see also Peter Abelard, *Sic et Non, PL* 178:1603.

18. St. Jerome, *Adversus Jovinianum, PL* 23:270–73, ch. 41.

19. St. Ambrose, *Concerning Virgins,* in *St. Ambrose: Select Works and Letters, NPNF,* 2d series, vol. 10, pp. 386–87.

20. St. Augustine, *The City of God,* ed. David Knowles, trans. Henry Bettenson (Harmondsworth, 1972), bk. 1, ch. 16, p. 26.

21. Ibid., bk. 1, chs. 17–18, pp. 26–28.

22. Ibid., bk. 1, ch. 19, pp. 30–31.

23. Ibid., bk. 1, ch. 25, p. 36.

24. St. Leo, *Epistola XII,* caps. 8 and 11, *PL* 54:653, 655. See also Burchard of Worms, *Decretorum liber octavus, PL* 140:806.

25. Aldhelm, *De laudibus virginitatis, PL* 89:103–62; *Aldhelm: The Prose Works,* trans. Lapidge and Herren; see also Sr. Mary Bryne, *The Tradition of the Nun in Medieval England* (Washington, D.C., 1932), pp. 25–43.

26. Aldhelm, *PL* 89:121, no. 23; *Aldhelm: The Prose Works,* trans. Lapidge and Herren, p. 81.

27. Aldhelm, *PL* 89:104, no. 2; *Aldhelm: The Prose Works,* trans. Lapidge and Herren, p. 60.

28. Aldhelm, *PL* 89:106, no. 5; *Aldhelm: The Prose Works,* trans. Lapidge and Herren, p. 62. One can also find this analogy of virginity to the "chaste bee" in the writings of St. Ambrose; see Ambrose, "Concerning Virgins," *NPNF,* 2d ser., vol. 10, p. 369. Peter Damian also notes in his *Bestiary,* dedicated to the monks of Monte-Cassino, the chastity of various species including the bee. According to Peter Damian, the ideal would be for humans to be able to give birth like these chaste animals—either through the mouth, ear, or any other way that did not involve sex. *Peter Damian, Letters 61–90,* Fathers of the Church, Medieval Continuation, trans. Owen J. Blum (Washington, D.C., 1992), vol. 3, letter 86, pp. 275–76.

29. *Aldhelm: The Poetic Works,* trans. Lapidge and Rosier, pp. 98–99; for instance, in Aldhelm's discussion of Judith he writes: "Thus pure chastity rejects in blessed triumph the vice of wicked flesh with its defiled filth, repulsing rivalling conflicts with virtuous arrows, lest the lurid poison of the brothel creep into the delicate fibres of the body and scorch the marrow with fire" (p. 159).

30. *Aldhelm: The Prose Works,* trans. Lapidge and Herren, p. 132; Aldhelm, *PL* 89:161–62, no. 60.

31. *Aldhelm: The Prose Works,* trans. Lapidge and Herren, p. 129; Aldhelm, *PL* 89:158, no. 58.

32. Ibid.

33. *Aldhelm: The Prose Works,* trans. Lapidge and Herren, p. 90; Aldhelm, *PL* 89:128, no. 31.

34. *Aldhelm: The Prose Works,* trans. Lapidge and Herren, pp. 90–91 (emphasis mine); Aldhelm, *PL* 89:128–29, no. 31.

35. *Aldhelm: The Prose Works,* trans. Lapidge and Herren, pp. 106–121; Aldhelm, *PL* 89:141–52, nos. 40–52.

36. *Judith,* in *Poems from the Old English,* trans. Burton Raffel (Lincoln, 1960). See also Bugge, *Virginitas,* p. 51.

37. Albert S. Cook, ed. *Judith: An Old English Epic Fragment* (Boston, 1888), pp. xxiv–xxv.

38. Sr. Mary Bryne, *The Tradition of the Nun,* pp. 51–52, 60. See also the perceptive study by Shari Horner, "Spiritual Truth and Sexual Violence: The Old English *Juliana,* Anglo-Saxon Nuns, and the Discourse of Female Monastic Enclosure," *Signs: Journal of Women in Culture and Society* 19, no. 3 (1994): 658–75.

39. Katharina M. Wilson, ed., *Medieval Women Writers* (Athens, Ga., 1984), pp. 30–31; Hrotswitha of Gandersheim, "The Prefaces of Roswitha," in *The Plays of Roswitha,* trans. Christopher St. John (New York, 1966), p. xxvi.

40. *The Plays of Roswitha,* p. xxvii. See also Peter Dronke, *Women Writers of the Middle Ages: A Critical Study of Texts from Perpetua (d. 203) to Marguerite Porete (d. 1310)* (Cambridge and New York, 1984), pp. 55–83; Katharina M. Wilson, ed. *Medieval Women Writers,* pp. 30–63; Kathryn Gravdal, *Ravishing Maidens: Writing Rape in Medieval French Literature and Law* (Philadelphia, 1991), pp. 21–41. Gravdal notes that "Hrotsvitha takes up the rape plot in her stories of women saints, but it is sexual violence with a difference. Hrotsvitha transforms the rape plot to combat the contradictions of patristic thought: that woman is sexuality because she is sinful, and sinful because she is sexuality. The paradox of Hrotsvitha's dogma is that she fiercely defends the patristic ideal of virginity, but does so to demonstrate the strength and purity of female nature, rather than any corruption that must be overcome. Hrotsvitha depicts male aggression and violence against women, then focuses on the alternatives of women as they respond to such objectification. In her *opera* the troping of sexual assault becomes a way to represent female power, virtue, courage, and superiority" (pp. 27–28). She also notes, "Like other hagiographers, Hrotsvitha uses sexual violence as a vehicle for *imitatio Christi:* the pure virgin becomes Christlike in her resistance to temptation" (p. 31). See also M. R. Sperberg-McQueen's important study, "Whose Body Is It? Chaste Strategies and the Reinforcement of Patriarchy in Three Plays by Hrotswitha von Gandersheim," in *Women in German Yearbook* 8 (1992): 47–71; and Sandro Sticca, "Sin and Salvation: The Dramatic Context

of Hrotswitha's Women," in *The Roles and Images of Women in the Middle Ages and Renaissance,* ed. Douglas Radcliff-Umstead (Pittsburgh, 1975), pp. 3–22.

41. Sperberg-McQueen, "Whose Body Is It?" pp. 54–55.

42. Ibid., p. 61.

43. Ibid., pp. 63–65.

44. Brigitte Cazelles in her study *The Lady as Saint: A Collection of French Hagiographic Romances of the Thirteenth Century* (Philadelphia, 1991), p. 11, n. 11, has noted that even in the female-authored hagiographic poems or devotional chronicles, "they offer quite a conventional characterization of female sanctity, in conformity with the views expressed in the male hagiographic tradition. For example, the Benedictine author of the *Life of Saint Osyth* 'saw nothing strange in delivering an attack . . . on the frail nature of woman . . . in a work devoted to the praise of one of the species'" (citing M. Dominica Legge, *Anglo-Norman Literature and Its Background* [Oxford, 1963], p. 261).

45. Tacitus, *The "Agricola" and the "Germania,"* trans. H. Mattingly, rev. S. A. Handford (Harmondsworth, 1970), pp. 117–18. See also *The Letters of Saint Boniface,* trans. Ephraim Emerton (New York, 1976), pp. 127–28: "In Old Saxony, if a virgin disgraces her father's house by adultery or if a married woman breaks the bond of wedlock and commits adultery, they sometimes compel her to hang herself with her own hand and then hang the seducer above the pyre on which she has been burned. Sometimes a troop of women get together and flog her through the towns, beating her with rods and stripping her to the waist, cutting her whole body with knives, pricking her with wounds, and sending her on bleeding and torn from town to town; . . . until finally they leave her dead or almost dead, that other women may be made to fear adultery and evil conduct." *The Burgundian Code* prescribes the following deterrent: "If the daughter of any native Burgundian before she is given in marriage unites herself secretly and disgracefully in adultery with either barbarian or Roman, and if afterward she brings a complaint, and the act is established as charged, let him who has been accused of her corruption, and as has been said, is convicted with certain proof, suffer no defamation of character (*calumnia*) upon payment of fifteen solidi. She indeed, defeated in her purpose by the vileness of her conduct, shall sustain the disgrace of lost chastity." *The Burgundian Code,* trans. Katherine Fischer Drew (Philadelphia, 1972), ch. 44, p. 51. Also many of the reparations in the Germanic law codes are based on actions which threatened the chastity or virtue of Germanic women.

46. This exemplum is cited, for example, by Giovanni Boccaccio in *Concerning Famous Women,* trans. Guido A. Guarino (New Brunswick, 1963), pp. 177–78.

47. *Vita Caesarii episcopi Arelatensis libri duo, MGH SRM* 3:470. *The Rule for Nuns of St. Caesarius of Arles,* trans. McCarthy, p. 171.

48. According to Caesarius's *vita,* he had originally constructed his convent outside the city walls of Arles, perhaps at Alyscamps. However, even before his work was fully complete, the monastery was totally destroyed by bar-

barian armies which attacked Arles. After this experience he rebuilt his new monastery for women within the safety of the city walls. *The Rule for Nuns,* trans. McCarthy, pp. 13–14; *MGH SRM* 3:467.

49. *The Rule for Nuns,* trans. McCarthy, p. 171.

50. St. Jerome, *Regula monacharum, PL* 30:414–15. I would like to express my thanks to Sara Richards for her translation of this section of the *Regula.* The preoccupation with the need to keep female religious out of sight, "hidden," and enclosed can also be noted in the legislation of the councils of the period. See Schulenburg, "Strict Active Enclosure and Its Effects on the Female Monastic Experience (ca. 500–1100)."

51. Gregory of Tours, *The History of the Franks,* bk. 4, ch. 47, p. 244.

52. *The Letters of Saint Boniface,* trans. Emerton, pp. 126, 129.

53. William of Malmesbury, *The History of the Kings of England,* chs. 157–58, pp. 139–40; Saint Aethelwold, *Regularis Concordia: The Monastic Agreement of the Monks and the Nuns of the English Nation,* ed. Thomas Symons (London, 1953), pp. 1–2.

54. *The Anglo-Saxon Chronicle,* trans. G. N. Garmonsway (London, 1975), p. 164.

55. Reinhold Rau, ed., *Quellen zur Karolingischen Reichsgeschichte* (Darmstadt, 1958), 2:342; *The Annals of St-Bertin: Ninth Century Histories,* trans. Janet L. Nelson (Manchester and New York, 1991), 1:39, 53.

56. Hincmar of Reims, *Ad Regem, De coercendo et exstirpando raptu viduarum, puellarum ac sanctimonialium, PL* 125:1017–36.

57. Wulfstan, "The Sermon of the Wolf to the English," in *English Historical Documents c. 500–1042,* ed. Dorothy Whitelock (New York, 1955), vol. 1, p. 857.

58. A few examples of legislation concerning the violation and abduction of female religious include: *Concilium Parisiense* (556–73), *MGH LEG III: Concilia* 1:144, no. 5; *Capitularia Merowingica Chlotherii II, Edictum* (614), *MGH LEG II: Capitularia regum francorum* 1:23, no. 18; *Concilium Clippiacense* (626–27), *MGH LEG III,* 1:200, no. 26; *Ansegisi Capitularium, MGH LEG II,* 1:408, no. 100; *Additamenta ad capit. Reg. Franciae Occident* (845), *MGH LEG II,* 2:414, no. 67; *Synodus Papiensis* (850), *MGH LEG II,* 2:119–20, no. 10; *Capitulare missorum Silvacense* (853), *MGH LEG II,* 2:271–72, no. 2; "The Laws of King Liutprand," in *The Lombard Laws,* trans. Katherine Fischer Drew (Philadelphia: University of Pennsylvania Press, 1973), ch. 95. XII, p. 185; "Laws of Alfred: (885–99)" in *English Historical Documents, ca. 500–1042,* ed. Dorothy Whitelock (New York, 1955) vol. 1, p. 375, nos. 8, 8.1, 8.2, 8.3; and the "Laws of Cnut" (1020–23), ibid., vol. 1, p. 426, no. 50.1. For an interesting look at the topic of rape in medieval French literature and law (with an emphasis on the twelfth century and later), see Kathryn Gravdal, *Ravishing Maidens: Writing Rape in Medieval French Literature and Law* (Philadelphia, 1991).

59. "The Laws of King Liutprand," in Drew, *The Lombard Laws,* ch. 30. I, pp. 159–60.

60. *Laws of the Alamans and Bavarians,* trans. Theodore John Rivers (Philadelphia, 1977), bk. 1, ch. 11, p. 122.

61. "Laws of Alfred," in Whitelock, *English Historical Documents,* p. 376, no. 18.

62. In regard to Caesarius's monastery at Arles see *The Rule for Nuns,* trans. McCarthy, pp. 13–14; *MGH SRM* 3:467; or for the moving of St. Salaberga's house from a site outside of the city of Langres to within the walls of Laon, see *Vita Sadalbergae, MGH SRM* 5:56–57. Also a similar shift in sites can be noted in an early convent for women originally built by Ebroin and his wife Leutradis outside the walls of Soissons, only later to be moved within the walls of the city. See Jean Verdon, "Recherches sur les monastères feminins dans la France du Nord aux IXe–XIe siècles," *Revue Mabillon* 59 (1976):55; David Knowles and R. Neville Hadcock, *Medieval Religious Houses,* pp. 78 (Tynemouth), 486 (Wytham).

63. Thomas Perkins, *The Abbey Churches of Bath and Malmesbury and the Church of Saint Laurence, Bradford-on-Avon* (London, 1901), p. 106. Whitelock, *English Historical Documents,* pp. 473–74; Rollason, *The Mildrith Legend,* p. 25.

64. The monks of Noirmoutier (near Nantes), in attempting to escape the Vikings (ca. 836), first fled up the Loire Valley to Saumur, then to Cunauld, then south to Poitou, then to the Massif Central, and finally after another stop they ended up at Tournus. David Herlihy, ed., *The History of Feudalism* (New York, 1970), p. 8. A. Hamilton Thompson, *Lindisfarne Priory, Northumberland,* Ministry of Public Bulding and Works (London, 1949), pp. 3–4.

65. *Sigeberti Chronica* (882–93), *MGH SS* 6:343.

66. *VSB* 10 (October 11): 346; *DSW* 1:118–19; E. de Moreau, *Histoire de l'église en Belgique: Circonscriptions ecclésiastiques, chapitres, abbayes, couvents en Belgique avant 1559* (Brussels, 1948), p. 251.

67. Rollason, *The Mildrith Legend,* p. 22–24.

68. Knowles and Hadcock, *Medieval Religious Houses,* pp. 78 (Tynemouth), 80 (Whitby); Debra Shipley and Mary Peplow, *England's Undiscovered Heritage: A Guide to 100 Unusual Sites and Monuments* (New York, 1988), p. 116.

69. Y. Chaussy et al., *L'Abbaye royale Notre-Dame de Jouarre* (Paris, 1961) vol. 1, p. 81.

70. *De S. Gudila Virgine, AASS, Ian. I* (Jan. 8), no. 37, p. 523, and no. 26, p. 528.

71. Rollason, *The Mildrith Legend,* pp. 26–27.

72. David Knowles, *The Monastic Order in England* (Cambridge, 1940), p. 101.

73. Knowles and Hadcock, *Medieval Religious Houses,* p. 261 (Minster). See also *The Victoria History of the Counties of England: Kent* (London, 1926) vol. 2, p. 149.

74. William Sidney Gibson, *The History of the Monastery Founded at Tynemouth* (London, 1846), pp. 15–16.

75. Knowles and Hadcock, *Medieval Religious Houses,* p. 256 (Barking).

76. *Liber Eliensis* (Camden Third Series, 92), ed. E. O. Blake (London, 1962), chs. 38–41, pp. 52–56. This source describes how the Danes invaded the area, carrying off many of the inhabitants as hostages and killing others.

"Ad cenobium autem virginum quod gloriosa virgo et sponsa Christi Aetheldreda construxerat tandem perveniens, pro dolor, invadit, sancta contami-
nat, conculcat ac diripit. Protenditur rabidorum gladius in lactea sacrataque
colla. Mactatur, ut victima innocua, sanctimonialium caterva et, quoscumque
repperit sacri desiderii fratres et sorores, absque ulla humanitatis considera-
tione precipiti peremit strage. Sicque monasterio quod vera Dei christicola
Aetheldreda construxerat cum virginibus et ornamentis et reliquiis sanctorum
sanctarumque combusto, civitate etiam spoliata et cremata, prede ubertate di-
tati omniaque eiusdem loci adimentes mobilia atque utensilia, inimici Domini
redierunt ad propria" (p. 55). See also William Dugdale, *Monasticon Anglicanum* (London, 1846), vol. 1, p. 458.

77. Knowles and Hadcock, *Medieval Religious Houses*, p. 70 (Minster-in-
Thanet). There are several examples of abbesses taken as captives by the invaders: Abbess Leofrun at Canterbury (1010), Abbess Edgiva of Leominster
(1046), etc. (*Anglo-Saxon Chronicle*, pp. 141, 164). The *Vita Rumoldi* describes the brutality of the Vikings toward the nun, Gerlendis, whom they
took captive (*De Sancto Rumoldo, AASS, Iul. I*, July 1, no. 212, p. 219). See
also Albert d'Haenens, *Les invasions normandes en Belgique aux IXe siècle*,
Université de Louvain recueil de travaux d'histoire et philologie, 4e série, fasc.
38 (Louvain, 1967), pp. 255, n. 292, 257.

78. *Bibliotheca Sanctorum* (Istituto Giovanni XXIII della Pontificia Università Lateranense; Rome, 1961–70) 9:1281–83; *De S. Ositha vel Osgitha
Virg. Mart., AASS, Oct. III*, Oct. 7, pp. 942–43.

79. St. Wiborada, *AASS, Mai. I*, May 2, pp. 289–313; *MGH SS* 4:
452–57. *DSW* 2:185; *Bibliotheca Sanctorum* 12:1072–73; *BHL* 2:1278; A.
Fah, *Die hl. Wiborada* (1926).

80. For an exhaustive study of St. Cyr and the heroics of Eusebia and her
nuns see Simon Verne, *Sainte Eusebie, abbesse, et ses quarante compagnes
martyres à Marseille* (Marseille, 1891). See also Gonzague de Rey, *Les saints
de l'église de Marseille* (Marseille, 1885), pp. 225–38; *De SS. Eusebia Abbatissa, AASS, Oct. IV*, October 8, pp. 292–95; H. Leclercq, *DACL*, 10:
2239–41.

81. De Rey, *Les saints*, pp. 227–28.

82. Roger of Wendover, *Flowers of History: Comprising the History of England from the Descent of the Saxons to A.D. 1235*, trans. J. A. Giles (London, 1849), vol. 1, p. 191. *AASS, Aug. V* (August 25), pp. 196–98; *BHL*
1:355.

83. Roger of Wendover, *Flowers of History*, pp. 191–92.

84. Fray Antonio de Yepes, *Cronica general de la Orden de San Benito*
(Madrid, 1959), 1:138. I wish to express my thanks to Heath Dillard for
bringing this reference to my attention. I would also like to thank Victoria J.
Meyer for her kindness in translating this episode. On St. Florentine's monas-
tery and Leander's Rule for nuns, see Ivan Gobry, *De saint Colomban à saint
Boniface* (Paris, 1985), pp. 275–78.

85. De Yepes, *Cronica general de la Orden de San Benito*, p. 138. A number of long-lived local traditions perpetuated this event of martyrdom: the
road from the main church of S. Cruz to the monastery of Ecija was called the

"Road of the Virgins" or the "Road of the Howling"; there was also a "Bridge of the Virgins" with Stations of the Cross; stones splashed with the blood of the virgins were kept at Old Palma; and a sixteenth-century vision of a procession of virgins with lighted candles was said to have been witnessed by Maria de la Cruz. Heath Dillard has noted the use of self-inflicted facial lacerations by women mourners and victims of assault in Castilian society (1100–1300). In pressing charges against the assailant, the self-inflicted scratches on women's cheeks served as evidence that they had been assaulted. "Clawing her cheeks, a rape victim made the customary sign of a woman in mourning, but now she grieved for the loss of her chastity and her honour." See pp. 183–84 in Dillard's *Daughters of the Reconquest, Women in Castilian Town and Society, 1100–1300* (Cambridge, 1984); see also pp. 96–97. Another ancient legend concerns the Benedictine nuns of the monastery of Sant Pere de les Puelles of Barcelona. During the invasion of al-Mansur's troops in ca. 985, a number of religious buildings in Barcelona were destroyed, including the convent of Sant Pere de les Puelles. According to a well-known early tradition, when the nuns learned of the Moors' imminent arrival, they feared that they would become captives and would be forced to join their harems. Thus, to save their virginal purity, they disfigured themselves; they made themselves repugnant by amputating their noses. When the invaders saw the nuns, they were said to be so furious that they did not rape them but rather decapitated them. Anna de Valldaura, *Tradicions Religioses de Catalunya* (Barcelona, 1948), p. 40. I would like to thank Carole Nicholas for bringing this case to my attention. At this writing I have only come across modern sources which mention this "ancient legend."

86. John W. Baldwin, *Masters, Princes and Merchants: The Social Views of Peter the Chanter and His Circle* (Princeton, 1970), 1:256; 2:183–84; Wogan-Browne, "Saints' Lives and the Female Reader," p. 326.

87. *De Venerabili Oda, AASS, Apr. II,* April 20, pp. 770–78. The venerable Oda's *vita* was written by a contemporary, Philip Harveng, abbot of Bonne-Esperance (p. 771).

88. Ibid., pp. 774–75.

89. *De B. Margarita Hungarica, AASS, Ian. III,* January 28, p. 518. I would like to thank Michael Goodich for his kindness in providing me with this reference. See also Goodich, *Vita Perfecta,* p. 116.

90. Drew, "Rothair's Edict," in Drew, *The Lombard Laws,* nos. 49, 50, 54, 82, 84, 106, and 108; Rivers, *Laws of the Alamans and Bavarians,* pp. 86–87, sec. 57, nos. 15–19; Katherine Fischer Drew, trans., *The Laws of the Salian Franks* (Philadelphia, 1991): "Pactus Legis Salicae," XXIX, no. 1, p. 92, no. 13, p. 93; "Capitulary VI," III, no. 6, p. 160; "Lex Salica Karolina," XVI[XXXI], no. 1 and no. 14, p. 184. There are a great many other examples of this common type of mutilation in the law codes. For a summary see: "Denasatus"/"Nasi abscissio," in Charles Du Fresne Du Cange, *Glossarium mediae et infimae Latinitatis* (Paris, 1938) 3:63. It is also interesting to note that in early Irish society we find references to a "nose tax"—eg., "An alms out of every nose in Fermoy." In *Wars of the Gaedhil with the Gaill,* an Irish authority comments on the fact that failure to pay this

tax was punished either by reduction into slavery, or *by having the tip of the nose cut off*. See *Anecdota Oxoniensia: Lives of Saints from The Book of Lismore*, trans. and ed. Whitley Stokes (Oxford, 1890), p. 348. We can also find in our sources a few examples of self-inflicted mutilations: "The Burgundian Penitential" (ca. 700–725) warns: "If anyone intentionally cuts off any member [of his body], he shall do penance for three years, one of these on bread and water." Or "The So-called Roman Penitential" (ca. 830) stipulates: "If anyone intentionally cuts off any of his own members, he shall do penance for three years, one year on bread and water." John T. McNeill and Helena M. Gamer, *Medieval Handbooks of Penance*, Records of Western Civilization Series (New York, 1938, 1990), pp. 275, 307.

91. Whitelock, *English Historical Documents*, vol. 1, p. 426. I would also like to thank Gerda Lerner for pointing out the fact that this punishment was really an ancient one and already existed in the Assyrian Code. Here the law stipulates that a man may cut off the nose of his wife if he catches her in adultery, but he must also turn the adulterer into a eunuch and disfigure his face. If he spares his wife, he must also acquit the man (MAL no. 15). "Middle Assyrian Laws," in *Ancient Near Eastern Texts Relating to the Old Testament*, ed. James Bennet Pritchard (Princeton, 1955). Similar provisions can be found in fourteenth-century Spain. Here a Jewish widow was charged with having sexual relations with a Gentile. The Jewish court ordered that her nose be cut off so as to disfigure her and make her no longer acceptable to her lover. Louis M. Epstein, *Sex Laws and Customs in Judaism* (New York, 1967), p. 173. Guido Ruggiero notes that in early Renaissance Venice, mutilation for crimes involving sexuality was very rare. He writes, "It is significant that facial mutilation by the commune was commonly used for serious crimes committed by females when a similar penalty for a man would be the loss of a hand. Apparently a woman's worth in this male-oriented society was seen in her beauty while a man's was seen in his working ability." See footnote 13, p. 205, in Ruggiero's *Violence in Early Renaissance Venice* (New Brunswick, 1980). See especially his chapter on rape, pp. 156–70.

92. *Lex Pacis Castrensis* (1158) in *MGH LEG IV: Constitutiones et acta publica imperatorum et regum* 1:240, no. 7. I would like to thank Sarah Blanshei for the following disfigurement citation from the Statutes of Bologna, ca. 1250, where prostitutes were punished by having their noses cut off: "Statuimus et ordinamus quod publice meretrices et earum receptores seu receptrices non sinantur stare iuxta dictam ecclesiam sancti petri vel in illa contrata, et ad minus per XX domos iuxta ipsam ecclesiam ex omni parte vie et ex omni parte ipsius ecclesie stare non debeant; et si quis concesserit eis domum suam ad standum aliquo modo solvat nomine banni quociens invente fuerint I. libras bononenorum et plus arbitrio potestatis; et ganee seu meretrices capiantur et in prima vice fustigentur per Civitatem, et *in secunda incidatur ei aliquantulum de naso*." Luigi Frati, ed., *Statuti di Bologna dall-anno 1245 all-anno 1267* (Bologna, 1869), vol. 1, pp. 452–53 (emphasis added). The same punishment was reserved for prostitutes from Augsburg and Naples in the late Middle Ages. Iwan Bloch, *Die Prostitution* (Berlin, 1912), vol. 1, p. 813. Similarly, Roger of Sicily ordered that mothers who sold

their daughters into prostitution should have their noses cut off. James Brundage, *Law, Sex, and Christian Society in Medieval Europe* (Chicago and London, 1987), p. 392.

93. Wace, *Arthurian Chronicles*, trans. Eugene Mason (New York, 1962), p. 210.

94. Odericus Vitalis, *The Ecclesiastical History of Odericus Vitalis*, ed. and trans. Marjorie Chibnall (Oxford, 1969), vol. 6, bk. 12, p. 213. I would like to thank Penny Gold for this reference.

95. *Vita I S. Brigidae, AASS, Feb. I*, February 1, p. 120. Similarly the Irish St. Cranat (fl. sixth century) was said to have plucked out her eyes to avoid a forced marriage. Afterwards, when the threat of marriage was removed, her eyes were miraculously restored. James F. Kenney, *The Sources of the Early History of Ireland: Ecclesiastical* (Shannon, 1968), p. 406. Among other female saints in this miraculous tradition are Sts. Lucy, Alexandrina, and Odilia.

96. *Vitae Columbani abbatis discipulorumque eius libri duo auctore Iona, MGH SRM* 4:120–21.

97. *De S. Enimia Virgine, AASS, Oct. III*, October 6, p. 406.

98. *De S. Licinio, AASS, Feb. II*, February 13, p. 679.

99. *Vita Ansberti episcopi Rotomagensis, MGH SRM* 5:620–21.

100. *De S. Itisberga Virgine, AASS, Mai. V*, May 21, p. 46b; *DSW* 1: 403–4.

101. *De S. Ulphia, AASS, Ian. III*, January 31, p. 738.

102. On this topic see Jean Gessler, *La Légende de sainte Wilgeforte ou Ontcommer, la Vierge miraculeusement barbue* (Brussels, 1938); Gillian Edward, *Uncumber and Pantaloon* (New York, 1969); Bullough, *Sexual Variance in Society and History*, pp. 367–68; Bullough, "Transvestites in the Middle Ages," *American Journal of Sociology*, 79, no. 6: 1387; Vern L. and Bonnie Bullough, *Cross Dressing, Sex, and Gender* (Philadelphia, 1993), pp. 54–55. *DSW* 2:302–3; Butler 3:151–52.

103. *Saint Gregory the Great: Dialogues*, trans. Odo John Zimmerman, FC, (New York, 1959), vol. 39, bk. 4, ch. 14, pp. 205–6.

104. The name, Wilgefortis, may be derived from Vierge-forte (strong virgin) or Hilge vartz "holy face." Wilgefortis is known by a variety of other names which are based on Liberata, i.e., "the deliverer" and Uncumber (probably related to the German *Kummer,* meaning "trouble"). In England, Wilgefortis or Uncumber seems to have been especially invoked by women who wanted to get rid of their troublesome husbands. In this tradition, according to St. Thomas More, "For a peck of oats she would not fail to uncumber them of their husbands." See Gessler, *La Légende de sainte Wilgeforte ou Ontcommer*, pp. 65–67; Butler 3:151–52; Delehaye, *Cinq leçons sur la méthode hagiographique* (Brussels, 1934), p. 135; and Charles Cahier's comments on Wilgefortis in *Caracteristiques des saints dans l'art populaire* (Paris, 1867), especially pp. 121, 290, 569. See also, note 102. A wonderful statue depicting Wilgefortis reading a book can be found in Westminster Abbey. It is also interesting to note that we find among the "marvels" described by Gerald of

Wales (d. 1223) two cases of women with beards. In *The Topography of Ireland*, Gerald of Wales provides the following description: "Duvenald, king of Limerick, had a woman with a beard down to her navel, and, also, a crest like a colt of a year old, which reached from the top of her neck down her backbone, and was covered with hair. The woman, thus remarkable for two monstrous deformities, was, however, not an hermaphrodite, but in other respects had the parts of a woman; and she constantly attended the court, an object of ridicule as well as of wonder. The fact of her spine being covered with hair neither determined her gender to be male or female; and in wearing a long beard she followed the customs of her country, though it was unnatural in her. Also, within our time, a woman was seen attending the court of Connaught, who partook of the nature of both sexes, and was an hermaphrodite. On the right side of her face she had a long and thick beard, which covered both sides of her lips to the middle of her chin, like a man; on the left, her lips and chin were smooth and hairless, like a woman." *The Historical Works of Giraldus Cambrensis*, ed. Thomas Wright (London, 1905), p. 84. There is also a fascinating illustration of a bearded woman with a mane, shown with her distaff and spindle, in the British Library, London, (Royal MS 13.B.VIII, fo. 19), reproduced in *Medieval England 1066–1485*, ed. Edmund King (Oxford, 1988), p. 87. Also, for a delightful fictional account of a modern quest for the truth about "la femme à barbe"—St. Wilgefortis—see Robertson Davies, *Fifth Business* (Penguin Books: Harmondsworth, 1977), book 1 of his *Deptford Trilogy*.

105. *De S. Paula, Cognomenta Barbata, virgine Abulensi in Hispania*, *AASS*, Feb. *III*, February 20, p. 177. See also Bullough, "Transvestites in the Middle Ages," p. 1388.

106. *Mayo Clinic Family Health Book*, ed. David E. Larson (New York, 1990), pp. 1184–85, 722. Another hypothesis attempts to identify these early bearded female saints with the ailment of anorexia nervosa. According to this theory, an endocrine disorder (amenorrhoea) produces a hormonal imbalance among some anorexic patients with the result that hair develops on the upper lip and chin, as well as a layer of lanugo or downy hair on the back, arms, legs, and side of the face. J. Hubert Lacey, "Anorexia Nervosa and a Bearded Female Saint," *British Medical Journal*, 285 (18–25 Dec., 1982): 1816–17. I would like to thank Ellen Stephenson for this reference.

107. L. Gougaud, *Les saints irlandais hors d'Ireland* (1946), pp. 135–39. St. Maudez/Mande, *PB* 13 (Nov. 18):497; *BHL* 2:838.

108. "Rothair's Edict," in Drew, *The Lombard Laws*, no. 180, pp. 84–85 (emphasis mine).

109. See, for example, R. W. Southern's comments for the twelfth century, *Western Society and the Church in the Middle Ages: The Pelican History of the Church*, vol. 2 (Harmondsworth, 1970), pp. 311–12.

110. The findings of the anthropologist I. M. Lewis further corroborate the validity of this behavior. From a cross-cultural perspective he discusses certain types of marginal possession cults as forms of indirect protest used particularly by women. I. M. Lewis, *Ecstatic Religion: An Anthropological Study of*

Spirit Possession and Shamanism (Harmondsworth, 1971), especially pp. 31–32, 77, 147, 186, 191, 200. I would like to thank Susan Friedman for calling my attention to this work.

111. See Joyce Salisbury, *Church Fathers, Independent Virgins,* pp. 90, 103, 106–10; John Anson, "The Female Transvestite in Early Monasticism: The Origin and Development of a Motif," *Viator* 5 (1974): 1–32; Vern Bullough, "Transvestites in the Middle Ages," pp. 1381–94; Bullough and Bullough, *Cross Dressing, Sex, and Gender,* pp. 45–73.

112. Raymond Firth, *Symbols: Public and Private* (Ithaca, 1973), pp. 288–89, 298.

113. "Acts of Paul," in *The Apocryphal New Testament,* trans. Montague Rhodes James (Oxford, 1924) II:25; 277; II:40, 280; II:43, 281. For the life and miracles of St. Thecla, see Gilbert Dagron, *Vie et miracles de sainte Thecle,* Subsidia Hagiographica no. 62 (Brussels, 1978).

114. John Anson, "The Female Transvestite in Early Monasticism," p. 3. See also Evelyne Patlagean, "L'Histoire de la femme deguisée en moine et l'évolution de la sainteté féminine à Byzance," *Studi Medievali,* ser. 3, vol. 17, no. 2 (1976): 609.

115. Palladius, *The Lausiac History,* ch. 34, p. 97.

116. St. Jerome, *Letters and Select Works, NPNF,* 2d ser. vol. 6, letter 147, p. 292.

117. St. Jerome, *The Letters of St. Jerome,* trans. C. Mierow, *ACW* I, letter 22, p. 162.

118. Ambrose, *De lapsu virginis consecratae, PL* 16: bk. 1, cap. 8 (314), 35, 377–78.

119. Optatus, *De Schismate Donatistarum, PL,* 11, bk. 6 (95), 1074.

120. *Vita S. Ermelindis Virginis, AASS, Oct. XII,* October 29, p. 849.

121. *Vita Sanctae Gertrudis, MGH SRM* 2:456. ch. 2. "Ut non violatores animarum filiam suam ad inlecebras huius mundi voluptates per vim raperent, ferrum tonsoris arripuit et capillos sanctae puellae ad instar coronae abscisit." See also *SWDA,* p. 224.

122. *Vita S. Faronis, AASS, Oct. XII,* October 28, p. 598. *DSW* 1:123; *Vita S. Arnulphi episcopi, AASS, Iul. IV,* July 18, pp. 428, 442; *MGH SRM* 2:426–46.

123. See Anson, "The Female Transvestite in Early Monasticism"; Anson (p. 13) notes that the legends of female monk/saints generally shared a tripartite structure consisting of (1) flight from the world—often from unwanted suitors; (2) adoption of male disguise and seclusion; and (3) discovery and recognition. See also Patlagean, "L'Histoire de la femme déguisée en moine et l'évolution de la sainteté féminine à Byzance"; Bullough, "Transvestites in the Middle Ages"; Delcourt, "Le complex de Diane dans l'hagiographie chrétienne," *Revue de l'histoire des religions* 153 (1958):1–33; Delehaye, *The Legends of Saints,* pp. 150–56. See also Marina Warner's *Joan of Arc: The Image of Female Heroism* (London, 1981). There are also a number of recent studies on women dressing as men across history, especially as warriors in the "modern" eras. See for example, Bullough and Bullough, *Cross Dressing, Sex, and Gender;* Dianne Dugaw, *Dangerous Examples: Warrior Women and Pop-*

ular Balladry, 1600–1850 (Cambridge, 1989); Rudolf Dekker and Lotte van de Pol, *The Tradition of Female Cross-Dressing in Early Modern Europe* (New York, 1988); Julie Wheelwright, *Amazons and Military Maids: Women Who Dressed as Men in Pursuit of Life, Liberty and Happiness* (London, 1989).

124. Anson, "The Female Transvestite in Early Monasticism," p. 5. In this study Anson attempts "to pinpoint rather exactly what in the motif exercised the imagination of early monastic authors and led them to reproduce version after version. In a male society dedicated to celibacy as the highest virtue and so not surprisingly given to excesses of antifeminism, the fantasy of a holy woman disguised among their number represented, I shall suggest, a psychological opportunity to neutralize the threat of female temptation" (ibid.).

125. Paul E. Szarmach, "Aelfric's Women Saints: Eugenia," in *New Readings on Women in Old English Literature,* ed. Helen Damico and Alexandra Hennessey Olsen (Bloomington and Indianapolis, 1990), pp. 153–54; Giselle de Nie, "'Consciousness Fecund through God': From Male Fighter to Spiritual Bride-Mother in Late Antique Female Sanctity," in *Sanctity and Motherhood: Essays on Holy Mothers in the Middle Ages,* ed. Anneke B. Mulder-Bakker, Garland Medieval Casebooks, vol. 14 (New York and London, 1995), pp. 123–27.

126. De Nie, "'Consciousness Fecund through God,'" pp. 127–29. The special relevance which St. Eugenia held for female religious in this early period can also be seen in their church dedications. The *vita* of St. Eustadiola, for example, notes that "she dedicated the houses she possessed within the walls of Bourges as basilicas in honor of the Holy Mary Ever-virgin and the blessed martyr Eugenia." *SWDA,* p. 108.

127. Avitus, *Liber sextus de virginitate,* MGH AA 6:289–90; PL 59:378.

128. Fortunatus, *Opera Poetica, Carminum liber VIII,* poem 3, *De virginitate, MGH AA* 4:182; see also *Histoire de l'Abbaye Sainte-Croix de Poitiers,* p. 59.

129. *Aldhelm: The Prose Works,* trans. Lapidge and Herren, ch. 44, pp. 110–11; Aldhelm, *De Laudibus Virginitatis,* PL 89: 144–45, ch. 44.

130. Szarmach, "Aelfric's Women Saints: Eugenia," p. 154, see also p. 148; Skeat, *Aelfric's Lives of Saints,* pp. 29, 31, 39. Aelfric also includes among his female *exempla* of virile or transvestite saints, Eufrasia or Euphrosyne. According to the *vita,* she adopted the male monastic habit, requested that her hair be cut off, and entered a male monastery in order that her father would not find her and force her into an unwanted marriage. See Skeat, *Aelfric's Lives of Saints,* pp. 335–55.

131. Raymond van Dam, trans., *Gregory of Tours: Glory of the Confessors,* pp. 30–31; Gregory of Tours, *De Gloria Confessorum,* no. 16, MGH SRM 1:756–57. Another well-known account, in this popular tradition of the disguised monk, concerns St. Hildigund who assumed the name of Brother Joseph in a twelfth-century Cistercian community. See Bullough, *Sexual Variance,* p. 394; *DSW* 1:388–91.

132. *The Life of Christina of Markyate: A Twelfth Century Recluse,* ed.

C. H. Talbot (Oxford, 1959), ch. 33, pp. 90–91; ch. 34, pp. 92–93. Other examples of women adopting a male disguise: Empress St. Adelaide, to escape from prison; St. Aurelia (d. ca. 1027), to flee an unwanted marriage. *DSW* 1:5–9, 94. See also Bullough and Bullough, *Cross Dressing, Sex, and Gender*, pp. 51–73.

133. *Vita de S. Carilefo* (St. Calais), *AASS, Iul. I*, July 1, p. 87.

134. My next project, on medieval women and proscriptions of sacred space, contains a number of examples of these "audacious" women who dared to cross the boundaries and to trespass into male-defined, "sacred" space. In this context see also chapter 7, "Gender Relationships and Circles of Friendship."

135. Synod of Gangra, *Sacrorum conciliorum nova, et amplissima collectio*, J. Mansi, ed. (Florence, 1759, 1901), cn. 13, 1102; cn. 17, 1103 (emphasis mine).

136. *The Theodosian Code and Novels and the Sirmondian Constitutions*, trans. Clyde Pharr (Princeton, 1952), bk. 16, p. 445. The seriousness of this prohibition against women cutting off their hair can be seen in the following stipulation: "Moreover, if a bishop should permit a woman with shorn head to enter a church, even the bishop himself shall be expelled from his position and kept away, along with such comrades. Not only if he should recommend that this be done, but even if he should learn that it is being accomplished by any persons, or finally, that it has been done in any way whatsoever, he shall understand that nothing will exonerate him. This shall indisputably serve as a law for those who deserve correction and as a customary practice for those who have already received correction, so that the latter may have a witness, and the former may begin to fear judgement" (ibid.).

137. *Concilia Rispacense*, MGH LEG II 1:28(23), 211. "Ut sanctae moniales non induantur virilia indumenta, id est rocho vel fanones (fano pannus est), nisi tantum feminea vestimenta."

138. *Concilium Vernense*, MGH LEG II: *Capitularia regum Francorum*, 2:385, no. 7: "Si quae sanctimoniales causa religionis, ut eis falso videtur, vel virilem habitum sumunt vel crines adtondent, quia ignorantia magis, quam studio eas errare putamus, admonendas castigandasque decernimus; ne forte veteris ac novi instrumenti praevaricatrices iuxta Gangrensem gynodum severitate anathemaatis ab ecclesiae corpore praecidantur."

139. *Biblioteca Casinensis*, III, L. II, c. 102, cited in *Sainte Fare et Faremoutiers: Treize siècles de vie monastique* (Abbaye de Faremoutiers, 1956), p. 166.

140. Burchard of Worms, *Decretorum Libri XX, PL* 140, bk. 8, caps. 60, 62, p. 805.

141. Ivo of Chartres, *Decretum, PL* 161, pt. 7, caps. 78, 80, 81, p. 564; and pt. 8, cap. 320, p. 653. Gratian, *Decretum, PL* 187, pt. 1, dist. 30, caps. 2, 6, p. 165. See also Jenny Jochen's important study, "Before the Male Gaze: The Absence of the Female Body in Old Norse," in *Sex in the Middle Ages: A Book of Essays*, ed. Joyce E. Salisbury (New York and London, 1991), especially pp. 9–19. Jochens notes that in Old Norse society it was illegal for women and men to wear the clothing of the opposite sex. "If a woman dresses

in male clothing or cuts her hair like a man or carries weapons in order to be different from others, the punishment is the smaller outlawry (expatriation for three years). . . . The same is the case if men dress in female (Grágás lb.203–04)" (p. 9).

142. See Florence of Worcester, *The Chronicle of Florence of Worcester with the Two Continuations* [A.D. 1053], trans. Thomas Forester (London, 1854), p. 156. I would like to thank Andrew Larson for providing me with this reference. Gerald of Wales also notes in regard to the Welsh, "The men and women cut their hair close round to the ears and eyes. The women, after the manner of the Parthians, cover their heads with a large white veil, folded together in the form of a crown." *The Historical Works of Giraldus Cambrensis*, p. 494.

143. De Nie, " 'Consciousness Fecund through God,' " p. 127.

144. Bullough, "Transvestites in the Middle Ages," p. 1383. Male transvestites lost status and were strongly condemned as dangerous and sinful at this time. Consequently, there were no male transvestite saints (ibid.).

145. Wogan-Browne, " 'Clerc u lai, muïne u dame': women and Anglo-Norman hagiography in the twelfth and thirteenth centuries," in *Women and Literature in Britain, 1150–1500*, ed. Carol M. Meale (Cambridge, 1993), p. 71.

146. Wogan-Browne, "Saints' Lives and the Female Reader," p. 323.

147. See Barbara Newman, *Sister of Wisdom: St. Hildegard's Theology of the Feminine* (Berkeley, Los Angeles, London, 1987), especially pp. 151–52.

148. Hildegard of Bingen, *Scivias*, Classics of Western Spirituality, trans. Mother Columba Hart and Jane Bishop (New York and Mahwah, 1990), bk. 2, vision 6, no. 77, p. 278.

149. Bynum, *Holy Feast and Holy Fast*, especially p. 291; see also Jochens, "Before the Male Gaze," pp. 17–19.

150. Kieckhefer, *Unquiet Souls*, pp. 13–14.

151. *Eadmer's History of Recent Events in England (Historia Novorum in Anglia)*, trans. Geoffrey Bosanquet (London, 1964), bk. 3, p. 129.

152. Ibid., p. 127.

153. Ibid., pp. 128–30. See also R. W. Southern, *Saint Anselm and His Biographer: A Study of Monastic Life and Thought 1059–c. 1130* (Cambridge, 1963), p. 189.

154. Paul the Deacon, *History of the Langobards*, trans. William Dudley Foulke (Philadelphia, 1907), bk. 4, ch. 37, pp. 180–81, 183–84 (emphasis mine).

155. Christine de Pisan, *Here begynneth the boke of the Cyte of Ladyes*, trans. Brian Anslay (London, 1521), pt. 2, cap. 46; or Christine de Pizan, *The Book of the City of Ladies*, trans. Earl Jeffrey Richards (New York, 1982), p. 164; François de Billon, *Le Fort inexpugnable de l'honneur du sexe Féminin*, ed. M. A. Screech (New York, 1970), pp. 65–66. I would like to thank Ingrid Åkerlund for this reference. The continuity in these rather unusual tactics adopted to ward off rapists can be noted in a modern product which was marketed in the 1980s called "Skunk Oil" and advertised as a deterrent used to repel would-be rapists. "The product is a tiny plastic vial of synthetic skunk

oil to be pinned to a woman's undergarments. The vial can be crushed between two fingers with about the same force it takes to break a pencil. The resulting odor is so offensive and unexpected that in most cases the attacker will flee"—an uncanny counterpart to the early medieval "rotten chicken parts" repellent! "World of Women," *Milwaukee Sentinel,* March 3, 1980, p. 8. I would like to thank Willa Schmidt and Louise Coates of University of Wisconsin Memorial Library Reference Department and Annamarie Weis of the *Milwaukee Journal* for their help in locating this reference.

156. Peter Damian, Opusc. 47: "De Castitate et mediis eam tuendi," *PL* 145:711–12, ch. 1. In her *Book of the Experience of the True Faithful,* Angela of Foligno also specifically mentions the association of rotting meat and fish with human corruption. "I was not ashamed, however, to confess in front of everyone all the sins I had committed, I even enjoyed imagining how I could make public my iniquities, hypocrisies, and sins. I wanted to parade naked through towns and public squares with pieces of meat and fish hanging from my neck and to proclaim: 'Behold the lowest of women, full of malice and deceit, stinking with every vice and evil.'" *Angela of Foligno: Complete Works,* trans. by Paul Lachance (New York, 1993), p. 219. I thank Kathleen Kamerick, University of Iowa, for this reference. See also Bynum, *Holy Feast and Holy Fast,* p. 143.

157. David Hugh Farmer, *The Oxford Dictionary of Saints* (Oxford and New York, 1982), p. 117.

158. See note no. 80 for sources on the monastery of St. Cyr.

159. Delehaye, *Les Légendes hagiographiques,* pp. 52–53.

160. de Rey, *Les Saints,* p. 228; Verne, *Sainte Eusesbie,* p. 411.

161. Verne, *Sainte Eusesbie,* pp. 403–83.

162. See for example, Bede, *A History of the English Church and People,* bk. 4, ch. 19, p. 241.

163. de Rey, *Les Saints,* p. 228; Verne, *Sainte Eusesbie,* pp. 33–53, 346–49, 403–83, 611–13, 623–34, 676–87.

164. Josephine E. Vallerie, *Garin le Loheren,* According to Manuscript A (Bibliothèque de l'Arsenal 2983), *with Text, Introduction and Linguistic Study* (Ann Arbor, 1947), p. 240.

165. *Vitae Caesarii episcopi Arelatensis libri duo,* MGH SRM 3:494; Joan Evans, *Monastic Life at Cluny, 910–1157* (London, 1931), pp. 29–30; Schulenburg, "Strict Active Enclosure," pp. 64–65.

166. LeRoy G. Schultz, ed., *Rape Victimology* (Springfield, Ill., 1975), p. 381.

167. See especially Cyprian, *Saint Cyprian, Treatises: The Dress of Virgins,* ed. Roy J. Deferrari, trans. Angela Elizabeth Keenan (New York, 1958), ch. 5, pp. 35–36.

168. Fortunatus, *De Vita Sanctae Radegundis liber I,* chs. 25–26, MGH SRM 2:372–73.

169. *The Letters of St. Jerome,* no. 29, p. 164; nos. 39–40, pp. 176–78.

170. These saints, plus many others, were mutilated or lost their beauty in one way or another, only to be cured or to have their "features" miraculously restored. Sts. Rodena and Euphemia are two little-known early Christian

saints who allegedly cut off their noses and lips (Rodena also cut off her ears) to avoid forced marriages. And in the hagiographic tradition, their features were appropriately restored after their marriages were called off. St. Rodena, *De SS. Silvano et Silvestro Conf. ac Rodena Virg.*, AASS, Sept. VI, September 22, p. 405; *DSW* 1:291.

171. *De SS. Eusebia Abbatissa*, AASS, Oct. IV, October 8, p. 294.

172. Matthew of Westminster (based on Matthew of Paris), *The Flowers of History*, trans. C. D. Yonge (London, 1853), 1:410.

173. For further comments on this continuity in the heroics of virginity see Susan Brownmiller, *Against Our Will* (New York, 1975), and the Epilogue to the present volume. ;

174. Lewis, *Ecstatic Religion*, p. 33.

175. *The Letters of St. Jerome*, no. 41, p. 179; Aldhelm, *PL* 89:108, no. 7.

CHAPTER FOUR

1. *Caesarius of Arles, Sermons*, trans. Sr. Mary Magdeleine Mueller (New York, 1956), vol. 1, no. 6, ch. 7, p. 43.

2. The term "domestic proselytization" refers to the special evangelizing or apostolic role which women were encouraged to exercise within the confines of the "home" and family. Since women were limited by exclusion from the priesthood and formal preaching, this became an important "approved" outlet for their involvement in missionary activities. In many cases during this early period the influence of this role extended far beyond the "immediate family"; for it was assumed that after the conversion of the husband, nobleman, or king, the entire household and followers would then accept the new religion. This process of "domestic proselytization" has been treated by Godefroy Kurth, *Sainte Clotilde (Les Saints)*, 8th ed. (Paris, 1905), pp. 1–19.

3. Many general studies of the early missionary movement ignore or only briefly mention women's roles in conversion. For example, in the important study by James Campbell, "Observations on the Conversion of England," in *Essays in Anglo-Saxon History* (London and Ronceverte, 1986), pp. 69–84, he explores many aspects of conversion, including continental ties, without mentioning the influence of Bertha or the concept of "domestic proselytization." A number of scholars, however, have noted in their studies the important contribution which women made to the process of conversion. See, for example, W. H. C. Frend's monumental study, *The Rise of Christianity* (London, 1984), especially pp. 561–62, 887–89; J. N. Hillgarth, *The Conversion of Western Europe, 350–750* (Englewood Cliffs, 1969); S. Neill, *A History of Christian Missions* (Harmondsworth, 1964). See also, for example, Peter Hunter Blair, *An Introduction to Anglo-Saxon England* (Cambridge, 1970), William A. Chaney, *The Cult of Kingship in Anglo-Saxon England: The Transition from Paganism to Christianity* (Berkeley and Los Angeles, 1970); Henry Mayr-Harting, *The Coming of Christianity to England* (New York, 1972); John Godfrey, *The Church in Anglo-Saxon England* (Cambridge, 1962); Edward James, *The Franks* (Oxford and Cambridge, Mass., 1988). Several collections of essays focus on the early conversion of Europe: see *Studies in*

Church History 16 (1979); *Settimane di Studio del Centro Italiano di Studi sull'Alto Medioevo* (Spoleto), vol. 14 (1967) and *Revue du Nord* 68, no. 269 (Avril/Juin 1986). Several new studies have also focused specifically on the important role of women as proselytizers: see, for example, the studies by Jo Ann McNamara, "Living Sermons: Consecrated Women and the Conversion of Gaul," in *Peace Weavers,* pp. 19–37; Felice Lifshitz, "Les femmes missionnaires: l'exemple de la Gaule franque," *Revue d'Histoire Ecclésiastique* 83 (1988): 5–33; Janet L. Nelson, "Les femmes et l'évangelisation," *Revue du Nord* 68, no. 269 (Avril/Juin 1986): 471–85.

4. Albert I. Gordon, *The Nature of Conversion* (Boston, 1967), pp. 1–2.

5. Ibid., p. 2

6. James, *The Franks,* p. 123. See also, for example, Martin of Braga, "Reforming the Rustics (*De correctione rusticorum*)," *The Iberian Fathers,* vol. 1, *Martin of Braga, Paschasius of Dumium, Leander of Seville,* FC 62, trans. Claude W. Barlow (Washington, D.C., 1969), pp. 71–85; Edward James, *The Origins of France: From Clovis to the Capetians, 500–1000,* New Studies in Medieval History, ed. Maurice Keen (Houndmills and London, 1982), pp. 93–99.

7. See J. Nelson, "Queens as Jezebels: The Careers of Brunhild and Balthild in Merovingian History," in Derek Baker, *Medieval Women,* pp. 74–75; see also on the early methods of conversion, E. de Moreau, *Histoire de l'Eglise en Belgique,* 2d ed. (Brussels, 1945), vol. 1, esp. pp. 107–119.

8. P. G. Walsh, *Letters of St. Paulinus of Nola,* ACW 2 (Westminster, Maryland, and London, 1967), letter 31, p. 129 (emphasis mine). Eusebius, for example, credits Constantine for his formative role in Helena's conversion: Butler 3:347. See, for example, Hans A. Pohlsander, *Helena: Empress and Saint* (Chicago, 1995), and the classic studies by A. H. M. Jones, *Constantine and the Conversion of Europe* (New York, 1948, 1962), and Ferdinand Lot, *The End of the Ancient World and the Beginnings of the Middle Ages* (New York, 1961), pp. 29 ff.

9. See Kurth's study, *Sainte Clotilde.*

10. Gregory of Tours, *The History of the Franks,* trans. Lewis Thorpe, pp. 102, 141–43, 158, 166–67, 180–82, 185–86, 197; Bernard S. Bachrach, ed. and trans., *Liber Historiae Francorum* (henceforth cited as *LHF*), pp. 36ff.

11. *Vita Sanctae Chrothildis, MGH SRM* 2:341–48; *SWDA,* pp. 40–50.

12. Two contemporaries, Fortunatus and Sidonius Apollinaris, celebrated Caretena's virtues. In a letter written by Sidonius Apollinaris, in his praise for Caretena he recalled the memory of Tanaquil and the first Agrippina—two Roman women who strongly influenced their husbands. Sidonius Apollinaris, *Epistolae V,* 7, cited by Kurth, *Sainte Clotilde,* p. 24; *LHF,* ch. 11, p. 36. Kurth notes (pp. 24, 28) that Clotilda had a younger sister named Sedeleube. Some scholars have disputed the identification of Clotilda's mother with Caretena. See *SWDA,* p. 41, n. 13.

13. *LHF,* ch. 11, p. 36.

14. Ibid.

15. Ibid., pp. 36–37.

16. Ibid., ch. 12, pp. 38–39.

17. Ibid., ch. 12, pp. 39–40, and Gregory of Tours, *History of the Franks,* bk. 2, ch. 6, p. 166. J. B. Bury, in his *The Invasion of Europe by the Barbarians: A Series of Lectures* (London, 1928), p. 238, argues that this story of Gundobad's murder of Clotilda's parents is a later invention, used to justify the great war of 523 between the Burgundians and the Franks in which King Sigismund of Burgundy and his family perished; this war was especially tragic because of the close relationship of the royal families.

18. Clotilda's espousal of Catholicism rather than Arianism thus played an important role in the formation of this mixed marriage. Briefly, the heresy of Arianism arose from a dispute between the bishop of Alexandria and his priest Arius. Very generally, it focused on the divinity of Christ and the relationship between God the Father and God the Son. Although admitting that Christ was divine, Arius denied that he was of the same nature and substance as God. For Arius and his followers, Christ the Son then occupied a lesser or subordinate position in comparison to God the Father. See, for example, Henry Chadwick, *The Early Church: The Pelican History of the Church,* vol. 1 (Harmondsworth, 1967), pp. 124, 129–30, 133–36; Lot, *The End of the Ancient World and the Beginnings of the Middle Ages,* pp. 42 ff., 47, 278, 280, 289.

19. Bury, *The Invasion of Europe by the Barbarians,* p. 241.

20. Ibid.

21. *LHF,* ch. 12, p. 39.

22. Ibid., pp. 39–40.

23. Gregory of Tours, *History of the Franks,* bk. 2, ch. 29, pp. 141–42.

24. Ibid.

25. Ibid., p. 142.

26. Ibid., ch. 30, p. 143.

27. Ibid.

28. Ibid. (emphasis mine).

29. *LHF,* ch. 15, p. 45 (emphasis mine).

30. Ibid.; *History of the Franks,* bk. 2, ch. 30, p. 143.

31. *History of the Franks,* bk. 2, ch. 30, p. 143.

32. Ibid., ch. 31, p. 143.

33. Ibid., p. 144.

34. Ibid., pp. 144–45.

35. For an important discussion of the transition from paganism to Christianity see Chaney, *The Cult of Kingship in Anglo-Saxon England.*

36. *Vita Sanctae Chrothildis,* ch. 7, p. 344; *SWDA,* pp. 44–45.

37. Ibid., p. 345 (emphasis mine); *SWDA,* p. 45. On Clovis's conversion see also Georges Tessier's extensive study, *Le Baptême de Clovis* (Paris, 1964). This event appears to have been a popular theme in medieval French artwork. See Tessier, e.g., illus. 4–5. Two especially lovely gothic sculptural representations of the baptism of Clovis are found at the Cathedral of Reims (the coronation church of the French kings); they depict the king along with Sts. Remi and Clotilda (location: west facade and tympanum of the north transept).

38. *Vita Balthildis reginae,* ch. 18, *MGH SRM* 2:505–6; *SWDA,* p. 277.

39. Vincent de Beauvais, *Speculum Quadruplex sive Speculum Maius, Speculum Historiale* (Graz, 1965), bk. 21, pp. 819–20.

40. Christine de Pizan, *The Book of the City of Ladies,* trans. Earl Jeffrey Richards (New York, 1982), bk. 2, 35.1, p. 151. She continues her account of Clotilda's conversion of Clovis: "For after she had been enlightened by the Faith, like the good Christian and holy lady she was, she did not cease to prod and beg her lord to receive the holy Faith and be baptized. But he did not wish to assent, and on this account the lady never stopped praying to God in tears, fasts, and devotions to enlighten the king's heart. She prayed so much that our Lord took pity on her affliction and inspired King Clovis, so that once, having gone into battle against the king of the Germans and seeing the battle's fortunes turn against him, he lifted his eyes toward Heaven and in great devotion declared (just as God had wished to inspire him), 'All powerful God, *whom my wife, the queen, believes in and worships,* please help me in this battle, and I promise that I will accept your holy law.' No sooner had he spoken this vow than the battle turned in his favor and he won a complete victory. So he gave thanks to God and, upon returning, to the great joy and consolation of both himself and the queen, he was baptized, along with all the barons and then all the people. From that hour on, thanks to the prayers of this good and holy queen Clotilda, God has so generously bestowed His grace that the Faith has never been defeated in France" (pp. 151–52, emphasis mine).

41. Alan C. Kors and Edward Peters, *Witchcraft in Europe 1100–1700: A Documentary History* (Philadelphia, 1972), pp. 117, 120.

42. Ibid., p. 120.

43. Nicetius, *Epistulae Austrasicae, MGH, Epistolae Merowingici et Karolini aevi,* I: III, letter 8, pp. 119–22.

44. Ibid., p. 122.

45. Gregory the Great, Epistle 12 (To Theodelinda, Queen of the Lombards), in *Gregory the Great, Ephraim Syrus, Aphrahat, NPNF,* vol. 13, pt. 2 (New York, 1898), p. 106; Paul the Deacon, *History of the Lombards,* in Thomas Hodgkin, *Italy and Her Invaders: 600–744* (New York, 1880–89/1967), vol. 5, pp. 236–39, 281, 285–86, 418, 420, 447, 479–80; vol. 6, pp. 132, 138, 143, 160–62.

46. Gregory the Great, Epistle 12, p. 106.

47. Ibid., p. 107.

48. Paul the Deacon, *History of the Lombards,* in Hodgkin, *Italy and her Invaders,* vol. 6, p. 143 (emphasis mine).

49. Ibid., pp. 143–44; for a discussion of the Three Chapters Schism, see A. A. Vasiliev, *History of the Byzantine Empire* (Madison and Milwaukee, 1964) vol. 1, pp. 151–53.

50. Ibid., pp. 131–34.

51. Gregory of Tours, *History of the Franks,* bk. 3, ch. 1, p. 162; see also Wemple, *Women in Frankish Society,* pp. xii–xiii (genealogy chart).

52. Gregory of Tours, *History of the Franks,* bk. 3, ch. 10, p. 170 (emphasis mine).

53. Ibid. Gregory of Tours then elaborates on Childebert's extensive looting: "Along with the other treasure Childebert removed a most valuable col-

lection of church plate. He carried off sixty chalices, fifteen patens and twenty gospel bindings, all made of pure gold and adorned with precious gems. He did not have them broken up. He donated them all to various churches and monastery chapels" (pp. 170–71).

54. Ibid., bk. 5, ch. 38, pp. 301–2.

55. Kurth, *Sainte Clotilde*, pp. 13–14.

56. Gregory of Tours, *History of the Franks*, bk. 5, ch. 38, pp. 301–2.

57. Ibid., p. 302.

58. Ibid., bk. 5, ch. 38, pp. 302–3; bk. 8, ch. 28, p. 456.

59. Ibid., bk. 8, ch. 28, p. 456.

60. Bede, *A History of the English Church and People*, bk. 1, ch. 32, pp. 89–91; Gregory the Great, Epistle 29, *NPNF*, vol. 13, pt. 2, pp. 56–57.

61. Bede, bk. 1, ch. 25, p. 69.

62. Ibid.

63. Ibid., bk. 1, ch. 26, pp. 70–71.

64. Ibid., p. 192.

65. Gregory the Great, Epistle 29, pp. 56–57. See also Hollis, *Anglo-Saxon Women and the Church*, pp. 222–27, 237.

66. Bede, bk. 1, ch. 32, pp. 89–91.

67. On this very interesting dilemma see R. A. Markus, "The Chronology of the Gregorian Mission to England: Bede's Narrative and Gregory's Correspondence," *Journal of Ecclesiastical History* 14 (1963):16–30. Markus argues that Bede was not acquainted with this letter. See also H. Mayr-Harting, *The Coming of Christianity to Anglo-Saxon England*, pp. 266–69. This work suggests that King Ethelbert was already baptized prior to Augustine's mission to Kent or was sympathetic to the new faith. See Hollis, *Anglo-Saxon Women and the Church*, pp. 221–27, p. 225, note 104. I would also like to thank Richard Kieckhefer for his comments about Bede's primary interest in exhalting Gregory in regard to the conversion of England and for calling my attention to Johannes Haller's work *Das Papsttum: Idee und Wirklichkeit* (Basel, 1951), 1:364–87.

68. Gregory the Great, Epistle 29, pp. 56–57.

69. Bede, bk. 1, ch. 32, pp. 89–90. In another letter, written by Pope Gregory to the empress Leontia (wife of Phocas), the pope again cites the example of Helena (here in reference to the empress Pulcheria), whom Gregory invokes as a model for Leontia. (Gregory the Great, Epistle 39, *NPNF*, vol. 13, pt. 2, pp. 100–101.) See also Markus, "The Chronology of the Gregorian Mission to England," p. 21. Pope Gregory also reminds the king: "So it was that the devout Emperor Constantine in his day turned the Roman State from its ignorant worship of idols by his own submission to our mighty Lord and God Jesus Christ, and with his subjects accepted Him with all his heart. The result is that his glorious reputation has excelled that of all his predecessors, and he has outshone them in reputation as greatly as he surpassed them in good works. Now, therefore, let Your Majesty make all speed to bring to your subject princes and peoples the knowledge of the One God, Father, Son and Holy Spirit, so that your own merit and repute may excel that of all the former kings of your nation."

70. Gregory the Great, Epistle 29, p. 57.

71. Ibid. (emphasis mine).

72. Bede, *A History of the English Church and People,* bk. 1, ch. 25, p. 70.

73. For a translation of this letter to Brunhilda, see Arthur J. Mason, ed., *The Mission of St. Augustine to England according to the Original Documents: Being a Handbook for the Thirteenth Centenary* (Cambridge, 1897), pp. 33–35 (emphasis mine).

74. In this context, Gregory the Great's "commendatory letter" to Brunhilda, as noted, states that "it has reached us, that the English nation, by God's favour, desires to become Christian." In his companion letter to the brothers Theoderic and Theodebert, he says, "and it has reached us that the English nation, by the mercy of God, desires earnestly to be converted to the Christian faith, but that the priests in the neighbourhood take no notice, and hang back from kindling the desires of the English by exhortations of their own." Mason, *The Mission of St. Augustine to England,* pp. 31–35. It is difficult to know the origins of this request. However, since Bertha was already a practicing Christian who had her own bishop, Liudhard, with her in Canterbury, it is highly possible that she was responsible for initiating the request for this mission to England. See also Chaney, *The Cult of Kingship in Anglo-Saxon England,* p. 157. In her study *Anglo-Saxon Women and the Church,* Hollis notes that this assumption does not seem very plausible (p. 222).

75. Mason, *The Mission of St. Augustine to England,* pp. 44–45.

76. See *DSW* 1:117. William of Malmesbury in his *History of the Kings of England* also briefly describes the conversion of King Ethelbert. He notes Ethelbert's success in battle and subjugation of other kingdoms. He then explains: "And, in order to obtain foreign connexions, he entered into affinity with the king of France, by marrying his daughter." William of Malmesbury then attributes Ethelbert's original reception to the new faith to Bertha's bishop, Letard: "To this was added the very exemplary life of bishop Letard, who had come over with the queen, by which, though silently, he allured the king to the knowledge of Christ our Lord. Hence it arose that his mind already softened, easily yielded to the preaching of the blessed Augustine; and, first of all his race, he renounced the errors of paganism, that he might obscure by the glory of his faith those whom he surpassed in power" (no. 9, p. 12).

77. Bede, *A History of the English Church and People,* bk. 2, ch. 9, pp. 114–15.

78. Ibid., p. 115.

79. Ibid.

80. Ibid.

81. Ibid.

82. Ibid., bk. 2, ch. 9, p. 116.

83. Ibid., bk 2, ch. 9, p. 117.

84. Ibid., bk. 2, ch. 10, p. 118.

85. Ibid., bk. 2, ch. 11, p. 120.

86. Ibid.

87. Ibid., bk. 2, ch. 11, pp. 121–22.

88. Ibid., bk. 2, ch. 14, p. 128.

89. Ibid., bk. 2, ch. 14, p. 129.

90. Ibid., bk. 4, ch. 23, p. 246.

91. Ibid., bk. 2, ch. 14, p. 129.

92. Ibid., bk. 2, ch. 20, p. 139; See also *DSW* 1:278–79, for information on Ethelberga and her monastery at Lyming.

93. Hollis, *Anglo-Saxon Women and the Church*, p. 226.

94. Ibid., p. 225. Bede notes that at this time the Middle Angles were ruled by Peada, son of Penda and they "accepted the true Faith and its sacraments." Peada "went to Oswy king of the Northumbrians and requested the hand of his daughter Alchfled in marriage. Oswy, however, would not agree to this unless the king and his people accepted the Christian Faith and were baptized. So when Peada had received instruction in the true Faith, and had learned of the promises of the kingdom of heaven and of man's hope of resurrection and eternal life to come, he said that he would gladly become a Christian, even if he were refused the princess." Bede then adds that "He was chiefly influenced to accept the Faith by King Oswy's son Alchfrid, who was his kinsman and friend, and had married his sister Cyniburg, daughter of King Penda." Bede, *A History of the English Church and People*, bk. 3, ch. 21, pp. 176–77

95. *ODS*, p. 135.

96. *Roger of Wendover's Flowers of History*, trans. J. A. Giles (London, 1849), 1:245. Also noted by Hollis, *Anglo-Saxon Women and the Church*, p. 231, n. 129. Also in this tradition is the marriage arrangement which was said to have been negotiated between Charles the Simple and Rollo as part of the Treaty of Saint-Clair-sur-Epte (911). According to the chronicler Dudon de Saint-Quentin, the Archbishop Franco, in his capacity as intermediary, promised Rollo that he could marry the king's daughter, Gisela, on the condition that he receive baptism in the Catholic faith. When consulted by Rollo, the Norman nobility favored this union. They pointed out that Gisela possessed all of the positive characteristics of a noble bride: "Il est bon que tu t'unisses en mariage avec cette fille de roi. . . . Sa naissance est légitime du côté paternel comme du côté maternel; elle est de haute taille, et, d'après ce qu'on nous a dit, pleine de grâce . . . elle est prudente dans ses conseils, pleine d'expérience pour traiter les affaires de l'Etat, d'une conversation agréable, d'un caractère aimant, habituée aux travaux domestiques; bref, c'est la plus accomplie des jeunes filles." Historically, however, there seems to be some confusion in regard to the details of this event and whether Rollo actually married Gisela or Popa, who was said to be his wife. See Henri Prentout, *Étude critique sur Dudon de Saint-Quentin et son histoire des premiers ducs normands* (Paris, 1916), pp. 206–7. According to a later tradition, Eanswith (daughter of Eadbald and founder of one of the first Anglo-Saxon monasteries for women) was pursued in marriage by the king of Northumbria. He was a pagan and she agreed to marry him on the condition that his gods perform a certain miracle. When they failed, he had to withdraw his plans to marry her. Cited by L. Eckenstein, *Woman under Monasticism*, p. 83.

97. William of Malmesbury, *History of the Kings of England*, pp. 28–29, note 5.

98. Fell, *Women in Anglo-Saxon England*, p. 91; William of Malmesbury, *History of the Kings of England*, ch. 36, pp. 29–30.

99. William of Malmesbury, *History of the Kings of England*, ch. 37, pp. 31–32; Bede, *A History of the English Church and People*, bk. 5, ch. 7, pp. 280–81.

100. Bede, *A History of the English Church and People*, bk. 3, ch. 25, pp. 185–92. Hollis, *Anglo-Saxon Women and the Church*, pp. 237–41.

101. Hollis, p. 226.

102. Garmonsway, *The Anglo-Saxon Chronicle*, p. 210.

103. Ibid., pp. 201–2.

104. Turgot, *Life of Queen Margaret*, ch. 8, pp. 69–74.

105. A. O. Anderson, *Early Sources of Scottish History*, pp. 31–32; Baker, "A 'Nursery of Saints,'" pp. 137–38.

106. *DSW* 1:475–77; Butler 3:570; Kurth, *Sainte Clotilde*, pp. 15–16.

107. Kurth, *Sainte Clotilde*, p. 16.

108. See Francis Dvornik, *Byzantine Missions among the Slavs* (New Brunswick, 1970), pp. 267–68.

109. For St. Olga's conversion and baptism see Samuel Hazzard Cross and Olgerd P. Sherbowitz-Wetzor, trans., *The Russian Primary Chronicle: Laurentian Text* (The Medieval Academy of America: Publication no. 60) (Cambridge, Mass., 1953), especially pp. 239–40. I would like to thank Pat Herlihy for calling my attention to this source. See also Dvornik, *Byzantine Missions*, p. 268; Dvornik, *The Making of Central and Eastern Europe* (London, 1949), pp. 67–69; George Ostrogorsky, *History of the Byzantine State*, trans. Joan Hussey (New Brunswick, 1957), p. 251 and note 2; Kurth, *Sainte Clotilde*, pp. 16–18; Sr. Margaret Borkowska, "Slavic Women: Saints Olga and Anna," in *Vox Benedictina: A Journal of Translations from Monastic Sources* 2, no. 4 (Oct. 1985): 366; Ludmilla Koehler, "Saints and Witches," in *The Roles and Images of Women in the Middle Ages and Renaissance* (University of Pittsburgh Publications on the Middle Ages and Renaissance, vol. 3), ed. Douglas Radcliff Umstead (Pittsburgh, 1975), pp. 43–56. Of these, see especially Cross and Sherbowitz-Wetzor, Dvornik, and Ostrogorsky, who summarize this debate.

110. Cross and Sherbowitz-Wetzor, *The Russian Primary Chronicle*, p. 82.

111. Ibid., p. 83.

112. Ibid., p. 84.

113. Dvornik, *Byzantine Missions*, pp. 268–69.

114. Cross and Sherbowitz-Wetzor, *The Russian Primary Chronicle*, p. 86.

115. Ibid., pp. 86–87.

116. Ibid., p. 87.

117. Ostrogorsky, *History of the Byzantine State*, p. 251.

118. Borkowska, "Slavic Women: Saints Olga and Anna," p. 366.

119. Cross and Sherbowitz-Wetzor, *The Russian Primary Chronicle*, p. 112; Dvornik, *Byzantine Missions*, p. 270.

120. Cross and Sherbowitz-Wetzor, *The Russian Primary Chronicle*, pp. 111–12.

121. Ibid., p. 112.

122. Ibid., pp. 113, 116.

123. Dvornik, *Byzantine Missions,* p. 272.

124. Cross and Sherbowitz-Wetzor, *The Russian Primary Chronicle,* pp. 117–19, 124.

125. Ibid., p. 111.

126. Dvornik, *Byzantine Missions,* p. 272.

127. *DSW* 1:69.

128. *PB* 10, Sept. 2, p. 422; Butler 3, Sept. 2, p. 466.

129. Vincent of Beauvais, *Speculum Historiale,* bk. 25, ch. 9, p. 1005.

130. Augustine, *St Augustine: Confessions,* trans. R. S. Pine-Coffin (Baltimore, 1961), bk. 1, ch. 11, p. 32 (emphasis mine). See also Peter Brown, *Augustine of Hippo* (Berkeley and Los Angeles, 1970), pp. 28–34; Frend, *The Rise of Christianity,* p. 561.

131. *PB* 6, June 8, p. 519; Gildardus episcopus Rotomagensis, *AB* 8:393–404; *BHL* 1:527; Medardus episcopus Noviomensis, *AASS, Iun. II,* June 8, pp. 78–95, *BHL* 2:857.

132. *PB,* p. 519. See also Lifshitz, "Femmes missionaires: la Gaule franque," p. 16.

133. Butler 2, May 15, p. 322; *AASS, Mai. III,* May 15, pp. 502–5; *BHL* 2:1071–72; *DSW* 1:119–20 (St. Bertha, d. ca. 808).

134. For example, concerning St. Martin, Sulpicius Severus, et al., *The Western Fathers,* trans. F. R. Hoare, pp. 17–18; Frend, *The Rise of Christianity,* p. 562. St. Dympna, Butler 2, May 15, pp. 320–21; C. Horstmann, *The Lives of Women Saints of our Contrie of England,* pp. 43–49; *DSW* 1:246; *PB* 5, May 15, p. 551. St. Fursy, *AASS, Ian. II,* January 16, pp. 401–19; *BHL* 1:480–81. St. Rioc, *PB* 2, Feb. 12, p. 480.

135. See Lynn Thorndyke, trans., *University Records and Life in the Middle Ages,* Columbia University Records of Civilization (New York, 1944 [1972]), pp. 138–49.

136. Ibid., p. 138.

137. Ibid., p. 140.

138. Ibid., p. 148.

139. Ibid., p. 140.

140. Ibid.

141. Ibid., pp. 140–41.

142. For an interesting look at the use of wives as proselytizers in the late thirteenth-century Mongol Empire, see "Christian Wives of Mongol Rulers and Western Missionaries' Expectations in Asia," paper delivered by James D. Ryan at the Twenty-eighth International Congress on Medieval Studies, Kalamazoo, Michigan, May 9, 1993.

143. An early example of problems related to women's inability to be priests and to baptize their new converts can be seen in an incident from the Life of St. Brigid. As a result of Brigid's fame in effecting miracles, she was brought to a pagan man's new house in order to bless it. The man then explained that he had not been willing to accept baptism from St. Patrick but

would receive the new faith from Brigid. However, because she was a woman and was not an ordained priest, she was unable to baptize him and needed to call upon a bishop or priest to accomplish this. Stokes, *Lives of Saints from the Book of Lismore*, pp. 327–28. In another rendition, the hagiographer notes that "thereafter Patrick ordered Brigit and his [Bishop Bron's] successor that they should never be without an ordained person in their company: therefore Nat-Fraich took priest's orders." Stokes, p. 191.

144. McNamara, "Living Sermons," p. 24.

145. Christine de Pizan, *The Book of the City of Ladies*, bk. 2, 35.1, p. 151.

CHAPTER FIVE

1. For an insightful analysis of many of the complexities of early Christian and medieval motherhood see Clarissa Atkinson, *The Oldest Vocation: Christian Motherhood in the Middle Ages* (Ithaca and London, 1991). See also the important collection of essays edited by Anneke B. Mulder-Bakker, *Sanctity and Motherhood: Essays on Holy Mothers in the Middle Ages* (New York and London, 1995), as well as *Medieval Mothering*, edited by John Carmi Parsons and Bonnie Wheeler (New York and London, 1996). See also Bitel, *Land of Women*, pp. 84–110. For the history of childhood see Shulamith Shahar, *Childhood in the Middle Ages*, trans. Chaya Galai (London and New York, 1990, 1992); Philippe Ariès, *Centuries of Childhood: A Social History of Family Life*, trans. Robert Baldick (New York, 1962); and *The History of Childhood*, ed. Lloyd de Mause (New York, 1974).

2. Tertullian, "To His Wife," in *Treatises on Marriage and Remarriage*, trans. William P. Le Saint (Westminster, 1951), p. 17.

3. Tertullian, "Monogamy," in *Treatises on Marriage and Remarriage*, p. 107. He adds, "Let them provide for Antichrist, so that his savage cruelty may wanton all the more. He will give them midwives—the public executioners."

4. Tertullian, "To His Wife," in *Treatises on Marriage and Remarriage*, p. 17.

5. Leander of Seville, *The Training of Nuns*, in *Iberian Fathers*, 1 (FC 62):191, 193.

6. Caesarius of Arles, *Sermons*, FC 31, trans. Sr. Mary Magdeleine Mueller (New York, 1956), vol. 1, Sermon 51, pp. 257–58.

7. Jerome, *Commentarius in Epistolam ad Ephesios*, III, V (658), PL 26:533, cited by Bullough, "Transvestism in the Middle Ages," in *Sexual Practices and the Medieval Church*, ed. Vern L. Bullough and James Brundage (Buffalo, 1982), p. 45.

8. Jerome, "Against Helvidius," in *St. Jerome: Dogmatic and Polemical Works*, FC 53, trans. John N. Hritzu (Washington, D.C., 1965), ch. 21, p. 42.

9. Ibid., ch. 18, p. 38; ch. 20, pp. 40–41.

10. Jerome, letter "Ad matrem et filiam in Gallia commorantes," 117.4, cited and trans. by Clarissa Atkinson, *The Oldest Vocation*, p. 69; see also *Saint Jérôme, Lettres*, trans. Labourt, vol. 6, letter CXVII, p. 79.

11. *St. Jerome: Letters and Select Works, NPNF,* vol. 6, letter 108, ch. 6, p. 197; *Saint Jérôme, Lettres,* trans. Labourt vol. 5, letter CVIII, ch. 6, p. 164.

12. Fortunatus, *Opera Poetica,* ed. C. Nisard (Paris, 1887), bk. 8, poem 3, cited and trans. by Julia O'Faolain and Lauro Martines, eds., *Not in God's Image: Women in History from the Greeks to the Victorians* (New York, 1973), pp. 138–39.

13. Leander of Seville, *The Training of Nuns,* trans. Barlow, p. 191.

14. On this topic see especially Peter Browe, S.J., *Beiträge zur Sexualethik des Mittelalters,* in *Breslauer Studien zur historischen Theologie,* Band 23 (Breslau, 1932), pp. 1–35, 80–113. I would like to thank Carolly Erickson for this reference. See also Carolly Erickson, *The Medieval Vision: Essays in History and Perception* (New York, 1976), pp. 195–97.

15. Erickson, *The Medieval Vision,* p. 196. In this tradition Gregory the Great, while citing the Old Testament proscription that required women wait thirty-three days after the birth of a son and sixty-six days after the birth of a daughter before they could enter the temple, argued in an enlightened manner that this was to be "understood as an allegory, for were a woman to enter church and return thanks in the very hours of her delivery, she would do nothing wrong." "Pope Gregory's letter to S. Augustine," in Bede, *A History of the English Church and People,* bk. 1, ch. 27, VIII, pp. 76–79. The Penitential of Theodore of Tarsus is more restrictive in its warning that women who enter a church before purification after childbirth (a ritual done forty days after childbirth), shall do penance. Penitential of Theodore of Tarsus, no. 17. See Herm. Jos. Schmitz, *Die Bussbücher und das kanonische Bussverfahren* (Düsseldorf, 1898), II, nos. 125, 126, p. 536. See also J. T. McNeill and H. M. Gamer, *Medieval Handbooks of Penance. A Translation of the Principal Libri Poenitentiales and Selections from Related Documents,* Records of Civilization, Sources and Studies, 29 (New York, 1938), p. 197; Pierre Payer, *Sex and the Penitentials: The Development of a Sexual Code 550–1150* (Toronto, Buffalo, London, 1984), pp. 26, 36. Honorius of Autun (12th c.), citing Levit. *15,* also observes that after the birth of a child, women were not to enter the church because they were designated unclean and excluded from the heavenly temple. Because of this, Honorius explains, it was customary that women, joined by men, stand as penitents at the *foris* (porch area or door of the church). Honorius of Autun, *Gemma Animae, PL* 172, bk. 1, cap. 146, p. 589; see also Burchard of Worms, *Decretorum Libri XX, PL* 140, lib. 19, cap. 141, p. 1010. The topic of female pollution and the sacred is one of the areas that I will be exploring in my next study on medieval women and proscriptions of sacred space.

16. Honorius of Autun, *Gemma Animae, PL* 172, bk. 1, cap. 170, pp. 596–97; Browe, *Beiträge zur Sexualethik,* pp. 20, n. 24, 22. Charles Joseph Hefele and H. LeClercq, *Historie des conciles,* vol. 5, pt. 1, p. 113, ch. 9: Council of Rouen (1074); William Durandus, *The Symbolism of Church and Church Ornaments: A Translation of the First Book of the Rationale Divinorum Officiarum,* trans. John Mason Neale and Benjamin Webb (London, 1893), nos. 15 and 16, p. 86.

17. On this topic for early Ireland, see for example, Plummer, *Vitae Sanc-*

torum Hiberniae, vol. 1, esp. p. cx; or for Wales, *The Life of St. Cadoc* notes that "all kings, earls, and nobles, and also military officers, and domestics, be buried in the cemetery of thy Monastery at Llancarvan; that is, let every one be there buried, *except exiles, and women dying in child-bed"* (emphasis mine). W. J. Rees, *Lives of the Cambro British Saints,* p. 356. See also William Durandus, *Symbolism,* p. 86.

18. St. Jerome, "Letter CVII to Laeta," *NPNF,* vol. 6, ch. 6, p. 192. Citing 1 Timothy 2:15.

19. St. Jerome, "Letter VII. Ad Chromatium, Iovinum, Eusebium," *Select Letters of St. Jerome,* trans. F. A. Wright (Cambridge and London, 1980), letter 7, pp. 24–27: "Matrem communem, quae, cum vobis sanctitate societur, in eo vos praevenit, quia tales genuit, *cuius vere venter aureus potest dici,* eo salutamus honore, quo nostis" (emphasis mine).

20. Wemple, *Women in Frankish Society,* pp. 103, 258.

21. Ibid., p. 103. See Peter Dronke, *The Medieval Lyric* (New York, 1968), pp. 41–42.

22. *Cáin Adamnáin: An Old-Irish Treatise on the Law of Adamnan, Anecdota Oxoniensia,* trans. Kuno Meyer (Oxford, 1905), p. 5. See also Bitel, *Land of Women,* pp. 84–85.

23. See Wemple, *Women in Frankish Society,* p. 103; Mary Clayton, *The Cult of the Virgin Mary in Anglo-Saxon England:* Cambridge Studies in Anglo-Saxon England (Cambridge, 1990); Bitel, *Land of Women,* pp. 106–110; Ilene H. Forsyth, *The Throne of Wisdom: Wood Sculptures of the Madonna in Romanesque France* (Princeton, 1972); Mary Martin McLaughlin, "Survivors and Surrogates: Children and Parents from the Ninth to the Thirteenth Centuries," in *The History of Childhood,* ed. Lloyd de Mause (New York, 1974), pp. 132–33.

24. The Anglo-Saxon Dewsbury Cross, for example, provides a tender portrayal of the Christ child reaching to his mother's breast. See Clayton, *The Cult of the Virgin in Anglo-Saxon England,* p. 267.

25. Emile Mâle, *Notre-Dame de Chartres* (Paris, 1963), p. 9.

26. Clayton, *The Cult of the Virgin in Anglo-Saxon England,* esp. pp. 1–24, 52–178, 267–74.

27. On chaste marriage, see the fascinating study by Dyan Elliott, *Spiritual Marriage: Sexual Abstinence in Medieval Wedlock* (Princeton, 1993).

28. This high valuation can be seen, for example, in the writings of Tacitus, the laws of the period, etc. See also David Herlihy, *Medieval Households* (Cambridge, Mass., 1985), pp. 29–78; Wemple, *Women in Frankish Society,* pp. 27–123.

29. Drew, *The Laws of the Salian Franks,* p. 127; Herlihy, "Life Expectancies for Women in Medieval Society," in *The Role of Women in the Middle Ages,* ed. Rosmarie Thee Morewedge (Albany, 1975), pp. 8–9; Wemple, *Women in Frankish Society,* pp. 29, 213.

30. Herlihy, "Life Expectancies for Women in Medieval Society," pp. 1–20. However, it should also be mentioned that according to the Germanic codes, after menopause women continued to receive wergeld equal to that of men of their same class. In other words, after their reproductive usefulness

had passed, they were still viewed by the Germanic codes as highly valued members of their society. And although very high wergelds were attached to their childbearing years, their value was not predicated solely on this reproductive function. See also Carol J. Clover, "The Politics of Scarcity: Notes on the Sex Ratio in Early Scandinavia," in *New Readings on Women in Old English Literature*, ed. Helen Damico and Alexandra Hennessey Olsen (Bloomington and Indianapolis, 1990), pp. 100–134; Marcia Guttentag and Paul F. Secord, *Too Many Women? The Sex Ratio Question* (Beverly Hills, 1983), pp. 53–58.

31. The three officially canonized women saints who lived during the period under consideration in this study were St. Wiborada, virgin martyr (d. 925, canonized 1047), St. Godeleva, married martyr (killed by her husband's men, d. 1070, canonized 1084), St. Adelaide, German Empress, the mother of Emma, Otto II, and St. Matilda, abbess of Quedlinburg, as well as three other children. Adelaide died in 999 and was canonized between 1084–1096. Folz, *Les saintes reines du moyen âge en occident*, pp. 77–78.

32. St. Godeleva/Godelieve: *AASS, Iul. II*, July 6, pp. 359–444; *PB* 8, July 6, p. 83; Wemple, *Women in Frankish Society*, p. 100; Corbet, *Les Saints ottoniens*, pp. 31, 59; St. Margaret of Scotland, Butler 2, June 10, p. 515.

33. See individual *vitae*, in the *Bibliotheca sanctorum, Butler's Lives of the Saints, The Oxford Dictionary of Saints (ODS), Les Petits Bollandistes (PB)*, and Dunbar's *Dictionary of Saintly Women (DSW)*. See also J. C. Russell, who notes that "normally, given the death rate of women, one married at thirty might expect to have an average of four children, at twenty-five an average of five, and at twenty an average of six." "Population in Europe, 500–1500," in *The Fontana Economic History of Europe: The Middle Ages*, ed. Carlo M. Cipolla (Glasgow, 1972), p. 61.

34. St. Bilhild, *DSW* 1:123; *BHL* 1:198. St. Eustadiola, abbess of Bituricensis, *AASS, Iun. II*, June 8, pp. 131–33; *DSW*, 1:298–99.

35. Einhard and Notker the Stammerer, *Two Lives of Charlemagne*, trans. Lewis Thorpe (Harmondsworth, 1969), p. 185. See, concerning St. Protagie, chapter 4, "Marriage and Domestic Proselytization."

36. St. Notburga, *AASS, Ian. III*, January 26, pp. 365–66; *DSW* 2:110–11; Eckenstein, *Woman under Monasticism*, p. 34. In this same tradition is the story surrounding St. Quiteria's birth (2d c.). She is said to be one of nine daughters born to Lucius Caius Attilius (governor of Lusitania and Galicia) and his wife Calfia. *DSW* 2:173.

37. *AASS, Sept. VI*, September 22, 451–53; *DSW* 1:478–79; Butler 3, July 20, p. 151.

38. Eckenstein, *Woman under Monasticism*, p. 34; *DSW* 1:2.

39. Plummer, *Vitae Sanctorum Hiberniae*, vol. 1, pp. clvii–clviii.

40. Ibid., p. cxxxvii, n. 9; p. clviii, n. 2.

41. According to the Life of St. Maedoc of Ferns, the parents of the future saint went to Drumlane to fast with the purpose of obtaining an heir. Here the mother of the saint saw a vision of the moon entering the mouth of her husband and her husband saw a star entering the mouth of his wife. This was interpreted to mean that an eminent birth would emerge from this couple.

Plummer, *Lives of Irish Saints,* vol. 2, p. 177. Telach, the mother of St. Findian of Clonard, had a vision at the time of her pregnancy of a flame of fire which came "into her mouth and went back in the form of a bright bird." Whitley Stokes, *Lives of Saints from the Book of Lismore,* p. 222. The story of St. Willibrord's conception relates: "Now it happened that his wife, Willibrord's mother, saw a vision in her sleep during the dead of night. It seemed to her as though she were looking at a new moon in the sky, which grew before her eyes until it became full. Then, as she gazed spellbound, suddenly it fell from its course and dropped into her mouth. She swallowed it, and her body glowed with the splendor of the moon. Then she awoke, terribly frightened. When she told the dream to a certain devout priest he asked her if she had had her customary relations with her husband on the night that the vision had come to her. She said that she had, and then he told her: 'The moon which you saw grow from small to large is a son whom you conceived that very night and who will dispel the gloomy darkness of error with the light of truth.'" Clinton Albertson, *Anglo-Saxon Saints and Heroes* (New York, 1967), p. 279.

42. Plummer, *Vitae Sanctorum Hiberniae,* vol. 1, p. clviii.

43. Ibid., n. 4; Stokes, *Martyrology of Oengus,* 246–47.

44. Stokes, *Martyrology of Oengus,* pp. 135–37; see also Henken, *The Welsh Saints,* pp. 23–25.

45. Gerard Sitwell, trans., *St. Odo of Cluny: Being the Life of St. Odo of Cluny by John of Salerno and the Life of St. Gerarld of Aurillac by St. Odo* (London and New York, 1958), bk. 1, ch. 2, p. 95.

46. Jonas of Bobbio, *The Life of St. Columban,* trans. Carleton, ch. 22, p. 13.

47. *St. Odo of Cluny,* trans. Sitwell, bk. 1, ch. 5, p. 8.

48. *Vita Bennonis II Episcopi Osnabrugensis by Norberto abbate Iburgensi,* ch. 1, *MGH SS,* 12:61.

49. See Elissa R. Henken, *The Welsh Saints: A Study in Patterned Lives* (Cambridge, 1991), pp. 24, 207. For the remarkable birth of St. Beino—whose parents were aged and without heirs, for they had slept together twelve years without sexual intercourse—see W. J. Rees, ed. and trans., "The Life of St. Beino," in *Lives of the Cambro British Saints,* pp. 299–300.

50. *Vita Sadalbergae abbatissae Laudunensis,* ch. 11, *MGH SRM* 5:55–56. There has been some question, however, about the reliability of this *vita.* As noted by Suzanne Wemple: "To provide a role model for this kind of filial behavior, the biographer of Salaberga, writing in the early ninth century, some 150 years after her death, deprived the saint of her virginity, inventing two husbands and five children for her. Salaberga's purported marriages were arranged by her father 'against her wishes,' the biographer was careful to say. Her first union ended abruptly with the death of her husband two months after the nuptials." In her second marriage we are told that, "pressured by his parents and ordered by the king, Baldwin married Salaberga for the sake of procreating children. The union, fruitless at first, was eventually blessed by five children, each dedicated to God by the parents. When her obligation to bear and raise children had been finally met, Salaberga was able to fulfill her wish of founding and leading a convent." Wemple, *Women in Frankish Soci-*

ety, p. 153. See also *SWDA,* p. 176.

51. Rudolf, *The Life of St. Leoba,* pp. 210–11.

52. Included in this tradition of miracle babies are Sts. Remi, Donatus, Samson, Maedoc of Ferns, Berach, Lioba, Odo of Cluny, Hildegund, Sirude, Odilia, and others.

53. Weinstein and Bell, *Saints and Society,* pp. 20, 23.

54. Réau, *Iconographie de l'art chrétien,* vol. 1, p. 388.

55. Ibid., vol. 2, p. 800.

56. Eckenstein, *Woman under Monasticism,* p. 7.

57. Rees, *Lives of the Cambro British Saints,* p. 527.

58. Réau, *Iconographie de l'art chrétien,* vol. 3, p. 1151.

59. *DSW* 1:470–71.

60. Eckenstein, *Woman under Monasticism,* p. 31.

61. J. Gessler, *La Légende de sainte Wilgeforte ou Ontcommer,* p. 18; Butler (July 20) 3:151; Réau, *Iconographie de l'art chrétien,* vol. 3, p. 1344. St. Brigid was also looked to as a fertility specialist. She was called upon by her maternal aunt who "had long been barren." Brigid then fasted for three days in the church at Kildare and then blessed her aunt's womb. She later had three sons. Stokes, *Lives of Saints from the Book of Lismore,* p. 335. Another episode in the Life of Saint Brigid also notes her success in bringing about the miracle of fertility: "Quadam vero nocte fuit quidam vir cum sua uxore in hospitio cum S. Brigida; et ille rogavit eam, ut signaret vulvam uxoris, ut filium haberet: et ita facit. Et statim uxor ejus dormiente illo cum ea concepit; et inde natus est Echenus praecipuus Sanctus." *AASS, Feb. I,* February 1, ch. 16, p. 133. See also on fertility miracles, Rees, *Lives of the Cambro British Saints,* pp. 331–32; Gregory of Tours, *Libri Miraculorum,* vol. 2, bk. 4, ch. 11, pp. 286–89; bk. 4, ch. 23, pp. 302–3; *The Life of King Edward,* pp. 61–62.

62. *Rhigyfarch's Life of St. David,* trans. J. W. James (Cardiff, 1967), ch. 4, p. 30.

63. See the Life of St. Kentigern by Jocelinus, a monk of Furness, and a fragment of the Life of St. Kentigern by a cleric of St. Kentigern, in *The Lives of S. Ninian and S. Kentigern,* vol. 5 in *The Historians of Scotland,* ed. Alexander Penrose Forbes (Edinburgh, 1874), pp. 34–35, 126–28. See also Henken, *The Welsh Saints: A Study in Patterned Lives,* p. 24. Jenny Jochens has also noted that Old Norse law prohibited a man to "disguise himself in the female head-dress or dress in female clothing [in order to seduce a woman]." The punishment for this behavior was lesser outlawry. Jochens, "Before the Male Gaze," p. 17.

64. See André Wilmart, "La Légende de Sainte Edith en prose et vers par le moine Goscelin," *AB* 56 (1938): 5–101, 265–307; Farmer, *The Oxford Dictionary of Saints,* pp. 411–12; Butler 3:571. See also Susan Millinger, "Humility and Power," in *Distant Echoes,* pp. 115–29.

65. Plummer, "Life of Brendan of Clonfert," *Lives of Irish Saints,* vol. 2, pp. 44–45. These miracles which focus on the breasts of the future saints' mothers underscore the maternal functions to be assumed by these women in nursing their own infants, as well as the belief in the special, or even miracu-

lous, quality of their milk. Other visions which appeared to the mothers of saints can be seen in the Life of St. Columba (Adomnan, *Adomnan's Life of Columba,* pp. 465–66); the Life of St. Columbanus (Jonas, *Life of St. Columban,* ch. 6, p. 2); the Life of St. Mochuda (Plummer, *Lives of Irish Saints,* vol. 2, ch. 4, p. 282); the Life of St. Prix (*PB1,* Jan. 25, p. 604).

66. Bede, *A History of the English Church and People,* bk. 4, ch. 23, p. 248.

67. Stokes, *Lives of Saints from the Book of Lismore,* p. 222.

68. Wulfstan of Winchester, *The Life of St. Aethelwold,* ed. Michael Lapidge and Michael Winterbottom (Oxford, 1991), pp. 4–5.

69. *SS. Bernardi vita prima,* ch. 1, *PL* 185:227–28. For other prenatal "speaking" miracles: see St. Finchua (Stokes, *Lives of Saints from the Book of Lismore,* chs. 2812, 2824, pp. 231–32); St. Bairre of Cork (Plummer, *Lives of Irish Saints,* vol. 2, p. 11); St. Patrick, while still in the womb, was also said to have saved his mother from being poisoned (Stokes, *Lives of Saints from the Book of Lismore,* ch. 52, p. 150).

70. Plummer, *Lives of Irish Saints,* vol. 2, p. 121; *AASS, Mar. I,* March 1, pp. 94–96; *PB3,* March 1, p. 90.

71. *Rhigyfarch's Life of St. David,* ch. 6, p. 32. In the early thirteenth century, Gerald of Wales noted that "the stone is preserved in the church (of St. David's) to this day among the relics, and the marks of the five fingers appear impressed on the flint as though it were in wax" (*The Historical Works of Giraldus Cambrensis,* trans. Thomas Wright, p. 341).

72. Plummer, *Lives of Irish Saints,* vol. 2, p. 185.

73. Plummer, *Vitae Sanctorum Hiberniae,* vol. 1, p. 34. A number of other *vitae* note saints born on stones as well as sacred stones associated with births and future miracles. See, e.g., *The Most Ancient Lives of Saint Patrick,* ed. James O'Leary (New York, 1897), pp. 137–38. The Life of Maedoc of Ferns notes that "the first miracle of Maedoc after his birth was that on the stone on which he was carried to his baptism folk would be ferried backwards and forwards as in any ferry-boat." Plummer, *Lives of Irish Saints,* vol. 2, p. 185. Other *vitae* note the miraculous footprints of saints, their horses, oxen, etc., in stones. For a number of examples of this motif, see Henken, *The Welsh Saints: A Study in Patterned Lives.*

74. In a miracle attributed to the Virgin of Rocamadour, cited by Renate Blumenfeld-Kosinski, we find perhaps a "record" in pregnancy and the duration of labor. In this case the woman was said to have been pregnant for almost thirty months! For much of this time the unfortunate woman had been in labor and was unable to give birth. According to the account, "Miraculously the stomach of the poor woman opened, contrary to nature and without the help of a doctor. The dead and already putrid child was extracted in pieces and the mother was completely healed. She came to the church of Rocamadour to give thanks to her benefactress. And since she belonged to that uncouth nation that does not know any shame she gladly showed her still open wound. She did not stop singing the praise of the powerful Virgin." Renate Blumenfeld-Kosinski, *Not of Woman Born: Representations of Cae-*

sarean Birth in Medieval and Renaissance Culture (Ithaca and London, 1990), pp. 121–22. See also Ronald C. Finucane, *Miracles and Pilgrims: Popular Beliefs in Medieval England* (Totowa, 1977), p. 106.

75. See individual saints in Réau, *Iconographie de l'art chrétien; Bibliotheca sanctorum; Les Petits Bollandistes; Butler's Lives of the Saints;* Dunbar, *Dictionary of Saintly Women;* Farmer, *The Oxford Dictionary of Saints.*

76. See for St. Ghislain, *PB* 12, Oct. 9, p. 211, Butler, 4, Oct. 9, p. 71; or for St. Brigid, we learn that she gave her girdle to a woman who had always been in poverty. She assured her "that it would heal whatsoever disease or illness to which it was applied. And it was so done, and thus the woman used to make her livelihood thenceforward" (Stokes, *Lives of Saints from the Book of Lismore,* p. 192).

77. Gottfried and Theoderic, *The Life of Holy Hildegard,* trans. by Aldegundis Führkötter and James McGrath, ed. Mary Palmquist (Collegeville, 1995), pp. 78–79.

78. St. Margaret or Marina, *DSW,* 2:11–12; Butler, 3, July 20, pp. 152–53; see also Mary Clayton and Hugh Magennis, *The Old English Lives of St. Margaret* (Cambridge, 1994), pp. 3–71; Blumenfeld-Kosinski, *Not of Woman Born,* pp. 7–11, 121. The story of St. Margaret, and her special concern for women in childbirth, can also be found in the popular *Golden Legend* by Jacobus of Voragine.

79. *Matthew Paris's English History from the Year 1235 to 1273,* trans. J. A. Giles (London, 1852), 1:290 (emphasis mine). Evidence of the cult of St. Margaret in late Anglo-Saxon England can be found in a variety of sources, including, as noted by Mary Clayton and Hugh Magennis, "calendars, litanies, masses, relics, inclusion in collections of saints' lives as well as the vernacular evidence of the entry in the *Old English Martyrology* and the three lives." They also suggest that veneration of Margaret in the second half of the eleventh century may be related to the special respect shown for Margaret, queen-saint of Scotland. Nevertheless, it was only in the twelfth century that Margaret became especially popular in the West as patron saint of childbirth. Clayton and Magennis, *The Old English Lives of St. Margaret,* pp. 1–6, 72–83. See also C. H. Talbot, *Medicine in Medieval England* (London, 1967); Peter Biller, "Childbirth in the Middle Ages," *History Today* 36 (August 1986):48.

80. Réau, *Iconographie de l'art chrétien,* vol. 3, p. 879. It is interesting to note that in response to the heavy demand for St. Margaret's miraculous belt or girdle, the original somehow multiplied. According to Réau, in France alone there were at least four belts attributed to St. Margaret: two in Paris (one in the Abbey of St-Germain-des-Près and the other in the Monastery de Feuillants), another at Amiens, and a fourth at Dol. In Paris the saint's belt was especially popular and known for working miracles. Réau also notes that in the topography of Paris, near the old wall of the Abbey of St-Germain, was the Court of the Dragon, named for the symbol of St. Margaret. Sauval in the *Antiquités de Paris* (1724) observed that "La ceinture de sainte Marguerite attire quantité de monde le jour de sa fête et le faubourg est rempli de femmes

grosses" (Réau, p. 879); see also Blumenfeld-Kosinski, *Not of Woman Born*, pp. 7–9.

81. Réau, *Iconographie de l'art chrétien*, 3:879.
82. Mâle, *Notre-Dame de Chartres*, pp. 9–10.
83. Jacobus de Voragine, *The Golden Legend*, 6:134; see also *MGH SRM* 3:396–99.
84. Plummer, *Vitae Sanctorum Hiberniae*, vol. 2, ch. 1, p. 107: "Hic lapis multis confert sanitatem corporalem, et specialiter mulieribus in puerperio laborantibus, si ex locione eius biberint aquam, singulare dat presidium."
85. *AASS, Apr. III*, April 22, p. 70.
86. *PB* 3, March 1, pp. 90–91.
87. Plummer, *Vitae Sanctorum Hiberniae*, 2:110.
88. See Salisbury, *Church Fathers, Independent Virgins*, p. 112.
89. Blumenfeld-Kosinski, *Not of Woman Born*, p. 123.
90. Ibid. (emphasis mine).
91. Ibid., p. 124.
92. Ibid., pp. 122–23.
93. Ibid., p. 123.
94. Gregory of Tours, *Life of the Fathers*, trans. Edward James, ch. 17, p. 114; see also early miracles in the Lives of the following saints: St. Brigid (Stokes, *Lives of Saints from the Book of Lismore*, p. 184); St. Ambrose (Sulpicius Severus, et al., *The Western Fathers: Being the Lives of Martin of Tours, Ambrose, Augustine of Hippo, Honoratus of Arles, and Germanus of Auxerre*, trans. F. R. Hoare [New York, 1954/1965], ch. 3, pp. 150–51); and St. Gervais, *PB* 8, July 6, p. 70; *AASS, Iul. II*, July 6, pp. 314–15; *BHL* 1:524.
95. *PB* 4, April 19, p. 492; *AASS, Apr. II*, April 19, pp. 647–64.
96. Whitley Stokes, "Life of S. Fechin of Fore," *Revue Celtique* 12 (1891): 323.
97. For the procedure of namegiving of the Germanic nobility before the eleventh century, see Karl F. Werner, "Liens de parenté et noms de personne. Un problème historique et méthodologique," *Famille et parenté dans l'occident médiéval*, Collection de l'Ecole française de Rome, vol. 30 (Rome, 1977), pp. 13–18, 25–34. On godparents and baptismal sponsorship, see Joseph H. Lynch, *Godparents in Early Medieval Europe* (Princeton, 1986), especially pp. 168, 172–73.
98. Michael Swanton, trans., *Three Lives of the Last Englishmen*, Garland Library of Medieval Literature, vol. 10, Ser. B (New York, 1984), p. 92.
99. Fell, "Hild, Abbess of Streonæshalch," p. 78.
100. *Vita Corbiani episcopi Baiuvariorum auctore Arbeone*, ch. 1, *MGH SRM* 6:561. "Illius vero post obitum venerandus vir Dei natus est et genitoris sortitus vocabulum ex sacro fontis sumpsit lavacro; isdem unigenitus dum fuisset, viduata mulier tante dilectionis soboli caris in suum Conabatur filium vertere vocabulum; in cuius usitato nomine adherebat infantulum, *ut patrinomiae privaretur vocationi, ut matrinomius existeret Corbinianus* [my emphasis]."
101. *PB* 4, March 29, p. 52; *PB* 11, Oct. 2, p. 654.

102. James F. Kenney, *The Sources for the Early History of Ireland, Ecclesiastical: An Introduction and Guide* (Shannon, 1968), p. 354.

103. J.N. Hillgarth, ed. *Christianity and Paganism, 350–750: The Conversion of Western Europe* (Philadelphia, 1969, 1986), p. 140.

104. Stokes, *Martyrology of Oengus*, pp. 48–49.

105. *Vita Sadalbergae*, ch. 11, pp. 55–56; *SWDA*, p. 184.

106. Rudolf, *Life of St. Leoba*, p. 211 (emphasis mine).

107. *AASS Mai VII*, May 30, pp. 267–74; *PB*, 6, May 30, p. 308.

108. *PB*, 9, August 15, p. 572; *VSB*, 8:274.

109. Baker, "A 'Nursery of Saints,'" pp. 126, 138.

110. Albertson, *Anglo-Saxon Saints and Heroes*, p. 279.

111. See, for example, *Aldhelm: The Prose Works*, trans. Lapidge and Herren, p. 59; for the naming of children in modern times and the adoption of saints' names see Réau, *Iconographie de l'art Chrétien*, 1:382.

112. *AASS Ian. III*, January 25, ch. 1, p. 252.

113. Ibid.

114. G. G. Coulton, ed., *Life in the Middle Ages* (New York, 1930), vol. 4, pp. 79–80; case also cited by M. McLaughlin, "Survivors and Surrogates," pp. 114–15.

115. *PB* 11, Oct. 1, p. 588.

116. *PB* 11, Sept. 17, p. 172.

117. See M. McLaughlin, "Survivors and Surrogates," pp. 115–16, 149–50; Janet L. Nelson, "Parents, Children, and the Church in the Earlier Middle Ages," in *The Church and Childhood: Studies in Church History* (Oxford, 1994), 31:92. On wet-nursing, see also for the later period, Christiane Klapisch-Zuber, "Blood Parents and Milk Parents: Wet Nursing in Florence, 1300–1530," in *Women, Family, and Ritual in Renaissance Italy* (Chicago and London, 1985), pp. 132–64; Caroline Walker Bynum, "Jesus as Mother and Abbot as Mother: Some Themes in Twelfth-Century Cistercian Writing," *Harvard Theological Review* 70 (1977): 257–84. For the use of milk in bathing the newborn, and the special milk required by a saint, see St. Brigid (Stokes, *Lives of Saints from the Book of Lismore*, pp. 184–185, 318). A special white cow was used to feed St. Coemgen (Plummer, *Lives of Irish Saints*, vol. 2, p. 122). Also the Life of St. Udalric, tenth-century bishop of Augsburg, notes that as an infant he was so puny and weak that he nearly died. Fortunately, on the advice of a churchman, he was weaned twelve weeks after his birth. Soon after this he grew stronger and became a very attractive infant. *PB* 8, July 4, p. 27.

118. *PB* 10, Sept. 1, p. 397.

119. *PB* 4, April 19, p. 492.

120. Marbod of Rennes, *Vita S. Roberti Cassae Dei*, PL 171:1507; see M. McLaughlin, "Survivors and Surrogates," p. 150, n. 62.

121. *AASS, Apr. II*, April 13, p. 139; *SS. Bernardi vita prima*, ch. 1, PL 185:227: "Propter quod etiam aliensis uberibus nutriendos committere illustris femina refugiebat, quasi cum lacte materno materni quodammodo boni infudens eis naturam." See also McLaughlin, "Survivors and Surrogates,"

especially pp. 115–17, 150. Again, it is interesting to note that most of these *vitae* that emphasize the special need for the mothers to nurse their infants concern saintly *sons:* I have come across only a few Lives that mention similar maternal requirements or commitments for their daughters (e.g., St. Procule). In fact several of the *vitae* which mention the nursing of the infant female saints note the use of wet-nurses either within the family or outside the family home. As Christiane Klapisch-Zuber and David Herlihy have suggested for the late Middle Ages (and which might also be applicable to this earlier period), "Or, il semble que les filles étaient plus volontiers que les garçons données en nourrice hors de leur famille et que les riches envoyaient *à balia* leurs enfants plus souvent que les pauvres. L'oubli lie au placement en nourrice hors de la famille a donc pu affecter un peu plus les effectifs feminins; il explique peut-être le déséquilibré entre les sexes particulierement accentué chez les jeunes enfants des familles les plus fortunées. . . ." David Herlihy and Christiane Klapisch-Zuber, *Les Toscans et leurs familles: Une étude du catasto florentin de 1427* (Paris, 1978), p. 330.

122. See István P. Bejczy, "The *Sacra Infantia* in Medieval Hagiography," in *The Church and Childhood: Studies in Church History* (Oxford, 1994), 31:145; the story of Nicholas as recorded, for example, by Jacobus de Voragine, *The Golden Legend,* 2:110; Butler 4, Dec. 6, p. 504.

123. Plummer, *Lives of Irish Saints,* vol. 2, p. 152.

124. *PB* 8, July 9, p. 189.

125. Bejczy, "The *Sacra Infantia* in Medieval Hagiography," p. 146.

126. See for example, Plummer, *Vitae Sanctorum Hiberniae,* vol. 1, p. clviii, n. 2.

127. Gregory of Tours, *Glory of the Confessors,* trans. Van Dam, ch. 82, pp. 88–89.

128. Stokes, *Lives of Saints from the Book of Lismore,* p. 237.

129. Plummer, *Lives of Irish Saints,* vol. 2, pp. 167–68.

130. Plummer, *Vitae Sanctorum Hiberniae,* vol. 1, p. 76. See also Herlihy, *Medieval Households,* p. 42.

131. *Vita Odiliae abbatissae Hohenburgensis,* ch. 10, *MGH SRM* 6:42–43.

132. Réau, *Iconographie de l'art chrétien,* vol. 1, p. 388; *DSW* 1:21–22.

133. Réau, *Iconographie de l'art chrétien,* vol. 1, p. 388.

134. Butler 3, Sept. 1, 457–58; Réau, *Iconographie de l'art chrétien,* vol. 2, p. 595.

135. *PB* 12, Oct. 9, pp. 219–20.

136. See, for example, Herlihy, "Life Expectancies for Women," p. 8. See also Theodore John Rivers, trans. *Laws of the Alamans and Bavarians* (Philadelphia, 1977), LXXXVIII, p. 98: "[Concerning an abortion in a woman.] 1. If anyone causes an abortion in a pregnant woman so that you can immediately recognize whether [the offspring] would have been a boy or a girl: if it was to be a boy, let him compensate with twelve solidi; however, if a girl, [let him compensate] with twenty-four [solidi]. 2. If whether [the fetus is male or female] cannot be immediately recognized, and [the fetus] has not

changed the shape of the mother's body, let him compensate with twelve solidi. If he seeks more, let him clear himself with oathtakers."

137. See Emily Coleman, "Infanticide in the Early Middle Ages," in
Women in Medieval Society, ed. Susan Mosher Stuard (Philadelphia, 1976),
p. 60.

138. See Coleman, "Infanticide in the Early Middle Ages," p. 55; Carol J.
Clover, "The Politics of Scarcity." Herlihy and Klapisch-Zuber also note this
decided preference for male rather than female offspring for late medieval
Tuscany. See Herlihy and Klapisch-Zuber, *Les Toscans et leurs familles,*
p. 554.

139. *Vita Sancti Eligi,* lib. II, ch. 32, *MGH SRM* 4:717. "Regina . . .
verens ne filiam ederet, et ab hoc regnum succumberet."

140. Ibid.

141. Plummer, *Lives of Irish Saints,* vol. 2, p. 8 (emphasis mine).

142. G. G. Coulton, *Life in the Middle Ages* (New York and Cambridge,
1930), pp. 8–9. Another example in this tradition of miraculous sex-change
or "engendering change" in infants was said to have occurred in the early thirteenth century. It concerns a Spanish noblewoman who prayed to St. Dominic
that she would give birth to a son, who she then promised would be given to
the Dominican order. However, when she was told by the midwives that she
had given birth to a daughter, she became distraught and continuously prayed
and cried. After some time, we learn, a "fortuitous change" occurred in the
infant's sex, namely, it had become a male! According to the miracle story,
"posse tamen illum suis apud Deum precibus de femina marem facere; et hoc
mira cum fiducia, nec minore impetrandi spe, dum peteret, exauditam: nam
cum infantem sibi porrigi ab obstetricibus petisset, stupentibus omnibus, quae
paulo ante feminam esse viderant, marem esse deprehendit; quem sanctis edu-
catum moribus, ubi adolevit, in monasterio Praedicatorum Deo ac beato Do-
minico dedicavit." *AASS, Aug. I,* August 4, p. 652. Shulamith Shahar mentions this example in her article, "Infancy in the Lives of Saints," *The Journal
of Psychohistory,* 10:3 (Winter, 1983): 300.

143. See Coleman, "Female Infanticide in the Early Middle Ages," and
Clover, "The Politics of Scarcity." For the later period see also Herlihy and
Klapisch-Zuber, *Les Toscans et leurs familles,* especially pp. 338–40; R. C.
Trexler, "Infanticide in Florence: New Sources and First Results," *History of
Childhood Quarterly* 2 (1975): 98–116, and "The Foundlings of Florence:
1395–1455," in the *History of Childhood Quarterly* 1 (1973):259–84.

144. For example, Regino of Prüm in his collection of canonical decrees
warns women not to kill their infants, but rather to leave them at the church
doors: "We advise all priests to announce publicly to their congregations that
if any woman should conceive and give birth as the result of a clandestine affair, she must not kill her son or daughter . . . but should have the baby carried to the doors of the church and left there, so that it can be brought to the
priest in the morning and taken in and brought up by some one of the faithful.
She will thus avoid being guilty of murder and, even worse, of parricide."
J. Boswell, *The Kindness of Strangers* (New York, 1988), p. 223, citing *De*

synodalibus causes et disciplinis ecclesiasticis, ed. F. Wasserschleben (Leipzig, 1840), 2.68.

145. Caesarius of Arles, *Sermons,* vol. 1 (*FC* 31), Sermon 51, pp. 258–59.

146. Ibid., vol. 3 (*FC* 66), Sermon 200, p. 61.

147. Ibid., vol. 1, Sermon 52, p. 261. St. Jerome in his famous Letter to Eustochium (22) also notes the practice of infanticide among "fallen virgins": "I cannot bring myself to speak of the many virgins who daily fall and are lost to the bosom of the church, their mother. . . . You may see many women widows before wedded, who try to conceal their miserable fall by a lying garb. Unless they are betrayed by swelling wombs or by the crying of their infants, they walk abroad with tripping feet and heads in the air. Some go so far as to take potions, that they may insure barrenness, and thus murder human beings almost before their conception. Some, when they find themselves with child through their sin, use drugs to procure abortion, and when (as often happens) they die with their offspring, they enter the lower world laden with the guilt not only of adultery against Christ but also of suicide and child murder." *NPNF,* 6:27.

148. *Vita Germani Episcopi Parisiaci auctore Venantio Fortunato, MGH SRM,* 7:372.

149. Ibid., p. 373. See also *PB* 6, May 28, p. 264.

150. Plummer, *Lives of Irish Saints,* vol. 2, p. 39.

151. *AASS, Mar. III,* March 26, p. 642. *Vita S. Liutbirgae, MGH SS* 4:158–64. Here translated by Herlihy, *Medieval Households,* pp. 53–54.

152. *AASS, Mar. III,* March 26, pp. 642. In regard to the "nursing horn," Mary McLaughlin notes that the earliest example of its use comes from the Life of St. Liudger and that it "was a small polished cow's horn pierced at the small end, to which were fastened two small pieces of parchment like the fingers of a glove through which the milk in the horn could be sucked." McLaughlin, "Survivors and Surrogates," p. 151, n. 75. See also Herlihy, *Medieval Households,* pp. 53–54.

153. See *Vita Odiliae abbatissae Hohenburgensis, MGH SRM* 6:38–39.

154. The story of his birth and early rejection by his mother are told in his *vita* by John of Lodi, *AASS, Feb. III,* February 23, p. 423. These events are also treated in some detail by McLaughlin, "Survivors and Surrogates," pp. 101–5. See also Shahar, "Infancy in the Lives of Saints," p. 282; Shahar, *Childhood in the Middle Ages,* p. 42.

155. *AASS, Feb. III,* February 23, p. 423. McLaughlin, "Survivors and Surrogates," especially pp. 103–4.

156. Ibid.

157. Gregory of Tours, *Libri miraculorum: Les Livres des miracles,* trad. H. L. Bordier (Paris, 1860), vol. 2, bk. 2, ch. 24, pp. 130–33; see also Caesarius of Arles, who warns in one of his sermons: "Above all, no one should know his wife when Sunday or other feasts come around. Similar precautions should be taken as often as women menstruate, for the Prophet says: 'Do not come near to a menstruous woman.' If a man is aware that his wife is in this condition but refuses to control himself on a Sunday or feast, the children

who are then conceived will be born as lepers, or epileptics, or perhaps even demoniacs" (Caesarius of Arles, *Sermons,* vol. 1, *FC* 31, Sermon 44, p. 225).

158. *DSW* 1:450–51.

159. *AASS, Feb. I,* Feb. 1, no. 60, ch. 10, p. 169. "Alio quoque die quaedam mulier venit ad S. Brigidam, dicens: Domina de hoc filio meo quid faciam? nam pene abortivus est, et caecus a nativitate, habens tabulatam faciem; et ideo pater ejus volebat occidere eum. Tunc B. Brigida mulieris miserta, jussit faciem pueruli in aqua propinqua lavari: et statim factus est sanus. Domino donante salutem propter S. Brigidam. Ille vocabatur Crimthanus, qui vixit multum tempus." There are a number of other references to infanticide used as a measure to dispose of infants conceived through immoral or incestuous relationships, e.g., St. Barr. See Plummer, *Vitae Sanctorum Hiberniae,* vol. 1, p. 65.

160. "Penitential of Theodore," in *Die Bussbücher und das kanonische Bussverfahren,* ed. Schmitz (XXVIII) XIII. 1. "Pater filium (suum) necessitate coactus potestatem habet tradere in (servitium VII) servitio (XIV) septem annos (nam). Deinde sine voluntate filii licentiam tradendi non habet" (p. 579).

161. *Vita S. Balthildis reginae, MGH SRM* 2:483; see also *SWDA,* pp. 268–69.

162. Stokes, *Lives of Saints from the Book of Lismore,* pp. 187–88. Also, according to tradition, St. Patrick had been captured and sold into slavery; similarly, the mother of St. Patrick and her sister were said to have been sold at the command of their father. O'Leary, *The Most Ancient Lives of St. Patrick,* p. 135.

163. Stokes, *Martyrology of Oengus,* pp. 242–43.

164. Ibid., pp. 180–81.

165. *AASS, Iul. II,* July 6, pp. 333–37; *PB* 8, July 6, pp. 74–75; here translated by John Boswell, *The Kindness of Strangers* (New York, 1988), p. 218.

166. *PB* 5, April 25, p. 36; *MGH SS* 15:452–54.

167. See Coleman, "Infanticide in the Early Middle Ages"; Boswell, *The Kindness of Strangers,* pp. 41–45, 157–61. For demographic implications see Herlihy, "Life Expectancies for Women in the Middle Ages"; Guttentag and Secord, *Too Many Women? The Sex Ratio Question;* Wemple, *Women in Frankish Society,* pp. 101–2, 72.

168. See Boswell, *The Kindness of Strangers.*

169. Coleman, "Female Infanticide in the Early Middle Ages," p. 60. Moreover, in light of continual problems regarding food shortages, famine, and malnutrition, female infants seem to have been further disadvantaged when compared to their brothers. Emily Coleman has noted, for example, that among the peasant population reflected in the early ninth-century polyptych of Saint-Victor of Marseilles, baby boys were given a definite nutritive edge over their sisters: that is, male infants were nursed for two years while female children were weaned after only one year. Thus this gender-based practice which encouraged the survival of male infants could further endanger the lives of female infants by making them much more susceptible to disease, mal-

nutrition, and starvation. It has also been suggested in a study of infanticide among "primitive" people, that infanticide was primarily adopted in cases where there was another young sibling who was still being nursed by the mother and was not thought to be ready for weaning (Coleman, p. 69, n. 48).

170. Further corroboration of this tradition can be found in the Icelandic Saga of "Gunnlaug Serpent-Tongue." Here the father specifies that if his wife gave birth to a girl, she must expose it; however a boy required that she rear it. The Saga also notes that "those men who have few possessions, but yet have many dependents on their lands, had their children exposed." Cited by Coleman, "Infanticide in the Early Middle Ages," p. 58.

171. See McLaughlin, "Survivors and Surrogates," p. 155, n. 99.

172. For the use of infanticide and the ensuing scandal which it could cause at a female monastery, see Rudolf, *Life of St. Leoba*, pp. 216–18. In this case, a poor crippled girl who lived off the alms of Leoba's monastery gave birth to a child. She got rid of the unwanted infant by throwing it into a pool at night. When the corpse of the child was discovered the following day, the villagers believed that it was an illegitimate child of one of the nuns of the convent. And only after some time, through the intecession of a "miracle" by St. Leoba, did the guilty party confess to her crime. It is interesting that the outrage of the villagers was more concerned with the fact that the infant's body had been thrown into a pond adjoining their mill (and thus polluting the water), as well as with the perceived hypocrisy of the nuns, than with the actual act of infanticide.

173. "The Penitential of Theodore," McNeill and Gamer, *Medieval Handbooks of Penance*, nos. 25, 26, p. 197.

174. Boswell, *The Kindness of Strangers*, p. 220, citing *Poenitentiale Valicellanum* 1.40, in H. J. Schmitz, *Die Bussbücher und die Bussdisciplin der Kirche* 1.285.

175. For St. Hildegard, see Einhard and Notker the Stammerer, *Two Lives of Charlemagne*, trans. Lewis Thorpe (Harmondsworth, 1969), n. 43, p. 185; St. Evrard and Itta, *PB* 4, April 7, p. 265; St. Monegund, Gregory of Tours, *Life of the Fathers*, ch. 19, pp. 124–30; see also individual *vitae; Butler's Lives of the Saints;* Dunbar, *A Dictionary of Saintly Women.*

176. See the classic study by Philippe Ariès, *Centuries of Childhood: A Social History of Family Life*, trans. Robert Baldick (New York, 1962), esp. pp. 33–49. Arguments against this theory can be found in David Herlihy's "Medieval Children," in *Essays in Medieval Civilization*, eds. B. K. Lackner and K. R. Philip (Austin, 1978), pp. 109–41. Here he argues that the "social and psychological investments in children were growing substantially from approximately the eleventh and twelfth centuries, through to the end of the Middle Ages and doubtlessly beyond" (p. 120). See also Shulamith Shahar, *The Fourth Estate: A History of Women in the Middle Ages*, p. 236; Shahar, *Childhood in the Middle Ages*, pp. 1–4; Jacques Le Goff, "Petits enfants dans la littérature des XIIᵉ–XIIIᵉ siècles," *Annales de démographie historique* (1973): 129–32; Paul Spagnoli's review, "Philippe Ariès, Historian of the Family," *Journal of Family History* 6, 4 (1981) 434–41; Boswell, *The Kindness of Strangers*, pp. 36–39 and n. 83 (for a summary of these issues), and

Barbara A. Hanawalt, *The Ties That Bound: Peasant Families in Medieval England* (New York and Oxford, 1986), pp. 171–87.

177. St. Jerome, "Letter XXXIX to Paula," in *NPNF*, vol. 6, ch. 5, p. 53.

178. Gregory of Tours, *History of the Franks*, bk. 2, ch. 29, p. 142.

179. *SWDA*, p. 210.

180. Finucane, *Miracles and Pilgrims*, p. 109, 181; see also Eddius Stephanus, *Life of Wilfrid*, p. 151.

181. Finucane, *Miracles and Pilgrims*, p. 109.

182. See, for instance, *PB* 9, Aug. 15, p. 572; Nelson, "Parents, Children, and the Church," p. 93.

183. Gregory of Tours, *Life of the Fathers*, ch. 19, pp. 124, 130.

184. Boswell, *The Kindness of Strangers*; see especially pp. 228–55.

185. *PB* 2, Feb. 5, p. 301.

186. *PB* 1, Jan. 1, p. 30.

187. *VSB* 5 (May 12):243; *SWDA*, pp. 199, 203–4.

188. *PB* 11, Sept. 26, p. 418.

189. *PB* 14, Dec. 12, pp. 216–17.

190. *PB* 4, April 19, p. 492.

191. Turgot, *Life of Queen Margaret*, ch. 5, p. 66. He also notes in regard to the children's proper behavior: "They were ever kind and peaceful among themselves, and the younger everywhere showed honour to the elder. Thus even at the celebration of mass, when they went forward after their parents to the offering, the younger by no means ventured to go before the elder; but in the order of age the elder used to precede the younger" (p. 66).

192. Ibid.

193. Compare Jerome's praise of Paula (for leaving her family), at note no. 11, above. We also see this type of behavior commended in later Lives such as that of Yvette of Huy (d. 1228), widow, recluse, and mother of three, who left her children behind to retire to a leper colony. See Hugh of Floreffe, *Vita de B. Juetta sive Jutta, Vidua Reclusa, Hui in Belgio, AASS, Ian. II,* January 13, pp. 151–52. However, for this early period there are a number of Lives which show exemplary mothers delaying their own career plans in order to continue caring for their children. The Life of St. Rictrude, widow, nun of Marchiennes (d. ca. 688), notes that before her husband's death she occupied herself with the education of her children in Christian wisdom and virtues. As a widow she continued to occupy herself with the care of her children and her servants and the practice of charity. She consulted St. Amand regarding her wish to retire from the world and to dedicate herself to a religious life. However, following Amand's advice, Rictrude decided to delay her departure until her son was old enough to be admitted to the Frankish court. *AASS, Mai. III,* May 12, pp. 81–88; *VSB* 5 (May 12):242–43. In the same tradition St. Waldetrude, mother of Saints Landry, Dentelin, Adeltrude, and Madelberta, delayed her entry into monastic life in order to dedicate herself to her children's upbringing and education. *DSW* 2:298–99.

194. St. Rictrude: *AASS, Mai. III,* May 12, pp. 78–98; *DSW* 2:187–88; *SWDA*, p. 209. St. Bertha of Blangy: *AASS, Iul. II,* July 4, pp. 49–54; *AASS B.* 6:562–69; *DSW* 1:118–19.

195. *Vita Sanctae Geretrudis,* pp. 454–57; *SWDA,* p. 224.

196. *Vita Sadalbergae abbatissae Laudunensis, MGH SRM* 5:55–60. Again there seems to be some disagreement among scholars about Salaberga's status and whether her marriage and five children were simply invented by a Carolingian forger. See Wemple, *Women in Frankish Society,* p. 100; *SWDA,* pp. 176, 292.

197. St. Rupertus, *AASS, Mai. III,* May 15, pp. 502–5; *PL* 197:1083–1092; *BHL* 2:1071–72; *DSW* 1:119–20.

198. G. G. Coulton, *A Medieval Garner* (London, 1910), p. 83.

199. McLaughlin, "Survivors and Surrogates," p. 103.

200. *AASS, Ian. I,* January 3, pp. 138–47; *MGH SRM* 3:215–38; *PB* 1, (Jan. 3):94; Heinzelmann and Poulin, *Les Vies anciennes de sainte Geneviève de Paris,* p. 87.

201. *AASS, Mar. II,* March 14, pp. 447–50; *AASS B.* 4:557–64; *BHL* 1:410–11; *DSW* 1:297–98, *SWDA,* pp. 213–17.

202. *SWDA,* pp. 215–17.

203. C. H. Talbot, ed., *The Life of Christina of Markyate: A Twelfth Century Recluse* (Oxford, 1959), pp. 72–73, 75; see also Jacobus de Voragine, *The Golden Legend,* 7:219–20, which describes the beating of St. Aldegund by her mother. According to this story, Aldegund's mother gave her some material to make clothing for her future husband. Aldegund instead made chrisms, or little caps worn by infants when they were baptized. In her anger, her mother beat her daughter with a stick, and Aldegund fled into the forest, where she remained hidden until after her mother's death.

204. *Vita Auct. Laurentio Dunelmensi,* ch. 5, *AASS, Feb. I* (February 1), p. 175.

205. *DSW* 1:477; Butler 1, Jan. 23, p. 157.

206. Eddius Stephanus, *Life of Wilfrid,* ch. 2, p. 135.

207. Butler 1, March 18, p. 627.

208. William of Malmesbury, *History of the Kings,* pp. 142–43 (emphasis mine).

209. See chapter 4 on women as domestic proselytizers; Gregory of Tours, *History of the Franks,* bk. 5, ch. 38, p. 302.

210. Georges Duby in his work *The Knight, The Lady and the Priest: The Making of Modern Marriage in Medieval France,* trans. Barbara Bray (Harmondsworth, 1983) also discusses this case in some length. See especially pp. 130–35 (quote, p. 132).

211. *De S. Godeleva virg. et mart, AASS, Iul. II,* July 6, pp. 359–444.

212. *PB* 6, May 28, p. 264. See also *MGH SMR,* 7:373.

213. Bede, *A History of the English Church and People,* bk. 4, ch. 23, p. 248; 4, 6, 218; 4, 7, 218; 4, 19, 239.

214. Baudonivia, *De vita Sanctae Radegundis liber II,* ch. 8, p. 383; *SWDA,* p. 91.

215. Gregory of Tours, *The History of the Franks,* bk. 9, ch. 39, p. 528; Gregory of Tours, *Glory of the Confessors,* ch. 104, p. 106. The *vita* of the abbess St. Bertilla also describes her important role as mother of her community. On her death the monks and nuns clamored: "Nutrix pia, mater optima,

cur nos deseris, et cui nos relinquis, quos tanto tempore dulci et materno affectu nutristi?" *Vita Bertilae Abbatissae Calensis*, p. 108, no. 8.

216. *Vita S. Balthildis reginae*, ch. 4, pp. 485–86; ch. 6, p. 488; ch. 9,
p. 494; ch. 11, p. 497; *SWDA*, pp. 270–71, 273–74.

217. See Thomas Head, "Hrotsvit's *Primordia* and the Historical Traditions of Monastic Communities," in *Hrotsvit of Gandersheim: Rara avis in
Saxonia?* Medieval and Renaissance Monograph Series, vol. 7, ed. Katharina
Wilson (Ann Arbor, 1987), p. 148, here citing *Primordia coenobii Gandeshemensis*, in *Hrotsvithae Opere*, Helena Homeyer, ed. (Munich, 1970), lines
417–29, p. 466.

218. Corbet, *Les Saints ottoniens*, pp. 131, 200, 201. See also Corbet on
Sts. Oda, Edith, and Adelaide and their roles as mothers.

219. See M. Stoeckle, *Studien über Ideale in Frauenviten*, pp. 74–75;
Mater Spiritualis, trans. Dick.

220. *Mater Spiritualis: The Life of Adelheid of Vilich*, trans. Dick, ch. 4, p. 27;
ch. 6, pp. 28–31; *Vita Adelheidis Abbatissae Vilicensis, MGH, SS*, 15: 755–63.

221. Turgot, *Life of Queen Margaret*, pp. 75, 78.

222. See Boswell, *The Kindness of Strangers*, p. 228; also J. F. Niermeyer,
Mediae Latinitatis Lexicon Minus (Leiden, 1954–58), fasc. VIII, "oblatio,"
p. 728.

223. Herlihy, *Medieval Households*, pp. 39, 41–42, 54–55. See also Bitel,
Land of Women, pp. 96–97.

224. John Ryan, *Irish Monasticism: Origins and Early Development*
(Dublin and Cork, 1931), p. 139. See also Bitel, *Land of Women*, pp. 93–103.

225. Plummer, *Vitae Sanctorum Hiberniae*, vol. 1, ch. 3, p. 99.

226. Plummer, *Lives of Irish Saints*, vol. 2, pp. 45–46.

227. Ibid., p. 47.

228. Ibid., pp. 62, 80.

229. Plummer, *Vitae Sanctorum Hiberniae*, vol. 2, esp. pp. 164–67. The
Life of Maedoc of Ferns notes another of Ita's foster children. Maedoc was
visiting the neighborhood of Ita's church when he heard bells tolling. He
learned that the reason for this was that "a foster child of Ita, a virgin who
was a dearly-loved favourite of hers," had died. Ita wanted Maedoc to come
to her monastery to use his skills to bring the girl back to life. Instead, he sent
one of his disciples in his place, who took the saint's holy staff with him. This
he laid on the nun's breast and, according to the legend, she arose at once in
the presence of all and was restored to health. Plummer, *Lives of Irish Saints*,
vol. 2, p. 231.

230. Stokes, *Martyrology of Oengus*, pp. 44–45.

231. Ibid., pp. 172–73. The Life of St. Patrick notes that after his baptism
his "mother's sister took him in fosterage, for she herself was barren. Then she
fostered Patrick in Nemptor till he was a lad." Thus, many of St. Patrick's
early miracles concerned his foster mother and her household. In contrast, his
biological parents seemed to play only a peripheral role in his life. Stokes,
Lives of Saints from the Book of Lismore, pp. 151–67.

232. Plummer, *Lives of Irish Saints*, vol. 2, p. 186.

233. *Two Lives of Saint Cuthbert*, trans. Colgrave, pp. 89–91.

234. Plummer, *Vitae Sanctorum Hiberniae*, vol. 2, pp. 262, 266.

235. *Vita I S. Brigidae virg.*, ch. 16, *AASS, Feb. I* (Feb. 1), pp. 132–33.

236. *Vita S. Balthildis reginae*, ch. 4, pp. 485–86; ch. 14, p. 500; *SWDA,* p. 276 and n. 53.

237. Gregory of Tours, *History of the Franks*, bk. 9, ch. 42, p. 535.

238. Fortunatus, *Opera poetica, Carminum liber XI*, poem 3, *MGH AA* 4:259. "Mater optima, decens, voto laetare beato, / gaude: natalem filia dulcis habet. / hanc tibi non uterus natam, sed gratia fecit; / non caro, sed Christus hanc in amore dedit."

There are many examples in the *vitae* of abbesses raising their spiritual daughters: St. Waldetrude, abbess and founder of Mons, raised her niece, Ulftrude, from the cradle. Ulftrude then succeeded her as abbess of Mons at the age of twenty. *DSW* 2:299. Waldetrude's biological daughter, St. Adeltrude, was in turn entrusted to her maternal aunt (St. Aldegund, abbess of Maubeuge) who educated her and taught her the rule. *AASS, Ian. III,* January 30, ch. 4, pp. 654, 659. See also *SWDA*, pp. 235–63. St. Elfleda, at scarcely a year old, was given by her parents as a victory thank-offering to the service of God. She was entrusted to Abbess Hilda, then living at Hartlepool, who was a cousin of Elfleda's mother. Elfleda lived for almost sixty years at the monastery of Whitby and succeeded Hilda as abbess. Bede, *A History of the English Church and People*, bk. 3, ch. 24, pp. 183–84. St. Odilia, founding abbess of Hohenbourg, also raised three of her brother Adelard's daughters. In time all three became abbesses and won recognition of sanctity: St. Eugenia succeeded Odilia as abbess of Hohenbourg; St. Attala became abbess of St. Etienne, Strasbourg; and St. Gundelind was named abbess of Nidermünster. *MGH SRM* ch. 19, 6:47–48. The holy hermit St. Ulphe or Ulphia (eighth century) was foster mother to St. Aurea. *PB* 12, Oct. 5, p. 87; *DSW,* 2:277–78; see also M. Abbé Corblet, *Hagiographie du diocèse d'Amiens;* or Adelheid of Vilich raised and educated her sister's daughter at the monastery of Vilich. She then became Adelheid's successor as abbess of Vilich. *Mater Spiritualis: The Life of Adelheid of Vilich,* trans. Dick, p. 35.

239. *Ex vita Sanctae Liutbirgae*, ch. 7, *MGH SS* 7:160: "Unum ergo tibi iterum iterumque commendo, quod fidei tuae mater tua committit, et speciali summopere petitione ac materno affectu deposcit; est, filiam ut meam dilectam Liutbirgam, quam promissione fidei adoptavi mihi in filiam . . ."

240. *AASS, Mai. I,* May 2, pp. 295–96, 307–8; the *vitae* note that she also instructed and befriended St. Udalric, pp. 292, 306.

241. For those parents who entered monastic life with their children, the seventh-century Rule of St. Fructuosus notes that the children were to become permanent inmates of the monastery and be subjected to monastic disipline. For parents and children to converse, they needed special authorization from the abbot; however, very young children were allowed to see their parents and speak with them when they wished. See Boswell, *The Kindness of Strangers,* p. 255, n. 92.

242. McLaughlin, "Survivors and Surrogates," pp. 132–34.

243. Bynum, "Jesus as Mother and Abbot as Mother," p. 274.

244. The *vitae* of this period, particularly those of the early hermits or

monks, frequently portray a fear of female sexuality and practices of avoidance of women—even one's own mother. According to a popular story from the Life of St. Arsenius, a desert father and early abbot, one of the fathers found it necessary at one point to carry his aged mother across a river. In making preparations for the crossing, he began to wrap his hands in his mantle. His mother then asked, "Wherefore hast thou covered thy hands so, my son?" He responded that "the body of woman is as fire that burneth, and because the mind of other women should not come in my remembrance, therefore I do it." Jacobus Voragine, *The Golden Legend*, vol. 7, p. 81. The Life of St. John of Reomay, abbot of Moutier-Saint-Jean (d. ca. 544), recounts that when his mother came to visit him at his monastery, he refused to see her or converse with her. Nevertheless, in response to her requests, he consented to walk past the crowd of people of which she was a part so that she might see him from a distance. He also warned her that she would not see him again until they met in heaven. *MGH SRM* 3:502ff.; *PB* 2, Jan. 28, p. 77. Similarly St. Sour, hermit and abbot of Terrasson (6th c.), refused to see his mother when she came to visit him in his cell. *AASS, Feb. I*, February 1, pp. 199–206; *PB* 2, Feb. 1, p. 192. A moving episode in the Life of St. Columbanus describes his departure from Ireland and the difficulty he experienced in leaving his mother. "His mother in anguish begged him not to leave her. But he said: 'Hast thou not heard, 'He that loveth father or mother more than me is not worthy of me?' He begged his mother, who placed herself in his way and held the door, to let him go. Weeping and stretched upon the floor, she said she would not permit it. Then leaping over both threshold and mother he asked his mother not to give way to her grief; she would never see him again in this life, but wherever the way of salvation led him, there he would go." *Life of St. Columban, by the Monk Jonas*, in *Translations and Reprints from the Original Sources of European History*, ed. Carleton (Philadelphia, 1902), 2:4.

245. See, for example, the important precedent established by Monica, mother of St. Augustine. As noted by Clarissa Atkinson, Monica became "a model of Christian motherhood and a saint for Christian mothers." Clarissa W. Atkinson, "'Your Servant, My Mother': The Figure of Saint Monica in the Ideology of Christian Motherhood," in *Immaculate and Powerful: The Female in Sacred Image and Social Reality*, The Harvard Women's Studies in Religion Series (Boston, 1985), p. 139. In her persistence in winning him over to Catholicism, in fighting for her son's soul, she remained a very real presence in his life. According to his *Confessions*, in his departure from Carthage to Rome, "She [Monica] wept bitterly to see me go and followed me to the water's edge, clinging to me with all her strength in the hope that I would either come home or take her with me. . . . The next morning [after Augustine had secretly sailed away] she was wild with grief, pouring her sighs and sorrows in your ear, because she thought you had not listened to her prayer. . . . You used her too jealous love for her son as a scourge of sorrow for her just punishment. For as mothers do, and far more than most, she loved to have me with her." We learn, however, that Monica was not easily dissuaded; she followed Augustine to Italy and there she died after having witnessed his conversion. At the end of her life, Monica is said to have admitted to Augustine that he

had been her main reason for living. Augustine, *Confessions,* bk. 5, ch. 8, pp. 100–101; bk. 9, ch. 10–11, pp. 196–200. Monica's purpose and life were thus defined by her single-minded commitment to her son; what we know about her comes from Augustine's observations in his *confessions.* Her sanctity was thus predicated on his fame and success. See also Clarissia W. Atkinson, *The Oldest Vocation,* pp. 144–93; Margaret R. Miles, "Infancy, Parenting, and Nourishment in Augustine's *Confessions," Journal of the American Academy of Religion* 50 (1982): 349–62; Peter Brown, *Augustine of Hippo* (Berkeley and Los Angeles, 1970), especially pp. 28–34.

246. Anneke B. Mulder-Bakker, ed., *Sanctity and Motherhood,* p. 4.

247. An example of the special "sin" associated with motherhood, as well as the double message for women fostered by the Church, can be found in an incident concerning Hugh of St. Victor (d. 1141). Hugh is said to have reported that when his mother was dying, she was reminded of the story that *"our birth had been a crime."* When asked if she *repented,* she responded that she could not in light of "the renown that we had acquired." M. le Vte. de Vaublanc, *La France au temps des Croisades* (Paris, 1846), vol. 3, p. 7. (Emphasis mine.)

CHAPTER SIX

1. Luke 14, 26.

2. Matthew 19, 29. These admonitions are also frequently cited in the *vitae* and other didactic works of the period.

3. See for example: *St. Benedict's Rule for Monasteries,* trans. Leonard J. Doyle (Collegeville, Minn., 1948), ch. 69, pp. 96–97; John Cassian, *Institutions Cenobitiques, Sources Chrétiennes,* 109, ed. and trans. J. Cl. Guy (Paris, 1965), pp. 444–45. See Louis Leloir, "Woman and the Desert Fathers," trans. Jacqueline M. E. Owen and Margot H. King, in *Vox Benedictina,* 3, no. 3 (July 1986), p. 208; *The Rule of Donatus of Besançon,* trans. McNamara and Halborg, pp. 39–40, 61, 63–64, 71; *The Rule for Nuns of St. Caesarius of Arles,* trans. McCarthy, pp. 186–87, 174, 188–89.

4. *Vita Auct. Hartmanno mon. S. Galli, AASS, Mai. I,* May 2, p. 289.

5. On sibling relationships in the Roman world, see the excellent study by Judith P. Hallett, *Fathers and Daughters in Roman Society: Women and the Elite Family* (Princeton, 1984), pp. 150–201, especially pp. 178–91.

6. *The Life of Pachomius (Vita Prima Graeca),* Society of Biblical Literature, Texts and Translations, 7, trans. Apostolos N. Athanassakis (Missoula, 1975), ch. 32, p. 45.

7. See for example, St. Ambrose, *Concerning Virgins* in *St. Ambrose: Select Works and Letters, NPNF,* vol. 10; in addition, Ambrose wrote a number of personal letters to his sister Marcellina. Letter no. 61 (June 20, 386) is addressed "To the lady his sister, dearer than life and eyes, a brother." *Saint Ambrose, Letters,* trans. Sr. Mary Melchior Beyenka, *FC* 26 (New York, 1954), letters 60–62, pp. 365–97; see also Augustine's letter to the consecrated virgins of his sister's monastery, "Letter 211," in *St. Augustine: Let-*

ters, FC 32, vol. 5 (204–270), trans. Sr. Wilfrid Parsons (New York, 1956), pp. 38–51.

8. Avitus, *Liber sextus de virginitate, MGH AA* 6:279; or *PL* 59: 372: "Quod sequimus tamen, hoc tuum est: conversio fratrum exemplo debenda pio."

9. Pope St. Gregory the Great, *Life and Miracles of St. Benedict* (Book 2 of the *Dialogues*), trans. Odo J. Zimmerman and Benedict R. Avery (Collegeville, Minn., n.d.), ch. 33–34, pp. 67–70.

10. *Caesarius of Arles: Life, Testament, Letters,* Translated Texts for Historians, vol. 19, trans. William E. Klingshirn (Liverpool, 1994), ch. 28, pp. 22–23; ch. 35, pp. 26–27; chs. 57–58, pp. 38–39. See *Vitae Caesarii Episcopi Arelatensis libri duo,* ch. 35, *MGH SRM* 3:470; see also McCarthy, *The Rule for Nuns of St. Caesarius of Arles;* and the excellent study by William E. Klingshirn, *Caesarius of Arles: The Making of a Christian Community in Late Antique Gaul* (Cambridge, 1994).

11. For a recent translation of the *regula,* see Jo Ann McNamara and John E. Halborg, *The Rule of Donatus of Besançon.*

12. Leander of Seville, *The Training of Nuns and the Contempt of the World,* in *Iberian Fathers,* vol. 1, *Martin of Braga, Paschasius of Dumium, Leander of Seville, FC* 62, trans. Claude W. Barlow (Washington, D.C., 1969), pp. 183–228.

13. I would like to thank Penelope Johnson for her comments in regard to this relationship.

14. See Wemple, *Women in Frankish Society,* pp. 142, 159–62, 170, 289; Mary Bateson, "Origin and Early History of Double Monasteries," *Transactions of the Royal Historical Society* 13 (London, 1899). See also chapters 2 and 3, above, for more detail on this important topic.

15. St. Burgundofara and Burgundofaro, Jonas, *Vitae Columbani abbatis discipulorumque eius, MGH SRM* 4:61–108 (Liber I: Vita Burgundofarae et Miracula Evoriacensia), or *PL* 87:1070–82. For the Life of St. Faro, see *MGH SRM* 5:171–206; see also H. M. Delsart, *Sainte Fare, sa vie et son culte* (1911); and especially *Sainte Fare et Faremoutiers* (L'Abbaye de Faremoutiers, 1956).

16. Sr. Telchilde de Montesses, *Jouarre: ses cryptes, son église, son abbaye* (Les presses monastiques, Yonne, 1976), pp. 3–6; de Rohan-Chabot Maillé, *Les cryptes de Jouarre* (Paris, 1971).

17. *English Historical Documents,* ed. D. C. Douglas, vol. 1, c. 500–1042, ed. Dorothy Whitelock (London, 1955), p. 446.

18. Bede, *History of the English Church and People,* bk. 4, ch. 6, p. 218.

19. *The Saint of London: The Life and Miracles of St. Erkenwald,* Text and Translation, Medieval & Renaissance Texts & Studies, 58, trans. E. Gordon Whatley (Binghamton, 1989), miracle 18, pp. 160–63.

20. *The Saint of London: The Life and Miracles of St. Erkenwald,* p. 19.

21. Bede, *History of the English Church and People,* bk. 3, ch. 11, p. 159.

22. Gregory of Tours, *Life of the Fathers,* pp. 34, 137.

23. Stokes, *Lives of Saints from the Book of Lismore,* pp. 226–27.

24. *De sanctis virginibus, Bova abbatissa et Doda sanctimoniali, Remis in Gallia, AASS, Apr. III,* April 24, pp. 286–88.

25. *VSB* 5, May 12, p. 242; Butler 2, May 12, p. 287.

26. *PB* 7, June 30, p. 514.

27. *PB* 11, Sept. 28, p. 492.

28. Wemple, *Women in Frankish Society,* p. 161, no. 79, p. 287.

29. *VSB* 8, Aug. 25, p. 478.

30. *PB* 8, July 22, pp. 612–13.

31. *VSB* 6, June 30, p. 524.

32. Butler 1, March 13, p. 584.

33. *Vita S. Opportunae abbatissae, AASS, Apr. III,* April 22, pp. 62–66.

34. *VSB* 1, March 26, p. 562; Butler 1, March 26, p. 686. Another important brother and sister dyad who held power during this period was that of Adalhard, Abbot of Corbie (d. ca. 827) and his sister, Theodrada, Abbess of Soissons. Butler 1, Jan. 2, pp. 22–23; *AASS, Ian. I,* Jan. 2, pp. 96–103.

35. Butler 2, May 28, p. 411.

36. *VSB* 6, June 21, p. 342.

37. *Vita de S. Hugone, AASS, Apr. III,* April 29, pp. 640, 641, 645; Butler 2, April 29, p. 289; R. W. Southern, *Western Society and the Church in the Middle Ages: The Pelican History of the Church,* vol. 2 (Harmondsworth, 1970), pp. 310–11.

38. I would like to thank Richard Kieckhefer for his observations on the importance of these "etiological legends" acccounting for or lending further dignity to relationships between monasteries. In light of these many saintly dyads and their establishment of a variety of twin, affiliated, or dependent houses, this interesting topic needs to be studied further. In this same tradition of brother-sister saints see, for example, the sister of St. Bernard of Clairvaux. Jean Leclercq, *Women and Saint Bernard of Clairvaux,* Cistercian Studies Series: 104 (Kalamazoo, 1989), p. 55. Or the sister of Aelred of Rievaulx, A. Squire, *Aelred of Rievaulx: A Study* (London, 1969), pp. 118 ff; and Aelred of Rievaulx, "A Rule of Life for a Recluse," in *Aelred of Rievaulx: Treatises and Pastoral Prayer* (Kalamazoo, 1971).

39. Wemple, *Women in Frankish Society,* p. 162.

40. Butler 2, May 5, p. 238; *AASS, Mai. II,* May 5, pp. 53–54; St. Rictrudis: *AASS, Mai. III,* May 12, pp. 81–88; *BHL* 2:844.

41. *MGH SS* vol. 15, pt. 1, pp. 86–106; Butler 1, Feb. 25, pp. 415–16; *DSW* 2:297.

42. *De sanctis virginibus Herlinde et Reinula seu Renilde abbatissis Masaci in Belgio, AASS, Mar. III,* March 22, pp. 384–87.

43. Bede, *A History of the English Church and People,* pp. 239, 345. See also C. J. Stranks, *St. Etheldreda: Queen and Abbess* (Dean & Chp. of Ely, 1975), p. 26.

44. See Eckenstein, *Woman under Monasticism,* p. 159; *DSW* 1:360. Wemple, *Women in Frankish Society,* p. 280, n. 17; Suzanne Fonay Wemple, "Monastic Life of Women from the Merovingians to the Ottonians," in *Hrotsvit of Gandersheim: Rara Avis in Saxonia?* Medieval and Renaissance

Monograph Series, vol. 7, ed. Katharina Wilson (Ann Arbor, 1987), pp. 43–44.

45. See *Vita Adelheidis abbatissae Vilicensis auct. Bertha, MGH SS* 15: 760–61. See also *Mater Spiritualis*, trans. Dick, pp. 29–30, 90–93.

46. *Vita Odiliae abbatissae Hohenburgensis*, ch. 19, pp. 47–48.

47. Plummer, *Vitae Sanctorum Hiberniae*, vol. 2, *vita sancti Endei abbatis de Arann*, ch. 2–4, 6, 8–12, pp. 60–66; *DSW* 1:305–7; see also Bitel, *Land of Women*, p. 191.

48. *Vita S. Aldegundis virginis, AASS, Ian. III*, January 30, pp. 651, 657; see also *MGH SRM* 6:87–88; *Vita S. Waldetrudis, AASS Belgii selecta* 4:439–48; *SWDA*, ch. 4, p. 240.

49. *VSB* 8, Aug. 25, p. 481.

50. Butler 1, May 12, p. 574.

51. Stokes, *Lives of Saints from the Book of Lismore*, p. 227.

52. See, for example, the correspondence of Boniface with Abbess Eangyth and her daughter Heaburg and their questions in regard to travel to Rome: "that we have long wished to go to Rome, once mistress of the world, as many of our friends, both relatives and strangers, have done." Emerton, *The Letters of Saint Boniface*, pp. 36–40; also 56–57, 114. In this context Boniface strongly urges Cuthbert to forbid Anglo-Saxon women to make frequent visits to Rome. Ibid., p. 140. Canons of church councils similarly attempted to curtail travel, especially by female religious. For example, the Council of Frioul (796 or 797), no. 12, notes that no nun is to go on pilgrimage to Rome or elsewhere. Hefele and Leclercq, *Histoire des conciles* 3/2, p. 1095. I plan to deal with this topic in more detail in my next book on gender and proscriptions of sacred space.

53. *PB* 11, Oct. 8, p. 177.

54. *VSB* 2, Feb. 5, p. 122.

55. *DSW* 1:136; *BHL* 2:838.

56. *DSW* 1:44–45.

57. *AASS, Mai. I*, May 2, *Auctore Hartmanno monacho S. Galli fere coaevo*, ch. 8, p. 190.

58. *VSB* 8, Aug. 10, p. 184.

59. *PB* 6, June 8, pp. 529–30; Butler 3, Sept. 1, pp. 460–61; *DSW* 2:237–38.

60. *DSW* 2:295.

61. *VSB* 10, Oct. 13, p. 406.

62. *MGH SS*, vol. 15, pt. 1, 86–106; Butler 1:415–16 (Feb. 25); *DSW* 2:297–98.

63. Plummer, *Vitae Sanctorum Hiberniae*, vol. 1, *Vita prima sancti Brendani abbatis de Cluain Ferta*, ch. 4, pp. 99–100; Plummer, *Lives of Irish Saints*, vol. 2, p. 46.

64. Plummer, *Vitae Sanctorum Hiberniae*, vol. 1, ch. 26, p. 162.

65. On this interesting debate, see Fr. Pearse Aidan Cusack, "St. Scholastica: Myth or Real Person?" *The Downside Review* 92, 308 (July 1974): 145–59; J. H. Wansbrough, "St. Gregory's Intention in the Stories of St.

Scholastica and St. Benedict," *Revue Benedictine* 75 (1965): 145–51; Paul Meyvaert's comments, review of William D. McCready's *Signs of Sanctity: Miracles in the Thoughts of Gregory the Great*, *Speculum* 66, no. 2 (April 1991): 449.

66. Meyvaert, p. 449.

67. "St. Scholastica by Gregory the Great, Aldhelm and Paul the Deacon," trans. Mary Forman and Margot H. King, *Vox Benedictina: A Journal of Feminine and Monastic Spirituality* 7, no. 3 (July 1990): 230.

68. Gregory the Great, *Life and Miracles of St. Benedict*, ch. 33, pp. 67–69; ch. 34, pp. 69–70. Forman and King, "St. Scholastica," p. 235.

69. Leander of Seville, *The Training of Nuns*, pp. 189, 194.

70. *Vita SS. Bovae et Dodae*, AASS April III (April 24), pp. 287–88.

71. *Vita S. Hiltrudis virginis*, AASS Sept. VII (Sept. 27), pp. 462–63.

72. Dronke, *Women Writers of the Middle Ages*, pp. 30–32.

73. Ibid., p. 31.

74. Ibid., p. 32.

75. Ibid., p. 31.

76. Ibid., p. 32.

77. Emerton, *The Letters of St. Boniface*, p. 34.

78. Ibid., pp. 34–35.

79. *Vita sanctae Hathumodae*, ch. 5, p. 1177.

80. *Vita S. Aldegundis virginis*, p. 654; *SWDA*, p. 240, n. 22, p. 250.

81. *SWDA*, pp. 260–61.

82. There are a number of instances in the *vitae* that show the cruel side of these saintly brothers toward their sisters. While *The Acts of St. Patrick* note that he healed his young sister of a head injury and she was "then of good stature," according to *The Tripartite Life* she later committed adultery and became pregnant. Enraged, Patrick had his chariot run over her three times bringing about her death. O'Leary, *The Most Ancient Lives of Saint Patrick*, pp. 119, 141. According to one tradition in the Life of St. Brigid, the saint's stepbrothers attempted, through the use of force, to persuade their sister to renounce her intentions to pursue a life of virginity and to accept marriage. *AASS, Feb. I*, February 1, see pp. 121, 177. The *vita* of the virgin-martyr Sperie (d. ca. 760) notes her brother's role in attempting to force Sperie into an unwanted marriage. The end result was that she was killed by her fiancé for her refusal to marry him. *PB* 12 (Oct. 12):299–303. A later example of conflict between siblings concerns St. Bernard of Clairvaux, his brother Andrew, and their sister Humbeline. According to a story related by William of St. Thierry, Humbeline was viewed by her brothers as being overly secular, for she was "married in the world and given to things of the world." On a visit to her brother Bernard, who was a young reform abbot at Clairvaux, as well as to her other brothers who had entered the monastery, she arrived with an elegant retinue. Bernard, "hating and loathing her as if she were a snare of the devil set on luring souls, refused to go out to see her." Humbeline complained about her treatment. Andrew, the doorkeeper of the monastery, "seems to have rebuked her with being a parcel of dung, because of her elegant clothes." And, according to the story, because of the strong disapproval of her "world-

liness" voiced by her brothers, she underwent a dramatic conversion and decided to change her lifestyle. *Vita prima,* bk. 1, ch. 6, 30, *PL* 185:244–45. See Leclercq, *Women and St. Bernard of Clairvaux,* pp. 121–22.

83. This legend is related in some detail by Dunbar, *DSW* 1:89–90; see also *BHL* 2:1156. *AASS, Feb. II* (February 9), pp. 297–300; Colganus, *Act. SS. Hiberniae,* pp. 278–81.

84. *DSW* 1:89–90.

85. Ibid.

86. *The Life of Pachomius,* trans. Athanassakis, ch. 32, p. 45.

87. Ibid.

88. Ibid.

89. *Early Christian Biographies, FC* 15, trans. Roy Deferrari (New York, 1952), ch. 26, p. 105 (emphasis mine).

90. John Cassian, "The Institutes of John Cassian," *NPNF,* vol. 11, ch. 18, p. 279 (emphasis mine).

91. F. Martine, *Vies des Pères du Jura, SC,* no. 142 (Paris, 1968), pp. 268–69; Gregory of Tours, *Life of the Fathers,* pp. 34, 137.

92. Plummer, *Vitae Sanctorum Hiberniae,* vol. 2, ch. 9, p. 64.

93. *Ingulf's Chronicle of the Abbey of Croyland with the Continuations by Peter of Blois and Anonymous Writers,* trans. Henry T. Riley (London, 1854), p. 4.

94. *Felix's Life of Saint Guthlac,* trans. Bertram Colgrave (Cambridge and New York, 1956), ch. 50, pp. 154–55.

95. Ibid., p. 24.

96. See, for example, the diocesan statute of Theodulph (Bishop of Orleans 798–818): c. 12 stipulates that no woman relative was to reside with a priest; the second statute of Theodulf reiterates this regulation stating that all women were forbidden to live with a priest because of the dangers associated with this. Carlo de Clercq, *La Législation religieuse franque de Clovis à Charlemagne (507–814)* (Louvain and Paris, 1936), pp. 261–62.

97. There is also mention of incest and marriage between brother and sister in the Germanic codes. *The Salic Laws,* for example, stipulate, "He who enters into a profane marriage with his sister . . . shall be separated from this union and the children will not be legitimate heirs, and will be marked by disgrace." Drew, *The Laws of the Salian Franks,* XXIII (XIV), 16, p. 190. Similarly "The Penitential of Theodore" (668–90) warns: "He who commits fornication with his sister shall do penance for fifteen years in the way in which it is stated above of his mother." McNeill and Gamer, *Medieval Handbooks of Penance,* n. 17, p. 186. However, the early Germanic and Celtic legends contain a fair number of cases of incest between brother and sister with their heroes and saints born of these incestuous relations. See Plummer, *Vitae Sanctorum Hiberniae,* vol. 1, pp. cvi, n. 5, cxxv, n. 2. As pointed out by Suzanne Wemple, according to one of the court poets in Louis the Pious's entourage, the Bretons were Christians in name only, for they practiced incest—"brothers sleep with sisters and rape their sisters-in-law." Wemple, *Women in Frankish Society,* p. 116; Herlihy, *Medieval Households,* especially pp. 37, 61.

98. The Council of Nantes (658) warns that the mother, sister, or aunt of a priest was not to reside in the same dwelling with him because of reports of dreadful incest. Hefele and Leclercq, *Histoire des conciles,* 3/1, p. 297; or the Council of Cologne (late 9th c.) notes that priests were not to have any women with them, for they sinned even with their own sisters. Hefele and Leclercq, *Histoire des conciles,* 4/2, p. 691. See also Wemple, *Women in Frankish Society,* pp. 146, 276–77.

99. Hincmar, *De divortio,* PL 125:629–41. The events of this notorious case have been analyzed in some detail by Wemple, *Women in Frankish Society,* pp. 84–87, 90–91, 104, 171, 248, ns. 56, 58. See also Pauline Stafford, "Family Politics in the Early Middle Ages," in *Medieval Women,* ed. Derek Baker (Oxford, 1978), p. 90; Frances and Joseph Gies, *Marriage and the Family in the Middle Ages* (New York and Cambridge, 1987), pp. 88–94.

100. *Vita auctore Harmanno monacho S. Galli,* AASS, Mai. I, May 2, pp. 289–98.

101. Ibid., pp. 289–90.

102. Ibid., p. 290.

103. Ibid.

104. Ibid.

105. *Vita et miracula auct. Hepidamno mon. Sangallensi,* AASS, Mai I, May 2, p. 302.

106. Ibid.

107. Ibid., pp. 302–4, 309–10.

108. *La Vie Latine de Sainte Céronne,* ed. Dolbeau, AB 104 (1986): 65, 70–72.

109. Ibid., pp. 72–73.

110. Ibid., p. 73.

111. Ibid.

112. Ibid., pp. 73–74.

113. Ibid., pp. 74–75.

114. Ibid., p. 66.

115. Ibid.; see pp. 66, 69, 72 (*parili consensu* and *parilem conversationem*).

116. During this period the popular legend of Charlemagne's "secret sin"—the grievous sin he was too ashamed to name, his incestuous relationship with his sister—appears. This story is told in the Life of St. Giles/Aegidius (d. 721/725), which was written in the tenth or eleventh century. According to this legend the abbot-saint Giles was Charlemagne's confessor. The king had sent for him in order to unburden his conscience; however, he was unable to confess to the abbot his horrible sin. While St. Giles celebrated Mass on the following Sunday, an angel appeared to the saint and placed on the altar a scroll with the king's sin written on it. The scroll also related that Charlemagne would be forgiven through St. Giles's intercession, as long as the king did penance and did not commit this sin in the future. After Mass, St. Giles handed the scroll to Charlemagne to read; he then fell at the abbot's feet and begged him to intercede for him. St. Giles then prayed, commending the king to God, and he warned him to refrain from that sin in the future. *AASS Sept. I,* Sept. 1, pp. 299–303; Butler 3, Sept. 1, pp. 457; Robert Folz, *Le Souvenir et*

la légende de Charlemagne dans l'Empire germanique médiéval (Paris, 1950), pp. 167–68. The events of this story are also vividly captured in the famous Charlemagne window of Chartres Cathedral.

117. Gregory the Great, *Life and Miracles of St. Benedict*, trans. Zimmerman and Avery, ch. 34, pp. 69–70.

118. *SWDA*, p. 261.

119. *Vita S. Aldegundis virginis*, AASS, Ian. III, Jan. 30, pp. 655, 661. *SWDA*, p. 252. According to tradition, St. Lutrude was also very close to her sister, St. Pusinna, who lived in Picardy. Aware of her imminent death, Pusinna wished to see Lutrude one last time. Although Pusinna had not spoken for five days, she made signs to inquire if her sister was coming. When Lutrude arrived, Pusinna sat up and thanked God. She told Lutrude that she could now die a happy death since she had seen her sister once again, and she begged that she remain there until after her burial. The sisters held each other and prayed and wept, and Pusinna died in Lutrude's arms. Lutrude then buried Pusinna at Corbie in Picardy. *AASS, Sept. VI*, Sept. 22, pp. 451–53; *AASS, Apr. III*, April 22, pp. 167–72; *DSW* 1:479.

120. Cited by Eleanor Shipley Duckett, *The Wandering Saints of the Early Middle Ages* (New York, 1954), p. 78; see also *Vita S. Brendani Clonfertensis e codice Dubliniensi*, AB 48:99f.

121. Martine, *Vies des Pères du Jura*, pp. 304–7, n. 1, pp. 306–7; see also Gregory of Tours, *Life of the Fathers*, p. 34.

122. *Vita SS. Bovae et Dodae*, AASS, Apr. III, April 12, pp. 291–92.

123. *VSB* 6, June 30, p. 524.

124. Butler 1, March 26, p. 686; *VSB* 3, March 26, p. 562; Emma Mason, *St. Wulfstan of Worcester, c. 1008–1095* (Oxford, 1990), p. 255.

125. *SWDA*, p. 69; see Karen Cherewatuk's important study, "Radegund and Epistolary Tradition," in *Dear Sister: Medieval Women and the Epistolary Genre*, eds. Karen Cherewatuk and Ulrike Wiethaus (Philadelphia, 1993), pp. 26–33.

126. *SWDA*, p. 69.

127. Ibid., pp. 294–96.

128. *Vita S. Opportunae abbatissae*, pp. 65–66.

129. Plummer, *Vitae Sanctorum Hiberniae*, vol. 2, *Vita sancti Munnu*, ch. 10, p. 230. The *vita* of St. Molua notes how on one of the saint's visits he returned home only to find his sister, Croin, lying dead on a bier, surrounded by her weeping nuns, and being carried to her grave. Molua prayed at the bier, and, according to legend, his sister rose up from the dead and blessed everyone. After Molua wished her well and provided a blessing and prayer, she chose to die again (*remori*). Plummer, *Vita Sanctorum Hiberniae*, vol. 2, *Vita sancti Moluae*, ch. 39, p. 220.

130. *Felix's "Life of Saint Guthlac,"* ch. 50, p. 157.

131. Ibid., ch. 50, pp. 155–57.

132. Ibid., ch. 50, pp. 159–61.

133. Ibid., ch. 53, pp. 169–71.

134. Ibid., ch. 51, pp. 161–63.

135. *Ingulf's Chronicle of the Abbey of Croyland*, trans. Riley, p. 4.

136. Ibid.

137. Bede, *A History of the English Church and People*, bk. 4, ch. 19, p. 239.

138. Ibid., pp. 239–40.

139. Ibid., p. 240.

140. Ibid., pp. 240–41.

141. Stranks, *St. Etheldreda Queen and Abbess*, p. 26.

142. Butler 1, Feb. 25, pp. 415–16.

143. *Vita S. Maura, AASS, Sept. VI*, Sept. 21, p. 275.

144. Leander of Seville, *The Training of Nuns*, pp. 188–89.

145. Ibid., p. 189.

146. Vauchez, *La Sainteté en Occident*, especially pp. 209–215, Vauchez, "'Beata Stirps': Sainteté et lignage en occident," in *Famille et parenté dans l'occident médiéval* (Actes du Colloque de Paris, 6–8 juin, 1974). Collection de l'École Française de Rome 30, communications et débats par Georges Duby et Jaques Le Goff (Rome, 1977), pp. 397–406. See also Laurent Theis, "Saints sans famille? Quelques remarques sur la famille dans le monde franc à travers les sources hagiographiques," *Revue Historique* 255 (1976): 3–20.

CHAPTER SEVEN

1. Robert R. Bell, *Worlds of Friendship* (Beverly Hills and London, 1981), especially pp. 55–73.

2. Aristotle, *Nic. Ethics* VIII, 7, pp. 227–28, cited by Rosemary Rader, *Breaking Boundaries: Male/Female Friendship in Early Christian Communities* (New York, 1983), p. 27.

3. Bell, *Worlds of Friendship*, pp. 55–73; Rader, *Breaking Boundaries*, p. 22.

4. For women's friendships (especially cross-sex friendships) in the early Christian world, see Rosemary Rader, *Breaking Boundaries;* Elizabeth Clark, *Jerome, Chrysostom, and Friends* (Lewiston, N.Y., 1979). For the medieval world, see Frederick Joseph Cowrie, *Boniface (ca. 675–754) and His Friends: A Communion of Saints* (doctoral dissertation, Saint Louis University, 1975); Brian Patrick McGuire, "The Cistercians and the Transformation of Monastic Friendships," *Analecta Cisterciensia*, 37 (1981) 1–63; Brian Patrick McGuire, *Friendship and Community: The Monastic Experience, 350–1250* (Kalamazoo, 1988); Adele M. Fiske, *Friends and Friendship in the Monastic Tradition*, Cidoc Cuaderno no. 51 (Cuernavaca, Mexico, 1970); *Aelred of Rievaulx, Spiritual Friendship*, Cistercian Father Series, no. 5, trans. Mary Eugenia Laker (Washington, D.C., 1974); "Amitié," in *Dict. de Sp.*, ed. M. Viller (Paris, 1937), 1:500–29. For same-sex friendships, see Judith Brown, *Immodest Acts: The Life of a Lesbian Nun in Renaissance Italy* (New York and Oxford, 1986), and also Carroll Smith-Rosenberg's early study on female friendships in American History, "The Female World of Love and Ritual: Relations between Women in Nineteenth-century America," *Signs*, I, no. 1 (Autumn, 1975): 1–29.

5. Gerhart Ladner, "Introduction," in Fiske, *Friends and Friendship in the Monastic Tradition*, p. 6.

6. Bell, *Worlds of Friendship*, pp. 10–11.

7. Ibid., pp. 10, 23.

8. McGuire, *Friendship and Community*, pp. xiv–xv.

9. See, for example, *Aelred of Rievaulx, Spiritual Friendship;* McGuire, *Friendship and Community*, especially pp. xi–l; Fiske, *Friends and Friendship in the Monastic Tradition.*

10. Rader, *Breaking Boundaries*, p. 5.

11. Ibid., pp. 19–20.

12. See Brundage, *Law, Sex, and Christian Society in Medieval Europe,* p. 428.

13. *The Rule for Nuns of St. Caesarius of Arles*, trans. McCarthy, no. 51, p. 188.

14. Caesarius of Arles, *Oeuvres pour les moniales: Sources chrétiennes,* vol. 1 of *Césaire d'Arles: Oeuvres monastiques,* trans. A. de Vogüé and J. Courreau (Paris, 1988), "Lettre aux moniales," pp. 329–33. See also *Caesarius of Arles: Life, Testament, Letters,* trans. William E. Klingshirn, pp. 131–39.

15. Caesarius of Arles, *Oeuvres pour les moniales,* "Ecrits de l'abbesse Césarie," pp. 492–93.

16. There are many canons of church councils which prohibit the *mulieres subintroductae* relationship; see, for example, the Council of Bordeaux (660–73) which threatens all clerks with punishment who live with sisters *agapetes* or *mulieres subintroductae,* Hefele and Leclercq, III/1, p. 299. Similar warnings can be found in the Council of Frioul (796–97), no. 4, Hefele and Leclercq, III/2, p. 1094; the Council of Arles (813), no. 22, Hefele and Leclercq, III/2, p. 1137; or the Council of Rouen (1073), no. 15, Hefele and Leclercq, IV/2, p. 1282. See Roger E. Reynolds, "*Virgines subintroductae* in Celtic Christianity," *Harvard Theological Review* 61 (1968): 547–66; L. Gougaud, "Mulierum Consortia: Etude sur le syneisaktisme chez les ascètes celtiques," *Eriu* 9 (1921–23): 147–56; Elizabeth Clark, "John Chrysostom and the *subintroductae,*" in *Ascetic Piety and Women's Faith: Essays on Late Ancient Christianity* (New York and Toronto, 1986), pp. 265–90; H. Achelis, *Virgines subintroductae* (Leipzig, 1902). See also, on the dangers of double houses, Hefele and Leclercq, III/2, no. 20, pp. 790–92; Wemple, *Women in Frankish Society,* pp. 159–62, 170, 289, no. 91; Mary Bateson, "Origin and Early History of Double Monasteries," *Transactions of the Royal Historical Society,* n.s. 13 (London, 1899): 137–98.

17. Bede, *A History of the English Church and People*, bk. 4, ch. 25, pp. 255–56. The *vita* of the Irish saint Daig also notes that St. Daig's double community came under suspicion. It was only through a miracle, which was accomplished by the nuns carrying hot coals in their robes without causing any damage to their clothing, that they were able to convince a monastic team of investigators of their innocence. However, St. Daig ultimately removed the nuns from his monastery and established a separate affiliated community for them. See Bitel, *Land of Women,* p. 197.

18. A number of church councils stipulate that foundations of nuns and those of monks must be physically separated from one another. The Council of Agde, Languedoc (506), is the one that warns that convents of nuns are not to be found in the neighborhood of monasteries of monks as much because of the ruses of Satan as the rumors that would result from this. Hefele and Leclercq, II/2, n. 28, p. 991. The Council of Seville (619) contends that monasteries of women in the Betique are to be administered and ruled by monks and that these monks must live at a distance from the nuns. Hefele and Leclercq, III/1, n. 11, p. 258. Odericus Vitalis, in his *History of the Church* notes that no woman is allowed to come to the island of Thorney "except for prayer, nor is any woman allowed to stay there for any reason whatsoever; but the monks have taken care that all dwellings of women must be at least nine miles distant." Odericus Vitalis, lib. 11, c. 17, *PL* 188:837, cited by G. G. Coulton, *Five Centuries of Religion: The Friars and the Dead Weight of Tradition, 1200–1400 A.D.* (Cambridge, 1927), vol. 2, Appendix 37, p. 648. (My present project on women and proscriptions of sacred space explores in some detail this topic of gendered space within the monastic environment.)

19. See Payer, *Sex and the Penitentials,* especially pp. 38–39. Heavy penances, for example, were exacted for a priest having intercourse with a nun *(cum ancilla dei)*—10–11 years (Payer, p. 38). "The Burgundian Penitential" warns: "If anyone commits fornication with a nun or a woman vowed to God, as in the above decision each shall do penance according to his order." McNeill and Gamer, *Medieval Handbooks of Penance,* no. 13, p. 275; see also Payer, pp. 38–39.

20. For a discussion of this famous formula, see Kathleen Hughes, *The Church in Early Irish Society* (London, 1966), pp. 69–80; James Henthorn Todd, *St. Patrick Apostle of Ireland* (Dublin, 1864), pp. 88–90; see also chapter 2, "The Making of the *Mulier Sancta.*"

21. Peter Brown, *The Body and Society,* especially pp. 213–40.

22. E. J. Gwynn and W. J. Purton, eds. and trans., "The Monastery of Tallaght," *Proceedings of the Royal Irish Academy* 29c (1911): 151; see also Hughes, *The Church in Early Irish Society,* p. 177.

23. Plummer, *Vitae Sanctae Hiberniae,* vol. 1, p. cxxi, n. 5; Brown, *The Body and Society,* p. 242.

24. *Rhigyfarch's Life of St. David,* chs. 17–20, p. 35. In Teilo's Life, Teilo and David are approached by the maidservants of the housekeeper of a Pictish prince who conduct themselves in a lewd manner before the saints. On this recurrent theme of employing naked women as a means of constraint against a saint, see Henken, *The Welsh Saints,* pp. 35–36.

25. Jonas of Bobbio, *Life of St. Columban,* ch. 7, p. 3; ch. 8, pp. 3–4.

26. *AASS, Iul. I,* July 1, pp. 80–87; *MGH SRM* 3:389–94; *PB* 8, July 1, pp. 557–62.

27. Ibid.

28. *AASS, Oct. XI,* October 25, p. 691; see also *BHL* 1:537–38.

29. *AASS, Aug. VI,* August 30, pp. 598–620.

30. Mabillon, *Annales ordinis S. Benedicti occidentalium,* V, p. 269.

31. See F. Martine, *Vie des Pères du Jura;* on the monastery of LaBalme and St. Romanus, see n. 1, pp. 266–67, and n. 1, pp. 306–7.

32. Gregory of Tours, *Life of the Fathers,* bk. 1, ch. 6, p. 34.

33. Ibid., and p. 137, n. 11.

34. Gregory the Great, *Dialogues, FC* 39, dialogue 1, p. 16. See also William D. McCready, *Signs of Sanctity: Miracles in the Thought of Gregory the Great,* Pontifical Institute of Mediaeval Studies: Studies and Texts 91 (Toronto, 1989), pp. 85–86.

35. Gregory the Great, *Life and Miracles of St. Benedict,* trans. Zimmerman and Avery, ch. 2, pp. 7–8.

36. *Three Lives of the Last Englishmen,* pp. 94–95; see also pp. 99–100 where Wulfstan is again confronted by female temptation.

37. See, for example, the cases of Sts. Leoban, Odilo of Cluny, and William Firmatus. St. Leoban: *AASS, Oct. VI,* October 13, p. 227; St. Odilo of Cluny: Dom Jacques Hourlier, *Saint Odilon, Abbé de Cluny,* Bibliothèque de la revue d'histoire ecclésiastique, no. 40 (Louvain, 1964), pp. 130–31; St. William Firmatus: *AASS, Apr. III,* April 24, ch. 8, pp. 337–38. See also Dominique Iogna-Prat, "La femme dans la perspective pénitentielle des ermites du Bas-Maine (fin XIème–début XIIème siècle)," *Revue d'histoire de la spiritualité* 53 (1977): 57–62; and Schulenburg, "Saints and Sex, ca. 500–1100: Striding Down the Nettled Path of Life," in *Sex in the Middle Ages: A Book of Essays,* Garland Medieval Casebooks, vol. 3, ed. Joyce E. Salisbury (New York and London, 1991), pp. 203–31.

38. Giraldi Cambrensis, *Gemma ecclesiastica* in *Rerum Britannicarum mediiaevi scriptores (Rolls Series),* ed. J. S. Brewer (London, 1862), 21, 2, ch. 10, p. 216. See also Louis Gougaud, *Devotional and Ascetic Practices in the Middle Ages,* trans. G. C. Bateman (London, 1927), especially pp. 159–78.

39. Rees, *Lives of the Cambro British Saints,* p. 431.

40. Louis Gougaud, "Mulierum Consortia," *Eriu* 9 (1921–1923): 147–48.

41. *La plus ancienne vie de Saint Wandrille (dite Vita prima),* trans. Jean Laporte (Caudebec-en-Caux, 1979), ch. 8, p. 11.

42. *AASS, Feb. III,* February 23, ch. 2, p. 424.

43. *SS. Bernardi vita prima,* bk. 1, ch. 3, *PL* 185:230 (1065); see also Jean Leclercq's comments in *Women and St. Bernard of Clairvaux,* pp. 116–17.

44. See Reynolds, "*Virgines Subintroductae* in Celtic Christianity," pp. 559, 563; Todd, *St. Patrick,* p. 91, n. 1; for Aldhelm see William of Malmesbury, *De Gestis Pontificum Anglorum: Libri quinque,* ed. N. E. S. A. Hamilton (London, 1870; reprint, 1964), pt. 3, no. 213, pp. 358–59. Giraldus Cambrensis warned, "Let us not presume to attempt such things, therefore, according to the example of St. Aldhelm of Malmesbury, who, it is said, lay between two maidens every night, one on one side and the other on the other side, so that he might be defamed by men, but his continence rewarded the more copiously in the future by God, who understood his conscience." Cited by Reynolds, "*Virgines Subintroductae,*" p. 563; Gougaud, "Mulierum

Consortia," pp. 148–50; Giraldus Cambrensis, *Gemma Ecclesiastica*, ed. J. S. Brewer (London, 1862), II, 15, pp. 236–37; for Robert of Arbrissel, see especially Jacques Dalarun, "Robert d'Arbrissel et les femmes," *Annales, Economies, Sociétés, Civilisations*, 39, no. 6 (Nov–Dec., 1984): 1140–60; Gougaud, "Mulierum Consortia," pp. 150–51.

45. It is especially in the Romanesque art of the eleventh and twelfth centuries, frequently reflecting the ideas and imagination of monastic reformers, that we see a proliferation of frightening images of woman as the handmaiden of the devil; woman representing *luxuria*, or lust, with her nude body being attacked by snakes. See Emile Mâle, *Religious Art in France: The Twelfth Century: A Study of the Origins of Medieval Iconography* (The Bollingen Series XC: 1), trans. Marthiel Mathews (Princeton, 1978), especially pp. 372–76; Chiara Frugoni, "L'iconographie de la femme au cours des Xe–XIIe siècles," in *La femme dans la civilisation des Xe–XIIIe siècle* (Poitiers, 1977), pp. 87–98; also Chiara Frugoni, "The Imagined Woman," in *A History of Women in the West: II Silences of the Middle Ages*, eds. Georges Duby and Michelle Perrot (Cambridge, Mass., and London, 1992), pp. 336–422.

46. Cited by Thomas Merton, trans., *The Wisdom of the Desert: Sayings from the Desert Fathers of the Fourth Century* (Norfolk, Conn., 1973), ch. 21, p. 32; see also Helen Waddell, *The Desert Fathers* (1936).

47. Examples of extremes of behavior dictated by the necessity of avoiding females can be found in a number of the *vitae* of the desert fathers. See, in Benedicta Ward, trans., *The Sayings of the Desert Fathers* (London and Oxford, 1975): Arsenius, ch. 28, pp. 13–14; Eudeman, ch. 1, p. 64; Sisoes, ch. 3, p. 213.

48. *AASS, Feb. I*, February 1, ch. 12, p. 129.

49. Ibid. For additional comments on this episode, see also S. Baring-Gould, *Virgin Saints and Martyrs*, (New York, 1901), pp. 164–65.

50. Stokes, *Lives of Saints from the Book of Lismore*, pp. 219–20. Here I have taken the liberty to alter and modernize the translation provided by Stokes.

51. See, for example, the case of a strictly enclosed female hermit who avoided all men and even refused to see St. Martin during his visit to the region. Sulpicius Severus et al., *The Western Fathers*, trans. and ed. by F. R. Hoare, pp. 117–18. The abbess-saint Monnine never looked a man in the face although she led a very public life and was said to have traveled to Rome three times. See Ryan, *Irish Monasticism*, p. 138; St. Moninna/Darerca, *AASS, Iul. II*, July 6, pp. 290–312; Conchubranus, *Vita Sanctae Monennae, Proceedings of the Royal Irish Academy* 28 (1910): 202–38; *BHL* 1:316–17. Similarly, the Lives of St. Brigid note that she followed certain acts of proper deportment when in the presence of men, e.g., she never washed her hands, feet, or head among men. Stokes, *Lives of Saints from the Book of Lismore*, pp. 197–98.

52. See, especially, Elizabeth Clark, *Jerome, Chrysostom, and Friends,* and Rader, *Breaking Boundaries.*

53. *Die ältere Wormser Briefsammlung*, bearbeitet von Walther Bulst, *MGH Die Briefe der Deutschen Kaiserzeit* 3 (Weimar, 1949), letter 45, pp.

82–83. This letter is cited by Brian McGuire (*Friendship and Community,* pp. 188, 203), who also points out that after defending spiritual love among men and women, the bishop then asks the abbess/nun for a special favor "that only she can grant because of her political influence" (p. 188).

54. J. N. D. Kelly, *Jerome: His Life, Writings, and Controversies,* pp. 113–14.

55. *AASS, Feb. I,* February 1, pp. 119–85; Baring-Gould, *Virgin Saints and Martyrs,* pp. 161, 169; James O'Leary, *The Most Ancient Lives of Saint Patrick,* 7th ed. (New York, 1897), pp. 243–44, 339–41; Plummer, *Lives of Irish Saints,* vol. 2, pp. 83–84, 118; Stokes, *Lives of Saints from the Book of Lismore,* p. 225. (According to Jocelin's later *Life and Acts of St. Patrick,* Brigid is described as St. Patrick's contemporary. Patrick was said to have died ca. 461 and the date assigned to St. Brigid's death is ca. 525.)

56. Stokes, *Lives of Saints from the Book of Lismore,* pp. 199–200.

57. Plummer, *Vitae Sanctorum Hiberniae,* vol. 2, pp. 116–30; see also *DSW* 1:418–21.

58. Plummer, *Lives of Irish Saints,* vol. 2, pp. 45–46.

59. Plummer, *Vitae Sanctorum Hiberniae,* vol. 2, p. 120.

60. *SWDA,* p. 28.

61. There are still extant some fifty-five letters and poems, written by Fortunatus and addressed to Radegund and Agnes. Fortunatus, *Carminum liber XI,* poems 2–23, *MGH AA* 4:258–67; Fortunatus, *De vita Sanctae Radegundis liber I.* See also Jean Leclercq, "Les relations entre Venance Fortunat et Radegonde," in *La Riche personnalité de Sainte Radegonde: Conférences et Homélies du XIVe Centenaire de sa mort (587–1987),* pp. 57–76; and Cherewatuk, "Radegund and Epistolary Tradition," pp. 20–45.

62. Judith W. George, *Venantius Fortunatus: A Latin Poet in Merovingian Gaul* (Oxford, 1992), p. 170.

63. Fortunatus, *Carminum liber XI,* poem 6, *MGH AA* 4:260; see also poem 2, p. 258, poem 3, p. 259, poem 7, p. 261. Leclercq, "Relations entre Venance Fortunat et Radegonde," pp. 66–67.

64. Fortunatus, poem 6, *MGH AA* 4:260. Leclercq, pp. 66–67.

65. Fortunatus, poem 6, *MGH AA* 4:265. Leclercq, p. 67.

66. George, *Venantius Fortunatus,* p. 173.

67. Brian Brennan suggests that caution may have caused the nuns to exclude Fortunatus from their company for a period of time. See Brennan, "St. Radegund and Poitiers," p. 342.

68. Fortunatus, *Carminum liber XI,* poem 7, *MGH AA* 4:261; see also Cristiani, "La Sainteté féminine du haute moyen âge," p. 408, n. 84.

69. See René Aigrain, *Sainte Radegonde,* 2d ed. (Paris, 1918), pp. 152–53; George, *Venantius Fortunatus,* p. 168.

70. Baudonivia, *De vita Sanctae Radegundis liber II,* ch. 4, p. 381. See also *SWDA,* p. 88.

71. *AASS, Aug. III,* August 13, pp. 38–46.

72. Gregory of Tours, *Glory of the Confessors,* trans. van Dam, no. 104, pp. 107–8.

73. *Vita S. Eligii,* ch. 32, *MGH SRM* 4:717.

74. Ibid., p. 721.

75. Ibid., pp. 651ff.

76. *Vita S. Gisleni Confessoris, AASS, Oct. IV,* October 9, pp. 1023, 1033.

77. Ibid., p. 1023. According to our sources there was "a bond of the closest relationship and friendship between Gislenus and the two sisters Waldetrude and Aldegunde." To provide support for building the bridge, St. Aldegunde donated two villas in Basiaco to the Monastery of Celle; St. Waldetrude also donated the villa of Frameraies as well as that of the Oratory of St. Quintine where St. Gislenus and St. Waldetrude used to meet to discuss spiritual matters when they were impaired by old age and no longer able to travel long distances.

78. *VSB* 3, March 25, p. 548.

79. *AASS, Oct. IV,* October 9, pp. 1023, 1030; *SWDA,* p. 247. Also, for the special friendship of Sts. Ida and Gertrude of Nivelles with Sts. Amand, Foillan, and Ultan see *Vita Sanctae Geretrudis, MGH SMR* 2:449–51, 455, 457; *SWDA,* pp. 224, 227–28.

When St. Gertrude was on her deathbed, she sent one of her monks to Fosse to tell St. Ultan of her fears and to inquire as to whether God had revealed to him the time of her death. He responded posthaste with a message that she would die the next day with the saints and angels awaiting her soul. According to the *vita,* this message from her friend brought Gertrude joy and comfort in her last hours. *Vita Sanctae Geretrudis,* pp. 462–63; *SWDA,* pp. 227–28.

80. Bede, *A History of the English Church and People,* bk 4, ch. 23, pp. 246–47.

81. *Two Lives of St. Cuthbert,* trans. Colgrave, ch. 6, pp. 102–5; ch. 24, pp. 234–39; ch. 10, pp. 126–29. For a detailed discussion of these Lives, see Hollis, *Anglo-Saxon Women and the Church,* pp. 102, 128–29, 189–90, 199–207. She notes the special friendships of Cuthbert with several women religious recorded in the anonymous Lindisfarne Life in comparison to Bede's rewriting of this Life in which he "is at pains to reduce these friendships to purely official interactions" (p. 102).

82. *Two Lives of St. Cuthbert,* ch. 23, pp. 230–33.

83. See Eckenstein, *Woman under Monasticism,* p. 106, citing D. H. Haigh, "On the Monasteries of St Heiu and St Hild," *Yorkshire Archaeological Journal,* 3:375; *DSW* 1:255.

84. *Two Lives of St. Cuthbert,* ch. 10, pp. 188–89.

85. Ibid., ch. 35, pp. 264–65.

86. Ibid., ch. 37, pp. 272–73.

87. *Liber Eliensis,* Camden Third Series, vol. 92, ed. E. O. Blake (London, 1962), bk. 1, ch. 9, p. 24.

88. Bede, *A History of the English Church and People,* bk. 4, ch. 19, pp. 238–39.

89. *Liber Eliensis,* bk. 1, ch. 15, p. 33; bk. 1, ch. 16, p. 34; bk. 1, ch. 19, pp. 37–38.

90. Eddius Stephanus, *Life of Wilfrid* in *Lives of the Saints,* trans. J. F. Webb (Harmondsworth, 1965), ch. 22, p. 154. We also learn that St. Wilfrid

attended the translation of St. Etheldreda. The priest, Huna, was another important person in Etheldreda's life. He joined her almost as soon as she arrived at Ely and assisted her and her community until her death. Huna and a monk of the double monastery of Ely performed Etheldreda's burial rites. After this final service to his friend and spiritual mother, Huna retired to lead the anchoritic life on a small island in the fens. There he gained a reputation for holiness and at his death he was recognized as a saint. See C. J. Stranks, *St. Etheldreda Queen and Abbess* (Ely, 1975), pp. 20–23.

91. Eddius Stephanus, *Life of Wilfrid*, ch. 39, p. 171.

92. Ibid., ch. 39, p. 172.

93. Ibid., ch. 43, p. 176; ch. 59, p. 195; ch. 60, pp. 196–98. The Life of Wilfrid mentions another of the saint's special friends, Abbess Cynithrith. We learn that after Wilfrid's death, Abbot Bacula had spread out the saint's robe on the ground and the brothers then laid Wilfrid's body on it: here the holy man's body was washed and clothed. Later the abbot asked his servant to take the cloak to "Wilfrid's abbess, Cynithrith." Cynithrith was told to keep it as it was, folded up, until the abbot should visit her. Apparently at first she did as she was told, but later decided to have the cloak washed. A poor nun in the convent, hearing that the robe was being washed, asked that she might bathe her withered hand in the washing water as she had "unshakeable faith in the power of this water, mixed as it is with the saint's sweat." The abbess then assisted the nun: she "plunged it [her lifeless hand] into the warm soapy water and rubbed it with the cloak. And, lo and behold, the fingers straightened out, the hand regained its vitality, and she got back the use of her whole arm." Stephanus then draws the comparison: "Like Moerisa, the woman in the gospel who was cured of an issue of blood by touching the hem of Christ's garment, her faith had made her whole." Eddius Stephanus, *Life of Wilfrid*, ch. 66, p. 204.

94. Bede, *A History of the English Church and People*, bk. 4, ch. 26, p. 258.

95. *Aldhelm: The Prose Works*, trans. Lapidge and Herren, p. 59.

96. Ibid., pp. 59–60, 131–32.

97. Ibid., p. 167.

98. *Felix's Life of Saint Guthlac*, ch. 20–24, pp. 84–87.

99. Ibid., ch. 48, pp. 146–47.

100. For this topic see especially Cowrie, *Boniface (ca. 675–754) and His Friends; The Letters of Saint Boniface*, ed. Emerton; McGuire, *Friendship and Community*, especially pp. 105–15; Hollis, *Anglo-Saxon Women and the Church*, especially pp. 130–50, 317. Ivan Gobry, *De saint Colomban à saint Boniface*, vol. 3 of *Les moines en Occident* (Poitiers, 1987), pp. 411–36.

101. *The Letters of Saint Boniface*, ed. Emerton, no. 29, pp. 59–60.

102. Rudolf, *Life of St. Leoba*, p. 214.

103. This arrangement is noted in some detail in the *vita*: "Sometimes she came to the Monastery of Fulda to say her prayers, a privilege never granted to any woman either before or since, because from the day that monks began to dwell there entrance was always forbidden to women. Permission was only granted to her, for the simple reason that the holy martyr St. Boniface had

commended her to the seniors of the monastery and because he had ordered her remains to be buried there." Rudolf, *Life of St. Leoba*, p. 223.

104. Ibid., pp. 221–22.

105. Ibid.

106. *The Letters of Saint Boniface*, ed. Emerton, pp. 38, 40. See also McGuire, *Friendship and Community*, pp. 108–10.

107. *The Letters of St. Boniface*, ed. Emerton, p. 40.

108. Ibid., pp. 40–41.

109. Ibid., p. 57.

110. Ibid., pp. 177–78.

111. Ibid., p. 171.

112. Ibid., pp. 34–35.

113. Ibid., pp. 121, 60–61.

114. Ibid., pp. 64–65.

115. Ibid., pp. 77–78.

116. *The English Correspondence of Saint Boniface*, trans. Edward Kylie (London, 1911), pp. 108–9. I have modernized the translation provided by Kylie.

117. Ibid., pp. 98–102. Here I have modernized Kylie's translation.

118. *Vita Sanctae Hathumodae*, PL 137:1173. See also Eckenstein, *Woman under Monasticism*, p. 156.

119. "Dialogus Agii de Obitu Sanctae Hathumodae Abbatissae," *PL* 137:1185–86, trans. Eckenstein, *Woman under Monasticism*, p. 158. From his writings it is difficult to know Agius's exact relationship to Hathumoda. Wemple notes that he was her brother (*Women in Frankish Society*, p. 297, n. 193). Corbet, *Les Saints ottoniens*, notes that he was "un proche—et peut-être même un parent—de la défunte et de sa famille" (p. 45, and notes nos. 16–17).

120. Schulenburg, "Women's Monastic Communities, 500–1100: Patterns of Expansion and Decline," *Signs* 14, no. 2 (Winter, 1989), especially pp. 279–82.

121. *AASS, Mai. IV*, May 19, p. 362–63.

122. Translation adapted from Horstmann, *The Lives of Women Saints of our Contrie of England*, pp. 103–4; see also Millinger, "Anglo-Saxon Nuns," p. 122.

123. "The Life of St. Dunstan," in *English Historical Documents c. 500–1042*, vol. 1, ed. Dorothy Whitelock (New York, 1955), ch. 12, p. 827; *AASS, Mai. IV*, May 19, p. 349.

124. *AASS, Oct. XII*, Oct. 29, pp. 918–26; Knowles, *The Monastic Order in England*, pp. 38–59; Farmer, *Oxford Dictionary of Saints*, pp. 140–42.

125. *Mater Spiritualis: The Life of Adelheid of Vilich*, trans. Dick, ch. 6, p. 30.

126. Turgot, *Life of Queen Margaret*, p. 59.

127. Ibid., p. 67 (emphasis mine).

128. Ibid., p. 69.

129. Ibid., p. 75.

130. Ibid.

131. Ibid., p. 81 (emphasis mine).

132. Ibid., p. 82.

133. Ibid.

134. Ibid. Turgot also notes Margaret's friendship with other holy men, especially those embracing the eremitic life (p. 76). The special ties joining Margaret and the royal house of Scotland with Durham should be underscored. Turgot, her adviser and biographer, was prior of Durham (1087–1109), and her chaplain became a monk there after Margaret's death. Durham was the final resting place of St. Cuthbert, and according to Reginald of Durham, St. Cuthbert was St. Margaret's favorite saint and held a special place of honor for the queen. She had read his *vita* and he had been especially responsive to her requests for assistance. St. Margaret also gave Durham many important donations, including beautiful ornaments, a gospel book, and a precious cope, as well as the cross decorated with pearls which Margaret had held while on her deathbed. Reginald of Durham, *Libellus de . . . Cuthberti virtutibus,* ch. 98, p. 218. See also Malcolm Baker, "Bede's *Life of St. Cuthbert,*" p. 48. D. H. Farmer has suggested that in light of St. Margaret's special ties with St. Cuthbert and Durham, as well as her well-known zeal in acquiring books, Bede's *Life of St. Cuthbert* (today found in University College, Oxford) was written for her use. See Malcolm Baker, "Bede's *Life of St. Cuthbert,*" p. 48.

135. Goscelin, "The Liber Confortatorius of Goscelin of Saint Bertin," ed. C. H. Talbot, in *Analecta Monastica,* Studia Anselmiana 37, 3d series (Rome, 1955):1–117, on Eve and Goscelin, see introduction, pp. 1–25; see the extensive studies of Eve and Goscelin by André Wilmart, "Eve et Goscelin (I)" and "Eve et Goscelin (II)," *Revue Bénédictine* 46 (1934): 414–38; 50 (1938): 42–83. This friendship is also discussed in some detail by Sharon K. Elkins in her *Holy Women of Twelfth-Century England* (Chapel Hill and London, 1988), pp. 21–27; see also McGuire, *Friendship and Community,* pp. 201–4.

136. Elkins, *Holy Women of Twelfth-Century England,* p. 22; Goscelin, "The Liber Confortatorius," pp. 26–28.

137. Elkins, p. 23; Wilmart, "Eve et Goscelin (II)," p. 62; Goscelin, "The Liber Confortatorius," pp. 37, 42.

138. Wilmart, "Eve et Goscelin (II)," p. 63; Goscelin, "The Liber Confortatorius," pp. 42–45.

139. Wilmart, "Eve et Goscelin (II)," p. 63; Goscelin, "The Liber Confortatorius," p. 45.

140. Wilmart, "Eve et Goscelin (II)," p. 63.

141. Ibid., p. 80; Elkins, *Holy Women of Twelfth-Century England,* pp. 23–24; Goscelin, "The Liber Confortatorius," p. 113.

142. Wilmart, "Eve et Goscelin (II)," p. 81; Goscelin, "The Liber Confortatorius," p. 115.

143. Elkins, *Holy Women of Twelfth-Century England,* p. 23.

144. Wilmart, "Eve et Goscelin (II)," p. 82; Goscelin, "The Liber Confortatorius," pp. 115–17.

145. McGuire, *Friendship and Community,* p. 203. McGuire asks, "What did Eve think about all these passionate statements? She is silent, as are so

many of the women in history whose existence is known only through what men wrote. One suspects that her flight from England may have been inspired by a desire to get away from so dominating and dependent a figure as Goscelin" (p. 203).

146. Wilmart, "Eve et Goscelin (I)," pp. 428–29 and p. 429, n. 2; Elkins, *Holy Women of Twelfth-Century England,* p. 26.

147. Elkins, *Holy Women of Twelfth-Century England,* p. 26; Wilmart, "Eve et Goscelin (I)," p. 429. Elkins also mentions a letter dated to 1102 written by Geoffrey, abbot of Vendôme to Eve and Hervey, which expressed his approval of their friendship. He notes: "Who is perfect in love, let them not fear" (Elkins, pp. 26–27).

148. Elkins, *Holy Women of Twelfth-Century England,* p. 26. See also Christina of Markyate's close cross-sex spiritual friendships, pp. 33–42; *The Life of Christina of Markyate,* trans. Talbot.

149. See Jean Leclercq, "S. Pierre Damien et les femmes," *Studia Monastica* 15 (1973): 43–55; Jo Ann McNamara, "Chaste Marriage and Clerical Celibacy," in *Sexual Practices and the Medieval Church,* ed. Vern L. Bullough and James Brundage (Buffalo, 1982), pp. 32–33. In letter 51 (1057) written by Peter Damian to Duchess Beatrice of Tuscany, he rejoices over the duke and duchess's agreement that they would live in continence. He also encourages Beatrice to follow noble models of generosity to the Church "grant land and you will snatch heaven away." She was to especially look to the *exempla* of the lives of holy queens and empresses which would teach her the practice of virtue proper to her calling. He included among these role models Galla, wife of the emperor Theodosius; Guilla, the mother of Marquis Hugh; and St. Helena, mother of Constantine. Peter Damian, *Letters,* trans. Owen J. Blum, FC, *Mediaeval Continuation* (Washington, D.C., 1990), 2:335–40.

150. Peter Damian, *Letters,* 1:27–28.

151. McNamara, "Chaste Marriage and Clerical Celibacy," p. 33.

152. Ibid., citing *Epistolae collectae,* 11, ed. Jaffe, 532, Dec. 16, 1074, *PL,* 145. In addition to these many examples of spiritual friendship between prominent churchmen and women, the sources of the period also provide evidence of a wide range of close working relationships formulated between female and male religious. We see, for example, cases in which monks sought refuge with nuns. During the Viking invasions we learn that the monks of St. Wandrille were forced to flee from their monastery, and according to the miracles of St. Bertha of Blangy, from 868 to 885 they stayed with the nuns of Blangy. See Elisabeth M. C. van Houts, "Historiography and Hagiography at Saint-Wandrille: The 'Inventio et Miracula Sancti Vulfranni,'" *Anglo-Norman Studies* (1989, 1990), 12:234. Some of these relationships, as Lisa Bitel has noted in her study of women in early Ireland, concerned the production of cloth and the sewing of clothing by nuns for their male colleagues. For example, the nuns of St. Samthann's monastery were sent a boatload of raw wool from the monastery of Iona presumably for the purpose of making cloth; a female disciple of St. Mochta, who had been raised from the dead by the holy man, spent some thirty years making clothes for Mochta's monks; or the Irish nun, Ciar, also made special clothing for St. Coemgen. See Bitel,

Land of Women, p. 266, n. 98, p. 185. According to the *Martyrology of Oengus*, the Irish nun-saint Ernait was a cook and robe-maker for St. Columba and his disciples of Iona. Stokes, *Martyrology of Oengus*, p. 43; see also Bitel, *Land of Women*, pp. 128–29. We also learn that the convent of St. Moduca and the male community under St. Buite (Monasterboice) were joined together in a "formal alliance" which involved the nuns and monks praying for one another, and the nuns washing the monks' clothing. Bitel, *Land of Women*, p. 185. The Merovingian affiliated foundations of Jumièges and Pavilly also had a similar arrangement. By common agreement the nuns of Pavilly were charged with the laundry of the monks of Jumièges. And, according to tradition, they found at that time a donkey who was intelligent enough to carry on its own the laundry from one abbey to the other—a distance of some six leagues. Aloys Aubertin, *Abbaye de Jumièges* (Jumièges, 1973), p. 28.

153. We learn, for example, that the abbot-saints Majolus or Mayeul and Odilo of Cluny were friends of the empress St. Adelaide. They served as her confessors; they offered her advice and supported her in her misfortunes. Odilo wrote a short *vita* of Adelaide based on information which she herself related to him. Adelaide in turn proved to be an especially generous patron of Cluny and the Church in general. St. Eumagne was also a friend of the empress, and he was named abbot of one of the monasteries which she founded. See Odilo of Cluny, *Vita Sanctae Adalheidis Imperatricis*, pp. 353ff; Corbet, *Les Saints ottoniens*, pp. 81–110; Butler 4, Dec. 16, 572–73; *DSW* 1:9.

154. See Geneviève Bührer-Thierry, "La reine adultère," *Cahiers de Civilisation Médiévale*, 35 (1992): 299–312, in which she notes the increase in the number of accusations of adultery against queens of the ninth century as a reflection of the important role assumed by the royal wife in political life. See also chapter 6, above, and the increased concern with problems of incest.

155. Folz, *Les Saintes Reines*, pp. 47–48.

156. Ibid.; see also Bührer-Thierry, "La reine adultère," pp. 307–9.

157. See *The Historical Works of Simeon of Durham:* The Church Historians of England, trans. Joseph Stevenson (London, 1855), vol. 3, pt. 2, chs. 40–42, pp. 699–703; Victoria Tudor, "The Misogyny of Saint Cuthbert," *Archaeologia Aeliana*, 5th series, 12 (1984), pp. 157–67; and Victoria Tudor, "The Cult of St. Cuthbert in the Twelfth Century: The Evidence of Reginald of Durham," in *Saint Cuthbert, His Cult and His Community to AD 1200*, ed. Gerald Bonner, David Rollason, Clare Stancliffe (Woodbridge, Suffolk, and Wolfeboro, New Hampshire, 1989), pp. 447–67; see also, for examples of Cuthbert's "historical" friendship with women, *Two Lives of St. Cuthbert*.

158. *The Historical Works of Simeon of Durham*, ch. 40, pp. 699–700.

159. Ibid., ch. 41, p. 701; A. J. Piper, "The First Generations of Durham: Monks and the Cult of St. Cuthbert," in *St. Cuthbert, His Cult and His Community*, pp. 437, 441.

160. As cited by Tudor, "The Misogyny of Saint Cuthbert," p. 159.

161. Ibid., pp. 159, 166.

162. Ibid., p. 159. Tudor notes briefly: "The precise manner in which the

idea was conceived and then spread abroad is probably beyond reconstruction but it is quite possible that the belief in Cuthbert's antifeminism arose, as it were, naturally in the monastic community and that no conscious attempt was ever made to deceive. Some encouragement may have come from the bishop who brought the Benedictine monks to Durham and who had spent part of his career in the monastery of St. Carileph in Maine." I would argue that this tie of the reform bishop William with St. Calais (and his strong antifeminist policy) was crucial in this radical transformation of St. Cuthbert; thus the new bishop's early misogynist conditioning needs to be underscored. From later sources we also learn that the memory of Calais' continuing importance at Durham and his notorious misogynism were perpetuated, for example, on the late medieval screen of the altar of St. Jerome and St. Benedict in Durham Cathedral. Here, according to the *Rites of Durham,* was a statue to St. Calais with the following inscription below: "SANCTUS KARILEPHUS in Arvernensi territorio clarissimis parentibus ortus, postea in monasterio Casagaia juxta urbem Cenomanicam, quod ipse fundavit, monachus et Abbas effectus, regem Francie Hildebertum ejusque familiam de quodam vase parvulo semel vino impleto sed meritis ejusdem Sancti semper exuberante habundantissime refecit. *Reginam Francie eum visitare affectans non permisit, sed insuper ingressum mulierum ab ecclesia sua imperpetuum interdixit. Unde mulier quedam veste virili induta ejus ecclesiam ausu temerario ingressa, continuo est cecata.* Ex historia aurea sub anno gracie 512, ca. 62." *Rites of Durham: Being A Description or Brief Declaration of All the Ancient Monuments, Rites, & Customs Belonging or Being Within the Monastical Church of Durham Before the Suppression. Written 1593.* Surtees Society, vol 107 (Durham and Edinburgh, 1902), pp. 133–34 (emphasis mine). I discuss this important shift in more detail in my study of proscriptions of sacred space.

163. Tudor, "The Misogyny of Saint Cuthbert"; see also Joan Nicholson, "*Feminae gloriosae:* Women in the Age of Bede," in *Medieval Women,* ed. Derek Baker, especially p. 28.

164. *The Historical Works of Simeon of Durham,* trans. Stevenson, ch. 22, pp. 657–58.

165. *Rites of Durham,* ch. 17, p. 35.

166. Ibid., ch. 22, p. 43.

167. Victoria Tudor has noted how the misogynist image projected of Cuthbert, and the gender-based policy of keeping females from approaching the tomb, affected the clientele of the cult center and the saint's miracles for women. The area *outside* of the west doors at Durham seems to have been publicized as the location for female cures. Most women, however, seem to have flocked to the nearby shrine of St. Godric of Finchale. See Tudor, "The Cult of St Cuthbert in the Twelfth Century," pp. 456–58. See also Schulenburg, "Saints, Gender, and the Production of Miracles in Medieval Europe," paper presented at the Ninth Berkshire Conference on the History of Women, Vassar College, June 13, 1993.

168. Nicholson, "*Feminae gloriosae:* Women in the Age of Bede," p. 28; see also Hollis, *Anglo-Saxon Women and the Church,* pp. 128–29, 189–90, 199–207, 317.

169. *The Historical Works of Simeon of Durham,* chs. 23, 24, pp. 658–59; 46, pp. 682–83; Reginald of Durham, *Libellus de . . . Cuthberti virtutibus,* ch. 74, pp. 151–54; see also Tudor, "The Misogyny of Saint Cuthbert," pp. 159–61, and "The Cult of St. Cuthbert in the Twelfth Century," pp. 456–58.

170. For these misogynist episodes in the Life of St. Calais, see *AASS, Iul. I* (July 1), pp. 86–87; *MGH SRM* 3:393.

171. See also Hollis, *Anglo-Saxon Women and the Church,* p. 102.

172. See for example, Waldabertus, *Regula ad virgines,* ch. 23, *PL* 88:1070: "De non defendenda proxima vel consanguinea in monasterio"; *The Rule of a Certain Father to the Virgins,* trans. Jo Ann McNamara and John Halborg, ch. 23, p. 100.

173. *The Rule of Donatus of Besançon,* trans. McNamara and Halborg, ch. 1, p. 34.

174. *Regula Monacharum,* "De ordine in operibus Abbatissae," ch. 16, *PL* 30:405–6.

175. *St. Augustine: Letters,* vol. 5 (204–270), trans. Parsons, *FC* 32, Letter 211, p. 50.

176. *The Rule for Nuns of St. Caesarius of Arles,* no. 51, p. 188 (emphasis mine).

177. Aurelian, *Regula ad virgines,* ch. 11, *PL* 68:401.

178. Donatus, *Regula ad virgines,* ch. 32. "Ut nulla alterius teneat manum, nec juvenculae se invicem appellent." "Prohibetur ne pro dilectione aliqua ulla alterius teneat manum, sive steterit, sive ambulaverit, sive sederit. Quod si fecerit, duodecim percussionibus emendetur. Juvenculae, quibus imponitur terminus, ut non se appellent invicem, si transgressae fuerint, quadraginta percussionibus poeniteat." *PL* 87:284. See also *The Rule of Donatus of Besançon,* trans. McNamara and Halborg, ch. 32, p. 51.

179. *The Rule for Nuns of St. Caesarius of Arles,* ch. 25, p. 178.

180. *St. Augustine: Letters,* trans. Parsons, Letter 211, p. 48.

181. Leander of Seville, *The Training of Nuns,* ch. 30 (20), pp. 224–25; *Sancti Leandri Regula,* ch. 20, *PL* 72:891.

182. *The Rule for Nuns of St. Caesarius of Arles,* ch. 9, p. 174.

183. Donatus, *Regula ad virgines,* ch. 65, *PL* 87:293; *The Rule of Donatus of Besançon,* trans. McNamara and Halborg, ch. 65, p. 67.

184. Waldabertus, *Regula ad virgines,* ch. 14, *PL* 88:1065 (emphasis mine). See also *The Rule of a Certain Father to the Virgins,* trans. McNamara and Halborg, ch. 14, pp. 92–93.

185. *The Rule of a Certain Father to the Virgins,* trans. McNamara and Halborg, ch. 2, p. 78; see also Waldabertus, *Regula ad virgines,* ch. 2, *PL* 88:1055.

186. *Concilia Antiqua Galliae,* ed. Jacques Sirmond (Paris, 1629, reprint 1970), vol. 2. Council of Aix (Concilium Aquisgranense, 816), no. 10, p. 419: "Omnes in dormitorio dormiant, singulae scilicet in singulis lectis." No. 17, p. 421: "Caveatur etiam ab illis, ut nihil inhonestum, aut indecens in dormitorio geratur: nec aliqua aliquam inquietate praesumat, nec ad verba inutilia, & otiosa prorumpere cogat. Si qua vero id fecerit, severissima invectione

corripiatur. Lucerna quoque noctis tempore in eodem dormitorio iugiter ardeat." No. 18, pp. 421–42: ". . . in dormitorio aliquid indecens aut inhonestum, verbis aut actibus perpetraverit, alibi quam in dormitorio absque causa inevitabili dormire praesumpserit, sororibus caritatis officio servire neglexerit."

187. Pierre Payer, *Sex and the Penitentials: The Development of a Sexual Code, 550–1150* (Toronto, Buffalo, London, 1984); see especially pp. 43, 68, 92, 93, 95, 99, 100, 102, 108, 112, 138; concerning lesbian nuns, pp. 43, 99.

188. McNeill and Gamer, *Medieval Handbooks of Penance,* p. 185.

189. "Si mulier cum muliere fornicans, III. annos." A. W. Haddan and W. Stubbs, *Councils and Ecclesiastical Documents Relating to Great Britain and Ireland* 3, no. 23 (Oxford, 1871, reprint 1964): 328.

190. Payer, *Sex and the Penitentials,* pp. 40, 43; "Si monachus cum monacha, annos VII," Haddan and Stubbs, *Councils and Ecclesiastical Documents,* 3, no. 11, p. 328.

191. "Si sanctaemoniales cum sanctaemoniale per machinam, annos VII," Haddan and Stubbs, *Councils and Ecclesiastical Documents,* 3, no. 24, p. 328; see Payer, *Sex and the Penitentials,* pp. 43, 172, n. 136. Payer notes that this text will also be repeated in later collections. The ninth-century Penitential of Pseudo-Theodore also censures the use of an instrument (*molimen*) by a woman acting alone or with another woman. Payer, p. 61.

192. E. Ann Matter, "My Sister, My Spouse: Woman-Identified Women in Medieval Christianity," *Journal of Feminist Studies in Religion* 2, no. 2 (Fall, 1986): 88–93.

193. See John Boswell, *Christianity, Social Tolerance, and Homosexuality: Gay People in Western Europe from the Beginning of the Christian Era to the Fourteenth Century* (Chicago, 1980), p. 204, n. 132; Payer, *Sex and the Penitentials,* p. 138; Matter, "My Sister, My Spouse," p. 89.

194. Payer, *Sex and the Penitentials,* pp. 99–100; Burchard of Worms, *Decretum,* 17.27–29; *PL* 140:924.

195. Cited by Louis Crompton, "The Myth of Lesbian Impunity: Capital Laws from 1270 to 1791," *Journal of Homosexuality* 6, nos. 1–2 (fall–winter 1980–81):14.

196. Ibid. See also Judith Brown, *Immodest Acts: The Life of a Lesbian Nun in Renaissance Italy* (New York and Oxford, 1986), pp. 6–7.

197. Philippe Ariès and Georges Duby, eds., *A History of Private Life II: Revelations of the Medieval World,* trans. Arthur Goldhammer (Cambridge, Mass., and London, 1988), p. 80. See *AASS, Iul. II,* July 6, pp. 424–25.

198. Peter Dronke, *Women Writers of the Middle Ages,* pp. 154–59; Peter Dronke, *Medieval Latin and the Rise of European Love-Lyric,* 2d ed. (Oxford, 1968), pp. 476–82.

199. Butler 4, Nov. 19, p. 389; *DSW* 1:262–63.

200. See for example, Rader, *Breaking Boundaries,* especially pp. 93, 111; also Dronke, *Women Writers of the Middle Ages,* pp. 26–35; Cherewatuk and Wiethaus, *Dear Sister,* especially pp. 1–19.

201. Dronke, *Women Writers of the Middle Ages,* p. 31; see also the Council of 789 (Capitula de diversis rebus), "III. . . . & nulla Abbatissa foras

Monasterium exire praesumat sine nostra iussione, nec sibi subditas facere permittat: & earum claustra sint bene firmata, & nullatenus vvinileodes scribere vel mittere praesumant." Sirmond, *Concilia Antiqua Galliae*, vol. 2, p. 157.

202. Although there are many examples of early Christian cross-sex friendships which served as models for these relationships among holy men and women in later ages, early female same-sex exempla are more difficult to discover. One especially dramatic same-sex example can be found in the bond of friendship and spiritual equality of the early Christian martyrs, Perpetua and her slave, Felicitas. In the story of their martyrdom, after Perpetua had been attacked and wounded by the heifer, she got up "and seeing that Felicitas had been crushed to the ground, she went over to her, gave her hand, and lifted her up. Then the two stood side by side." *The Martyrdom of Saints Perpetua and Felicitas*, in *Acts of the Christian Martyrs*, ch. 20, p. 129; Rader, *Breaking Boundaries*, p. 61.

203. *AASS, Feb. I*, February 1, ch. 16, pp. 132–33.

204. Ibid., ch. 17, p. 134. We also find mention in one of St. Brigid's *vitae* that she frequently spent time at night (when it was snowy and icy) praying in pools of cold water. And according to the Life she accomplished this ritual "cum quadam puella" who remains unnamed. Ibid., ch. 16, p. 132.

205. Cited by Bitel, *Land of Women*, pp. 188–89. See *Conchubrani Vita Sanctae Monennae*, ed. Mario Esposito in *Proceedings of the Royal Irish Academy* 28 (1910), bk. 2, ch. 9, pp. 222–23.

206. Ibid.

207. Gregory of Tours, *History of the Franks*, bk. 9, ch. 41, pp. 535–36.

208. Fortunatus, *Carminum liber XI*, poem 3, *MGH AA* 4:259; *Carm. Appendix*, 20; see also Aigrain, *Sainte Radegonde*, p. 151.

209. *Vita S. Balthildis Reginae*, ch. 7, pp. 489–90; ch. 11, p. 497, ch. 13, pp. 499–500; *SWDA*, pp. 271, 274–76.

210. *Vita S. Balthildis Reginae*, ch. 14, pp. 500–501; *SWDA*, p. 276.

211. *AASS, Iul. II*, July 4, pp. 49–54; *AASS B.*, 6:562–69; see also *DSW* 1:118–19.

212. See also Wilhelm Levison, *England and the Continent in the Eighth Century* (Oxford, 1946), p. 77; *DSW* 2:247; Eckenstein, *Woman under Monasticism*, pp. 135, 138–39.

213. Rudolf, *The Life of St. Leoba*, p. 223.

214. Ibid., pp. 222–23.

215. Ibid., pp. 223–24.

216. Hollis, *Anglo-Saxon Women and the Church*, p. 298.

217. Ibid. Hollis also suggests that Rudolf, the author of Leoba's *vita*, in his attempt to neutralize Boniface's kindred-soul relation with Leoba, has redirected this close friendship to Leoba and a member of her own sex, Queen Hildegard (pp. 297–99).

218. Janet L. Nelson, "Women at the Court of Charlemagne: A Case of Monstrous Regiment?" in *Medieval Queenship*, ed. John Carmi Parsons (New York, 1993), p. 53.

219. Rudolf, *The Life of St. Leoba*, p. 224. Also later when the church was enlarged, Leoba's tomb was moved to the west porch.

220. *AASS, Mar. II,* March 14, p. 364; *DSW* 2:70.
221. Gregory the Great, *Dialogues,* trans. Zimmerman, pp. 296–97.
222. Ibid.
223. *Vite Sanctae Geretrudis (De virtutibus Sanctae Geretrudis),* ch. 2, pp. 465–66; see also *SWDA,* pp. 229–30.
224. Ibid.
225. Bede, *A History of the English Church and People,* bk. 4, ch. 23, p. 249.
226. Ibid., p. 250.
227. *AASS, Sept. VI* (September 21), ch. 17, p. 278.
228. *Vite Sanctae Geretrudis (De virtutibus Sanctae Geretrudis),* ch. 10, p. 469; see also *SWDA,* pp. 232–33.
229. Medard Barth, "Die Legende und Verehrung del hl. Attala, der ersten Aebtissin von St. Stephan in Strassburg," *Archiv für Elsässische Kirchengeschichte,* 2 (1927):123–25; *BHL* 1:120.

CHAPTER EIGHT

1. J. C. Russell, *Late Ancient and Medieval Population,* Transactions of the American Philosophical Society (Philadelphia, 1958), p. 33. See also for longevity in the Middle Ages: *Aging and the Aged in Medieval Europe,* ed. Michael M. Sheehan (Toronto, 1990), and Shulamith Shahar, *Growing Old in the Middle Ages: 'Winter clothes us in shadow and pain,'* trans. Yael Lotan (London and New York, 1997). (Shahar's work was published after the completion of my manuscript.)
2. Sorokin, *Altruistic Love,* p. 103.
3. Ibid.
4. For Methuselah, see Genesis 5:27, and for Jacob, Gen. 47:28. In this same tradition, Mahalalel was said to have lived 895 years (Gen. 5:17); Enoch, 365 years (Gen. 5:23); Lamech, 777 years (Gen. 5:31); Noah, 950 years (Gen. 9:29); Abraham, 175 years (Gen. 25:7).
5. Delooz, *Sociologie et canonisations,* p. 289.
6. Bede, *A History of the English Church and People,* bk. 4, ch. 23, pp. 245–56.
7. J. C. Russell, "Population in Europe 500–1500," in *The Fontana Economic History of Europe: The Middle Ages,* ed. Carlo M. Cipolla (Glasgow, 1972), p. 44.
8. Herlihy, "Life Expectancies for Women in Medieval Society," pp. 1–22.
9. Wemple, *Women in Frankish Society,* p. 101.
10. Leyser, *Rule and Conflict in an Early Medieval Society,* p. 52; Wemple, *Women in Frankish Society,* pp. 101–2.
11. Leyser, *Rule and Conflict in an Early Medieval Society,* pp. 49–59.
12. Wemple, *Women in Frankish Society,* pp. 101–2. See also Paul Edward Dutton, "Beyond the Topos of Senescence: The Political Problems of the Aged Carolingian Rulers," in *Aging and the Aged in Medieval Europe,* pp. 75–94.
13. Wemple, *Women in Frankish Society,* p. 102.
14. "By her [Hildegard] Charlemagne had four sons and four daughters,

according to Paul the Deacon: one son, the twin of Lewis, called Lothair, died as a baby and is not mentioned by Einhard; two daughters, Hildigard and Adelhard, died as babies, so that Einhard seems to err in one of his names, unless there were really five daughters." *Einhard and Notker the Stammerer: Two Lives of Charlemagne,* trans. Thorpe, n. 43, p. 185; Wemple, *Women in Frankish Society,* p. 100; *DWS,* 1:360; Hildegard's epitaph notes sadly: "Alas, alas, O mother of Kings, the glory and the pain." Paul the Deacon, *Gesta Episcoporum Mettensium, MGH SS,* 2:266 (line 40), cited by Janet L. Nelson, "Women at the Court of Charlemagne," p. 53.

15. *The Rule for Nuns of St. Caesarius of Arles,* ch. 4, p. 171.

16. *The Rule of Donatus of Besançon,* ch. 6, p. 39.

17. *St. Benedict's Rule for Monasteries,* ch. 58, p. 79.

18. *Sainte Fare et Faremoutiers,* p. 166.

19. See P. Loret, "The Discernment of Vocations," in *Religious Sisters* (Westminster, Maryland, 1952), p. 216.

20. Roberta Gilchrist's important archaeological work on English nunneries of the central and late Middle Ages might, however, lead us to an opposite conclusion in regard to the longevity of female religious. Her studies point to the rather poor sanitation and hygienic levels found at most English convents. Gilchrist argues: "In addition to reflecting lack of resources, the meagre sanitation afforded to most nunneries may have possessed a deeper meaning. Poor sanitation and relatively lax disposal of domestic refuse may comment on the different value which male and female religious communities placed on cleanliness. Whereas monasteries outstripped their richest patrons in latrine facilities, nunneries were content with garderobes or single drains." She suggests that one possible explanation for this difference might be "that religious women embraced poor sanitation as an element of eremitic living, since uncleanness seems to have been valued as a sign of asceticism." Roberta Gilchrist, *Gender and Material Culture: The Archaeology of Religious Women* (London and New York, 1994), pp. 125–26; see also pp. 89, 113–15.

21. *St. Augustine: Letters,* vol. 5, FC 32, letter 211, p. 48.

22. *The Rule for Nuns of St. Caesarius of Arles,* p. 180.

23. *The Rule of Donatus of Besançon,* ch. 12, p. 42.

24. Fortunatus, *De vita Sanctae Radegundis liber I,* ch. 29, pp. 373–74.

25. *The Rule for Nuns of St. Caesarius of Arles;* six chapters concern the care of the infirm and elderly: ch. 22, p. 177; ch. 30, p. 180; ch. 31, p. 180; ch. 32, p. 181; ch. 42, p. 184; ch. 71, pp. 203–4.

26. Ibid., ch. 32, pp. 180–81; ch. 71, pp. 203–204.

27. *The Rule of Donatus of Besançon,* ch. 12, p. 42.

28. *The Rule for Nuns of St. Caesarius of Arles,* ch. 33, p. 181.

29. Ibid., ch. 8, p. 173; ch. 16, p. 175.

30. Sorokin, *Altruistic Love,* p. 104.

31. Vern Bullough and Cameron Campbell, "Female Longevity and Diet in the Middle Ages," *Speculum* 55/2 (1980): 319.

32. Ibid., pp. 319–25.

33. Michel Rouche, "La faim à l'époque carolingienne: essai sur quelques types de rations alimentaires," *Revue Historique* 250 (1973): 308, 314–15,

317–18. See also *De Institutione Sanctimonialium,* Council of Aix (Concilium Aquisgranense, 816), in Sirmond, *Concilia Antiqua Galliae,* vol. 2, ch. 13, p. 420, which stipulates the nourishment required for female religious; and Jean Verdon, "Notes sur le rôle économique des monastères feminins en France dans la seconde moitié du IXe et au début du Xe siècle," *Revue Mabillon* 58 (1975): 332, 338.

34. *De Institutione Sanctimonialium,* p. 420.

35. Stokes, *Lives of Saints from the Book of Lismore,* ch. 1355, pp. 188–89; ch. 1368, p. 189; ch. 1595, p. 195. Here we note, for example, the saint's profligate behavior and the critical response of her nuns: "Little good have we from thy compassion to everyone, and we ourselves in need of food and raiment!"

36. *AASS, Iul. II,* July 6, pp. 291, 294, 298–99, 305; see also Ryan, *Irish Monasticism,* pp. 137–38; *Conchubrani Vita Sanctae Monennae,* ed. Mario Esposito in *Proceedings of the Royal Irish Academy,* 28 (1910), bk. 3, ch. 2, p. 229. See also Ryan, *Irish Monasticism,* pp. 137–38. Despite the frequent references by hagiographers to the poverty of their women saints and of their religious communities, Lisa Bitel has argued that in fact some of the early Irish female monasteries were fairly wealthy and managed very well. She notes: "When Samthann's hagiographer, like those of Brigit, Moninne, and many other male and female saints, pleaded poverty for his subject, he must have been describing the spiritual poverty appropriate to Christian professionals rather than an actual lack of goods and land. The very vitae these women merited argue for the prosperity of their houses." Lisa Bitel, *Land of Women,* p. 173. See also Gilchrist's observations on the wealth and status of women's houses in England, *Gender and Material Culture,* pp. 24–25, 41–44, 89–90, 105, 125–26, 131, 136, 168, 190.

37. Gregory of Tours, *History of the Franks,* bk. 10, ch. 16, p. 572.

38. *AASS, Ian. I,* Jan. 8, no. 38, p. 523, no. 26, p. 528; *AASS, Feb. I,* Feb. 3, p. 384.

39. *AASS, Feb. I,* Feb. 3, pp. 380–84; *AASS B.* 5:264–71; see also R. Podevyn, "Etude Critique sur la vita Gudulae," *Revue Belge de philologie et d'histoire* 21 (1923): 634.

40. *The Letters of Saint Boniface,* trans. Emerton, p. 37.

41. Dom Y. Chassey, et al., eds. *L'Abbaye royale Notre-Dame de Jouarre* (Paris, 1961), pp. 72–73.

42. Schulenburg, "Strict Active Enclosure," pp. 75–79.

43. On this topic, see especially Jo Ann McNamara, "A Legacy of Miracles," pp. 36–52.

44. See Bynum, *Holy Feast and Holy Fast;* Bell, *Holy Anorexia;* Weinstein and Bell, *Saints and Society,* pp. 24, 154 (table 18, p. 234, notes that penitential asceticism, which included fasting, was much more common among women saints); Kieckhefer, *Unquiet Souls,* especially pp. 25–27, 40, 45, 82, 140–42, 183, 191; Vauchez, *La Sainteté en occident,* pp. 224, 226, 347–48, 405–6, 450–51.

45. I would like to thank Richard Kieckhefer for his helpful comments on this topic.

46. "Jeûne," *Dictionnaire de Spiritualité; Ascetique et Mystique, Doctrine et Histoire*, M. Viller et al., eds. (Paris, 1974) 8:1164.

47. Ibid., pp. 1164–1179; F. Cabrol and H. Leclercq, "Jeûnes," *Dictionnaire Archéologie Chrétienne et de Liturgie* (Paris, 1927), 7, II:2481–2501. One especially interesting case of the use of fasting can be found in the Life of St. Genovefa. "When it was noised abroad that Attila the King of the Huns, overcome with savage rage, was laying waste the province of Gaul, the terror-stricken citizens of Paris sought to save their goods and money from his power by moving them to other, safer cities. But Genovefa summoned the matrons of the city and persuaded them to undertake a series of fasts, prayers, and vigils in order to ward off the threatening disaster, as Esther and Judith had done in the past. Agreeing with Genovefa, the women gave themselves up to God and labored for days in the baptistery—fasting, praying and keeping watch as she directed." *SWDA*, p. 23.

48. Bell, *Holy Anorexia*, p. 16.

49. "Jeûne," *Dict. Sp.*, 8:1178. See Bynum, *Holy Feast and Holy Fast*, pp. 36–37 citing the translation by Herbert Musurillo, "The Problem of Ascetical Fasting in the Greek Patristic Writers," *Traditio* 12 (1956): 17.

50. *St. Augustine: Letters*, vol. 5, FC, vol. 32, letter 211, p. 43.

51. See Bynum, *Holy Feast and Holy Fast*; Bell, *Holy Anorexia*.

52. St. Jerome, *Letters and Select Works*, NPNF, vol. 6, "Letter CVIII to Eustochium," p. 196.

53. Ibid., p. 204.

54. Jerome, *The Letters of St. Jerome*, ACW 1, "Letter 22 to Eustochium," ch. 11, p. 143.

55. Ibid., p. 148.

56. Ibid., p. 149.

57. St. Jerome, "Letter CVII to Laeta," in *Letters and Select Works*, NPNF, vol. 6, pp. 193–94.

58. St. Jerome, "Letter XXIV to Marcella," ibid., p. 43 (emphasis mine).

59. St. Jerome, "Letter XXXIX to Paula," ibid., p. 49.

60. Ibid., p. 53 (emphasis mine).

61. *Vitae Caesarii Episcopi Arelatensis libri duo*, bk. 1, ch. 58, p. 481; see also *Caesarius of Arles: Life, Testament, Letters*, trans. William Klingshirn, p. 39.

62. *The Rule for Nuns of St. Caesarius of Arles*, pp. 87, 151, ch. 67, pp. 196–97, ch. 71, pp. 202–4.

63. Ibid., pp. 197, 202 n. 76, ch. 42, p. 184.

64. *The Rule of Donatus of Besançon*, ch. 36, p. 52, ch. 12, pp. 42–43, ch. 76, pp. 72–73.

65. *Rule of Caesarius*, ch. 30, p. 180; *Rule of Donatus*, ch. 24, p. 48.

66. Plummer, *Vitae Sanctorum Hiberniae*, vol. 2, p. 119. See also Diane P. Hall, "Gender and Sanctity in the Hagiography of Early Medieval Irish Women" (M.A. thesis, University of Melbourne, 1992), especially pp. 89–100.

67. Hall, "Gender and Sanctity," pp. 93–94; *Conchubrani Vita Sanctae Monennae*, bk. 3, ch. 2, p. 229.

68. *PB* 1, Jan. 3, p. 95; see also *SWDA*, p. 24.

69. Gregory of Tours, *Life of the Fathers*, p. 95; *SWDA*, pp. 54–55.

70. Fortunatus, *De vita Sanctae Radegundis liber I*, ch. 4, p. 366; Aigrain, *Sainte Radegonde*, pp. 158–59; *SWDA*, pp. 72–73.

71. Fortunatus, *De vita Sanctae Radegundis liber I*, ch. 15, p. 369; *SWDA*, p. 76.

72. Fortunatus, *De vita Sanctae Radegundis liber I*, chs. 21–22, pp. 371–72; *SWDA*, pp. 79–80. For the entire period of Lent Radegund consumed only approximately 2 *sestaria* or pints of water. *SWDA*, p. 79, n. 67.

73. Fortunatus, *Carminum liber XI*, poem 4, *MGH AA* 4:259.

74. Caesaria, "Dominabus sanctis Richildae et Radegundi Caesaria exigua" (Epistola), in *Caesaire d'Arles Oeuvres Monastiques I: Oeuvres pour les Moniales*, SC 345, trans. Adalbert de Vogué and Joel Courreau (Paris, 1988), pp. 486–89.

75. *Vita Sanctae Geretrudis*, ch. 6, p. 459; *SWDA*, p. 226.

76. Ibid., ch. 7, p. 461; *SWDA*, p. 227.

77. *PB* 2, Feb. 3, p. 250; *AASS, Feb. I*, Feb. 3, p. 380.

78. *AASS, Apr. III*, April 22, ch. 1, p. 64.

79. *AASS, Sept. VI*, September 21, pp. 273, 276.

80. *Vita S. Liutbirgae*, *MGH SS*, 4, pp. 163–64.

81. Turgot, *Life of Queen Margaret*, ch. 10, p. 79.

82. *PB* 4, April 19, p. 492.

83. For the later Middle Ages, see Bynum, *Holy Feast and Holy Fast*, and Bell, *Holy Anorexia*. There are two other very interesting examples of religiously motivated fasting in the sources of this early period. One concerns a ninth-century teen-aged girl who lived in the vicinity of Toul. As recorded in the *Royal Frankish Annals*, after receiving Holy Communion she was said to have fasted (i.e., to have taken no bodily nourishment) for three full years (823–825). After that time she started to take food and eat. *Royal Frankish Annals*, in Bernhard Walter Scholz, trans., *Carolingian Chronicles: Royal Frankish Annals and Nithard's Histories* (Ann Arbor, 1970), p. 118 (year 825). The other incident is described in some detail in the miracles of St. Walburga, abbess of Heidenheim, d. ca. 780. This fascinating case concerned a servant named Frideride who was initially afflicted by an embarrassing ravenous hunger. However, after having been given a piece of consecrated bread by the priest, Mundus, her appetite was extinguished. And for the next three years she followed a life of extreme fasting, without taking any "meat or drink." "Ex Wolfhardi Haserensis miraculis S. Waldburgis Monheimensibus," *MGH SS*, vol. 15, pt. 1, ch. 12, pp. 554–55; *The Lives of Women Saints of Our Contrie of England*, ed. Horstmann, pp. 84–86.

84. Stephanus Hilpisch, *History of Benedictine Nuns*, trans. Sr. M. Joanne Muggli (Collegeville, Minn., 1958), p. 43, n. 6.

85. Bede, *A History of the English Church and People*, bk. 5, ch. 3, pp. 273–74.

86. *Duplex legationis edictum 789*, *MGH, LEG* II, *Capitularia Regum Francorum* I, no. 19, p. 63.

87. Bynum, *Holy Feast and Holy Fast*; Bell, *Holy Anorexia*; Elizabeth

Alvilda Petroff, ed., *Medieval Women's Visionary Literature* (Oxford and New York, 1986), pp. 35–44.

88. St. Jerome, "Letter LXV to Asella," *NPNF*, vol. 6, ch. 3, p. 59; "Letter 22 to Eustochium," *ACW* I, ch. 18, p. 149.

89. St. Jerome, "Letter XXIV to Marcella," *NPNF*, vol. 6, ch. 5, p. 43.

90. St. Gregory the Great, *Dialogues*, *FC* 39, bk. 4, ch. 17, p. 211.

91. Fortunatus, *De vita Sanctae Radegundis liber I*, ch. 5, p. 367; *SWDA*, p. 73.

92. Baudonivia, *De vita Sanctae Radegundis liber II*, ch. 9, p. 384; *SWDA*, p. 92.

93. Baudonivia, *De vita Sanctae Radegundis liber II*, ch. 8, p. 383; *SWDA*, p. 91. In addition to depriving themselves of sleep through prayer and vigils, a number of other women saints made their beds into instruments of torture and self-mortification. The fourth-century St. Febronia had a small wooden bench constructed which was three cubits long and six palms wide; here she allowed herself to sleep for a restricted amount of time. Sometimes she chose to sleep on the bare ground. *AASS, Iun. VII*, June 25, p. 17. Also in this tradition St. Macrina (d. ca. 379), sister of Sts. Basil the Great and Gregory of Nyssa, in her final illness chose not to sleep on a bed but rather on the ground where "there was a board covered with a coarse cloth, and another board supported her head, designed to be used instead of a pillow, supporting the sinews of her neck slantwise and conveniently supporting the neck." Gregory of Nyssa, *Saint Gregory of Nyssa Ascetical Works*, trans. by Virginia Woods Callahan, *FC* 58 (Washington, D.C., 1967), p. 175. In his description of the ascetic life adopted by the virgin Asella, St. Jerome notes that "lying on the dry ground did not affect her limbs, and the rough sackcloth that she wore failed to make her skin either foul or rough." Jerome, "Letter XXIV to Marcella," *NPNF*, vol. 6, p. 43.

94. *Vita Rusticulae*, ch. 7, *MGH SRM* 4:343; *SWDA*, p. 126.

95. Bede, *History of the English Church and People*, bk. 4, ch. 19, p. 239.

96. *PB* 2, Feb. 3, p. 250.

97. *AASS, Mai. I*, May 2, ch. 2, p. 291.

98. Fortunatus, *De vita Sanctae Radegundis liber I*, ch. 25, pp. 372–73; *SWDA*, p. 81.

99. Fortunatus, *De vita Sanctae Radegundis liber I*, ch. 26, p. 373; *SWDA*, p. 81.

100. Louis Gougaud, *Ermites et Reclus: Etudes sur d'anciennes formes de vie religieuse* (Vienne, 1928), p. 55; Margot H. King, "The Desert Mothers: A Survey of The Feminine Anchoretic Tradition in Western Europe," in *Matrologia Latina* (Saskatoon, 1985); Ann K. Warren, "The Nun as Anchoress: England, 1100–1500," in *Distant Echoes: Medieval Religious Women*, ed. John M. Nichols and Lillian T. Shank, pp. 197–212; Ann K. Warren, *Anchorites and Their Patrons in Medieval England* (Berkeley, Los Angeles, and London, 1985); Elkins, *Holy Women of Twelfth-Century England*; Patricia J. F. Rosof, "Anchoresses in Twelfth and Thirteenth Century Society" (Ph.D. dissertation, New York, 1978).

101. Gregory of Tours, *Glory of the Confessors,* ch. 33, p. 46; Gregory of Tours, *Life of the Fathers,* ch. 19, pp. 124–30.

102. *AASS, Sept. VII,* September 27, ch. 10, p. 463; *DSW* 1:392.

103. *AASS, Iul. II,* July 4, p. 53.

104. Gregory of Tours, *History of the Franks,* bk. 6, ch. 29, pp. 357–58. An interesting work of historical fiction which focuses on this event is Julia O'Faolain's *Women in the Wall* (New York, 1973).

105. *Vita S. Liutbirgae, MGH SS,* 4:163.

106. *AASS, Mai. I,* May 2, ch. 2, pp. 291–92; *DSW,* 2:290–91.

107. On Eve of Wilton, see especially Elkins, *Holy Women of Twelfth-Century England,* pp. 19–27; Goscelin, "The Liber confortatorius of Goscelin of Saint Bertin," ed. C. H. Talbot, in *Analecta Monastica,* ed. M. M. Lebreton, J. Leclercq, and C. H. Talbot. Studia Anselmiana 37, no. 3 (Rome, 1955): 1–117, especially pp. 1–22; Wilmart, "Eve et Goscelin (I)," and "Eve et Goscelin (II),"; Hilary, *Versus et ludi,* ed. J. J. Champollion-Figeac (Paris, 1838). See also ch. 7: "Gender Relationships and Circles of Friendship among the *Mulieres Sanctae.*"

108. *The Martyrology of Oengus,* ed. Stokes, pp. 42–45; see also Hall, "Gender and Sanctity," p. 63.

109. Bede, *A History of the English Church and People,* bk. 4, ch. 23, p. 249 (emphasis mine).

110. Ibid., bk. 4, ch. 9, pp. 220–21.

111. *AASS, Ian. III,* January 30, ch. 28, p. 661.

112. Turgot, *Life of Queen Margaret,* p. 79.

113. See Bynum, "Fast, Feast, and Flesh: The Religious Significance of Food to Medieval Women," *Representations* 11 (Summer, 1985), pp. 13–14; see also her *Holy Feast and Holy Fast* and "Women's Stories, Women's Symbols: A Critique of Victor Turner's Theory of Liminality," in Frank Reynolds and Robert Moore, eds., *Anthropology and the Study of Religion* (Chicago, 1984), p. 118; Kieckhefer, *Unquiet Souls,* pp. 89–121.

114. Fortunatus, *De vita Sanctae Radegundis liber I,* ch. 26, p. 373; Baudonivia, *De vita Sanctae Radegundis liber II,* ch. 16, pp. 388–89; *SWDA,* p. 81, 96–99. See also chapter 2, above, and Isabel Moreira, "*Provisatrix Optima:* St. Radegund of Poitiers' Relic Petitions to the East," *Journal of Medieval History* 19 (1993), 285–305. Queen Margaret of Scotland also had a strong devotion to the crucifixion. As she lay dying, she commanded Turgot to bring her the cross that she called the Black Cross. When it was brought out of the case where it had been enclosed and taken to her "she received it with reverence; and set to embracing and kissing it, and signing with it very frequently her eyes and face." Turgot, *Life of Queen Margaret,* p. 84.

115. Fortunatus, *De vita Sanctae Radegundis liber I,* ch. 26, p. 373; *SWDA,* p. 81.

116. *Vita Bertilae abbatissae Calensis,* ch. 8, p. 108; translation based on *SWDA,* p. 287.

117. *AASS, Apr. III,* April 22, ch. 3, p. 63.

118. Gwynn and Purton, eds. and trans. "The Monastery of Tallaght," ch. 60, p. 149 (emphasis mine).

119. St. Jerome, "Against Helvidius," in *St Jerome: Dogmatic and Polemical Works,* trans. John N. Hritzu, *FC* 53 (Washington, D.C., 1965), p. 41.

120. Bynum, "Fast, Feast, and Flesh," p. 11; also *Holy Feast and Holy Fast,* p. 214, citing Albert the Great, *De animalibus libri XXVI nach der Cölner Urschrift,* vol. 1, Beiträge zur Geschichte der Philosophie des Mittelalters: Texte und Untersuchungen 15 (Münster, 1916), bk. 9, tract 1, ch. 2, p. 682. Caroline Bynum has also noted that according to Hildegard of Bingen, the menstrual flow of virgins was less than that of nonvirgins. Although Hildegard did not attribute this to diet, as Bynum has pointed out, "it may, however, have been an empirically sound observation because of the effects of restricted food intake on the nuns she observed." Bynum, *Holy Feast and Holy Fast,* n. 105, pp. 393–94.

121. See chapter 3, "At What Cost Virginity?" See also Lewis, *Ecstatic Religion.*

122. *Aldhelm: The Prose Works,* trans. Lapidge and Herren, ch. XIV, p. 71 (emphasis mine).

123. *Vita Sanctae Geretrudis,* ch. 6, p. 461; *SWDA,* p. 227.

124. *DSW* 1:84–85.

125. *AASS, Mar. II,* March 14, pp. 447–50; *DSW* 1:298.

126. *AASS, Sept. VI,* September 21, p. 271.

127. *Vita Sanctae Hathumodae,* ch. 9, p. 1184; Dunbar, *DSW* 1:360, notes that Hathumoda's mother lived to 109 years of age; according to Eckenstein, *Woman under Monasticism,* p. 159, she died at 107.

128. *ODS,* p. 120.

129. St. Jerome, "Letter XXIV to Marcella," *NPNF,* vol. 6, ch. 4, p. 43.

130. Shankar Vedantam, "Science Finds Ways to Slow Aging, but They Won't Be Fun," *Wisconsin State Journal,* June 2, 1996, pp. 1A, 8A, citing studies by George Roth, NIA.

131. *PB* 1, Jan. 3, p. 92.

132. Radegund appears to have been approximately 62 to 69 years of age at the time of her death. According to René Aigrain and Elmond-René Laband, Radegund lived from ca. 520 to ca. 587; *SWDA,* ca. 525–587; Butler and Farmer (*ODS*), ca. 518–587.

133. *SWDA,* pp. 109–10.

134. *Vita Bertilae abbatissae Calensis,* ch. 7, p. 108; de Montessus, *Jouarre: ses cryptes, son église, son abbaye,* p. 43.

135. *Vita Rusticulae,* ch. 22, p. 348.

136. *PB* 1, Jan. 4, p. 132.

137. Rudolf, *Life of St. Leoba,* p. 223.

138. *ODS,* pp. 262–63; Baker, "'A Nursery of Saints': St. Margaret of Scotland Reconsidered," p. 134, n. 113, p. 138.

139. As noted by Lisa Bitel, the eighth-century Irish tracts which assigned legal compensation for injuries "accorded women and children less medical attention than men, just as they gave noble patients more compensation than ailing peasants. Doctors were to feed women patients, for example, half or less of the rations prescribed for men, on the specious assumption that women required and deserved less food than men." Bitel, *Land of Women,* p. 21.

140. In Peter Abelard's detailed Rule for the Paraclete, for example, he extols the virtues of age and experience in regard to the selection of the abbess. Here he cites Ecclesiasticus: "How beautiful is the judgement of grey hairs and counsel taken from the old! How beautiful the wisdom of the aged, how glorious their understanding and counsel! Long experience is the old man's crown and his pride is the fear of the Lord." Or "Speak, if you are old, for it is your privilege. . . . If you are young, speak in your own case, but not much." *The Letters of Abelard and Heloise,* trans. Betty Radice (Harmondsworth, 1974), p. 200.

EPILOGUE

1. See, for example, the early classic study by Doris Stenton, *The English Woman in History* (New York, 1957, 1977). She argued that "enough has been said to show that in Anglo-Saxon England men and women lived on terms of rough equality with each other" (p. 28). This evaluation of the early period of English History as a kind of "golden age" for women has been questioned by a number of modern studies.

2. Olwen Hufton, "Women in History: Early Modern Europe," *Past and Present* 101 (1983): 126.

3. Judith M. Bennett, *Women in the Medieval English Countryside: Gender and Household in Brigstock before the Plague* (New York and Oxford, 1987), pp. 4–8.

4. For an interesting look at an earlier development, see also Elizabeth A. Clark, "Patrons, Not Priests: Gender and Power in Late Ancient Christianity," *Gender and History,* 2/3 (Autumn, 1990): pp. 252–73.

5. Barbara Newman, *Sister of Wisdom,* pp. 152–53.

6. Gregory of Tours, *History of the Franks,* bk. 9, ch. 42, p. 535.

7. Ibid., bk. 9, ch. 42, p. 538.

8. Gregory of Tours, *Glory of the Confessors,* no. 104, p. 108 (emphasis mine).

9. Head, "Hrotsvit's *Primordia* and the Historical Traditions of Monastic Communities," p. 153.

10. Fortunatus, *De vita Sanctae Radegundis liber I,* chs. 27–38, pp. 373–76; Baudonivia, *De vita Sanctae Radegundis liber II,* chs. 11–12, 15, 17, 24–28, pp. 385–87, 389–90, 393–95; *SWDA,* pp. 82–86, 93–94, 96, 99–100, 103–05.

11. Baudonivia, *De vita Sanctae Radegundis liber II,* ch. 27, p. 394; *SWDA,* pp. 104–5; on this incident see Brennan, "St. Radegund and the Early Development of Her Cult at Poitiers," pp. 352–54. In addition to showing Radegund's special powers, Brennan argues that this episode should be read in the political context of the competition between these two cult centers.

12. Aigrain, *Sainte Radegonde,* pp. 179–80. Brennan notes that although Radegund was a Thuringian princess by birth, she became transformed into a French royal saint. "By a somewhat ironic twist this Thuringian princess was invoked by the women of Poitiers to protect their city aginst the Germans dur-

ing the Franco-Prussian War." Brennan, "St. Radegund and the Early Development of Her Cult at Poitiers," p. 340.

13. *SWDA*, pp. 299–303.

14. Ibid., pp. 318–25.

15. Ibid., pp. 324–25; *AASS, Feb. II*, February 10, p. 426. See Wemple, *Women in Frankish Society*, p. 41 and p. 223, n. 80. *SWDA*, pp. 318–25. Austreberta's miraculous cure of a woman with cancer of the breast is especially moving. "The mother of a rich and noble family, who had formerly enjoyed the friendship of God's holy woman, was struck by the pestiferous and incurable disease which doctors call cancer. For nine years it tore at her chest until her breast was nearly consumed. On the day when the holy deposition of the blessed virgin is celebrated, she came and prostrated herself with devotion and faith before the venerated one's sepulchre. With many tears flowing because of her suffering she prayed intently for a long time. Then on another day, after she had returned home, the wound putrefying in her flesh was pulled out by the roots, a flood of bloody matter streamed out and within a few days she was restored to health" (*SWDA*, ch. 13, p. 322).

16. *AASS, Mai. I*, May 2, ch. 1, no. 2, p. 300. "Nam Theutonica locutione prolatum, Mulierum consilium sonat."

17. Kieckhefer, *Unquiet Souls*, pp. 12–14.

18. Atkinson, Buchanan, and Miles, *Immaculate and Powerful*, pp. 1–14; Ashley and Sheingorn, eds., *Interpreting Cultural Symbols*, especially pp. 1–6.

19. Kieckhefer, *Unquiet Souls*, pp. 12–14.

20. Atkinson, Buchanan, and Miles, *Immaculate and Powerful*, pp. 1–14; Ashley and Sheingorn, eds. *Interpreting Cultural Symbols*, pp. 1–6; see also Jocelyn Wogan-Browne's important studies, "Queens, Virgins, and Mothers: Hagiographic Representations of the Abbess and Her Powers in Twelfth- and Thirteenth-Century Britain," " 'Clerc u lai, muïne u dame': Women and Anglo-Norman Hagiography in the Twelfth and Thirteenth Centuries," and "Saints' Lives and the Female Reader."

21. For the *vita* as a "clear mirror," see *SWDA*, p. 288. See also Bennett, *Women in the Medieval English Countryside*, p. 5; Geary, *Living with the Dead in the Middle Ages*, pp. 9–29.

22. Another important all-female hagiography is Osbern Bokenham's *Legendys of Hooly Wummen* (1443?–1447?), see Sheila Delany, trans., *A Legend of Holy Women: A Translation of Osbern Bokenham's Legends of Holy Women* (Notre Dame and London, 1992). This work contains the stories of thirteen women saints from the gospels, apocrypha, martyrologies, and the thirteenth-century St. Elizabeth of Hungary. There are, however, no representatives of *mulieres sanctae* from the early medieval period in this collection.

23. See especially Kenneth L. Woodward, *Making Saints: How the Catholic Church Determines Who Becomes a Saint, Who Doesn't, and Why* (New York and London, 1990), pp. 16, 77–126. See also Alan Riding, "Vatican 'Saint Factory': Is It Working Too Hard?" *New York Times International*,

Saturday, April 15, 1989, p. Y5. I would like to thank Jim Brundage for this reference.

24. William D. Montalbano, "The Pope's Passion for New Saints," *Los Angeles Times,* Thursday, Jan. 5, 1995, pp. A1, A6.

25. See Riding, "Vatican 'Saint Factory,' " p. Y5; Montalbano, "The Pope's Passion for New Saints," p. A1; also Woodward, *Making Saints,* p. 120.

26. On beatification and canonization, see Vauchez, *La Sainteté en occident,* pp. 1–162; Delooz, "Pour une étude sociologique de la sainteté canonisée dans l'église catholique," pp. 17–43; Delooz, *Sociologie et canonisations;* Kemp, *Canonization and Authority in the Western Church;* also for the modern period, Woodward, *Making Saints,* pp. 121, 377–80.

27. Montalbano, "The Pope's Passion for New Saints," p. A6.

28. We see in various sources which describe the process of canonization a differential treatment of potential saints and their miracles based on gender. For example: "au XIXe siècle, cette abondance de miracles féminins inquietait un apologiste comme le chanoine Moigno. En étudiant les miracles retenus pour la béatification et la canonisation de Benoît-Joseph Labre (trois pour l'une et deux pour l'autre), il fut gêné d'avoir affaire à cinq guérisons féminines et il s'en ouvrit à Léon XIII, lequel lui rétorqua: 'Quand il s'agit de miracles féminins, comme il vous plait de les appeler, la Sacrée Congrégation des Rites est encore plus sur ses gardes et plus sévère; elle exige une surabondance de preuve extraordinaire, et, s'il était possible, le miracle serait rendu encore plus certain.' " F. Moigno, *Les splendeurs de la foi* 5:XXVII, cited by Delooz, *Sociologie et canonisations,* p. 121, n. 1.

29. Bitel, *Land of Women,* p. 188 citing W. W. Heist, ed. *Vitae Sanctorum Hiberniae.* Subsidia Hagiographica, 28 (Brussels, 1965), p. 129. The complex problem of "female miracles" versus "male miracles" needs to be further explored for the medieval period. It is also interesting that a number of the *vitae* of women saints argue that miracles per se were not essential for a holy life, rather deeds were more admirable than miracles. For example, see Turgot, *Life of Queen Margaret,* p. 80. For a discussion of the issue of saints and saints' Lives without miracles, see Giulia Barone, "Une hagiographie sans miracles: observations en marge de quelques vies du XIe siècle," in *Les fonctions des saints dans le monde occidental (IIIe–XIIIe siècle),* Collection de l'École française de Rome 149 (Rome, 1991), pp. 435–46.

30. Susan Brownmiller, *Against Our Will: Men, Women and Rape* (New York, 1975), pp. 332, 68. This type of behavior has also been verified by my colleague, Rosemarie Lester (Department of Liberal Studies, University of Wisconsin-Madison), who lived in Berlin during World War II. She noted that as young girls they blackened their faces to avoid being raped.

31. See Mary Beth Rose, "Introduction," *Women in the Middle Ages and Renaissance,* pp. xviii–xix.

32. Butler 3, July 6, pp. 28–29.

33. This modern day "use" of Saint Maria Goretti was related to me by Eileen Seifert (Department of English, DePaul University) and concerned her own experiences in a Catholic girls' high school in Pittsburgh.

34. This incident was told to me by Karen Lindsey, a journalist from Cambridge, Massachusetts, at the Seventh Berkshire Conference on the History of Women, Wellesley College, June 19–21, 1987. She was amazed at the uncanny resemblance of responses required for the maintenance of virginity as advocated by the medieval church (with its cases of self-mutilation, etc.) and the modern Catholic Church.

35. I would like to thank Dale Bauer (Department of English and Women's Studies, University of Wisconsin-Madison) for providing me with this information.

36. Petroff, *Body and Soul,* p. 161.

37. Matthew of Westminster (Matthew of Paris), *The Flowers of History,* I, p. 410.

Selected Bibliography

PRIMARY SOURCES

Acts of the Christian Martyrs, The. Edited and translated by Herbert Musurillo. Oxford, 1972.

Adelheide. *Vita Adelheidis Abbatissae Vilicensis Auct. Bertha. MGH SS* 15: 755–63; *AASS* Feb. I: 721–27. (See also *Mater Spiritualis: The Life of Adelheid of Vilich.*)

Adomnan. *Adomnan's Life of Columba.* Edited and translated by Alan Orr Anderson and Marjorie Ogilvie Anderson. London, 1961.

Aelfric's Lives of Saints. Edited and translated by W. W. Skeat. 2 vols. in 4. The Early English Text Society. London, 1881.

Aethelwold, Saint. *Regularis Concordia: The Monastic Agreement of the Monks and Nuns of the English Nation.* Edited by Thomas Symons. London, 1953.

Agius. "Dialogus Agii: De obitu sanctae Hathumodae abbatissa." *PL* 137: 1183–95.

Aldegund. *Vita Aldegundis, abbatissae Malbodiensis. MGH SRM* 6:70–90; *AASS* Ian. III: 651–70; *AASS B* 4:315–36. (See also *Sainted Women of the Dark Ages,* pp. 235–54.)

Aldhelm. *De Laudibus Virginitatis, PL* 89:103–62.

———. *De Laudibus Virginum, PL* 89:237–80.

———. *De virginitate.* In *Aldhelm: The Prose Works.*

———. *Aldhelm: The Poetic Works.* Translated by Michael Lapidge and James L. Rosier. Cambridge, 1985.

———. *Aldhelm: The Prose Works.* Edited and translated by Michael Lapidge and Michael Herren. Totowa, 1989.

Ambrose. *St. Ambrose: Select Works and Letters.* Translated by H. de Romestin. A Select Library of Nicene and Post-Nicene Fathers of the Christian Church, 2d series, edited by Philip Schaff and Henry Wace, vol. 10. New York, 1896; rpt. Grand Rapids, Mich., 1955.

———. *De lapsu virginis consecratae. PL* 16:367–84.

———. *Saint Ambrose, Letters.* Translated by Sr. Mary Melchior Beyenka. The Fathers of the Church. New York, 1954.

Anecdota Oxoniensia: Lives of the Saints from the Book of Lismore. Translated by Whitley Stokes. Oxford, 1890.

Anglo-Saxon Chronicle, The. Translated and edited by G. N. Garmonsway. London and New York, 1972.

Anglo-Saxon Missionaries in Germany, The. Translated and edited by C. H. Talbot. New York, 1954.

Anglo-Saxon Saints and Heroes. Edited by Clinton Albertson. New York, 1967.

Annales ordinis S. Benedicti occidentalium. 6 vols. Edited by Jean Mabillon. Lucca, 1739.

Annals of St-Bertin, The. Translated and annotated by Janet L. Nelson. *Ninth Century Histories,* vol. 1. Manchester and New York, 1991.

Ansbert. *Vita Ansberti episcopi Rotomagensis. MGH SRM* 5:613–43.

Arnulf. *Vita S. Arnulphi episcopi Mettensis. AASS* Iul. IV: 434–47; *MGH SRM* 2:432–46.

Augustine. *Concerning the City of God against the Pagans.* Edited by David Knowles, translated by Henry Bettenson. Harmondsworth, 1972.

———. *Confessions.* Translated by R. S. Pine-Coffin. Baltimore, 1961.

———. *St. Augustine: Letters.* Translated by Sr. Wilfrid Parsons. The Fathers of the Church, a New Translation, vol. 32. New York, 1956.

Aurelian of Arles. *Regula ad virgines. PL* 68:399–406.

Austreberta. *Vita S. Austrebertae virginis. AASS* Feb. II: 419–27. (See also *Sainted Women of the Dark Ages,* pp. 304–25.)

Avitus of Vienne. *Poematum liber sextus de virginitate. MGH AA* 6:275–94; *PL* 59:369–82.

Balthild. *Vita S. Balthildis Reginae. MGH SRM* 2:477–508. (See also *Sainted Women of the Dark Ages,* pp. 264–78.)

Baudonivia. *De Vita Sanctae Radegundis, Liber II. MGH SRM* 2:377–95.

Bede. *A History of the English Church and People.* Translated by Leo Sherley-Price, revised by R. E. Latham. Harmondsworth, 1955, 1968.

———. *Life of St. Cuthbert.* In *Two Lives of Saint Cuthbert,* translated by Bertram Colgrave. Cambridge, 1940, rpt. 1985.

Benedict. *Saint Benedict's "Rule for Monasteries."* Translated by Leonard J. Doyle. Collegeville, Minn., 1948.

Benno. *Vita S. Bennonis II Episcopi Osnabrugensis. MGH SS* 12:60–84.

Berlinde. *Vita S. Berlindis v. Merbecae in Brabantia. AASS B* 5:264–71; *AASS* Feb. I: 383–85.

Bernard. *Vita Prima, libris quinque. PL* 185:225–366.

Bertha. *Vita Adelheidis Abbatissae Vilicensis Auctore Bertha. MGH SS* 15:755–63; *AASS* Feb. I:721–27. (See also *Mater Spiritualis: The Life of Adelheid of Vilich.*)

———. *Vita S. Bertae Abbatissae Blangiacenis. AASS* Iul. II: 49–60.

Bertilla. *Vita Bertilae Abbatissae Calensis. MGH SRM* 6:95–109. (See also *Sainted Women of the Dark Ages,* pp. 279–88.)

Bokenbam, Osbern. *A Legend of Holy Women.* Translated by Sheila Delaney. Notre Dame and London, 1992.

Boniface. *The Letters of Saint Boniface.* Translated by Ephraim Emerton. New York, 1976.

———. *The English Correspondence of Saint Boniface.* Translated by Edward Kylie. London, 1911.

———. *Vitae Sancti Bonifatii archiepiscopi Moguntini. MGH Script* II: 333–53; *AASS* Iun. I:452–75.

Book of Sainte Foy, The. Trans. by Pamela Sheingorn. Philadelphia, 1995.

Bova. *De sanctis virginibus, Bova abbatissa et Doda sanctimoniali, Remis in Gallia. AASS* Apr. III:286–88.

Brendan. *Life of Brendan of Clonfert.* In *Lives of the Saints,* edited and translated by Charles Plummer, 2:44–96. Oxford, 1922.

Brigid. *Vitae S. Brigidae Virginis. AASS* Feb. I: 119–85. (See also *The Life of Saint Brigit* in *Lives of Saints from the Book of Lismore.*)

Burgundian Code, The. Translated by Katherine Fischer Drew. Philadelphia, 1972.

Burgundofara. *Vita S. Columbani abbatis discipulorumque eius libri duo auctore Iona. MGH SRM* 4:130–43. (See also *Sainted Women of the Dark Ages,* pp. 155–75.)

Caesarius of Arles. *Life, Testament, Letters.* Translated by William E. Klingshirn. Translated Texts for Historians, vol. 19. Liverpool, 1994.

———. *Oeuvres monastiques I: Oeuvres pour les moniales. SC* 345. Translated by Adalbert de Vogüé and Joel Courreau. Paris, 1988.

———. *Regula ad virgines. PL* 67:1103–21.

———. *The Rule for Nuns of St. Caesarius of Arles: A Translation with a Critical Introduction* by Maria Caritas McCarthy. Catholic University of America, Studies in Mediaeval History, n.s. 16. Washington, D.C., 1960.

———. *Sermons.* Translated by Sr. Mary Magdeleine Mueller. The Fathers of the Church, a New Translation, vols. 31, 47, 66. New York, 1956, 1964, 1973.

———. *Vita Caesarii episcopi Arelatensis libri duo. MGH SRM* 3:457–501; *PL* 67:1001–42.

Cáin Adamnáin: An Old-Irish Treatise on the Law of Adamnan. Anecdota Oxoniensia. Edited and translated by Kuno Meyer. Oxford, 1905.

Carileffus/Calais. *Vita S. Carileffi (St. Calais). AASS* Iul. I: 80–90.

Cassian, John. *Institutions Cénobitiques. SC* 109. Edited and translated by J. Cl. Guy. Paris, 1965.

Cerona. *La Vie latine de Sainte Céronne.* Edited by François Dolbeau. *Analecta Bollandiana* 104 (1986):68–78.

Christine de Pizan. *The Book of the City of Ladies.* Translated by Earl Jeffrey Richards. New York, 1982.

Chrothild. *Vita Sanctae Chrothildis reginae francorum. MGH SRM* 2:342–48; *AASS* Iun. I: 290–91. (See also *Sainted Women of the Dark Ages,* pp. 38–50.)

Columbanus. *Vita Columbani abbatis discipulorumque eius libri duo auctore Iona. MGH SRM* 4:61–108.

"Conchubranus Vita Sanctae Monennae." Edited by Mario Esposito. *Proceedings of the Royal Irish Academy* 28 (1910): 202–51.

Concilia Antiqua Galliae. 3 vols. Edited by Jacques Sirmond. Paris, 1629, rpt. Scientia Verlag Aalen, 1970.

Councils and Ecclesiastical Documents relating to Great Britain and Ireland. 3 vols. Edited by Arthur West Haddan and William Stubbs. Oxford, 1869–78; rpt. 1964.

Cunegund. *Vita S. Cunegundis. MGH SRM* 4:821–24; *AASS* Mar. I: 271–78.

Cuthbert. *Two Lives of Saint Cuthbert.* Translated by Bertram Colgrave. Cambridge, 1940, rpt. 1985.

Cyprian. *Saint Cyprian, Treatises: The Dress of Virgins.* Edited by Roy J. Deferrari and translated by Angela Elizabeth Kennan. New York, 1958.

David. *Rhigyfarch's Life of St. David.* Translated by J. W. James. Cardiff, 1967.

Doda. See Bova.

Donatus. *Regula ad virgines. PL* 87:273–98.

———. *The Rule of Donatus of Besançon.* 2d ed. Translated by Jo Ann McNamara and John E. Halborg. Peregrina Translations Series, no. 5. Toronto, 1993.

Durandus, William. *The Symbolism of Church and Church Ornaments: A Translation of the First Book of the Rationale Divinorum Officiarum.* Translated by John Mason Neale and Benjamin Webb. London, 1893.

Eadmer's History of Recent Events in England: Historia Novorum in Anglia. Translated by Geoffrey Bosanquet. London, 1964.

Early Christian Biographies. Translated by Roy Deferrari. The Fathers of the Church, a New Translation, vol. 15. New York, 1952.

Eddius Stephanus. *Life of Wilfrid.* In *Lives of the Saints,* translated by J. F. Webb. Harmondsworth, 1965.

Einhard and Notker the Stammerer. *Two Lives of Charlemagne.* Translated by Lewis Thorpe. Harmondsworth, 1969.

Eloi/Eligius. *Vita Sancti Eligii episcopi Noviomensis. MGH SRM* 4:663–741.

English Historical Documents. Vol. 1: c. 500–1042. Edited by Dorothy Whitelock. New York, 1955.

Erkenwald. *The Saint of London: The Life and Miracles of St. Erkenwald.* Edited and translated by E. Gordon Whatley. Binghamton, 1989.

Ermelinde. *Vita S. Ermelindis Virginis. AASS* Oct. XII: 849–55.

Eustadiola. *Vita S. Eustadiolae. AASS* Iun. II: 132–34. (See also *Sainted Women of the Dark Ages,* pp. 106–11.)

Faro. *Vita S. Faronis episcopi Meldensis. AASS* Oct. XII: 609–19.

Felix's Life of Saint Guthlac. Translated by Bertram Colgrave. Cambridge and New York, 1956.

Florence of Worcester. *The Chronicle of Florence of Worcester with the Two Continuations.* Translated by Thomas Forester. London, 1854.

Fortunatus, Venantius. *Carminum Lib. VIII, MGH AA4,* part 1: 178–200.

———. *De Vita Sanctae Radegundis liber I. MGH SRM* 2:364–77.

———. *Vita Sancti Germani. MGH AA4,* part 2: 11–27.

Furseus. *Vita Virtutesque Fursei Abbatis Latiniacensis. MGH SRM* 4:434–49; *AASS* Ian. II: 401–19.

Genovefa. *Vita S. Genovefae. MGH SRM* 3:204–38. (See also *Sainted Women of the Dark Ages,* pp. 17–37.)

Germain. *Vita S. Germani Episcopi Parisiaci* (Auct. Venantio Fortunato). *MGH AA* 4, 2, 11–27; *AASS* Mai VI: 768–77.

Gertrude of Nivelles. *Vita Sanctae Geretrudis Nivialensis. MGH SRM* 2: 453–64. (See also *Sainted Women of the Dark Ages,* pp. 220–34.)

Gildard. *Vita Sancti Gildardi episcopi Rothomagensis. Analecta Bollandiana* 8:393–405.

Giraldus Cambrensis. *The Historical Works of Giraldus Cambrensis.* Revised and edited by Thomas Wright. London, 1905.

Gislenus. *Vita S. Gisleni Confessoris. AASS* Oct. IV: 1030–34.

Glodesind. *Vita S. Glodesindis. AASS* Iul. VI: 198–224. (See also *Sainted Women of the Dark Ages,* pp. 137–54.)

Godeberta. *Vita S. Godeberthae. AASS* Apr. II: 32–36.

Godeleva. *Vita S. Godelevae. AASS* Iul. II: 359–444.

Goscelin of Canterbury. "La Légende de Sainte Edith en prose et en vers par le moine Goscelin." Edited and translated by André Wilmart. *Analecta Bollandiana* 56 (1938): 5–101, 265–307.

———. "The Liber confortatorius of Goscelin of Saint Bertin." Edited by C. H. Talbot. In *Analecta Monastica* 3:1–117. Studia Anselmiana 37. Rome, 1955.

———. "La Vie de Sainte Vulfhilde par Goscelin de Cantorbéry." Edited by M. Esposito. *Analecta Bollandiana* 32 (1913):10–26.

Gottfried and Theoderic. *The Life of Holy Hildegard.* Translated by Aldegundis Führkötter and James McGrath; edited by Mary Palmquist. Collegeville, Minn., 1995.

Gregory the Great. *Saint Gregory the Great: Dialogues.* Translated by Odo John Zimmerman. The Fathers of the Church, a New Translation, vol. 39. New York, 1959.

———. *Dialogorum libri IV. PL* 77:149–430.

———. *Life and Miracles of St. Benedict* (Book 2 of the *Dialogues*). Translated by Odo J. Zimmerman and Benedict R. Avery (Collegeville, Minn., n.d.).

Gregory of Nyssa. *Saint Gregory of Nyssa, Ascetical Works.* Translated by Virginia Woods Callahan. The Fathers of the Church, a New Translation, vol. 58. Washington, D.C., 1967.

Gregory of Tours. *Life of the Fathers.* Translated by Edward James. Translated Texts for Historians, Latin Series 1. Liverpool, 1985.

———. *De Gloria Confessorum. MGH SRM* 1:747–820.

———. *Glory of the Confessors.* Translated by Raymond Van Dam. Translated Texts for Historians, Latin Series 4. Liverpool, 1988.

———. *History of the Franks.* Translated by Lewis Thorpe. Harmondsworth, 1974.

———. *Libri Miraculorum: Les Livres des miracles.* 4 vols. Edited and translated by H. L. Bordier. Paris, 1857–64.

Gudila. *Vita S. Gudilae virginis. AASS* Ian. I: 514–30; *AASS B* 5:689–734.

Guthlac. *Felix's Life of Saint Guthlac*. Translated by Bertram Colgrave. Cambridge and New York, 1956.

Hartmannus. *Vita S. Wiboradae: Vita Auct. Hartmanno Mon. Sangallensi*. AASS Mai. I: 289–98; Mabillon, *AASS OSB* 5:44–60.

Hathumoda. *Dialogus Agii: De Obitu Sanctae Hathumodae Abbatissae*. PL 137:1183–95.

———. *Vita Sanctae Hathumodae*. PL 137:1169–84; MGH SS 4:166–75.

Hepidannus. *Vita S. Wiboradae: Vita et Miracula Auct. Hepidanno Mon. Sangallensi*. AASS Mai. I: 298–313; Mabillon, *AASS OSB* 5:60–66.

Herlindis and Renildis. *Vita Ss. Herlindis [Harlindis] et Renildis [Renula]*. AASS Mar. III: 383–89.

Hildegard of Bingen. *Scivias*. Translated by Mother Columba Hart and Jane Bishop. The Classics of Western Spirituality. New York and Mahwah, 1990.

Hillgarth, J. N., ed. *Christianity and Paganism, 350–750*. Philadelphia, 1969; rev. ed. 1986.

Hiltrudis. *Vita S. Hiltrudis*. AASS Sept. VII: 461–68.

Hincmar of Reims. *Ad Regem, De coercendo et exstirpando raptu viduarum, puellarum ac sanctimonialium*. PL 125:1017–36.

Holy Women of Byzantium: Ten Saints' Lives in English Translation. Edited by Alice-Mary Talbot. Washington, D.C., 1996.

Hrotswitha of Gandersheim. *Carmen de Primordiis Coenobii Gandersheiim*. PL 137:1135–48.

———. *The Dramas of Hrotsvit of Gandersheim*. Trans. Katharina Wilson. Saskatoon, 1985.

———. *Hrotsvithae Opera*. Edited by Helena Homeyer. Munich, 1970.

———. *The Plays of Roswitha*. Translated by Christopher St. John. New York, 1966.

Hucbald. "Prologue to the *Vitae Rictrudis Sanctimonialis Marchianensis*." MGH SRM 6:91–94.

———. *Vita S. Aldegundis—Vita Auct. Hucbaldo Elnonensi*. AASS Ian. III: 655–62; PL 132:857–76.

———. *Vita S. Rictrudis*. AASS Mai. III:81–88; AASS B 4:488–503; PL 132:829–48.

Hugo. *Vita S. Hugonis*. AASS Apr. III: 656–69; MGH SS 15:937–40.

Ingulf's Chronicle of the Abbey of Croyland with the Continuations by Peter of Blois and Anonymous Writers. Translated by Henry T. Riley. London, 1854.

Ita. *Vita Sancte Ite Virginis*. In *Vitae Sanctorum Hiberniae*, edited by Charles Plummer, 2:116–30. Oxford, 1910.

Jacobus de Voragine. *The Golden Legend, or the Lives of the Saints, as Englished by William Caxton*. 7 vols. Translated by William Caxton. London 1900–39; New York, 1973.

———. *The Golden Legend: Readings on the Saints*. Translated by William Granger Ryan. 2 vols. Princeton, 1993.

Jerome. *Saint Jerome: Dogmatic and Polemical Works*. Translated by John N.

Hritzu. The Fathers of the Church, a New Translation, vol. 53. Washington, D.C., 1965.

———. *St. Jerome: Letters and Select Works*. Translated by W. H. Fremantle. A Select Library of Nicene and Post-Nicene Fathers of the Christian Church, 2d series, vol. 6. New York, Oxford, and London, 1893; rpt. Grand Rapids, Mich., n.d.

———. *Letters of St. Jerome, The*. Translated by Charles Christopher Mierow. ACW, Westminster, Md., 1963.

———. *Saint Jérôme: Lettres*. Edited and translated by Jérôme Labourt. Collection des Universités de France. Paris, 1955.

———. *Regula monacharum*. PL 30:391–426.

———. *Select Letters of St. Jerome*. Translated by F. A. Wright. Cambridge, Mass., and London, 1933.

Jonas of Bobbio. *Vitae sanctorum: Vitae S. Columbani disciplorumque eius*. MGH SRM 4:61–152.

———. *Life of St. Columban*. Edited by Dana Carleton. Philadelphia, 1902.

———. "Life of Columbanus, The." In *Monks, Bishops, and Pagans: Christian Culture in Gaul and Italy, 500–700*. Edited by Edward Peters. Philadelphia, 1975.

Laws of the Alamans and Bavarians. Translated by Theodore John Rivers. Philadelphia, 1977.

Laws of the Salian Franks, The. Translated and edited by Katherine Fischer Drew. Philadelphia, 1991.

Leander of Seville. *Sancti Leandri Regula*. PL 72:873–94.

———. "The Training of Nuns and the Contempt of the World." In *Martin of Braga, Paschasius of Dumium, Leander of Seville*. Vol. 1 of *Iberian Fathers*.

"Legende und Verehrung der hl. Attala, der ersten Aebtissin von St. Stephan in Strassburg, Die." Edited by Von Medard Barth. *Archiv für elsässische Kirchengeschichte* 2 (1927): 89–198 (*vita*, 110–59).

Leoba. "The *Life of St. Leoba* by Rudolf, monk of Fulda." In *The Anglo-Saxon Missionaries in Germany*, translated and edited by C. H. Talbot. New York, 1954.

Letters of St. Paulinus of Nola. 2 vols. Translated and annotated by P. G. Walsh. ACW, Westminster, Maryland, and London, 1966–67.

Liber Historiae Francorum. Edited and translated by Bernard S. Bachrach. Lawrence, Kans., 1973.

Life in the Middle Ages. The Cambridge Anthologies. Translated by G. G. Coulton. New York and Cambridge, 1910; rpt. 1930.

Life of Christina of Markyate, The: A Twelfth Century Recluse. Edited and translated by C. H. Talbot. Oxford, 1959.

Life of King Edward who rests at Westminster, The, attributed to a monk of St. Bertin. Edited and translated by Frank Barlow. London, Edinburgh, 1962.

Life of Melania the Younger, The. Edited and translated by Elizabeth A. Clark. New York, 1984.

Life of Pachomius (Vita Prima Graeca), The. Translated by Apostolos N. Athanassakis. Early Christian Literature Series 2, Texts and Translations, 7. Missoula, 1975.

Life of Saint Brigit, The. In *Anecdota Oxoniensia: Lives of Saints from the Book of Lismore,* translated by Whitley Stokes. Oxford, 1890.

"*Life of St. Leoba, The,* by Rudolf, monk of Fulda." In *The Anglo-Saxon Missionaries in Germany.* Translated and edited by C. H. Talbot. New York, 1954.

Liutberga. *Vita S. Liutbirgae. MGH SS* 4:158–64.

Lives of Irish Saints. 2 vols. Edited and translated by Charles Plummer. Oxford, 1922.

Lives of S. Ninian and S. Kentigern. Vol. 5 of *The Historians of Scotland.* Edited and translated by Alexander Penrose Forbes. Edinburgh, 1874.

Lives of the Cambro British Saints. Edited and translated by W. J. Rees. Llandovery, 1853.

Lives of the Saints from the Book of Lismore (Anecdota Oxoniensia). Edited by Whitley Stokes. Oxford, 1890.

Lives of Women Saints of our Contrie of England, The, c. 1610–1615. Edited by C. Horstmann. London, 1886.

Lombard Laws, The. Translated by Katherine Fischer Drew. Philadelphia, 1973.

Marbod of Rennes. *Vita S. Roberti Cassae Dei. PL* 171:1505–18.

Margaret of Scotland. Turgot, *Life of Queen Margaret.* In *Early Sources of Scottish History: A.D. 500–1286,* translated by Alan Orr Anderson; pp. 59–88. Edinburgh and London, 1922.

Martin of Braga, Paschasius of Dumium, Leander of Seville. Vol. 1 of *The Iberian Fathers.* Translated by Claude W. Barlow. The Fathers of the Church, a New Translation, vol. 62. Washington, D.C., 1969.

Martyrology of Oengus the Culdee, The. Edited by Whitley Stokes. London, 1905.

Mater Spiritualis: The Life of Adelheid of Vilich. Edited and translated by Madelyn Bergen Dick. Toronto, 1994.

Matthew of Westminster [Matthew of Paris]. *The Flowers of History.* 2 vols. Translated by C. D. Yonge. London, 1853.

Maura. *Vita S. Maurae. AASS* Sept. VI: 275–78.

Medieval Handbooks of Penance: A translation of the principal libri poenitentiales and selections from related documents. Edited and translated by J. T. McNeill and H. M. Gamer. Records of Western Civilization Series, Sources and Studies, 29. New York, 1938; rpt. 1990.

Mission of St. Augustine to England according to the Original Documents, The: Being a Handbook for the Thirteenth Centenary. Edited and translated by Arthur J. Mason. Cambridge, 1897.

"Monastery of Tallaght, The." Edited and translated by E. J. Gwynn and W. J. Purton. *Proceedings of the Royal Irish Academy* 29 (1911): 115–79.

Most Ancient Lives of Saint Patrick, The. Edited by James O'Leary. New York, 1897.

Odilia. *Vita Odiliae abbatissae Hohenburgensis. MGH SRM,* 6:24–50.

Odilo of Cluny. *Vita Sanctae Adalheidis Imperatricis.* In *Bibliotheca Cluniacensis,* edited by Martinus Marrier and Andreas Quercetanus, pp. 354–69. Brussels and Paris, 1915.

Opportuna. *Vita S. Opportunae abbatissae. AASS* Apr. III: 62–72.

Ordericus Vitalis. *The Ecclesiastical History of Odericus Vitalis.* 6 vols. Edited and translated by Marjorie Chibnall. Oxford, 1969–80.

Pachomius. *The Life of Pachomius (Vita Prima Graeca).* Early Christian Literature Series 2, Texts and Translations 7. Translated by Apostolos N. Athanassakis. Missoula, 1975.

Palladius. *The Lausiac History.* Translated by Robert J. Meyer. ACW, London, 1965.

Patrick. *The Most Ancient Lives of St. Patrick.* 7th ed. Edited and translated by James O'Leary. New York, 1897.

Peter Damian. *The Letters of Peter Damian.* 3 vols. Translated by Owen J. Blum. The Fathers of the Church, Mediaeval Continuation. Washington, D.C., 1989–92.

Pizan, Christine de. *The Book of the City of Ladies.* Translated by Earl Jeffrey Richards. New York, 1982.

Radegund. Venantius Fortunatus. *De Vita Sanctae Radegundis liber I. MGH SRM* 2:364–77. (See also *Sainted Women of the Dark Ages,* pp. 70–86.)

———. Baudonivia. *De Vita Sanctae Radegundis, Liber II. MGH SRM* 2:377–95. (See also *Sainted Women of the Dark Ages,* pp. 86–105.)

Reginald of Durham. *Libellus de Admirandis Beati Cuthberti Virtutibus.* Surtees Society. London, 1958.

Regula Monacharum (previously attributed to St. Jerome). *PL* 30:391–426.

Reineldis. *Vita S. Reineldis/Raineldis Virg. Mart. AASS* Iul. IV: 176–78.

Renildis. See Herlindis.

Rhigyfarch's Life of St. David. Translated by J. W. James. Cardiff, 1967.

Richardis. *Vita S. Richardis. AASS* Sept. V: 794–98.

Rites of Durham: Being a Description or Brief Declaration of All the Ancient Monuments, Rites, & Customs Belonging or Being Within the Monastical Church of Durham Before the Suppression. Written 1593. Surtees Society, vol. 107. Durham and Edinburgh, 1902.

Roger of Wendover. *Flowers of History: Comprising the History of England from the Descent of the Saxons to A.D. 1235.* Translated by J. A. Giles. 2 vols. London, 1849.

Royal Frankish Annals. In *Carolingian Chronicles: Royal Frankish Annals and Nithard's Histories,* translated by Bernhard Walter Scholz. Ann Arbor, 1970.

Rudolf. "*The Life of St. Leoba* by Rudolf, monk of Fulda." In *The Anglo-Saxon Missionaries in Germany,* edited and translated by C. H. Talbot. New York, 1954.

Rule of a Certain Father to the Virgins. Tentatively attributed to Waldebert of Luxeuil. 2d ed. Translated by Jo Ann McNamara and John E. Halborg. Peregrina Translations Series, no. 5. Toronto, 1993.

Russian Primary Chronicle, The: Laurentian Text. Translated by Samuel Hazzard Cross and Olgerd P. Sherbowitz-Wetzor. The Medieval Academy of America, Publication 60. Cambridge, Mass., 1953.

Rusticula. *Vita Rusticulae sive Marciae Abbatissae Arelatensis. MGH SRM* 4:339–51. (See also *Sainted Women of the Dark Ages,* pp. 119–36.)

Sadalberga. *Vita Sadalbergae Abbatissae Laudunensis. MGH SRM* 5:40–66. (See also *Sainted Women of the Dark Ages,* pp. 176–94.)

Saint of London, The: The Life and Miracles of St. Erkenwald. Edited and translated by E. Gordon Whatley. Binghamton, 1989.

St. Odo of Cluny: Being the Life of St. Odo of Cluny by John of Salerno and the Life of St. Gerald of Aurillac by St. Odo. Translated by Dom Gerard Sitwell. London and New York, 1958.

Sainted Women of the Dark Ages (SWDA). Edited and translated by Jo Ann McNamara and John E. Halborg with E. Gordon Whatley. Durham and London, 1992.

Simeon of Durham. *The Historical Works of Simeon of Durham.* Translated by Joseph Stevenson. The Church Historians of England. London, 1855.

Sulpicius Severus. *Vita Martini (Vie de Saint Martin).* 3 vols. Edited and translated by Jacques Fontaine. *SC,* vols. 133–35. Paris, 1967–69.

Sulpicius Severus et al. *The Western Fathers, Being the Lives of Martin of Tours, Ambrose, Augustine of Hippo, Honoratus of Arles, and Germanus of Auxerre.* Translated by F. R. Hoare. New York, 1954; rpt. 1965.

Tacitus. *The "Agricola" and the "Germania."* Translated by H. Mattingly; revised by S. A. Handford. Harmondsworth, 1970.

Tertullian. *Treatises on Marriage and Remarriage.* Translated by William P. Le Saint. Westminster, 1951.

Thomas of Ely. *Liber Eliensis.* Edited by E. O. Blake. Camden Third Series, vol. 92. London, 1962.

Three Lives of the Last Englishmen. Translated by Michael Swanton. Garland Library of Medieval Literature, ser. B, vol. 10. New York, 1984.

Tripartite Life of Patrick, The, with Other Documents Relating to that Saint. Edited by Whitley Stokes. London, 1887.

Turgot, *Life of Queen Margaret.* In *Early Sources of Scottish History: A.D. 500–1286,* translated by Alan Orr Anderson; pp. 59–88. Edinburgh and London, 1922.

Two Lives of Saint Cuthbert. Translated by Bertram Colgrave. Cambridge, 1940; rpt. 1985.

Vies des Pères du Jura. Edited by F. Martine. *SC* 142. Paris, 1968.

Vincent of Beauvais. *Speculum Quadruplex sive Speculum Maius, Speculum Historiale.* 4 vols. Graz, 1965.

Vitae Sanctorum Hiberniae. Edited by Charles Plummer. 2 vols. Oxford, 1910.

Waddell, Helen, trans. *The Desert Fathers.* London, 1936.

Walburga. *Vita et miracula de S. Waldburgis abb. Heidenheimensis. MGH SS* XV: 538–55; *AASS* Febr. III: 529–74.

Waldabert of Luxeuil. *Regula cuiusdam patris ad virgines. PL* 88:1053–70. (See also *Rule of a Certain Father to the Virgins.*)

Waldetrude. *Vita S. Waldetrudis*. *AASS* Apr. I: 828–32; *AASS Belgii selecta* 4:439–48. (See also *Sainted Women of the Dark Ages*, pp. 254–63.)

Wandrille. *La plus ancienne vie de Saint Wandrille dite "Vita prima."* Editions de Fontenelle. Translated by Jean Laporte. Yvetot, 1979.

Ward, Benedicta, trans. *The Sayings of the Desert Fathers*. London and Oxford, 1975.

Wiborada. *Vita S. Wiboradae: Vita Auct. Hartmanno Mon. Sangallensi*. *AASS* Mai. I: 289–98; Mabillon, *AASS OSB* 5:44–60.

———. *Vita S. Wiboradae: Vita et Miracula Auct. Hepidanno Mon. Sangallensi*. *AASS* Mai. I: 298–313; Mabillon, *AASS OSB* 5:60–66.

William of Malmesbury. *The History of the Kings of England*. Vol. 3, pt. 1, of *The Church Historians of England*. 5 vols., translated by J. Sharpe; revised by J. Stevenson. London, 1854.

Wulfstan of Winchester. *The Life of St. Aethelwold*. Edited and translated by Michael Lapidge and Michael Winterbottom. Oxford, 1991.

Yepes, Fray Antonio de. *Cronica general de la Orden de San Benito*. 3 vols. Madrid, 1959.

SECONDARY SOURCES

Abou-El-Haj, Barbara. *The Medieval Cult of Saints: Formations and Transformations*. Cambridge, 1994.

Aigrain, René. *L'Hagiographie: Ses sources, ses méthodes, son histoire*. Paris, 1953.

———. *Sainte Radegonde (vers 520–587); "Les Saints."* 2d ed. Paris, 1918.

Anson, John. "The Female Transvestite in Early Monasticism: The Origin and Development of a Motif." *Viator* 5 (1974): 1–32.

Ariès, Philippe. *Centuries of Childhood: A Social History of Family Life*. Translated by Robert Baldick. New York, 1962.

Ashley, Kathleen, and Pamela Sheingorn, eds. *Interpreting Cultural Symbols: Saint Anne in Late Medieval Society*. Athens, Ga., and London, 1990.

Aspegren, Kerstin. *The Male Woman: A Feminine Ideal in the Early Church*. Acta Universitatis Upsaliensis, Uppsula Women's Studies: A. Women in Religion, 4. Uppsala, 1990.

Atkinson, Clarissa. *The Oldest Vocation: Christian Motherhood in the Middle Ages*. Ithaca and London, 1991.

———. "'Your Servant, My Mother': The Figure of Saint Monica in the Ideology of Christian Motherhood." In *Immaculate and Powerful*, edited by Atkinson, Buchanan, and Miles, pp. 139–72.

Atkinson, Clarissa, C. Buchanan, and M. Miles, eds. *Immaculate and Powerful: The Female in Sacred Image and Reality*. The Harvard Women's Studies in Religion Series, Boston, 1985.

Babut, Ernest Ch. *Saint Martin de Tours*. Paris, 1912.

Baker, Derek, ed. *Medieval Women*. Studies in Church History, Subsidia, no. 1. Oxford, 1978.

———. "A 'Nursery of Saints': St. Margaret of Scotland Reconsidered." In Baker, *Medieval Women*.

Baker, Malcolm. "Medieval Illustrations of Bede's *Life of St. Cuthbert.*" *Journal of Warburg and Courtauld Institutes* 41 (1978): 16–49.

Baring-Gould, Sabine. *Virgin Saints and Martyrs.* New York, 1901.

Barth, Von Medard. "Die Legende und Verehrung der hl. Attala, der ersten Aebtissin von St. Stephan in Strassburg." *Archiv für Elsässische Kirchengeschichte* 2 (1927): 89–198.

Bateson, Mary. "Origin and Early History of Double Monasteries." *Transactions of the Royal Historical Society,* n.s. 13, pp. 137–98. London, 1899.

Bekker-Nielsen, Hans, Peter Foote, et al., eds. *Hagiography and Medieval Literature: A Symposium.* Odense, 1981.

Bell, Robert R. *Worlds of Friendship.* Beverly Hills and London, 1981.

Bell, Rudolf. *Holy Anorexia.* Chicago, 1985.

Bennett, Judith M. *Women in the Medieval English Countryside: Gender and Household in Brigstock before the Plague.* New York and Oxford, 1987.

Berger, Pamela. *The Goddess Obscured: Transformation of the Grain Protectress from Goddess to Saint.* Boston, 1985.

Bitel, Lisa M. *Isle of the Saints: Monastic Settlement and Christian Community in Early Ireland.* Ithaca and London, 1990.

———. *Land of Women: Tales of Sex and Gender from Early Ireland.* Ithaca and London, 1996.

Blumenfeld-Kosinski, Renate. *Not of Woman Born: Representations of Caesarian Birth in Medieval and Renaissance Culture.* Ithaca and London, 1990.

Blumenfeld-Kosinski, Renate, and Timea Szell, eds. *Images of Sainthood in Medieval Europe.* Ithaca and London, 1991.

Bonner, Gerald, David Rollason, and Clare Stancliffe. *St. Cuthbert, His Cult and His Community to AD 1200.* Woodbridge and Wolfeboro, 1989.

Borkowska, Sr. Margaret. "Slavic Women: Saints Olga and Anna." *Vox Benedictina: A Journal of Translations from Monastic Sources* 2:4 (1985): 363–68.

Boswell, John. *Christianity, Social Tolerance, and Homosexuality: Gay People in Western Europe from the Beginning of the Christian Era to the Fourteenth Century.* Chicago, 1980.

———. *The Kindness of Strangers: The Abandonment of Children in Western Europe from Late Antiquity to the Renaissance.* New York, 1988.

Braunfels, W. *Monasteries of Western Europe: The Architecture of the Orders.* London, 1972.

Brennan, Brian. "St. Radegund and the Early Development of Her Cult at Poitiers." *Journal of Religious History* 13 (1985): 340–54.

Browe, Peter, S.J. *Beiträge zur Sexualethik des Mittelalters.* In Breslauer Studien zur historischen Theologie, 23. Breslau, 1932.

Brown, Judith. *Immodest Acts: The Life of a Lesbian Nun in Renaissance Italy.* New York and Oxford, 1986.

Brown, Peter. *Augustine of Hippo.* Berkeley and Los Angeles, 1970.

———. *The Body and Society: Men, Women, and Sexual Renunciation in Early Christianity.* New York, 1988.

————. *The Cult of Saints: Its Rise and Function in Latin Christianity.* Chicago, 1981.

————. *Society and the Holy in Late Antiquity.* Berkeley and Los Angeles, 1982.

Brownmiller, Susan. *Against Our Will: Men, Women and Rape.* New York, 1975.

Brundage, James A. *Law, Sex, and Christian Society in Medieval Europe.* Chicago and London, 1987.

Bryne, Sr. Mary. *The Tradition of the Nun in Medieval England.* Washington, D.C., 1932.

Bugge, John. *Virginitas: An Essay in the History of a Medieval Ideal.* The Hague, 1975.

Bührer-Thierry, Geneviève. "La reine adultère." *Cahiers de Civilisation Médiévale* 35 (1992): 299–312.

Bullough, Vern. *Sexual Variance in Society and History.* Chicago, 1976.

————. "Transvestites in the Middle Ages." *American Journal of Sociology* 79, no. 6 (1974): 1381–94.

Bullough, Vern, and James A. Brundage, eds. *Sexual Practices and the Medieval Church.* Buffalo, 1982.

Bullough, Vern, and Bonnie Bullough. *Cross Dressing, Sex, and Gender.* Philadelphia, 1993.

Bullough, Vern, and Cameron Campbell. "Female Longevity and Diet in the Middle Ages." *Speculum* 55, no. 2 (1980): 317–25.

Bury, J. B. *The Invasion of Europe by the Barbarians: A Series of Lectures.* London, 1928.

Bynum, Caroline Walker. "Fast, Feast, and Flesh: The Religious Significance of Food to Medieval Women." *Representations* 11 (Summer 1985): 1–25.

————. *Fragmentation and Redemption: Essays on Gender and the Human Body in Medieval Religion.* New York, 1992.

————. *Holy Feast and Holy Fast: The Religious Significance of Food to Medieval Women.* Berkeley, 1987.

————. *Jesus as Mother: Studies in the Spirituality of the High Middle Ages.* Berkeley, Los Angeles and London, 1982.

————. "Women's Stories, Women's Symbols: A Critique of Victor Turner's Theory of Liminality." In *Anthropology and the Study of Religion,* edited by Frank Reynolds and Robert Moore, pp. 105–25. Chicago, 1984.

Cahier, Charles. *Caractéristiques des saints dans l'art populaire.* Paris, 1867.

Campbell, James. "Observations on the Conversion of England." In *Essays in Anglo-Saxon History,* pp. 69–84. London and Ronceverte, 1986.

Carrasco, Magdalena Elizabeth. "Spirituality in Context: The Romanesque Illustrated Life of St. Radegund of Poitiers (Poitiers, Bibl. Mun., MS 250)." *The Art Bulletin* 72, no. 3 (September 1990): 414–35.

Cazelles, Brigitte. *The Lady as Saint: A Collection of French Hagiographic Romances of the Thirteenth Century.* Philadelphia, 1991.

Chadwick, Henry. *The Early Church: The Pelican History of The Church,* vol. 1. Harmondsworth, 1967.

Chance, Jane. *Woman as Hero in Old English Literature.* Syracuse, 1986.

Chaney, William A. *The Cult of Kingship in Anglo-Saxon England: The Transition from Paganism to Christianity.* Berkeley and Los Angeles, 1970.

Chaussy, Dom Yves, et al. *L'Abbaye royale Notre-Dame de Jouarre.* 2 vols. Paris, 1961.

Cherewatuk, Karen. "Radegund and Epistolary Tradition." In Cherewatuk and Wiethaus, eds., *Dear Sister.*

Cherewatuk, Karen, and Ulrike Wiethaus, eds. *Dear Sister: Medieval Women and the Epistolary Tradition.* Philadelphia, 1993.

Christie, A. G. I. *English Medieval Embroidery.* Oxford, 1938.

Clark, Elizabeth A. *Jerome, Chrysostom, and Friends.* Lewiston, N.Y., 1979.

———. "John Chrysostom and the *subintroductae.*" In *Ascetic Piety and Women's Faith: Essays on Late Ancient Christianity,* edited by Elizabeth A. Clark, pp. 265–90. New York and Toronto, 1986.

———. "Patrons, Not Priests: Gender and Power in Late Ancient Christianity." *Gender and History* 2, no. 3 (1990): 252–64.

Clayton, Mary. *The Cult of the Virgin Mary in Anglo-Saxon England.* Cambridge and New York, 1990.

Clayton, Mary and Hugh Magennis, *The Old English Lives of St Margaret.* Cambridge and New York, 1994.

Clercq, Carlo de. *La législation religieuse franque de Clovis à Charlemagne (507–814).* Louvain and Paris, 1936.

Clover, Carol J. "The Politics of Scarcity: Notes on the Sex Ratio in Early Scandinavia." In *New Readings on Women in Old English Literature,* edited by Helen Damico and Alexandra Hennessey Olsen, pp. 100–34. Bloomington and Indianapolis, 1990.

Coleman, Emily. "Infanticide in the Early Middle Ages." In *Women in Medieval Society,* edited by Susan Mosher Stuard, pp. 47–70. Philadelphia, 1976.

Coon, Lynda L., Katherine J. Haldane, and Elisabeth W. Sommer, eds. *That Gentle Strength: Historical Perspectives on Women in Christianity.* Charlottesville and London, 1990.

Corbet, Patrick. *Les Saints ottoniens: Sainteté dynastique, sainteté royale, et sainteté féminine autour de l'an Mil.* Beihefte der Francia 15. Sigmaringen, 1986.

Coudanne, Louise. "Baudonivia, moniale de Sainte-Croix et biographe de sainte Radegonde." *Etudes mérovingiennes. Actes des Journées de Poitiers, 1952,* pp. 45–51. Poitiers, 1953.

Cowrie, Frederick Joseph. *Boniface (ca. 675–754) and His Friends: A Communion of Saints.* Ph.D. dissertation, Saint Louis University, 1975.

Cristiani, Marta. "La Sainteté féminine du haut moyen âge: Biographie et valeurs." In *Les fonctions des saints dans le monde occidental (IIIe–XIIIe siècle),* pp. 385–434. Collection de l'Ecole française de Rome, 149. Rome, 1991.

Cusack, Fr. Pearse Aidan. "St. Scholastica: Myth or Real Person?" *Downside Review* 92, no. 308 (July 1974): 145–59.

Dalarun, Jacques. "Robert d'Arbrissel et les femmes." *Annales: Économies, sociétés, civilisations* 39, no. 6 (1984): 1140–60.

Delaruelle, Etienne. "Sainte Radegonde, son type de sainteté et la chrétienté de son temps." In *Études mérovingiennes. Actes des Journées de Poitiers, 1952*, pp. 65–74. Poitiers, 1953.

Delcourt, Marie. "Le complexe de Diane dans l'hagiographie chrétienne." *Révue de l'histoire des religions* 153 (1958): 1–33.

Delehaye, Hippolyte. *Cinq leçons sur la méthode hagiographique.* Brussels, 1934.

———. *Les Légendes hagiographiques.* 2d ed. Brussels, 1906. Translated by Donald Attwater as *The Legends of the Saints.* New York, 1962.

———. "Loca sanctorum." *Analecta Bollandiana* 48 (1930): 5–64.

———. *Sanctus: Essai sur le culte des saints dans l'antiquité.* Brussels, 1927.

Delooz, Pierre. *Sociologie et canonisations.* Collection scientifique de la faculté de droit de l'Université de Liège, no. 30. Liège and The Hague, 1969.

———. "Pour une étude sociologique de la sainteté canonisée dans l'église catholique." *Archives de Sociologie des Religions* 13 (1962): 24–43.

Delsart, H. M. *Ste. Fare et Faremoutiers.* L'Abbaye de Faremoutiers, 1956.

Doherty, Charles. "Some Aspects of Hagiography as a Source for Economic History." *Peritia: Journal of the Medieval Academy of Ireland* 1 (1982): 300–28.

Dronke, Peter. *Women Writers of the Middle Ages: A Critical Study of Texts from Perpetua (203) to Marguerite Porete (1310).* Cambridge, 1984.

Dubois, Jacques, and Jean-Loup Lemaitre. *Sources et méthodes de l'hagiographie médiévale.* Paris, 1993.

Duby, Georges. *The Knight, The Lady, and The Priest: The Making of Modern Marriage in Medieval France.* Translated by Barbara Bray. Harmondsworth, 1983.

Duckett, Eleanor Shipley. *The Wandering Saints of the Early Middle Ages.* New York, 1954.

Dugdale, William. *Monasticon Anglicanum.* London, 1846.

Dumm, Demetrius. *The Theological Basis of Virginity according to St. Jerome.* Latrobe, Penn., 1961.

Dvornik, Francis. *Byzantine Missions among the Slavs.* New Brunswick, 1970.

———. *The Making of Central and Eastern Europe.* London, 1949.

Eckenstein, Lina. *Woman under Monasticism: Chapters on Saint-lore and Convent Life between A.D. 500 and A.D. 1500.* Cambridge, 1896; rpt. New York, 1963.

Elkins, Sharon. *Holy Women of Twelfth-Century England.* Chapel Hill and London, 1988.

Elliott, Alison Goddard. *Roads to Paradise: Reading the Lives of the Early Saints.* Hanover and London, 1987.

Elliott, Dyan. *Spiritual Marriage: Sexual Abstinence in Medieval Wedlock.* Princeton, 1993.

Erickson, Carolly. *The Medieval Vision: Essays in History and Perception.* New York, 1976.

Erler, Mary, and Maryanne Kowaleski, eds. *Women and Power in the Middle Ages.* Athens, Ga., and London, 1988.

Facinger, Marion. "A Study of Medieval Queenship: Capetian France 987–1237." *Studies in Medieval and Renaissance History* 5 (1968): 3–48.

Farmer, Sharon. *Communities of Saint Martin: Legend and Ritual in Medieval Tours.* Ithaca and London, 1991.

Fell, Christine. *Women in Anglo-Saxon England.* Oxford, 1984.

———. "Hild, abbess of Streonæshalch." In *Hagiography and Medieval Literature: A Symposium,* ed. Hans Bekker-Nielson, Peter Foote, et al., pp. 76–99.

Fichtenau, Heinrich. *Living in the Tenth Century: Mentalities and Social Orders.* Translated by Patrick J. Geary. Chicago and London, 1991.

Finucane, Ronald C. *Miracles and Pilgrims: Popular Beliefs in Medieval England.* Totowa, N.J., 1977.

Firth, Raymond. *Symbols: Public and Private.* Ithaca, 1973.

Fisher, A. L. "Women and Gender in Palladius' *Lausiac History.*" *Studia Monastica* 33 (1991): 23–50.

Fiske, Adele M. *Friends and Friendships in the Monastic Tradition.* Cidoc Cuaderno 51. Cuernavaca, Mexico, 1970.

Folz, Robert. *Les Saintes Reines du Moyen Age en Occident (VIe–XIIIe siècles).* Subsidia Hagiographica 76. Brussels, 1992.

———. *Les Saints Rois du Moyen Age en Occident (VIe–XIIIe siècles).* Subsidia Hagiographica 68. Brussels, 1984.

———. *Le Souvenir et la légende de Charlemagne dans l'empire germanique médiéval.* Paris, 1950.

Les Fonctions des saints dans le monde occidental (IIIe–XIIIe siècle). Collection de l'École française de Rome, 149. Rome, 1991.

Fontaine, Jacques. "Hagiographie et politique, de Sulpice Sévère à Venance Fortunat." *Revue d'Histoire de l'Eglise de France* 62, no. 168 (1975):113–140.

Fouracre, Paul. "Merovingian History and Merovingian Historiography," *Past and Present* 127 (1990): 3–38.

Frend, W. H. C. *The Rise of Christianity.* London, 1984.

Frugoni, Chiara. "The Imagined Woman." In *Silences of the Medieval Ages.* Vol. 2 of *A History of Women in the West,* edited by Georges Duby and Michelle Perrot, pp. 336–422. Cambridge, Mass., and London, 1992.

———. "L'iconographie de la femme au cours des Xe–XIIe siècles." In *La Femme dans la civilisation des Xe–XIIIe siècle,* pp. 177–188. Procedings of a colloquium held at Poitiers (September 1976). *Cahiers de civilisation médiévale,* 20. Poitiers, 1977.

Gäbe, Sabine. "Radegundis: sancta, regina, ancilla: Zum Heiligkeitsideal der Radegundisviten von Fortunat und Baudonivia." *Francia* 16:1 (1989): 1–30.

Gaiffier, Baudouin de. *Recueil d'Hagiographie. Subsidia Hagiographica* 61. Brussels, 1977.

———. "Hagiographie et historiographie." In *La Storiografia altomedievale, Settimane di studio del centro italiano di studi sull'alto medioevo, XVII,* vol. 1, pp. 139–66, 179–96. Spoleto, 1970.

———. "Mentalité de l'hagiographie médiévale d'après quelques travaux récents." *Analecta Bollandiana* 86 (1968): 391–99.

———. *Etudes critiques d'hagiographie et d'iconologie.* Subsidia Hagiographica 43. Brussels, 1967.

Gajano, Sofia Boesch, ed. *Agiografia altomedioevale.* Bologna, 1976.

Geary, Patrick J. *Furta Sacra: Thefts of Relics in the Central Middle Ages.* Rev. ed. Princeton, 1990.

———. *Living with the Dead in the Middle Ages.* Ithaca and London, 1994.

———. *Phantoms of Remembrance: Memory and Oblivion at the End of the First Millennium.* Princeton, 1994.

George, Judith W. *Venantius Fortunatus: A Latin Poet in Merovingian Gaul.* Oxford, 1992.

Gessler, Jean. *La Légende de sainte Wilgeforte ou Ontcommer, la Vierge miraculeusement barbue.* Brussels, 1938.

Gibson, William Sidney. *The History of the Monastery Founded at Tynemouth.* London, 1846.

Gies, Frances and Joseph. *Marriage and the Family in the Middle Ages.* New York and Cambridge, 1987.

Gilchrist, Roberta. *Gender and Material Culture: The Archaeology of Religious Women.* London and New York, 1994.

Ginot, Émile. "Le manuscrit Sainte Radegonde de Poitiers et ses peintures du XIe siècle." *Bulletin de la Société Française de Reproductions de Manuscrits à Peintures* 4 (1914–20): 9–80.

Glasser, Marc. "Marriage in Medieval Hagiography." *Studies in Medieval and Renaissance History* 4, o.s. 14 (1981): 3–34.

Gobry, Ivan. *De saint Colomban à saint Boniface.* Vol. 3 of *Les Moines en Occident.* 3 vols. Paris, 1985.

Goodich, Michael. "*Ancilla Dei:* The Servant as Saint in the Late Middle Ages." In *Women of the Medieval World,* edited by Julius Kirshner and Suzanne F. Wemple, pp. 119–36. Oxford and New York, 1985.

———. "The Contours of Female Piety in Later Medieval Hagiography." *Church History* 50 (1981): 20–32.

———. *Violence and Miracle in the Fourteenth Century: Private Grief and Public Salvation.* Chicago and London, 1995.

———. *Vita Perfecta: The Ideal of Sainthood in the Thirteenth Century.* Stuttgart, 1982.

Gordon, Albert I. *The Nature of Conversion.* Boston, 1967.

Gougaud, Louis. *Ermites et reclus: Etudes sur d'anciennes formes de vie religieuse.* Vienne, 1928.

———. *Devotional and Ascetic Practices in the Middle Ages.* Translated by G. C. Bateman. London, 1927.

———. "Mulierum Consortia: Etude sur le syneisaktisme chez les ascètes celtiques." *Eriu* 9 (1921–1923): 147–56.

Graus, Frantisek. *Volk, Herrscher und Heiliger im Reich der Merowinger.* Studien zur Hagiographie der Merowingerzeit. Prague, 1965.

Gravdal, Kathryn. *Ravishing Maidens: Writing Rape in Medieval French Literature and Law.* Philadelphia, 1991.

Gurevich, Aron. *Medieval Popular Culture: Problems of Belief and Perception.* Translated by Janos M. Bak and Paul A. Hollingsworth. Cambridge Studies in Oral Literature and Literate Culture, 14. Cambridge and New York, 1988.

Guttentag, Marcia, and Paul F. Secord. *Too Many Women? The Sex Ratio Question.* Beverly Hills, 1983.

Hagiographie, cultures et sociétés IVᵉ–XIIᵉ siècles. Actes du Colloque organisé à Nanterre et à Paris (2–5 mai 1979). Edited by Evelyne Patlagean and Pierre Riché. Paris, 1981.

Hall, Diane P. *Gender and Sanctity in the Hagiography of Early Medieval Irish Women.* M.A. thesis, University of Melbourne, 1992.

Hallett, Judith P. *Fathers and Daughters in Roman Society: Women and the Elite Family.* Princeton, 1984.

Hanawalt, Barbara. *The Ties That Bound: Peasant Families in Medieval England.* New York and Oxford, 1986.

Head, Thomas. *Hagiography and the Cult of Saints: The Diocese of Orleans, 800–1200.* Cambridge Studies in Medieval Life and Thought. Cambridge and New York, 1990.

———. "Hrotsvit's *Primordia* and the Historical Tradition of Monastic Communities." In *Hrotsvit of Gandersheim: Rara Avis in Saxonia?* edited by Katharina M. Wilson, pp. 143–64. Ann Arbor, 1987.

Hefele, Karl Joseph von. *Histoire des conciles d'après les documents originaux.* Vols. 1–5. Translated from the German and revised by H. LeClercq. Paris, 1907–12.

Heffernan, Thomas J. *Sacred Biography: Saints and Their Biographers in the Middle Ages.* New York and Oxford, 1988.

Heinzelmann, Martin. "Une source de base de la littérature hagiographique latine: le recueil de miracles." In *Hagiographie, cultures et sociétés IVᵉ–XIIᵉ siècles.* Actes du Colloque organisé à Nanterre et à Paris (2–5 mai 1979). Paris, 1981, pp. 235–259.

———. *Manuscrits hagiographiques et travail des hagiographes.* Sigmaringen, 1992.

Heinzelmann, Martin, and Joseph-Claude Poulin. *Les Vies anciennes de sainte Geneviève de Paris: Etudes critiques:* Bibliothèque de l'Ecole des Hautes Etudes, 329. Paris, 1986.

Henken, Elissa R. *Traditions of the Welsh Saints.* Woodbridge, 1987.

———. *The Welsh Saints: A Study in Patterned Lives.* Cambridge, 1991.

Herlihy, David. "Did Women Have a Renaissance? A Reconsideration." In *Mediaevalia et Humanistica: Studies in Medieval and Renaissance Culture* n. s. 13, (1985): 1–22.

———. "Land, Family, and Women in Continental Europe, 701–1200." *Traditio* 18 (1962): 89–120.

———. "Life Expectancies for Women in Medieval Society." In *The Role of Women in the Middle Ages,* edited by Rosmarie Morewedge, pp. 1–22. Albany, 1975.

———. "Medieval Children." In *The Walter Prescott Webb Memorial Lec-*

tures: Essays on Medieval Civilization, edited by B. K. Lackner and K. R. Philip, pp. 109–42. Austin, 1978.

———. *Medieval Households.* Cambridge, Mass., and London, 1985.

———. *Opera Muliebria: Women and Work in Medieval Europe.* New York, 1990.

———. *Women, Family and Society in Medieval Europe: Historical Essays, 1978–1991.* Edited by A. Molho. Providence and Oxford, 1995.

Herlihy, David, and Christiane Klapisch-Zuber. *Les Toscans et leurs familles.* Paris, 1978.

Higounet, Charles. "Les saints mérovingiens d'Aquitaine dans la toponymie." In *Etudes mérovingiennes: Actes des Journées de Poitiers, 1952,* pp. 157–67. Poitiers, 1953.

Hilpisch, Stephanus. *History of Benedictine Nuns.* Translated by Sr. M. Moanne Muggli. Collegeville, Minn., 1958.

Hodgkin, Thomas. *Italy and Her Invaders: 600–744.* 8 vols. New York, 1885–99; rpt. 1967.

Hoebanx, Jean-Jacques. *L'Abbaye de Nivelles des origines au XIVe siècle.* Mémoires de l'Académie Royale de Belgique, 46 no. 4. Brussels, 1952.

Hollis, Stephanie. *Anglo-Saxon Women and the Church: Sharing a Common Fate.* Woodbridge, Suffolk, and Rochester, N.Y., 1992.

Horner, Shari. "Spiritual Truth and Sexual Violence: The Old English *Juliana,* Anglo-Saxon Nuns, and the Discourse of Female Monastic Enclosure." *Signs: Journal of Women in Culture and Society* 19, no. 3 (1994): 658–75.

Hourlier, Dom Jacques. *Saint Odilon, Abbé de Cluny.* Bibliothèque de la revue d'histoire ecclésiastique 40. Louvain, 1964.

Hrotsvit of Gandersheim: Rara Avis in Saxonia? A collection of essays compiled and edited by Katharina M. Wilson in Medieval and Renaissance Monograph Series, 7. Ann Arbor, 1987.

Hubert, Jean. "L'Erémitisme et archéologie." In *L'Eremetismo in occidente nei secoli XI e XII,* pp. 462–90. Milan, Università Catt. del Sacro Cuore, Contributi, Ser. 3, Var. 4; Studi Medioevali, Misc. 4. Milan, 1965.

Hughes, Diane Owen. "From Brideprice to Dowry in Mediterranean Europe." *Journal of Family History* 3 (1978): 262–96.

Hughes, Kathleen. *The Church in Early Irish Society.* London, 1966.

———. *Early Christian Ireland: An Introduction to the Sources.* Ithaca, 1972.

Huneycutt, Lois L. "The Idea of the Perfect Princess: The *Life of St. Margaret* in the Reign of Matilda II (1100–1118)," in *Anglo-Norman Studies* 12: *Proceedings of the Battle Conference, 1989,* ed. Marjorie Chibnall, pp. 81–97. Woodbridge, 1990.

Iogna-Prat, Dominique. "La femme dans la perspective pénitentielle des ermites du Bas-Maine (fin XIème–début XIIème siècle)." *Revue d'histoire de la spiritualité* 53 (1977): 47–64.

James, Edward. "Archaeology and the Merovingian Monastery." In *Columbanus and Merovingian Monasticism,* edited by H. B. Clarke and Mary Brennan, pp. 33–55. BAR International Series 114. 1981.

———. *The Franks.* Oxford and Cambridge, Mass., 1988.
———. *The Origins of France: From Clovis to the Capetians, 500–1000.* New Studies in Medieval History, edited by Maurice Keen. Houndmills and London, 1982.
Jochens, Jenny. "Before the Male Gaze: The Absence of the Female Body in Old Norse." In *Sex in the Middle Ages: A Book of Essays,* edited by Joyce E. Salisbury, pp. 3–29. New York and London, 1991.
Johnson, Penelope. *Equal in Monastic Profession: Religious Women in Medieval France.* Chicago and London, 1991.
Jones, A. H. M. *Constantine and the Conversion of Europe.* New York, 1948, 1962.
Kelly, J. N. D. *Jerome: His Life, Writings, and Controversies.* New York, 1975.
Kemp, Eric Waldram. *Canonization and Authority in the Western Church.* London, 1948.
Kenney, J. F. *The Sources for the Early History of Ireland: An Introduction and Guide:* vol. 2 *Ecclesiastical.* New York, 1929.
Kieckhefer, Richard. "Imitators of Christ: Sainthood in the Christian Tradition." In *Sainthood: Its Manifestations in World Religions,* edited by Richard Kieckhefer and George D. Bond, pp. 1–42. Berkeley, Los Angeles, and London, 1988.
———. *Unquiet Souls: Fourteenth-Century Saints and Their Religious Milieu.* Chicago, 1984.
King, Margot H. "The Desert Mothers: A Survey of the Feminine Anchoritic Tradition in Western Europe." In *Matrologia Latina,* Saskatoon, 1985.
Kleinberg, Aviad M. *Prophets in Their Own Country: Living Saints and the Making of Sainthood in the Later Middle Ages.* Chicago and London, 1992.
———. "Proving Sanctity: Selection and Authentication of Saints in the Later Middle Ages." *Viator* 20 (1989): 183–205.
Klingshirn, William E. *Caesarius of Arles: The Making of a Christian Community in Late Antique Gaul.* Cambridge and New York, 1994.
Knowles, David. *Christian Monasticism.* New York, 1969.
———. *The Monastic Order in England.* Cambridge, 1940.
Knowles, David, and R. Neville Hadcock. *Medieval Religious Houses: England and Wales.* London, 1971.
Kurth, Godefroy. *Sainte Clotilde.* Paris, 1905.
Labande-Mailfert, Y., R. Favreau, et al. *Histoire de l'Abbaye Sainte-Croix de Poitiers: Quatorze siècles de vie monastique.* Mémoires de la Société des Antiquaires de l'Ouest, 4me série, vol. 19. 1986–1987.
Leclercq, Jean. "Les relations entre Venance Fortunat et Radegonde." In *La Riche Personnalité de Sainte Radegonde: Conférences et homélies prononcées à Poitiers à l'occasion du XIVe centenaire de sa mort (587–1987),* pp. 57–76. Poitiers, 1988.
———. "S. Pierre Damien et les femmes." *Studia Monastica* 15 (1973): 43–55.

————. *Women and Saint Bernard of Clairvaux.* Cistercian Studies Series 104. Kalamazoo, Mich., 1989.

Leloir, Louis. "Woman and the Desert Fathers." Translated by Jacqueline M. E. Owen and Margot H. King. *Vox Benedictina* 3, no. 3 (1986):207–27.

Levison, William. *England and the Continent in the Eighth Century.* Oxford, 1946.

Lewis, I. M. *Ecstatic Religion: An Anthropological Study of Spirit Possession and Shamanism.* Harmondsworth, 1971.

Leyser, Karl J. *Rule and Conflict in an Early Medieval Society: Ottonian Saxony.* London, 1979.

Lifshitz, Felice. "Les femmes missionnaires: l'exemple de la Gaule Franque." *Revue d'histoire ecclésiastique* 83 (1988): 5–33.

Lynch, Joseph H. *Godparents in Early Medieval Europe.* Princeton, 1986.

McCready, William D. *Signs of Sanctity: Miracles in the Thought of Gregory the Great.* Pontifical Institute of Medieval Studies. Studies and Texts 91. Toronto, 1989.

McGuire, Brian Patrick. *Friendship and Community: The Monastic Experience, 350–1250.* Kalamazoo. Mich., 1988.

————. "The Cistercians and the Transformation of Monastic Friendships." *Analecta Cisterciensia* 37 (1981): 1–63.

McKitterick, Rosamond. *The Carolingians and the Written Word.* Cambridge and New York, 1989.

————. "Nuns' Scriptoria in England and Francia in the Eighth Century." *Francia* 19, no. 1 (1992): 1–35.

————. "Women in the Ottonian Church: An Iconographic Perspective." In *Women in the Church,* edited by W. J. Sheils and Diana Wood, pp. 79–100. Studies in Church History, 27. Oxford, 1990.

McLaughlin, Eleanor. "Women, Power and the Pursuit of Holiness in Medieval Christianity." In *Women of Spirit: Female Leadership in the Jewish and Christian Traditions,* edited by Eleanor McLaughlin and Rosemary Reuther, pp. 99–130. New York, 1979.

McLaughlin, Eleanor, and Rosemary Reuther, eds. *Women of Spirit: Female Leadership in the Jewish and Christian Traditions.* New York, 1979.

McLaughlin, Mary Martin. "Survivors and Surrogates: Children and Parents from the Ninth to the Thirteenth Centuries." In *The History of Childhood,* edited by Lloyd de Mause, pp. 101–81. New York, 1974.

McNamara, Jo Ann. "Chaste Marriage and Clerical Celibacy." In *Sexual Practices and the Medieval Church,* edited by Vern L. Bullough and James A. Brundage, pp. 22–33. Buffalo, 1982.

————. "A Legacy of Miracles: Hagiography and Nunneries in Merovingian Gaul." In *Women of the Medieval World: Essays in Honor of John H. Mundy,* edited by Julius Kirshner and Suzanne F. Wemple, pp. 36–52. Oxford and New York, 1985.

————. "Living Sermons: Consecrated Women and the Conversion of Gaul." In *Peace Weavers: Medieval Religious Women II,* edited by John A. Nichols and Lillian Thomas Shank, pp. 19–37. Kalamazoo, 1987.

———. "A New Song: Celibate Women of the First Three Christian Centuries." *Women and History*, nos. 6 and 7, 1983.

———. "The Ordeal of Community: Hagiography and Discipline in Merovingian Convents." In *Vox Benedictina: A Journal of Feminine & Monastic Spirituality* 3, no. 4 (1986): 293–326.

———. "Sexual Equality and the Cult of Virginity in Early Christian Thought." *Feminist Studies* 3, nos. 3–4 (1976): 145–58.

McNamara, Jo Ann, and Suzanne Fonay Wemple. "The Power of Women Through the Family in Medieval Europe: 500–1100." In *Clio's Consciousness Raised: New Perspectives on the History of Women*, edited by M. Hartman and L. W. Banner, pp. 103–18. New York, 1974.

———. "Sanctity and Power: The Dual Pursuit of Medieval Women," In *Becoming Visible: Women in European History*, edited by R. Bridenthal and C. Koonz, pp. 90–118. Boston, 1977.

Maillé, Geneviève Aliette (de Rohan-Chabot), marquise de. *Les Cryptes de Jouarre*. Paris, 1971.

Mâle, Emile. *Religious Art in France. The Twelfth Century: A Study of the Origins of Medieval Iconography*. Translated by Marthiel Mathews. Bollingen Series XC.1. Princeton, 1978.

Markus, R. A. "The Chronology of the Gregorian Mission to England: Bede's Narrative and Gregory's Correspondence." *Journal of Ecclesiatical History* 14 (1963): 16–30.

Matter, E. Ann. "My Sister, My Spouse: Woman-Identified Women in Medieval Christianity." *Journal of Feminist Studies in Religion* 2, no. 2 (Fall 1986): 81–93.

Mayr-Harting, Henry. *The Coming of Christianity to Anglo-Saxon England*. London, 1972.

Mecklin, John M. *The Passing of the Saint: A Study of a Cultural Type*. Chicago, 1940.

Metz, René. "Le Statut de la femme en droit canonique médiéval." *Recueils de la Société Jean Bodin pour l'histoire comparative des institutions: La Femme* 12, pt. 2 (1962): 59–113.

Meyer, Mark A. "Women and the Tenth Century English Monastic Reform." *Revue Bénédictine* 87 (1977): 34–61.

Miles, Margaret R. "Infancy, Parenting, and Nourishment in Augustine's *Confessions. Journal of the American Academy of Religion* 50 (1982): 349–62.

Millinger, Susan. "Humility and Power: Anglo-Saxon Nuns in Anglo-Norman Hagiography." In *Distant Echoes: Medieval Religious Women*, edited by John Nichols and Lillian T. Shank, pp. 115–29. Kalamazoo, Mich., 1984.

Montessus, Sr. Telchilde, de. *Jouarre: ses cryptes, son église, son abbaye*. Yonne, 1976.

Moore, R. I. *The Formation of a Persecuting Society: Power and Deviance in Western Europe, 950–1250*. London and New York, 1987.

———. "Family, Community, and Cult on the Eve of the Gregorian Reform." *Transactions of the Royal Historical Society*, 5th series, vol. 30, pp. 49–69. London, 1980.

Moreau, Edouard de. *Histoire de l'Eglise en Belgique*. 2 vols. 2d ed. Brussels, 1945.

Moreira, Isabel. "*Provisatrix optima*: St. Radegund of Poitiers' relic petitions to the East." *Journal of Medieval History* 19 (1993): 285–305.

Morris, Joan. *The Lady was a Bishop. The Hidden History of Women with Clerical Ordination and the Jurisdiction of Bishops*. New York and London, 1973.

Mulder-Bakker, Anneke B., ed. *Sanctity and Motherhood: Essays on Holy Mothers in the Middle Ages*. New York and London, 1995.

Murray, Alexander. *Reason and Society in the Middle Ages*. Oxford, 1978.

Neill, S. *A History of Christian Missions*. Harmondsworth, 1964.

Nelson, Janet L. "Les femmes et l'évangélisation." *Revue du Nord* 69, no. 269 (1986): 471–85.

———. "Parents, Children, and the Church in the Earlier Middle Ages." In *The Church and Childhood*, edited by Diana Wood, pp. 81–114. Studies in Church History, 31. Oxford and Cambridge, Mass., 1994.

———. "Queens as Jezebels: The Careers of Brunhild and Balthild in Merovingian History." In Baker, *Medieval Women*, pp. 31–77.

———. "Women and the Word in the Earlier Middle Ages." In *Women in the Church*, edited by W. J. Sheils and Diana Wood, pp. 53–78. Studies in Church History, 27. Oxford, 1990.

———. "Women at the Court of Charlemagne: A Case of Monstrous Regiment." In *Medieval Queenship*, edited by John Carmi Parsons, pp. 43–61. New York, 1993.

Newman, Barbara. *From Virile Woman to WomanChrist: Studies in Medieval Religion and Literature*. Philadelphia, 1995.

———. *Sister of Wisdom: St. Hildegard's Theology of the Feminine*. Berkeley, Los Angeles, and London, 1987.

Nichols, John A. and Lillian Thomas Shank, eds. *Distant Echoes*. Vol. 1 of *Medieval Religious Women*. Kalamazoo, Mich., 1984.

———. *Peace Weavers*. Vol. 2 of *Medieval Religious Women*. Kalamazoo, Mich., 1987.

Nicholson, Joan. "*Feminae gloriosae*: Women in the Age of Bede." In Baker, *Medieval Women*, pp. 15–29.

Nie, Giselle de. "'Consciousness Fecund through God': From Male Fighter to Spiritual Bride-Mother in Late Antique Female Society." In *Sanctity and Motherhood: Essays on Holy Mothers in the Middle Ages*, edited by Anneke B. Mulder-Bakker, pp. 100–61. New York and London, 1995.

———. *Views from a Many-Windowed Tower: Studies of Imagination in the Works of Gregory of Tours*. Amsterdam, 1987.

Ortner, Sherry, and Harriet Whitehead, eds. *Sexual Meanings: The Cultural Construction of Gender and Sexuality*. Cambridge and New York, 1981.

Patlagean, Evelyne. "Ancienne hagiographie byzantine et histoire sociale." *Annales: Économies, sociétés, civilisations* 23 (1968): 106–26. Translated in Wilson, *Saints and Their Cults*, pp. 101–21.

———. "L'Histoire de la femme déguisée en moine et l'évolution de la sainteté féminine à Byzance." *Studi Medievali*, series 3, 17:2 (1976):597–623.

Patlagean, Evelyne, and Pierre Riché, eds. *Hagiographie, cultures et sociétés, IVe–XIIe siècles*. Actes du Colloque organisé à Nanterre et à Paris (2–5 mai, 1979). Paris, 1981.

Payer, Pierre. *Sex and the Penitentials: The Development of a Sexual Code 550–1150*. Toronto, Buffalo, and London, 1984.

Peers, C., and C. A. Ralegh Radford. "The Saxon Monastery of Whitby." *Archaelogia* 89 (1943): 27–88.

Pernoud, Régine. *Les Saints au Moyen Age: La Sainteté d'hier est-elle pour aujourd'hui?*. Paris, 1984.

Petroff, Elizabeth Alvilda. *Body and Soul: Essays on Medieval Women and Mysticism*. New York and Oxford, 1994.

———. *Consolation of the Blessed*. New York, 1979.

———. *Medieval Women's Visionary Literature*. New York, 1986.

Piper, A. J. "The First Generations of Durham Monks and the Cult of Saint Cuthbert." In *Saint Cuthbert, His Cult and His Community to AD 1200*, edited by Gerald Bonner, David Rollason, and Clare Stancliffe, pp. 437–46. Woodbridge, Suffolk, and Wolfeboro, N.H., 1989.

Podevyn, R. "Etude critique sur la vita Gudulae." *Revue Belge de philologie et d'histoire* 2 (1923): 619–41.

Poulin, Joseph-Claude. *L'Idéal de sainteté dans l'Aquitaine carolingienne d'après les sources hagiographiques (750–950)*. Quebec, 1975.

Prinz, Friedrich. *Frühes Mönchtum im Frankenreich. Kultur und Gesellschaft in Gallien, den Rheinlanden und Bayern am Beispiel der monastischen Entwicklung (4. bis 8. Jahrhundert)*. Munich and Vienna, 1965.

Rader, Rosemary. *Breaking Boundaries: Male/Female Friendship in Early Christian Communities*. New York, 1983.

Réau, Louis. *Iconographie de l'art chrétien*. 3 vols. Paris, 1955–59.

Rey, Gonzague de. *Les Saints de l'église de Marseille*. Marseille, 1885.

Reynolds, Roger E. "*Virgines subintroductae* in Celtic Christianity." *Harvard Theological Review* 61 (1968): 547–66.

La Riche Personnalité de Sainte Radegonde. Conférences et homélies prononcées à Poitiers à l'occasion du XIVe centenaire de sa mort (587–1987). Poitiers, 1988.

Ridyard, Susan J. *The Royal Saints of Anglo-Saxon England: A Study of West Saxon and East Anglian Cults*. Cambridge Studies in Medieval Life and Thought. Cambridge and New York, 1988.

Roisin, Simone. *L'Hagiographie cistercienne dans le diocèse de Liège au XIIIe siècle*. Louvain, 1947.

Rollason, David. *The Mildrith Legend: A Study in Early Medieval Hagiography in England*. Leicester, 1982.

———. *Saints and Relics in Anglo-Saxon England*. Oxford and Cambridge, Mass., 1989.

Rosaldo, Michelle Zimbalist and Louise Lamphere, eds. *Women, Culture and Society*. Stanford, 1974.

Rose, Mary Beth, ed. *Women in the Middle Ages and Renaissance: Literary and Historical Perspectives*. Syracuse, 1986.

Rouche, Michel. "La faim à l'époque carolingienne: Essai sur quelques types de rations alimentaires." *Revue Historique* CCL (1973): 295–320.

———. "Miracles, maladies et psychologie de la foi à l'époque carolingienne en Francie." In *Hagiographie, cultures et sociétés IVe–XIIe siècles,* edited by Evelyne Patlagean and Pierre Riché, pp. 319–38. Paris, 1981.

Ruether, Rosemary Radford, ed. *Religion and Sexism: Images of Women in the Jewish and Christian Traditions.* New York, 1974.

Russell, J. C. *Late Ancient and Medieval Population. Transactions of the American Philosophical Society.* Philadelphia, 1958.

Ryan, John. *Irish Monasticism: Origins and Early Development.* Dublin and Cork, 1931.

Sainte Fare et Faremoutiers: Treize siècles de vie monastique. Abbaye de Faremoutiers, 1956.

Salisbury, Joyce E. *Church Fathers, Independent Virgins.* London and New York, 1991.

———. "Fruitful in Singleness." *Journal of Medieval History* 8 (1982): 97–106.

Schmitt, Jean-Claude. "Note critique: la fabrique des saints." *Annales: Économies, sociétés, civilisations,* 39 (mars–avril 1984):286–300.

Schulenburg, Jane Tibbetts. "The Heroics of Virginity: Brides of Christ and Sacrificial Mutilation." In *Women in the Middle Ages and the Renaissance: Literary and Historical Perspectives,* edited by Mary Beth Rose, pp. 26–72. Syracuse, 1986.

———. "Saints and Sex, ca. 500–1100: Striding Down the Nettled Path of Life." In *Sex in the Middle Ages: A Book of Essays,* edited by Joyce E. Salisbury, pp. 203–31. Garland Medieval Casebooks, vol. 3. New York and London, 1991.

———. "Sexism and the Celestial Gynaeceum—from 500–1200." *Journal of Medieval History* 4 (1978): 117–33.

———. "Strict Active Enclosure and Its Effects on the Female Monastic Experience (ca. 500–1100)." In Nichols and Thomas, *Distant Echoes,* pp. 51–86.

———. "Women's Monastic Communities, 500–1100: Patterns of Expansion and Decline." *Signs: Journal of Women in Culture and Society* 14, no. 2 (1989): 261–92.

Schultz, LeRoy G., ed. *Rape Victimology.* Springfield, Ill., 1975.

Scott, F. S. "The Hildithryth Stone and the other Hartlepool Name-Stones." *Archaeologia Aeliana,* 4th series, 24 (1956): 196–212.

Shahar, Shulamith. *Childhood in the Middle Ages.* Translated by Chaya Galai. London and New York, 1990.

———. *The Fourth Estate: A History of Women in the Middle Ages.* Translated by Chaya Galai. London, 1983.

———. "Infancy in the Lives of Saints." *The Journal of Psychohistory* 10:3 (Winter 1983): 281–309 .

Sharpe, Richard. *Medieval Irish Saints' Lives: An Introduction to Vitae Sanctorum Hiberniae.* Oxford, 1991.

Sheehan, Michael M., ed. *Aging and the Aged in Medieval Europe.* Toronto, 1990.

Sheingorn, Pamela. "The Saints in Medieval Culture: Recent Scholarship." *Envoi: A Review Journal of Medieval Literature* 2, no. 1 (Spring 1990): 1–29.

Sigal, Pierre-André. *L'Homme et le miracle dans la France médiévale (XIe–XIIe siècle).* Paris, 1985.

Smith, Julia M. H. "Oracle and Written: Saints, Miracles, and Relics in Brittany, c. 850–1250." *Speculum* 65 (1990): 309–43.

———. "The Problem of Female Sanctity in Carolingian Europe c. 780–920." *Past and Present: A Journal of Historical Studies* 146 (1995): 3–37.

Smith-Rosenberg, Carroll. "The Female World of Love and Ritual: Relations Between Women in Nineteenth-Century America." *Signs: Journal of Women in Culture and Society* 1, no. 1 (1975): 1–29.

Sorokin, Pitirim A. *Altruistic Love: A Study of American "Good Neighbors" and Christian Saints.* Boston, 1950.

Southern, R. W. *The Making of the Middle Ages.* New Haven and London, 1953.

———. *Saint Anselm and His Biographer: A Study of Monastic Life and Thought 1059–c. 1130.* Cambridge, 1963.

———. *Western Society and the Church in the Middle Ages.* Pelican History of the Church, 2. Harmondsworth, 1970.

Sperberg-McQueen, M. R. "Whose Body Is It? Chaste Strategies and the Reinforcement of Patriarchy in Three Plays by Hrotswitha von Gandersheim." In *Women in German Yearbook* 8 (1992): 47–71.

Stafford, Pauline. *Queens, Concubines, and Dowagers: The King's Wife in the Early Middle Ages.* Athens, Ga., 1983.

———. "Sons and Mothers: Family Politics in the Early Middle Ages." In Baker, *Medieval Women*, pp. 79–100.

Sticca, Sandro. "Sin and Salvation: The Dramatic Context of Hrotswitha's Women." In *The Roles and Images of Women in the Middle Ages and Renaissance,* edited by Douglas Radcliff-Umstead, pp. 3–22. Pittsburgh, 1975.

Stoeckle, Maria. *Studien über Ideale in Frauenviten des VII.–X. Jahrhunderts.* Munich, 1957.

Stranks, C. J. *St. Ethelreda, Queen and Abbess.* Ely, 1975.

Stuard, Susan Mosher. "The Dominion of Gender: Women's Fortunes in the High Middle Ages." In *Becoming Visible: Women in European History,* 2d ed., edited by R. Bridenthal, C. Koonz, and S. Stuard, pp. 152–72. Boston, 1987.

Stuard, Susan Mosher, ed. *Women in Medieval Society.* Philadelphia, 1976.

Sumption, Jonathon. *Pilgrimage: An Image of Mediaeval Religion.* London, 1975.

Szarmach, Paul E. "Aelfric's Women Saints: Eugenia." In *New Readings on Women in Old English Literature,* edited by Helen Damico and Alexandra Hennessey Olsen, pp. 146–57. Bloomington and Indianapolis, 1990.

Tessier, George. *Le Baptême de Clovis.* Paris, 1964.

Theis, Laurent. "Saints sans famille? Quelques remarques sur la famille dans le monde franc à travers les sources hagiographiques." *Revue Historique* 255 (1976): 3–20.

Thompson, A. Hamilton. *Lindisfarne Priory, Northumberland.* Ministry of Public Building and Works. London, 1949.

Thompson, Sally. *Women Religious: The Founding of English Nunneries after the Norman Conquest.* Oxford, 1991.

Todd, James Henthorn. *St. Patrick Apostle of Ireland: A Memoir of His Life and Mission.* Dublin, 1864.

Tudor, Victoria. "The Cult of St. Cuthbert in the Twelfth Century: The Evidence of Reginald of Durham." In *Saint Cuthbert, His Cult and His Community to AD 1200,* edited by Gerald Bonner, David Rollason, and Clare Stancliffe, pp. 447–67. Woodbridge and Wolfeboro, N.H., 1989.

———. "The Misogyny of Saint Cuthbert." *Archaeologia Aeliana,* 5th series, 12 (1984): 157–67.

Van Dam, Raymond. *Saints and Their Miracles in Late Antique Gaul.* Princeton, 1993.

Van der Essen, Léon. *Etude critique et littéraire sur les vitae des saints mérovingiens de l'ancienne Belgique.* Louvain and Paris, 1907.

Van't Spijker, Ineke. "Family Ties: Mothers and Virgins in the Ninth Century." In *Sanctity and Motherhood: Essays on Holy Mothers in the Middle Ages,* edited by Anneke B. Mulder-Bakker, pp. 164–90. New York and London, 1995.

Vauchez, André. "'Beata Stirps': Sainteté et lignage en occident." In *Famille et parenté dans l'occident médiéval (Actes du colloque de Paris, 6–8 juin, 1974),* pp. 397–406. Collection de l'Ecole Française de Rome 30, communications et débats par Georges Duby et Jacques Le Goff. Rome, 1977.

———. *La Sainteté en occident aux derniers siècles du moyen âge: d'après les procès de canonisation et les documents hagiographiques.* Bibliothèque des Ecoles françaises d'Athènes et de Rome, 241. Rome, 1981.

Verdon, Jean. "Les Moniales dans la France de l'Ouest aux XIe et XIIe siècles: Etude d'histoire sociale." *Cahiers de civilisation médiévale* 19 (1976): 247–64.

———. "Notes sur le rôle économique des monastères féminins en France dans la second moitié du IXe et au début du Xe siècle." *Revue Mabillon* 58 (1975): 329–43.

———. "Recherches sur les monastères féminins dans la France du Nord aux IXe–XIe siècles." *Revue Mabillon* 59 (1976): 49–96.

———. "Recherches sur les monastères féminins dans la France du Sud aux IXe–XIe siècles." *Annales de Midi* 88 (1976): 117–38.

Verne, Simon. *Sainte Eusebie, abbesse, et ses quarantes compagnes martyrs à Marseille.* Marseille, 1891.

Vieillard-Troiekouroff, May. *Les Monuments religieux de la Gaule d'après les oeuvres de Grégoire de Tours.* Paris, 1976.

Wallace-Hadrill, J. M. *The Frankish Church.* Oxford, 1983.

Wansbrough, J. H. "St. Gregory's Intention in the Stories of St. Scholastica and St. Benedict." *Revue Bénédictine* 75 (1965): 145–51.

Ward, Benedicta. *Miracles and the Medieval Mind: Theory, Record, and Event, 1000–1215.* Philadelphia, 1982.

———. *Signs and Wonders: Saints, Miracles and Prayers from the 4th Century to the 14th.* Hampshire, U.K., and Brookfield, Vt., 1992.

Warner, Marina. *Joan of Arc: The Image of Female Heroism.* London, 1981.

Warren, Ann K. *Anchorites and Their Patrons in Medieval England.* Berkeley, Los Angeles, and London, 1985.

Weinstein, Donald, and Rudolf M. Bell. *Saints and Society: The Two Worlds of Western Christendom, 1000–1700.* Chicago, 1982.

Wemple, Suzanne Fonay. "Female Spirituality and Mysticism in Frankish Monasteries: Radegund, Balthild and Aldegund." In *Peace Weavers: Medieval Religious Women II,* edited by John A. Nichols and Lillian Thomas Shank, 39–53. Kalamazoo, 1987.

———. "Monastic Life of Women from the Merovingians to the Ottonians." In *Hrotsvit of Gandersheim: Rara Avis in Saxonia?,* edited by Katharina M. Wilson, pp. 35–54. Ann Arbor, 1987.

———. "Sanctity and Power: The Dual Pursuit of Early Medieval Women." In *Becoming Visible: Women in European History,* 2d ed., edited by R. Bridenthal, C. Koonz, and S. Stuard, pp. 130–51. Boston, 1987.

———. *Women in Frankish Society: Marriage and the Cloister, 500 to 900.* Philadelphia, 1981.

Wilmart, André. "Eve et Goscelin." *Revue Bénédictine* 46 (1934):414–38; 50 (1938):42–83.

Wilson, Katharina M., ed. *Hrotsvit of Gandersheim: Rara Avis in Saxonia?* Medieval and Renaissance Monograph Series 7. Ann Arbor, 1987.

———. *Medieval Women Writers.* Athens, Ga., 1984.

Wilson, Stephen, ed. *Saints and Their Cults: Studies in Religious Sociology, Folklore and History.* Cambridge, 1983.

Wogan-Browne, Jocelyn. " 'Clerc u lai, muïne u dame': Women and Anglo-Norman Hagiography." In *Women and Literature in Britain 1100–1500,* ed. Carol Meale, pp. 61–85. Cambridge, 1993.

———. "Queens, Virgins and Mothers: Hagiographic Representations of the Abbess and Her Powers in Twelfth- and Thirteenth-Century Britain." In *Women and Sovereignty,* edited by Louise Olga Fradenburg, pp. 14–35. *Cosmos,* vol. 7. Edinburgh, 1992.

———. "Saints Lives and the Female Reader," *Forum for Modern Language Studies* 27, no. 4 (1991): 314–32.

Wood, Ian N. "A Prelude to Columbanus: The Monastic Achievement in the Burgundian Territories." In *Columbanus and Merovingian Monasticism,* edited by H. B. Clarke and M. Brennan, pp. 3–32. BAR International Series 114. Oxford, 1981.

———. *The Merovingian Kingdoms 450–751.* London and New York, 1994.

Woodward, Kenneth L. *Making Saints: How the Catholic Church Determines Who Becomes a Saint, Who Doesn't, and Why.* New York and London, 1990.

Index

abandonment, of infants, 213, 242–43, 247–50, 489n.144

Abban, Saint (abbot of Magh Arnaide), 241

abbesses, 77, 400, 403; as administrators, 92–96; age of, 175; building campaigns of, 83–86; captive, 459n.77; consecration of, 92–94; elderly, 373; and fosterage, 267, 269; as founders of monasteries, 77–83; friendships of, 342–43, 349–50; and hagiography, 30; and invasions, 172; involvement in reform, 109; as mothers, 261–63, 494n.215, 496n.238; power of, 92–96, 112–15; queens as, 77, 79–82; as saints, 80–86; and sibling relationships, 278–79. *See also names of individual abbesses and monasteries*

abortion, 240, 242–44, 488n.136, 490n.147

Adalsind (abbess of Dorniaticum), 277

Adela, Saint (countess of Flanders and abbess of Meesene), 88

Adelaide, Saint (empress and widow), 38; age at marriage, 219; commissions *vita,* 38; and domestic sphere, 117; establishes monasteries, 71–72; friendships of, 517n.153; as mother, 220, 255, 481n.31; as peacemaker, 75

Adelheid, Saint (abbess of Vilich), 37, 39, 496n.238, *plate 2;* as abbess, 262–63, 278–79; friendships of, 338

Adelph, Saint, 31

Adeltrude, Saint (abbess of Maubeuge), 496n.238

Adelviva, Saint (mother of St. Poppo), 235

Adile, Saint (abbess of St. Martin du Mont [Namur] and sister of St. Bavo), 277

admiranda, 2, 166, 407, 420n.4

Adomnan/Adamnan, Law of, 216

adoption, 247–48. *See also* fosterage

adultery, 243, 344, 352–53, 490n.147, 517n.154

Aed, Saint (Irish bishop), 228–29

Aelffled/Elfleda, Saint (abbess of Whitby), 95, 99, 328, 330, 496n.238, *plate 20*

Aelfric, 34, 136, 160, 465n.130

Aelfthryth (queen of England), 141

Aethelred II (king of England), 142

Aethelwold. *See* Ethelwold

Aethelwynn (friend of St. Dunstan), 337–38

affection: parental, 250–51, 253, 261–64, 268, 492n.176; in sibling relationships, 282–86. *See also* friendship

Agatha, Saint (virgin martyr), 174, 239